The Editor

JOHN G. PETERS is a University Distinguished Research Professor of English at the University of North Texas. He is the author of *Joseph Conrad's Critical Reception*, *The Cambridge Introduction to Joseph Conrad*, and *Conrad and Impressionism*. He is editor of *Joseph Conrad: The Contemporary Reviews (Volume 2)*, *A Historical Guide to Joseph Conrad*, and *Conrad in the Public Eye*.

NORTON CRITICAL EDITIONS
Modernist & Contemporary Eras

For a complete list of Norton Critical Editions, visit
wwnorton.com/nortoncriticals

A NORTON CRITICAL EDITION

Joseph Conrad

THE SECRET SHARER
AND OTHER STORIES

AUTHORITATIVE TEXTS
BACKGROUNDS AND CONTEXTS
CRITICISM

Edited by

JOHN G. PETERS
UNIVERSITY OF NORTH TEXAS

W · W · NORTON & COMPANY · *New York* · *London*

W. W. Norton & Company has been independent since its founding in 1923, when William Warder Norton and Mary D. Herter Norton first published lectures delivered at the People's Institute, the adult education division of New York City's Cooper Union. The firm soon expanded its program beyond the Institute, publishing books by celebrated academics from America and abroad. By midcentury, the two major pillars of Norton's publishing program—trade books and college texts—were firmly established. In the 1950s, the Norton family transferred control of the company to its employees, and today—with a staff of four hundred and a comparable number of trade, college, and professional titles published each year—W. W. Norton & Company stands as the largest and oldest publishing house owned wholly by its employees.

Manufacturing by Maple Press
Book design by Antonina Krass
Production manager: Vanessa Nuttry

Library of Congress Cataloging-in-Publication Data

Conrad, Joseph, 1857–1924.
    [Short stories. Selections]
    The secret sharer and other stories : authoritative texts, backgrounds and contexts criticism / Joseph Conrad ; edited by John G. Peters, University of North Texas. —First edition.
        pages cm. —(A Norton critical edition)
    Includes bibliographical references.

    ISBN: 978-0-393-93633-9 (pbk.)

    1. Sea stories, English.   2. Adventure stories, English.   3. Conrad, Joseph, 1857–1924. Secret sharer.   4. Conrad, Joseph, 1857–1924—Criticism and interpretation.   I. Peters, John G. (John Gerard) editor.   II. Title.
    PR6005.O4A6 2015
    823'.912—dc23

                                                                    2014038354

W. W. Norton & Company, Inc., 500 Fifth Avenue, New York, N.Y. 10110
www.wwnorton.com

W. W. Norton & Company Ltd., Castle House, 75/76 Wells Street,
London W1T 3QT

1 2 3 4 5 6 7 8 9 0

Contents

Contemporary Reviews

viii CONTENTS

Preface

I have selected the stories for this edition based on the connection Conrad himself saw among them. In his "Author's Note" to *Twixt Land and Sea* (p. 3), he refers to his two "Calm-pieces"—*The Secret Sharer* (1910) and *The Shadow-Line* (1917)—and his two "Storm-pieces"—*The Nigger of the "Narcissus"* (1897) and *Typhoon* (1902)—and I have sequenced the stories in the order Conrad lists them. Beyond this connection, other important elements link these tales. They are, of course, all directly tied to the sea, and in each the calm or storm plays a crucial role in its movement. The men must confront not only the difficulties of existing in an inexplicable universe but also the challenges posed by the elements of an indifferent natural world where humanity occupies no central position but is merely an insignificant entity among so many other insignificant entities. The dangers the calm and storm pose occur by chance, and humanity must respond with the full knowledge that there is no reason for the trials they face.

These tales also mark important moments in Conrad's literary career. *The Nigger of the "Narcissus"* was Conrad's first work to achieve nearly universal acclaim. With this story, Conrad arrived as a literary force, and the story ushered in his period of artistic maturity. *Typhoon* comes several years later, with Conrad's literary reputation now established, and revealed his remarkable descriptive powers (something that attracted so much early attention), solidifying his place in the world of letters. The term *genius*, previously spoken periodically in connection with Conrad's works, became commonplace after *Typhoon*. In contrast, *The Secret Sharer* appears at the end of what many feel was Conrad's highest artistic achievement, and even if one sees his later career not as a decline in ability but a shift in direction, what cannot be debated is that the works that followed this tale are different in emphasis, direction, and perhaps even conception of the world. The one exception is *The Shadow-Line*, which most see sharing much more with Conrad's earlier fiction than with such novels as *Chance* (1914), *Victory* (1915), *The Arrow of Gold* (1919), and *The Rescue* (1920), which precede and follow it. For many, *The Shadow-Line* provides a final glimpse of an earlier Conrad, perhaps because Conrad conceived of the tale nearly twenty years earlier (CL 2:167). Whatever the reason, *The Shadow-Line* resembles the other tales in this volume more than it does Conrad's contemporaneous writings.

Finally, all of these tales are based on Conrad's own experience. *The Shadow-Line* is the most autobiographical, Conrad himself referring to it as "exact autobiography" (CL 6:37; see p. 375); this is something of an overstatement but is not far from the truth. *The Secret Sharer* is similarly based on Conrad's first command, and although not as autobiographical as *The Shadow-Line*, it nevertheless records Conrad's insecurities and uncertainty in his new position of command. *The Nigger of the "Narcissus"* also follows Conrad's experiences, but here he conflates his experience aboard the *Narcissus* with that of other ships, and while *Typhoon* is directly based on Conrad's past, it is the least autobiographical of these tales; nevertheless, he drew on characters he knew and on his experience at sea. Of course, in all these tales, Conrad weds personal experience with creative imagination. Still, Conrad's life reflects profoundly on these tales, just as these tales reflect profoundly on his life.

Concerning the stories individually, *The Secret Sharer* is nearly unique in Conrad's literary career. Conrad famously struggled to write and struggled with doubt about the quality of his works, particularly while he was writing them. In contrast, he wrote *The Secret Sharer* quickly and had a great deal of confidence in its success (CL 5:128), and most later commentators have agreed, ranking it as his best or nearly best short story. The tale investigates the problem of self-knowledge, as the new captain must confront his feelings of inadequacy in his new position while at the same time proving himself adequate to fulfill that position. Tied to this issue is the relationship of self to Other, particularly the Other-self and how this exchange contributes to the search for self-knowledge as well as to the process of maturation.

The Shadow-Line investigates that imperceptible migration between youth and maturity, the moment one crosses the shadow line that separates the two. Conrad is thinking of his experience when he assumed command of the *Otago* and was forced to cross that line, but in dedicating the tale not only to his son, Borys, who was fighting in World War I, but also to all those like him, he universalizes the experience, reflecting the journey that all must make as each crosses that shadow line and becomes an adult. Furthermore, as in the other stories, Conrad explores how human beings confront the indifferent world around them, creating meaning for their existence while knowing there are no certainties—only contingencies. Conrad finds value in the human endeavor not only to endure and survive but to live consciously with fidelity to truths that are not absolute but merely relative.

Almost universally hailed by early and later commentators as Conrad's first masterpiece and one of his finest works, *The Nigger of the "Narcissus"* was regularly taught and reprinted in numerous editions. In the past fifteen years, however, its unfortunate title has caused it to fall off the map.[1] The story still receives its fair share of commentary (though far less than it once did), but it has become nearly extinct in the classroom. A victim of linguistic evolution, the story's use of what has become an increasingly intolerable racial epithet makes it extremely problematic to teach. Despite this stigma, it remains an important part of Conrad's oeuvre and certainly belongs in any discussion of Conrad's most important works, let alone his most important sea tales. Along with its remarkable descriptions of the storm, the story embodies an essential component of Conrad's philosophy: solidarity. The situation aboard the *Narcissus* is a microcosm for the human condition: just as the men must cooperate and show solidarity to survive in the face of a natural world indifferent to their plight, so also must humanity exhibit solidarity to survive in an inexplicable universe. Furthermore, Conrad investigates how humanity copes when confronted with the reality of imminent death and the doubt as to whether anything lies beyond that boundary.

Typhoon reflects many of the ideas appearing in the other stories: the necessity for solidarity and fidelity, as well as the precarious place humanity occupies in an indifferent universe. In addition, *Typhoon* presents a quiet heroism. MacWhirr, Jukes, the engineers, and the rest of the crew (except the second mate) all perform their duties and together bring the ship, though battered, safely through the typhoon, once again providing a microcosm of the human condition. At the same time, the second mate (like Donkin in *The Nigger of the "Narcissus"*) reveals the danger and corroding effect of those who fail to demonstrate solidarity to the group and fidelity to its values.

In selecting background materials, I included relevant correspondence, as well as contemporary reviews of these works (both British and American). In addition, I selected various documents related to Conrad's sources. Regarding the commentary, I attempted to strike a balance between established opinions and innovative approaches. For each story, I have included early commentary that gives a strong reading and provides the basis for later responses. The early commentary serves as opening remarks in the critical conversation.

---

1. For more on this, see my "'What's in a Name'?: Joseph Conrad's *The Nigger of the 'Narcissus,'*" *L'Epoque Conradienne* 33 (2007): 41–48.

I feel these are among the first important comments on the stories and ones to which subsequent commentary either directly or indirectly responds. For the remaining critical material, I sought views that identified important aspects of these works that have engendered further comment or identified significant issues (such as colonialism, narrative, gender, and race) that appear in these tales and elsewhere in Conrad's works. The criticism includes both new voices and established voices, and I selected commentary that represents a broad cross-section: early views, later views, and recent views.

Throughout the background and commentary section, I supplied page references in square brackets for quotations from these tales where the authors have not included them. In those instances where page numbers have been supplied to other editions, I have replaced them with corresponding page references to this edition. However, I have not altered the quoted passages themselves. I have also corrected any typographical or other obvious errors. Finally, I have regularized quotations from Conrad's letters, changing all references to citations from the authoritative Cambridge University Press edition. Similarly, I have regularized quotations from Conrad's other works, changing page references to citations from the Cambridge University Press edition where available and to the Doubleday uniform edition where no Cambridge edition exists. The only exceptions are *Heart of Darkness* and *Lord Jim*, where I have changed page references to citations from their Norton Critical Editions. In all of these instances, I have also supplied abbreviated titles with the page references. (Abbreviations are listed on pp. xv–xvii.) Along with these emendations, I have supplied missing bibliographic information from footnotes (where applicable), and for the sake of space I have abbreviated or deleted some footnotes. Finally, I have included a fair number of cross-references because, as with any collection of stories, people may not read all four tales. Consequently, the first time a word, phrase, or reference appears, I have glossed it with a footnote. If it appears again in the same work or the reviews or correspondence concerning that work, I do not cross-reference it. However, if the term appears in one of the other stories or the reviews for that story, I have inserted a cross reference.

Acknowledgments

I would like to thank the numerous Conrad scholars who have provided help, information, and suggestions, in particular, Mark Larabee, Peter Lancelot Mallios, Brian Richardson, J. H. Stape, Allan H. Simmons, Debra Romanick Baldwin, and Christopher GoGwilt. I would also like to thank the librarians at the Interlibrary Loan Department of the University of North Texas, in particular Pamela Johnson and Lynne Wright, for obtaining materials necessary for this edition. The Office of the Vice President for Research also provided aid in the form of a small grant to help with proofreading. Catherine Tisch, at Kent State University's Institute for Bibliography & Editing, was extremely helpful in supplying various editions of the works in this edition, which were instrumental in the textual editing of this volume.

I am also indebted to the following editors for the textual and annotating work they have done in their editions of the works included in this Norton Critical Edition: Jacques Berthoud, *The Nigger of the "Narcissus"* (Oxford, 1984) and *The Shadow-Line* (Penguin, 1986); Jeremy Hawthorn, *The Shadow-Line* (Oxford, 2003); Paul Kirschner, *Typhoon and Other Stories* (Penguin, 1992); J. H. Stape, *Typhoon and Other Stories* (Penguin, 2007); Brian Unsworth and Nels Pearson, *Typhoon and Other Stories* (Modern Library, 2003); Robert Kimbrough, *The Nigger of the "Narcissus"* (Norton, 1979); Cedric Watts, *The Nigger of the "Narcissus"* (Penguin, 1987) and *Typhoon and Other Tales* (Oxford, 2002); Jacques Berthoud, Laura L. Davis, and S. W. Reid, *'Twixt Land and Sea* (Cambridge, 2008); J. H. Stape and Allan H. Simmons, *The Shadow-Line* (Cambridge, 2013) and *The Nigger of the "Narcissus" and Other Stories* (Penguin, 2007); Allan H. Simmons, *The Nigger of the "Narcissus"* (Everyman, 1997); Norman Sherry, *The Nigger of the "Narcissus," Typhoon, Falk and Other Stories* (Everyman, 1974); Allan Ingram, *Selected Literary Criticism and The Shadow-Line* (Methuen, 1986).

Finally, I would like to thank my family for their support.

Abbreviations

Armstrong, Paul, ed. *Heart of Darkness* by Joseph   HD
Conrad. 4th ed. New York: W. W. Norton, 2006.

Berthoud, Jacques, ed. *The Nigger of the "Narcissus"*   BNN
by Joseph Conrad. Oxford: Oxford University Press,
1984.

Conrad, Joseph. *Chance.* Garden City, NY: C
Doubleday, Doran, 1928.

Conrad, Joseph. *Mirror of the Sea.* Garden City, NY: MS
Doubleday, Doran, 1928.

Conrad, Joseph. *Nostromo.* Garden City, NY: N
Doubleday, Doran, 1928.

Conrad, Joseph. *An Outcast of the Islands.* Garden   OI
City, NY: Doubleday, Doran, 1928.

Conrad, Joseph. *Typhoon and Other Stories.* Garden   TOS
City, NY: Doubleday, Doran, 1928.

Davies, Laurence, et al., eds. *The Collected Letters of*   CL
Joseph Conrad. 9 vols. Cambridge: Cambridge
University Press, 1983–2007.

Fachard, Alexandre, ed. *Within the Tides* by Joseph   WT
Conrad. Cambridge: Cambridge University Press,
2012.

Hawthorn, Jeremy, ed. *The Shadow-Line* by Joseph   HSL
Conrad. Oxford: Oxford University Press, 2003.

Ingram, Allan, ed. *Selected Literary Criticism and*   ISL
"The Shadow-Line" by Joseph Conrad. London:
Methuen, 1986.

Jean-Aubry, G. *Joseph Conrad: Life and Letters.*   JCLL
2 vols. Garden City, NY: Doubleday, Page, 1927.

Kimbrough, Robert, ed. *The Nigger of the "Narcissus"*   Kimbrough
by Joseph Conrad. New York: W. W. Norton, 1979.

Knowles, Owen, ed. *Youth, Heart of Darkness, The*   Y
End of the Tether by Joseph Conrad. Cambridge:
Cambridge University Press, 2010.

Larabee, Mark D. "'A Mysterious System':   Larabee
Topographical Fidelity and the Charting of
Imperialism in Joseph Conrad's Siamese Waters."
Studies in the Novel 32.3 (Fall 2000): 348–68.

Minamida, Seiji. "*The Shadow-Line*: Explanatory   MSL
Notes and Glossary." *Journal of the College of Arts
and Sciences Chiba University* B–21 (November
1988): 193–220.

Moser, Thomas, ed. *Lord Jim* by Joseph Conrad. 2nd   LJ
ed. New York: W. W. Norton, 1996.

Najder, Zdzisław, and J. H. Stape, eds. *A Personal*   PR
Record by Joseph Conrad. Cambridge: Cambridge
University Press, 2008.

Osborne, Roger, et al., eds. *Under Western Eyes* by   UWE
Joseph Conrad. Cambridge: Cambridge University
Press, 2013.

Sherry, Norman. *Conrad's Eastern World*. Cambridge: CEW
Cambridge University Press, 1966.

Sherry, Norman, ed. *The Nigger of the "Narcissus,"*   NNTF
Typhoon, Falk and Other Stories by Joseph Conrad.
London: Everyman, 1974.

Stape, J. H., ed. *The Nigger of the 'Narcissus' and*   NNOS
Other Stories by Joseph Conrad. London: Penguin
Books, 2007.

Stape, J. H., ed. *Notes on Life and Letters* by Joseph   NLL
Conrad. Cambridge: Cambridge University Press,
2004.

Stape, J. H., ed. *Typhoon and Other Stories* by Joseph   Stape
Conrad. London: Penguin Books, 2007.

Stape, J. H., and Owen Knowles, eds. *A Portrait in*   PL
Letters: Correspondence to and about Conrad.
Amsterdam: Rodopi, 1996.

Stape, J. H., and Allan H. Simmons, eds. *The*   SSSL
Shadow-Line by Joseph Conrad. Cambridge:
Cambridge University Press, 2013.

Stevens, Harold Ray, and J. H. Stape, eds. *Last*   LE
Essays by Joseph Conrad. Cambridge: Cambridge
University Press, 2010.

Unsworth, Barry, and Nels Pearson, eds. *Typhoon*   Pearson
and Other Stories by Joseph Conrad. New York:
Modern Library, 2003.

Watts, Cedric, ed. *The Nigger of the "Narcissus"* by   *WNN*
Joseph Conrad. London: Penguin Books, 1987.

Watts, Cedric, ed. *Typhoon and Other Stories* by   Watts
Joseph Conrad. Oxford: Oxford University Press,
2002.

Note on the Texts

Throughout this edition, I have used the first English book edition as my copy text for the stories and the first American edition for my copy text for the "Author's Note" for *The Shadow-Line*, *Typhoon*, and *The Secret Sharer*. For "To My Readers in America," the foreword to Nelson Doubleday's 1914 American reprint of *The Nigger of the "Narcissus,"* I have used the first American edition (1914) as my copy text, and for the copy text for the "Preface" to *The Nigger of the "Narcissus,"* I have used the first English book edition (privately printed in 1902 by J. Hovick). In each case, Conrad oversaw the publication of these editions. The case for the copy text for *The Nigger of the "Narcissus"* is more complex. For the 1979 Norton Critical Edition of *The Nigger of the "Narcissus,"* Robert Kimbrough used the 1921 Heinemann collected edition as his copy text because Conrad is known to have taken a much larger role in its production than with many other volumes of this collected edition, making a number of substantive changes in the process. Kimbrough's decision is reasonable because there is clear authorial intention in these changes. However, as with the other tales in this collection, I have chosen to use the first English book edition for *The Nigger of the "Narcissus."* Although many of the changes appearing in the 1921 Heinemann edition were made by Conrad, the author was at that point roughly twenty-five years removed from the original writing of the novel and was a different author. Some have seen his later career to have been one of artistic decline, while others have seen it to have been a change in artistic direction, but regardless of the reason Conrad was not the same writer who produced the 1897 *The Nigger of the "Narcissus."* And to reproduce something close to the original novel, I have chosen to go a different direction from Kimbrough. Nevertheless, I have considered the revisions in the 1921 Heinemann edition and have adopted them where it seemed appropriate.

Concerning changes to the copy texts, I have made emendations only where compelling evidence exists for a different reading from another version of a particular work, to correct obvious errors, for consistency, and where meaning was unclear (this latter only in the case of punctuation). As far as consistency is concerned, I have made such aspects as hyphenation, spelling, and capitalization consistent across the four tales included in this volume. For example, *pagoda* appears with greater frequency than does *Pagoda,* so I have used *pagoda* throughout. I have approached similar discrepancies similarly. Where no clear preference appeared, I have tried to determine common contemporary practice. Regarding ellipses, I have standardized Conrad's ellipses as ". . . " rather than the ". . . ." that he often employed.

The Texts of
THE SECRET SHARER
AND OTHER STORIES

Author's Note [to *'Twixt Land and Sea*]†

The only bond between these three stories is, so to speak, geographical, for their scene, be it land, be it sea, is situated in the same region which may be called the region of the Indian Ocean with its offshoots and prolongations north of the equator even as far as the Gulf of Siam.[1] In point of time they belong to the period immediately after the publication of that novel with the awkward title *Under Western Eyes* [1911] and, as far as the life of the writer is concerned, their appearance in a volume marks a definite change in the fortunes of his fiction. For there is no denying the fact that *Under Western Eyes* found no favour in the public eye, whereas the novel called *Chance* [1914] which followed *'Twixt Land and Sea* was received on its first appearance by many more readers than any other of my books.[2]

This volume of three tales was also well received, publicly and privately and from a publisher's point of view. This little success was a most timely tonic for my enfeebled bodily frame. For this may indeed be called the book of a man's convalescence, at least as to three-fourths of it; because "The Secret Sharer," the middle story, was written much earlier than the other two.[3]

For in truth the memories of *Under Western Eyes* are associated with the memory of a severe illness which seemed to wait like a tiger in the jungle on the turn of a path to jump on me the moment the last words of that novel were written. The memory of an illness is very much like the memory of a nightmare.[4] On emerging from it in a much enfeebled state I was inspired to direct my tottering steps

---

† Written in 1920 for the Doubleday, Page & Co. collected edition, *The Works of Joseph Conrad*. *'Twixt Land and Sea*, originally published in late 1912, included "The Secret Sharer" (1910), "A Smile of Fortune" (1911), and "Freya of the Seven Isles" (1912).
1. Now the Gulf of Thailand, an inlet of the South China Sea bordered by Thailand (formerly Siam), Cambodia, and Vietnam. See p. 335.
2. *Chance* was Conrad's first popular success, nearly twenty years after his first book, *Almayer's Folly* (1895), was published and thereafter cemented his popular success. In America especially, Conrad became so popular that Franklin P. Adams (1881–1960) coined the term *Conradicals* for his ardent followers, and it was literally front-page news when Conrad first visited America in May 1923, where he was greeted by throngs of reporters at the docks of New York City.
3. Written in November and December 1909, while Conrad was still at work on *Under Western Eyes*.
4. Conrad is not exaggerating. He experienced emotional exhaustion after completing many of his major works, but he suffered a complete breakdown following *Under Western Eyes*. In a letter to David Meldrum dated February 6, 1910, Conrad's wife, Jesse (1873–1936), wrote: "The novel is finished, but the penalty [*sic*] has to be paid. Months of nervous strain have ended in a complete nervous breakdown. Poor Conrad is very ill and Dr. [Clifford] Hackney [1874–1956] says it will be a long time before he is fit for anything requiring mental exertion. . . . There is the M.S. complete but uncorrected and his fierce refusal to let even I touch it. It lays on a table at the foot of his bed and he lives mixed up in the scenes and holds converse with the characters" (*Letters to William Blackwood and David S. Meldrum*, ed. William Blackburn [Duke University Press, 1958], 192).

toward the Indian Ocean, a complete change of surroundings and atmosphere from the Lake of Geneva, as nobody would deny. * * * Who will dare say after this that the change of air had not been an immense success?

The origins of the middle story, "The Secret Sharer," are quite other [than that of "A Smile of Fortune"]. It was written much earlier and was published first in *Harper's Magazine*, during the early part, I think, of 1911. Or perhaps the latter part? My memory on that point is hazy.[5] The basic fact of the tale I had in my possession for a good many years. It was in truth the common possession of the whole fleet of merchant ships trading to India, China, and Australia: a great company the last years of which coincided with my first years on the wider seas. The fact itself happened on board a very distinguished member of it, *Cutty Sark*[6] by name and belonging to Mr. Willis, a notable ship-owner in his day, one of the kind (they are all underground now) who used personally to see his ships start on their voyages to those distant shores where they showed worthily the honoured house-flag of their owner. I am glad I was not too late to get at least one glimpse of Mr. Willis on a very wet and gloomy morning watching from the pier head of the New South Dock[7] one of his clippers starting on a China voyage—an imposing figure of a man under the invariable white hat so well known in the Port of London, waiting till the head of his ship had swung down-stream before giving her a dignified wave of a big gloved hand. For all I know it may have been the *Cutty Sark* herself though certainly not on that fatal voyage. I do not know the date of the occurrence[8] on which the scheme of "The Secret Sharer" is founded; it came to light and even got into newspapers about the middle eighties, though I had heard of it before, as it were privately, among the officers of the great wool fleet in which my first years in deep water were served. It came to light under circumstances dramatic enough, I think, but which have nothing to do with my story. In the more specially maritime part of my writings this bit of presentation may take its place as one of my two Calm-pieces. For, if there is to be any classification by subjects, I have done two Storm-pieces in *The Nigger of the "Narcissus"* and in "Typhoon"; and two Calm-pieces: this one and *The Shadow Line*, a book which belongs to a later period.

5. The story, illustrated by W. J. Aylward (1875–1956), actually appeared in the August and September 1910 issues of *Harper's Magazine*, a prominent magazine established in 1850 and still being published.
6. Built for John Willis (1817–1899) in 1869, it served a variety of nautical purposes until 1954 and is now part of the National Maritime Museum in Greenwich, London. "The fact itself": the story is loosely based on an actual event; see Sankey, pp. 421–31.
7. The East India South Dock on the River Thames, first opened in 1829.
8. The wool trade of 1883 to 1894, when clipper ships were heavily employed bringing wool from Australia to England. "Date of the occurrence": the August 4, 1882, issue of *The Times* (London) lists the date as August 9 or 10, 1880 (p. 4); see p. 433.

Notwithstanding their autobiographical form the above two stories are not the record of personal experience. Their quality, such as it is, depends on something larger if less precise: on the character, vision and sentiment of the first twenty independent years of my life. * * *

But I am glad to think that the two women in this book: Alice ["A Smile of Fortune"], the sullen, passive victim of her fate, and the actively individual Freya ["Freya of the Seven Isles"], so determined to be the mistress of her own destiny, must have evoked some sympathies because of all my volumes of short stories this was the one for which there was the greatest immediate demand.

1920.

J. C.

What does the ship represent?

What does Leggatt represent?

the ocean?

the wind?

the big, dark island?

The Secret Sharer
An Episode from the Coast

I

On my right hand there were lines of fishing-stakes resembling a mysterious system of half-submerged bamboo fences, incomprehensible in its division of the domain of tropical fishes, and crazy of aspect as if abandoned forever by some nomad tribe of fishermen now gone to the other end of the ocean; for there was no sign of human habitation as far as the eye could reach. To the left a group of barren islets, suggesting ruins of stone walls, towers, and blockhouses, had its foundations set in a blue sea that itself looked solid, so still and stable did it lie below my feet; even the track of light from the westering sun shone smoothly, without that animated glitter which tells of an imperceptible ripple. And when I turned my head to take a parting glance at the tug which had just left us anchored outside the bar,[1] I saw the straight line of the flat shore joined to the stable sea, edge to edge, with a perfect and unmarked closeness, in one levelled floor half brown, half blue under the enormous dome of the sky. Corresponding in their insignificance to the islets of the sea, two small clumps of trees, one on each side of the only fault in the impeccable joint, marked the mouth of the river Meinam we had just left on the first preparatory stage of our homeward journey; and, far back on the inland level, a larger and loftier mass, the grove surrounding the great Paknam pagoda,[2] was the only thing on which the eye could rest from the vain task of exploring the monotonous sweep of the horizon. Here and there gleams as of a few scattered pieces of silver marked the windings of the great river; and on the nearest of them, just within the bar, the tug steaming right into the land became lost to my sight, hull and funnel and masts, as though the impassive

1. The sand bar at mouth of the Meinam (or Menam) River (now Chao Phraya River).
2. A pagoda is a pyramid-shaped Buddhist temple. The River Meinam (or Menam; now Chao Phraya River) is a major river in western Thailand that flows from north to south and through Bangkok, emptying into the Gulf of Thailand. The Paknam pagoda (Prah Samut Chedi or Phra Chedi Klang Nam), located several miles upriver, in the Samut Prakam province, was in built in 1827–28 on an island, which, because of silt accumulation, has now become a peninsula. See p. 489.

7

earth had swallowed her up without an effort, without a tremor. My eye followed the light cloud of her smoke, now here, now there, above the plain, according to the devious curves of the stream, but always fainter and farther away, till I lost it at last behind the mitre-shaped hill of the great pagoda.[3] And then I was left alone with my ship, anchored at the head of the Gulf of Siam.

She floated at the starting-point of a long journey, very still in an immense stillness, the shadows of her spars flung far to the eastward by the setting sun. At that moment I was alone on her decks. There was not a sound in her—and around us nothing moved, nothing lived, not a canoe on the water, not a bird in the air, not a cloud in the sky. In this breathless pause at the threshold of a long passage we seemed to be measuring our fitness for a long and arduous enterprise, the appointed task of both our existences to be carried out, far from all human eyes, with only sky and sea for spectators and for judges.

There must have been some glare in the air to interfere with one's sight, because it was only just before the sun left us that my roaming eyes made out beyond the highest ridge of the principal islet of the group something which did away with the solemnity of perfect solitude. The tide of darkness flowed on swiftly; and with tropical suddenness[4] a swarm of stars came out above the shadowy earth, while I lingered yet, my hand resting lightly on my ship's rail as if on the shoulder of a trusted friend. But, with all that multitude of celestial bodies staring down at one, the comfort of quiet communion with her was gone for good. And there were also disturbing sounds by this time—voices, footsteps forward; the steward flitted along the main deck, a busily ministering spirit; a hand-bell tinkled urgently under the poop-deck. . . .

I found my two officers waiting for me near the supper table, in the lighted cuddy. We sat down at once, and as I helped the chief mate, I said:

"Are you aware that there is a ship anchored inside the islands? I saw her mastheads above the ridge as the sun went down."

He raised sharply his simple face, overcharged by a terrible growth of whisker, and emitted his usual ejaculations: "Bless my soul, sir! You don't say so!"

My second mate was a round-cheeked, silent young man, grave beyond his years, I thought; but as our eyes happened to meet I detected a slight quiver on his lips. I looked down at once. It was not

---

3. According to Stape and Simmons (*NNOS*), Conrad appears to be conflating two separate pagodas: the Prah Samut Chedi and the Golden Mount pagoda (Wat Saket); see also Larabee, pp. 484–89, on the confusion surrounding this pagoda. "Mitre": a tall, cleft headdress worn by a bishop.
4. Closer to the equator, twilight is shorter because the sun's descent is more vertical than elsewhere.

my part to encourage sneering on board my ship. It must be said, too, that I knew very little of my officers. In consequence of certain events of no particular significance, except to myself, I had been appointed to the command only a fortnight before. Neither did I know much of the hands forward.[5] All these people had been together for eighteen months or so, and my position was that of the only stranger on board.[6] I mention this because it has some bearing on what is to follow. But what I felt most was my being a stranger to the ship; and if all the truth must be told, I was somewhat of a stranger to myself. The youngest man on board (barring the second mate), and untried as yet by a position of the fullest responsibility, I was willing to take the adequacy of the others for granted. They had simply to be equal to their tasks; but I wondered how far I should turn out faithful to that ideal conception of one's own personality every man sets up for himself secretly. *how good am I, really.*

Meantime the chief mate, with an almost visible effect of collaboration on the part of his round eyes and frightful whiskers, was trying to evolve a theory of the anchored ship. His dominant trait was to take all things into earnest consideration. He was of a painstaking turn of mind. As he used to say, he "liked to account to himself" for practically everything that came in his way, down to a miserable scorpion he had found in his cabin a week before. The why and the wherefore of that scorpion—how it got on board and came to select his room rather than the pantry (which was a dark place and more what a scorpion would be partial to), and how on earth it managed to drown itself in the inkwell of his writing-desk—had exercised him infinitely. The ship within the islands was much more easily accounted for; and just as we were about to rise from table he made his pronouncement. She was, he doubted not, a ship from home lately arrived. Probably she drew too much water to cross the bar except at the top of spring tides. Therefore she went into that natural harbour to wait for a few days in preference to remaining in an open roadstead.

"That's so," confirmed the second mate, suddenly, in his slightly hoarse voice. "She draws over twenty feet. She's the Liverpool[7] ship *Sephora* with a cargo of coal. Hundred and twenty-three days from Cardiff."[8]

an outsider to others and himself. / Needs a reason for everything, will be logical, but will follow some kind of order

5. The crew (hands) have their quarters in the forward part of the ship, in contrast to the officers.
6. The captain's appointment bears some similarity to Conrad's appointment as captain of the *Otago* in 1888.
7. A prominent port city on the west coast of the United Kingdom, on the River Mersey and Liverpool Bay; see p. 336.
8. Another major port and the capital of Wales, located in southeast Wales on the Bristol Channel, which separates south Wales from Devon and Somerset in southwest England.

We looked at him in surprise.

"The tugboat skipper told me when he came on board for your letters, sir," explained the young man. "He expects to take her up the river the day after to-morrow."

After thus overwhelming us with the extent of his information he slipped out of the cabin. The mate observed regretfully that he "could not account for that young fellow's whims." What prevented him telling us all about it at once, he wanted to know.

I detained him as he was making a move. For the last two days the crew had had plenty of hard work, and the night before they had very little sleep. I felt painfully that I—a stranger—was doing something unusual when I directed him to let all hands turn in without setting an anchor-watch. I proposed to keep on deck myself till one o'clock or thereabouts. I would get the second mate to relieve me at that hour.

"He will turn out the cook and the steward at four," I concluded, "and then give you a call. Of course at the slightest sign of any sort of wind we'll have the hands up and make a start at once."

He concealed his astonishment. "Very well, sir." Outside the cuddy he put his head in the second mate's door to inform him of my unheard-of caprice to take a five hours' anchor-watch on myself. I heard the other raise his voice incredulously— "What? The captain himself?" Then a few more murmurs, a door closed, then another. A few moments later I went on deck.

My strangeness, which had made me sleepless, had prompted that unconventional arrangement, as if I had expected in those solitary hours of the night to get on terms with the ship of which I knew nothing, manned by men of whom I knew very little more. Fast alongside a wharf, littered like any ship in port with a tangle of unrelated things, invaded by unrelated shore people, I had hardly seen her yet properly. Now, as she lay cleared for sea, the stretch of her main deck seemed to me very fine under the stars. Very fine, very roomy for her size, and very inviting. I descended the poop and paced the waist, my mind picturing to myself the coming passage through the Malay Archipelago,[9] down the Indian Ocean, and up the Atlantic. All its phases were familiar enough to me, every characteristic, all the alternatives which were likely to face me on the high seas—everything! . . . except the novel responsibility of command. But I took heart from the reasonable thought that the ship was like other ships, the men like other men, and that the sea was not likely to keep any special surprises expressly for my discomfiture.[1]

9. The extensive archipelago of islands lying between mainland Southeast Asia and Australia. See p. 335.
1. Traditionally meaning utter disappointment, confusion, and perplexity, but here probably less strongly meaning merely discomfort or unease.

land /civilization = storm /chaos

still seas = easy life

Arrived at that comforting conclusion, I bethought myself of a cigar and went below to get it. All was still down there. Everybody at the after-end of the ship was sleeping profoundly. I came out again on the quarter-deck, agreeably at ease in my sleeping-suit[2] on that warm breathless night, barefooted, a glowing cigar in my teeth, and, going forward, I was met by the profound silence of the fore-end of the ship. Only as I passed the door of the forecastle I heard a deep, quiet, trustful sigh of some sleeper inside. And suddenly I rejoiced in the great security of the sea as compared with the unrest of the land, in my choice of that untempted life presenting no disquieting problems, invested with an elementary moral beauty by the absolute straightforwardness of its appeal and by the singleness of its purpose.

peace disturbed by worrying — about how he is perceived — even in his good intentions

The riding-light in the fore-rigging burned with a clear, untroubled, as if symbolic, flame, confident and bright in the mysterious shades of the night. Passing on my way aft along the other side of the ship, I observed that the rope side-ladder, put over, no doubt, for the master of the tug when he came to fetch away our letters, had not been hauled in as it should have been. I became annoyed at this, for exactitude in small matters is the very soul of discipline. Then I reflected that I had myself peremptorily dismissed my officers from duty, and by my own act had prevented the anchor-watch being formally set and things properly attended to. I asked myself whether it was wise ever to interfere with the established routine of duties even from the kindest of motives. My action might have made me appear eccentric. Goodness only knew how that absurdly whiskered mate would "account" for my conduct, and what the whole ship thought of that informality of their new captain. I was vexed with myself.

Not from compunction certainly, but, as it were mechanically, I proceeded to get the ladder in myself. Now a side-ladder of that sort is a light affair and comes in easily, yet my vigorous tug, which should have brought it flying on board, merely recoiled upon my body in a totally unexpected jerk. What the devil! . . . I was so astounded by the immovableness of that ladder that I remained stock-still, trying to account for it to myself like that imbecile mate of mine. In the end, of course, I put my head over the rail.

The side of the ship made an opaque belt of shadow on the darkling glassy shimmer of the sea. But I saw at once something elongated and pale floating very close to the ladder. Before I could form a guess a faint flash of phosphorescent light, which seemed to issue suddenly

---

2. A two-piece sleeping outfit rather than the more usual one-piece nightgown worn in the 19th century.

from the naked body of a man, flickered in the sleeping water with
the elusive, silent play of summer lightning[3] in a night sky. With a
gasp I saw revealed to my stare a pair of feet, the long legs, a broad
livid[4] back immersed right up to the neck in a greenish cadaverous
glow. One hand, awash, clutched the bottom rung of the ladder. He
was complete but for the head. A headless corpse! The cigar dropped
out of my gaping mouth with a tiny plop and a short hiss quite audible in the absolute stillness of all things under heaven. At that I suppose he raised up his face, a dimly pale oval in the shadow of the
ship's side. But even then I could only barely make out down there
the shape of his black-haired head. However, it was enough for
the horrid, frost-bound sensation which had gripped me about the
chest to pass off. The moment of vain exclamations was past, too. I
only climbed on the spare spar and leaned over the rail as far as I
could, to bring my eyes nearer to that mystery floating alongside.

As he hung by the ladder, like a resting swimmer, the sea-lightning
played about his limbs at every stir; and he appeared in it ghastly,
silvery, fish-like. He remained as mute as a fish, too. He made no
motion to get out of the water, either. It was inconceivable that he
should not attempt to come on board, and strangely troubling to suspect that perhaps he did not want to. And my first words were
prompted by just that troubled incertitude.

"What's the matter?" I asked in my ordinary tone, speaking down
to the face upturned exactly under mine.

"Cramp," it answered, no louder. Then slightly anxious, "I say, no
need to call any one."

"I was not going to," I said.

"Are you alone on deck?"

"Yes."

I had somehow the impression that he was on the point of letting
go the ladder to swim away beyond my ken[5]—mysterious as he came.
But, for the moment, this being appearing as if he had risen from
the bottom of the sea (it was certainly the nearest land to the
ship) wanted only to know the time. I told him. And he, down
there, tentatively:

"I suppose your captain's turned in?"

"I am sure he isn't," I said.

He seemed to struggle with himself, for I heard something like
the low, bitter murmur of doubt. "What's the good?" His next words
came out with a hesitating effort.

3. Or sheet lightning, which appears sheet-like through cloud reflection, often occurring
   in hot weather (or during equatorial storms) and often without audible thunder.
4. Pale.
5. Vision or range of sight.

"Look here, my man. Could you call him out quietly?"

I thought the time had come to declare myself.

"*I* am the captain."

I heard a "By Jove!"[6] whispered at the level of the water. The phosphorescence flashed in the swirl of the water all about his limbs, his other hand seized the ladder.

"My name's Leggatt."[7]

The voice was calm and resolute. A good voice. The self-possession of that man had somehow induced a corresponding state in myself. It was very quietly that I remarked:

"You must be a good swimmer."

"Yes. I've been in the water practically since nine o'clock. The question for me now is whether I am to let go this ladder and go on swimming till I sink from exhaustion, or—to come on board here."

I felt this was no mere formula of desperate speech, but a real alternative in the view of a strong soul. I should have gathered from this that he was young; indeed, it is only the young who are ever confronted by such clear issues. But at the time it was pure intuition on my part. A mysterious communication was established already between us two—in the face of that silent, darkened tropical sea. I was young, too; young enough to make no comment. The man in the water began suddenly to climb up the ladder, and I hastened away from the rail to fetch some clothes.

Before entering the cabin I stood still, listening in the lobby at the foot of the stairs. A faint snore came through the closed door of the chief mate's room. The second mate's door was on the hook, but the darkness in there was absolutely soundless. He, too, was young and could sleep like a stone. Remained the steward, but he was not likely to wake up before he was called. I got a sleeping-suit out of my room and, coming back on deck, saw the naked man from the sea sitting on the main-hatch, glimmering white in the darkness, his elbows on his knees and his head in his hands. In a moment he had concealed his damp body in a sleeping-suit of the same grey-stripe pattern as the one I was wearing and followed me like my double on the poop. Together we moved right aft, barefooted, silent.

"What is it?" I asked in a deadened voice, taking the lighted lamp out of the binnacle, and raising it to his face.

"An ugly business."

He had rather regular features; a good mouth; light eyes under somewhat heavy, dark eyebrows; a smooth, square forehead; no growth on his cheeks; a small, brown moustache, and a well-shaped,

6. Another name for Jupiter, chief god of the Romans (Zeus in Greek mythology).
7. Loosely based on Sidney Smith (c. 1850–1922), chief mate of the *Cutty Sark* in 1880; see Sankey, pp. 421–26.

round chin. His expression was concentrated, meditative, under the inspecting light of the lamp I held up to his face; such as a man thinking hard in solitude might wear. My sleeping-suit was just right for his size. A well-knit young fellow of twenty-five at most. He caught his lower lip with the edge of white, even teeth.

"Yes," I said, replacing the lamp in the binnacle. The warm, heavy tropical night closed upon his head again.

"There's a ship over there," he murmured.

"Yes, I know. The *Sephora*. Did you know of us?"

"Hadn't the slightest idea. I am the mate of her—" He paused and corrected himself. "I should say I *was*."

"Aha! Something wrong?"

"Yes. Very wrong indeed. I've killed a man."

"What do you mean? Just now?"

"No, on the passage. Weeks ago. Thirty-nine south.[8] When I say a man—"

"Fit of temper," I suggested, confidently.

The shadowy, dark head, like mine, seemed to nod imperceptibly above the ghostly grey of my sleeping-suit. It was, in the night, as though I had been faced by my own reflection in the depths of a sombre and immense mirror.

"A pretty thing to have to own up to for a *Conway*[9] boy," murmured my double, distinctly.

"You're a *Conway* boy?"

"I am," he said, as if startled. Then, slowly . . . "Perhaps you too—"

It was so; but being a couple of years older I had left before he joined. After a quick interchange of dates a silence fell; and I thought suddenly of my absurd mate with his terrific whiskers and the "Bless my soul—you don't say so" type of intellect. My double gave me an inkling of his thoughts by saying:

"My father's a parson in Norfolk.[1] Do you see me before a judge and jury on that charge? For myself I can't see the necessity. There are fellows that an angel from heaven— And I am not that. He was one of those creatures that are just simmering all the time with a silly sort of wickedness.[2] Miserable devils that have no business to live at all. He wouldn't do his duty and wouldn't let anybody else do theirs. But what's the good of talking! You know well enough the sort of ill-conditioned snarling cur—"

8. Probably below the Cape of Good Hope, a cape near the southernmost part of the African continent; see p. 173, n. 4 and p. 336.
9. In 1859 established as a training vessel on the River Mersey near Liverpool.
1. A coastal county in eastern England.
2. Leggatt's victim is based on John Francis (d. 1880), whom Smith killed during the *Cutty Sark*'s voyage to the Far East in 1880. Unlike in "The Secret Sharer," the incident occurred during fair weather; see Sankey, p. 426.

He appealed to me as if our experiences had been as identical as our clothes. And I knew well enough the pestiferous danger of such a character where there are no means of legal repression. And I knew well enough also that my double there was no homicidal ruffian. I did not think of asking him for details, and he told me the story roughly in brusque, disconnected sentences. I needed no more. I saw it all going on as though I were myself inside that other sleeping-suit.

"It happened while we were setting a reefed foresail, at dusk. Reefed foresail! You understand the sort of weather. The only sail we had left to keep the ship running; so you may guess what it had been like for days. Anxious sort of job, that. He gave me some of his cursed insolence at the sheet. I tell you I was overdone with this terrific weather that seemed to have no end to it. Terrific, I tell you—and a deep ship. I believe the fellow himself was half crazed with funk.[3] It was no time for gentlemanly reproof, so I turned round and felled him like an ox. He up and at me. We closed just as an awful sea made for the ship. All hands saw it coming and took to the rigging, but I had him by the throat,[4] and went on shaking him like a rat, the men above us yelling, 'Look out! look out!' Then a crash as if the sky had fallen on my head. They say that for over ten minutes hardly anything was to be seen of the ship—just the three masts and a bit of the forecastle-head and of the poop all awash driving along in a smother of foam. It was a miracle that they found us, jammed together behind the forebits. It's clear that I meant business, because I was holding him by the throat still when they picked us up. He was black in the face. It was too much for them. It seems they rushed us aft together, gripped as we were, screaming 'Murder!' like a lot of lunatics, and broke into the cuddy. And the ship running for her life, touch and go all the time, any minute her last in a sea fit to turn your hair grey only a-looking at it. I understand that the skipper, too, started raving like the rest of them. The man had been deprived of sleep for more than a week, and to have this sprung on him at the height of a furious gale nearly drove him out of his mind. I wonder they didn't fling me overboard after getting the carcass of their precious ship-mate out of my fingers. They had rather a job to separate us, I've been told. A sufficiently fierce story to make an old judge and a respectable jury sit up a bit. The first thing I heard when I came to myself was the maddening howling of that endless gale, and on that[5] the voice of the old man. He was hanging on to my bunk, staring into my face out of his sou'wester.[6]

3. Cowering fear, panic, or shrinking terror.
4. In the *Cutty Sark* incident, Smith struck Francis over the head with a capstan bar; see Sankey, p. 426.
5. I.e., on top of that, over that.
6. A large, waterproof hat.

'Mr. Leggatt, you have killed a man. You can act no longer as chief mate of this ship.' "

His care to subdue his voice made it sound monotonous. He rested a hand on the end of the skylight to steady himself with, and all that time did not stir a limb, so far as I could see. "Nice little tale for a quiet tea-party," he concluded in the same tone.

One of my hands, too, rested on the end of the skylight; neither did I stir a limb, so far as I knew. We stood less than a foot from each other. It occurred to me that if old "Bless my soul—you don't say so" were to put his head up the companion and catch sight of us, he would think he was seeing double, or imagine himself come upon a scene of weird witchcraft; the strange captain having a quiet confabulation by the wheel with his own grey ghost. I became very much concerned to prevent anything of the sort. I heard the other's soothing undertone.

"My father's a parson in Norfolk," it said. Evidently he had forgotten he had told me this important fact before. Truly a nice little tale.

"You had better slip down into my stateroom now," I said, moving off stealthily. My double followed my movements; our bare feet made no sound; I let him in, closed the door with care, and, after giving a call to the second mate, returned on deck for my relief.[7]

"Not much sign of any wind yet," I remarked when he approached.

"No, sir. Not much," he assented, sleepily, in his hoarse voice, with just enough deference, no more, and barely suppressing a yawn.

"Well, that's all you have to look out for. You have got your orders."

"Yes, sir."

I paced a turn or two on the poop and saw him take up his position face forward with his elbow in the ratlines of the mizzen-rigging before I went below. The mate's faint snoring was still going on peacefully. The cuddy lamp was burning over the table on which stood a vase with flowers, a polite attention from the ship's provision merchant—the last flowers we should see for the next three months at the very least. Two bunches of bananas hung from the beam symmetrically, one on each side of the rudder-casing. Everything was as before in the ship—except that two of her captain's sleeping-suits were simultaneously in use, one motionless in the cuddy, the other keeping very still in the captain's stateroom.

It must be explained here that my cabin had the form of the capital letter L, the door being within the angle and opening into the short part of the letter. A couch was to the left, the bed-place to the right; my writing-desk and the chronometers' table faced the door. But any one

7. To relieve the captain from his time on watch.

opening it, unless he stepped right inside, had no view of what I call the long (or vertical) part of the letter. It contained some lockers surmounted by a bookcase; and a few clothes, a thick jacket or two, caps, oilskin[8] coat, and such like, hung on hooks. There was at the bottom of that part a door opening into my bath-room, which could be entered also directly from the saloon. But that way was never used.

The mysterious arrival had discovered the advantage of this particular shape. Entering my room, lighted strongly by a big bulkhead lamp swung on gimbals above my writing-desk, I did not see him anywhere till he stepped out quietly from behind the coats hung in the recessed part.

"I heard somebody moving about, and went in there at once," he whispered.

I, too, spoke under my breath.

"Nobody is likely to come in here without knocking and getting permission."

He nodded. His face was thin and the sunburn faded, as though he had been ill. And no wonder. He had been, I heard presently, kept under arrest in his cabin for nearly seven weeks. But there was nothing sickly in his eyes or in his expression. He was not a bit like me, really; yet, as we stood leaning over my bed-place, whispering side by side, with our dark heads together and our backs to the door, anybody bold enough to open it stealthily would have been treated to the uncanny sight of a double captain busy talking in whispers with his other self.

"But all this doesn't tell me how you came to hang on to our side-ladder," I inquired, in the hardly audible murmurs we used, after he had told me something more of the proceedings on board the *Sephora* once the bad weather was over.

"When we sighted Java Head[9] I had had time to think all those matters out several times over. I had six weeks of doing nothing else, and with only an hour or so every evening for a tramp on the quarter-deck."

He whispered, his arms folded on the side of my bed-place, staring through the open port. And I could imagine perfectly the manner of this thinking out—a stubborn if not a steadfast operation; something of which I should have been perfectly incapable.

"I reckoned it would be dark before we closed with the land," he continued, so low that I had to strain my hearing, near as we were to each other, shoulder touching shoulder almost. "So I asked to

---

8. Cloth made waterproof with oil.
9. The northwest corner of Java, an island in the Malay Archipelago and part of present-day southern Indonesia. See p. 336.

speak to the old man. He always seemed very sick when he came to
see me—as if he could not look me in the face. You know, that foresail saved the ship. She was too deep to have run long under bare
poles. And it was I that managed to set it for him. Anyway, he came.
When I had him in my cabin—he stood by the door looking at me
as if I had the halter[1] round my neck already— I asked him right
away to leave my cabin door unlocked at night while the ship was
going through Sunda Straits.[2] There would be the Java coast within
two or three miles, off Angier Point.[3] I wanted nothing more. I've
had a prize for swimming my second year in the *Conway*."

"I can believe it," I breathed out.

"God only knows why they locked me in every night. To see some
of their faces you'd have thought they were afraid I'd go about at
night strangling people. Am I a murdering brute? Do I look it? By
Jove! if I had been he wouldn't have trusted himself like that into my
room. You'll say I might have chucked him aside and bolted out,
there and then—it was dark already. Well, no. And for the same reason I wouldn't think of trying to smash the door. There would have
been a rush to stop me at the noise, and I did not mean to get into
a confounded scrimmage. Somebody else might have got killed—for
I would not have broken out only to get chucked back, and I did not
want any more of that work. He refused,[4] looking more sick than ever.
He was afraid of the men, and also of that old second mate of his who
had been sailing with him for years—a grey-headed old humbug; and
his steward, too, had been with him devil knows how long—seventeen
years or more—a dogmatic sort of loafer who hated me like poison,
just because I was the chief mate. No chief mate ever made more
than one voyage in the *Sephora*, you know. Those two old chaps ran
the ship. Devil only knows what the skipper wasn't afraid of (all his
nerve went to pieces altogether in that hellish spell of bad weather
we had)—of what the law would do to him—of his wife, perhaps.
Oh, yes! she's on board. Though I don't think she would have med-
dled. She would have been only too glad to have me out of the
ship in any way. The 'brand of Cain'[5] business, don't you see.

1. A noose for hanging.
2. Between the islands of Sumatra and Java in the Malay Archipelago and connecting the
   Indian Ocean to the Java Sea. See p. 336.
3. Also Anjer Point, the westernmost point of Java.
4. In the actual incident, Captain James Wallace (d. 1880) allowed Smith to escape; consequently, the crew refused to work, and in the end Wallace committed suicide by
   jumping overboard; see Sankey, pp. 427–29.
5. Reference to the story of Cain's slaying his brother Abel; see Genesis 4:14–15: "Behold,
   thou hast driven me out this day from the face of the earth; and from thy face shall I be
   hid; and I shall be a fugitive and a vagabond in the earth; and it shall come to pass, that
   every one that findeth me shall slay me. And the Lord said unto him, Therefore whosoever slayeth Cain, vengeance shall be taken on him sevenfold. And the Lord set a mark
   upon Cain, lest any finding him should kill him."

That's all right. I was ready enough to go off wandering on the face of the earth—and that was price enough to pay for an Abel of that sort. Anyhow, he wouldn't listen to me. 'This thing must take its course. I represent the law here.' He was shaking like a leaf. 'So you won't?' 'No!' 'Then I hope you will be able to sleep on that,' I said, and turned my back on him. 'I wonder that *you* can,' cries he, and locks the door.

"Well, after that, I couldn't. Not very well. That was three weeks ago. We have had a slow passage through the Java Sea; drifted about Carimata[6] for ten days. When we anchored here they thought, I suppose, it was all right. The nearest land (and that's five miles) is the ship's destination; the Consul[7] would soon set about catching me; and there would have been no object in bolting to these islets there. I don't suppose there's a drop of water on them. I don't know how it was, but to-night that steward, after bringing me my supper, went out to let me eat it, and left the door unlocked. And I ate it—all there was, too. After I had finished I strolled out on the quarter-deck. I don't know that I meant to do anything. A breath of fresh air was all I wanted, I believe. Then a sudden temptation came over me. I kicked off my slippers and was in the water before I had made up my mind fairly. Somebody heard the splash and they raised an awful hullabaloo. 'He's gone! Lower the boats! He's committed suicide! No, he's swimming.' Certainly I was swimming. It's not so easy for a swimmer like me to commit suicide by drowning. I landed on the nearest islet before the boat left the ship's side. I heard them pulling about in the dark, hailing, and so on, but after a bit they gave up. Everything quieted down and the anchorage became as still as death. I sat down on a stone and began to think. I felt certain they would start searching for me at daylight. There was no place to hide on those stony things—and if there had been, what would have been the good? But now I was clear of that ship, I was not going back. So after a while I took off all my clothes, tied them up in a bundle with a stone inside, and dropped them in the deep water on the outer side of that islet. That was suicide enough for me. Let them think what they liked, but I didn't mean to drown myself. I meant to swim till I sank—but that's not the same thing. I struck out for another of these little islands, and it was from that one that I first saw your riding-light. Something to swim for. I went on easily, and on the way I came upon a flat rock a foot or two above water. In the daytime, I dare say, you might make

6. Or Karimata, an island in the Malay Archipelago forty miles off the west coast of Borneo. The Java Sea is a shallow sea in the Malay Archipelago bordered by the islands of Borneo on the north, Java on the south, Sumatra on the west, and Sulawesi on the east.
7. Short for Consul-General, an official residing in a foreign port to protect the home country's commercial interests, settle disputes, and assist in the various issues concerning the commerce between the two countries.

it out with a glass[8] from your poop. I scrambled up on it and rested myself for a bit. Then I made another start. That last spell must have been over a mile."

His whisper was getting fainter and fainter, and all the time he stared straight out through the port-hole, in which there was not even a star to be seen. I had not interrupted him. There was something that made comment impossible in his narrative, or perhaps in himself; a sort of feeling, a quality, which I can't find a name for. And when he ceased, all I found was a futile whisper: "So you swam for our light?"

"Yes—straight for it. It was something to swim for. I couldn't see any stars low down because the coast was in the way, and I couldn't see the land, either. The water was like glass. One might have been swimming in a confounded thousand-feet deep cistern with no place for scrambling out anywhere; but what I didn't like was the notion of swimming round and round like a crazed bullock before I gave out; and as I didn't mean to go back . . . No. Do you see me being hauled back, stark naked, off one of these little islands by the scruff of the neck and fighting like a wild beast? Somebody would have got killed for certain, and I did not want any of that. So I went on. Then your ladder—"

"Why didn't you hail the ship?" I asked, a little louder.

He touched my shoulder lightly. Lazy footsteps came right over our heads and stopped. The second mate had crossed from the other side of the poop and might have been hanging over the rail, for all we knew.

"He couldn't hear us talking—could he?" My double breathed into my very ear, anxiously.

His anxiety was an answer, a sufficient answer, to the question I had put to him. An answer containing all the difficulty of that situation. I closed the port-hole quietly, to make sure. A louder word might have been overheard.

"Who's that?" he whispered then.

"My second mate. But I don't know much more of the fellow than you do."

And I told him a little about myself. I had been appointed to take charge while I least expected anything of the sort, not quite a fortnight ago. I didn't know either the ship or the people. Hadn't had the time in port to look about me or size anybody up. And as to the crew, all they knew was that I was appointed to take the ship home. For the rest, I was almost as much of a stranger on board as himself,

8. A telescope or spyglass.

I said. And at the moment I felt it most acutely. I felt that it would take very little to make me a suspect person in the eyes of the ship's company.

He had turned about meantime; and we, the two strangers in the ship, faced each other in identical attitudes.

"Your ladder—" he murmured, after a silence. "Who'd have thought of finding a ladder hanging over at night in a ship anchored out here! I felt just then a very unpleasant faintness. After the life I've been leading for nine weeks, anybody would have got out of condition. I wasn't capable of swimming round as far as your rudder-chains. And, lo and behold! there was a ladder to get hold of. After I gripped it I said to myself, 'What's the good?' When I saw a man's head looking over I thought I would swim away presently and leave him shouting—in whatever language it was. I didn't mind being looked at. I—I liked it. And then you speaking to me so quietly—as if you had expected me—made me hold on a little longer. It had been a confounded lonely time— I don't mean while swimming. I was glad to talk a little to somebody that didn't belong to the Sephora. As to asking for the captain, that was a mere impulse. It could have been no use, with all the ship knowing about me and the other people pretty certain to be round here in the morning. I don't know— I wanted to be seen, to talk with somebody, before I went on. I don't know what I would have said. . . . 'Fine night, isn't it?' or something of the sort."

"Do you think they will be round here presently?" I asked with some incredulity.

"Quite likely," he said, faintly.

He looked extremely haggard all of a sudden. His head rolled on his shoulders.

"H'm. We shall see then. Meantime get into that bed," I whispered. "Want help? There."

It was a rather high bed-place with a set of drawers underneath. This amazing swimmer really needed the lift I gave him by seizing his leg. He tumbled in, rolled over on his back, and flung one arm across his eyes. And then, with his face nearly hidden, he must have looked exactly as I used to look in that bed. I gazed upon my other self for a while before drawing across carefully the two green serge curtains which ran on a brass rod. I thought for a moment of pinning them together for greater safety, but I sat down on the couch, and once there I felt unwilling to rise and hunt for a pin. I would do it in a moment. I was extremely tired, in a peculiarly intimate way, by the strain of stealthiness, by the effort of whispering and the general secrecy of this excitement. It was three o'clock by now and I had been on my feet since nine, but I was not sleepy; I could not have gone to sleep. I sat there, fagged out,[9] looking at the curtains, trying to clear my mind of the confused sensation of being in two places at once, and greatly bothered by an exasperating knocking in my head. It was a relief to discover suddenly that it was not in my head at all, but on the outside of the door. Before I could collect myself the words "Come in" were out of my mouth, and the steward entered with a tray, bringing in my morning coffee. I had slept, after all, and I was so frightened that I shouted, "This way! I am here, steward," as though he had been miles away. He put down the tray on the table next the couch and only then said, very quietly, "I can see you are here, sir." I felt him give me a keen look, but I dared not meet his eyes just then. He must have wondered why I had drawn the curtains of my bed before going to sleep on the couch. He went out, hooking the door open as usual.

I heard the crew washing decks above me. I knew I would have been told at once if there had been any wind. Calm, I thought, and I was doubly vexed. Indeed, I felt dual more than ever. The steward reappeared suddenly in the doorway. I jumped up from the couch so quickly that he gave a start.

"What do you want here?"

"Close your port, sir—they are washing decks."

"It is closed," I said, reddening.

"Very well, sir." But he did not move from the doorway and returned my stare in an extraordinary, equivocal manner for a time. Then his eyes wavered, all his expression changed, and in a voice unusually gentle, almost coaxingly:

"May I come in to take the empty cup away, sir?"

"Of course!" I turned my back on him while he popped in and out. Then I unhooked and closed the door and even pushed the bolt. This sort of thing could not go on very long. The cabin was as hot as an oven, too. I took a peep at my double, and discovered that he had not moved, his arm was still over his eyes; but his chest heaved; his hair was wet; his chin glistened with perspiration. I reached over him and opened the port.

"I must show myself on deck," I reflected.

Of course, theoretically, I could do what I liked, with no one to say nay to me within the whole circle of the horizon; but to lock my cabin door and take the key away I did not dare. Directly I put my head out of the companion I saw the group of my two officers, the second mate barefooted, the chief mate in long india-rubber[1] boots, near the break of the poop, and the steward half-way down the poop ladder talking to them eagerly. He happened to catch sight of me and dived,

9. Fatigued or exhausted (slang).
1. Natural rubber or caoutchouc, obtained from the latex of certain trees or plants.

the second ran down on the main deck shouting some order or other, and the chief mate came to meet me, touching his cap.

There was a sort of curiosity in his eye that I did not like. I don't know whether the steward had told them that I was "queer" only, or downright drunk, but I know the man meant to have a good look at me. I watched him coming with a smile which, as he got into point-blank range, took effect and froze his very whiskers. I did not give him time to open his lips.

"Square the yards by lifts and braces before the hands go to breakfast."

It was the first particular order I had given on board that ship; and I stayed on deck to see it executed, too. I had felt the need of asserting myself without loss of time. That sneering young cub[2] got taken down a peg or two on that occasion, and I also seized the opportunity of having a good look at the face of every foremast man as they filed past me to go to the after-braces. At breakfast time, eating nothing myself, I presided with such frigid dignity that the two mates were only too glad to escape from the cabin as soon as decency permitted; and all the time the dual working of my mind distracted me almost to the point of insanity. I was constantly watching myself, my secret self, as dependent on my actions as my own personality, sleeping in that bed, behind that door which faced me as I sat at the head of the table. It was very much like being mad, only it was worse because one was aware of it.

I had to shake him for a solid minute, but when at last he opened his eyes it was in the full possession of his senses, with an inquiring look.

"All's well so far," I whispered. "Now you must vanish into the bath-room."

He did so, as noiseless as a ghost, and I then rang for the steward, and facing him boldly, directed him to tidy up my stateroom while I was having my bath—"and be quick about it." As my tone admitted of no excuses, he said, "Yes, sir," and ran off to fetch his dust-pan and brushes. I took a bath and did most of my dressing, splashing, and whistling softly for the steward's edification, while the secret sharer of my life stood drawn up bolt upright in that little space, his face looking very sunken in daylight, his eyelids lowered under the stern, dark line of his eyebrows drawn together by a slight frown.

When I left him there to go back to my room the steward was finishing dusting. I sent for the mate and engaged him in some insignificant conversation. It was, as it were, trifling with the terrific character of his whiskers; but my object was to give him an opportunity for a good look at my cabin. And then I could at last shut, with a clear

2. Awkward, uncouth, or undeveloped youth.

conscience, the door of my stateroom and get my double back into the recessed part. There was nothing else for it. He had to sit still on a small folding-stool, half smothered by the heavy coats hanging there. We listened to the steward going into the bath-room out of the saloon, filling the water-bottles there, scrubbing the bath, setting things to rights, whisk, bang, clatter—out again into the saloon—turn the key—click. Such was my scheme for keeping my second self invisible. Nothing better could be contrived under the circumstances. And there we sat; I at my writing-desk ready to appear busy with some papers, he behind me, out of sight of the door. It would not have been prudent to talk in daytime; and I could not have stood the excitement of that queer sense of whispering to myself. Now and then, glancing over my shoulder, I saw him far back there, sitting rigidly on the low stool, his bare feet close together, his arms folded, his head hanging on his breast—and perfectly still. Anybody would have taken him for me.

I was fascinated by it myself. Every moment I had to glance over my shoulder. I was looking at him when a voice outside the door said:

"Beg pardon, sir."

"Well!" . . . I kept my eyes on him, and so, when the voice outside the door announced, "There's a ship's boat coming our way, sir," I saw him give a start—the first movement he had made for hours. But he did not raise his bowed head.

"All right. Get the ladder over."

I hesitated. Should I whisper something to him? But what? His immobility seemed to have been never disturbed. What could I tell him he did not know already? . . . Finally I went on deck.

II

The skipper of the *Sephora* had a thin red whisker all round his face, and the sort of complexion that goes with hair of that colour; also the particular, rather smeary shade of blue in the eyes. He was not exactly a showy figure; his shoulders were high, his stature but middling—one leg slightly more bandy than the other. He shook hands, looking vaguely around. A spiritless tenacity was his main characteristic, I judged. I behaved with a politeness which seemed to disconcert him. Perhaps he was shy. He mumbled to me as if he were ashamed of what he was saying; gave his name (it was something like Archbold—but at this distance of years I hardly am sure), his ship's name, and a few other particulars of that sort, in the manner of a criminal making a reluctant and doleful confession. He had had terrible weather on the passage out—terrible—terrible—wife aboard, too.

By this time we were seated in the cabin and the steward brought in a tray with a bottle and glasses. "Thanks! No." Never took liquor. Would have some water, though. He drank two tumblerfuls. Terrible thirsty work. Ever since daylight had been exploring the islands round his ship.

"What was that for—fun?" I asked, with an appearance of polite interest.

"No!" He sighed. "Painful duty."

As he persisted in his mumbling and I wanted my double to hear every word, I hit upon the notion of informing him that I regretted to say I was hard of hearing.

"Such a young man, too!" he nodded, keeping his smeary blue, unintelligent eyes fastened upon me. What was the cause of it—some disease? he inquired, without the least sympathy and as if he thought that, if so, I'd got no more than I deserved.

"Yes; disease," I admitted in a cheerful tone which seemed to shock him. But my point was gained, because he had to raise his voice to give me his tale. It is not worth while to record that version. It was just over two months since all this had happened, and he had thought so much about it that he seemed completely muddled as to its bearings, but still immensely impressed.

"What would you think of such a thing happening on board your own ship? I've had the *Sephora* for these fifteen years. I am a well-known shipmaster."

He was densely distressed—and perhaps I should have sympathised with him if I had been able to detach my mental vision from the unsuspected sharer of my cabin as though he were my second self. There he was on the other side of the bulkhead, four or five feet from us, no more, as we sat in the saloon. I looked politely at Captain Archbold (if that was his name), but it was the other I saw, in a grey sleeping-suit, seated on a low stool, his bare feet close together, his arms folded, and every word said between us falling into the ears of his dark head bowed on his chest.

"I have been at sea now, man and boy, for seven-and-thirty years, and I've never heard of such a thing happening in an English ship. And that it should be my ship. Wife on board, too."

I was hardly listening to him.

"Don't you think," I said, "that the heavy sea which, you told me, came aboard just then might have killed the man? I have seen the sheer weight of a sea kill a man very neatly, by simply breaking his neck."

"Good God!" he uttered, impressively, fixing his smeary blue eyes on me. "The sea! No man killed by the sea ever looked like that." He seemed positively scandalised at my suggestion. And as I gazed

at him, certainly not prepared for anything original on his part, he
advanced his head close to mine and thrust his tongue out at me so
suddenly that I couldn't help starting back.

After scoring over my calmness in this graphic way he nodded
wisely. If I had seen the sight, he assured me, I would never forget it
as long as I lived. The weather was too bad to give the corpse a
proper sea burial. So next day at dawn they took it up on the poop,
covering its face with a bit of bunting; he read a short prayer, and
then, just as it was, in its oilskins and long boots,[3] they launched it
amongst those mountainous seas that seemed ready every moment
to swallow up the ship herself and the terrified lives on board of her.

"That reefed foresail saved you," I threw in.

"Under God—it did," he exclaimed fervently. "It was by a special
mercy, I firmly believe, that it stood some of those hurricane squalls."

"It was the setting of that sail which—" I began.

"God's own hand in it," he interrupted me. "Nothing less could
have done it. I don't mind telling you that I hardly dared give the
order. It seemed impossible that we could touch anything without
losing it, and then our last hope would have been gone."

The terror of that gale was on him yet. I let him go on for a bit,
then said, casually—as if returning to a minor subject:

"You were very anxious to give up your mate to the shore people,
I believe?"

He was. To the law. His obscure tenacity on that point had in it
something incomprehensible and a little awful; something, as it
were, mystical, quite apart from his anxiety that he should not be
suspected of "countenancing any doings of that sort." Seven-and-
thirty virtuous years at sea, of which over twenty of immaculate
command, and the last fifteen in the *Sephora*, seemed to have laid
him under some pitiless obligation.

"And you know," he went on, groping shamefacedly amongst his
feelings, "I did not engage that young fellow. His people had some
interest with my owners. I was in a way forced to take him on. He
looked very smart, very gentlemanly, and all that. But do you know—I
never liked him, somehow. I am a plain man. You see, he wasn't
exactly the sort for the chief mate of a ship like the *Sephora*."

I had become so connected in thoughts and impressions with the
secret sharer of my cabin that I felt as if I, personally, were being
given to understand that I, too, was not the sort that would have
done for the chief mate of a ship like the *Sephora*. I had no doubt of
it in my mind.

---

3. Waterproof boots that reach to the thigh.

"Not at all the style of man. You understand," he insisted, super-fluously, looking hard at me.

I smiled urbanely. He seemed at a loss for a while.

"I suppose I must report a suicide."

"Beg pardon?"

"Sui-cide! That's what I'll have to write to my owners directly I get in."

"Unless you manage to recover him before to-morrow," I assented, dispassionately. . . . "I mean, alive."

He mumbled something which I really did not catch, and I turned my ear to him in a puzzled manner. He fairly bawled:

"The land—I say, the mainland is at least seven miles off my anchorage."

"About that."

My lack of excitement, of curiosity, of surprise, of any sort of pro-nounced interest, began to arouse his distrust. But except for the felicitous pretence of deafness I had not tried to pretend anything. I had felt utterly incapable of playing the part of ignorance properly, and therefore was afraid to try. It is also certain that he had brought some ready-made suspicions with him, and that he viewed my polite-ness as a strange and unnatural phenomenon. And yet how else could I have received him? Not heartily! That was impossible for psy-chological reasons, which I need not state here. My only object was to keep off his inquiries. Surlily? Yes, but surliness might have provoked a point-blank question. From its novelty to him and from its nature, punctilious courtesy was the manner best calculated to restrain the man. But there was the danger of his breaking through my defence bluntly. I could not, I think, have met him by a direct lie, also for psychological (not moral) reasons. If he had only known how afraid I was of his putting my feeling of identity with the other to the test! But, strangely enough—(I thought of it only afterward)—I believe that he was not a little disconcerted by the reverse side of that weird situation, by something in me that reminded him of the man he was seeking—suggested a mysterious similitude to the young fellow he had distrusted and disliked from the first.

However that might have been, the silence was not very pro-longed. He took another oblique step.

"I reckon I had no more than a two-mile pull to your ship. Not a bit more."

"And quite enough, too, in this awful heat," I said.

Another pause full of mistrust followed. Necessity, they say, is mother of invention, but fear, too, is not barren of ingenious sugges-tions. And I was afraid he would ask me point blank for news of my other self.

"Nice little saloon, isn't it?" I remarked, as if noticing for the first time the way his eyes roamed from one closed door to the other. "And very well fitted out, too. Here, for instance," I continued, reaching over the back of my seat negligently and flinging the door open, "is my bath-room."

He made an eager movement, but hardly gave it a glance. I got up, shut the door of the bath-room, and invited him to have a look round, as if I were very proud of my accommodation. He had to rise and be shown round, but he went through the business without any raptures whatever.

"And now we'll have a look at my stateroom," I declared, in a voice as loud as I dared to make it, crossing the cabin to the starboard side with purposely heavy steps.

He followed me in and gazed around. My intelligent double had vanished. I played my part.

"Very convenient—isn't it?"

"Very nice. Very comf . . ." He didn't finish, and went out brusquely as if to escape from some unrighteous wiles of mine. But it was not to be. I had been too frightened not to feel vengeful; I felt I had him on the run, and I meant to keep him on the run. My polite insistence must have had something menacing in it, because he gave in suddenly. And I did not let him off a single item; mates' rooms, pantry, storerooms, the very sail-locker which was also under the poop—he had to look into them all. When at last I showed him out on the quarter-deck he drew a long, spiritless sigh, and mumbled dismally that he must really be going back to his ship now. I desired my mate, who had joined us, to see to the captain's boat.

The man of whiskers gave a blast on the whistle which he used to wear hanging round his neck, and yelled, "*Sephora*'s away!" My double down there in my cabin must have heard, and certainly could not feel more relieved than I. Four fellows came running out from somewhere forward and went over the side, while my own men, appearing on deck too, lined the rail. I escorted my visitor to the gangway ceremoniously, and nearly overdid it. He was a tenacious beast. On the very ladder he lingered, and in that unique, guiltily conscientious manner of sticking to the point:

"I say . . . you . . . you don't think that—"

I covered his voice loudly:

"Certainly not. . . . I am delighted. Good-bye."

I had an idea of what he meant to say, and just saved myself by the privilege of defective hearing. He was too shaken generally to insist, but my mate, close witness of that parting, looked mystified and his face took on a thoughtful cast. As I did not want to appear as if I wished to avoid all communication with my officers, he had the opportunity to address me.

"Seems a very nice man. His boat's crew told our chaps a very extraordinary story, if what I am told by the steward is true. I suppose you had it from the captain, sir?"

"Yes. I had a story from the captain."

"A very horrible affair—isn't it, sir?"

"It is."

"Beats all these tales we hear about murders in Yankee ships."[4]

"I don't think it beats them. I don't think it resembles them in the least."

"Bless my soul—you don't say so! But of course I've no acquaintance whatever with American ships, not I, so I couldn't go against your knowledge. It's horrible enough for me. . . . But the queerest part is that those fellows seemed to have some idea the man was hidden aboard here. They had really. Did you ever hear of such a thing?"

"Preposterous—isn't it?"

We were walking to and fro athwart the quarter-deck. Not one of the crew forward could be seen (the day was Sunday), and the mate pursued:

"There was some little dispute about it. Our chaps took offence. 'As if we would harbour a thing like that,' they said. 'Wouldn't you like to look for him in our coal-hole?' Quite a tiff. But they made it up in the end. I suppose he did drown himself. Don't you, sir?"

"I don't suppose anything."

"You have no doubt in the matter, sir?"

"None whatever."

I left him suddenly. I felt I was producing a bad impression, but with my double down there it was most trying to be on deck. And it was almost as trying to be below. Altogether a nerve-trying situation. But on the whole I felt less torn in two when I was with him. There was no one in the whole ship whom I dared take into my confidence. Since the hands had got to know his story, it would have been impossible to pass him off for any one else, and an accidental discovery was to be dreaded now more than ever. . . .

The steward being engaged in laying the table for dinner, we could talk only with our eyes when I first went down. Later in the afternoon we had a cautious try at whispering. The Sunday quietness of the ship was against us; the stillness of air and water around her was against us; the elements, the men were against us—everything was against us in our secret partnership; time itself—for this could not go on forever. The very trust in Providence was, I suppose, denied to his guilt. Shall I confess that this thought cast me down very

---

4. Harsh discipline aboard American ships was notorious in the 19th century.

much? And as to the chapter of accidents which counts for so much in the book of success, I could only hope that it was closed. For what favourable accident could be expected?

"Did you hear everything?" were my first words as soon as we took up our position side by side, leaning over my bed-place.

He had. And the proof of it was his earnest whisper, "The man told you he hardly dared to give the order."

I understood the reference to be to that saving foresail.

"Yes. He was afraid of it being lost in the setting."

"I assure you he never gave the order. He may think he did, but he never gave it. He stood there with me on the break of the poop after the main-topsail blew away, and whimpered about our last hope—positively whimpered about it and nothing else—and the night coming on! To hear one's skipper go on like that in such weather was enough to drive any fellow out of his mind. It worked me up into a sort of desperation. I just took it into my own hands and went away from him, boiling, and— But what's the use telling you? *You* know! . . . Do you think that if I had not been pretty fierce with them I should have got the men to do anything? Not it! The boss'n perhaps? Perhaps! It wasn't a heavy sea—it was a sea gone mad! I suppose the end of the world will be something like that; and a man may have the heart to see it coming once and be done with it—but to have to face it day after day— I don't blame anybody. I was precious little better than the rest. Only—I was an officer of that old coal-waggon, anyhow—"

"I quite understand," I conveyed that sincere assurance into his ear. He was out of breath with whispering; I could hear him pant slightly. It was all very simple. The same strung-up force which had given twenty-four men a chance, at least, for their lives, had, in a sort of recoil, crushed an unworthy mutinous existence.

But I had no leisure to weigh the merits of the matter—footsteps in the saloon, a heavy knock. "There's enough wind to get under way with, sir." Here was the call of a new claim upon my thoughts and even upon my feelings.

"Turn the hands up," I cried through the door. "I'll be on deck directly."

I was going out to make the acquaintance of my ship. Before I left the cabin our eyes met—the eyes of the only two strangers on board. I pointed to the recessed part where the little camp-stool awaited him and laid my finger on my lips. He made a gesture—somewhat vague—a little mysterious, accompanied by a faint smile, as if of regret.

This is not the place to enlarge upon the sensations of a man who feels for the first time a ship move under his feet to his own independent word. In my case they were not unalloyed. I was not wholly alone with my command; for there was that stranger in my cabin. Or rather, I was not completely and wholly with her. Part of me was absent. That mental feeling of being in two places at once affected me physically as if the mood of secrecy had penetrated my very soul. Before an hour had elapsed since the ship had begun to move, having occasion to ask the mate (he stood by my side) to take a compass bearing of the pagoda,[5] I caught myself reaching up to his ear in whispers. I say I caught myself, but enough had escaped to startle the man. I can't describe it otherwise than by saying that he shied. A grave, preoccupied manner, as though he were in possession of some perplexing intelligence, did not leave him henceforth. A little later I moved away from the rail to look at the compass with such a stealthy gait that the helmsman noticed it—and I could not help noticing the unusual roundness of his eyes. These are trifling instances, though it's to no commander's advantage to be suspected of ludicrous eccentricities. But I was also more seriously affected. There are to a seaman certain words, gestures, that should in given conditions come as naturally, as instinctively as the winking of a menaced eye. A certain order should spring on to his lips without thinking; a certain sign should get itself made, so to speak, without reflection. But all unconscious alertness had abandoned me. I had to make an effort of will to recall myself back (from the cabin) to the conditions of the moment. I felt that I was appearing an irresolute commander to those people who were watching me more or less critically.

And, besides, there were the scares. On the second day out, for instance, coming off the deck in the afternoon (I had straw slippers on my bare feet) I stopped at the open pantry door and spoke to the steward. He was doing something there with his back to me. At the sound of my voice he nearly jumped out of his skin, as the saying is, and incidentally broke a cup.

"What on earth's the matter with you?" I asked, astonished.

He was extremely confused. "Beg your pardon, sir. I made sure you were in your cabin."

"You see I wasn't."

"No, sir. I could have sworn I had heard you moving in there not a moment ago. It's most extraordinary . . . very sorry, sir."

I passed on with an inward shudder. I was so identified with my secret double that I did not even mention the fact in those scanty, fearful whispers we exchanged. I suppose he had made some slight noise of some kind or other. It would have been miraculous if he hadn't at one time or another. And yet, haggard as he appeared, he looked always perfectly self-controlled, more than calm—almost

5. I.e., the Paknam pagoda; see p. 7, n. 2.

invulnerable. On my suggestion he remained almost entirely in the bath-room, which, upon the whole, was the safest place. There could be really no shadow of an excuse for any one ever wanting to go in there, once the steward had done with it. It was a very tiny place. Sometimes he reclined on the floor, his legs bent, his head sustained on one elbow. At others I would find him on the camp-stool, sitting in his grey sleeping-suit and with his cropped dark hair like a patient, unmoved convict. At night I would smuggle him into my bed-place, and we would whisper together, with the regular footfalls of the officer of the watch passing and repassing over our heads. It was an infinitely miserable time. It was lucky that some tins of fine preserves were stowed in a locker in my stateroom; hard bread I could always get hold of; and so he lived on stewed chicken, paté de foie gras, asparagus, cooked oysters, sardines—on all sorts of abominable sham delicacies out of tins. My early morning coffee he always drank; and it was all I dared do for him in that respect.

Every day there was the horrible manœuvring to go through so that my room and then the bath-room should be done in the usual way. I came to hate the sight of the steward, to abhor the voice of that harmless man. I felt that it was he who would bring on the disaster of discovery. It hung like a sword over our heads.[6]

The fourth day out, I think (we were then working down the east side of the Gulf of Siam,[7] tack for tack, in light winds and smooth water)—the fourth day, I say, of this miserable juggling with the unavoidable, as we sat at our evening meal, that man, whose slightest movement I dreaded, after putting down the dishes ran up on deck busily. This could not be dangerous. Presently he came down again; and then it appeared that he had remembered a coat of mine which I had thrown over a rail to dry after having been wetted in a shower which had passed over the ship in the afternoon. Sitting stolidly at the head of the table I became terrified at the sight of the garment on his arm. Of course he made for my door. There was no time to lose.

"Steward," I thundered. My nerves were so shaken that I could not govern my voice and conceal my agitation. This was the sort of thing that made my terrifically whiskered mate tap his forehead with his forefinger. I had detected him using that gesture while talking on deck with a confidential air to the carpenter. It was too far to hear a word, but I had no doubt that this pantomime could only refer to the strange new captain.

6. An allusion to the story of Damocles, who after praising the happiness of his sovereign Dionysius II (c. 397–343 B.C.E.) was invited to dinner and seated beneath a sword suspended by a single hair, indicating the precarious nature of the happiness of those who hold political power; see Cicero's (106–43 B.C.E.) *Tusculanæ disputationes* (V. 61–62).
7. The east side of the Bight of Bangkok, the upper part of the Gulf of Thailand. See p. 483.

"Yes, sir," the pale-faced steward turned resignedly to me. It was this maddening course of being shouted at, checked without rhyme or reason, arbitrarily chased out of my cabin, suddenly called into it, sent flying out of his pantry on incomprehensible errands, that accounted for the growing wretchedness of his expression.

"Where are you going with that coat?"

"To your room, sir."

"Is there another shower coming?"

"I'm sure I don't know, sir. Shall I go up again and see, sir?"

"No! never mind."

My object was attained, as of course my other self in there would have heard everything that passed. During this interlude my two officers never raised their eyes off their respective plates; but the lip of that confounded cub, the second mate, quivered visibly.

I expected the steward to hook my coat on and come out at once. He was very slow about it; but I dominated my nervousness sufficiently not to shout after him. Suddenly I became aware (it could be heard plainly enough) that the fellow for some reason or other was opening the door of the bath-room. It was the end. The place was literally not big enough to swing a cat in. My voice died in my throat and I went stony all over. I expected to hear a yell of surprise and terror, and made a movement, but had not the strength to get on my legs. Everything remained still. Had my second self taken the poor wretch by the throat? I don't know what I would have done next moment if I had not seen the steward come out of my room, close the door, and then stand quietly by the sideboard.

"Saved," I thought. "But, no! Lost! Gone! He was gone!"

I laid my knife and fork down and leaned back in my chair. My head swam. After a while, when sufficiently recovered to speak in a steady voice, I instructed my mate to put the ship round at eight o'clock himself.

"I won't come on deck," I went on. "I think I'll turn in, and unless the wind shifts I don't want to be disturbed before midnight. I feel a bit seedy."

"You did look middling bad a little while ago," the chief mate remarked without showing any great concern.

They both went out, and I stared at the steward clearing the table. There was nothing to be read on that wretched man's face. But why did he avoid my eyes I asked myself. Then I thought I should like to hear the sound of his voice.

"Steward!"

"Sir!" Startled as usual.

"Where did you hang up that coat?"

"In the bath-room, sir." The usual anxious tone. "It's not quite dry yet, sir."

For some time longer I sat in the cuddy. Had my double vanished as he had come? But of his coming there was an explanation, whereas his disappearance would be inexplicable. . . . I went slowly into my dark room, shut the door, lighted the lamp, and for a time dared not turn round. When at last I did I saw him standing bolt-upright in the narrow recessed part. It would not be true to say I had a shock, but an irresistible doubt of his bodily existence flitted through my mind. Can it be, I asked myself, that he is not visible to other eyes than mine? It was like being haunted. Motionless, with a grave face, he raised his hands slightly at me in a gesture which meant clearly, "Heavens! what a narrow escape!" Narrow indeed. I think I had come creeping quietly as near insanity as any man who has not actually gone over the border. That gesture restrained me, so to speak.

The mate with the terrific whiskers was now putting the ship on the other tack. In the moment of profound silence which follows upon the hands going to their stations I heard on the poop his raised voice: "Hard alee!" and the distant shout of the order repeated on the main deck. The sails, in that light breeze, made but a faint fluttering noise. It ceased. The ship was coming round slowly; I held my breath in the renewed stillness of expectation; one wouldn't have thought that there was a single living soul on her decks. A sudden brisk shout, "Mainsail haul!" broke the spell, and in the noisy cries and rush overhead of the men running away with the main-brace we two, down in my cabin, came together in our usual position by the bed-place.

He did not wait for my question. "I heard him fumbling here and just managed to squat myself down in the bath," he whispered to me. "The fellow only opened the door and put his arm in to hang the coat up. All the same—"

"I never thought of that," I whispered back, even more appalled than before at the closeness of the shave, and marvelling at that something unyielding in his character which was carrying him through so finely. There was no agitation in his whisper. Whoever was being driven distracted, it was not he. He was sane. And the proof of his sanity was continued when he took up the whispering again.

"It would never do for me to come to life again."

It was something that a ghost might have said. But what he was alluding to was his old captain's reluctant admission of the theory of suicide. It would obviously serve his turn—if I had understood at all the view which seemed to govern the unalterable purpose of his action.

"You must maroon me as soon as ever you can get amongst these islands off the Cambodge shore,"[8] he went on.

8. Cambodian shore. See p. 483.

"Maroon you! We are not living in a boy's adventure tale," I protested. His scornful whispering took me up.

"We aren't indeed! There's nothing of a boy's tale in this. But there's
nothing else for it. I want no more. You don't suppose I am afraid of
what can be done to me? Prison or gallows or whatever they may
please. But you don't see me coming back to explain such things to
an old fellow in a wig and twelve respectable tradesmen,[9] do you?
What can they know whether I am guilty or not—or of *what* I am
guilty, either? That's my affair. What does the Bible say? 'Driven off
the face of the earth.'[1] Very well. I am off the face of the earth now.
As I came at night so I shall go."

"Impossible!" I murmured. "You can't."

"Can't? . . . Not naked like a soul on the Day of Judgment.[2] I shall
freeze on to this sleeping-suit. The Last Day[3] is not yet—and . . .
you have understood thoroughly. Didn't you?"

I felt suddenly ashamed of myself. I may say truly that I
understood—and my hesitation in letting that man swim away from
my ship's side had been a mere sham sentiment, a sort of cowardice.

"It can't be done now till next night," I breathed out. "The ship is
on the off-shore tack and the wind may fail us."

"As long as I know that you understand," he whispered. "But of
course you do. It's a great satisfaction to have got somebody to
understand. You seem to have been there on purpose."[4] And in the
same whisper, as if we two whenever we talked had to say things to
each other which were not fit for the world to hear, he added, "It's
very wonderful."

We remained side by side talking in our secret way—but sometimes silent or just exchanging a whispered word or two at long
intervals. And as usual he stared through the port. A breath of wind
came now and again into our faces. The ship might have been
moored in dock, so gently and on an even keel she slipped through
the water, that did not murmur even at our passage, shadowy and
silent like a phantom sea.

At midnight I went on deck, and to my mate's great surprise put
the ship round on the other tack. His terrible whiskers flitted round
me in silent criticism. I certainly should not have done it if it had
been only a question of getting out of that sleepy gulf as quickly as
possible. I believe he told the second mate, who relieved him, that

9. Judge and jury. In England, judges wear traditional wigs.
1. Another reference to Genesis 4:14; see p. 18, n. 5.
2. Reference to Ecclesiastes 5:15: "As he came forth of his mother's womb, naked shall he
   return to go as he came, and shall take nothing of his labour, which he may carry away
   in his hand"; see also Revelation 16:15 and Job 1:21.
3. According to the Bible, the Day of Judgment is to occur on the last day, at which time
   human beings will be judged and receive their reward or punishment.
4. I.e., providentially.

it was a great want of judgment. The other only yawned. That intolerable cub shuffled about so sleepily and lolled against the rails in
such a slack, improper fashion that I came down on him sharply.

"Aren't you properly awake yet?"

"Yes, sir! I am awake."

"Well, then, be good enough to hold yourself as if you were. And
keep a look-out. If there's any current we'll be closing with some
islands before day-light."

The east side of the gulf is fringed with islands, some solitary,
others in groups. On the blue background of the high coast they
seem to float on silvery patches of calm water, arid and grey, or dark
green and rounded like clumps of evergreen bushes, with the larger
ones, a mile or two long, showing the outlines of ridges, ribs of grey
rock under the dank mantle of matted leafage. Unknown to trade,
to travel, almost to geography, the manner of life they harbour is an
unsolved secret. There must be villages—settlements of fishermen
at least—on the largest of them, and some communication with the
world is probably kept up by native craft. But all that forenoon, as
we headed for them, fanned along by the faintest of breezes, I saw
no sign of man or canoe in the field of the telescope I kept on pointing at the scattered group.

At noon I gave no orders for a change of course, and the mate's
whiskers became much concerned and seemed to be offering themselves unduly to my notice. At last I said:

"I am going to stand right in. Quite in—as far as I can take her."

The stare of extreme surprise imparted an air of ferocity also to
his eyes, and he looked truly terrific for a moment.

"We're not doing well in the middle of the gulf," I continued,
casually. "I am going to look for the land breezes to-night."

"Bless my soul! Do you mean, sir, in the dark amongst the lot of
all them islands and reefs and shoals?"

"Well—if there are any regular land breezes at all on this coast
one must get close inshore to find them, mustn't one?"

"Bless my soul!" he exclaimed again under his breath. All that
afternoon he wore a dreamy, contemplative appearance which in
him was a mark of perplexity. After dinner I went into my stateroom
as if I meant to take some rest. There we two bent our dark heads
over a half-unrolled chart lying on my bed.

"There," I said. "It's got to be Koh-ring.[5] I've been looking at it ever
since sunrise. It has got two hills and a low point. It must be inhabited. And on the coast opposite there is what looks like the mouth of

5. Various scholars have suggested the island may be based on Koh Ryn or Koh Rin (12°8′
   N 100°7′ E).

a biggish river—with some town, no doubt, not far up. It's the best chance for you that I can see."

"Anything. Koh-ring let it be."

He looked thoughtfully at the chart as if surveying chances and distances from a lofty height—and following with his eyes his own figure wandering on the blank land of Cochin-China,[6] and then passing off that piece of paper clean out of sight into uncharted regions. And it was as if the ship had two captains to plan her course for her. I had been so worried and restless running up and down that I had not had the patience to dress that day. I had remained in my sleeping-suit, with straw slippers and a soft floppy hat. The closeness of the heat in the gulf had been most oppressive, and the crew were used to see me wandering in that airy attire.

"She will clear the south point as she heads now," I whispered into his ear. "Goodness only knows when, though, but certainly after dark. I'll edge her in to half a mile, as far as I may be able to judge in the dark—"

"Be careful," he murmured, warningly—and I realised suddenly that all my future, the only future for which I was fit, would perhaps go irretrievably to pieces in any mishap to my first command. I could not stop a moment longer in the room. I motioned him to get out of sight and made my way on the poop. That unplayful cub had the watch. I walked up and down for a while thinking things out, then beckoned him over.

"Send a couple of hands to open the two quarter-deck ports," I said, mildly.

He actually had the impudence, or else so forgot himself in his wonder at such an incomprehensible order, as to repeat:

"Open the quarter-deck ports! What for, sir?"

"The only reason you need concern yourself about is because I tell you to do so. Have them open wide and fastened properly."

He reddened and went off, but I believe made some jeering remark to the carpenter as to the sensible practice of ventilating a ship's quarter-deck. I know he popped into the mate's cabin to impart the fact to him because the whiskers came on deck, as it were by chance, and stole glances at me from below—for signs of lunacy or drunkenness, I suppose.

A little before supper, feeling more restless than ever, I rejoined, for a moment, my second self. And to find him sitting so quietly was surprising, like something against nature, inhuman.

I developed my plan in a hurried whisper.

"I shall stand in as close as I dare and then put her round. I shall presently find means to smuggle you out of here into the sail-locker,

6. The southern portion of Vietnam; at this time, it was a French colony. See p. 335.

which communicates with the lobby. But there is an opening, a sort of square for hauling the sails out, which gives straight on the quarter-deck and which is never closed in fine weather, so as to give air to the sails. When the ship's way is deadened in stays and all the hands are aft at the main-braces you shall have a clear road to slip out and get overboard through the open quarter-deck port. I've had them both fastened up. Use a rope's end to lower yourself into the water so as to avoid a splash—you know. It could be heard and cause some beastly complication."

He kept silent for a while, then whispered, "I understand."

"I won't be there to see you go," I began with an effort. "The rest . . . I only hope I have understood, too."

"You have. From first to last"—and for the first time there seemed to be a faltering, something strained in his whisper. He caught hold of my arm, but the ringing of the supper bell made me start. He didn't, though; he only released his grip.

After supper I didn't come below again till well past eight o'clock. The faint, steady breeze was loaded with dew; and the wet, darkened sails held all there was of propelling power in it. The night, clear and starry, sparkled darkly, and the opaque, lightless patches shifting slowly against the low stars were the drifting islets. On the port bow there was a big one more distant and shadowily imposing by the great space of sky it eclipsed.

On opening the door I had a back view of my very own self looking at a chart. He had come out of the recess and was standing near the table.

"Quite dark enough," I whispered.

He stepped back and leaned against my bed with a level, quiet glance. I sat on the couch. We had nothing to say to each other. Over our heads the officer of the watch moved here and there. Then I heard him move quickly. I knew what that meant. He was making for the companion; and presently his voice was outside my door.

"We are drawing in pretty fast, sir. Land looks rather close."

"Very well," I answered. "I am coming on deck directly."

I waited till he was gone out of the cuddy, then rose. My double moved too. The time had come to exchange our last whispers, for neither of us was ever to hear each other's natural voice.

"Look here!" I opened a drawer and took out three sovereigns.[7] "Take this, anyhow. I've got six and I'd give you the lot, only I must keep a little money to buy some fruit and vegetables for the crew from native boats as we go through Sunda Straits."

He shook his head.

---

7. Gold coin equivalent to one pound in the 19th century under the former British monetary system.

"Take it," I urged him, whispering desperately. "No one can tell what—"

He smiled and slapped meaningly the only pocket of the sleeping-jacket. It was not safe, certainly. But I produced a large old silk handkerchief of mine, and tying the three pieces of gold in a corner, pressed it on him. He was touched, I suppose, because he took it at last and tied it quickly round his waist under the jacket, on his bare skin.

Our eyes met; several seconds elapsed, till, our glances still mingled, I extended my hand and turned the lamp out. Then I passed through the cuddy, leaving the door of my room wide open. . . . "Steward!"

He was still lingering in the pantry in the greatness of his zeal, giving a rub-up to a plated cruet stand[8] the last thing before going to bed. Being careful not to wake up the mate, whose room was opposite, I spoke in an undertone.

He looked round anxiously. "Sir!"

"Can you get me a little hot water from the galley?"

"I am afraid, sir, the galley fire's been out for some time now."

"Go and see."

He fled up the stairs.

"Now," I whispered, loudly, into the saloon—too loudly, perhaps, but I was afraid I couldn't make a sound. He was by my side in an instant—the double captain slipped past the stairs—through a tiny dark passage . . . a sliding door. We were in the sail-locker, scrambling on our knees over the sails. A sudden thought struck me. I saw myself wandering barefooted, bareheaded, the sun beating on my dark poll. I snatched off my floppy hat and tried hurriedly in the dark to ram it on my other self. He dodged and fended off silently. I wondered what he thought had come to me before he understood and suddenly desisted. Our hands met gropingly, lingered united in a steady, motionless clasp for a second. . . . No word was breathed by either of us when they separated.

I was standing quietly by the pantry door when the steward returned.

"Sorry, sir. Kettle barely warm. Shall I light the spirit-lamp?"[9]

"Never mind."

I came out on deck slowly. It was now a matter of conscience to shave the land as close as possible—for now he must go overboard whenever the ship was put in stays. Must! There could be no going back for him. After a moment I walked over to leeward and my heart

---

8. A silver-plated frame or stand for holding glass bottles of condiments.
9. A lamp fueled by methylated or other spirits and used for heating.

flew into my mouth at the nearness of the land on the bow. Under any other circumstances I would not have held on a minute longer. The second mate had followed me anxiously.

I looked on till I felt I could command my voice.

"She will weather," I said then in a quiet tone.

"Are you going to try that, sir?" he stammered out incredulously.

I took no notice of him and raised my tone just enough to be heard by the helmsman.

"Keep her good full."

"Good full, sir."

The wind fanned my cheek, the sails slept, the world was silent. The strain of watching the dark loom of the land grow bigger and denser was too much for me. I had shut my eyes—because the ship must go closer. She must! The stillness was intolerable. Were we standing still?

When I opened my eyes the second view started my heart with a thump. The black southern hill of Koh-ring seemed to hang right over the ship like a towering fragment of the everlasting night. On that enormous mass of blackness there was not a gleam to be seen, not a sound to be heard. It was gliding irresistibly toward us and yet seemed already within reach of the hand. I saw the vague figures of the watch grouped in the waist, gazing in awed silence.

"Are you going on, sir," inquired an unsteady voice at my elbow.

I ignored it. I had to go on.

"Keep her full. Don't check her way. That won't do now," I said, warningly.

"I can't see the sails very well," the helmsman answered me, in strange, quavering tones.

Was she close enough? Already she was, I won't say in the shadow of the land, but in the very blackness of it, already swallowed up as it were, gone too close to be recalled, gone from me altogether.

"Give the mate a call," I said to the young man who stood at my elbow as still as death. "And turn all hands up."

My tone had a borrowed loudness reverberated from the height of the land. Several voices cried out together: "We are all on deck, sir."

Then stillness again, with the great shadow gliding closer, towering higher, without a light, without a sound. Such a hush had fallen on the ship that she might have been a bark of the dead floating in slowly under the very gate of Erebus.[1]

"My God! Where are we?"

---

1. In Greek mythology, the son of Chaos and associated with the region of the Hades, the Greek underworld, where the dead arrive after being ferried across the River Styx by Charon, Erebus's son.

It was the mate moaning at my elbow. He was thunderstruck, and as it were deprived of the moral support of his whiskers. He clapped his hands and absolutely cried out, "Lost!"

"Be quiet," I said, sternly.

He lowered his tone, but I saw the shadowy gesture of his despair. "What are we doing here?"

"Looking for the land wind."

He made as if to tear his hair, and addressed me recklessly.

"She will never get out. You have done it, sir. I knew it'd end in something like this. She will never weather, and you are too close now to stay. She'll drift ashore before she's round. O my God!"

I caught his arm as he was raising it to batter his poor devoted head, and shook it violently.

"She's ashore already," he wailed, trying to tear himself away.

"Is she? . . . Keep good full there!"

"Good full, sir," cried the helmsman in a frightened, thin, child-like voice.

I hadn't let go the mate's arm and went on shaking it. "Ready about, do you hear? You go forward"—shake—"and stop there"—shake—"and hold your noise"—shake—"and see these head sheets properly overhauled"—shake, shake—shake.

And all the time I dared not look toward the land lest my heart should fail me. I released my grip at last and he ran forward as if fleeing for dear life.

I wondered what my double there in the sail-locker thought of this commotion. He was able to hear everything—and perhaps he was able to understand why, on my conscience, it had to be thus close—no less. My first order "Hard alee!" re-echoed ominously under the towering shadow of Koh-ring as if I had shouted in a mountain gorge. And then I watched the land intently. In that smooth water and light wind it was impossible to feel the ship coming-to. No! I could not feel her. And my second self was making now ready to slip out and lower himself overboard. Perhaps he was gone already . . . ?

The great black mass brooding over our very mastheads began to pivot away from the ship's side silently. And now I forgot the secret stranger ready to depart, and remembered only that I was a total stranger to the ship. I did not know her. Would she do it? How was she to be handled?

I swung the main yard and waited helplessly. She was perhaps stopped, and her very fate hung in the balance, with the black mass of Koh-ring like the gate of the everlasting night towering over her taffrail. What would she do now? Had she way on her yet? I stepped to the side swiftly, and on the shadowy water I could see nothing except a faint phosphorescent flash revealing the glassy smoothness of the sleeping surface. It was impossible to tell—and I had not

learned yet the feel of my ship. Was she moving? What I needed
was something easily seen, a piece of paper, which I could throw overboard and watch. I had nothing on me. To run down for it I didn't
dare. There was no time. All at once my strained, yearning stare
distinguished a white object floating within a yard of the ship's side.
White on the black water. A phosphorescent flash passed under it.
What was that thing? . . . I recognised my own floppy hat. It must
have fallen off his head . . . and he didn't bother. Now I had what I
wanted—the saving mark for my eyes. But I hardly thought of my
other self, now gone from the ship, to be hidden forever from all
friendly faces, to be a fugitive and a vagabond on the earth, with no
brand of the curse on his sane forehead to stay a slaying hand[2] . . .
too proud to explain.

And I watched the hat—the expression of my sudden pity for his
mere flesh. It had been meant to save his homeless head from the
dangers of the sun. And now—behold—it was saving the ship, by
serving me for a mark to help out the ignorance of my strangeness.
Ha! It was drifting forward, warning me just in time that the ship
had gathered sternway.

"Shift the helm," I said in a low voice to the seaman standing still
like a statue.

The man's eyes glistened wildly in the binnacle light as he jumped
round to the other side and spun round the wheel.

I walked to the break of the poop. On the overshadowed deck all
hands stood by the forebraces waiting for my order. The stars ahead
seemed to be gliding from right to left. And all was so still in the
world that I heard the quiet remark "She's round," passed in a tone
of intense relief between two seamen.

"Let go and haul."

The foreyards ran round with a great noise, amidst cheery cries.
And now the frightful whiskers made themselves heard giving various orders. Already the ship was drawing ahead. And I was alone
with her. Nothing! no one in the world should stand now between us,
throwing a shadow on the way of silent knowledge and mute affection, the perfect communion of a seaman with his first command.

Walking to the taffrail, I was in time to make out, on the very edge
of a darkness thrown by a towering black mass like the very gateway
of Erebus—yes, I was in time to catch an evanescent glimpse of my
white hat left behind to mark the spot where the secret sharer of
my cabin and of my thoughts, as though he were my second self, had
lowered himself into the water to take his punishment: a free man,
a proud swimmer striking out for a new destiny.

---

2. Another reference to Cain's plight in Genesis 4:15; see p. 18, n. 5.

Author's Note [to *The Shadow-Line*]†

This story, which I admit to be in its brevity a fairly complex piece of work, was not intended to touch on the supernatural. Yet more than one critic has been inclined to take it in that way, seeing in it an attempt on my part to give the fullest scope to my imagination by taking it beyond the confines of the world of the living, suffering humanity.[1] But as a matter of fact my imagination is not made of stuff so elastic as all that. I believe that if I attempted to put the strain of the Supernatural on it it would fail deplorably and exhibit an unlovely gap. But I could never have attempted such a thing, because all my moral and intellectual being is penetrated by an invincible conviction that whatever falls under the dominion of our senses must be in nature and, however exceptional, cannot differ in its essence from all the other effects of the visible and tangible world of which we are a self-conscious part. The world of the living contains enough marvels and mysteries as it is; marvels and mysteries acting upon our emotions and intelligence in ways so inexplicable that it would almost justify the conception of life as an enchanted state. No, I am too firm in my consciousness of the marvellous to be ever fascinated by the mere supernatural, which (take it any way you like) is but a manufactured article, the fabrication of minds insensitive to the intimate delicacies of our relation to the dead and to the living, in their countless multitudes; a desecration of our tenderest memories; an outrage on our dignity.

Whatever my native modesty may be it will never condescend so low as to seek help for my imagination within those vain imaginings common to all ages and that in themselves are enough to fill all lovers of mankind with unutterable sadness. As to the effect of a mental or moral shock on a common mind that is quite a legitimate subject for study and description. Mr. Burns' moral being receives a severe shock in his relations with his late captain, and this in his diseased state turns into a mere superstitious fancy compounded of fear and animosity. This fact is one of the elements of the story, but there is nothing supernatural in it, nothing so to speak from beyond the confines of this world, which in all conscience holds enough mystery and terror in itself.

---

† Written in 1920 for the Doubleday, Page & Co. collected edition, *The Works of Joseph Conrad*. *The Shadow-Line* was originally published in 1917.
1. Conrad is responding to the emphasis various reviewers placed on the supernatural in the book, perhaps foremost among them Arthur Waugh's review in *The Outlook* (March 31, 1917, pp. 301–2).

Perhaps if I had published this tale, which I have had for a long time in my mind, under the title of *First Command*[2] no suggestion of the Supernatural would have been found in it by any impartial reader, critical or otherwise. I will not consider here the origins of the feeling in which its actual title, *The Shadow-Line*, occurred to my mind. Primarily the aim of this piece of writing was the presentation of certain facts which certainly were associated with the change from youth, care-free and fervent, to the more self-conscious and more poignant period of maturer life. Nobody can doubt that before the supreme trial of a whole generation[3] I had an acute consciousness of the minute and insignificant character of my own obscure experience. There could be no question here of any parallelism. That notion never entered my head. But there was a feeling of identity, though with an enormous difference of scale—as of one single drop measured against the bitter and stormy immensity of an ocean. And this was very natural too. For when we begin to meditate on the meaning of our own past it seems to fill all the world in its profundity and its magnitude. This book was written in the last three months of the year 1916.[4] Of all the subjects of which a writer of tales is more or less conscious within himself this is the only one I found it possible to attempt at the time. The depth and the nature of the mood with which I approached it is best expressed perhaps in the dedication which strikes me now as a most disproportionate thing—as another instance of the overwhelming greatness of our own emotion to ourselves.

This much having been said I may pass on now to a few remarks about the mere material of the story. As to locality it belongs to that part of the Eastern Seas from which I have carried away into my writing life the greatest number of suggestions. From my statement that I thought of this story for a long time under the title of *First Command* the reader may guess that it is concerned with my personal experience. And as a matter of fact it *is* personal experience seen in perspective with the eye of the mind and coloured by that affection one can't help feeling for such events of one's life as one has no reason to be ashamed of. And that affection is as intense (I appeal here to universal experience) as the shame, and almost the anguish with which one remembers some unfortunate occurrences, down to mere mistakes in speech, that have been perpetrated by one in the past. The effect of perspective in memory is to make things loom large because the essentials stand out isolated from

---

2. Conrad first mentions this title in a letter to William Blackwood dated February 14, 1899: "I thought of two other stories (more in the 'note' of my 'Maga' [*Blackwood's Magazine*] work) one of them being called *First Command*. . . ." (*CL* 2:167).
3. World War I (1914–18).
4. Actually, it was 1915, and the writing took closer to seven months.

their surroundings of insignificant daily facts which have naturally faded out of one's mind. I remember that period of my sea-life with pleasure because begun inauspiciously it turned out in the end a success from a personal point of view, leaving a tangible proof in the terms of the letter[5] the owners of the ship wrote to me two years afterwards when I resigned my command in order to come home. This resignation marked the beginning of another phase of my sea-man's life, its terminal phase, if I may say so, which in its own way has coloured another portion of my writings. I didn't know then how near its end my sea-life was, and therefore I felt no sorrow except at parting with the ship. I was sorry also to break my connection with the firm which owned her and who were pleased to receive with friendly kindness and give their confidence to a man who had entered their service in an accidental manner and in very adverse circum-stances. Without disparaging the earnestness of my purpose I sus-pect now that luck had no small part in the success of the trust reposed in me. And one cannot help remembering with pleasure the time when one's best efforts were seconded by a run of luck.

The words *"Worthy of my undying regard"* selected by me for the motto on the title page are quoted from the text of the book itself [see p. 114]; and, though one of my critics surmised that they applied to the ship,[6] it is evident from the place where they stand that they refer to the men of that ship's company: complete strangers to their new captain and yet who stood by him so well during those twenty days that seemed to have been passed on the brink of a slow and agonizing destruction. And *that* is the greatest memory of all! For surely it is a great thing to have commanded a handful of men worthy of one's undying regard.

1920.

J. C.

---

5. In a letter dated April 2, 1889, Henry Simpson & Sons, owners of the *Otago*, which Con-rad commanded from 1888 to 1889, wrote: "[W]e entertain a high opinion of your ability in the capacity you now vacate, of your attainments generally, and shall be glad to learn of your future success" (*PL* 5; see p. 365).

6. Conrad is almost certainly referring to the unsigned review in *The Saturday Review* (March 24, 1917), which states: "On the title-page of this book is the sentence, 'Worthy of my undying regard,' and underneath stands no human name, but a ship with sails set. Here once more Mr. Conrad shows that he loves a ship as a lover does his mistress, and so his latest book is an essential piece of himself, a return to earlier triumphs" (p. 282).

The Shadow-Line
A Confession

"Worthy of my undying regard"[1]

To Borys and all others who like himself have crossed in early
youth the shadow-line of their generation with love[2]

. . . —*D'autres fois, calme plat, grand miroir*
 De mon désespoir.

Baudelaire.[3]

I

Only the young have such moments. I don't mean the very young.
No. The very young have, properly speaking, no moments. It is the
privilege of early youth to live in advance of its days in all the beautiful continuity of hope which knows no pauses and no introspection.

One closes behind one the little gate of mere boyishness—and
enters an enchanted garden. Its very shades glow with promise. Every
turn of the path has its seduction. And it isn't because it is an
undiscovered country.[4] One knows well enough that all mankind had
streamed that way. It is the charm of universal experience from which
one expects an uncommon or personal sensation—a bit of one's own.

One goes on recognising the landmarks of the predecessors,
excited, amused, taking the hard luck and the good luck together—
the kicks and the halfpence,[5] as the saying is—the picturesque common lot that holds so many possibilities for the deserving or perhaps
for the lucky. Yes. One goes on. And the time, too, goes on—till one
perceives ahead a shadow-line warning one that the region of early
youth, too, must be left behind.

1. A quotation taken from *The Shadow-Line* itself; see p. 114.
2. Dedicated to Conrad's son, Borys (1898–1978), who enlisted to fight in World War I in
September 1915.
3. From "La Musique" by Charles Baudelaire (1821–1867), a sonnet from his collection
Les Fleurs de Mal (*The Flowers of Evil*, 1857). The lines can be translated "At other
times, dead calm, large mirror / Of my despair."
4. Probably an allusion to *Hamlet* 3.1.81–82: "The undiscovered country from whose
bourn / No traveller returns."
5. More trouble than it's worth.

This is the period of life in which such moments of which I have spoken are likely to come. What moments? Why, the moments of boredom, of weariness, of dissatisfaction. Rash moments. I mean moments when the still young are inclined to commit rash actions, such as getting married suddenly or else throwing up a job for no reason.

This is not a marriage story. It wasn't so bad as that with me. My action, rash as it was, had more the character of divorce—almost of desertion. For no reason on which a sensible person could put a finger I threw up my job—chucked my berth—left the ship of which the worst that could be said was that she was a steamship and therefore, perhaps, not entitled to that blind loyalty[6] which. . . . However, it's no use trying to put a gloss on what even at the time I myself half suspected to be a caprice.

It was in an Eastern port.[7] She was an Eastern ship, inasmuch as then she belonged to that port. She traded among dark islands on a blue reef-scarred sea, with the Red Ensign over the taffrail and at her masthead a house-flag, also red, but with a green border and with a white crescent[8] in it. For an Arab owned her, and a Syed[9] at that. Hence the green border on the flag. He was the head of a great House of Straits Arabs, but as loyal a subject of the complex British Empire as you could find east of the Suez Canal.[1] World politics did not trouble him at all, but he had a great occult power amongst his own people.

It was all one to us who owned the ship. He had to employ white men in the shipping part of his business, and many of those he so employed

---

6. Conrad, like many sailors of his generation, had an attachment to sailing vessels and considered steamships a lesser class of vessels. In his *The Mirror of the Sea* (1906), he says:

   The taking of a modern steamship about the world * * * has not the same quality of intimacy with nature, which, after all, is an indispensable condition to the building up of an art. It is less personal and a more exact calling; less arduous, but also less gratifying in the lack of close communion between the artist and the medium of his art. It is, in short, less a matter of love. Its effects are measured exactly in time and space as no effect of an art can be (MS 30).

7. Singapore, a port city on the southern tip of the Malay Peninsula. See p. 483. Conrad draws on his experience as first mate aboard the *Vidar* (1887–88), a position he similarly suddenly gave up, presumably with no particularly good reason.

8. A symbol for Islam, as is the color green, which is closely associated with the green dome on the prophet's mosque in Medina, Saudi Arabia. "Red Ensign": the official flag of the British Merchant Marine service. Red is thus associated with the Merchant Marine.

9. Or Sayyid; a title designating a man who traces his ancestry to Muhammad through his grandsons Hasan ibn Ali and Husayn ibn Ali but also simply a title of honor. Sayyid Mohsin Bin Saleh Ja'fri (1809–1894), the owner of the *Vidar*, is the model for this character.

1. The canal connecting the Mediterranean Sea to the Red Sea, which was completed in 1869 to provide an alternative to the long trip around Africa to get to the East. "Straits Arabs": Arabs living in the British Straits Settlements colony primarily located on the Malay Peninsula and consisting of Penang, Singapore, Malacca (Melaka), and the Dinding (Manjung). See p. 483.

had never set eyes on him from the first to the last day. I myself saw him but once, quite accidentally on a wharf—an old, dark little man blind in one eye, in a snowy robe and yellow slippers. He was having his hand severely kissed by a crowd of Malay pilgrims to whom he had done some favour, in the way of food and money. His alms-giving, I have heard, was most extensive, covering almost the whole Archipelago.[2] For isn't it said that "The charitable man is the friend of Allah"?[3]

Excellent (and picturesque) Arab owner, about whom one needed not to trouble one's head, a most excellent Scottish ship—for she was that from the keel up—excellent sea-boat, easy to keep clean, most handy in every way, and if it had not been for her internal pro-pulsion, worthy of any man's love; I cherish to this day a profound respect for her memory. As to the kind of trade she was engaged in and the character of my shipmates, I could not have been happier if I had had the life and the men made to my order by a benevolent Enchanter.

And suddenly I left all this. I left it in that, to us, inconsequential manner in which a bird flies away from a comfortable branch. It was as though all unknowing I had heard a whisper or seen some-thing. Well—perhaps! One day I was perfectly right and the next everything was gone—glamour, flavour, interest, contentment—everything. It was one of these moments, you know. The green sick-ness[4] of late youth descended on me and carried me off. Carried me off that ship, I mean.

We were only four white men on board, with a large crew of Kalashes and two Malay petty officers. The Captain[5] stared hard as if wondering what ailed me. But he was a sailor, and he, too, had been young at one time. Presently a smile came to lurk under his thick iron-grey moustache, and he observed that, of course, if I felt I must go he couldn't keep me by main force. And it was arranged that I should be paid off the next morning. As I was going out of the chart-room he added suddenly, in a peculiar wistful tone, that he hoped I would find what I was so anxious to go and look for. A soft, cryptic utterance which seemed to reach deeper than any diamond-hard tool could have done. I do believe he understood my case.

2. I.e., the Malay Archipelago.
3. Not a direct quote from the Qur'an or the *Hadith*, but charity's importance is empha-sized throughout both.
4. Chlorosis, an anemia that affects young girls in puberty, causing a greenish tint to the skin. Conrad, though, is using the term figuratively to refer to an illness associated with youth.
5. Captain Kent is modeled on James Craig (1846–1929), captain of the *Vidar* while Con-rad served as first mate.

But the second engineer[6] attacked me differently. He was a sturdy young Scot, with a smooth face and light eyes. His honest red countenance emerged out of the engine-room companion and then the whole robust man, with shirt sleeves turned up, wiping slowly the massive fore-arms with a lump of cotton-waste.[7] And his light eyes expressed bitter distaste, as though our friendship had turned to ashes. He said weightily: "Oh! Aye! I've been thinking it was about time for you to run away home and get married to some silly girl."

It was tacitly understood in the port that John Nieven was a fierce mysogynist; and the absurd character of the sally convinced me that he meant to be nasty—very nasty—had meant to say the most crushing thing he could think of. My laugh sounded deprecatory. Nobody but a friend could be so angry as that. I became a little crestfallen. Our chief engineer[8] also took a characteristic view of my action, but in a kindlier spirit.

He was young, too, but very thin, and with a mist of fluffy brown beard all round his haggard face. All day long, at sea or in harbour, he could be seen walking hastily up and down the after-deck, wearing an intense, spiritually rapt expression, which was caused by a perpetual consciousness of unpleasant physical sensations in his internal economy. For he was a confirmed dyspeptic. His view of my case was very simple. He said it was nothing but deranged liver. Of course! He suggested I should stay for another trip and meantime dose myself with a certain patent medicine in which his own belief was absolute. "I'll tell you what I'll do. I'll buy you two bottles, out of my own pocket. There. I can't say fairer than that, can I?"

I believe he would have perpetrated the atrocity (or generosity) at the merest sign of weakening on my part. By that time, however, I was more discontented, disgusted, and dogged than ever. The past eighteen months, so full of new and varied experience, appeared a dreary, prosaic waste of days. I felt—how shall I express it?—that there was no truth to be got out of them.

What truth? I should have been hard put to it to explain. Probably, if pressed, I would have burst into tears simply. I was young enough for that.

Next day the Captain and I transacted our business in the Harbour Office. It was a lofty, big, cool, white room, where the screened light of day glowed serenely. Everybody in it—the officials, the public—were in white. Only the heavy polished desks gleamed darkly

---

6. John Nieven, the second engineer, is modeled after John C. Niven (1853–1926), who was the second engineer of the *Vidar* during Conrad's time with the ship.
7. Refuse yarn from cotton manufacturing for cleaning machinery and other uses.
8. Modeled after John Allen, first engineer of the *Vidar* during Conrad's time aboard.

in a central avenue, and some papers lying on them were blue. Enormous punkahs[9] sent from on high a gentle draught through that immaculate interior and upon our perspiring heads.

The official behind the desk we approached grinned amiably and kept it up till, in answer to his perfunctory question, "Sign off and on again?" my Captain answered, "No! Signing off for good." And then his grin vanished in sudden solemnity. He did not look at me again till he handed me my papers with a sorrowful expression, as if they had been my passports for Hades.

While I was putting them away he murmured some question to the Captain, and I heard the latter answer good-humouredly:

"No. He leaves us to go home."

"Oh!" the other exclaimed, nodding mournfully over my sad condition.

I didn't know him outside the official building, but he leaned forward over the desk to shake hands with me, compassionately, as one would with some poor devil going out to be hanged; and I am afraid I performed my part ungraciously, in the hardened manner of an impenitent criminal.

No homeward-bound mail-boat was due for three or four days. Being now a man without a ship, and having for a time broken my connection with the sea—become, in fact, a mere potential passenger—it would have been more appropriate perhaps if I had gone to stay at an hotel.[1] There it was, too, within a stone's throw of the Harbour Office, low, but somehow palatial, displaying its white, pillared pavilions surrounded by trim grass plots. I would have felt a passenger indeed in there! I gave it a hostile glance and directed my steps towards the Officers' Sailors' Home.[2]

I walked in the sunshine, disregarding it, and in the shade of the big trees on the Esplanade without enjoying it. The heat of the tropical East descended through the leafy boughs, enveloping my thinly-clad body, clinging to my rebellious discontent, as if to rob it of its freedom.

The Officers' Home was a large bungalow with a wide verandah and a curiously suburban-looking little garden of bushes and a few trees between it and the street. That institution partook somewhat of the character of a residential club, but with a slightly Governmental flavour about it, because it was administered by the

---

9. Large fans made of cloth or canvas on a rectangular frame and suspended from the ceiling, operated either manually by a cord or electrically (Hindi).
1. Given its location, Conrad perhaps has in mind the Hôtel de l'Europe, which opened in 1857.
2. Modeled after the Sailor's Home in Singapore, founded in 1851.

Harbour Office. Its manager was officially styled Chief Steward.[3] He was an unhappy, wizened little man, who if put into a jockey's rig[4] would have looked the part to perfection. But it was obvious that at some time or other in his life, in some capacity or other, he had been connected with the sea. Possibly in the comprehensive capacity of a failure.

I should have thought his employment a very easy one, but he used to affirm for some reason or other that his job would be the death of him some day. It was rather mysterious. Perhaps everything naturally was too much trouble for him. He certainly seemed to hate having people in the house.

On entering it I thought he must be feeling pleased. It was as still as a tomb. I could see no one in the living rooms; and the verandah, too, was empty, except for a man at the far end dozing prone in a long chair. At the noise of my footsteps he opened one horribly fish-like eye. He was a stranger to me. I retreated from there, and, crossing the dining-room—a very bare apartment with a motionless punkah hanging over the centre table—I knocked at a door labelled in black letters: "Chief Steward."

The answer to my knock being a vexed and doleful plaint: "Oh, dear! Oh, dear! What is it now?" I went in at once.

It was a strange room to find in the tropics. Twilight and stuffiness reigned in there. The fellow had hung enormously ample, dusty, cheap lace curtains over his windows, which were shut. Piles of cardboard boxes, such as milliners and dressmakers use in Europe, cumbered the corners; and by some means he had procured for himself the sort of furniture that might have come out of a respectable parlour in the East-end of London[5]—a horsehair sofa, arm-chairs of the same. I glimpsed grimy antimacassars[6] scattered over that horrid upholstery, which was awe-inspiring, insomuch that one could not guess what mysterious accident, need, or fancy had collected it there. Its owner had taken off his tunic, and in white trousers and a thin short-sleeved singlet prowled behind the chair-backs nursing his meagre elbows.

An exclamation of dismay escaped him when he heard that I had come for a stay; but he could not deny that there were plenty of vacant rooms.

---

3. Modeled after Charles Phillips (1834–1904). In a letter to W. G. St. Clair (March 31, 1917), Conrad wrote of the steward, "He was a meagre wizened creature, always bemoaning his fate, and did try to do me an unfriendly turn for some reason or other" (CL 6:62; see p. 377).
4. A jockey's clothes, outfit.
5. At the time, a poor, working-class area of London.
6. Coverings to protect furniture against Macassar hair oil or other soiling.

"Very well. Can you give me the one I had before?"

He emitted a faint moan from behind a pile of cardboard boxes on the table, which might have contained gloves or handkerchiefs or neckties. I wonder what the fellow did keep in them? There was a smell of decaying coral, of Oriental dust, of zoological specimens in that den of his. I could only see the top of his head and his unhappy eyes levelled at me over the barrier.

"It's only for a couple of days," I said, intending to cheer him up.

"Perhaps you would like to pay in advance?" he suggested eagerly.

"Certainly not!" I burst out directly I could speak. "Never heard of such a thing! This is the most infernal[7] cheek. . . ."

He had seized his head in both hands—a gesture of despair which checked my indignation.

"Oh, dear! Oh, dear! Don't fly out like this. I am asking everybody."

"I don't believe it," I said bluntly.

"Well, I am going to. And if you gentlemen all agreed to pay in advance I could make Hamilton[8] pay up too. He's always turning up ashore dead broke, and even when he has some money he won't settle his bills. I don't know what to do with him. He swears at me and tells me I can't chuck a white man out into the street here. So if you only would. . . ."

I was amazed. Incredulous too. I suspected the fellow of gratuitous impertinence. I told him with marked emphasis that I would see him and Hamilton hanged first, and requested him to conduct me to my room with no more of his nonsense. He produced then a key from somewhere and led the way out of his lair, giving me a vicious sidelong look in passing.

"Anyone I know staying here?" I asked him before he left my room.

He had recovered his usual pained impatient tone, and said that Captain Giles was there, back from a Sulu Sea[9] trip. Two other guests were staying also. He paused. And, of course, Hamilton, he added.

"Oh, yes! Hamilton," I said, and the miserable creature took himself off with a final groan.

---

7. Probably a euphemism for *damned*. Early in Conrad's writing career, he was sometimes criticized for profanity in his works. For example, in a review of *The Nigger of the "Narcissus,"* the anonymous reviewer referred to the language of the sailors as "[s]trong, brutal, and in many places absolutely repellent by reason of the robustness of the adjectives employed" ("A Tale of the Sea," *The Literary World*, December 7, 1898, p. 78). Subsequently, Conrad often employed euphemisms instead.

8. Norman Sherry speculates that a certain C. Hamilton may have been the model for Hamilton (*CEW* 214), who also appears in Conrad's "The End of the Tether" (1902).

9. In the Pacific Ocean bordered by Borneo, the Philippines, and the Sulu Archipelago. See p. 335. "Captain Giles": in letters to Sir Sidney Colvin (February 27, 1917, *CL* 6:37) and W. G. St. Clair, *CL* 6:62; see pp. 375 and 377), Conrad identifies a Captain Patterson as the model for Captain Giles.

His impudence still rankled when I came into the dining-room at tiffin time. He was there on duty overlooking the Chinamen servants. The tiffin was laid on one end only of the long table, and the punkah was stirring the hot air lazily—mostly above a barren waste of polished wood.

We were four around the cloth. The dozing stranger from the chair was one. Both his eyes were partly opened now, but they did not seem to see anything. He was supine. The dignified person next him, with short side whiskers and a carefully scraped chin, was, of course, Hamilton. I have never seen any one so full of dignity for the station in life Providence had been pleased to place him in. I had been told that he regarded me as a rank outsider. He raised not only his eyes, but his eyebrows as well, at the sound I made pulling back my chair.

Captain Giles was at the head of the table. I exchanged a few words of greeting with him and sat down on his left. Stout and pale, with a great shiny dome of a bald forehead and prominent brown eyes, he might have been anything but a seaman. You would not have been surprised to learn that he was an architect. To me (I know how absurd it is) to me he looked like a churchwarden.[1] He had the appearance of a man from whom you would expect sound advice, moral sentiments, with perhaps a platitude or two thrown in on occasion, not from a desire to dazzle, but from honest conviction.

Though very well known and appreciated in the shipping world, he had no regular employment. He did not want it. He had his own peculiar position. He was an expert. An expert in—how shall I say it?—in intricate navigation. He was supposed to know more about remote and imperfectly charted parts of the Archipelago than any man living. His brain must have been a perfect warehouse of reefs, positions, bearings, images of headlands, shapes of obscure coasts, aspects of innumerable islands, desert and otherwise. Any ship, for instance, bound on a trip to Palawan[2] or somewhere that way would have Captain Giles on board, either in temporary command or "to assist the master." It was said that he had a retaining fee from a wealthy firm of Chinese steamship owners,[3] in view of such services. Besides, he was always ready to relieve any man who wished to take a spell ashore for a time. No owner was ever known to object to an arrangement of that sort. For it seemed to be the established opinion at the port that Captain Giles was as good as the best, if not a little better. But in Hamilton's view he was an "outsider." I believe that for

---

1. In the Anglican Church, an elected lay member of a congregation who maintains church property and order in the church.
2. A large island of the Philippines that divides the Sulu Sea from the South China Sea. See p. 335.
3. Stape and Simmons (*SSSL*) suggest that this may refer to the Singapore-based Kim Seng Shipping Company, for which Captain Patterson worked.

Hamilton the generalisation "outsider" covered the whole lot of us; though I suppose that he made some distinctions in his mind.

I didn't try to make conversation with Captain Giles, whom I had not seen more than twice in my life. But, of course, he knew who I was. After a while, inclining his big shiny head my way, he addressed me first in his friendly fashion. He presumed from seeing me there, he said, that I had come ashore for a couple of days' leave.

He was a low-voiced man. I spoke a little louder, saying that: No—I had left the ship for good.

"A free man for a bit," was his comment.

"I suppose I may call myself that—since eleven o'clock," I said.

Hamilton had stopped eating at the sound of our voices. He laid down his knife and fork gently, got up, and muttering something about "this infernal heat cutting one's appetite," went out of the room. Almost immediately we heard him leave the house down the veran-dah steps.

On this Captain Giles remarked easily that the fellow had no doubt gone off to look after my old job. The Chief Steward, who had been leaning against the wall, brought his face of an unhappy goat nearer to the table and addressed us dolefully. His object was to unburden himself of his eternal grievance against Hamilton. The man kept him in hot water with the Harbour Office as to the state of his accounts. He wished to goodness he would get my job, though in truth what would it be? Temporary relief at best.

I said: "You needn't worry. He won't get my job. My successor is on board already."

He was surprised, and I believe his face fell a little at the news. Captain Giles gave a soft laugh. We got up and went out on the verandah, leaving the supine stranger to be dealt with by the China-men. The last thing I saw they had put a plate with a slice of pine-apple on it before him and stood back to watch what would happen. But the experiment seemed a failure. He sat insensible.

It was imparted to me in a low voice by Captain Giles that this was an officer of some Rajah's[4] yacht which had come into our port to be dry-docked. Must have been "seeing life" last night, he added, wrinkling his nose in an intimate, confidential way which pleased me vastly. For Captain Giles had prestige. He was credited with wonderful adventures and with some mysterious tragedy in his life. And no man had a word to say against him. He continued:

"I remember him first coming ashore here some years ago. Seems only the other day. He was a nice boy. Oh! these nice boys!"

---

4. Originally an Indian prince or king, but later it came to be used more generically for any ruler in the East (Hindi).

I could not help laughing aloud. He looked startled, then joined in the laugh. "No! No! I didn't mean that,"[5] he cried. "What I meant is that some of them do go soft mighty quick out here."

Jocularly I suggested the beastly heat as the first cause. But Captain Giles disclosed himself possessed of a deeper philosophy. Things out East were made easy for white men. That was all right. The difficulty was to go on keeping white, and some of these nice boys did not know how. He gave me a searching look, and in a benevolent, heavy-uncle manner asked point blank:

"Why did you throw up your berth?"

I became angry all of a sudden; for you can understand how exasperating such a question was to a man who didn't know. I said to myself that I ought to shut up that moralist; and to him aloud I said with challenging politeness:

"Why . . . ? Do you disapprove?"

He was too disconcerted to do more than mutter confusedly: "I! . . . In a general way . . ." and then gave me up. But he retired in good order, under the cover of a heavily humorous remark that he, too, was getting soft, and that this was his time for taking his little siesta—when he was on shore. "Very bad habit. Very bad habit."

The simplicity of the man would have disarmed a touchiness even more youthful than mine. So when next day at tiffin he bent his head towards me and said that he had met my late Captain last evening, adding in an undertone: "He's very sorry you left. He had never had a mate that suited him so well," I answered him earnestly, without any affectation, that I certainly hadn't been so comfortable in any ship or with any commander in all my sea-going days.

"Well—then," he murmured.

"Haven't you heard, Captain Giles, that I intend to go home?"

"Yes," he said benevolently. "I have heard that sort of thing so often before."

"What of that?" I cried. I thought he was the most dull, unimaginative man I had ever met. I don't know what more I would have said, but the much-belated Hamilton came in just then and took his usual seat. So I dropped into a mumble.

"Anyhow, you shall see it done this time."

Hamilton, beautifully shaved, gave Captain Giles a curt nod, but didn't even condescend to raise his eyebrows at me; and when he spoke it was only to tell the Chief Steward that the food on his plate wasn't fit to be set before a gentleman. The individual addressed seemed much too unhappy to groan. He only cast his eyes up to the punkah and that was all.

---

5. Stape and Simmons (*SSSL*) suggest that the narrator infers an unintended homosexual meaning for the term *nice boys*.

Captain Giles and I got up from the table, and the stranger next to Hamilton followed our example, manœuvring himself to his feet with difficulty. He, poor fellow, not because he was hungry but I verily believe only to recover his self-respect, had tried to put some of that unworthy food into his mouth. But after dropping his fork twice and generally making a failure of it, he had sat still with an air of intense mortification combined with a ghastly glazed stare. Both Giles and I had avoided looking his way at table.

On the verandah he stopped short on purpose to address to us anxiously a long remark which I failed to understand completely. It sounded like some horrible unknown language. But when Captain Giles, after only an instant for reflection, answered him with homely[6] friendliness, "Aye, to be sure. You are right there," he appeared very much gratified indeed, and went away (pretty straight too) to seek a distant long chair.

"What was he trying to say?" I asked with disgust.

"I don't know. Mustn't be down too much on a fellow. He's feeling pretty wretched, you may be sure; and to-morrow he'll feel worse yet."

Judging by the man's appearance it seemed impossible. I wondered what sort of complicated debauch had reduced him to that unspeakable condition. Captain Giles' benevolence was spoiled by a curious air of complacency which I disliked. I said with a little laugh:

"Well, he will have you to look after him."

He made a deprecatory gesture, sat down, and took up a paper. I did the same. The papers were old and uninteresting, filled up mostly with dreary stereotyped descriptions of Queen Victoria's first jubilee celebrations.[7] Probably we should have quickly fallen into a tropical afternoon doze if it had not been for Hamilton's voice raised in the dining-room. He was finishing his tiffin there. The big double doors stood wide open permanently, and he could not have had any idea how near to the doorway our chairs were placed. He was heard in a loud, supercilious tone answering some statement ventured by the Chief Steward.

"I am not going to be rushed into anything. They will be glad enough to get a gentleman I imagine. There is no hurry."

A loud whispering from the steward succeeded and then again Hamilton was heard with even intenser scorn.

"What? That young ass who fancies himself for having been chief mate with Kent so long? . . . Preposterous."

Giles and I looked at each other. Kent being the name of my late commander, Captain Giles' whisper, "He's talking of you," seemed

6. In the sense of familiar or reminding one of home rather than unattractive.
7. The Golden Jubilee celebrations, commemorating Victoria's fifty years of reigning, occurred in 1887.

to me sheer waste of breath. The Chief Steward must have stuck to
his point whatever it was, because Hamilton was heard again more
supercilious, if possible, and also very emphatic:

"Rubbish, my good man! One doesn't *compete* with a rank outsider like that. There's plenty of time."

Then there was pushing of chairs, footsteps in the next room, and
plaintive expostulations from the Steward, who was pursuing Hamilton, even out of doors through the main entrance.

"That's a very insulting sort of man," remarked Captain Giles—
superfluously, I thought. "Very insulting. You haven't offended him
in some way, have you?"

"Never spoke to him in my life," I said grumpily. "Can't imagine
what he means by competing. He has been trying for my job after I
left—and didn't get it. But that isn't exactly competition."

Captain Giles balanced his big benevolent head thoughtfully.
"He didn't get it," he repeated very slowly. "No, not likely either, with
Kent. Kent is no end sorry you left him. He gives you the name of a
good seaman too."

I flung away the paper I was still holding. I sat up, I slapped the
table with my open palm. I wanted to know why he would keep harp-
ing on that, my absolutely private affair. It was exasperating, really.

Captain Giles silenced me by the perfect equanimity of his gaze.
"Nothing to be annoyed about," he murmured reasonably, with an
evident desire to soothe the childish irritation he had aroused. And
he was really a man of an appearance so inoffensive that I tried to
explain myself as much as I could. I told him that I did not want to
hear any more about what was past and gone. It had been very nice
while it lasted, but now it was done with I preferred not to talk about
it or even think about it. I had made up my mind to go home.

He listened to the whole tirade in a particular, lending-the-ear
attitude, as if trying to detect a false note in it somewhere; then
straightened himself up and appeared to ponder sagaciously over
the matter.

"Yes. You told me you meant to go home. Anything in view there?"

Instead of telling him that it was none of his business I said
sullenly:

"Nothing that I know of."

I had indeed considered that rather blank side of the situation I had
created for myself by leaving suddenly my very satisfactory employment. And I was not very pleased with it. I had it on the tip of my
tongue to say that common sense had nothing to do with my action,
and that therefore it didn't deserve the interest Captain Giles seemed
to be taking in it. But he was puffing at a short wooden pipe now, and
looked so guileless, dense, and commonplace, that it seemed hardly
worth while to puzzle him either with truth or sarcasm.

He blew a cloud of smoke, then surprised me by a very abrupt: "Paid your passage money yet?"

Overcome by the shameless pertinacity of a man to whom it was rather difficult to be rude, I replied with exaggerated meekness that I had not done so yet. I thought there would be plenty of time to do that to-morrow.

And I was about to turn away, withdrawing my privacy from his fatuous, objectless attempts to test what sort of stuff it was made of, when he laid down his pipe in an extremely significant manner, you know, as if a critical moment had come, and leaned sideways over the table between us.

"Oh! You haven't yet!" He dropped his voice mysteriously. "Well, then I think you ought to know that there's something going on here."

I had never in my life felt more detached from all earthly goings on. Freed from the sea for a time, I preserved the sailor's consciousness of complete independence from all land affairs. How could they concern me? I gazed at Captain Giles' animation with scorn rather than with curiosity.

To his obviously preparatory question whether our steward had spoken to me that day I said he hadn't. And what's more he would have had precious little encouragement if he had tried to. I didn't want the fellow to speak to me at all.

Unrebuked by my petulance, Captain Giles, with an air of immense sagacity, began to tell me a minute tale about a Harbour Office peon.[8] It was absolutely pointless. A peon was seen walking that morning on the verandah with a letter in his hand. It was in an official envelope. As the habit of these fellows is, he had shown it to the first white man he came across. That man was our friend in the armchair. He, as I knew, was not in a state to interest himself in any sublunary matters. He could only wave the peon away. The peon then wandered on along the verandah and came upon Captain Giles, who was there by an extraordinary chance. . . .

At this point he stopped with a profound look. The letter, he continued, was addressed to the Chief Steward. Now what could Captain Ellis,[9] the Master Attendant, want to write to the Steward for? The fellow went every morning, anyhow, to the Harbour Office with his report, for orders or what not. He hadn't been back more than an hour before there was an office peon chasing him with a note. Now what was that for?

---

8. An attendant, messenger, orderly, or footman (Spanish). In this instance, almost certainly a native Malay.
9. Based on Captain Henry Ellis (1835–1908), the master attendant in Singapore from 1873 until 1888 who appointed Conrad captain of the *Otago* shortly before he retired. He appears in *Lord Jim* (1900), "Falk" (1903), and "The End of the Tether" as Captain Elliot.

And he began to speculate. It was not for this—and it could not be for that. As to that other thing it was unthinkable.

The fatuousness of all this made me stare. If the man had not been somehow a sympathetic personality I would have resented it like an insult. As it was, I felt only sorry for him. Something remarkably earnest in his gaze prevented me from laughing in his face. Neither did I yawn at him. I just stared.

His tone became a shade more mysterious. Directly the fellow (meaning the Steward) got that note he rushed for his hat and bolted out of the house. But it wasn't because the note called him to the Harbour Office. He didn't go there. He was not absent long enough for that. He came darting back in no time, flung his hat away, and raced about the dining-room moaning and slapping his forehead. All these exciting facts and manifestations had been observed by Captain Giles. He had, it seems, been meditating upon them ever since.

I began to pity him profoundly. And in a tone which I tried to make as little sarcastic as possible I said that I was glad he had found something to occupy his morning hours.

With his disarming simplicity he made me observe, as if it were a matter of some consequence, how strange it was that he should have spent the morning indoors at all. He generally was out before tiffin, visiting various offices, seeing his friends in the harbour, and so on. He had felt out of sorts somewhat on rising. Nothing much. Just enough to make him feel lazy.

All this with a sustained, holding stare which, in conjunction with the general inanity of the discourse, conveyed the impression of mild, dreary lunacy. And when he hitched his chair a little and dropped his voice to the low note of mystery, it flashed upon me that high professional reputation was not necessarily a guarantee of sound mind.

It never occurred to me then that I didn't know in what soundness of mind exactly consisted and what a delicate and, upon the whole, unimportant matter it was. With some idea of not hurting his feelings I blinked at him in an interested manner. But when he proceeded to ask me mysteriously whether I remembered what had passed just now between that Steward of ours and "that man Hamilton," I only grunted sour assent and turned away my head.

"Aye. But do you remember every word?" he insisted tactfully.

"I don't know. It's none of my business," I snapped out, consigning, moreover, the Steward and Hamilton aloud to eternal perdition.[1]

I meant to be very energetic and final, but Captain Giles continued to gaze at me thoughtfully. Nothing could stop him. He went

1. Probably a euphemism for *damnation*.

on to point out that my personality was involved in that conversation. When I tried to preserve the semblance of unconcern he became positively cruel. I heard what the man had said? Yes? What did I think of it then?—he wanted to know.

Captain Giles' appearance excluding the suspicion of mere sly malice, I came to the conclusion that he was simply the most tactless idiot on earth. I almost despised myself for the weakness of attempting to enlighten his common understanding. I started to explain that I did not think anything whatever. Hamilton was not worth a thought. What such an offensive loafer . . . —"Aye! that he is," interjected Captain Giles— . . . thought or said was below any decent man's contempt, and I did not propose to take the slightest notice of it.

This attitude seemed to me so simple and obvious that I was really astonished at Giles giving no sign of assent. Such perfect stupidity was almost interesting.

"What would you like me to do?" I asked laughing. "I can't start a row with him because of the opinion he has formed of me. Of course, I've heard of the contemptuous way he alludes to me. But he doesn't intrude his contempt on my notice. He has never expressed it in my hearing. For even just now he didn't know we could hear him. I should only make myself ridiculous."

That hopeless Giles went on puffing at his pipe moodily. All at once his face cleared, and he spoke.

"You missed my point."

"Have I? I am very glad to hear it," I said.

With increasing animation he stated again that I had missed his point. Entirely. And in a tone of growing self-conscious complacency he told me that few things escaped his attention, and he was rather used to think them out, and generally from his experience of life and men arrived at the right conclusion.

This bit of self-praise, of course, fitted excellently the laborious inanity of the whole conversation. The whole thing strengthened in me that obscure feeling of life being but a waste of days, which, half-unconsciously, had driven me out of a comfortable berth, away from men I liked, to flee from the menace of emptiness . . . and to find inanity at the first turn. Here was a man of recognised character and achievement disclosed as an absurd and dreary chatterer. And it was probably like this everywhere—from east to west, from the bottom to the top of the social scale.

A great discouragement fell on me. A spiritual drowsiness. Giles' voice was going on complacently; the very voice of the universal hollow conceit. And I was no longer angry with it. There was nothing original, nothing new, startling, informing to expect from the world: no opportunities to find out something about oneself, no wisdom to acquire, no fun to enjoy. Everything was stupid and overrated, even as Captain Giles was. So be it.

The name of Hamilton suddenly caught my ear and roused me up.

"I thought we had done with him," I said, with the greatest possible distaste.

"Yes. But considering what we happened to hear just now I think you ought to do it."

"Ought to do it?" I sat up bewildered. "Do what?"

Captain Giles confronted me very much surprised.

"Why! Do what I have been advising you to try. You go and ask the Steward what there was in that letter from the Harbour Office. Ask him straight out."

I remained speechless for a time. Here was something unexpected and original enough to be altogether incomprehensible. I murmured, astounded.

"But I thought it was Hamilton that you . . ."

"Exactly. Don't you let him. You do what I tell you. You tackle that Steward. You'll make him jump, I bet," insisted Captain Giles, waving his smouldering pipe impressively at me. Then he took three rapid puffs at it.

His aspect of triumphant acuteness was indescribable. Yet the man remained a strangely sympathetic creature. Benevolence radiated from him ridiculously, mildly, impressively. It was irritating, too. But I pointed out coldly, as one who deals with the incomprehensible, that I didn't see any reason to expose myself to a snub from the fellow. He was a very unsatisfactory steward and a miserable wretch besides, but I would just as soon think of tweaking his nose.

"Tweaking his nose," said Captain Giles in a scandalised tone. "Much use it would be to you."

That remark was so irrelevant that one could make no answer to it. But the sense of the absurdity was beginning at last to exercise its well-known fascination. I felt I must not let the man talk to me any more. I got up, observing curtly that he was too much for me—that I couldn't make him out.

Before I had time to move away he spoke again in a changed tone of obstinacy and puffing nervously at his pipe.

"Well—he's a—no account cuss—anyhow. You just—ask him. That's all."

That new manner impressed me—or rather made me pause. But sanity asserting its sway at once I left the verandah after giving him a mirthless smile. In a few strides I found myself in the dining-room, now cleared and empty. But during that short time various thoughts occurred to me, such as: that Giles had been making fun of me, expecting some amusement at my expense;

that I probably looked silly and gullible; that I knew very little of life. . . .

The door facing me across the dining-room flew open to my extreme surprise. It was the door inscribed with the word "Steward" and the man himself ran out of his stuffy Philistinish[2] lair in his absurd hunted animal manner, making for the garden door.

To this day I don't know what made me call after him: "I say! Wait a minute." Perhaps it was the sidelong glance he gave me; or possibly I was yet under the influence of Captain Giles' mysterious earnestness. Well, it was an impulse of some sort; an effect of that force somewhere within our lives which shapes them this way or that.[3] For if these words had not escaped from my lips (my will had nothing to do with that) my existence would, to be sure, have been still a seaman's existence, but directed on now to me utterly inconceivable lines.

No. My will had nothing to do with it. Indeed, no sooner had I made that fateful noise than I became extremely sorry for it. Had the man stopped and faced me I would have had to retire in disorder. For I had no notion to carry out Captain Giles' idiotic joke, either at my own expense or at the expense of the Steward.

But here the old human instinct of the chase came into play. He pretended to be deaf, and I, without thinking a second about it, dashed along my own side of the dining table and cut him off at the very door.

"Why can't you answer when you are spoken to?" I asked roughly.

He leaned against the lintel[4] of the door. He looked extremely wretched. Human nature is, I fear, not very nice right through. There are ugly spots in it. I found myself growing angry, and that, I believe, only because my quarry looked so woe-begone. Miserable beggar![5]

I went for him without more ado. "I understand there was an official communication to the Home from the Harbour Office this morning. Is that so?"

Instead of telling me to mind my own business, as he might have done, he began to whine with an undertone of impudence. He couldn't see me anywhere this morning. He couldn't be expected to run all over the town after me.

"Who wants you to?" I cried. And then my eyes became opened to the inwardness of things and speeches the triviality of which had been so baffling and tiresome.

2. A Philistine is an uneducated or uncultured person. This use of the term predates Matthew Arnold's *Culture and Anarchy: An Essay in Political and Social Criticism* (1869), but Arnold popularized its usage.
3. Hawthorn (*HSL*) sees a possible allusion to *Hamlet* 5.2.10–11: "There's a divinity that shapes our ends, / Rough-hew them how we will—."
4. Stape and Simmons (*SSSL*) note the looser use of this word at the time to include the entire door-frame, as opposed to its more narrow usage, which refers to only the top of the door frame.
5. Fellow or chap, sometimes used contemptuously.

I told him I wanted to know what was in that letter. My sternness of tone and behaviour was only half assumed. Curiosity can be a very fierce sentiment—at times.

He took refuge in a silly, muttering sulkiness. It was nothing to me, he mumbled. I had told him I was going home. And since I was going home he didn't see why he should. . . .

That was the line of his argument, and it was irrelevant enough to be almost insulting. Insulting to one's intelligence, I mean.

In that twilight region between youth and maturity, in which I had my being then, one is peculiarly sensitive to that kind of insult. I am afraid my behaviour to the Steward became very rough indeed. But it wasn't in him to face out anything or anybody. Drug habit or solitary tippling, perhaps. And when I forgot myself so far as to swear at him he broke down and began to shriek.

I don't mean to say that he made a great outcry. It was a cynical shrieking confession, only faint—piteously faint. It wasn't very coherent either, but sufficiently so to strike me dumb at first. I turned my eyes from him in righteous indignation, and perceived Captain Giles in the verandah doorway surveying quietly the scene, his own handiwork, if I may express it in that way. His smouldering black pipe was very noticeable in his big, paternal fist. So, too, was the glitter of his heavy gold watch-chain across the breast of his white tunic. He exhaled an atmosphere of virtuous sagacity thick enough for any innocent soul to fly to confidently. I flew to him.

"You would never believe it," I cried. "It was a notification that a master is wanted for some ship. There's a command apparently going about and this fellow puts the thing in his pocket."

The Steward screamed out in accents of loud despair, "You will be the death of me!"

The mighty slap he gave his wretched forehead was very loud, too. But when I turned to look at him he was no longer there. He had rushed away somewhere out of sight. This sudden disappearance made me laugh.

This was the end of the incident—for me. Captain Giles, however, staring at the place where the Steward had been, began to haul at his gorgeous gold chain till at last the watch came up from the deep pocket like solid truth from a well.[6] Solemnly he lowered it down again and only then said:

"Just three o'clock. You will be in time—if you don't lose any, that is."

"In time for what?" I asked.

---

6. An allusion to the saying that truth is found in a deep well. The origins of this idea are often attributed to the Greek philosopher Democritus (c. 460–c. 370 B.C.E.).

"Good Lord! For the Harbour Office. This must be looked into."

Strictly speaking, he was right. But I've never had much taste for investigation, for showing people up and all that, no doubt, ethically meritorious kind of work. And my view of the episode was purely ethical. If any one had to be the death of the Steward I didn't see why it shouldn't be Captain Giles himself, a man of age and standing, and a permanent resident. Whereas I, in comparison, felt myself a mere bird of passage in that port. In fact, it might have been said that I had already broken off my connection. I muttered that I didn't think—it was nothing to me. . . .

"Nothing!" repeated Captain Giles, giving some signs of quiet, deliberate indignation. "Kent warned me you were a peculiar young fellow. You will tell me next that a command is nothing to you—and after all the trouble I've taken, too!"

"The trouble!" I murmured, uncomprehending. What trouble? All I could remember was being mystified and bored by his conversation for a solid hour after tiffin. And he called that taking a lot of trouble.

He was looking at me with a self-complacency which would have been odious in any other man. All at once, as if a page of a book had been turned over disclosing a word which made plain all that had gone before, I perceived that this matter had also another than an ethical aspect.

And still I did not move. Captain Giles lost his patience a little. With an angry puff at his pipe he turned his back on my hesitation.

But it was not hesitation on my part. I had been, if I may express myself so, put out of gear mentally. But as soon as I had convinced myself that this stale, unprofitable world of my discontent[7] contained such a thing as a command to be seized, I recovered my powers of locomotion.

It's a good step from the Officers' Home to the Harbour Office; but with the magic word "Command" in my head I found myself suddenly on the quay as if transported there in the twinkling of an eye,[8] before a portal of dressed white stone above a flight of shallow white steps.

All this seemed to glide towards me swiftly. The whole great roadstead to the right was just a mere flicker of blue, and the dim cool hall swallowed me up out of the heat and glare of which I had not been aware till the very moment I passed in from it.

---

7. Possible allusion to *Hamlet* 1.2.133–134: "How weary, stale, flat and unprofitable / Seems to me all the uses of this world!"
8. Cf. 1 Corinthians 15:52: "In a moment, in the twinkling of an eye, at the last trump: for the trumpet shall sound, and the dead shall be raised incorruptible, and we shall be changed."

The broad inner staircase insinuated itself under my feet somehow. Command is a strong magic. The first human beings I perceived
distinctly since I had parted with the indignant back of Captain
Giles were the crew of the harbour steam-launch lounging on the
spacious landing about the curtained archway of the shipping office.

It was there that my buoyancy abandoned me. The atmosphere of
officialdom would kill anything that breathes the air of human
endeavour, would extinguish hope and fear alike in the supremacy of
paper and ink. I passed heavily under the curtain which the Malay
coxswain of the harbour launch raised for me. There was nobody in
the office except the clerks, writing in two industrious rows. But the
head shipping-master[9] hopped down from his elevation and hurried
along on the thick mats to meet me in the broad central passage.

He had a Scottish name, but his complexion was of a rich olive
hue, his short beard was jet black, and his eyes, also black, had a
languishing expression. He asked confidentially:

"You want to see Him?"

All lightness of spirit and body having departed from me at the
touch of officialdom, I looked at the scribe without animation and
asked in my turn wearily:

"What do you think? Is it any use?"

"My goodness! He has asked for you twice to-day."

This emphatic He was the supreme authority, the Marine Superintendent, the Harbour-Master—a very great person in the eyes of
every single quill-driver[1] in the room. But that was nothing to the
opinion he had of his own greatness.

Captain Ellis looked upon himself as a sort of divine (pagan)
emanation, the deputy-Neptune[2] for the circumambient seas. If he
did not actually rule the waves,[3] he pretended to rule the fate of the
mortals whose lives were cast upon the waters.

This uplifting illusion made him inquisitorial and peremptory.
And as his temperament was choleric[4] there were fellows who were
actually afraid of him. He was redoubtable, not in virtue of his
office, but because of his unwarrantable assumptions. I had never
had anything to do with him before.

I said: "Oh! He has asked for me twice. Then perhaps I had better go in."

9. Ingram (ISL) argues that Mr. R., as he is called later, is the character Archie Ruthvel of
    Lord Jim.
1. Pejorative term for a clerk.
2. Roman god of the seas.
3. Hawthorn (HSL) sees an allusion to the patriotic song "Rule, Britannia" by James
    Thomson (1700–1748) and Thomas Arne (1710–1778), which includes the refrain:
    "Rule, Britannia! Britannia rule the waves!"
4. Hot, wrathful, irascible.

"You must! You must!"

The shipping-master led the way with a mincing gait round the whole system of desks to a tall and important-looking door, which he opened with a deferential action of the arm.

He stepped right in (but without letting go of the handle) and, after gazing reverently down the room for a while, beckoned me in by a silent jerk of the head. Then he slipped out at once and shut the door after me most delicately.

Three lofty windows gave on the harbour. There was nothing in them but the dark-blue sparkling sea and the paler luminous blue of the sky. My eye caught in the depths and distances of these blue tones the white speck of some big ship just arrived and about to anchor in the outer roadstead. A ship from home—after perhaps ninety days at sea. There is something touching about a ship coming in from sea and folding her white wings[5] for a rest.

The next thing I saw was the top-knot of silver hair surmounting Captain Ellis' smooth red face, which would have been apoplectic if it hadn't had such a fresh appearance.

Our deputy-Neptune had no beard on his chin, and there was no trident to be seen standing in a corner anywhere, like an umbrella. But his hand was holding a pen—the official pen, far mightier than the sword[6] in making or marring the fortune of simple toiling men. He was looking over his shoulder at my advance.

When I had come well within range he saluted me by a nerve-shattering: "Where have you been all this time?"

As it was no concern of his I did not take the slightest notice of the shot. I said simply that I had heard there was a master needed for some vessel, and being a sailing-ship man I thought I would apply. . . .

He interrupted me. "Why! Hang it! *You* are the right man for that job—if there had been twenty others after it. But no fear of that. They are all afraid to catch hold. That's what's the matter."

He was very irritated. I said innocently: "Are they, sir. I wonder why?"

"Why!" he fumed. "Afraid of the sails. Afraid of a white crew. Too much trouble. Too much work. Too long out here. Easy life and deck-chairs more their mark. Here I sit with the Consul-General's cable[7]

5. A common metaphor for a ship's sails.
6. Cf. "The pen is mightier than the sword" (act 2, scene 2) from the 1839 play *Richelieu; Or the Conspiracy* by Edward Bulwer-Lytton (1803–1873).
7. A telegraph cable message. "Consul-General": see p. 19, n. 7; the Consul-General in Bangkok during the time *The Shadow-Line* is set was Edward Blencowe Gould (1847–1916), whom Conrad knew (*CL* 6:62; see p. 378).

before me, and the only man fit for the job not to be found anywhere. I began to think you were funking[8] it too. . . ."

"I haven't been long getting to the office," I remarked calmly.

"You have a good name out here, though," he growled savagely without looking at me.

"I am very glad to hear it from you, sir," I said.

"Yes. But you are not on the spot when you are wanted. You know you weren't. That steward of yours wouldn't dare to neglect a message from this office. Where the devil did you hide yourself for the best part of the day?"

I only smiled kindly down on him, and he seemed to recollect himself, and asked me to take a seat. He explained that the master of a British ship having died in Bankok[9] the Consul-General had cabled to him a request for a competent man to be sent out to take command.

Apparently, in his mind, I was the man from the first, though for the looks of the thing the notification addressed to the Sailors' Home was general. An agreement had already been prepared. He gave it to me to read, and when I handed it back to him with the remark that I accepted its terms, the deputy-Neptune signed it, stamped it with his own exalted hand, folded it in four (it was a sheet of blue foolscap[1]), and presented it to me—a gift of extraordinary potency, for, as I put it in my pocket, my head swam a little.

"This is your appointment to the command," he said with a certain gravity. "An official appointment binding the owners to conditions which you have accepted. Now—when will you be ready to go?"

I said I would be ready that very day if necessary. He caught me at my word with great readiness. The steamer *Melita*[2] was leaving for Bankok that evening about seven. He would request her captain officially to give me a passage and wait for me till ten o'clock.

Then he rose from his office chair, and I got up too. My head swam, there was no doubt about it, and I felt a heaviness of limbs as if they had grown bigger since I had sat down on that chair. I made my bow.

A subtle change in Captain Ellis' manner became perceptible as though he had laid aside the trident of deputy-Neptune. In reality, it was only his official pen that he had dropped on getting up.

---

8. See p. 15, n. 3.
9. Or Bangkok; the capital of Thailand (formerly Siam), located on the Menam River (now Chao Phraya River) in southern Thailand. See p. 486. Conrad's spelling is idiosyncratic.
1. A sheet of writing paper roughly 16¾ inches by 13½ inches, originally called such for the watermark in the shape of a fool's cap which appeared on it. Foolscap for purposes other than writing came in other sizes.
2. The name of the steamer that conveyed Conrad from Singapore to Bangkok to take command of the *Otago* in January 1888. See p. 363.

II

He shook hands with me: "Well, there you are, on your own, appointed officially under my responsibility."

He was actually walking with me to the door. What a distance off it seemed! I moved like a man in bonds. But we reached it at last. I opened it with the sensation of dealing with mere dream-stuff,[3] and then at the last moment the fellowship of seamen asserted itself, stronger than the difference of age and station. It asserted itself in Captain Ellis' voice.

"Good-bye—and good luck to you," he said so heartily that I could only give him a grateful glance. Then I turned and went out, never to see him again in my life. I had not made three steps into the outer office when I heard behind my back a gruff, loud, authoritative voice, the voice of our deputy-Neptune.

It was addressing the head shipping-master, who, having let me in, had, apparently, remained hovering in the middle distance ever since.

"Mr. R.,[4] let the harbour launch have steam up to take the captain here on board the *Melita* at half-past nine to-night."

I was amazed at the startled assent of R.'s "Yes, sir." He ran before me out on the landing. My new dignity sat yet so lightly on me that I was not aware that it was I, the Captain, the object of this last graciousness. It seemed as if all of a sudden a pair of wings had grown on my shoulders. I merely skimmed along the polished floor.

But R. was impressed.

"I say!" he exclaimed on the landing, while the Malay crew of the steam-launch standing by looked stonily at the man for whom they were going to be kept on duty so late, away from their gambling, from their girls, or their pure domestic joys. "I say! His own launch. What have you done to him?"

His stare was full of respectful curiosity. I was quite confounded.

"Was it for me? I hadn't the slightest notion," I stammered out.

He nodded many times. "Yes. And the last person who had it before you was a Duke.[5] So, there!"

I think he expected me to faint on the spot. But I was in too much of a hurry for emotional displays. My feelings were already in such a whirl that this staggering information did not seem to make the slightest difference. It fell into the seething cauldron of my brain,

---

3. Possible allusion to *The Tempest* 4.1.156–57: "We are such stuff / As dreams are made on."
4. See p. 66, n. 9.
5. Stape and Simmons (*SSSL*) suggest that this is George Granville Leveson Gower (1828–1892), third Duke of Sutherland.

and I carried it off with me after a short but effusive passage of leave-taking with R.

The favour of the great throws an aureole round the fortunate object of its selection. That excellent man inquired whether he could do anything for me. He had known me only by sight, and he was well aware he would never see me again; I was, in common with the other seamen of the port, merely a subject for official writing, filling up of forms with all the artificial superiority of a man of pen and ink to the men who grapple with realities outside the consecrated walls of official buildings. What ghosts we must have been to him! Mere symbols to juggle with in books and heavy registers, without brains and muscles and perplexities; something hardly useful and decidedly inferior.

And he—the office hours being over—wanted to know if he could be of any use to me!

I ought, properly speaking—I ought to have been moved to tears. But I did not even think of it. It was only another miraculous manifestation of that day of miracles. I parted from him as if he had been a mere symbol. I floated down the staircase. I floated out of the official and imposing portal. I went on floating along.

I use that word rather than the word "flew," because I have a distinct impression that, though uplifted by my aroused youth, my movements were deliberate enough. To that mixed white, brown, and yellow portion of mankind, out abroad on their own affairs, I presented the appearance of a man walking rather sedately. And nothing in the way of abstraction could have equalled my deep detachment from the forms and colours of this world. It was, as it were, absolute.

And yet, suddenly, I recognised Hamilton. I recognised him without effort, without a shock, without a start. There he was, strolling towards the Harbour Office with his stiff, arrogant dignity. His red face made him noticeable at a distance. It flamed, over there, on the shady side of the street.

He had perceived me too. Something (unconscious exuberance of spirits perhaps) moved me to wave my hand to him elaborately. This lapse from good taste happened before I was aware that I was capable of it.

The impact of my impudence stopped him short, much as a bullet might have done. I verily believe he staggered, though as far as I could see he didn't actually fall. I had gone past in a moment and did not turn my head. I had forgotten his existence.

The next ten minutes might have been ten seconds or ten centuries for all my consciousness had to do with it. People might have been falling dead around me, houses crumbling, guns firing, I wouldn't have known. I was thinking: "By Jove! I have got it." *It* being the command. It had come about in a way utterly unforeseen in my modest day-dreams.

I perceived that my imagination had been running in conventional channels and that my hopes had always been drab stuff. I had envisaged a command as a result of a slow course of promotion in the employ of some highly respectable firm. The reward of faithful service. Well, faithful service was all right. One would naturally give that for one's own sake, for the sake of the ship, for the love of the life of one's choice; not for the sake of the reward.

There is something distasteful in the notion of a reward.

And now here I had my command, absolutely in my pocket, in a way undeniable indeed, but most unexpected; beyond my imaginings, outside all reasonable expectations, and even notwithstanding the existence of some sort of obscure intrigue to keep it away from me. It is true that the intrigue was feeble, but it helped the feeling of wonder—as if I had been specially destined for that ship I did not know, by some power higher than the prosaic agencies of the commercial world.

A strange sense of exultation began to creep into me. If I had worked for that command ten years or more there would have been nothing of the kind. I was a little frightened.

"Let us be calm," I said to myself.

Outside the door of the Officers' Home the wretched Steward seemed to be waiting for me. There was a broad flight of a few steps, and he ran to and fro on the top of it as if chained there. A distressed cur. He looked as though his throat were too dry for him to bark.

I regret to say I stopped before going in. There had been a revolution in my moral nature. He waited open-mouthed, breathless, while I looked at him for half a minute.

"And you thought you could keep me out of it," I said scathingly.

"You said you were going home," he squeaked miserably. "You said so. You said so."

"I wonder what Captain Ellis will have to say to that excuse," I uttered slowly with a sinister meaning.

His lower jaw had been trembling all the time and his voice was like the bleating of a sick goat.

"You have given me away? You have done for me?"

Neither his distress nor yet the sheer absurdity of it was able to disarm me. It was the first instance of harm being attempted to be done to me—at any rate, the first I had ever found out. And I was still young enough, still too much on this side of the shadow-line, not to be surprised and indignant at such things.

I gazed at him inflexibly. Let the beggar suffer. He slapped his forehead and I passed in, pursued, into the dining-room, by his screech:

"I always said you'd be the death of me."

This clamour not only overtook me, but went ahead as it were on to the verandah and brought out Captain Giles.

He stood before me in the doorway in all the commonplace solidity of his wisdom. The gold chain glittered on his breast. He clutched a smouldering pipe.

I extended my hand to him warmly and he seemed surprised, but did respond heartily enough in the end, with a faint smile of superior knowledge which cut my thanks short as if with a knife. I don't think that more than one word came out. And even for that one, judging by the temperature of my face, I had blushed as if for a bad action. Assuming a detached tone, I wondered how on earth he had managed to spot the little underhand game that had been going on.

He murmured complacently that there were but few things done in the town that he could not see the inside of. And as to this house, he had been using it off and on for nearly ten years. Nothing that went on in it could escape his great experience. It had been no trouble to him. No trouble at all.

Then in his quiet thick tone he wanted to know if I had complained formally of the Steward's action.

I said that I hadn't—though, indeed, it was not for want of opportunity. Captain Ellis had gone for me bald-headed[6] in a most ridiculous fashion for being out of the way when wanted.

"Funny old gentleman," interjected Captain Giles. "What did you say to that?"

"I said simply that I came along the very moment I heard of his message. Nothing more. I didn't want to hurt the Steward. I would scorn to harm such an object. No. I made no complaint, but I believe he thinks I've done so. Let him think. He's got a fright that he won't forget in a hurry, for Captain Ellis would kick him out into the middle of Asia. . . ."

"Wait a moment," said Captain Giles, leaving me suddenly. I sat down feeling very tired, mostly in my head. Before I could start a train of thought he stood again before me, murmuring the excuse that he had to go and put the fellow's mind at ease.

I looked up with surprise. But in reality I was indifferent. He explained that he had found the Steward lying face downwards on the horsehair sofa. He was all right now.

"He would not have died of fright," I said contemptuously.

"No. But he might have taken an overdose out of one of them little bottles he keeps in his room," Captain Giles argued seriously. "The confounded fool has tried to poison himself once—a couple of years ago."

6. Without thought of the consequences.

"Really," I said without emotion. "He doesn't seem very fit to live, anyhow."

"As to that, it may be said of a good many."

"Don't exaggerate like this!" I protested, laughing irritably. "But I wonder what this part of the world would do if you were to leave off looking after it, Captain Giles? Here you have got me a command and saved the Steward's life in one afternoon. Though why you should have taken all that interest in either of us is more than I can understand."

Captain Giles remained silent for a minute. Then gravely:

"He's not a bad steward really. He can find a good cook, at any rate. And, what's more, he can keep him when found. I remember the cooks we had here before his time. . . ."

I must have made a movement of impatience, because he interrupted himself with an apology for keeping me yarning there, while no doubt I needed all my time to get ready.

What I really needed was to be alone for a bit. I seized this opening hastily. My bedroom was a quiet refuge in an apparently uninhabited wing of the building. Having absolutely nothing to do (for I had not unpacked my things), I sat down on the bed and abandoned myself to the influences of the hour. To the unexpected influences. . . .

And first I wondered at my state of mind. Why was I not more surprised? Why? Here I was, invested with a command in the twinkling of an eye, not in the common course of human affairs, but more as if by enchantment. I ought to have been lost in astonishment. But I wasn't. I was very much like people in fairy tales. Nothing ever astonishes them. When a fully appointed gala coach is produced out of a pumpkin to take her to a ball Cinderella does not exclaim. She gets in quietly and drives away to her high fortune.

Captain Ellis (a fierce sort of fairy) had produced a command out of a drawer almost as unexpectedly as in a fairy tale. But a command is an abstract idea, and it seemed a sort of "lesser marvel" till it flashed upon me that it involved the concrete existence of a ship.

A ship! My ship! She was mine, more absolutely mine for possession and care than anything in the world; an object of responsibility and devotion. She was there waiting for me, spellbound, unable to move, to live, to get out into the world (till I came), like an enchanted princess.[7] Her call had come to me as if from the clouds. I had never suspected her existence. I didn't know how she looked, I had

7. Stape and Simmons (*SSSL*) see an allusion to Charles Perrault's fairy tale "The Sleeping Beauty" (1697).

barely heard her name, and yet we were indissolubly united for a certain portion of our future, to sink or swim together!

A sudden passion of anxious impatience rushed through my veins and gave me such a sense of the intensity of existence as I have never felt before or since. I discovered how much of a seaman I was, in heart, in mind, and, as it were, physically—a man exclusively of sea and ships; the sea the only world that counted, and the ships the test of manliness, of temperament, of courage and fidelity—and of love.

I had an exquisite moment. It was unique also. Jumping up from my seat, I paced up and down my room for a long time. But when I came into the dining-room I behaved with sufficient composure. Only I couldn't eat anything at dinner.

Having declared my intention not to drive but to walk down to the quay, I must render the wretched Steward justice that he bestirred himself to find me some coolies[8] for the luggage. They departed, carrying all my worldly possessions (except a little money I had in my pocket) slung from a long pole. Captain Giles volunteered to walk down with me.

We followed the sombre, shaded alley across the Esplanade. It was moderately cool there under the trees. Captain Giles remarked, with a sudden laugh: "I know who's jolly thankful at having seen the last of you."

I guessed that he meant the Steward. The fellow had borne himself to me in a sulkily frightened manner at the last. I expressed my wonder that he should have tried to do me a bad turn for no reason at all.

"Don't you see that what he wanted was to get rid of our friend Hamilton by dodging him in front of you for that job? That would have removed him for good, see?"

"Heavens!" I exclaimed, feeling humiliated somehow. "Can it be possible? What a fool he must be! That overbearing, impudent loafer! Why! He couldn't . . . And yet he's nearly done it, I believe; for the Harbour Office was bound to send somebody."

"Aye. A fool like our Steward can be dangerous sometimes," declared Captain Giles sententiously. "Just because he is a fool," he added, imparting further instruction in his complacent low tones. "For," he continued in the manner of a set demonstration, "no sensible person would risk being kicked out of the only berth between himself and starvation just to get rid of a simple annoyance—a small worry. Would he now?"

"Well, no," I conceded, restraining a desire to laugh at that something mysteriously earnest in delivering the conclusions of his wisdom as though it were the product of prohibited operations. "But that fellow looks as if he were rather crazy. He must be."

---

8. Unskilled laborers of the Far East (Hindi).

"As to that, I believe everybody in the world is a little mad," he announced quietly.

"You make no exceptions?" I inquired, just to hear his answer.

He kept silent for a little while, then got home in an effective manner.

"Why! Kent says that even of you."

"Does he?" I retorted, extremely embittered all at once against my former captain. "There's nothing of that in the written character[9] from him which I've got in my pocket. Has he given you any instances of my lunacy?"

Captain Giles explained in a conciliating tone that it had been only a friendly remark in reference to my abrupt leaving the ship for no apparent reason.

I muttered grumpily: "Oh! leaving his ship," and mended my pace. He kept up by my side in the deep gloom of the avenue as if it were his conscientious duty to see me out of the colony as an undesirable character. He panted a little, which was rather pathetic in a way. But I was not moved. On the contrary. His discomfort gave me a sort of malicious pleasure.

Presently I relented, slowed down, and said:

"What I really wanted was to get a fresh grip. I felt it was time. Is that so very mad?"

He made no answer. We were issuing from the avenue. On the bridge over the canal a dark, irresolute figure seemed to be awaiting something or somebody.

It was a Malay policeman, barefooted, in his blue uniform. The silver band on his little round cap shone dimly in the light of the street lamp. He peered in our direction timidly.

Before we could come up to him he turned about and walked in front of us in the direction of the jetty. The distance was some hundred yards; and then I found my coolies squatting on their heels. They had kept the pole on their shoulders, and all my worldly goods, still tied to the pole, were resting on the ground between them. As far as the eye could reach along the quay there was not another soul abroad except the police peon, who saluted us.

It seems he had detained the coolies as suspicious characters, and had forbidden them the jetty. But at a sign from me he took off the embargo with alacrity. The two patient fellows, rising together with a faint grunt, trotted off along the planks, and I prepared to take my leave of Captain Giles, who stood there with an air as though his mission were drawing to a close. It could not be denied that he

9. A document of discharge, speaking to a sailor's character regarding his conduct and ability.

had done it all. And while I hesitated about an appropriate sentence he made himself heard:

"I expect you'll have your hands pretty full of tangled up business."

I asked him what made him think so; and he answered that it was his general experience of the world. Ship a long time away from her port, owners inaccessible by cable,[1] and the only man who could explain matters dead and buried.

"And you yourself new to the business in a way," he concluded in a sort of unanswerable tone.

"Don't insist," I said. "I know it only too well. I only wish you could impart to me some small portion of your experience before I go. As it can't be done in ten minutes I had better not begin to ask you. There's that harbour launch waiting for me too. But I won't feel really at peace till I have that ship of mine out in the Indian Ocean."

He remarked casually that from Bankok to the Indian Ocean was a pretty long step. And this murmur, like a dim flash from a dark lantern,[2] showed me for a moment the broad belt of islands and reefs between that unknown ship, which was mine, and the freedom of the great waters of the globe.

But I felt no apprehension. I was familiar enough with the Archipelago by that time. Extreme patience and extreme care would see me through the region of broken land, of faint airs and of dead water to where I would feel at last my command swing on the great swell and list over to the great breath of regular winds, that would give her the feeling of a large, more intense life. The road would be long. All roads are long that lead towards one's heart's desire. But this road my mind's eye could see on a chart, professionally, with all its complications and difficulties, yet simple enough in a way. One is a seaman or one is not. And I had no doubt of being one.

The only part I was a stranger to was the Gulf of Siam.[3] And I mentioned this to Captain Giles. Not that I was concerned very much. It belonged to the same region the nature of which I knew, into whose very soul I seemed to have looked during the last months of that existence with which I had broken now, suddenly, as one parts with some enchanting company.

"The gulf . . . Ay! A funny piece of water—that," said Captain Giles.

---

1. According to Minamida, there was in fact a cable from Bankok to Adelaide and one from Bankok to Singapore, with Singapore connected to the rest of the world (*MSL* 197). Larabee, however, argues that there was no cable from Bankok to Singapore; see p. 490.
2. A lantern with a sliding mechanism to conceal its light.
3. See p. 3, n. 1.

Funny, in this connection, was a vague word. The whole thing sounded like an opinion uttered by a cautious person mindful of actions for slander.

I didn't inquire as to the nature of that funniness. There was really no time. But at the very last he volunteered a warning.

"Whatever you do keep to the east side of it. The west side is dangerous at this time of the year. Don't let anything tempt you over. You'll find nothing but trouble there."

Though I could hardly imagine what could tempt me to involve my ship amongst the currents and reefs of the Malay shore,[4] I thanked him for the advice.

He gripped my extended arm warmly, and the end of our acquaintance came suddenly in the words: "Good-night."

That was all he said: "Good-night." Nothing more. I don't know what I intended to say, but surprise made me swallow it, whatever it was. I choked slightly, and then exclaimed with a sort of nervous haste: "Oh! Good-night, Captain Giles, good-night."

His movements were always deliberate, but his back had receded some distance along the deserted quay before I collected myself enough to follow his example and made a half-turn in the direction of the jetty.

Only my movements were not deliberate. I hurried down to the steps and leaped into the launch. Before I had fairly landed in her stern sheets the slim little craft darted away from the jetty with a sudden swirl of her propeller and the hard rapid puffing of the exhaust in her vaguely gleaming brass funnel amidships.

The misty churning at her stern was the only sound in the world. The shore lay plunged in the silence of the deepest slumber. I watched the town recede still and soundless in the hot night, till the abrupt hail, "Steam-launch, ahoy!" made me spin round face forward. We were close to a white, ghostly steamer. Lights shone on her decks, in her port-holes. And the same voice shouted from her: "Is that our passenger?"

"It is," I yelled.

Her crew had been obviously on the jump.[5] I could hear them running about. The modern spirit of haste was loudly vocal in the orders to "Heave away on the cable"—to "Lower the side-ladder," and in urgent requests to me to "Come along, sir! We have been delayed three hours for you. . . . Our time is seven o'clock, you know!"

I stepped on the deck. I said "No! I don't know." The spirit of modern hurry was embodied in a thin, long-armed, long-legged man,[6]

---

4. Actually, the Siamese shore.
5. On the move; abruptly or swiftly.
6. The captain of the *Melita* is listed as either Captain Moretz or Captain Morck, depending on the source (*CEW* 217).

with a closely-clipped grey beard. His meagre hand was hot and dry. He declared feverishly:

"I am hanged if I would have waited another five minutes— harbour-master or no harbour-master."

"That's your own business," I said. "I didn't ask you to wait for me."

"I hope you don't expect any supper," he burst out. "This isn't a boarding-house afloat. You are the first passenger I ever had in my life and I hope to goodness you will be the last."

I made no answer to this hospitable communication; and, indeed, he didn't wait for any, bolting away on to his bridge to get his ship under way.

For the four days he had me on board he did not depart from that half-hostile attitude. His ship having been delayed three hours on my account he couldn't forgive me for not being a more distinguished person. He was not exactly outspoken about it, but that feeling of annoyed wonder was peeping out perpetually in his talk.

He was absurd.

He was also a man of much experience, which he liked to trot out; but no greater contrast with Captain Giles could have been imagined. He would have amused me if I had wanted to be amused. But I did not want to be amused. I was like a lover looking forward to a meeting. Human hostility was nothing to me. I thought of my unknown ship. It was amusement enough, torment enough, occupation enough.

He perceived my state, for his wits were sufficiently sharp for that, and he poked sly fun at my preoccupation in the manner some nasty, cynical old men assume towards the dreams and illusions of youth. I, on my side, refrained from questioning him as to the appearance of my ship, though I knew that being in Bankok every month or so he must have known her by sight. I was not going to expose the ship, my ship! to some slighting reference.

He was the first really unsympathetic man I had ever come in contact with. My education was far from being finished, though I didn't know it. No! I didn't know it.

All I knew was that he disliked me and had some contempt for my person. Why? Apparently because his ship had been delayed three hours on my account. Who was I to have such a thing done for me? Such a thing had never been done for him. It was a sort of jealous indignation.

My expectation, mingled with fear, was wrought to its highest pitch. How slow had been the days of the passage and how soon they were over. One morning, early, we crossed the bar, and while the sun was rising splendidly over the flat spaces of the land we steamed up the innumerable bends, passed under the shadow of the great gilt pagoda,[7] and reached the outskirts of the town.

There it was, spread largely on both banks, the Oriental capital which had as yet suffered no white conqueror; an expanse of brown houses of bamboo, of mats, of leaves, of a vegetable-matter style of architecture, sprung out of the brown soil on the banks of the muddy river.[8] It was amazing to think that in those miles of human habitations there was not probably half a dozen pounds of nails. Some of those houses of sticks and grass, like the nests of an aquatic race, clung to the low shores. Others seemed to grow out of the water; others again floated in long anchored rows in the very middle of the stream. Here and there in the distance, above the crowded mob of low, brown roof ridges; towered great piles of masonry, King's Palace,[9] temples, gorgeous and dilapidated, crumbling under the vertical sunlight, tremendous, overpowering, almost palpable, which seemed to enter one's breast with the breath of one's nostrils and soak into one's limbs through every pore of one's skin.

The ridiculous victim of jealousy had for some reason or other to stop his engines just then. The steamer drifted slowly up with the tide. Oblivious of my new surroundings I walked the deck, in anxious, deadened abstraction, a commingling of romantic reverie with a very practical survey of my qualifications. For the time was approaching for me to behold my command and to prove my worth in the ultimate test of my profession.

Suddenly I heard myself called by that imbecile. He was beckoning me to come up on his bridge.

I didn't care very much for that, but as it seemed that he had something particular to say I went up the ladder.

He laid his hand on my shoulder and gave me a slight turn, pointing with his other arm at the same time.

"There! That's your ship, Captain," he said.

I felt a thump in my breast—only one, as if my heart had then ceased to beat. There were ten or more ships moored along the bank, and the one he meant was partly hidden from my sight by her next astern. He said: "We'll drift abreast her in a moment."

What was his tone? Mocking? Threatening? Or only indifferent? I could not tell. I suspected some malice in this unexpected manifestation of interest.

---

7. Probably Wat Saket, or the pagoda on the Golden Mount; see also p. 8, n. 3. "Crossed the bar": see p. 7, n. 1.
8. The Menam River (now Chao Phraya River); see p. 7, n. 2. "Suffered no white conqueror": unlike the rest of Southeast Asia, Siam remained uncolonized throughout the colonial period.
9. The Grand Palace, begun in 1782, was the main residence of the king until 1925.

He left me, and I leaned over the rail of the bridge looking over the side. I dared not raise my eyes. Yet it had to be done—and, indeed, I could not have helped myself. I believe I trembled.

But directly my eyes had rested on my ship all my fear vanished. It went off swiftly, like a bad dream. Only that a dream leaves no shame behind it, and that I felt a momentary shame at my unworthy suspicions.

Yes, there she was.[1] Her hull, her rigging filled my eye with a great content. That feeling of life-emptiness which had made me so restless for the last few months lost its bitter plausibility, its evil influence, dissolved in a flow of joyous emotion.

At the first glance I saw that she was a high-class vessel, a harmonious creature in the lines of her fine body, in the proportioned tallness of her spars. Whatever her age and her history, she had preserved the stamp of her origin. She was one of those craft that, in virtue of their design and complete finish, will never look old. Amongst her companions moored to the bank, and all bigger than herself, she looked like a creature of high breed—an Arab steed in a string of cart-horses.

A voice behind me said in a nasty equivocal tone: "I hope you are satisfied with her, Captain." I did not even turn my head. It was the master of the steamer, and whatever he meant, whatever he thought of her, I knew that, like some rare women, she was one of those creatures whose mere existence is enough to awaken an unselfish delight. One feels that it is good to be in the world in which she has her being.

That illusion of life and character which charms one in men's finest handiwork radiated from her. An enormous baulk of teakwood timber swung over her hatchway; lifeless matter, looking heavier and bigger than anything aboard of her. When they started lowering it the surge of the tackle sent a quiver through her from water-line to the trucks up the fine nerves of her rigging, as though she had shuddered at the weight. It seemed cruel to load her so. . . .

Half-an-hour later, putting my foot on her deck for the first time, I received the feeling of deep physical satisfaction. Nothing could equal the fullness of that moment, the ideal completeness of that emotional experience which had come to me without the preliminary toil and disenchantments of an obscure career.

My rapid glance ran over her, enveloped, appropriated the form concreting the abstract sentiment of my command. A lot of details

---

1. The *Otago*, upon which this ship is based, was a 367-ton iron barque built in Glasgow in 1869 by Alexander Stephen & Sons. It was owned by Henry Simpson & Sons of Port Adelaide while Conrad commanded the *Otago*.

perceptible to a seaman struck my eye vividly in that instant. For the rest, I saw her disengaged from the material conditions of her being. The shore to which she was moored was as if it did not exist. What were to me all the countries of the globe? In all the parts of the world washed by navigable waters our relation to each other would be the same—and more intimate than there are words to express in the language. Apart from that, every scene and episode would be a mere passing show. The very gang of yellow coolies busy about the main-hatch was less substantial than the stuff dreams are made of.[2] For who on earth would dream of Chinamen? . . .

I went aft, ascended the poop, where, under the awning, gleamed the brasses of the yacht-like fittings, the polished surfaces of the rails, the glass of the skylights. Right aft two seamen, busy cleaning the steering-gear, with the reflected ripples of light running play-fully up their bent backs, went on with their work, unaware of me and of the almost affectionate glance I threw at them in passing towards the companion-way of the cabin.

The doors stood wide open, the slide was pushed right back. The half-turn of the staircase cut off the view of the lobby. A low hum-ming ascended from below, but it stopped abruptly at the sound of my descending footsteps.

III

The first thing I saw down there was the upper part of a man's body projecting backwards, as it were, from one of the doors at the foot of the stairs. His eyes looked at me very wide and still. In one hand he held a dinner plate, in the other a cloth.

"I am your new Captain," I said quietly.

In a moment, in the twinkling of an eye, he had got rid of the plate and the cloth and jumped to open the cabin door. As soon as I passed into the saloon he vanished, but only to reappear instantly, buttoning up a jacket he had put on with the swiftness of a "quick-change" artist.[3]

"Where's the chief mate?" I asked.

"In the hold, I think, sir. I saw him go down the after-hatch ten minutes ago."

"Tell him I am on board."

The mahogany table under the skylight shone in the twilight like a dark pool of water. The sideboard, surmounted by a wide looking-glass in an ormolu[4] frame, had a marble top. It bore a pair of

2. See p. 69, n. 3.
3. A theater or musical-hall performer who changes costumes quickly to change parts.
4. A gold-colored alloy for decorating furniture. "Sideboard": a piece of dining-room furni-ture with cabinets and shelves.

silver-plated lamps and some other pieces—obviously a harbour display. The saloon itself was panelled in two kinds of wood in the excellent, simple taste prevailing when the ship was built.

I sat down in the arm-chair at the head of the table—the captain's chair, with a small tell-tale compass swung above it—a mute reminder of unremitting vigilance.

A succession of men had sat in that chair. I became aware of that thought suddenly, vividly, as though each had left a little of himself between the four walls of these ornate bulkheads; as if a sort of composite soul, the soul of command, had whispered suddenly to mine of long days at sea and of anxious moments.

"You, too!" it seemed to say, "you, too, shall taste of that peace and that unrest in a searching intimacy with your own self—obscure as we were and as supreme in the face of all the winds and all the seas, in an immensity that receives no impress, preserves no memories, and keeps no reckoning of lives."

Deep within the tarnished ormolu frame, in the hot half-light sifted through the awning, I saw my own face propped between my hands. And I stared back at myself with the perfect detachment of distance, rather with curiosity than with any other feeling, except of some sympathy for this latest representative of what for all intents and purposes was a dynasty; continuous not in blood, indeed, but in its experience, in its training, in its conception of duty, and in the blessed simplicity of its traditional point of view on life.

It struck me that this quietly staring man whom I was watching, both as if he were myself and somebody else, was not exactly a lonely figure. He had his place in a line of men whom he did not know, of whom he had never heard; but who were fashioned by the same influences, whose souls in relation to their humble life's work had no secrets for him.

Suddenly I perceived that there was another man in the saloon, standing a little on one side and looking intently at me. The chief mate. His long, red moustache determined the character of his physiognomy,[5] which struck me as pugnacious in (strange to say) a ghastly sort of way.

How long had he been there looking at me, appraising me in my unguarded day-dreaming state? I would have been more disconcerted if, having the clock set in the top of the mirror-frame right in front of me, I had not noticed that its long hand had hardly moved at all.

I could not have been in that cabin more than two minutes altogether. Say three. . . . So he could not have been watching me

---

5. Facial features or countenance, historically sometimes seen as an indication of one's mind or character.

more than a mere fraction of a minute, luckily. Still, I regretted the occurrence.

But I showed nothing of it as I rose leisurely (it had to be leisurely) and greeted him with perfect friendliness.

There was something reluctant and at the same time attentive in his bearing. His name was Burns.[6] We left the cabin and went round the ship together. His face in the full light of day appeared very worn, meagre, even haggard. Somehow I had a delicacy as to looking too often at him; his eyes, on the contrary, remained fairly glued on my face. They were greenish and had an expectant expression.

He answered all my questions readily enough, but my ear seemed to catch a tone of unwillingness. The second officer,[7] with three or four hands, was busy forward. The mate mentioned his name and I nodded to him in passing. He was very young. He struck me as rather a cub.[8]

When we returned below I sat down on one end of a deep, semicircular, or, rather, semi-oval settee, upholstered in red plush. It extended right across the whole after-end of the cabin. Mr. Burns, motioned to sit down, dropped into one of the swivel-chairs round the table, and kept his eyes on me as persistently as ever, and with that strange air as if all this were make-believe and he expected me to get up, burst into a laugh, slap him on the back, and vanish from the cabin.

There was an odd stress in the situation which began to make me uncomfortable. I tried to react against this vague feeling.

"It's only my inexperience," I thought.

In the face of that man, several years, I judged, older than myself, I became aware of what I had left already behind me—my youth. And that was indeed poor comfort. Youth is a fine thing, a mighty power—as long as one does not think of it. I felt I was becoming self-conscious. Almost against my will I assumed a moody gravity. I said: "I see you have kept her in very good order, Mr. Burns."

Directly I had uttered these words I asked myself angrily why the deuce did I want to say that? Mr. Burns in answer had only blinked at me. What on earth did he mean?

I fell back on a question which had been in my thoughts for a long time—the most natural question on the lips of any seaman

---

6. Modeled somewhat after Charles Born (1854–1902), who served as Conrad's first mate aboard the *Otago*. Burns also appears in "A Smile of Fortune." Somewhat different incarnations of him appear as Jones in *Lord Jim* and as the unnamed chief mates in "Falk" and "The Secret Sharer."
7. The second mate aboard the *Otago* was Isaac Jackson, who was twenty-three when Conrad assumed command.
8. See p. 23, n. 2.

whatever joining a ship. I voiced it (confound this self-consciousness) in a *dégagé*[9] cheerful tone: "I suppose she can travel—what?"

Now a question like this might have been answered normally, either in accents of apologetic sorrow or with a visibly suppressed pride, in a "I don't want to boast, but you shall see" sort of tone. There are sailors, too, who would have been roughly outspoken: "Lazy brute," or openly delighted: "She's a flyer." Two ways, if four manners.

But Mr. Burns found another way, a way of his own which had, at all events, the merit of saving his breath, if no other.

Again he did not say anything. He only frowned. And it was an angry frown. I waited. Nothing more came.

"What's the matter? . . . Can't you tell after being nearly two years in the ship?" I addressed him sharply.

He looked as startled for a moment as though he had discovered my presence only that very moment. But this passed off almost at once. He put on an air of indifference. But I suppose he thought it better to say something. He said that a ship needed, just like a man, the chance to show the best she could do, and that this ship had never had a chance since he had been on board of her. Not that he could remember. The last captain.[1] . . . He paused.

"Has he been so very unlucky?" I asked with frank incredulity. Mr. Burns turned his eyes away from me. No, the late captain was not an unlucky man. One couldn't say that. But he had not seemed to want to make use of his luck.

Mr. Burns—man of enigmatic moods—made this statement with an inanimate face and staring wilfully at the rudder-casing. The statement itself was obscurely suggestive. I asked quietly:

"Where did he die?"

"In this saloon. Just where you are sitting now," answered Mr. Burns.

I repressed a silly impulse to jump up; but upon the whole I was relieved to hear that he had not died in the bed which was now to be mine. I pointed out to the chief mate that what I really wanted to know was where he had buried his late captain.

Mr. Burns said that it was at the entrance to the gulf. A roomy grave; a sufficient answer. But the mate, overcoming visibly something within him—something like a curious reluctance to believe in my advent (as an irrevocable fact, at any rate), did not stop at that—though, indeed, he may have wished to do so.

---

9. Easy, casual, unrestrained (French).
1. John Snadden (1837–1887), who died on December 8, 1887, while at sea, was Conrad's immediate predecessor as captain of the *Otago*, but the fictional captain appears to bear no other resemblance to Snadden.

As a compromise with his feelings, I believe, he addressed himself persistently to the rudder-casing, so that to me he had the appearance of a man talking in solitude, a little unconsciously, however.

His tale was that at seven bells in the forenoon watch he had all hands mustered on the quarter-deck and told them that they had better go down to say good-bye to the captain.

Those words, as if grudged to an intruding personage, were enough for me to evoke vividly that strange ceremony: The bare-footed, bare-headed seamen crowding shyly into that cabin, a small mob pressed against that sideboard, uncomfortable rather than moved, shirts open on sunburnt chests, weather-beaten faces, and all staring at the dying man with the same grave and expectant expression.

"Was he conscious?" I asked.

"He didn't speak, but he moved his eyes to look at them," said the mate.

After waiting a moment Mr. Burns motioned the crew to leave the cabin, but he detained the two eldest men to stay with the captain while he went on deck with his sextant to "take the sun." It was getting towards noon and he was anxious to obtain a good observation for latitude. When he returned below to put his sextant away he found that the two men had retreated out into the lobby. Through the open door he had a view of the captain lying easy against the pillows. He had "passed away" while Mr. Burns was taking his observation. As near noon as possible. He had hardly changed his position.

Mr. Burns sighed, glanced at me inquisitively, as much as to say, "Aren't you going yet?" and then turned his thoughts from his new captain back to the old, who, being dead, had no authority, was not in anybody's way, and was much easier to deal with.

Mr. Burns dealt with him at some length. He was a peculiar man—of sixty-five about—iron grey, hard-faced, obstinate, and uncommunicative. He used to keep the ship loafing at sea for inscrutable reasons. Would come on deck at night sometimes, take some sail off her, God only knows why or wherefore, then go below, shut himself up in his cabin, and play on the violin for hours—till daybreak perhaps. In fact, he spent most of his time day or night playing the violin. That was when the fit took him.[2] Very loud, too.

It came to this, that Mr. Burns mustered his courage one day and remonstrated earnestly with the captain. Neither he nor the second mate could get a wink of sleep in their watches below for the noise. . . . And how could they be expected to keep awake while on duty? he pleaded. The answer of that stern man was that if he and the second mate didn't like the noise, they were welcome to pack up their

2. Whenever he was in the mood.

traps[3] and walk over the side. When this alternative was offered the ship happened to be 600 miles from the nearest land.

Mr. Burns at this point looked at me with an air of curiosity. I began to think that my predecessor was a remarkably peculiar old man.

But I had to hear stranger things yet. It came out that this stern, grim, wind-tanned, rough, sea-salted, taciturn sailor of sixty-five was not only an artist, but a lover as well. In Haiphong,[4] when they got there after a course of most unprofitable peregrinations (during which the ship was nearly lost twice), he got himself, in Mr. Burns' own words, "mixed up" with some woman. Mr. Burns had had no personal knowledge of that affair, but positive evidence of it existed in the shape of a photograph taken in Haiphong. Mr. Burns found it in one of the drawers in the captain's room.

In due course I, too, saw that amazing human document (I even threw it overboard later). There he sat, with his hands reposing on his knees, bald, squat, grey, bristly, recalling a wild boar somehow; and by his side towered an awful, mature, white female with rapacious nostrils and a cheaply ill-omened stare in her enormous eyes. She was disguised in some semi-oriental, vulgar, fancy costume. She resembled a low-class medium or one of those women who tell fortunes by cards for half-a-crown.[5] And yet she was striking. A professional sorceress from the slums. It was incomprehensible. There was something awful in the thought that she was the last reflection of the world of passion for the fierce soul which seemed to look at one out of the sardonically savage face of that old seaman. However, I noticed that she was holding some musical instrument—guitar or mandoline—in her hand. Perhaps that was the secret of her sortilege.[6]

For Mr. Burns that photograph explained why the unloaded ship was kept sweltering at anchor for three weeks in a pestilential hot harbour without air. They lay there and gasped. The captain, appearing now and then on short visits, mumbled to Mr. Burns unlikely tales about some letters he was waiting for.

Suddenly, after vanishing for a week, he came on board in the middle of the night and took the ship out to sea with the first break of dawn. Daylight showed him looking wild and ill. The mere getting clear of the land took two days, and somehow or other they bumped slightly on a reef. However, no leak developed, and the

---

3. Luggage or personal belongings.
4. Haiphong is a port city in northern Vietnam on the Red River Delta in the Gulf of Tonkin. See p. 335.
5. A coin worth two shillings and six pence in the former British monetary system.
6. Strictly speaking, divination through drawing or casting lots, but in this instance more generally referring to magic or sorcery.

captain, growling "no matter," informed Mr. Burns that he had made up his mind to take the ship to Hong-Kong[7] and dry-dock her there.

At this Mr. Burns was plunged into despair. For indeed, to beat up to Hong-Kong against a fierce monsoon, with a ship not sufficiently ballasted and with her supply of water not completed, was an insane project.

But the captain growled peremptorily, "Stick her at it," and Mr. Burns, dismayed and enraged, stuck her at it, and kept her at it, blowing away sails, straining the spars, exhausting the crew—nearly maddened by the absolute conviction that the attempt was impossible and was bound to end in some catastrophe.

Meantime the captain, shut up in his cabin and wedged in a corner of his settee against the crazy bounding of the ship, played the violin—or, at any rate, made continuous noise on it.

When he appeared on deck he would not speak and not always answer when spoken to. It was obvious that he was ill in some mysterious manner, and beginning to break up.

As the days went by the sounds of the violin became less and less loud, till at last only a feeble scratching would meet Mr. Burns' ear as he stood in the saloon listening outside the door of the captain's state-room.

One afternoon in perfect desperation he burst into that room and made such a scene, tearing his hair and shouting such horrid imprecations that he cowed the contemptuous spirit of the sick man. The water-tanks were low, they had not gained 50 miles in a fortnight. She would never reach Hong-Kong.

It was like fighting desperately towards destruction for the ship and the men. This was evident without argument. Mr. Burns, losing all restraint, put his face close to his Captain's and fairly yelled: "You, sir, are going out of the world. But I can't wait till you are dead before I put the helm up. You must do it yourself. You must do it now!"

The man on the couch snarled in contempt:

"So I am going out of the world—am I?"

"Yes, sir—you haven't many days left in it," said Mr. Burns calming down. "One can see it by your face."

"My face, eh? . . . Well, put the helm up and be damned to you."

Burns flew on deck, got the ship before the wind, then came down again, composed but resolute.

---

7. A city on the southern coast of China. It was ceded to Great Britain in 1842 as part of the Treaty of Nanking. The territory was expanded twice, in 1860 and 1898, when the arrangement was changed to a ninety-nine-year lease. The lease expired in 1997, and Hong Kong returned to Chinese control. See p. 335.

"I've shaped a course for Pulo Condor,[8] sir," he said. "When we make it, if you are still with us, you'll tell me into what port you wish me to take the ship and I'll do it."

The old man gave him a look of savage spite, and said these atrocious words in deadly, slow tones:

"If I had my wish, neither the ship nor any of you would ever reach a port. And I hope you won't."

Mr. Burns was profoundly shocked. I believe he was positively frightened at the time. It seems, however, that he managed to produce such an effective laugh that it was the old man's turn to be frightened. He shrank within himself and turned his back on him.

"And his head was not gone then," Mr. Burns assured me excitedly. "He meant every word of it."

Such was practically the late captain's last speech. No connected sentence passed his lips afterwards. That night he used the last of his strength to throw his fiddle over the side. No one had actually seen him in the act, but after his death Mr. Burns couldn't find the thing anywhere. The empty case was very much in evidence, but the fiddle was clearly not in the ship. And where else could it have gone to but overboard?

"Threw his violin overboard!" I exclaimed.

"He did," cried Mr. Burns excitedly. "And it's my belief he would have tried to take the ship down with him if it had been in human power. He never meant her to see home again. He wouldn't write to his owners, he never wrote to his old wife either—he wasn't going to. He had made up his mind to cut adrift from everything. That's what it was. He didn't care for business, or freights, or for making a passage—or anything. He meant to have gone wandering about the world till he lost her with all hands."

Mr. Burns looked like a man who had escaped great danger. For a little he would have exclaimed: "If it hadn't been for me!" And the transparent innocence of his indignant eyes was underlined quaintly by the arrogant pair of moustaches which he proceeded to twist, and as if extend, horizontally.

I might have smiled if I had not been busy with my own sensations, which were not those of Mr. Burns. I was already the man in command. My sensations could not be like those of any other man on board. In that community I stood, like a king in his country, in a class all by myself. I mean an hereditary king, not a mere elected head of a state. I was brought there to rule by an agency as remote from the people and as inscrutable almost to them as the Grace of God.

---

8. Or Puolo Condor, an island (now named Côn So'n Island) off the southern coast of Vietnam. See p. 335.

And like a member of a dynasty, feeling a semi-mystical bond with the dead, I was profoundly shocked by my immediate predecessor.

That man had been in all essentials but his age just such another man as myself. Yet the end of his life was a complete act of treason, the betrayal of a tradition which seemed to me as imperative as any guide on earth could be. It appeared that even at sea a man could become the victim of evil spirits. I felt on my face the breath of unknown powers that shape our destinies.[9]

Not to let the silence last too long I asked Mr. Burns if he had written to his captain's wife. He shook his head. He had written to nobody.

In a moment he became sombre. He never thought of writing. It took him all his time to watch incessantly the loading of the ship by a rascally Chinese stevedore. In this Mr. Burns gave me the first glimpse of the real chief mate's soul which dwelt uneasily in his body.

He mused, then hastened on with gloomy force.

"Yes! The captain died as near noon as possible. I looked through his papers in the afternoon. I read the service over him at sunset and then I stuck the ship's head north and brought her in here. I—brought—her—in."

He struck the table with his fist.

"She would hardly have come in by herself," I observed. "But why didn't you make for Singapore instead?"

His eyes wavered. "The nearest port," he muttered sullenly.

I had framed the question in perfect innocence, but this answer (the difference in distance was insignificant) and his manner offered me a clue to the simple truth. He took the ship to a port where he expected to be confirmed in his temporary command from lack of a qualified master to put over his head. Whereas Singapore, he surmised justly, would be full of qualified men. But his naïve reasoning forgot to take into account the telegraph cable[1] reposing on the bottom of the very Gulf up which he had turned that ship which he imagined himself to have saved from destruction. Hence the bitter flavour of our interview. I tasted it more and more distinctly—and it was less and less to my taste.

"Look here, Mr. Burns," I began, very firmly. "You may as well understand that I did not run after this command. It was pushed in my way. I've accepted it. I am here to take the ship home first of all, and you may be sure that I shall see to it that every one of you on board here does his duty to that end. This is all I have to say—for the present."

9. See p. 63, n. 3.
1. See p. 76, n. 1. Like Burns, Charles Born brought the *Otago* into Bangkok after Captain Snadden's death rather than sailing to Singapore, arriving there December 20, 1887.

He was on his feet by this time, but instead of taking his dismissal he remained with trembling, indignant lips, and looking at me hard as though, really, after this, there was nothing for me to do in common decency but to vanish from his outraged sight. Like all very simple emotional states this was moving. I felt sorry for him—almost sympathetic, till (seeing that I did not vanish) he spoke in a tone of forced restraint.

"If I hadn't a wife and a child at home you may be sure, sir, I would have asked you to let me go the very minute you came on board."

I answered him with a matter-of-course calmness as though some remote third person were in question.

"And I, Mr. Burns, would not have let you go. You have signed the ship's articles as chief officer, and till they are terminated at the final port of discharge I shall expect you to attend to your duty and give me the benefit of your experience to the best of your ability."

Stony incredulity lingered in his eyes; but it broke down before my friendly attitude. With a slight upward toss of his arms (I got to know that gesture well afterwards) he bolted out of the cabin.

We might have saved ourselves that little passage of harmless sparring. Before many days had elapsed it was Mr. Burns who was pleading with me anxiously not to leave him behind; while I could only return him but doubtful answers. The whole thing took on a somewhat tragic complexion.

And this horrible problem was only an extraneous episode, a mere complication in the general problem of how to get that ship—which was mine with her appurtenances and her men, with her body and her spirit now slumbering in that pestilential river—how to get her out to sea.

Mr. Burns, while still acting captain, had hastened to sign a charter-party which in an ideal world without guile would have been an excellent document. Directly I ran my eye over it I foresaw trouble ahead unless the people of the other part were quite exceptionally fair-minded and open to argument.

Mr. Burns, to whom I imparted my fears, chose to take great umbrage at them. He looked at me with that usual incredulous stare, and said bitterly:

"I suppose, sir, you want to make out I've acted like a fool?"

I told him, with my systematic kindliness which always seemed to augment his surprise, that I did not want to make out anything. I would leave that to the future.

And, sure enough, the future brought in a lot of trouble. There were days when I used to remember Captain Giles with nothing short of abhorrence. His confounded acuteness had let me in for this job; while his prophecy that I "would have my hands full" coming true, made it appear as if done on purpose to play an evil joke on my young innocence.

Yes. I had my hands full of complications which were most valuable as "experience." People have a great opinion of the advantages of experience. But in that connection experience means always something disagreeable as opposed to the charm and innocence of illusions.

I must say I was losing mine rapidly. But on these instructive complications I must not enlarge more than to say that they could all be resumed[2] in the one word: Delay.

A mankind which has invented the proverb, "Time is money,"[3] will understand my vexation. The word "Delay" entered the secret chamber of my brain, resounded there like a tolling bell which maddens the ear, affected all my senses, took on a black colouring, a bitter taste, a deadly meaning.

"I am really sorry to see you worried like this. Indeed, I am . . ."

It was the only humane speech I used to hear at that time. And it came from a doctor,[4] appropriately enough.

A doctor is humane by definition. But that man was so in reality. His speech was not professional. I was not ill. But other people were, and that was the reason of his visiting the ship.

He was the doctor of our Legation and, of course, of the Consulate[5] too. He looked after the ship's health, which generally was poor, and trembling, as it were, on the verge of a break-up. Yes. The men ailed. And thus time was not only money, but life as well.

I had never seen such a steady ship's company. As the doctor remarked to me: "You seem to have a most respectable lot of seamen." Not only were they consistently sober, but they did not even want to go ashore. Care was taken to expose them as little as possible to the sun. They were employed on light work under the awnings. And the humane doctor commended me.

"Your arrangements appear to me to be very judicious, my dear Captain."

It is difficult to express how much that pronouncement comforted me. The Doctor's round full face framed in a light-coloured whisker was the perfection of a dignified amenity. He was the only human being in the world who seemed to take the slightest interest in me. He would generally sit in the cabin for half an hour or so at every visit.

2. Summarized.
3. A phrase attributed to Benjamin Franklin (1706–1790) that appears in his *Advice to a Young Tradesman, Written by an Old One* (1748).
4. Modeled after William Willis (1837–1894), who was the physician to the British Legation in Siam and attended the sick crew of the *Otago* while in Bangkok.
5. The Consul-General and accompanying staff; see p. 19, n. 7.

I said to him one day:

"I suppose the only thing now is to take care of them as you are doing, till I can get the ship to sea?"

He inclined his head, shutting his eyes under the large spectacles, and murmured:

"The sea . . . undoubtedly."

The first member of the crew fairly knocked over was the steward—the first man to whom I had spoken on board. He was taken ashore (with choleraic symptoms) and died there at the end of a week.[6] Then, while I was still under the startling impression of this first home-thrust of the climate, Mr. Burns gave up and went to bed in a raging fever without saying a word to anybody.

I believe he had partly fretted himself into that illness; the climate did the rest with the swiftness of an invisible monster ambushed in the air, in the water, in the mud of the river-bank. Mr. Burns was a predestined victim.

I discovered him lying on his back, glaring sullenly and radiating heat on one like a small furnace. He would hardly answer my questions, and only grumbled: Couldn't a man take an afternoon off duty with a bad headache—for once?

That evening, as I sat in the saloon after dinner, I could hear him muttering continuously in his room. Ransome, who was clearing the table, said to me:

"I am afraid, sir, I won't be able to give the mate all the attention he's likely to need. I will have to be forward in the galley a great part of my time."

Ransome was the cook. The mate had pointed him out to me the first day, standing on the deck, his arms crossed on his broad chest, gazing on the river.

Even at a distance his well-proportioned figure, something thoroughly sailor-like in his poise, made him noticeable. On nearer view the intelligent, quiet eyes, a well-bred face, the disciplined independence of his manner made up an attractive personality. When, in addition, Mr. Burns told me that he was the best seaman in the ship, I expressed my surprise that in his earliest prime and of such appearance he should sign on as cook on board a ship.

"It's his heart," Mr. Burns had said. "There's something wrong with it. He mustn't exert himself too much or he may drop dead suddenly."

6. John Carlson (1859–1888), the *Otago*'s cook and steward, died of cholera on January 16, 1888, about a week before Conrad assumed command; he was replaced by Pat Conroy, who was nineteen at the time.

And he was the only one the climate had not touched—perhaps because, carrying a deadly enemy in his breast, he had schooled himself into a systematic control of feelings and movements. When one was in the secret this was apparent in his manner. After the poor steward died, and as he could not be replaced by a white man in this Oriental port, Ransome had volunteered to do the double work.

"I can do it all right, sir, as long as I go about it quietly," he had assured me.

But obviously he couldn't be expected to take up sick-nursing in addition. Moreover, the doctor peremptorily ordered Mr. Burns ashore.

With a seaman on each side holding him up under the arms, the mate went over the gangway more sullen than ever. We built him up with pillows in the gharry,[7] and he made an effort to say brokenly:

"Now—you've got—what you wanted—got me out of the ship."

"You were never more mistaken in your life, Mr. Burns," I said quietly, duly smiling at him; and the trap[8] drove off to a sort of sanatorium, a pavilion of bricks which the doctor had in the grounds of his residence.

I visited Mr. Burns regularly. After the first few days, when he didn't know anybody, he received me as if I had come either to gloat over a crushed enemy or else to curry favour with a deeply-wronged person. It was either one or the other, just as it happened according to his fantastic sick-room moods. Whichever it was, he managed to convey it to me even during the period when he appeared almost too weak to talk. I treated him to my invariable kindliness.

Then one day, suddenly, a surge of downright panic burst through all this craziness.

If I left him behind in this deadly place he would die. He felt it, he was certain of it. But I wouldn't have the heart to leave him ashore. He had a wife and child in Sydney.[9]

He produced his wasted fore-arms from under the sheet which covered him and clasped his fleshless claws. He would die! He would die here. . . .

He absolutely managed to sit up, but only for a moment, and when he fell back I really thought that he would die there and then. I called to the Bengali dispenser,[1] and hastened away from the room.

Next day he upset me thoroughly by renewing his entreaties. I returned an evasive answer, and left him the picture of ghastly

7. Horse-drawn carriage or cart (Hindi).
8. Light two- or four-wheeled horse-drawn carriage.
9. A port city on the southeastern coast of Australia.
1. A person who makes up medical prescriptions and dispenses them. Bengal is an area of the Indian subcontinent that is now divided between northeastern India and Bangladesh.

despair. The day after I went in with reluctance, and he attacked me at once in a much stronger voice and with an abundance of argument which was quite startling. He presented his case with a sort of crazy vigour, and asked me finally how would I like to have a man's death on my conscience? He wanted me to promise that I would not sail without him.

I said that I really must consult the doctor first. He cried out at that. The doctor! Never! That would be a death sentence.

The effort had exhausted him. He closed his eyes, but went on rambling in a low voice. I had hated him from the start. The late captain had hated him too. Had wished him dead. Had wished all hands dead. . . .

"What do you want to stand in with that wicked corpse for, sir? He'll have you too," he ended, blinking his glazed eyes vacantly.

"Mr. Burns," I cried, very much discomposed, "what on earth are you talking about?"

He seemed to come to himself, though he was too weak to start.

"I don't know," he said languidly. "But don't ask that doctor, sir. You and I are sailors. Don't ask him, sir. Some day perhaps you will have a wife and child yourself."

And again he pleaded for the promise that I would not leave him behind. I had the firmness of mind not to give it to him. Afterwards this sternness seemed criminal; for my mind was made up. That prostrated man, with hardly strength enough to breathe and ravaged by a passion of fear, was irresistible. And, besides, he had happened to hit on the right words. He and I were sailors. That was a claim, for I had no other family. As to the wife-and-child (some day) argument it had no force. It sounded merely bizarre.

I could imagine no claim that would be stronger and more absorbing than the claim of that ship, of these men snared in the river by silly commercial complications, as if in some poisonous trap.

However, I had nearly fought my way out. Out to sea. The sea—which was pure, safe, and friendly. Three days more.

That thought sustained and carried me on my way back to the ship. In the saloon the doctor's voice greeted me, and his large form followed his voice, issuing out of the starboard spare cabin where the ship's medicine chest was kept securely lashed in the bed-place.

Finding that I was not on board he had gone in there, he said, to inspect the supply of drugs, bandages, and so on. Everything was complete and in order.

I thanked him; I had just been thinking of asking him to do that very thing, as in a couple of days, as he knew, we were going to sea, where all our troubles of every sort would be over at last.

He listened gravely and made no answer. But when I opened to him my mind as to Mr. Burns he sat down by my side, and, laying his hand on my knee amicably, begged me to think what it was I was exposing myself to.

The man was just strong enough to bear being moved and no more. But he couldn't stand a return of the fever. I had before me a passage of sixty days perhaps, beginning with intricate navigation and ending probably with a lot of bad weather. Could I run the risk of having to go through it single-handed, with no chief officer and with a second quite a youth? . . .

He might have added that it was my first command too. He did probably think of that fact, for he checked himself. It was very present to my mind.

He advised me earnestly to cable to Singapore for a chief officer, even if I had to delay my sailing for a week.

"Not a day," I said. The very thought gave me the shivers. The hands seemed fairly fit, all of them, and this was the time to get them away. Once at sea I was not afraid of facing anything. The sea was now the only remedy for all my troubles.

The doctor's glasses were directed at me like two lamps searching the genuineness of my resolution. He opened his lips as if to argue further, but shut them again without saying anything. I had a vision of poor Burns so vivid in his exhaustion, helplessness, and anguish, that it moved me more than the reality I had come away from only an hour before. It was purged from the drawbacks of his personality, and I could not resist it.

"Look here," I said. "Unless you tell me officially that the man must not be moved I'll make arrangements to have him brought on board to-morrow, and shall take the ship out of the river next morning, even if I have to anchor outside the bar for a couple of days to get her ready for sea."

"Oh! I'll make all the arrangements myself," said the doctor at once. "I spoke as I did only as a friend—as a well-wisher, and that sort of thing."

He rose in his dignified simplicity and gave me a warm handshake, rather solemnly, I thought. But he was as good as his word. When Mr. Burns appeared at the gangway carried on a stretcher, the doctor himself walked by its side. The programme had been altered in so far that this transportation had been left to the last moment, on the very morning of our departure.

It was barely an hour after sunrise. The doctor waved his big arm to me from the shore and walked back at once to his trap, which had followed him empty to the river-side. Mr. Burns, carried across the quarter-deck, had the appearance of being absolutely lifeless. Ransome went down to settle him in his cabin. I had to remain on deck to look after the ship, for the tug had got hold of our tow-rope already.

The splash of our shore-fasts falling in the water produced a complete change of feeling in me. It was like the imperfect relief of awakening from a nightmare. But when the ship's head swung down the river away from that town, Oriental and squalid, I missed the expected elation of that striven-for moment. What there was, undoubtedly, was a relaxation of tension which translated itself into a sense of weariness after an inglorious fight.

About mid-day we anchored a mile outside the bar. The afternoon was busy for all hands.[2] Watching the work from the poop, where I remained all the time, I detected in it some of the languor of the six weeks spent in the steaming heat of the river.[3] The first breeze would blow that away. Now the calm was complete. I judged that the second officer—a callow youth with an unpromising face— was not, to put it mildly, of that invaluable stuff from which a commander's right hand is made. But I was glad to catch along the main deck a few smiles on those seamen's faces at which I had hardly had time to have a good look as yet. Having thrown off the mortal coil of shore affairs,[4] I felt myself familiar with them and yet a little strange, like a long-lost wanderer among his kin.

Ransome flitted continually to and fro between the galley and the cabin. It was a pleasure to look at him. The man positively had grace. He alone of all the crew had not had a day's illness in port. But with the knowledge of that uneasy heart within his breast I could detect the restraint he put on the natural sailor-like agility of his movements. It was as though he had something very fragile or very explosive to carry about his person and was all the time aware of it.

I had occasion to address him once or twice. He answered me in his pleasant quiet voice and with a faint, slightly wistful smile. Mr. Burns appeared to be resting. He seemed fairly comfortable.

After sunset I came out on deck again to meet only a still void. The thin, featureless crust of the coast could not be distinguished. The darkness had risen around the ship like a mysterious emanation from the dumb and lonely waters. I leaned on the rail and turned my ear to the shadows of the night. Not a sound. My command might have been a planet flying vertiginously on its appointed path in a space of infinite silence. I clung to the rail as if my sense of balance were leaving me for good. How absurd. I hailed nervously.

"On deck there!"

---

2. Along with Conrad, Born, Jackson, and Conroy, the crew of the *Otago* consisted of T. Nils Kristian (nineteen), O. W. Leonard (thirty), Daniel Hatson (twenty-four), R. Haith (thirty-one), and J. Scarfe (nineteen).
3. The *Otago* left on February 9, 1888, with Conrad at command, some six weeks after it arrived in Bangkok.
4. Cf. *Hamlet* 3.1.69: "When we have shuffled off this mortal coil."

The immediate answer, "Yes, sir," broke the spell. The anchor-watch man ran up the poop ladder smartly. I told him to report at once the slightest sign of a breeze coming.

Going below I looked in on Mr. Burns. In fact, I could not avoid seeing him, for his door stood open. The man was so wasted that, in that white cabin, under a white sheet, and with his diminished head sunk in the white pillow, his red moustaches captured one's eyes exclusively, like something artificial—a pair of moustaches from a shop exhibited there in the harsh light of the bulkhead lamp without a shade.

While I stared with a sort of wonder he asserted himself by opening his eyes and even moving them in my direction. A minute stir.

"Dead calm, Mr. Burns," I said resignedly.

In an unexpectedly distinct voice Mr. Burns began a rambling speech. Its tone was very strange, not as if affected by his illness, but as if of a different nature. It sounded unearthly. As to the matter, I seemed to make out that it was the fault of the "old man"—the late captain—ambushed down there under the sea with some evil intention. It was a weird story.

I listened to the end; then stepping into the cabin I laid my hand on the mate's forehead. It was cool. He was light-headed only from extreme weakness. Suddenly he seemed to become aware of me, and in his own voice—of course, very feeble—he asked regretfully:

"Is there no chance at all to get under way, sir?"

"What's the good of letting go our hold of the ground only to drift, Mr. Burns?" I answered.

He sighed, and I left him to his immobility. His hold on life was as slender as his hold on sanity. I was oppressed by my lonely responsibilities. I went into my cabin to seek relief in a few hours' sleep, but almost before I closed my eyes the man on deck came down reporting a light breeze. Enough to get under way with, he said.

And it was no more than just enough. I ordered the windlass manned, the sails loosed, and the topsails set. But by the time I had cast the ship I could hardly feel any breath of wind. Nevertheless, I trimmed the yards and put everything on her. I was not going to give up the attempt.

IV

With her anchor at the bow and clothed in canvas to her very trucks, my command seemed to stand as motionless as a model ship set on the gleams and shadows of polished marble.[5] It was impossible to

5. Hawthorne (*HSL*) sees an echo of lines from "The Rime of the Ancient Mariner" (1798) by Samuel Taylor Coleridge (1772–1834): "Day after day, day after day, / We stuck, nor breath nor motion; / As idle as a painted ship / Upon a painted ocean" (lines 115–18).

distinguish land from water in the enigmatical tranquillity of the immense forces of the world. A sudden impatience possessed me.

"Won't she answer the helm at all?" I said irritably to the man whose strong brown hands grasping the spokes of the wheel stood out lighted on the darkness; like a symbol of mankind's claim to the direction of its own fate.

He answered me:

"Yes, sir. She's coming-to slowly."

"Let her head come up to south."

"Aye, aye, sir."

I paced the poop. There was not a sound but that of my footsteps, till the man spoke again.

"She is at south now, sir."

I felt a slight tightness of the chest before I gave out the first course of my first command to the silent night, heavy with dew and sparkling with stars. There was a finality in the act committing me to the endless vigilance of my lonely task.

"Steady her head at that," I said at last. "The course is south."

"South, sir," echoed the man.

I sent below the second mate and his watch and remained in charge, walking the deck through the chill, somnolent hours that precede the dawn.

Slight puffs came and went, and whenever they were strong enough to wake up the black water the murmur alongside ran through my very heart in a delicate crescendo of delight and died away swiftly. I was bitterly tired. The very stars seemed weary of waiting for day-break. It came at last with a mother-of-pearl sheen at the zenith, such as I had never seen before in the tropics, unglowing, almost grey, with a strange reminder of high latitudes.

The voice of the look-out man hailed from forward:

"Land on the port bow, sir."

"All right."

Leaning on the rail I never even raised my eyes. The motion of the ship was imperceptible. Presently Ransome brought me the cup of morning coffee. After I had drunk it I looked ahead, and in the still streak of very bright pale orange light I saw the land profiled flatly as if cut out of black paper and seeming to float on the water as light as cork. But the rising sun turned it into mere dark vapour, a doubtful, massive shadow trembling in the hot glare.

The watch finished washing the decks. I went below and stopped at Mr. Burns' door (he could not bear to have it shut), but hesitated to speak to him till he moved his eyes. I gave him the news.

"Sighted Cape Liant[6] at daylight. About fifteen miles."

He moved his lips then, but I heard no sound till I put my ear down, and caught the peevish comment: "This is crawling. . . . No luck."

"Better luck than standing still, anyhow," I pointed out resignedly, and left him to whatever thoughts or fancies haunted his hopeless prostration.

Later that morning, when relieved by my second officer, I threw myself on my couch and for some three hours or so I really found oblivion. It was so perfect that on waking up I wondered where I was. Then came the immense relief of the thought: on board my ship! At sea! At sea!

Through the port-holes I beheld an unruffled, sun-smitten horizon. The horizon of a windless day. But its spaciousness alone was enough to give me a sense of a fortunate escape, a momentary exultation of freedom.

I stepped out into the saloon with my heart lighter than it had been for days. Ransome was at the sideboard preparing to lay the table for the first sea dinner of the passage. He turned his head, and something in his eyes checked my modest elation.

Instinctively I asked: "What is it now?" not expecting in the least the answer I got. It was given with that sort of contained serenity which was characteristic of the man.

"I am afraid we haven't left all sickness behind us, sir."

"We haven't! What's the matter?"

He told me then that two of our men had been taken bad with fever in the night. One of them was burning and the other was shivering, but he thought that it was pretty much the same thing. I thought so too. I felt shocked by the news. "One burning, the other shivering, you say? No. We haven't left the sickness behind. Do they look very ill?"

"Middling bad, sir." Ransome's eyes gazed steadily into mine. We exchanged smiles. Ransome's a little wistful, as usual, mine no doubt grim enough, to correspond with my secret exasperation.

I asked:

"Was there any wind at all this morning?"

"Can hardly say that, sir. We've moved all the time though. The land ahead seems a little nearer."

That was it. A little nearer. Whereas if we had only had a little more wind, only a very little more, we might, we should, have been abreast of Cape Liant by this time and increasing our distance from that contaminated shore. And it was not only the distance. It seemed

---

6. In southern Thailand (12°6′, 100°97′ E), marking the division between the Gulf of Thailand and the Bight of Bangkok. See p. 483.

to me that a stronger breeze would have blown away the infection which clung to the ship. It obviously did cling to the ship. Two men. One burning, one shivering. I felt a distinct reluctance to go and look at them. What was the good? Poison is poison. Tropical fever is tropical fever. But that it should have stretched its claw after us over the sea seemed to me an extraordinary and unfair licence. I could hardly believe that it could be anything worse than the last desperate pluck of the evil from which we were escaping into the clean breath of the sea. If only that breath had been a little stronger. However, there was the quinine against the fever. I went into the spare cabin where the medicine chest was kept to prepare two doses. I opened it full of faith as a man opens a miraculous shrine. The upper part was inhabited by a collection of bottles, all square-shouldered and as like each other as peas. Under that orderly array there were two drawers, stuffed as full of things as one could imagine—paper packages, bandages, card-board boxes officially labelled. The lower of the two, in one of its compartments, contained our provision of quinine.

There were five bottles, all round and all of a size. One was about a third full. The other four remained still wrapped up in paper and sealed. But I did not expect to see an envelope lying on top of them. A square envelope, belonging, in fact, to the ship's stationery.

It lay so that I could see it was not closed down, and on picking it up and turning it over I perceived that it was addressed to myself. It contained a half-sheet of notepaper, which I unfolded with a queer sense of dealing with the uncanny, but without any excitement as people meet and do extraordinary things in a dream.

"My dear Captain," it began, but I ran to the signature. The writer was the doctor. The date was that of the day on which, returning from my visit to Mr. Burns in the hospital, I had found the excellent doctor waiting for me in the cabin; and when he told me that he had been putting in time inspecting the medicine chest for me. How bizarre! While expecting me to come in at any moment he had been amusing himself by writing me a letter, and then as I came in had hastened to stuff it into the medicine-chest drawer. A rather incredible proceeding. I turned to the text in wonder.

In a large, hurried, but legible hand the good, sympathetic man for some reason, either of kindness or more likely impelled by the irresistible desire to express his opinion, with which he didn't want to damp my hopes before, was warning me not to put any trust in the beneficial effects of a change from land to sea. "I didn't want to add to your worries by discouraging your hopes," he wrote. "I am afraid that, medically speaking, the end of your troubles is not yet." In short, he expected me to have to fight a probable return of tropical illness. Fortunately I had a good provision of quinine. I should put my trust in that, and administer it steadily, when the ship's health would certainly improve.

I crumpled up the letter and rammed it into my pocket. Ransome carried off two big doses to the men forward. As to myself, I did not go on deck as yet. I went instead to the door of Mr. Burns' room, and gave him that news too.

It was impossible to say the effect it had on him. At first I thought that he was speechless. His head lay sunk in the pillow. He moved his lips enough, however, to assure me that he was getting much stronger; a statement shockingly untrue on the face of it.

That afternoon I took my watch as a matter of course. A great over-heated stillness enveloped the ship and seemed to hold her motionless in a flaming ambience composed in two shades of blue. Faint, hot puffs eddied nervelessly from her sails. And yet she moved. She must have. For, as the sun was setting, we had drawn abreast of Cape Liant and dropped it behind us: an ominous retreating shadow in the last gleams of twilight.

In the evening, under the crude glare of his lamp, Mr. Burns seemed to have come more to the surface of his bedding. It was as if a depressing hand had been lifted off him. He answered my few words by a comparatively long, connected speech. He asserted himself strongly. If he escaped being smothered by this stagnant heat, he said, he was confident that in a very few days he would be able to come up on deck and help me.

While he was speaking I trembled lest this effort of energy should leave him lifeless before my eyes. But I cannot deny that there was something comforting in his willingness. I made a suitable reply, but pointed out to him that the only thing that could really help us was wind—a fair wind.

He rolled his head impatiently on the pillow. And it was not comforting in the least to hear him begin to mutter crazily about the late captain, that old man buried in latitude 8°20′,[7] right in our way—ambushed at the entrance of the Gulf.

"Are you still thinking of your late Captain, Mr. Burns?" I said. "I imagine the dead feel no animosity against the living. They care nothing for them."

"You don't know that one," he breathed out feebly.

"No. I didn't know him, and he didn't know me. And so he can't have any grievance against me, anyway."

"Yes. But there's all the rest of us on board," he insisted.

---

7. Sherry notes that in the manuscript for Conrad's "Falk" Captain Snadden was buried at sea off the coast of Cochinchina (now southern Vietnam) rather than at the mouth of the Gulf of Thailand (*CEW* 223).

I felt the inexpugnable strength of common sense being insidiously menaced by this gruesome, by this insane delusion. And I said:

"You mustn't talk so much. You will tire yourself."

"And there is the ship herself," he persisted in a whisper.

"Now, not a word more," I said, stepping in and laying my hand on his cool forehead. It proved to me that this atrocious absurdity was rooted in the man himself and not in the disease, which, apparently, had emptied him of every power, mental and physical, except that one fixed idea.

I avoided giving Mr. Burns any opening for conversation for the next few days. I merely used to throw him a hasty, cheery word when passing his door. I believe that if he had had the strength he would have called out after me more than once. But he hadn't the strength. Ransome, however, observed to me one afternoon that the mate "seemed to be picking up wonderfully."

"Did he talk any nonsense to you of late?" I asked casually.

"No, sir." Ransome was startled by the direct question; but, after a pause, he added equably: "He told me this morning, sir, that he was sorry he had to bury our late Captain right in the ship's way, as one may say, out of the Gulf."

"Isn't this nonsense enough for you?" I asked, looking confidently at the intelligent, quiet face on which the secret uneasiness in the man's breast had thrown a transparent veil of care.

Ransome didn't know. He had not given a thought to the matter. And with a faint smile he flitted away from me on his never-ending duties, with his usual guarded activity.

Two more days passed. We had advanced a little way—a very little way—into the larger space of the Gulf of Siam. Seizing eagerly upon the elation of the first command thrown into my lap, by the agency of Captain Giles, I had yet an uneasy feeling that such luck as this has got perhaps to be paid for in some way. I had held, professionally, a review of my chances. I was competent enough for that. At least, I thought so. I had a general sense of my preparedness which only a man pursuing a calling he loves can know. That feeling seemed to me the most natural thing in the world. As natural as breathing. I imagined I could not have lived without it.

I don't know what I expected. Perhaps nothing else than that special intensity of existence which is the quintessence of youthful aspirations. Whatever I expected I did not expect to be beset by hurricanes. I knew better than that. In the Gulf of Siam there are no hurricanes. But neither did I expect to find myself bound hand and foot to the hopeless extent which was revealed to me as the days went on.

Not that the evil spell held us always motionless. Mysterious currents drifted us here and there, with a stealthy power made manifest by the changing vistas of the islands fringing the east shore of the Gulf. And there were winds too, fitful and deceitful. They raised hopes only to dash them into the bitterest disappointment, promises of advance ending in lost ground, expiring in sighs, dying into dumb stillness in which the currents had it all their own way— their own inimical way.

The Island of Koh-ring, a great, black, upheaved ridge amongst a lot of tiny islets, lying upon the glassy water like a triton amongst minnows,[8] seemed to be the centre of the fatal circle. It seemed impossible to get away from it. Day after day it remained in sight. More than once, in a favourable breeze, I would take its bearing in the fast ebbing twilight, thinking that it was for the last time. Vain hope. A night of fitful airs would undo the gains of temporary favour, and the rising sun would throw out the black relief of Koh-ring, looking more barren, inhospitable, and grim than ever.

"It's like being bewitched, upon my word," I said once to Mr. Burns, from my usual position in the doorway.

He was sitting up in his bed-place. He was progressing towards the world of living men; if he could hardly have been said to have rejoined it yet. He nodded to me his frail and bony head in a wisely mysterious assent.

"Oh, yes, I know what you mean," I said.

"But you cannot expect me to believe that a dead man has the power to put out of joint the meteorology of this part of the world. Though indeed it seems to have gone utterly wrong. The land and sea breezes have got broken up into small pieces. We cannot depend upon them for five minutes together."

"It won't be very long now before I can come up on deck," muttered Mr. Burns, "and then we shall see."

Whether he meant this for a promise to grapple with supernatural evil I couldn't tell. At any rate, it wasn't the kind of assistance I needed. On the other hand, I had been living on deck practically night and day so as to take advantage of every chance to get my ship a little more to the southward. The mate, I could see, was extremely weak yet, and not quite rid of his delusion, which to me appeared but a symptom of his disease. At all events, the hopefulness of an invalid was not to be discouraged. I said:

"You will be most welcome there, I am sure, Mr. Burns. If you go on improving at this rate you'll be presently one of the healthiest men in the ship."

---

8. Cf. Shakespeare's *Coriolanus* 3.1.92: "Hear you this Triton of the minnows?" In Greek mythology, Triton (son of Poseidon and Amphitrite) is a god and the messenger of the sea. For Koh-ring, see p. 36, n. 5.

This pleased him, but his extreme emaciation converted his self-satisfied smile into a ghastly exhibition of long teeth under the red moustache.

"Aren't the fellows improving, sir?" he asked soberly, with an extremely sensible expression of anxiety on his face.

I answered him only with a vague gesture and went away from the door. The fact was that disease played with us capriciously very much as the winds did. It would go from one man to another with a lighter or heavier touch, which always left its mark behind, staggering some, knocking others over for a time, leaving this one, returning to another, so that all of them had now an invalidish aspect and a hunted, apprehensive look in their eyes; while Ransome and I, the only two completely untouched, went amongst them assiduously distributing quinine. It was a double fight. The adverse weather held us in front and the disease pressed on our rear. I must say that the men were very good. The constant toil of trimming the yards they faced willingly. But all spring was out of their limbs, and as I looked at them from the poop I could not keep from my mind the dreadful impression that they were moving in poisoned air.

Down below, in his cabin, Mr. Burns had advanced so far as not only to be able to sit up, but even to draw up his legs. Clasping them with bony arms, like an animated skeleton, he emitted deep, impatient sighs.

"The great thing to do, sir," he would tell me on every occasion, when I gave him the chance, "the great thing is to get the ship past 8° 20′ of latitude. Once she's past that we're all right."

At first I used only to smile at him, though, God knows, I had not much heart left for smiles. But at last I lost my patience.

"Oh, yes. The latitude 8° 20′. That's where you buried your late Captain, isn't it?" Then with severity: "Don't you think, Mr. Burns, it's about time you dropped all that nonsense?"

He rolled at me his deep-sunken eyes in a glance of invincible obstinacy. But for the rest, he only muttered, just loud enough for me to hear, something about "Not surprised . . . find . . . play us some beastly trick yet. . . ."

Such passages as this were not exactly wholesome for my resolution. The stress of adversity was beginning to tell on me. At the same time I felt a contempt for that obscure weakness of my soul. I said to myself disdainfully that it should take much more than that to affect in the smallest degree my fortitude.

I didn't know then how soon and from what unexpected direction it would be attacked.

It was the very next day. The sun had risen clear of the southern shoulder of Koh-ring, which still hung, like an evil attendant, on our port quarter. It was intensely hateful to my sight. During the night we had been heading all round the compass, trimming the yards again and again, to what I fear must have been for the most part imaginary puffs of air. Then just about sunrise we got for an hour an inexplicable, steady breeze, right in our teeth. There was no sense in it. It fitted neither with the season of the year, nor with the secular[9] experience of seamen as recorded in books, nor with the aspect of the sky. Only purposeful malevolence could account for it. It sent us travelling at a great pace away from our proper course; and if we had been out on pleasure sailing bent it would have been a delightful breeze, with the awakened sparkle of the sea, with the sense of motion and a feeling of unwonted freshness. Then all at once, as if disdaining to carry farther the sorry jest, it dropped and died out completely in less than five minutes. The ship's head swung where it listed;[1] the stilled sea took on the polish of a steel plate in the calm.

I went below, not because I meant to take some rest, but simply because I couldn't bear to look at it just then. The indefatigable Ransome was busy in the saloon. It had become a regular practice with him to give me an informal health report in the morning. He turned away from the sideboard with his usual pleasant, quiet gaze. No shadow rested on his intelligent forehead.

"There are a good many of them middling bad this morning, sir," he said in a calm tone.

"What? All knocked out?"

"Only two actually in their bunks, sir, but . . ."

"It's the last night that has done for them. We have had to pull and haul all the blessed[2] time."

"I heard, sir. I had a mind to come out and help only, you know. . . ."

"Certainly not. You mustn't. . . . The fellows lie at night about the decks, too. It isn't good for them."

Ransome assented. But men couldn't be looked after like children. Moreover, one could hardly blame them for trying for such coolness and such air as there was to be found on deck. He himself, of course, knew better.

He was, indeed, a reasonable man. Yet it would have been hard to say that the others were not. The last few days had been for us like the ordeal of the fiery furnace.[3] One really couldn't quarrel with their common, imprudent humanity making the best of the moments of relief, when the night brought in the illusion of coolness and the starlight twinkled through the heavy, dew-laden air. Moreover, most of them were so weakened that hardly anything could be done without

9. In the more obscure meaning of *centuries old.*
1. In the archaic sense of *wished.* Cf. John 3:8: "The wind bloweth where it listeth."
2. Probably a euphemism for *damned.*
3. Cf. Daniel 1–3, in which three Israelites (Shadrach, Meshach and Abednego) survive a fiery furnace through the protection of the God of Israel.

everybody that could totter mustering on the braces. No, it was no use remonstrating with them. But I fully believed that quinine was of very great use indeed.

I believed in it. I pinned my faith to it. It would save the men, the ship, break the spell by its medicinal virtue, make time of no account, the weather but a passing worry, and, like a magic powder working against mysterious malefices, secure the first passage of my first command against the evil powers of calms and pestilence. I looked upon it as more precious than gold, and unlike gold, of which there ever hardly seems to be enough anywhere, the ship had a sufficient store of it. I went in to get it with the purpose of weighing out doses. I stretched my hand with the feeling of a man reaching for an unfailing panacea, took up a fresh bottle and unrolled the wrapper, noticing as I did so that the ends, both top and bottom, had come unsealed. . . .

But why record all the swift steps of the appalling discovery. You have guessed the truth already. There was the wrapper, the bottle, and the white powder inside, some sort of powder! But it wasn't quinine. One look at it was quite enough. I remember that at the very moment of picking up the bottle, before I even dealt with the wrapper, the weight of the object I had in my hand gave me an instant of premonition. Quinine is as light as feathers; and my nerves must have been exasperated into an extraordinary sensibility. I let the bottle smash itself on the floor. The stuff, whatever it was, felt gritty under the sole of my shoe. I snatched up the next bottle and then the next. The weight alone told the tale. One after another they fell, breaking at my feet, not because I threw them down in my dismay, but slipping through my fingers as if this disclosure were too much for my strength.

It is a fact that the very greatness of a mental shock helps one to bear up against it, by producing a sort of temporary insensibility. I came out of the state-room stunned, as if something heavy had dropped on my head. From the other side of the saloon, across the table, Ransome, with a duster in his hand, stared open-mouthed. I don't think that I looked wild. It is quite possible that I appeared to be in a hurry because I was instinctively hastening up on deck. An example this of training become instinct. The difficulties, the dangers, the problems of a ship at sea must be met on deck.

To this fact, as it were of nature, I responded instinctively; which may be taken as a proof that for a moment I must have been robbed of my reason.

I was certainly off my balance, a prey to impulse, for at the bottom of the stairs I turned and flung myself at the doorway of Mr. Burns' cabin. The wildness of his aspect checked my mental disorder. He was sitting up in his bunk, his body looking immensely long, his head drooping a little sideways, with affected complacency. He flourished, in his trembling hand, on the end of a forearm no thicker than a stout walking-stick, a shining pair of scissors which he tried before my very eyes to jab at his throat.

I was to a certain extent horrified; but it was rather a secondary sort of effect, not really strong enough to make me yell at him in some such manner as: "Stop!" . . . "Heavens!" . . .

"What are you doing?"

In reality he was simply overtaxing his returning strength in a shaky attempt to clip off the thick growth of his red beard. A large towel was spread over his lap, and a shower of stiff hairs, like bits of copper wire, was descending on it at every snip of the scissors.

He turned to me his face grotesque beyond the fantasies of mad dreams, one cheek all bushy as if with a swollen flame, the other denuded and sunken, with the untouched long moustache on that side asserting itself, lonely and fierce. And while he stared thunderstruck, with the gaping scissors on his fingers, I shouted my discovery at him fiendishly, in six words, without comment.

V

I heard the clatter of the scissors escaping from his hand, noted the perilous heave of his whole person over the edge of the bunk after them, and then, returning to my first purpose, pursued my course on to the deck. The sparkle of the sea filled my eyes. It was gorgeous and barren, monotonous and without hope under the empty curve of the sky. The sails hung motionless and slack, the very folds of their sagging surfaces moved no more than carved granite. The impetuosity of my advent made the man at the helm start slightly. A block aloft squeaked incomprehensibly, for what on earth could have made it do so? It was a whistling note like a bird's. For a long, long time I faced an empty world, steeped in an infinity of silence, through which the sunshine poured and flowed for some mysterious purpose. Then I heard Ransome's voice at my elbow.

"I have put Mr. Burns back to bed, sir."

"You have."

"Well, sir, he got out, all of a sudden, but when he let go of the edge of his bunk he fell down. He isn't light-headed, though, it seems to me."

"No," I said dully, without looking at Ransome. He waited for a moment, then, cautiously as if not to give offence: "I don't think we need lose much of that stuff, sir," he said. "I can sweep it up, every bit of it almost, and then we could sift the glass out. I will go about it at once. It will not make the breakfast late, not ten minutes."

"Oh, yes," I said bitterly. "Let the breakfast wait, sweep up every bit of it, and then throw the damned lot overboard!"

The profound silence returned, and when I looked over my shoulder Ransome—the intelligent, serene Ransome—had vanished from my side. The intense loneliness of the sea acted like poison on my brain. When I turned my eyes to the ship, I had a morbid vision of her as a floating grave. Who hasn't heard of ships found drifting, haphazard, with their crews all dead?[4] I looked at the seaman at the helm, I had an impulse to speak to him, and, indeed, his face took on an expectant cast as if he had guessed my intention. But in the end I went below, thinking I would be alone with the greatness of my trouble for a little while. But through his open door Mr. Burns saw me come down, and addressed me grumpily: "Well, sir?"

I went in. "It isn't well at all," I said.

Mr. Burns, re-established in his bed-place, was concealing his hirsute cheek in the palm of his hand.

"That confounded fellow has taken away the scissors from me," were the next words he said.

The tension I was suffering from was so great that it was perhaps just as well that Mr. Burns had started on this grievance. He seemed very sore about it and grumbled, "Does he think I am mad, or what?"

"I don't think so, Mr. Burns," I said. I looked upon him at that moment as a model of self-possession. I even conceived on that account a sort of admiration for that man, who had (apart from the intense materiality of what was left of his beard) come as near to being a disembodied spirit as any man can do and live. I noticed the preternatural sharpness of the ridge of his nose, the deep cavities of his temples, and I envied him. He was so reduced that he would probably die very soon. Enviable man! So near extinction—while I had to bear within me a tumult of suffering vitality, doubt, confusion, self-reproach, and an indefinite reluctance to meet the horrid logic of the situation. I could not help muttering: "I feel as if I were going mad myself."

Mr. Burns glared spectrally, but was otherwise wonderfully composed.

"I always thought he would play us some deadly trick," he said, with a peculiar emphasis on the *he*.

---

4. Here and elsewhere, Conrad alludes to tales—such as Coleridge's "The Rime of the Ancient Mariner"; the opera *The Flying Dutchman* (1841), by Richard Wagner (1813–1883); and *The Phantom Ship* (1839), by Frederick Marrayat (1792–1848)—that chronicle a ship unable to reach port because of the transgression of one of its crew.

It gave me a mental shock, but I had neither the mind, nor the heart, nor the spirit to argue with him. My form of sickness was indifference. The creeping paralysis of a hopeless outlook. So I only gazed at him. Mr. Burns broke into further speech.

"Eh? What? No! You won't believe it? Well, how do you account for this? How do you think it could have happened?"

"Happened?" I repeated dully. "Why, yes, how in the name of the infernal powers did this thing happen?"

Indeed, on thinking it out, it seemed incomprehensible that it should be just like this: the bottles emptied, refilled, rewrapped, and replaced. A sort of plot, a sinister attempt to deceive, a thing resembling sly vengeance—but for what?—or else a fiendish joke. But Mr. Burns was in possession of a theory. It was simple, and he uttered it solemnly in a hollow voice.

"I suppose they have given him about fifteen pounds in Haiphong for that little lot."

"Mr. Burns!" I cried.

He nodded grotesquely over his raised legs, like two broomsticks in the pyjamas, with enormous bare feet at the end.

"Why not? The stuff is pretty expensive in this part of the world, and they were very short of it in Tonkin.[5] And what did he care? You have not known him. I have, and I have defied him. He feared neither God, nor devil, nor man, nor wind, nor sea, nor his own conscience. And I believe he hated everybody and everything. But I think he was afraid to die. I believe I am the only man who ever stood up to him. I faced him in that cabin where you live now, when he was sick, and I cowed him then. He thought I was going to twist his neck for him. If he had had his way we would have been beating up against the North-East monsoon,[6] as long as he lived and afterwards too, for ages and ages. Acting the Flying Dutchman in the China Sea![7] Ha! Ha!"

"But why should he replace the bottles like this?" . . . I began.

"Why shouldn't he? Why should he want to throw the bottles away? They fit the drawer. They belong to the medicine chest."

"And they were wrapped up," I cried.

"Well, the wrappers were there. Did it from habit, I suppose, and as to refilling, there is always a lot of stuff they send in paper parcels

5. The northern part of Vietnam, one of the three protectorates under French rule (the others being Annam and Cochinchina). See p. 335.
6. A wind that blows to the northeast in southeast Asia from roughly December to March. Its complement is the southwest monsoon, which blows southwest from roughly June to September. These monsoon winds strongly affect the weather of the region.
7. I.e., the South China Sea, a marginal sea in the Pacific Ocean bordered on the east by the Philippines, the north by China, the south by Indonesia, and the west by the Malay Peninsula. See p. 335. "Flying Dutchman": see p. 108, n. 4.

that burst after a time. And then, who can tell? I suppose you didn't taste it, sir? But, of course, you are sure . . ."

"No," I said. "I didn't taste it. It is all overboard now."

Behind me, a soft, cultivated voice said: "I have tasted it. It seemed a mixture of all sorts, sweetish, saltish, very horrible."

Ransome, stepping out of the pantry, had been listening for some time, as it was very excusable in him to do.

"A dirty trick," said Mr. Burns. "I always said he would."

The magnitude of my indignation was unbounded. And the kind, sympathetic doctor too. The only sympathetic man I ever knew . . . instead of writing that warning letter, the very refinement of sympathy, why didn't the man make a proper inspection? But, as a matter of fact, it was hardly fair to blame the doctor. The fittings were in order and the medicine chest is an officially arranged affair. There was nothing really to arouse the slightest suspicion. The person I could never forgive was myself. Nothing should ever be taken for granted. The seed of everlasting remorse was sown in my breast.

"I feel it's all my fault," I exclaimed, "mine, and nobody else's. That's how I feel. I shall never forgive myself."

"That's very foolish, sir," said Mr. Burns fiercely.

And after this effort he fell back exhausted on his bed. He closed his eyes, he panted; this affair, this abominable surprise had shaken him up too. As I turned away I perceived Ransome looking at me blankly. He appreciated what it meant, but he managed to produce his pleasant, wistful smile. Then he stepped back into his pantry, and I rushed up on deck again to see whether there was any wind, any breath under the sky, any stir of the air, any sign of hope. The deadly stillness met me again. Nothing was changed except that there was a different man at the wheel. He looked ill. His whole figure drooped, and he seemed rather to cling to the spokes than hold them with a controlling grip. I said to him:

"You are not fit to be here."

"I can manage, sir," he said feebly.

As a matter of fact, there was nothing for him to do. The ship had no steerage way. She lay with her head to the westward, the everlasting Koh-ring visible over the stern, with a few small islets, black spots in the great blaze, swimming before my troubled eyes. And but for those bits of land there was no speck on the sky, no speck on the water, no shape of vapour, no wisp of smoke, no sail, no boat, no stir of humanity, no sign of life, nothing!

The first question was, what to do? What could one do? The first thing to do obviously was to tell the men. I did it that very day. I wasn't going to let the knowledge simply get about. I would face them. They were assembled on the quarter-deck for the purpose. Just before I stepped out to speak to them I discovered that life could hold terrible moments. No confessed criminal had ever been so oppressed by his sense of guilt. This is why, perhaps, my face was set hard and my voice curt and unemotional while I made my declaration that I could do nothing more for the sick, in the way of drugs. As to such care as could be given them they knew they had had it.

I would have held them justified in tearing me limb from limb. The silence which followed upon my words was almost harder to bear than the angriest uproar. I was crushed by the infinite depth of its reproach. But, as a matter of fact, I was mistaken. In a voice which I had great difficulty in keeping firm, I went on: "I suppose, men, you have understood what I said, and you know what it means."

A voice or two were heard: "Yes, sir. . . . We understand."

They had kept silent simply because they thought that they were not called upon to say anything; and when I told them that I intended to run into Singapore and that the best chance for the ship and the men was in the efforts all of us, sick and well, must make to get her along out of this, I received the encouragement of a low assenting murmur and of a louder voice exclaiming: "Surely there is a way out of this blamed[8] hole."

Here is an extract from the notes I wrote at the time.

"We have lost Koh-ring at last. For many days now I don't think I have been two hours below altogether. I remain on deck, of course, night and day, and the nights and the days wheel over us in succession, whether long or short, who can say? All sense of time is lost in the monotony of expectation, of hope, and of desire—which is only one: Get the ship to the southward! Get the ship to the southward! The effect is curiously mechanical; the sun climbs and descends, the night swings over our heads as if somebody below the horizon were turning a crank.[9] It is the pettiest, the most aimless! . . . and all through that miserable performance I go on, tramping, tramping the deck. How many miles have I walked on the poop of that ship! A stubborn pilgrimage of sheer restlessness, diversified by short excursions below to look upon Mr. Burns. I don't know whether it is an illusion, but he seems to become more substantial from day to day. He doesn't say much, for, indeed, the situation doesn't lend itself to idle remarks. I notice this even with the men as I watch them moving or sitting about the decks. They don't talk to each other. It strikes me that if there exists an invisible ear catching the whispers of the earth, it will find this ship the most silent spot on it. . . .

8. Probably another euphemism for *damned*.
9. Ingram (*ISL*) sees an echo of "The Rime of the Ancient Mariner": "The sun came up upon the left, / Out of the sea came he! / And he shone bright, and on the right / Went down into the sea" (lines 25–29).

"No, Mr. Burns has not much to say to me. He sits in his bunk with his beard gone, his moustaches flaming, and with an air of silent determination on his chalky physiognomy. Ransome tells me he devours all the food that is given him to the last scrap, but that, apparently, he sleeps very little. Even at night, when I go below to fill my pipe, I notice that, though dozing flat on his back, he still looks very determined. From the side glance he gives me when awake it seems as though he were annoyed at being interrupted in some arduous mental operation; and as I emerge on deck the ordered arrangement of the stars meets my eye, unclouded, infinitely wearisome. There they are: stars, sun, sea, light, darkness, space, great waters; the formidable Work of the Seven Days,[1] into which mankind seems to have blundered unbidden. Or else decoyed. Even as I have been decoyed into this awful, this death-haunted command. . . ."

The only spot of light in the ship at night was that of the compass-lamps, lighting up the faces of the succeeding helmsmen; for the rest we were lost in the darkness, I walking the poop and the men lying about the decks. They were all so reduced by sickness that no watches could be kept. Those who were able to walk remained all the time on duty, lying about in the shadows of the main deck, till my voice raised for an order would bring them to their enfeebled feet, a tottering little group, moving patiently about the ship, with hardly a murmur, a whisper amongst them all. And every time I had to raise my voice it was with a pang of remorse and pity.

Then about four o'clock in the morning a light would gleam forward in the galley. The unfailing Ransome with the uneasy heart, immune, serene, and active, was getting ready the early coffee for the men. Presently he would bring me a cup up on the poop, and it was then that I allowed myself to drop into my deck chair for a couple of hours of real sleep. No doubt I must have been snatching short dozes when leaning against the rail for a moment in sheer exhaustion; but, honestly, I was not aware of them, except in the painful form of convulsive starts that seemed to come on me even while I walked. From about five, however, until after seven I would sleep openly under the fading stars.

I would say to the helmsman: "Call me at need," and drop into that chair and close my eyes, feeling that there was no more sleep for me on earth. And then I would know nothing till, some time between seven and eight, I would feel a touch on my shoulder and look up at Ransome's face, with its faint, wistful smile and friendly, grey eyes, as though he were tenderly amused at my slumbers. Occasionally the

---

1. A reference to God's creation of heaven and the earth in seven days in Genesis 1–2.

second mate would come up and relieve me at early coffee time. But it didn't really matter. Generally it was a dead calm, or else faint airs so changing and fugitive that it really wasn't worth while to touch a brace for them. If the air steadied at all the seaman at the helm could be trusted for a warning shout: "Ship's all aback, sir!" which like a trumpet-call would make me spring a foot above the deck. Those were the words which it seemed to me would have made me spring up from eternal sleep. But this was not often. I have never met since such breathless sunrises. And if the second mate happened to be there (he had generally one day in three free of fever) I would find him sitting on the skylight half-senseless, as it were, and with an idiotic gaze fastened on some object near by—a rope, a cleat, a belaying-pin, a ringbolt.

That young man was rather troublesome. He remained cubbish in his sufferings. He seemed to have become completely imbecile; and when the return of fever drove him to his cabin below the next thing would be that we would miss him from there. The first time it happened Ransome and I were very much alarmed. We started a quiet search and ultimately Ransome discovered him curled up in the sail-locker, which opened into the lobby by a sliding-door. When remonstrated with, he muttered sulkily, "It's cool in there." That wasn't true. It was only dark there.

The fundamental defects of his face were not improved by its uniform livid[2] hue. It was not so with many of the men. The wastage of ill-health seemed to idealise the general character of the features, bringing out the unsuspected nobility of some, the strength of others, and in one case revealing an essentially comic aspect. He was a short, gingery, active man with a nose and chin of the Punch[3] type, and whom his shipmates called "Frenchy." I don't know why. He may have been a Frenchman, but I have never heard him utter a single word in French.

To see him coming aft to the wheel comforted one. The blue dungaree trousers turned up the calf, one leg a little higher than the other, the clean check shirt, the white canvas cap, evidently made by himself, made up a whole of peculiar smartness, and the persistent jauntiness of his gait, even, poor fellow, when he couldn't help tottering, told of his invincible spirit. There was also a man called Gambril.[4] He was the only grizzled person in the ship. His face was of an austere type. But if I remember all their faces,

---

2. See p. 12, n. 4.
3. A character from the popular puppet show *Punch and Judy* who has a hunched back and whose nose nearly touches his chin. He is a violent character who liberally uses a stick on other characters. "Gingery": sandy or ginger-colored hair or complexion; full of vigor, high spirited; hot spiced.
4. Gambril also appears in Conrad's "Falk."

wasting tragically before my eyes, most of their names have vanished from my memory.

The words that passed between us were few and puerile in regard of the situation. I had to force myself to look them in the face. I expected to meet reproachful glances.[5] There were none. The expression of suffering in their eyes was indeed hard enough to bear. But that they couldn't help. For the rest, I ask myself whether it was the temper of their souls or the sympathy of their imagination that made them so wonderful, so worthy of my undying regard.[6]

For myself, neither my soul was highly tempered, nor my imagination properly under control. There were moments when I felt, not only that I would go mad, but that I had gone mad already; so that I dared not open my lips for fear of betraying myself by some insane shriek. Luckily I had only orders to give, and an order has a steadying influence upon him who has to give it. Moreover, the seaman, the officer of the watch, in me was sufficiently sane. I was like a mad carpenter making a box. Were he ever so convinced that he was King of Jerusalem,[7] the box he would make would be a sane box. What I feared was a shrill note escaping me involuntarily and upsetting my balance. Luckily, again, there was no necessity to raise one's voice. The brooding stillness of the world seemed sensitive to the slightest sound like a whispering gallery.[8] The conversational tone would almost carry a word from one end of the ship to the other. The terrible thing was that the only voice that I ever heard was my own. At night especially it reverberated very lonely amongst the planes of the unstirring sails.

Mr. Burns, still keeping to his bed with that air of secret determination, was moved to grumble at many things. Our interviews were short five-minute affairs, but fairly frequent. I was everlastingly diving down below to get a light, though I did not consume much tobacco at that time. The pipe was always going out; for in truth my mind was not composed enough to enable me to get a decent smoke. Likewise, for most of the time during the twenty-four hours I could have struck matches on deck and held them aloft till the flame burnt my fingers. But I always used to run below. It was a change. It was the only break in the incessant strain; and, of course, Mr. Burns through the open door could see me come in and go out every time.

5. Hawthorne (*HSL*) sees another echo from "The Rime of the Ancient Mariner": "Each turned his face with a ghastly pang, / And cursed me with his eye" (lines 214–15).
6. This phrase serves as the epigraph to the novel.
7. The kings of Jerusalem ruled the conquered territories in the Middle East after the First Crusade in 1099 until 1291.
8. A gallery in which the acoustics allow for whispers to be heard in other parts of the room.

With his knees gathered up under his chin and staring with his greenish eyes over them, he was a weird figure, and with my knowledge of the crazy notion in his head, not a very attractive one for me. Still, I had to speak to him now and then, and one day he complained that the ship was very silent. For hours and hours, he said, he was lying there, not hearing a sound, till he did not know what to do with himself.

"When Ransome happens to be forward in his galley everything's so still that one might think everybody in the ship was dead," he grumbled. "The only voice I do hear sometimes is yours, sir, and that isn't enough to cheer me up. What's the matter with the men? Isn't there one left that can sing out[9] at the ropes?"

"Not one, Mr. Burns," I said. "There is no breath to spare on board this ship for that. Are you aware that there are times when I can't muster more than three hands to do anything?"

He asked swiftly but fearfully:

"Nobody dead yet, sir?"

"No."

"It wouldn't do," Mr. Burns declared forcibly. "Mustn't let him. If he gets hold of one he will get them all."

I cried out angrily at this. I believe I even swore at the disturbing effect of these words. They attacked all the self-possession that was left to me. In my endless vigil in the face of the enemy I had been haunted by gruesome images enough. I had had visions of a ship drifting in calms and swinging in light airs, with all her crew dying slowly about her decks. Such things had been known to happen.

Mr. Burns met my outburst by a mysterious silence.

"Look here," I said. "You don't believe yourself what you say. You can't. It's impossible. It isn't the sort of thing I have a right to expect from you. My position's bad enough without being worried with your silly fancies."

He remained unmoved. On account of the way in which the light fell on his head I could not be sure whether he had smiled faintly or not. I changed my tone.

"Listen," I said. "It's getting so desperate that I had thought for a moment, since we can't make our way south, whether I wouldn't try to steer west and make an attempt to reach the mail-boat track. We could always get some quinine from her, at least. What do you think?"

He cried out: "No, no, no. Don't do that, sir. You mustn't for a moment give up facing that old ruffian. If you do he will get the upper hand of us."

I left him. He was impossible. It was like a case of possession. His protest, however, was essentially quite sound. As a matter of fact,

9. A reference to the sea chanties sailors would sing while working.

my notion of heading out west on the chance of sighting a problem-
atical steamer could not bear calm examination. On the side where
we were we had enough wind, at least from time to time, to struggle
on towards the south. Enough, at least, to keep hope alive. But suppose that I had used those capricious gusts of wind to sail away to
the westward, into some region where there was not a breath of air
for days on end, what then? Perhaps my appalling vision of a ship
floating with a dead crew[1] would become a reality for the discovery
weeks afterwards by some horror-stricken mariners.

That afternoon Ransome brought me up a cup of tea, and while
waiting there, tray in hand, he remarked in the exactly right tone of
sympathy:

"You are holding out well, sir."

"Yes," I said. "You and I seem to have been forgotten."

"Forgotten, sir?"

"Yes, by the fever-devil who has got on board this ship," I said.

Ransome gave me one of his attractive, intelligent, quick glances
and went away with the tray. It occurred to me that I had been talking somewhat in Mr. Burns' manner. It annoyed me. Yet often in
darker moments I forgot myself into an attitude towards our troubles more fit for a contest against a living enemy.

Yes. The fever-devil had not laid his hand yet either on Ransome or
on me. But he might at any time. It was one of those thoughts one
had to fight down, keep at arm's length at any cost. It was unbearable
to contemplate the possibility of Ransome, the housekeeper of the
ship, being laid low. And what would happen to my command if I got
knocked over, with Mr. Burns too weak to stand without holding on
to his bed-place and the second mate reduced to a state of permanent
imbecility? It was impossible to imagine, or, rather, it was only too
easy to imagine.

I was alone on the poop. The ship having no steerage way, I had
sent the helmsman away to sit down or lie down somewhere in the
shade. The men's strength was so reduced that all unnecessary calls
on it had to be avoided. It was the austere Gambril with the grizzly
beard. He went away readily enough, but he was so weakened by
repeated bouts of fever, poor fellow, that in order to get down the
poop ladder he had to turn sideways and hang on with both hands
to the brass rail. It was just simply heart-breaking to watch. Yet he
was neither very much worse nor much better than most of the
half-dozen miserable victims I could muster up on deck.

It was a terribly lifeless afternoon. For several days in succession
low clouds had appeared in the distance, white masses with dark

1. See p. 108, n. 4.

convolutions resting on the water, motionless, almost solid, and yet all the time changing their aspects subtly. Towards evening they vanished as a rule. But this day they awaited the setting sun, which glowed and smouldered sulkily amongst them before it sank down. The punctual and wearisome stars reappeared over our mastheads, but the air remained stagnant and oppressive.

The unfailing Ransome lighted the binnacle lamps and glided, all shadowy, up to me.

"Will you go down and try to eat something, sir?" he suggested.

His low voice startled me. I had been standing looking out over the rail, saying nothing, feeling nothing, not even the weariness of my limbs, overcome by the evil spell.

"Ransome," I asked abruptly, "how long have I been on deck? I am losing the notion of time."

"Fourteen days, sir," he said. "It was a fortnight last Monday since we left the anchorage."

His equable voice sounded mournful somehow. He waited a bit, then added: "It's the first time that it looks as if we were to have some rain."

I noticed then the broad shadow on the horizon extinguishing the low stars completely, while those overhead, when I looked up, seemed to shine down on us through a veil of smoke.

How it got there, how it had crept up so high, I couldn't say. It had an ominous appearance. The air did not stir. At a renewed invitation from Ransome I did go down into the cabin to—in his words—"try and eat something." I don't know that the trial was very successful. I suppose at that period I did exist on food in the usual way; but the memory is now that in those days life was sustained on invincible anguish, as a sort of infernal stimulant exciting and consuming at the same time.

It's the only period of my life in which I attempted to keep a diary. No, not the only one. Years later, in conditions of moral isolation, I did put down on paper the thoughts and events of a score of days. But this was the first time. I don't remember how it came about or how the pocket-book and the pencil came into my hands. It's inconceivable that I should have looked for them on purpose. I suppose they saved me from the crazy trick of talking to myself.

Strangely enough, in both cases I took to that sort of thing in circumstances in which I did not expect, in colloquial phrase, "to come out of it." Neither could I expect the record to outlast me. This shows that it was purely a personal need for intimate relief and not a call of egotism.

Here I must give another sample of it, a few detached lines, now looking very ghostly to my own eyes, out of the part scribbled that very evening:—

"There is something going on in the sky like a decomposition, like a corruption of the air, which remains as still as ever. After all, mere clouds, which may or may not hold wind or rain. Strange that it should trouble me so. I feel as if all my sins had found me out.[2] But I suppose the trouble is that the ship is still lying motionless, not under command; and that I have nothing to do to keep my imagination from running wild amongst the disastrous images of the worst that may befall us. What's going to happen? Probably nothing. Or anything. It may be a furious squall coming, butt-end foremost. And on deck there are five men with the vitality and the strength of, say, two. We may have all our sails blown away. Every stitch of canvas has been on her since we broke ground at the mouth of the Mei-nam, fifteen days ago . . . or fifteen centuries. It seems to me that all my life before that momentous day is infinitely remote, a fading memory of light-hearted youth, something on the other side of a shadow. Yes, sails may very well be blown away. And that would be like a death sentence on the men. We haven't strength enough on board to bend another suit; incredible thought, but it is true. Or we may even get dismasted. Ships have been dismasted in squalls simply because they weren't handled quick enough, and we have no power to whirl the yards around. It's like being bound hand and foot preparatory to having one's throat cut. And what appals me most of all is that I shrink from going on deck to face it. It's due to the ship, it's due to the men who are there on deck—some of them, ready to put out the last remnant of their strength at a word from me. And I am shrinking from it. From the mere vision. My first command. Now I understand that strange sense of insecurity in my past. I always suspected that I might be no good. And here is proof positive. I am shirking it. I am no good."

At that moment, or, perhaps, the moment after, I became aware of Ransome standing in the cabin. Something in his expression startled me. It had a meaning which I could not make out. I exclaimed:

"Somebody's dead."

It was his turn then to look startled.

"Dead? Not that I know of, sir. I have been in the forecastle only ten minutes ago and there was no dead man there then."

"You did give me a scare," I said.

His voice was extremely pleasant to listen to. He explained that he had come down below to close Mr. Burns' port in case it should come on to rain. He did not know that I was in the cabin, he added.

"How does it look outside?" I asked him.

2. Cf. Numbers 32:23: "be sure your sin will find you out."

"Very black indeed, sir. There is something in it for certain."

"In what quarter?"

"All round, sir."

I repeated idly: "All round. For certain," with my elbows on the table.

Ransome lingered in the cabin as if he had something to do there, but hesitated about doing it. I said suddenly:

"You think I ought to be on deck?"

He answered at once but without any particular emphasis or accent: "I do, sir."

I got to my feet briskly, and he made way for me to go out. As I passed through the lobby I heard Mr. Burns' voice saying:

"Shut the door of my room, will you, steward?" And Ransome's rather surprised: "Certainly, sir."

I thought that all my feelings had been dulled into complete indifference. But I found it as trying as ever to be on deck. The impenetrable blackness beset the ship so close that it seemed that by thrusting one's hand over the side one could touch some unearthly substance. There was in it an effect of inconceivable terror and of inexpressible mystery. The few stars overhead shed a dim light upon the ship alone, with no gleams of any kind upon the water, in detached shafts piercing an atmosphere which had turned to soot. It was something I had never seen before, giving no hint of the direction from which any change would come, the closing in of a menace from all sides.

There was still no man at the helm. The immobility of all things was perfect. If the air had turned black, the sea, for all I knew, might have turned solid. It was no good looking in any direction, watching for any sign, speculating upon the nearness of the moment. When the time came the blackness would overwhelm silently the bit of starlight falling upon the ship, and the end of all things[3] would come without a sigh, stir, or murmur of any kind, and all our hearts would cease to beat like run-down clocks.

It was impossible to shake off that sense of finality. The quietness that came over me was like a foretaste of annihilation. It gave me a sort of comfort, as though my soul had become suddenly reconciled to an eternity of blind stillness.

The seaman's instinct alone survived whole in my moral dissolution. I descended the ladder to the quarter-deck. The starlight seemed to die out before reaching that spot, but when I asked quietly: "Are you there, men?" my eyes made out shadowy forms starting up around me, very few, very indistinct; and a voice spoke: "All here, sir." Another amended anxiously:

3. The end of the world, a contrast to the "Work of Seven Days." See p. 112, n. 1.

"All that are any good for anything, sir."

Both voices were very quiet and unringing; without any special character of readiness or discouragement. Very matter-of-fact voices.

"We must try to haul this mainsail close up," I said.

The shadows swayed away from me without a word. Those men were the ghosts of themselves,[4] and their weight on a rope could be no more than the weight of a bunch of ghosts. Indeed, if ever a sail was hauled up by sheer spiritual strength it must have been that sail, for, properly speaking, there was not muscle enough for the task in the whole ship, let alone the miserable lot of us on deck. Of course, I took the lead in the work myself. They wandered feebly after me from rope to rope, stumbling and panting. They toiled like Titans.[5] We were an hour at it at least, and all the time the black universe made no sound. When the last leech-line was made fast, my eyes, accustomed to the darkness, made out the shapes of exhausted men drooping over the rails, collapsed on hatches. One hung over the after-capstan, sobbing for breath; and I stood amongst them like a tower of strength, impervious to disease and feeling only the sickness of my soul. I waited for some time fighting against the weight of my sins, against my sense of unworthiness, and then I said:

"Now, men, we'll go aft and square the main yard. That's about all we can do for the ship; and for the rest she must take her chance."

VI

As we all went up it occurred to me that there ought to be a man at the helm. I raised my voice not much above a whisper, and, noiselessly, an uncomplaining spirit in a fever-wasted body appeared in the light aft, the head with hollow eyes illuminated against the blackness which had swallowed up our world—and the universe. The bared fore-arm extended over the upper spokes seemed to shine with a light of its own.

I murmured to that luminous appearance:

"Keep the helm right amidships."

It answered in a tone of patient suffering:

"Right amidships, sir."

Then I descended to the quarter-deck. It was impossible to tell whence the blow would come. To look round the ship was to look into a bottomless, black pit. The eye lost itself in inconceivable depths.

I wanted to ascertain whether the ropes had been picked up off the deck. One could only do that by feeling with one's feet. In my

---

4. Cf. "The Rime of the Ancient Mariner": "We were a ghastly crew" (line 340).
5. In Greek mythology, the twelve sons and daughters of Uranus and Gaea, rulers of the universe.

cautious progress I came against a man in whom I recognised Ransome. He possessed an unimpaired physical solidity which was manifest to me at the contact. He was leaning against the quarter-deck capstan and kept silent. It was like a revelation. He was the collapsed figure sobbing for breath I had noticed before we went on the poop.

"You have been helping with the mainsail!" I exclaimed in a low tone.

"Yes, sir," sounded his quiet voice.

"Man! What were you thinking of? You mustn't do that sort of thing."

After a pause he assented. "I suppose I mustn't." Then after another short silence he added: "I am all right now," quickly, between the tell-tale gasps.

I could neither hear nor see anybody else; but when I spoke up, answering sad murmurs filled the quarter-deck, and its shadows seemed to shift here and there. I ordered all the halyards laid down on deck clear for running.

"I'll see to that, sir," volunteered Ransome in his natural, pleasant tone, which comforted one and aroused one's compassion too, somehow.

That man ought to have been in his bed, resting, and my plain duty was to send him there. But perhaps he would not have obeyed me. I had not the strength of mind to try. All I said was:

"Go about it quietly, Ransome."

Returning on the poop I approached Gambril. His face, set with hollow shadows in the light, looked awful, finally silenced. I asked him how he felt, but hardly expected an answer. Therefore I was astonished at his comparative loquacity.

"Them shakes leaves me as weak as a kitten, sir," he said, preserving finely that air of unconsciousness as to anything but his business a helmsman should never lose. "And before I can pick up my strength that there hot fit comes along and knocks me over again."

He sighed. There was no complaint in his tone, but the bare words were enough to give me a horrible pang of self-reproach. It held me dumb for a time. When the tormenting sensation had passed off I asked:

"Do you feel strong enough to prevent the rudder taking charge if she gets sternway on her? It wouldn't do to get something smashed about the steering-gear now. We've enough difficulties to cope with as it is."

He answered with just a shade of weariness that he was strong enough to hang on. He could promise me that she shouldn't take the wheel out of his hands. More he couldn't say.

At that moment Ransome appeared quite close to me, stepping out of the darkness into visibility suddenly, as if just created with his composed face and pleasant voice.

Every rope on deck, he said, was laid down clear for running, as far as one could make certain by feeling. It was impossible to see anything. Frenchy had stationed himself forward. He said he had a jump or two left in him yet.

Here a faint smile altered for an instant the clear, firm design of Ransome's lips. With his serious clear, grey eyes, his serene temperament, he was a priceless man altogether. Soul as firm as the muscles of his body.

He was the only man on board (except me, but I had to preserve my liberty of movement) who had a sufficiency of muscular strength to trust to. For a moment I thought I had better ask him to take the wheel. But the dreadful knowledge of the enemy he had to carry about him made me hesitate. In my ignorance of physiology it occurred to me that he might die suddenly, from excitement, at a critical moment.

While this gruesome fear restrained the ready words on the tip of my tongue, Ransome stepped back two paces and vanished from my sight.

At once an uneasiness possessed me, as if some support had been withdrawn. I moved forward too, outside the circle of light, into the darkness that stood in front of me like a wall. In one stride I penetrated it. Such must have been the darkness before creation.[6] It had closed behind me. I knew I was invisible to the man at the helm. Neither could I see anything. He was alone, I was alone, every man was alone where he stood. And every form was gone too, spar, sail, fittings, rails; everything was blotted out in the dreadful smoothness of that absolute night.

A flash of lightning would have been a relief—I mean physically. I would have prayed for it if it hadn't been for my shrinking apprehension of the thunder. In the tension of silence I was suffering from it seemed to me that the first crash must turn me into dust.

And thunder was, most likely, what would happen next. Stiff all over and hardly breathing, I waited with a horribly strained expectation. Nothing happened. It was maddening. But a dull, growing ache in the lower part of my face made me aware that I had been grinding my teeth madly enough, for God knows how long.

It's extraordinary I should not have heard myself doing it; but I hadn't. By an effort which absorbed all my faculties I managed to keep my jaw still. It required much attention, and while thus engaged I became bothered by curious, irregular sounds of faint tapping on the deck. They could be heard single, in pairs, in groups. While I wondered at this mysterious devilry, I received a slight blow under

---

6. A reference to Genesis 1:2: "And the earth was without form, and void; and darkness was upon the face of the deep."

the left eye and felt an enormous tear run down my cheek. Rain-drops. Enormous. Forerunners of something. Tap. Tap. Tap. . . .

I turned about, and, addressing Gambril earnestly, entreated him to "hang on to the wheel." But I could hardly speak from emotion. The fatal moment had come. I held my breath. The tapping had stopped as unexpectedly as it had begun, and there was a renewed moment of intolerable suspense; something like an additional turn of the racking screw.[7] I don't suppose I would have ever screamed, but I remember my conviction that there was nothing else for it but to scream.

Suddenly—how am I to convey it? Well, suddenly the darkness turned into water. This is the only suitable figure.[8] A heavy shower, a downpour, comes along, making a noise. You hear its approach on the sea, in the air too, I verily believe. But this was different. With no preliminary whisper or rustle, without a splash, and even without the ghost of impact, I became instantaneously soaked to the skin. Not a very difficult matter, since I was wearing only my sleeping suit. My hair got full of water in an instant, water streamed on my skin, it filled my nose, my ears, my eyes. In a fraction of a second I swallowed quite a lot of it.

As to Gambril, he was fairly choked. He coughed pitifully, the broken cough of a sick man; and I beheld him as one sees a fish in an aquarium by the light of an electric bulb, an elusive, phosphorescent shape. Only he did not glide away. But something else happened. Both binnacle lamps went out. I suppose the water forced itself into them, though I wouldn't have thought that possible, for they fitted into the cowl perfectly.

The last gleam of light in the universe had gone, pursued by a low exclamation of dismay from Gambril. I groped for him and seized his arm. How startlingly wasted it was.

"Never mind," I said. "You don't want the light. All you need to do is to keep the wind when it comes, at the back of your head. You understand?"

"Aye, aye, sir. . . . But I should like to have a light," he added nervously.

All that time the ship lay as steady as a rock. The noise of the water pouring off the sails and spars, flowing over the break of the poop, had stopped short. The poop scuppers gurgled and sobbed for a little while longer, and then perfect silence, joined to perfect immobility, proclaimed the yet unbroken spell of our helplessness, poised on the edge of some violent issue, lurking in the dark.

7. Probably a reference to the thumbscrew, a medieval instrument of torture, or Conrad might have in mind the rack, another instrument of torture, or he may be conflating the two.
8. I.e., figure of speech.

I started forward restlessly. I did not need my sight to pace the poop of my ill-starred first command with perfect assurance. Every square foot of her decks was impressed indelibly on my brain, to the very grain and knots of the planks. Yet, all of a sudden, I fell clean over something, landing full length on my hands and face.

It was something big and alive. Not a dog—more like a sheep, rather. But there were no animals in the ship. How could an animal. . . . It was an added and fantastic horror which I could not resist. The hair of my head stirred even as I picked myself up, awfully scared; not as a man is scared while his judgment, his reason still try to resist, but completely, boundlessly, and, as it were, innocently scared—like a little child.

I could see It—that Thing! The darkness, of which so much had just turned into water, had thinned down a little. There It was! But I did not hit upon the notion of Mr. Burns issuing out of the companion on all fours till he attempted to stand up, and even then the idea of a bear crossed my mind first.

He growled like one when I seized him round the body. He had buttoned himself up into an enormous winter overcoat of some woolly material, the weight of which was too much for his reduced state. I could hardly feel the incredibly thin lath of his body, lost within the thick stuff, but his growl had depth and substance: Confounded dumb ship with a craven, tip-toeing crowd. Why couldn't they stamp and go with a brace? Wasn't there one God-forsaken lubber in the lot fit to raise a yell on a rope?

"Skulking's no good, sir," he attacked me directly. "You can't slink past the old murderous ruffian. It isn't the way. You must go for him boldly—as I did. Boldness is what you want. Show him that you don't care for any of his damned tricks. Kick up a jolly old row."

"Good God, Mr. Burns," I said angrily. "What on earth are you up to? What do you mean by coming up on deck in this state?"

"Just that! Boldness. The only way to scare the old bullying rascal."

I pushed him, still growling, against the rail. "Hold on to it," I said roughly. I did not know what to do with him. I left him in a hurry, to go to Gambril, who had called faintly that he believed there was some wind aloft. Indeed, my own ears had caught a feeble flutter of wet canvas, high up overhead, the jingle of a slack chain sheet. . . .

These were eerie, disturbing, alarming sounds in the dead stillness of the air around me. All the instances I had heard of topmasts being whipped out of a ship while there was not wind enough on her deck to blow out a match rushed into my memory.

"I can't see the upper sails, sir," declared Gambril shakily.

"Don't move the helm. You'll be all right," I said confidently.

The poor man's nerve was gone. I was not in much better case.[9] It was the moment of breaking strain and was relieved by the abrupt sensation of the ship moving forward as if of herself under my feet.[1] I heard plainly the soughing of the wind aloft, the low cracks of the upper spars taking the strain, long before I could feel the least draught on my face turned aft, anxious and sightless like the face of a blind man.

Suddenly a louder sounding note filled our ears, the darkness started streaming against our bodies, chilling them exceedingly. Both of us, Gambril and I, shivered violently in our clinging, soaked garments of thin cotton. I said to him:

"You are all right now, my man. All you've got to do is to keep the wind at the back of your head. Surely you are up to that. A child could steer this ship in smooth water."

He muttered: "Aye! A healthy child." And I felt ashamed of having been passed over by the fever which had been preying on every man's strength but mine, in order that my remorse might be the more bitter, the feeling of unworthiness more poignant, and the sense of responsibility heavier to bear.

The ship had gathered great way on her almost at once on the calm water. I felt her slipping through it with no other noise but a mysterious rustle alongside. Otherwise she had no motion at all, neither lift nor roll. It was a disheartening steadiness which had lasted for eighteen days now; for never, never had we had wind enough in that time to raise the slightest run of the sea. The breeze freshened suddenly. I thought it was high time to get Mr. Burns off the deck. He worried me. I looked upon him as a lunatic who would be very likely to start roaming over the ship and break a limb or fall overboard.

I was truly glad to find he had remained holding on where I had left him, sensibly enough. He was, however, muttering to himself ominously.

This was discouraging. I remarked in a matter-of-fact tone:

"We have never had so much wind as this since we left the roads."

"There's some heart in it too," he growled judiciously. It was a remark of a perfectly sane seaman. But he added immediately: "It was about time I should come on deck. I've been nursing my strength for this—just for this. Do you see it, sir?"

I said I did, and proceeded to hint that it would be advisable for him to go below now and take a rest.

---

9. State or condition.
1. The ship's movement here reminds Ingram (*ISL*) of lines 383–92 of "The Rime of the Ancient Mariner."

His answer was an indignant: "Go below! Not if I know it, sir."

Very cheerful! He was a horrible nuisance. And all at once he started to argue. I could feel his crazy excitement in the dark.

"You don't know how to go about it, sir. How could you? All this whispering and tiptoeing is no good. You can't hope to slink past a cunning, wide-awake, evil brute like he was. You never heard him talk. Enough to make your hair stand on end. No! No! He wasn't mad. He was no more mad than I am. He was just downright wicked. Wicked so as to frighten most people. I will tell you what he was. He was nothing less than a thief and a murderer at heart. And do you think he's any different now because he's dead? Not he! His carcass lies a hundred fathom under, but he's just the same . . . in latitude 8° 20′ North."

He snorted defiantly. I noted with weary resignation that the breeze had got lighter while he raved. He was at it again.

"I ought to have thrown the beggar out of the ship over the rail like a dog. It was only on account of the men. . . . Fancy having to read the Burial Service over a brute like that! . . . 'Our departed brother'[2] . . . I could have laughed. That was what he couldn't bear. I suppose I am the only man that ever stood up to laugh at him. When he got sick it used to scare that . . . brother . . . Brother . . . Departed . . . Sooner call a shark brother."

The breeze had let go so suddenly that the way of the ship brought the wet sails heavily against the mast. The spell of deadly stillness had caught us up again. There seemed to be no escape.

"Hallo!" exclaimed Mr. Burns in a startled voice. "Calm again!"

I addressed him as though he had been sane.

"This is the sort of thing we've been having for seventeen days, Mr. Burns," I said with intense bitterness. "A puff, then a calm, and in a moment, you'll see, she'll be swinging on her heel with her head away from her course to the devil somewhere."

He caught at the word. "The old dodging Devil," he screamed piercingly, and burst into such a loud laugh as I had never heard before. It was a provoking, mocking peal, with a hair-raising, screeching over-note[3] of defiance. I stepped back utterly confounded.

Instantly there was a stir on the quarter-deck, murmurs of dismay. A distressed voice cried out in the dark below us: "Who's that gone crazy, now?"

Perhaps they thought it was their captain! Rush is not the word that could be applied to the utmost speed the poor fellows were up

---

2. Cf. the "Order for the Burial of the Dead at Sea" from *The Book of Common Prayer* (1623), which reads: "Forasmuch as it hath pleased Almighty God of his great mercy to take unto himself the soul of our dear *brother* here departed, we therefore commit *his* body to the sea."

3. Overtone.

to; but in an amazingly short time every man in the ship able to walk upright had found his way on to that poop.

I shouted to them: "It's the mate. Lay hold of him a couple of you. . . ."

I expected this performance to end in a ghastly sort of fight. But Mr. Burns cut his derisive screeching dead short and turned upon them fiercely, yelling:

"Aha! Dog-gone ye![4] You've found your tongues—have ye? I thought you were dumb. Well, then—laugh! Laugh—I tell you. Now then— all together. One, two, three—laugh!"

A moment of silence ensued, of silence so profound that you could have heard a pin drop on the deck. Then Ransome's unperturbed voice uttered pleasantly the words:

"I think he has fainted, sir—" The little motionless knot of men stirred, with low murmurs of relief. "I've got him under the arms. Get hold of his legs, some one."

Yes. It was a relief. He was silenced for a time—for a time. I could not have stood another peal of that insane screeching. I was sure of it; and just then Gambril, the austere Gambril, treated us to another vocal performance. He began to sing out for relief. His voice wailed pitifully in the darkness: "Come aft, somebody! I can't stand this. Here she'll be off again directly and I can't. . . ."

I dashed aft myself meeting on my way a hard gust of wind whose approach Gambril's ear had detected from afar and which filled the sails on the main in a series of muffled reports mingled with the low plaint of the spars. I was just in time to seize the wheel while Frenchy, who had followed me, caught up the collapsing Gambril. He hauled him out of the way, admonished him to lie still where he was, and then stepped up to relieve me, asking calmly:

"How am I to steer her, sir?"

"Dead before it, for the present. I'll get you a light in a moment."

But going forward I met Ransome bringing up the spare binnacle lamp. That man noticed everything, attended to everything, shed comfort around him as he moved. As he passed me he remarked in a soothing tone that the stars were coming out. They were. The breeze was sweeping clear the sooty sky, breaking through the indolent silence of the sea.

The barrier of awful stillness which had encompassed us for so many days as though we had been accursed was broken. I felt that. I let myself fall on to the skylight seat. A faint white ridge of foam, thin, very thin, broke alongside. The first for ages—for ages. I could have cheered, if it hadn't been for the sense of guilt which clung to all my thoughts secretly. Ransome stood before me.

4. A euphemism for *damn you!*

"What about the mate?" I asked anxiously. "Still unconscious?"

"Well, sir—it's funny." Ransome was evidently puzzled. "He hasn't spoken a word, and his eyes are shut. But it looks to me more like sound sleep than anything else."

I accepted this view as the least troublesome of any, or at any rate, least disturbing. Dead faint or deep slumber, Mr. Burns had to be left to himself for the present. Ransome remarked suddenly:

"I believe you want a coat, sir."

"I believe I do," I sighed out.

But I did not move. What I felt I wanted were new limbs. My arms and legs seemed utterly useless, fairly worn out. They didn't even ache. But I stood up all the same to put on the coat when Ransome brought it up. And when he suggested that he had better now "take Gambril forward," I said:

"All right. I'll help you to get him down on the main deck."

I found that I was quite able to help, too. We raised Gambril up between us. He tried to help himself along like a man, but all the time he was inquiring piteously:

"You won't let me go when we come to the ladder? You won't let me go when we come to the ladder?"

The breeze kept on freshening and blew true, true to a hair.[5] At daylight by careful manipulation of the helm we got the foreyards to run square by themselves (the water keeping smooth) and then went about hauling the ropes tight. Of the four men I had with me at night, I could see now only two. I didn't inquire as to the others. They had given in. For a time only I hoped.

Our various tasks forward occupied us for hours, the two men with me moved so slowly and had to rest so often. One of them remarked that "every blamed thing in the ship felt about a hundred times heavier than its proper weight." This was the only complaint uttered. I don't know what we should have done without Ransome. He worked with us, silent too, with a little smile frozen on his lips. From time to time I murmured to him: "Go steady"—"Take it easy, Ransome"—and received a quick glance in reply.

When we had done all we could do to make things safe, he disappeared into his galley. Some time afterwards, going forward for a look round, I caught sight of him through the open door. He sat upright on the locker in front of the stove, with his head leaning back against the bulkhead. His eyes were closed; his capable hands held open the front of his thin cotton shirt baring tragically his powerful chest, which heaved in painful and laboured gasps. He didn't hear me.

---

5. Extremely accurate.

I retreated quietly and went straight on to the poop to relieve Frenchy, who by that time was beginning to look very sick. He gave me the course with great formality and tried to go off with a jaunty step, but reeled widely twice before getting out of my sight.

And then I remained all alone aft, steering my ship, which ran before the wind with a buoyant lift now and then, and even rolling a little. Presently Ransome appeared before me with a tray. The sight of food made me ravenous all at once. He took the wheel while I sat down on the after grating to eat my breakfast.

"This breeze seems to have done for our crowd," he murmured. "It just laid them low—all hands."

"Yes," I said. "I suppose you and I are the only two fit men in the ship."

"Frenchy says there's still a jump left in him. I don't know. It can't be much," continued Ransome with his wistful smile. "Good little man that. But suppose, sir, that this wind flies round when we are close to the land—what are we going to do with her?"

"If the wind shifts round heavily after we close in with the land she will either run ashore or get dismasted or both. We won't be able to do anything with her. She's running away with us now. All we can do is to steer her. She's a ship without a crew."

"Yes. All laid low," repeated Ransome quietly. "I do give them a look-in forward every now and then, but it's precious little I can do for them."

"I, and the ship, and every one on board of her, are very much indebted to you, Ransome," I said warmly.

He made as though he had not heard me, and steered in silence till I was ready to relieve him. He surrendered the wheel, picked up the tray, and for a parting shot informed me that Mr. Burns was awake and seemed to have a mind to come up on deck.

"I don't know how to prevent him, sir. I can't very well stop down below all the time."

It was clear that he couldn't. And sure enough Mr. Burns came on deck dragging himself painfully aft in his enormous overcoat. I beheld him with a natural dread. To have him around and raving about the wiles of a dead man while I had to steer a wildly rushing ship full of dying men was a rather dreadful prospect.

But his first remarks were quite sensible in meaning and tone. Apparently he had no recollection of the night scene. And if he had he didn't betray himself once. Neither did he talk very much. He sat on the skylight looking desperately ill at first, but that strong breeze, before which the last remnant of my crew had wilted down, seemed to blow a fresh stock of vigour into his frame with every gust. One could almost see the process.

By way of sanity test I alluded on purpose to the late captain. I was delighted to find that Mr. Burns did not display undue interest in the subject. He ran over the old tale of that savage ruffian's iniquities with a certain vindictive gusto and then concluded unexpectedly:

"I do believe, sir, that his brain began to go a year or more before he died."

A wonderful recovery. I could hardly spare it as much admiration as it deserved, for I had to give all my mind to the steering.

In comparison with the hopeless languor of the preceding days this was dizzy speed. Two ridges of foam streamed from the ship's bows; the wind sang in a strenuous note which under other circumstances would have expressed to me all the joy of life. Whenever the hauled-up mainsail started trying to slat and bang itself to pieces in its gear, Mr. Burns would look at me apprehensively.

"What would you have me do, Mr. Burns? We can neither furl it nor set it. I only wish the old thing would thrash itself to pieces and be done with it. This beastly racket confuses me."

Mr. Burns wrung his hands, and cried out suddenly:

"How will you get the ship into harbour, sir, without men to handle her?"

And I couldn't tell him.

Well—it did get done about forty hours afterwards. By the exorcising virtue of Mr. Burns' awful laugh, the malicious spectre had been laid, the evil spell broken, the curse removed. We were now in the hands of a kind and energetic Providence. It was rushing us on. . . .

I shall never forget the last night, dark, windy, and starry. I steered. Mr. Burns, after having obtained from me a solemn promise to give him a kick if anything happened, went frankly to sleep on the deck close to the binnacle. Convalescents need sleep. Ransome, his back propped against the mizzenmast and a blanket over his legs, remained perfectly still, but I don't suppose he closed his eyes for a moment. That embodiment of jauntiness, Frenchy, still under the delusion that there was "a jump" left in him, had insisted on joining us; but mindful of discipline, had laid himself down as far on the forepart of the poop as he could get, alongside the bucket-rack.

And I steered, too tired for anxiety, too tired for connected thought. I had moments of grim exultation and then my heart would sink awfully at the thought of that forecastle at the other end of the dark deck, full of fever-stricken men—some of them dying. By my fault. But never mind. Remorse must wait. I had to steer.

In the small hours the breeze weakened, then failed altogether. About five it returned, gentle enough, enabling us to head for the roadstead. Daybreak found Mr. Burns sitting wedged up with coils of rope on the stern-grating, and from the depths of his overcoat steering the ship with very white bony hands; while Ransome and I rushed along the decks letting go all the sheets and halyards by the run. We dashed next up on to the forecastle-head. The perspiration of labour and sheer nervousness simply poured off our heads as we toiled to get the anchors cock-billed. I dared not look at Ransome as we worked side by side. We exchanged curt words; I could hear him panting close to me and I avoided turning my eyes his way for fear of seeing him fall down and expire in the act of putting out his strength—for what? Indeed for some distinct ideal.

The consummate seaman in him was aroused. He needed no directions. He knew what to do. Every effort, every movement was an act of consistent heroism. It was not for me to look at a man thus inspired.

At last all was ready, and I heard him say, "Hadn't I better go down and open the compressors now, sir?"

"Yes. Do," I said. And even then I did not glance his way. After a time his voice came up from the main deck:

"When you like, sir. All clear on the windlass here."

I made a sign to Mr. Burns to put the helm down and then I let both anchors go one after another, leaving the ship to take as much cable as she wanted. She took the best part of them both before she brought up. The loose sails coming aback ceased their maddening racket above my head. A perfect stillness reigned in the ship. And while I stood forward feeling a little giddy in that sudden peace, I caught faintly a moan or two and the incoherent mutterings of the sick in the forecastle.

As we had a signal for medical assistance flying[6] on the mizzen it is a fact that before the ship was fairly at rest three steam-launches from various men-of-war arrived alongside; and at least five naval surgeons clambered on board. They stood in a knot gazing up and down the empty main deck, then looked aloft—where not a man could be seen either.

I went towards them—a solitary figure in a blue and grey striped sleeping suit and a pipe-clayed cork helmet[7] on its head. Their disgust was extreme. They had expected surgical cases. Each one had brought his carving tools with him. But they soon got over their little disappointment. In less than five minutes one of the steam-launches was rushing shorewards to order a big boat and some hospital people for the removal of the crew. The big steam-pinnace went off to her ship to bring over a few bluejackets to furl my sails for me.

One of the surgeons[8] had remained on board. He came out of the forecastle looking impenetrable, and noticed my inquiring gaze.

6. A flag with a red rectangle in the middle inside a white border that is inside a blue border.
7. A pith helmet, whitened with pipe clay.
8. When the *Otago* arrived in Singapore on March 1, 1888, Dr. Thomas Crighton Muglis-ton (1854–1931) tended to the sick crew and had three men hospitalized (see *CEW* 247).

"There's nobody dead in there, if that's what you want to know," he said deliberately. Then added in a tone of wonder: "The whole crew!"

"And very bad?"

"And very bad," he repeated. His eyes were roaming all over the ship. "Heavens! What's that?"

"That," I said, glancing aft, "is Mr. Burns, my chief officer."

Mr. Burns with his moribund head nodding on the stalk of his lean neck was a sight for any one to exclaim at. The surgeon asked:

"Is he going to the hospital too?"

"Oh, no," I said jocosely. "Mr. Burns can't go on shore till the main-mast goes. I am very proud of him. He's my only convalescent."

"You look . . ." began the doctor staring at me. But I interrupted him angrily:

"I am not ill."

"No. . . . You look queer."

"Well, you see, I have been seventeen days on deck."

"Seventeen! . . . But you must have slept."

"I suppose I must have. I don't know. But I'm certain that I didn't sleep for the last forty hours."

"Phew! . . . You will be going ashore presently, I suppose?"

"As soon as ever I can. There's no end of business waiting for me there."

The surgeon released my hand, which he had taken while we talked, pulled out his pocket book, wrote in it rapidly, tore out the page, and offered it to me.

"I strongly advise you to get this prescription made up for yourself ashore. Unless I am much mistaken you will need it this evening."

"What is it then?" I asked with suspicion.

"Sleeping draught," answered the surgeon curtly; and moving with an air of interest towards Mr. Burns he engaged him in conversation.

As I went below to dress to go ashore, Ransome followed me. He begged my pardon; he wished, too, to be sent ashore and paid off.

I looked at him in surprise. He was waiting for my answer with an air of anxiety.

"You don't mean to leave the ship!" I cried out.

"I do really, sir. I want to go and be quiet somewhere. Anywhere. The hospital will do."

"But, Ransome," I said, "I hate the idea of parting with you."

"I must go," he broke in. "I have a right!" He gasped and a look of almost savage determination passed over his face. For an instant he was another being. And I saw under the worth and the comeliness of the man the humble reality of things. Life was a boon to him—this precarious hard life—and he was thoroughly alarmed about himself.

"Of course I shall pay you off if you wish it," I hastened to say. "Only I must ask you to remain on board till this afternoon. I can't leave Mr. Burns absolutely by himself in the ship for hours."

He softened at once and assured me with a smile and in his natural pleasant voice that he understood that very well.

When I returned on deck everything was ready for the removal of the men. It was the last ordeal of that episode which had been maturing and tempering my character—though I did not know it.

It was awful. They passed under my eyes one after another— each of them an embodied reproach of the bitterest kind,[9] till I felt a sort of revolt wake up in me. Poor Frenchy had gone suddenly under. He was carried past me insensible, his comic face horribly flushed and as if swollen, breathing stertorously. He looked more like Mr. Punch than ever; a disgracefully intoxicated Mr. Punch.

The austere Gambril, on the contrary, had improved temporarily. He insisted on walking on his own feet to the rail—of course with assistance on each side of him. But he gave way to a sudden panic at the moment of being swung over the side and began to wail pitifully:

"Don't let them drop me, sir. Don't let them drop me, sir!" While I kept on shouting to him in most soothing accents: "All right, Gambril. They won't! They won't!"

It was no doubt very ridiculous. The bluejackets on our deck were grinning quietly, while even Ransome himself (much to the fore in lending a hand) had to enlarge his wistful smile for a fleeting moment.

I left for the shore in the steam-pinnace, and on looking back beheld Mr. Burns actually standing up by the taffrail, still in his enormous woolly overcoat. The bright sunlight brought out his weirdness amazingly. He looked like a frightful and elaborate scarecrow set up on the poop of a death-stricken ship, to keep the seabirds from the corpses.

Our story had got about already in town and everybody on shore was most kind. The marine office let me off the port dues, and as there happened to be a shipwrecked crew staying in the Home I had no difficulty in obtaining as many men as I wanted.[1] But when I inquired if I could see Captain Ellis for a moment I was told in accents

9. Cf. "The Rime of the Ancient Mariner": "All fixed on me their stony eyes" (line 436).
1. Before continuing on to Sydney, Conrad also had to replace the sick members of his crew: Leonard, Scarfe, Kristian, and Conroy were replaced by H. Green (thirty-three), Thomas Smith (twenty-seven), Theodor Jensen (twenty-two), Richard Green (forty-eight), and Thomas Humphrey (twenty-two). "Port dues": The *Otago* was also let off paying port dues. In a letter to W. G. St. Clair (1849–1930), dated March 31, 1917, Conrad writes, "Yes, I remember [Deputy Harbour-Master Edward] Bradbury. It was he who let me off port-dues when I put into Singapore in distress with all my crew unfit for duty" (*CL* 6:62; see p. 377).

of pity for my ignorance that our deputy-Neptune had retired and gone home on a pension about three weeks after I left the port.[2] So I suppose that my appointment was the last act, outside the daily routine, of his official life.

It is strange how on coming ashore I was struck by the springy step, the lively eyes, the strong vitality of every one I met. It impressed me enormously. And amongst those I met there was Captain Giles of course. It would have been very extraordinary if I had not met him. A prolonged stroll in the business part of the town was the regular employment of all his mornings when he was ashore.

I caught the glitter of the gold watch-chain across his chest ever so far away. He radiated benevolence.

"What is it I hear?" he queried with a "kind uncle" smile, after shaking hands. "Twenty-one days from Bankok?"

"Is this all you've heard?" I said. "You must come to tiffin with me. I want you to know exactly what you have let me in for."

He hesitated for almost a minute.

"Well—I will," he decided condescendingly at last.

We turned into the hotel. I found to my surprise that I could eat quite a lot. Then over the cleared table-cloth I unfolded to Captain Giles all the story since I took command in all its professional and emotional aspects, while he smoked patiently the big cigar I had given him.

Then he observed sagely:

"You must feel jolly well tired by this time."

"No," I said. "Not tired. But I'll tell you, Captain Giles, how I feel. I feel old. And I must be. All of you on shore look to me just a lot of skittish youngsters that have never known a care in the world."

He didn't smile. He looked insufferably exemplary. He declared:

"That will pass. But you do look older—it's a fact."

"Aha!" I said.

"No ! No! The truth is that one must not make too much of anything in life, good or bad."

"Live at half-speed," I murmured perversely. "Not everybody can do that."

"You'll be glad enough presently if you can keep going even at that rate," he retorted with his air of conscious virtue. "And there's another thing: a man should stand up to his bad luck, to his mistakes, to his conscience, and all that sort of thing. Why—what else would you have to fight against?"

I kept silent. I don't know what he saw in my face, but he asked abruptly:

"Why—you aren't faint-hearted?"

"God only knows, Captain Giles," was my sincere answer.

2. Ellis retired on February 23, 1888.

"That's all right," he said calmly. "You will learn soon how not to be faint-hearted. A man has got to learn everything—and that's what so many of them youngsters don't understand."

"Well I am no longer a youngster."

"No," he conceded. "Are you leaving soon?"

"I am going on board directly," I said. "I shall pick up one of my anchors and heave in to half-cable on the other as soon as my new crew comes on board and I shall be off at daylight to-morrow."[3]

"You will?" grunted Captain Giles approvingly. "That's the way. You'll do."

"What did you expect? That I would want to take a week ashore for a rest?" I said, irritated by his tone. "There's no rest for me till she's out in the Indian Ocean and not much of it even then."

He puffed at the cigar moodily, as if transformed.

"Yes, that's what it amounts to," he said in a musing tone. It was as if a ponderous curtain had rolled up disclosing an unexpected Captain Giles. But it was only for a moment, merely the time to let him add: "Precious little rest in life for anybody. Better not think of it."

We rose, left the hotel, and parted from each other in the street with a warm handshake, just as he began to interest me for the first time in our intercourse.

The first thing I saw when I got back to the ship was Ransome on the quarter-deck sitting quietly on his neatly lashed sea-chest.

I beckoned him to follow me into the saloon where I sat down to write a letter of recommendation for him to a man I knew on shore.

When finished I pushed it across the table. "It may be of some good to you when you leave the hospital."

He took it, put it in his pocket. His eyes were looking away from me—nowhere. His face was anxiously set.

"How are you feeling now?" I asked.

"I don't feel bad now, sir," he answered stiffly. "But I am afraid of its coming on. . . ." The wistful smile came back on his lips for a moment. "I—I am in a blue funk[4] about my heart, sir."

I approached him with extended hand. His eyes, not looking at me, had a strained expression. He was like a man listening for a warning call.

"Won't you shake hands, Ransome?" I said gently.

He exclaimed, flushed up dusky red, gave my hand a hard wrench—and next moment, left alone in the cabin, I listened to him going up the companion stairs cautiously, step by step, in mortal fear of starting into sudden anger our common enemy it was his hard fate to carry consciously within his faithful breast.

---

3. The *Otago* left for Sydney on March 3, 1888, just two days after arriving in Singapore.
4. A condition of extreme dread or nervousness.

The Nigger of the "Narcissus"

To My Readers in America[†]

From that evening when James Wait joined the ship—late for the muster of the crew—to the moment when he left us in the open sea, shrouded in sailcloth, through the open port, I had much to do with him. He was in my watch.[1] A negro in a British forecastle is a lonely being. He has no chums. Yet James Wait, afraid of death and making her his accomplice, was an imposter of some character—mastering our compassion, in scornful of sentimentalism, triumphing over our suspicions.

But in the book he is nothing; he is merely the centre of the ship's collective psychology and the pivot of the action. Yet he, who in the family circle and amongst my friends is familiarly referred to as the Nigger, remains very precious to me. For the book written round him is not just the sort of thing that can be attempted more than once in a life-time. It is the book by which, not as a novelist perhaps, but as an artist striving for the utmost sincerity of expression, I am willing to stand or fall.[2] Its pages are the tribute of my unalterable and profound affection for the ships, the seamen, the winds and the great sea—the moulders of my youth, the companions of the best years of my life.

After writing the last words of that book, in the revulsion of feeling before the accomplished task, I understood that I had done with the sea, and that henceforth I had to be a writer. And almost without laying down the pen I wrote a preface, trying to express the spirit in which I was entering on the task of my new life. That preface on advice[3] (which I now think was wrong) was never published with the

---

[†] This foreword was included in the 1914 Nelson Doubleday edition of the novel.
1. G. Jean-Aubry recounts Conrad's experience with the real man on whom Wait is based; see p. 436.
2. In a letter to John Quinn (December 8, 1912), Conrad says something similar: "the story by which, as a creative artist, I stand or fall" (CL 5:145).
3. in a March 27, 1914, letter to Alfred A. Knopf (1892–1984), Conrad says, "In the matter of the preface: it was suppressed simply because the publisher here (Mr Heinemann) thought it would do no good to the book—I don't know on what grounds—and I simply took his opinion meekly" (CL 5:368).

book. But the late W. E. Henley, who had the courage at the time (1897) to serialize my *Nigger* in the *New Review* judged it worthy to be printed as an afterword at the end of the last instalment of the tale.[4]

I am glad that this book which means so much to me is coming out again, under its proper title of *The Nigger of the "Narcissus"*[5] and under the auspices of my good friends and publishers Messrs. Doubleday, Page & Co. into the light of publicity.

Half the span of a generation has passed since W. E. Henley, after reading two chapters, sent me a verbal message: "Tell Conrad that if the rest is up to the sample it shall certainly come out in the *New Review*." The most gratifying recollection of my writer's life![6]

And here is the Suppressed Preface.

Joseph Conrad.
1914.

4. Henley published the preface (as an afterword) in the *New Review*, but it did not appear with the novel in book form until the 1914 Doubleday edition. Henley (1849–1903) was a British poet, critic, and editor. "*New Review*": A prominent literary magazine that began in June 1889 and ended in December 1897. The novel appeared serially from August through December 1897 in the magazine, which Henley edited from January 1895 through December 1897.

5. The novel originally appeared in the United States under the title *Children of the Sea*. According to Hamlin Garland (1860–1940), Conrad told him, "America would not buy a book about niggers, so my publishers changed the title to 'Children of the Sea.' I accepted the change. I was in no situation to object" (*My Friendly Contemporaries: A Literary Log* [New York: Macmillan, 1932], 493).

6. Conrad does not exaggerate here. In a letter to Edward Garnett, dated December 7, 1896, he writes: "Now I have conquered Henley I ain't 'fraid of the divvle himself" (*CL* 1:323).

Preface

A work that aspires, however humbly, to the condition of art should carry its justification in every line. And art itself may be defined as a single-minded attempt to render the highest kind of justice to the visible universe, by bringing to light the truth, manifold and one, underlying its every aspect. It is an attempt to find in its forms, in its colours, in its light, in its shadows, in the aspects of matter and in the facts of life, what of each is fundamental, what is enduring and essential—their one illuminating and convincing quality—the very truth of their existence. The artist, then, like the thinker or the scientist, seeks the truth and makes his appeal. Impressed by the aspect of the world the thinker plunges into ideas, the scientist into facts—whence, presently, emerging they make their appeal to those qualities of our being that fit us best for the hazardous enterprise of living. They speak authoritatively to our common-sense, to our intelligence, to our desire of peace or to our desire of unrest; not seldom to our prejudices, sometimes to our fears, often to our egoism—but always to our credulity. And their words are heard with reverence, for their concern is with weighty matters: with the cultivation of our minds and the proper care of our bodies: with the attainment of our ambitions: with the perfection of the means and the glorification of our precious aims.

It is otherwise with the artist.

Confronted by the same enigmatical spectacle the artist descends within himself, and in that lonely region of stress and strife, if he be deserving and fortunate, he finds the terms of his appeal. His appeal is made to our less obvious capacities: to that part of our nature which, because of the warlike conditions of existence, is necessarily kept out of sight within the more resisting and hard qualities—like the vulnerable body within the steel armour. His appeal is less loud, more profound, less distinct, more stirring—and sooner forgotten. Yet its effect endures for ever. The changing wisdom of successive generations discards ideas, questions facts, demolishes theories. But the artist appeals to that part of our being which is not dependent on wisdom: to that in us which is a gift and not an acquisition—and, therefore, more permanently enduring. He speaks to our capacity for delight and wonder, to the sense of mystery surrounding our lives: to our sense of pity, and beauty, and pain: to the latent feeling of fellowship with all creation—and to the subtle but invincible, conviction of solidarity that knits together the loneliness of innumerable hearts: to the solidarity in dreams, in joy, in sorrow, in aspirations, in illusions, in hope, in fear, which binds men to each other, which binds together all humanity—the dead to the living and the living to the unborn.

It is only some such train of thought, or rather of feeling, that can in a measure explain the aim of the attempt, made in the tale which follows, to present an unrestful episode in the obscure lives of a few individuals out of all the disregarded multitude of the bewildered, the simple and the voiceless. For, if there is any part of truth in the belief confessed above, it becomes evident that there is not a place of splendour or a dark corner of the earth that does not deserve, if only a passing glance of wonder and pity. The motive, then, may be held to justify the matter of the work; but this preface, which is simply an avowal of endeavour, cannot end here—for the avowal is not yet complete.

Fiction—if it at all aspires to be art—appeals to temperament. And in truth it must be, like painting, like music, like all art, the appeal of one temperament to all the other innumerable temperaments whose subtle and resistless power endows passing events with their true meaning, and creates the moral, the emotional atmosphere of the place and time. Such an appeal to be effective must be an impression conveyed through the senses; and, in fact, it cannot be made in any other way, because temperament, whether individual or collective, is not amenable to persuasion. All art, therefore, appeals primarily to the senses, and the artistic aim when expressing itself in written words must also make its appeal through the senses, if its high desire is to reach the secret spring of responsive emotions. It must strenuously aspire to the plasticity of sculpture, to the colour of painting, and to the magic suggestiveness of music—which is the art of arts.[1] And it is only through complete, unswerving devotion to the perfect blending of form and substance; it is only through an unremitting, never-discouraged care for the shape and ring of sentences that an approach can be made to plasticity, to colour; and the light of magic suggestiveness may be brought to play for an evanescent instant over the commonplace surface of words: of the old, old words, worn thin, defaced by ages of careless usage.

The sincere endeavour to accomplish that creative task, to go as far on that road as his strength will carry him, to go undeterred by faltering, weariness or reproach, is the only valid justification for the worker in prose. And if his conscience is clear, his answer to those who, in the fulness of a wisdom which looks for immediate profit, demand specifically to be edified, consoled, amused; who demand to be promptly improved, or encouraged, or frightened, or shocked, or charmed,[2]

1. Probably an allusion to the passage "All art constantly aspires toward the condition of music" by Walter Pater (1839–1894); see *The Renaissance: Studies in Art and Poetry*, ed. Donald L. Hill (University of California Press, 1980), 106.
2. David R. Smith sese an echo of the preface to *Pierre et Jean* (1888) by Guy de Maupassant (1850–1894); see *Conrad's Manifesto: Preface to a Career* (Rosenbach Foundation, 1966), 62.

must run thus:— My task which I am trying to achieve is, by the power of the written word, to make you hear, to make you feel—it is, before all, to make you *see*. That—and no more, and it is everything. If I succeed, you shall find there according to your deserts; encouragement, consolation, fear, charm—all you demand; and, perhaps, also that glimpse of truth for which you have forgotten to ask.

To snatch in a moment of courage, from the remorseless rush of time, a passing phase of life is only the beginning of the task. The task approached in tenderness and faith is to hold up unquestioningly, without choice and without fear, the rescued fragment before all eyes and in the light of a sincere mood. It is to show its vibration, its colour, its form; and through its movement, its form, and its colour, reveal the substance of its truth—disclose its inspiring secret: the stress and passion within the core of each convincing moment.[3] In a single-minded attempt of that kind, if one be deserving and fortunate, one may perchance attain to such clearness of sincerity that at last the presented vision of regret or pity, of terror or mirth, shall awaken in the hearts of the beholders that feeling of unavoidable solidarity; of the solidarity in mysterious origin, in toil, in joy, in hope, in uncertain fate, which binds men to each other and all mankind to the visible world.

It is evident that he who, rightly or wrongly, holds by the convictions expressed above cannot be faithful to any one of the temporary formulas of his craft. The enduring part of them—the truth which each only imperfectly veils—should abide with him as the most precious of his possessions, but they all: Realism, Romanticism, Naturalism,[4] even the unofficial sentimentalism (which, like the poor, is exceedingly difficult to get rid of); all these gods must, after a short period of fellowship, abandon him—even on the very threshold of the temple—to the stammerings of his conscience and to the outspoken consciousness of the difficulties of his work. In that uneasy solitude the supreme cry of Art for Art,[5] itself, loses the exciting ring of its apparent immorality. It sounds far off. It has ceased to be a cry, and is heard only as a whisper, often incomprehensible, but at times, and faintly, encouraging.

3. A possible allusion to the "Conclusion" to Pater's *The Renaissance*.
4. All literary movements. Realism occurred from the 1840s to the 1880s and emphasized realistic representations of people and events. Romanticism occurred in England from the 1790s to the 1830s and emphasized emotion, nature, and individualism. Naturalism was an extension of Realism but was strongly influenced by evolutionary biology and emphasized the importance of heredity and environment. Naturalist works also tended to investigate the seamy side of society and were prominent in England from the 1880s to the 1920s.
5. A phrase often attributed to Théophile Gautier (1811–1872) and adopted by the Aesthetic movement (sometimes called the Decadent movement) of the 1890s. Its intent was to argue that art's purpose is not to instruct or serve some other utilitarian end, but that art is an end in and of itself.

Sometimes, stretched at ease in the shade of a roadside tree, we watch the motions of a labourer in a distant field, and after a time, begin to wonder languidly as to what the fellow may be at. We watch the movements of his body, the waving of his arms; we see him bend down, stand up, hesitate, begin again. It may add to the charm of an idle hour to be told the purpose of his exertions. If we know he is trying to lift a stone, to dig a ditch, to uproot a stump, we look with a more real interest at his efforts; we are disposed to condone the jar of his agitation upon the restfulness of the landscape; and even, if in a brotherly frame of mind, we may bring ourselves to forgive his failure. We understood his object, and, after all, the fellow has tried, and perhaps he had not the strength, and perhaps he had not the knowledge. We forgive, go on our way—and forget.

And so it is with the workman of art. Art is long and life is short,[6] and success is very far off. And thus, doubtful of strength to travel so far, we talk a little about the aim—the aim of art, which, like life itself, is inspiring, difficult—obscured by mists. It is not in the clear logic of a triumphant conclusion; it is not in the unveiling of one of those heartless secrets which are called the Laws of Nature. It is not less great, but only more difficult.

To arrest, for the space of a breath, the hands busy about the work of the earth, and compel men entranced by the sight of distant goals to glance for a moment at the surrounding vision of form and colour, of sunshine and shadows; to make them pause for a look, for a sigh, for a smile—such is the aim, difficult and evanescent, and reserved only for a very few to achieve. But sometimes, by the deserving and the fortunate, even that task is accomplished. And when it is accomplished—behold!—all the truth of life is there: a moment of vision, a sigh, a smile—and the return to an eternal rest.

---

6. A rendering of the aphorism *Ars longa, vita brevis*, the Latin translation of the opening lines of *Aphorismi* by Hippocrates (c. 460–c. 375 B.C.E.).

The Nigger of the "Narcissus"

A *Tale of the Sea*

". . . My Lord in his discourse discovered a great deal of love to this ship."

—*Diary of Samuel Pepys*[1]

To
Edward Garnett[2]
This Tale about My Friends of the Sea

I

Mr. Baker, chief mate of the ship *Narcissus*,[3] stepped in one stride out of his lighted cabin into the darkness of the quarter-deck. Above his head, on the break of the poop, the night-watchman rang a double stroke. It was nine o'clock. Mr. Baker, speaking up to the man above him, asked:—"Are all the hands aboard, Knowles?"

The man limped down the ladder, then said reflectively:—"I think so, sir. All our old chaps are there, and a lot of new men has come. . . . They must be all there."

"Tell the boatswain[4] to send all hands aft," went on Mr. Baker; "and tell one of the youngsters to bring a good lamp here. I want to muster our crowd."

The main deck was dark aft, but half-way from forward, through the open doors of the forecastle, two streaks of brilliant light cut the shadow of the quiet night that lay upon the ship. A hum of voices was heard there, while port and starboard, in the illuminated doorways, silhouettes of moving men appeared for a moment, very black, without relief, like figures cut out of sheet tin. The ship was ready for sea. The carpenter[5] had driven in the last wedge of the main-hatch battens, and, throwing down his maul, had wiped his face with great deliberation, just on the stroke of five. The decks had

<hr>

1. Pepys (1633–1703), an English diarist. This passage comes from the entry for March 30, 1660.
2. Garnett (1868–1937), an English critic and writer. He was one of the original referees of Conrad's first novel, *Almayer's Folly*, for the publisher T. Fisher Unwin and became a close friend and literary advisor to Conrad.
3. A 1,336-ton clipper ship built by Robert Duncan & Co. in Port Glasgow for Robert R. Paterson (d. 1895) of Greenock, Scotland, in 1876. The ship had a long career, serving a variety of nautical purposes into the 1930s. Conrad served as second mate from April to October 1884, sailing from Bombay (now Mumbai) to Dunkirk. The actual chief mate of the *Narcissus* was Hamilton Hart, born in Hull (c. 1842). The ship's name comes from the Greek mythological figure Narcissus, the son of the god Cephissus and the nymph Liriope. When Narcissus went to a pool of water and saw his reflection, he fell in love with himself and was unable to leave the pool, eventually dying.
4. The boatswain aboard the *Narcissus* was John Evans, born in Canada (c. 1850).
5. The carpenter aboard the *Narcissus* was E. Larsen, born in Norway (c. 1853).

been swept, the windlass oiled and made ready to heave up the anchor; the big tow-rope lay in long bights along one side of the main deck, with one end carried up and hung over the bows, in readiness for the tug that would come paddling and hissing noisily, hot and smoky, in the limpid, cool quietness of the early morning. The captain was ashore, where he had been engaging some new hands to make up his full crew;[6] and, the work of the day over, the ship's officers had kept out of the way, glad of a little breathing-time. Soon after dark the few liberty-men and the new hands began to arrive in shore-boats rowed by white-clad Asiatics, who clamoured fiercely for payment before coming alongside the gangway-ladder. The feverish and shrill babble of Eastern language struggled against the masterful tones of tipsy seamen, who argued against brazen claims and dishonest hopes by profane shouts. The resplendent and bestarred peace of the East was torn into squalid tatters by howls of rage and shrieks of lament raised over sums ranging from five annas to half a rupee; and every soul afloat in Bombay Harbour[7] became aware that the new hands were joining the *Narcissus*.

Gradually the distracting noise had subsided. The boats came no longer in splashing clusters of three or four together, but dropped alongside singly, in a subdued buzz of expostulation cut short by a "Not a pice[8] more! You go to the devil!" from some man staggering up the accommodation-ladder—a dark figure, with a long bag poised on the shoulder. In the forecastle the newcomers, upright and swaying amongst corded boxes and bundles of bedding, made friends with the old hands, who sat one above another in the two tiers of bunks, gazing at their future shipmates with glances critical but friendly. The two forecastle lamps were turned up high, and shed an intense hard glare; shore-going hard hats[9] were pushed far on the backs of heads, or rolled about on the deck amongst the chain-cables; white collars, undone, stuck out on each side of red faces; big arms in white sleeves gesticulated; the growling voices hummed steady amongst bursts of laughter and hoarse calls. "Here, sonny, take that bunk! . . . Don't you do it! . . . What's your last ship? . . . I know her. . . . Three years ago, in Puget Sound.[1] . . . This here berth leaks, I tell you! . . . Come on; give us a chance to swing that chest! . . . Did you bring

---

6. Captain Archibald Duncan, born in Campbeltown, Scotland, in 1844, commanded the actual voyage of the *Narcissus*. He had to take on additional men (including Conrad) to fill out his crew in Bombay (Mumbai).
7. Now Mumbai; a port city in western India on the Arabian Sea. See p. 336. "Five annas to half a rupee": in India, a rupee is equivalent to sixteen annas, and ten rupees were equivalent to one British pound.
8. Four pice make one anna.
9. A hat made of stiff felt, such as a bowler.
1. An extension of the Pacific Ocean, reaching into northwest Washington State, with port cities of Seattle and Tacoma.

a bottle, any of you shore toffs?[2] . . . Give us a bit of 'baccy.[3] . . . I
know her; her skipper drank himself to death. . . . He was a dandy
boy! . . . Liked his lotion[4] inside, he did! . . . No! . . . Hold your row,
you chaps! . . . I tell you, you came on board a hooker, where they get
their money's worth out of poor Jack,[5] by—! . . ."

A little fellow, called Craik and nicknamed Belfast,[6] abused the
ship violently, romancing on principle, just to give the new hands
something to think over. Archie,[7] sitting aslant on his sea-chest,
kept his knees out of the way, and pushed the needle steadily
through a white patch in a pair of blue trousers. Men in black jackets and stand-up collars, mixed with men bare-footed, bare-armed,
with coloured shirts open on hairy chests, pushed against one
another in the middle of the forecastle. The group swayed, reeled,
turning upon itself with the motion of a scrimmage, in a haze of
tobacco smoke. All were speaking together, swearing at every second word. A Russian Finn,[8] wearing a yellow shirt with pink stripes,
stared upwards, dreamy-eyed, from under a mop of tumbled hair.
Two young giants with smooth, baby faces—two Scandinavians[9]—
helped each other to spread their bedding, silent, and smiling placidly at the tempest of good-humoured and meaningless curses. Old
Singleton,[1] the oldest able seaman in the ship, sat apart on the deck
right under the lamps, stripped to the waist, tattooed like a canni-
bal chief all over his powerful chest and enormous biceps. Between
the blue and red patterns his white skin gleamed like satin; his bare
back was propped against the heel of the bowsprit, and he held a
book at arm's length before his big, sunburnt face. With his spectacles and a venerable white beard, he resembled a learned and
savage patriarch, the incarnation of barbarian wisdom serene in
the blasphemous turmoil of the world. He was intensely absorbed,
and, as he turned the pages an expression of grave surprise
would pass over his rugged features. He was reading *Pelham*.

2. A disparaging working-class colloquialism for stylishly dressed people (slang).
3. Chewing tobacco.
4. Alcohol.
5. Short for "Jack Tar," a familar name for common sailors.
6. Probably based in part on James Craig, who was born in Belfast (c. 1863) and sailed
   aboard the *Narcissus* with Conrad.
7. Probably based on Archibald McLean, born in Scotland (c. 1861), who also sailed with
   Conrad aboard the *Narcissus*.
8. In 1809 Russia conquered Finland, which remained under Russian occupation until
   the Russian Revolution of 1917. No Finns sailed on the actual voyage of the *Narcissus*.
9. Jean-Aubry notes that Conrad told him that the two Scandinavians (later identified in
   the novel as Norwegians) were from another ship on which Conrad served (see p. 436),
   but there were four Norwegians (one was the carpenter) in the crew who sailed with
   Conrad.
1. Apparently based on a man named Sullivan (see p. 436), but there was no Sullivan aboard
   the *Narcissus*; there was, however, a Daniel Sullivan (b. c. 1841), with whom Conrad
   sailed aboard the *Tilkhurst* in 1885, who may have been the model for Singleton.

The popularity of Bulwer Lytton[2] in the forecastles of Southern-going ships is a wonderful and bizarre phenomenon. What ideas do his polished and so curiously insincere sentences awaken in the simple minds of the big children who people those dark and wandering places of the earth?[3] What meaning can their rough, inexperienced souls find in the elegant verbiage of his pages? What excitement?—what forgetfulness?—what appeasement? Mystery! Is it the fascination of the incomprehensible?—is it the charm of the impossible? Or are those beings who exist beyond the pale of life stirred by his tales as by an enigmatical disclosure of a resplendent world that exists within the frontier of infamy and filth, within that border of dirt and hunger, of misery and dissipation, that comes down on all sides to the water's edge of the incorruptible ocean, and is the only thing they know of life, the only thing they see of surrounding land—those life-long prisoners of the sea? Mystery!

Singleton, who had sailed to the southward since the age of twelve, who in the last forty-five years had lived (as we had calculated from his papers) no more than forty months ashore—old Singleton, who boasted, with the mild composure of long years well spent, that generally from the day he was paid off from one ship till the day he shipped in another he seldom was in a condition to distinguish daylight—old Singleton sat unmoved in the clash of voices and cries, spelling through *Pelham* with slow labour, and lost in an absorption profound enough to resemble a trance. He breathed regularly. Every time he turned the book in his enormous and blackened hands the muscles of his big white arms rolled slightly under the smooth skin. Hidden by the white moustache, his lips, stained with tobacco-juice that trickled down the long beard, moved in inward whisper. His bleared eyes gazed fixedly from behind the glitter of black-rimmed glasses. Opposite to him, and on a level with his face, the ship's cat sat on the barrel of the windlass in the pose of a crouching chimera,[4] blinking its green eyes at its old friend. It seemed to meditate a leap on to the old man's lap over the bent back of the ordinary seaman who sat at Singleton's feet. Young Charley was lean and long-necked. The ridge of his backbone made a chain of small hills under the old shirt. His face of a street-boy—a face precocious, sagacious, and ironic, with deep downward folds on each side of the thin, wide mouth—hung low over his bony knees. He was learning to make a lanyard knot with a bit of an old rope. Small

2. Edward George Bulwer-Lytton (1803–1873; first Baron Lytton), English poet, playwright, politician, and popular novelist. His novel *Pelham, or Adventures of a Gentleman* (1828) was his first popular success.
3. A possible allusion to Psalms 74:20: "Have respect unto the covenant: for the dark places of the earth are full of the habitations of cruelty."
4. In Greek mythology, a monstrous fire-breathing female creature, part lion, part snake, part goat.

drops of perspiration stood out on his bulging forehead; he sniffed strongly from time to time, glancing out of the corners of his restless eyes at the old seaman, who took no notice of the puzzled youngster muttering at his work.

The noise increased. Little Belfast seemed, in the heavy heat of the forecastle, to boil with facetious fury. His eyes danced; in the crimson of his face, comical as a mask, the mouth yawned black, with strange grimaces. Facing him, a half-undressed man held his sides, and, throwing his head back, laughed with wet eyelashes. Others stared with amazed eyes. Men sitting doubled up in the upper bunks smoked short pipes, swinging bare brown feet above the heads of those who, sprawling below on sea-chests, listened, smiling stupidly or scornfully. Over the white rims of berths stuck out heads with blinking eyes; but the bodies were lost in the gloom of those places, that resembled narrow niches for coffins in a whitewashed and lighted mortuary. Voices buzzed louder. Archie, with compressed lips, drew himself in, seemed to shrink into a smaller space, and sewed steadily, industrious and dumb. Belfast shrieked like an inspired Dervish:[5]—". . . So I seez to him, boys, seez I, 'Beggin' yer pardon, sorr,' seez I to that second mate of that steamer—'beggin' your-r-r pardon, sorr, the Board of Trade[6] must 'ave been drunk when they granted you your certificate!' 'What do you say, you—!' seez he, comin' at me like a mad bull . . . all in his white clothes; and I up with my tar-pot and capsizes it all over his blamed[7] lovely face and his lovely jacket. . . . 'Take that!' seez I. 'I am a sailor, anyhow, you nosing, skipper-licking, useless, sooperfloos bridge-stanchion, you!' 'That's the kind of man I am!' shouts I. . . . You should have seed him skip, boys! Drowned, blind with tar, he was! So . . ."

"Don't 'ee believe him! He never upset no tar; I was there!" shouted somebody. The two Norwegians sat on a chest side by side, alike and placid, resembling a pair of love-birds on a perch, and with round eyes stared innocently; but the Russian Finn, in the racket of explosive shouts and rolling laughter, remained motionless, limp and dull, like a deaf man without a backbone. Near him Archie smiled at his needle. A broad-chested, slow-eyed newcomer spoke deliberately to Belfast during an exhausted lull in the noise:—"I wonder any of the mates here are alive yet with such a chap as you on board! I concloode they ain't that bad now, if you had the taming of them, sonny."

5. Literally, a Muslim friar who takes vows of poverty and an austere life. Some are known for their whirling or dancing and are called dervishes.
6. A ministry that regulated commerce and trade.
7. As noted earlier, Conrad was criticized by some reviewers for the mild profanity in the novel (see p. 53, n. 7). In a letter to Edward Garnett (October 11, 1897), Conrad also complains that his publisher, William Heinemann (1863–1920), "objects to the *bloody's* in the book. . . . So I struck 3 or 4 *bloody's* out. I am sure there is [*sic*] a couple left yet, but, damn it, I am not going to hunt 'em up" (*CL* 1:395).

"Not bad! Not bad!" screamed Belfast. "If it wasn't for us sticking together. . . . Not bad! They ain't never bad when they ain't got a chawnce, blast their black 'arts.[8] . . ." He foamed, whirling his arms, then suddenly grinned and, taking a tablet of black tobacco out of his pocket, bit a piece off with a funny show of ferocity. Another new hand—a man with shifty eyes and a yellow hatchet face, who had been listening open-mouthed in the shadow of the midship locker— observed in a squeaky voice:—"Well, it's a 'omeward trip, anyhow. Bad or good, I can do it hall on my 'ed—s'long as I get 'ome. And I can look after my rights! I will show 'em!" All the heads turned towards him. Only the ordinary seaman and the cat took no notice. He stood with arms akimbo, a little fellow with white eyelashes. He looked as if he had known all the degradations and all the furies. He looked as if he had been cuffed, kicked, rolled in the mud; he looked as if he had been scratched, spat upon, pelted with unmentionable filth . . . and he smiled with a sense of security at the faces around. His ears were bending down under the weight of his battered hard hat. The torn tails of his black coat flapped in fringes about the calves of his legs. He unbuttoned the only two buttons that remained and every one saw he had no shirt under it. It was his deserved misfortune that those rags which nobody could possibly be supposed to own looked on him as if they had been stolen. His neck was long and thin; his eyelids were red; rare hairs hung about his jaws; his shoulders were peaked and drooped like the broken wings of a bird; all his left side was caked with mud which showed that he had lately slept in a wet ditch. He had saved his inefficient carcass from violent destruction by running away from an American ship[9] where, in a moment of forgetful folly, he had dared to engage himself; and he had knocked about for a fortnight ashore in the native quarter, cadging for drinks, starving, sleeping on rubbish-heaps, wandering in sunshine: a startling visitor from a world of nightmares. He stood repulsive and smiling in the sudden silence. This clean white forecastle was his refuge; the place where he could be lazy; where he could wallow, and lie and eat—and curse the food he ate; where he could display his talents for shirking work, for cheating, for cadging; where he could find surely some one to wheedle and some one to bully—and where he would be paid for doing all this. They all knew him. Is there a spot on earth where such a man is unknown, an ominous survival testifying to the eternal fitness of lies and impudence? A taciturn long-armed shellback, with hooked fingers, who had been lying on his back smoking, turned in his bed

8. A euphemism for *damn their black hearts.*
9. See p. 29, n. 4.

to examine him dispassionately, then, over his head, sent a long jet of clear saliva towards the door. They all knew him! He was the man that cannot steer, that cannot splice, that dodges the work on dark nights; that, aloft, holds on frantically with both arms and legs, and swears at the wind, the sleet, the darkness; the man who curses the sea while others work. The man who is the last out and the first in when all hands are called. The man who can't do most things and won't do the rest. The pet of philanthropists and self-seeking landlubbers. The sympathetic and deserving creature that knows all about his rights, but knows nothing of courage, of endurance, and of the unexpressed faith, of the unspoken loyalty that knits together a ship's company. The independent offspring of the ignoble freedom of the slums full of disdain and hate for the austere servitude of the sea.

Some one cried at him: "What's your name?"—"Donkin," he said, looking round with cheerful effrontery.—"What are you?" asked another voice.—"Why, a sailor like you, old man," he replied, in a tone that meant to be hearty but was impudent.—"Blamme if you don't look a blamed sight worse than a broken-down fireman," was the comment in a convinced mutter. Charley lifted his head and piped in a cheeky voice: "He is a man and a sailor"—then wiping his nose with the back of his hand bent down industriously over his bit of rope. A few laughed. Others stared doubtfully. The ragged newcomer was indignant.—"That's a fine way to welcome a chap into a fo'c'sle," he snarled. "Are you men or a lot of 'artless cannybals?"—"Don't take your shirt off[1] for a word, shipmate," called out Belfast, jumping up in front, fiery, menacing, and friendly at the same time.—"Is that 'ere bloke blind?" asked the indomitable scarecrow, looking right and left with affected surprise. "Can't 'ee see I 'aven't got no shirt?"

He held both his arms out crosswise and shook the rags that hung over his bones with dramatic effect.

"'Cos why?" he continued very loud. "The bloody Yankees been tryin' to jump my guts hout 'cos I stood up for my rights like a good 'un. I ham a Henglishman, I ham. They set upon me an' I 'ad to run. That's why. A'n't yer never seed a man 'ard up? Yah! What kind of blamed ship is this? I'm dead broke. I 'aven't got nothink. No bag, no bed, no blanket, no shirt—not a bloomin' rag but what I stand in. But I 'ad the 'art to stand hup agin' them Yankees. 'As any of you 'art enough to spare a pair of old pants for a chum?"

He knew how to conquer the naïve instincts of that crowd. In a moment they gave him their compassion, jocularly, contemptuously, or surlily; and at first it took the shape of a blanket thrown at

1. Don't offer to fight.

him as he stood there with the white skin of his limbs showing his human kinship through the black fantasy of his rags. Then a pair of old shoes fell at his muddy feet. With a cry:—"From under," a rolled-up pair of trousers, heavy with tar stains, struck him on the shoulder. The gust of their benevolence sent a wave of sentimental pity through their doubting hearts. They were touched by their own readiness to alleviate a shipmate's misery. Voices cried:—"We will fit you out, old man." Murmurs: "Never seed seech a hard case. . . . Poor beggar.[2] . . . I've got an old singlet. . . . Will that be of any use to you? . . . Take it, matey. . . ." Those friendly murmurs filled the forecastle. He pawed around with his naked foot, gathering the things in a heap and looked about for more. Unemotional Archie perfunctorily contributed to the pile an old cloth cap with the peak torn off. Old Singleton, lost in the serene regions of fiction, read on unheeding. Charley, pitiless with the wisdom of youth, squeaked:— "If you want brass buttons for your new unyforms I've got two for you." The filthy object of universal charity shook his fist at the youngster.—"I'll make you keep this 'ere fo'c'sle clean, young feller," he snarled viciously. "Never you fear. I will learn you to be civil to an able seaman, you hignorant hass." He glared harmfully, but saw Singleton shut his book, and his little beady eyes began to roam from berth to berth.—"Take that bunk by the door there—it's pretty fair," suggested Belfast. So advised, he gathered the gifts at his feet, pressed them in a bundle against his breast, then looked cautiously at the Russian Finn, who stood on one side with an unconscious gaze, contemplating, perhaps, one of those weird visions that haunt the men of his race.[3]—"Get out of my road, Dutchy,"[4] said the victim of Yankee brutality. The Finn did not move—did not hear. "Get out, blast ye," shouted the other, shoving him aside with his elbow. "Get out, you blanked[5] deaf and dumb fool. Get out." The man staggered, recovered himself, and gazed at the speaker in silence.—"Those damned fur-riners should be kept hunder," opined the amiable Donkin to the forecastle. "If you don't teach 'em their place they put on you like hanythink." He flung all his worldly possessions into the empty bed-place, gauged with another shrewd look the risks of the proceeding, then leaped up to the Finn, who stood pensive and dull.—"I'll teach you to swell around,"[6] he yelled. "I'll plug your eyes for you, you blooming square-head."[7] Most of the men were now in their bunks and the two had the forecastle clear to themselves. The development

2. See p. 63, n. 5.
3. Finns (and Laplanders) were thought to be able to cast spells affecting storms, winds, and other phenomena.
4. A contemptuous name for a Dutchman or German.
5. Another substitution for profanity.
6. To act conceited or puffed up.
7. A person of Germanic extraction. "Blooming": a substitution for profanity.

of the destitute Donkin aroused interest. He danced all in tatters before the amazed Finn, squaring from a distance at the heavy, unmoved face. One or two men cried encouragingly: "Go it, White-chapel!"[8] settling themselves luxuriously in their beds to survey the fight. Others shouted: "Shut yer row! . . . Go an' put yer 'ed in a bag! . . . The hubbub was recommencing. Suddenly many heavy blows struck with a handspike on the deck above boomed like discharges of small cannon through the forecastle. Then the boatswain's voice rose outside the door with an authoritative note in its drawl:—"D'ye hear, below there? Lay aft! Lay aft to muster all hands!"

There was a moment of surprised stillness. Then the forecastle floor disappeared under men whose bare feet flopped on the planks as they sprang clear out of their berths. Caps were rooted for amongst tumbled blankets. Some, yawning, buttoned waistbands. Half-smoked pipes were knocked hurriedly against woodwork and stuffed under pillows. Voices growled:—"What's up? . . . Is there no rest for us?" Donkin yelped:—"If that's the way of this ship, we'll 'ave to change hall that. . . . You leave me alone. . . . I will soon. . . ." None of the crowd noticed him. They were lurching in twos and threes through the doors, after the manner of merchant Jacks who cannot go out of a door fairly, like mere landsmen. The votary of change followed them. Singleton, struggling into his jacket, came last, tall and fatherly, bearing high his head of a weather-beaten sage on the body of an old athlete. Only Charley remained alone in the white glare of the empty place, sitting between the two rows of iron links that stretched into the narrow gloom forward. He pulled hard at the strands in a hurried endeavour to finish his knot. Suddenly he started up, flung the rope at the cat, and skipped after the black tom that went off leaping sedately over chain compressors, with the tail carried stiff and upright, like a small flag pole.

Outside the glare of the steaming forecastle the serene purity of the night enveloped the seamen with its soothing breath, with its tepid breath flowing under the stars that hung countless above the mastheads in a thin cloud of luminous dust. On the town side the blackness of the water was streaked with trails of light which un-dulated gently on slight ripples, similar to filaments that float rooted to the shore. Rows of other lights stood away in straight lines as if drawn up on parade between towering buildings; but on the other side of the harbour sombre hills arched high their black spines, on which, here and there, the point of a star resembled a spark fallen from the sky. Far off, Byculla[9] way, the electric lamps at the dock gates shone on the end of lofty standards with a glow blinding and

8. A poor district of East London.
9. A neighborhood in south Mumbai.

frigid like captive ghosts of some evil moons. Scattered all over the dark polish of the roadstead, the ships at anchor floated in perfect stillness under the feeble gleam of their riding-lights, looming up, opaque and bulky, like strange and monumental structures abandoned by men to an everlasting repose.

Before the cabin door Mr. Baker was mustering the crew. As they stumbled and lurched along past the mainmast, they could see aft his round, broad face with a white paper before it, and beside his shoulder the sleepy head, with dropped eyelids, of the boy, who held, suspended at the end of his raised arm, the luminous globe of a lamp. Even before the shuffle of naked soles had ceased along the decks, the mate began to call over the names. He called distinctly in a serious tone befitting this roll-call to unquiet loneliness, to inglorious and obscure struggle, or to the more trying endurance of small privations and wearisome duties. As the chief mate read out a name, one of the men would answer: "Yes, sir!" or "Here!" and, detaching himself from the shadowy mob of heads visible above the blackness of starboard bulwarks, would step barefooted into the circle of light, and in two noiseless strides pass into the shadows on the port side of the quarter-deck. They answered in divers tones: in thick mutters, in clear, ringing voices; and some, as if the whole thing had been an outrage on their feelings, used an injured intonation: for discipline is not ceremonious in merchant ships, where the sense of hierarchy is weak, and where all feel themselves equal before the unconcerned immensity of the sea and the exacting appeal of the work.

Mr. Baker read on steadily:—"Hanssen—Campbell—Smith—Wamibo. Now, then, Wamibo. Why don't you answer? Always got to call your name twice." The Finn emitted at last an uncouth grunt, and, stepping out, passed through the patch of light, weird and gaudy, with the face of a man marching through a dream. The mate went on faster:—"Craik—Singleton—Donkin . . . O Lord!" he involuntarily ejaculated as the incredibly dilapidated figure appeared in the light. It stopped; it uncovered pale gums and long, upper teeth in a malevolent grin.—"Is there anythink wrong with me, Mister Mate?" it asked, with a flavour of insolence in the forced simplicity of its tone. On both sides of the deck subdued titters were heard.—"That'll do. Go over," growled Mr. Baker, fixing the new hand with steady blue eyes. And Donkin vanished suddenly out of the light into the dark group of mustered men, to be slapped on the back and to hear flattering whispers. Round him men muttered to one another:—"He ain't afeard, he'll give sport to 'em, see if he don't. . . . Reg'lar Punch and Judy[1] show. . . . Did ye see the mate start at him? . . . Well! Damme, if I ever! . . ."

1. See p. 113, n. 3.

The last man had gone over, and there was a moment of silence while the mate peered at his list.—"Sixteen, seventeen," he muttered. "I am one hand short, boss'n," he said aloud. The big west-countryman[2] at his elbow, swarthy and bearded like a gigantic Spaniard, said in a rumbling bass:—"There's no one left forward, sir. I had a look round. He ain't aboard, but he may turn up before daylight."—"Ay. He may or he may not," commented the mate; "can't make out that last name. It's all a smudge. . . . That will do, men. Go below."

The indistinct and motionless group stirred, broke up, began to move forward.

"Wait!" cried a deep, ringing voice.

All stood still. Mr. Baker, who had turned away yawning, spun round open-mouthed. At last, furious, he blurted out:—"What's this? Who said 'Wait'? What . . ."

But he saw a tall figure standing on the rail. It came down and pushed through the crowd, marching with a heavy tread towards the light on the quarter-deck. Then again the sonorous voice said with insistence:—"Wait!" The lamplight lit up the man's body. He was tall. His head was away up in the shadows of lifeboats that stood on skids above the deck. The whites of his eyes and his teeth gleamed distinctly, but the face was indistinguishable, his hands were big and seemed gloved.

Mr. Baker advanced intrepidly. "Who are you? How dare you . . ." he began.

The boy, amazed like the rest, raised the light to the man's face. It was black. A surprised hum—a faint hum that sounded like the suppressed mutter of the word "Nigger"—ran along the deck and escaped out into the night. The nigger seemed not to hear. He balanced himself where he stood in a swagger that marked time. After a moment he said calmly:—"My name is Wait—James Wait."[3]

"Oh!" said Mr. Baker. Then, after a few seconds of smouldering silence, his temper blazed out. "Ah! Your name is Wait. What of that? What do you want? What do you mean, coming shouting here?"

The nigger was calm, cool, towering, superb. The men had approached and stood behind him in a body. He overtopped the tallest by half a head. He said: "I belong to the ship." He enunciated distinctly, with soft precision. The deep, rolling tones of his voice filled the deck without effort. He was naturally scornful, unaffectedly condescending, as if from his height of six foot three he had surveyed all

2. A man from southwestern England (typically the historic counties of Cornwall, Devon, Dorset, Somerset, and Bristol, sometimes including Gloucestershire and Wiltshire counties).
3. Conrad claims to have taken the name from another man who served with him aboard the *Duke of Sutherland,* not the *Narcissus;* see p. 436.

the vastness of human folly and had made up his mind not to be too hard on it. He went on:—"The captain shipped me this morning. I couldn't get aboard sooner. I saw you all aft as I came up the ladder, and could see directly you were mustering the crew. Naturally I called out my name. I thought you had it on your list, and would understand. You misapprehended." He stopped short. The folly around him was confounded. He was right as ever, and as ever ready to forgive. The disdainful tones had ceased, and, breathing heavily, he stood still, surrounded by all these white men. He held his head up in the glare of the lamp—a head vigorously modelled into deep shadows and shining lights—a head powerful and misshapen with a tormented and flattened face—a face pathetic and brutal: the tragic, the mysterious, the repulsive mask of a nigger's soul.

Mr. Baker, recovering his composure, looked at the paper close. "Oh, yes; that's so. All right, Wait. Take your gear forward," he said.

Suddenly the nigger's eyes rolled wildly, became all whites. He put his hand to his side and coughed twice, a cough metallic, hollow, and tremendously loud; it resounded like two explosions in a vault; the dome of the sky rang to it, and the iron plates of the ship's bulwarks seemed to vibrate in unison; then he marched off forward with the others. The officers lingering by the cabin door could hear him say: "Won't some of you chaps lend a hand with my dunnage?[4] I've got a chest and a bag." The words, spoken sonorously, with an even intonation, were heard all over the ship, and the question was put in a manner that made refusal impossible. The short, quick shuffle of men carrying something heavy went away forward, but the tall figure of the nigger lingered by the main-hatch in a knot of smaller shapes. Again he was heard asking: "Is your cook a coloured gentleman?" Then a disappointed and disapproving "Ah! h'm!" was his comment upon the information that the cook happened to be a mere white man. Yet, as they went all together towards the forecastle, he condescended to put his head through the galley door and boom out inside a magnificent "Good evening, doctor!" that made all the saucepans ring. In the dim light the cook dozed on the coal-locker in front of the captain's supper. He jumped up as if he had been cut with a whip, and dashed wildly on deck to see the backs of several men going away laughing. Afterwards, when talking about that voyage, he used to say:—"The poor fellow had scared me. I thought I had seen the devil." The cook had been seven years in the ship with the same captain. He was a serious-minded man with a wife and three children, whose society he enjoyed on an average one month out of twelve. When on shore he took his family to church twice every Sunday. At sea he went to sleep every evening

4. Miscellaneous baggage or a sailor's loose clothes.

with his lamp turned up full, a pipe in his mouth, and an open Bible
in his hand. Some one had always to go during the night to put out
the light, take the book from his hand, and the pipe from between
his teeth. "For"—Belfast used to say, irritated and complaining—
"some night, you stupid cookie, you'll swallow your ould clay,[5] and we
will have no cook."—"Ah! sonny, I am ready for my Maker's call . . .
wish you all were," the other would answer with a benign serenity
that was altogether imbecile and touching. Belfast outside the galley
door danced with vexation. "You holy fool! I don't want you to die,"
he howled, looking up with furious, quivering face and tender eyes.
"What's the hurry? you blessed wooden-headed ould heretic, the
divvle will have you soon enough. Think of Us . . . of Us . . . of Us!"
And he would go away, stamping, spitting aside, disgusted and worried; while the other, stepping out, saucepan in hand, hot, begrimed,
and placid, watched with a superior, cock-sure smile the back of his
"queer little man" reeling in a rage. They were great friends.

Mr. Baker, lounging over the after-hatch, sniffed the humid night
in the company of the second mate.—"Those West India[6] niggers
run fine and large—some of them . . . Ough! . . . Don't they? A fine,
big man that, Mr. Creighton. Feel him on a rope. Hey? Ough! I will
take him into my watch, I think." The second mate, a fair, gentlemanly young fellow, with a resolute face and a splendid physique,
observed quietly that it was just about what he expected. There could
be felt in his tone some slight bitterness which Mr. Baker very kindly
set himself to argue away. "Come, come, young man," he said, grunting between the words. "Come! Don't be too greedy. You had that big
Finn in your watch all the voyage. I will do what's fair. You may have
those two young Scandinavians and I . . . Ough! . . . I get the nigger,
and will take that . . . Ough! that cheeky costermonger[7] chap in a
black frock-coat. I'll make him . . . Ough! . . . make him toe the mark,
or my . . . Ough! . . . name isn't Baker. Ough! Ough! Ough!"

He grunted thrice—ferociously. He had that trick of grunting so
between his words and at the end of sentences. It was a fine, effective grunt that went well with his menacing utterance, with his
heavy, bull-necked frame, his jerky, rolling gait; with his big, seamed
face, his steady eyes, and sardonic mouth. But its effect had been
long ago discounted by the men. They liked him; Belfast—who was
a favourite, and knew it—mimicked him, not quite behind his back.
Charley—but with greater caution—imitated his walk. Some of his
sayings became established, daily quotations in the forecastle. Popularity can go no farther! Besides, all hands were ready to admit

5. I.e., clay pipe.
6. The West Indies.
7. A street vendor of fruit, vegetables, etc., used contemptuously here.

that on a fitting occasion the mate could "jump down a fellow's throat in a reg'lar Western Ocean style."[8]

Now he was giving his last orders. "Ough! . . . You, Knowles! Call all hands at four. I want . . . Ough! . . . to heave short before the tug comes. Look out for the captain. I am going to lay down in my clothes. . . . Ough! . . . Call me when you see the boat coming. Ough! Ough! . . . The old man is sure to have something to say when he comes aboard," he remarked to Creighton. "Well, good-night. . . . Ough! A long day before us to-morrow. . . . Ough! . . . Better turn in now. Ough! Ough!"

Upon the dark deck a band of light flashed, then a door slammed, and Mr. Baker was gone into his neat cabin. Young Creighton stood leaning over the rail, and looked dreamily into the night of the East. And he saw in it a long country lane, a lane of waving leaves and dancing sunshine. He saw stirring boughs of old trees outspread, and framing in their arch the tender, the caressing blueness of an English sky. And through the arch a girl in a clear dress, smiling under a sunshade, seemed to be stepping out of the tender sky.

At the other end of the ship the forecastle, with only one lamp burning now, was going to sleep in a dim emptiness traversed by loud breathings, by sudden short sighs. The double row of berths yawned black, like graves tenanted by uneasy corpses. Here and there a curtain of gaudy chintz, half drawn, marked the resting-place of a sybarite. A leg hung over the edge very white and lifeless. An arm stuck straight out with a dark palm turned up, and thick fingers half closed. Two light snores, that did not synchronise, quarrelled in funny dialogue. Singleton stripped again—the old man suffered much from prickly heat—stood cooling his back in the doorway, with his arms crossed on his bare and adorned chest. His head touched the beam of the deck above. The nigger, half undressed, was busy casting adrift the lashing of his box, and spreading his bedding in an upper berth. He moved about in his socks, tall and noiseless, with a pair of braces[9] beating about his heels. Amongst the shadows of stanchions and bowsprit, Donkin munched a piece of hard ship's bread, sitting on the deck with upturned feet and restless eyes; he held the biscuit up before his mouth in the whole fist, and snapped his jaws at it with a raging face. Crumbs fell between his outspread legs. Then he got up.

"Where's our water-cask?" he asked in a contained voice.

8. The northern Atlantic Ocean, known for its changeable and violent weather.
9. Suspenders (British).

Singleton, without a word, pointed with a big hand that held a short smouldering pipe. Donkin bent over the cask, drank out of the tin, splashing the water, turned round and noticed the nigger looking at him over the shoulder with calm loftiness. He moved up sideways.

"There's a blooming supper for a man," he whispered bitterly. "My dorg at 'ome wouldn't 'ave it. It's fit enouf for you an' me. 'Ere's a big ship's fo'c'sle! . . . Not a blooming scrap of meat in the kids. I've looked in all the lockers. . . ."

The nigger stared like a man addressed unexpectedly in a foreign language. Donkin changed his tone:—"Giv' us a bit of 'baccy, mate," he breathed out confidentially, "I 'aven't 'ad smoke or chew for the last month. I am rampin' mad for it. Come on, old man!"

"Don't be familiar," said the nigger. Donkin started and sat down on a chest near by, out of sheer surprise. "We haven't kept pigs together,"[1] continued James Wait in a deep undertone. "Here's your tobacco." Then, after a pause, he asked:—"What ship?"—"*Golden State*,"[2] muttered Donkin indistinctly, biting the tobacco. The nigger whistled low.—"Ran?" he said curtly. Donkin nodded: one of his cheeks bulged out.—"In course I ran," he mumbled. "They booted the life hout of one Dago[3] chap on the passage 'ere, then started on me. I cleared hout 'ere."—"Left your dunnage behind?"—"Yes, dunnage and money," answered Donkin, raising his voice a little; "I got nothink. No clothes, no bed. A bandy-legged little Hirish chap 'ere 'as give me a blanket. . . . Think I'll go an' sleep in the fore-topmast staysail to-night."

He went on deck trailing behind his back a corner of the blanket, Singleton, without a glance, moved slightly aside to let him pass. The nigger put away his shore togs[4] and sat in clean working clothes on his box, one arm stretched over his knees. After staring at Singleton for some time he asked without emphasis:—"What kind of ship is this? Pretty fair? Eh?"

Singleton didn't stir. A long while after he said, with unmoved face:—"Ship! . . . Ships are all right. It is the men in them!"[5]

He went on smoking in the profound silence. The wisdom of half a century spent in listening to the thunder of the waves had spoken

---

1. According to Zygmunt Frajzyungier, Conrad is translating a Polish rebuke to someone who has assumed social equality ("James Wait's Polish Idiom," *Conradiana* 17.2 [Summer 1985]: 143–44).
2. Possibly the American clipper ship launched on July 12, 1851. It is unknown whether Conrad has this particular ship in mind or simply chose the name randomly.
3. A term for someone of Portuguese, Spanish, or Italian extraction.
4. Clothes (slang).
5. Apparently based on an actual incident. In *The Mirror of the Sea* (1906), Conrad writes, "Ships! exclaimed an elderly seaman in clean shore togs. * * * "ships are all right; it's the men in 'em" (*MS* 128–29).

unconsciously through his old lips. The cat purred on the windlass. Then James Wait had a fit of roaring, rattling cough, that shook him, tossed him like a hurricane, and flung him panting with staring eyes headlong on his sea-chest. Several men woke up. One said sleepily out of his bunk: "'Struth! what a blamed row!"—"I have a cold on my chest," gasped Wait.—"Cold! you call it," grumbled the man; "should think 'twas something more. . . ."—"Oh! you think so," said the nigger upright and loftily scornful again. He climbed into his berth and began coughing persistently while he put his head out to glare all round the forecastle. There was no further protest. He fell back on the pillow, and could be heard there wheezing regularly like a man oppressed in his sleep.

Singleton stood at the door with his face to the light and his back to the darkness. And alone in the dim emptiness of the sleeping forecastle he appeared bigger, colossal, very old; old as Father Time himself, who should have come there into this place as quiet as a sepulchre to contemplate with patient eyes the short victory of sleep, the consoler. Yet he was only a child of time, a lonely relic of a devoured and forgotten generation. He stood, still strong, as ever unthinking; a ready man with a vast empty past and with no future, with his childlike impulses and his man's passions already dead within his tattooed breast. The men who could understand his silence were gone—those men who knew how to exist beyond the pale of life and within sight of eternity. They had been strong, as those are strong who know neither doubts nor hopes. They had been impatient and enduring, turbulent and devoted, unruly and faithful. Well-meaning people had tried to represent those men as whining over every mouthful of their food; as going about their work in fear of their lives. But in truth they had been men who knew toil, privation, violence, debauchery—but knew not fear, and had no desire of spite in their hearts. Men hard to manage, but easy to inspire; voiceless men—but men enough to scorn in their hearts the sentimental voices that bewailed the hardness of their fate. It was a fate unique and their own; the capacity to bear it appeared to them the privilege of the chosen! Their generation lived inarticulate and indispensable, without knowing the sweetness of affections or the refuge of a home—and died free from the dark menace of a narrow grave. They were the everlasting children of the mysterious sea.[6] Their successors are the grown-up children of a discontented earth. They are less naughty, but less innocent; less profane, but perhaps also less believing; and if they had learned how to speak they have also learned how to whine. But the others were

---

6. This phrase provides the basis for the title of the first U.S. edition: *The Children of the Sea: A Tale of the Forecastle.*

strong and mute; they were effaced, bowed and enduring, like stone caryatides[7] that hold up in the night the lighted halls of a resplendent and glorious edifice. They are gone now—and it does not matter. The sea and the earth are unfaithful to their children: a truth, a faith, a generation of men goes—and is forgotten, and it does not matter! Except, perhaps, to the few of those who believed the truth, confessed the faith—or loved the men.

A breeze was coming. The ship that had been lying tide-rode swung to a heavier puff; and suddenly the slack of the chain-cable between the windlass and the hawse-pipe clinked, slipped forward an inch, and rose gently off the deck with a startling suggestion as of unsuspected life that had been lurking stealthily in the iron. In the hawse-pipe the grinding links sent through the ship a sound like a low groan of a man sighing under a burden. The strain came on the windlass, the chain tautened like a string, vibrated—and the handle of the screw-brake moved in slight jerks. Singleton stepped forward.

Till then he had been standing meditative and unthinking, reposeful and hopeless, with a face grim and blank—a sixty-year-old child of the mysterious sea. The thoughts of all his lifetime could have been expressed in six words, but the stir of those things that were as much part of his existence as his beating heart called up a gleam of alert understanding upon the sternness of his aged face. The flame of the lamp swayed, and the old man, with knitted and bushy eyebrows, stood over the brake, watchful and motionless in the wild saraband[8] of dancing shadows. Then the ship, obedient to the call of her anchor, forged ahead slightly and eased the strain. The cable relieved, hung down, and after swaying imperceptibly to and fro dropped with a loud tap on the hard wood planks. Singleton seized the high lever, and, by a violent throw forward of his body, wrung out another half-turn from the brake. He recovered himself, breathed largely, and remained for awhile glaring down at the powerful and compact engine that squatted on the deck at his feet, like some quiet monster—a creature amazing and tame.

"You . . . hold!" he growled at it masterfully, in the incult tangle of his white beard.

II

Next morning, at daylight, the *Narcissus* went to sea.

A slight haze blurred the horizon. Outside the harbour the measureless expanse of smooth water lay sparkling like a floor of jewels, and as empty as the sky. The short black tug gave a pluck to

7. Female figures used as supporting columns.
8. A stately, slow Spanish dance in triple time.

windward, in the usual way, then let go the rope, and hovered for a moment on the quarter with her engines stopped; while the slim, long hull of the ship moved ahead slowly under lower topsails. The loose upper canvas blew out in the breeze with soft round contours, resembling small white clouds snared in the maze of ropes. Then the sheets were hauled home, the yards hoisted, and the ship became a high and lonely pyramid, gliding, all shining and white, through the sunlit mist. The tug turned short round and went away towards the land. Twenty-six pairs of eyes watched her low broad stern crawling languidly over the smooth swell between the two paddle-wheels that turned fast, beating the water with fierce hurry. She resembled an enormous and aquatic black beetle, surprised by the light, overwhelmed by the sunshine, trying to escape with ineffectual effort into the distant gloom of the land. She left a lingering smudge of smoke on the sky, and two vanishing trails of foam on the water. On the place where she had stopped a round black patch of soot remained, undulating on the swell—an unclean mark of the creature's rest.

The *Narcissus* left alone, heading south, seemed to stand resplendent and still upon the restless sea, under the moving sun. Flakes of foam swept past her sides; the water struck her with flashing blows; the land glided away, slowly fading; a few birds screamed on motionless wings over the swaying mastheads. But soon the land disappeared, the birds went away; and to the west the pointed sail of an Arab dhow running for Bombay, rose triangular and upright above the sharp edge of the horizon, lingered, and vanished like an illusion. Then the ship's wake, long and straight, stretched itself out through a day of immense solitude. The setting sun, burning on the level of the water, flamed crimson below the blackness of heavy rain clouds. The sunset squall, coming up from behind, dissolved itself into the short deluge of a hissing shower. It left the ship glistening from trucks to water-line, and with darkened sails. She ran easily before a fair monsoon,[9] with her decks cleared for the night; and, moving along with her, was heard the sustained and monotonous swishing of the waves, mingled with the low whispers of men mustered aft for the setting of watches; the short plaint of some block aloft; or, now and then, a loud sigh of wind.

Mr. Baker, coming out of his cabin, called out the first name sharply before closing the door behind him. He was going to take charge of the deck. On the homeward trip, according to an old custom of the sea, the chief officer takes the first night-watch—from eight till midnight. So Mr. Baker, after he had heard the last "Yes, sir!" said moodily, "Relieve the wheel and look-out"; and climbed

9. See p. 109, n. 6.

with heavy feet the poop ladder to windward. Soon after Mr. Creighton came down, whistling softly, and went into the cabin. On the doorstep the steward lounged, in slippers, meditative, and with his shirt-sleeves rolled up to the armpits. On the main deck the cook, locking up the galley doors, had an altercation with young Charley about a pair of socks. He could be heard saying impressively, in the darkness amidships: "You don't deserve a kindness. I've been drying them for you, and now you complain about the holes—and you swear, too! Right in front of me! If I hadn't been a Christian— which you ain't, you young ruffian—I would give you a clout on the head. . . . Go away!" Men in couples or threes stood pensive or moved silently along the bulwarks in the waist. The first busy day of a homeward passage was sinking into the dull peace of resumed routine. Aft, on the high poop, Mr. Baker walked shuffling; grunted to himself in the pauses of his thoughts. Forward, the look-out man, erect between the flukes of the two anchors, hummed an endless tune, keeping his eyes fixed dutifully ahead in a vacant stare. A multitude of stars coming out into the clear night peopled the emptiness of the sky. They glittered, as if alive above the sea; they surrounded the running ship on all sides; more intense than the eyes of a staring crowd, and as inscrutable as the souls of men.

The passage had begun; and the ship, a fragment detached from the earth, went on lonely and swift like a small planet. Round her the abysses of sky and sea met in an unattainable frontier. A great circular solitude moved with her, ever changing and ever the same, always monotonous and always imposing. Now and then another wandering white speck, burdened with life, appeared far off— disappeared; intent on its own destiny. The sun looked upon her all day, and every morning rose with a burning, round stare of undying curiosity. She had her own future; she was alive with the lives of those beings who trod her decks; like that earth which had given her up to the sea, she had an intolerable load of regrets and hopes. On her lived timid truth and audacious lies; and, like the earth, she was unconscious, fair to see—and condemned by men to an ignoble fate. The august loneliness of her path lent dignity to the sordid inspiration of her pilgrimage. She drove foaming to the southward, as if guided by the courage of a high endeavour. The smiling greatness of the sea dwarfed the extent of time. The days raced after one another, brilliant and quick like the flashes of a lighthouse, and the nights, eventful and short, resembled fleeting dreams.

The men had shaken into their places, and the half-hourly voice of the bells ruled their life of unceasing care. Night and day the head and shoulders of a seaman could be seen aft by the wheel, outlined high against sunshine or starlight, very steady above the stir of revolving spokes. The faces changed, passing in rotation. Youthful faces, bearded faces, dark faces: faces serene, or faces moody, but all akin with the brotherhood of the sea; all with the same attentive expression of eyes, carefully watching the compass or the sails. Captain Allistoun, serious, and with an old red muffler round his throat, all day long pervaded the poop. At night, many times he rose out of the darkness of the companion, such as a phantom above a grave, and stood watchful and mute under the stars, his night-shirt fluttering like a flag—then, without a sound, sank down again. He was born on the shores of the Pentland Firth. In his youth he attained the rank of harpooner in Peterhead[1] whalers. When he spoke of that time his restless grey eyes became still and cold, like the loom of ice. Afterwards he went into the East Indian trade[2] for the sake of change. He had commanded the *Narcissus* since she was built. He loved his ship, and drove her unmercifully; for his secret ambition was to make her accomplish some day a brilliantly quick passage which would be mentioned in nautical papers. He pronounced his owner's name with a sardonic smile, spoke but seldom to his officers, and reproved errors in a gentle voice, with words that cut to the quick. His hair was iron-grey, his face hard and of the colour of pump-leather. He shaved every morning of his life—at six—but once (being caught in a fierce hurricane eighty miles southwest of Mauritius[3]) he had missed three consecutive days. He feared naught but an unforgiving God, and wished to end his days in a little house, with a plot of ground attached—far in the country—out of sight of the sea.

He, the ruler of that minute world, seldom descended from the Olympian heights of his poop. Below him—at his feet, so to speak—common mortals led their busy and insignificant lives. Along the main deck Mr. Baker grunted in a manner bloodthirsty and innocuous; and kept all our noses to the grindstone, being—as he once remarked—paid for doing that very thing. The men working about the deck were healthy and contented—as most seamen are, when once well out to sea. The true peace of God begins at any spot a thousand miles from the nearest land; and when He sends there the messengers of His might it is not in terrible wrath against crime, presumption, and folly, but paternally, to chasten simple

1. The easternmost port in Scotland, known for its whaling history. Aboard the *Loch Etive* (1880–81), Conrad sailed with a second mate, James W. Allestan, who was from Peterhead and may have suggested the name for Captain Allistoun. Pentland Firth is the strait between northeast Scotland and the Orkney Islands.
2. Established in 1600 by Queen Elizabeth I (1533–1603), the East India Company oversaw trade from the East until it was dissolved at the end of 1873.
3. An island in the Indian Ocean, east of Madagascar, a British colony from 1810 (when it was won from the French) until 1968. In 1888, while commander of the *Otago*, Conrad spent seven weeks in Mauritius awaiting repairs to his ship. See p. 336.

hearts—ignorant hearts that know nothing of life, and beat undisturbed by envy or greed.

In the evening the cleared decks had a reposeful aspect, resembling the autumn of the earth. The sun was sinking to rest, wrapped in a mantle of warm clouds. Forward, on the end of the spare spars, the boatswain and the carpenter sat together with crossed arms; two men friendly, powerful, and deep-chested. Beside them the short, dumpy sailmaker[4]—who had been in the Navy—related, between the whiffs of his pipe, impossible stories about Admirals. Couples tramped backwards and forwards, keeping step and balance without effort, in a confined space. Pigs grunted in the big pigstye. Belfast, leaning thoughtfully on his elbow, above the bars, communed with them through the silence of his meditation. Fellows with shirts open wide on sunburnt breasts sat upon the mooring bits, and all up the steps of the forecastle ladders. By the foremast a few discussed in a circle the characteristics of a gentleman. One said:— "It's money as does it." Another maintained:—"No, it's the way they speak." Lame Knowles stumped up with an unwashed face (he had the distinction of being the dirty man of the forecastle), and, showing a few yellow fangs in a shrewd smile, explained craftily that he "had seen some of their pants." The backsides of them—he had observed—were thinner than paper from constant sitting down in offices, yet otherwise they looked first-rate and would last for years. It was all appearance. "It was," he said, "bloomin' easy to be a gentleman when you had a clean job for life." They disputed endlessly, obstinate and childish; they repeated in shouts and with inflamed faces their amazing arguments; while the soft breeze, eddying down the enormous cavity of the foresail, that stood out distended above their bare heads, stirred the tumbled hair with a touch passing and light like an indulgent caress.

They were forgetting their toil, they were forgetting themselves. The cook approached to hear, and stood by, beaming with the inward consciousness of his faith, like a conceited saint unable to forget his glorious reward; Donkin, solitary and brooding over his wrongs on the forecastle-head, moved closer to catch the drift of the discussion below him; he turned his sallow face to the sea, and his thin nostrils moved, sniffing the breeze, as he lounged negligently by the rail. In the glow of sunset faces shone with interest, teeth flashed, eyes sparkled. The walking couples stood still suddenly, with broad grins; a man, bending over a washtub, sat up, entranced, with the soapsuds flecking his wet arms. Even the three petty officers listened leaning back, comfortably propped, and with superior smiles. Belfast left off scratching the ear of his favourite pig, and, open mouthed, tried

4. The sailmaker aboard the *Narcissus* was W. G. Allen, born in Penarth, Wales, about 1830.

with eager eyes to have his say. He lifted his arms, grimacing and baffled. From a distance Charley screamed at the ring:—"I know about gentlemen morn'n any of you. I've been hintymate with 'em. . . . I've blacked their boots." The cook, craning his neck to hear better, was scandalised. "Keep your mouth shut when your elders speak, you impudent young heathen—you." "All right, old Hallelujah,[5] I'm done," answered Charley, soothingly. At some opinion of dirty Knowles, delivered with an air of supernatural cunning, a ripple of laughter ran along, rose like a wave, burst with a startling roar. They stamped with both feet; they turned their shouting faces to the sky; many, spluttering, slapped their thighs; while one or two, bent double, gasped, hugging themselves with both arms like men in pain. The carpenter and the boatswain, without changing their attitude, shook with laughter where they sat; the sailmaker, charged with an anecdote about a Commodore, looked sulky; the cook was wiping his eyes with a greasy rag; and lame Knowles, astonished at his own success, stood in their midst showing a slow smile.

Suddenly the face of Donkin leaning highshouldered over the after-rail became grave. Something like a weak rattle was heard through the forecastle door. It became a murmur; it ended in a sighing groan. The washerman plunged both his arms into the tub abruptly; the cook became more crestfallen than an exposed backslider; the boatswain moved his shoulders uneasily; the carpenter got up with a spring and walked away—while the sailmaker seemed mentally to give his story up, and began to puff at his pipe with sombre determination. In the blackness of the doorway a pair of eyes glimmered white, and big, and staring. Then James Wait's head protruding, became visible, as if suspended between the two hands that grasped a doorpost on each side of the face. The tassel of his blue woollen night-cap, cocked forward, danced gaily over his left eyelid. He stepped out in a tottering stride. He looked powerful as ever, but showed a strange and affected unsteadiness in his gait; his face was perhaps a trifle thinner, and his eyes appeared rather startlingly prominent. He seemed to hasten the retreat of departing light by his very presence; the setting sun dipped sharply, as though fleeing before our nigger; a black mist emanated from him; a subtle and dismal influence; a something cold and gloomy that floated out and settled on all the faces like a mourning veil. The circle broke up. The joy of laughter died on stiffened lips. There was not a smile left among all the ship's company. Not a word was spoken. Many turned their backs, trying to look unconcerned; others, with averted heads, sent half-reluctant glances out of the corners of their eyes. They resembled criminals conscious of misdeeds more

5. Referring (perhaps idiosyncratically) to the cook's having strong religious beliefs.

than honest men distracted by doubt; only two or three stared
frankly, but stupidly, with lips slightly open. All expected James
Wait to say something, and, at the same time, had the air of knowing beforehand what he would say. He leaned his back against the
doorpost, and with heavy eyes swept over us a glance domineering
and pained, like a sick tyrant overawing a crowd of abject but
untrustworthy slaves.

No one went away. They waited in fascinated dread. He said ironically, with gasps between the words:—

"Thank you . . . chaps. You . . . are nice . . . and . . . quiet . . . you
are! Yelling so . . . before . . . the door . . ."

He made a longer pause, during which he worked his ribs in an
exaggerated labour of breathing. It was intolerable. Feet were shuffled. Belfast let out a groan; but Donkin above blinked his red eyelids with invisible eyelashes, and smiled bitterly over the nigger's
head.

The nigger went on again with surprising ease. He gasped no
more, and his voice rang, hollow and loud, as though he had been
talking in an empty cavern. He was contemptuously angry.

"I tried to get a wink of sleep. You know I can't sleep o' nights.
And you come jabbering near the door here like a blooming lot of
old women. . . . You think yourselves good shipmates. Do you? . . .
Much you care for a dying man!"

Belfast spun away from the pigstye. "Jimmy," he cried tremulously,
"if you hadn't been sick I would—"

He stopped. The nigger waited awhile, then said, in a gloomy
tone:—"You would. . . . What? Go an' fight another such one as yourself. Leave me alone. It won't be for long. I'll soon die. . . . It's coming
right enough!"

Men stood around very still, breathing lightly, and with exasperated eyes. It was just what they had expected, and hated to hear,
that idea of a stalking death, thrust at them many times a day like a
boast and like a menace by this obnoxious nigger. He seemed to
take a pride in that death which, so far, had attended only upon the
ease of his life; he was overbearing about it, as if no one else in the
world had ever been intimate with such a companion; he paraded it
unceasingly before us with an affectionate persistence that made its
presence indubitable, and at the same time incredible. No man could
be suspected of such monstrous friendship! Was he a reality—or was
he a sham—this ever-expected visitor of Jimmy's? We hesitated
between pity and mistrust, while, on the slightest provocation, he
shook before our eyes the bones of his bothersome and infamous
skeleton. He was for ever trotting him out. He would talk of that
coming death as though it had been already there, as if it had been
walking the deck outside, as if it would presently come in to sleep

in the only empty bunk; as if it had sat by his side at every meal. It interfered daily with our occupations, with our leisure, with our amusements. We had no songs and no music in the evening, because Jimmy (we all lovingly called him Jimmy, to conceal our hate of his accomplice) had managed, with that prospective decease of his, to disturb even Archie's mental balance. Archie was the owner of the concertina;[6] but after a couple of stinging lectures from Jimmy he refused to play any more. He said:—"Yon's an uncanny joker. I dinna ken what's wrang wi' him, but there's something verra wrang, verra wrang. It's nae[7] manner of use asking me. I won't play." Our singers became mute because Jimmy was a dying man. For the same reason no chap—as Knowles remarked—could "drive in a nail to hang his few poor rags upon," without being made aware of the enormity he committed in disturbing Jimmy's interminable last moments. At night, instead of the cheerful yell, "One bell! Turn out! Do you hear there? Hey! hey! hey! Show leg!" the watches were called man by man, in whispers, so as not to interfere with Jimmy's, possibly, last slumber on earth. True, he was always awake, and managed, as we sneaked out on deck, to plant in our backs some cutting remark that, for the moment, made us feel as if we had been brutes, and afterwards made us suspect ourselves of being fools. We spoke in low tones within that fo'c'sle as though it had been a church. We ate our meals in silence and dread, for Jimmy was capricious with his food, and railed bitterly at the salt meat, at the biscuits, at the tea, as at articles unfit for human consumption—"let alone for a dying man!" He would say:—"Can't you find a better slice of meat for a sick man who's trying to get home to be cured—or buried? But there! If I had a chance, you fellows would do away with it. You would poison me. Look at what you have given me!" We served him in his bed with rage and humility, as though we had been the base courtiers of a hated prince; and he rewarded us by his unconciliating criticism. He had found the secret of keeping for ever on the run the fundamental imbecility of mankind; he had the secret of life, that confounded dying man, and he made himself master of every moment of our existence. We grew desperate, and remained submissive. Emotional little Belfast was for ever on the verge of assault or on the verge of tears. One evening he confided to Archie:—"For a ha'penny I would knock his ugly black head off—the skulking dodger!"[8] And the straightforward Archie pretended to be

---

6. A portable musical instrument, usually shaped like a polygon, with bellows and keys. It bears some similarity to an accordion.
7. Conrad's rendition of Scots dialect: "dinna" (don't), "ken" (know), "wrang" (wrong), "verra" (very), "nae" (no).
8. One who avoids work in a sneaky manner (slang).

shocked! Such was the infernal spell which that casual St. Kitts⁹
nigger had cast upon our guileless manhood! But the same night
Belfast stole from the galley the officers' Sunday fruit pie, to tempt
the fastidious appetite of Jimmy. He endangered not only his long
friendship with the cook but also—as it appeared—his eternal wel-
fare. The cook was overwhelmed with grief; he did not know the
culprit but he knew that wickedness flourished; he knew that Satan
was abroad amongst those men, whom he looked upon as in some
way under his spiritual care. Whenever he saw three or four of us
standing together he would leave his stove, to run out and preach.
We fled from him; and only Charley (who knew the thief) affronted
the cook with a candid gaze which irritated the good man. "It's you, I
believe," he groaned, sorrowful, and with a patch of soot on his chin.
"It's you. You are a brand for the burning! No more of *your* socks in
my galley." Soon, unofficially, the information was spread about that,
should there be another case of stealing our marmalade (an extra
allowance: half a pound per man) would be stopped. Mr. Baker
ceased to heap jocular abuse upon his favourites, and grunted suspiciously at all. The captain's cold eyes, high up on the poop, glittered
mistrustful, as he surveyed us trooping in a small mob from halyards
to braces for the usual evening pull at all the ropes. Such stealing in
a merchant ship is difficult to check, and may be taken as a declaration by men of their dislike for their officers. It is a bad symptom. It
may end in God knows what trouble. The *Narcissus* was still a peaceful ship, but mutual confidence was shaken. Donkin did not conceal
his delight. We were dismayed.

Then illogical Belfast reproached our nigger with great fury. James
Wait, with his elbow on the pillow, choked, gasped out:—"Did I ask
you to bone¹ the dratted thing? Blow² your blamed pie. It has made
me worse—you little Irish lunatic, you!" Belfast, with scarlet face and
trembling lips, made a dash at him. Every man in the forecastle rose
with a shout. There was a moment of wild tumult. Some one shrieked
piercingly:—"Easy, Belfast! Easy! . . ." We expected Belfast to strangle Wait without more ado. Dust flew. We heard through it the nigger's cough, metallic and explosive like a gong. Next moment we
saw Belfast hanging over him. He was saying plaintively:—"Don't!
Don't, Jimmy! Don't be like that. An angel couldn't put up with ye—
sick as ye are." He looked round at us from Jimmy's bedside, his comical mouth twitching, and through tearful eyes; then he tried to put
straight the disarranged blankets. The unceasing whisper of the

9. Or Saint Christopher Island; in the West Indies in the Caribbean Sea, southeast of
   Puerto Rico. It was under British control until 1983.
1. To steal (slang).
2. Used in imprecations; perhaps another of Conrad's euphemisms for profanity.

sea filled the forecastle. Was James Wait frightened, or touched, or repentant? He lay on his back with a hand to his side, and as motionless as if his expected visitor had come at last. Belfast fumbled about his feet, repeating with emotion:—"Yes. We know. Ye are bad, but . . . Just say what ye want done, and . . . We all know ye are bad—very bad. . . ." No! Decidedly James Wait was not touched or repentant. Truth to say, he seemed rather startled. He sat up with incredible suddenness and ease. "Ah! You think I am bad, do you?" he said gloomily, in his clearest baritone voice (to hear him speak sometimes you would never think there was anything wrong with that man). "Do you? . . . Well, act according! Some of you haven't sense enough to put a blanket shipshape over a sick man. There! Leave it alone! I can die anyhow!" Belfast turned away limply with a gesture of discouragement. In the silence of the forecastle, full of interested men, Donkin pronounced distinctly:—"Well, I'm blowed!" and sniggered.[3] Wait looked at him. He looked at him in a quite friendly manner. Nobody could tell what would please our incomprehensible invalid: but for us the scorn of that snigger was hard to bear.

Donkin's position in the forecastle was distinguished but unsafe. He stood on the bad eminence of a general dislike. He was left alone; and in his isolation he could do nothing but think of the gales of the Cape of Good Hope and envy us the possession of warm clothing and waterproofs.[4] Our sea-boots, our oilskin[5] coats, our well-filled sea-chests, were to him so many causes for bitter meditation: he had none of those things, and he felt instinctively that no man, when the need arose, would offer to share them with him. He was impudently cringing to us and systematically insolent to the officers. He anticipated the best results, for himself, from such a line of conduct— and was mistaken. Such natures forget that under extreme provocation men will be just—whether they want to be so or not. Donkin's insolence to long-suffering Mr. Baker became at last intolerable to us, and we rejoiced when the mate, one dark night, tamed him for good. It was done neatly, with great decency and decorum, and with little noise. We had been called—just before midnight—to trim the yards, and Donkin—as usual—made insulting remarks. We stood sleepily in a row with the forebrace in our hands waiting for the next order, and heard in the darkness a scuffly trampling of feet, an exclamation of surprise, sounds of cuffs and slaps, suppressed, hissing whispers:—"Ah! Will you!" . . . "Don't! . . . Don't!" . . . "Then behave." . . . "Oh! Oh! . . ." Afterwards there were soft thuds mixed

3. Snickered.
4. Garments made waterproof by applying tar, rubber, or some other substance. For Cape of Good Hope, see p. 173, n. 4 and p. 336.
5. See p. 17, n. 8.

with the rattle of iron things as if a man's body had been tumbling helplessly amongst the main pump-rods. Before we could realise the situation, Mr. Baker's voice was heard very near and a little impatient:—"Haul away, men! Lay back on that rope!" And we did lay back on the rope with great alacrity. As if nothing had happened, the chief mate went on trimming the yards with his usual and exasperating fastidiousness. We didn't at the time see anything of Donkin, and did not care. Had the chief officer thrown him overboard, no man would have said as much as "Hallo! he's gone!" But, in truth, no great harm was done—even if Donkin did lose one of his front teeth. We perceived this in the morning, and preserved a ceremonious silence: the etiquette of the forecastle commanded us to be blind and dumb in such a case, and we cherished the decencies of our life more than ordinary landsmen respect theirs. Charley, with unpardonable want of *savoir vivre*,[6] yelled out:—"'Ave you been to your dentyst? . . . Hurt ye, didn't it?" He got a box on the ear from one of his best friends. The boy was surprised, and remained plunged in grief for at least three hours. We were sorry for him, but youth requires even more discipline than age. Donkin grinned venomously. From that day he became pitiless; told Jimmy that he was a "black fraud"; hinted to us that we were an imbecile lot, daily taken in by a vulgar nigger. And Jimmy seemed to like the fellow!

Singleton lived untouched by human emotions. Taciturn and unsmiling, he breathed amongst us—in that alone resembling the rest of the crowd. We were trying to be decent chaps, and found it jolly difficult; we oscillated between the desire of virtue and the fear of ridicule; we wished to save ourselves from the pain of remorse, but did not want to be made the contemptible dupes of our sentiment. Jimmy's hateful accomplice seemed to have blown with his impure breath undreamt-of subtleties into our hearts. We were disturbed and cowardly. That we knew. Singleton seemed to know nothing, understand nothing. We had thought him till then as wise as he looked, but now we dared, at times, suspect him of being stupid—from old age. One day, however, at dinner, as we sat on our boxes round a tin dish that stood on the deck within the circle of our feet, Jimmy expressed his general disgust with men and things in words that were particularly disgusting. Singleton lifted his head. We became mute. The old man, addressing Jimmy, asked:—"Are you dying?" Thus interrogated, James Wait appeared horribly startled and confused. We all were startled. Mouths remained open; hearts thumped; eyes blinked; a dropped tin fork rattled in the dish; a man rose as if to go out, and stood still. In less than a minute Jimmy pulled himself together.—"Why? Can't you see I am?" he answered

6. To know how to live (French).

shakily. Singleton lifted a piece of soaked biscuit ("his teeth"—he declared—"had no edge on them now") to his lips.—"Well, get on with your dying," he said with venerable mildness; "don't raise a blamed fuss with us over that job. We can't help you." Jimmy fell back in his bunk, and for a long time lay very still wiping the perspiration off his chin. The dinner-tins were put away quickly. On deck we discussed the incident in whispers. Some showed a chuckling exultation. Many looked grave. Wamibo, after long periods of staring dreaminess, attempted abortive smiles; and one of the young Scandinavians, much tormented by doubt, ventured in the second dog-watch to approach Singleton (the old man did not encourage us much to speak to him) and ask sheepishly:—"You think he will die?" Singleton looked up.—"Why, of course he will die," he said deliberately. This seemed decisive. It was promptly imparted to every one by him who had consulted the oracle.[7] Shy and eager, he would step up and with averted gaze recite his formula:—"Old Singleton says he will die." It was a relief! At last we knew that our compassion would not be misplaced, and we could again smile without misgivings—but we reckoned without Donkin. Donkin "didn't want to 'ave no truck with 'em dirty furriners." When Neillssen came to him with the news: "Singleton says he will die," he answered him by a spiteful "And so will you—you fat-headed Dutchman. Wish you Dutchmen were hall dead—'stead comin' takin' our money hinto your starvin' country." We were appalled. We perceived that after all Singleton's answer meant nothing. We began to hate him for making fun of us. All our certitudes were going; we were on doubtful terms with our officers; the cook had given us up for lost; we had overheard the boatswain's opinion that "we were a crowd of softies." We suspected Jimmy, one another, and even our very selves. We did not know what to do. At every insignificant turn of our humble life we met Jimmy overbearing and blocking the way, arm-in-arm with his awful and veiled familiar. It was a weird servitude.

It began a week after leaving Bombay and came on us stealthily like any other great misfortune. Every one had remarked that Jimmy from the first was very slack at his work; but we thought it simply the outcome of his philosophy of life. Donkin said:—"You put no more weight on a rope than a bloody sparrer."[8] He disdained him. Belfast, ready for a fight, exclaimed provokingly:—"You don't kill yourself, old man!"—"Would *you*?" he retorted with extreme scorn—and Belfast

---

7. In ancient Greece, the instrument through which the gods were believed to speak or prophesy.
8. Conrad's rendition of a Cockney accent for *sparrow*. In a September 1920 letter to C. S. Evans (1883–1944), Conrad acknowledged that he failed to represent a Cockney accent consistently accurately (*CL* 7:174).

retired. One morning, as we were washing decks, Mr. Baker called
to him:—"Bring your broom over here, Wait." He strolled languidly.
"Move yourself! Ough!" grunted Mr. Baker; "what's the matter with
your hind legs?" He stopped dead short. He gazed slowly with eyes
that bulged out, with an expression audacious and sad.—"It isn't
my legs," he said, "it's my lungs." Everybody listened.—"What's . . .
Ough! . . . What's wrong with them?" inquired Mr. Baker. All the
watch stood around on the wet deck, grinning, and with brooms
or buckets in their hands. He said mournfully:—"Going—or
gone. Can't you see I'm a dying man? I know it!" Mr. Baker was
disgusted.—"Then why the devil did you ship aboard here?"—"I
must live till I die—mustn't I?" he replied. The grins became
audible.—"Go off the deck—get out of my sight," said Mr. Baker. He
was nonplussed. It was an unique experience. James Wait, obedient, dropped his broom, and walked slowly forward. A burst of
laughter followed him. It was too funny. All hands laughed. . . .
They laughed! . . . Alas!

He became the tormentor of all our moments; he was worse than
a nightmare. You couldn't see that there was anything wrong with
him: a nigger does not show. He was not very fat—certainly—but
then he was no leaner than other niggers we had known. He
coughed often, but the most prejudiced person could perceive that,
mostly, he coughed when it suited his purpose. He wouldn't, or
couldn't, do his work—and he wouldn't lie-up. One day he would
skip aloft with the best of them, and next time we would be obliged
to risk our lives to get his limp body down. He was reported, he was
examined; he was remonstrated with, threatened, cajoled, lectured.
He was called into the cabin to interview the captain. There were
wild rumours. It was said he had cheeked the old man; it was said
he had frightened him. Charley maintained that the "skipper, wee-
pin' 'as giv' 'im 'is blessin' an' a pot of jam.'" Knowles had it from the
steward that the unspeakable Jimmy had been reeling against the
cabin furniture; that he had groaned; that he had complained of
general brutality and disbelief; and had ended by coughing all over
the old man's meteorological journals which were then spread on
the table. At any rate, Wait returned forward supported by the
steward, who, in a pained and shocked voice, entreated us:—"Here!
Catch hold of him, one of you. He is to lie-up." Jimmy drank a tin
mugful of coffee, and, after bullying first one and then another,
went to bed. He remained there most of the time, but when it suited
him would come on deck and appear amongst us. He was scornful
and brooding; he looked ahead upon the sea; and no one could tell
what was the meaning of that black man sitting apart in a meditative attitude and as motionless as a carving.

He refused steadily all medicine; he threw sago[9] and cornflour overboard till the steward got tired of bringing it to him. He asked for paregoric. They sent him a big bottle; enough to poison a wilderness of babies. He kept it between his mattress and the deal lining of the ship's side; and nobody ever saw him take a dose. Donkin abused him to his face, jeered at him while he gasped; and the same day Wait would lend him a warm jersey. Once Donkin reviled him for half an hour; reproached him with the extra work his malingering gave to the watch; and ended by calling him "a black-faced swine." Under the spell of our accursed perversity we were horror-struck. But Jimmy positively seemed to revel in that abuse. It made him look cheerful—and Donkin had a pair of old sea boots thrown at him. "Here, you East-end[1] trash," boomed Wait, "you may have that."

At last Mr. Baker had to tell the captain that James Wait was disturbing the peace of the ship. "Knock discipline on the head—he will, Ough," grunted Mr. Baker. As a matter of fact, the starboard-watch came as near as possible to refusing duty, when ordered one morning by the boatswain to wash out their forecastle. It appears Jimmy objected to a wet floor—and that morning we were in a compassionate mood. We thought the boatswain a brute, and, practically, told him so. Only Mr. Baker's delicate tact prevented an all-fired row: he refused to take us seriously. He came bustling forward, and called us many unpolite names, but in such a hearty and seamanlike manner that we began to feel ashamed of ourselves. In truth, we thought him much too good a sailor to annoy him willingly: and after all Jimmy might have been a fraud—probably was! The forecastle got a clean up that morning; but in the afternoon a sick-bay was fitted up in the deck-house. It was a nice little cabin opening on deck, and with two berths. Jimmy's belongings were transported there, and then—notwithstanding his protests—Jimmy himself. He said he couldn't walk. Four men carried him on a blanket. He complained that he would have to die there alone, like a dog. We grieved for him, and were delighted to have him removed from the forecastle. We attended him as before. The galley was next door, and the cook looked in many times a day. Wait became a little more cheerful. Knowles affirmed having heard him laugh to himself in peals one day. Others had seen him walking about on deck at night. His little place, with the door ajar on a long hook, was always full of tobacco smoke. We spoke through the crack cheerfully, sometimes abusively, as we passed by, intent on our work. He fascinated

9. A starch made from the pith of the trunks of certain palms and cycads and used primarily as a food item, often boiled in milk or water.
1. See p. 52, n. 5.

us. He would never let doubt die. He overshadowed the ship. Invulnerable in his promise of speedy corruption he trampled on our self-respect, he demonstrated to us daily our want of moral courage; he tainted our lives. Had we been a miserable gang of wretched immortals, unhallowed alike by hope and fear, he could not have lorded it over us with a more pitiless assertion of his sublime privilege.

III

Meantime the *Narcissus*, with square yards, ran out of the fair monsoon. She drifted slowly, swinging round and round the compass, through a few days of baffling light airs. Under the patter of short warm showers, grumbling men whirled the heavy yards from side to side; they caught hold of the soaked ropes with groans and sighs, while their officers, sulky and dripping with rain water, unceasingly ordered them about in wearied voices. During the short respites they looked with disgust into the smarting palms of their stiff hands, and asked one another bitterly:—"Who would be a sailor if he could be a farmer?" All the tempers were spoilt, and no man cared what he said. One black night, when the watch, panting in the heat and half-drowned with the rain, had been through four mortal hours hunted from brace to brace, Belfast declared that he would "chuck going to sea for ever and go in a steamer." This was excessive, no doubt. Captain Allistoun, with great self-control, would mutter sadly to Mr. Baker:—"It is not so bad—not so bad," when he had managed to shove, and dodge, and manœuvre his smart ship through sixty miles in twenty-four hours. From the door-step of the little cabin, Jimmy, chin in hand, watched our distasteful labours with insolent and melancholy eyes. We spoke to him gently—and out of his sight exchanged sour smiles.

Then, again, with a fair wind and under a clear sky, the ship went on piling up the South Latitude.[2] She passed outside Madagascar[3] and Mauritius without a glimpse of the land. Extra lashings were put on the spare spars. Hatches were looked to. The steward in his leisure moments and with a worried air tried to fit washboards to the cabin doors. Stout canvas was bent with care. Anxious eyes looked to the westward, towards the Cape of Storms.[4] The ship began to dip

---

2. South of the equator.
3. A large island off the east coast of Africa, a French colony from 1896 until 1960. See p. 336.
4. The original European name for the Cape of Good Hope. The Portuguese navigator Bartolomeu Dias (1450?–1500) first rounded the cape in 1488 and named it the Cape of Storms because of its stormy weather. King John II of Portugal (1455–1495) later renamed it the Cape of Good Hope because of its commercial significance. See p. 336.

into a southwest swell, and the softly luminous sky of low latitudes took on a harder sheen from day to day above our heads: it arched high above the ship, vibrating and pale, like an immense dome of steel, resonant with the deep voice of freshening gales. The sunshine gleamed cold on the white curls of black waves. Before the strong breath of westerly squalls[5] the ship, with reduced sail, lay slowly over, obstinate and yielding. She drove to and fro in the unceasing endeavour to fight her way through the invisible violence of the winds: she pitched headlong into dark smooth hollows; she struggled upwards over the snowy ridges of great running seas; she rolled, restless, from side to side, like a thing in pain. Enduring and valiant, she answered to the call of men; and her slim spars waving for ever in abrupt semicircles, seemed to beckon in vain for help towards the stormy sky.

It was a bad winter off the Cape that year. The relieved helmsmen came off flapping their arms, or ran stamping hard and blowing into swollen, red fingers. The watch on deck dodged the sting of cold sprays or, crouching in sheltered corners, watched dismally the high and merciless seas boarding the ship time after time in unappeasable fury. Water tumbled in cataracts over the forecastle doors. You had to dash through a waterfall to get into your damp bed. The men turned in wet and turned out stiff to face the redeeming and ruthless exactions of their glorious and obscure fate. Far aft, and peering watchfully to windward, the officers could be seen through the mist of squalls. They stood by the weather-rail, holding on grimly, straight and glistening in their long coats; then, at times, in the disordered plunges of the hard-driven ship, they appeared high up, attentive, tossing violently above the grey line of a clouded horizon, and in motionless attitudes.

They watched the weather and the ship as men on shore watch the momentous chances of fortune. Captain Allistoun never left the deck, as though he had been part of the ship's fittings. Now and then the steward, shivering, but always in shirt sleeves, would struggle towards him with some hot coffee, half of which the gale blew out of the cup before it reached the master's lips. He drank what was left gravely in one long gulp, while heavy sprays pattered loudly on his oilskin coat, the seas swishing broke about his high boots; and he never took his eyes off the ship. He watched her every motion; he kept his gaze riveted upon her as a loving man who watches the unselfish toil of a delicate woman upon the slender thread of whose existence is hung the whole meaning and joy of the

---

5. The prevailing winds in the Southern Hemisphere. They are particularly strong between the fortieth and fiftieth parallels, where they are known as the "roaring forties."

world. We all watched her. She was beautiful and had a weakness.[6]
We loved her no less for that. We admired her qualities aloud, we
boasted of them to one another, as though they had been our own,
and the consciousness of her only fault we kept buried in the silence
of our profound affection. She was born in the thundering peal of
hammers beating upon iron, in black eddies of smoke, under a grey
sky, on the banks of the Clyde.[7] The clamorous and sombre stream
gives birth to things of beauty that float away into the sunshine of
the world to be loved by men. The *Narcissus* was one of that perfect
brood. Less perfect than many perhaps, but she was ours, and, consequently, incomparable. We were proud of her. In Bombay, ignorant landlubbers alluded to her as that "pretty grey ship." Pretty! A
scurvy meed[8] of commendation! We knew she was the most magnificent sea-boat ever launched. We tried to forget that, like many
good sea-boats, she was at times rather crank.[9] She was exacting.
She wanted care in loading and handling, and no one knew exactly
how much care would be enough. Such are the imperfections of
mere men! The ship knew, and sometimes would correct the presumptuous human ignorance by the wholesome discipline of fear.
We had heard ominous stories about past voyages. The cook (tech-
nically a seaman, but in reality no sailor)—the cook, when unstrung
by some misfortune, such as the rolling over of a saucepan, would
mutter gloomily while he wiped the floor:—"There! Look at what
she has done! Some voy'ge she will drown all hands! You'll see if she
won't." To which the steward, snatching in the galley a moment
to draw breath in the hurry of his worried life, would remark
philosophically:—"Those that see won't tell, anyhow. I don't want
to see it." We derided those fears. Our hearts went out to the old man
when he pressed her hard so as to make her hold her own, hold to
every inch gained to windward; when he made her, under reefed
sails, leap obliquely at enormous waves. The men, knitted together
aft into a ready group by the first sharp order of an officer coming to
take charge of the deck in bad weather:—"Keep handy the watch,"
stood admiring her valiance. Their eyes blinked in the wind; their
dark faces were wet with drops of water more salt and bitter than
human tears; beards and moustaches, soaked, hung straight and

---

6. Instability is the ship's weakness; see p. 175, n. 9. In a December 13, 1920, letter to G. G.
   Frisbee (1874–1947), Conrad remarked of the *Narcissus* during his voyage aboard: "the
   trouble with the *Narcissus* was that she had not enough ballast put into her. Not my fault,
   as I did not join her, coming overland from Madras to Bombay, till the ground-tier was
   laid" (CL 7:218).
7. The River Clyde in south-central Scotland, known particularly for shipbuilding and
   trade.
8. A reward (archaic).
9. Tending to lean to one side.

dripping like fine seaweed. They were fantastically misshapen; in high boots, in hats like helmets, and swaying clumsily, stiff and bulky in glistening oilskins, they resembled men strangely equipped for some fabulous adventure. Whenever she rose easily to a towering green sea, elbows dug ribs, faces brightened, lips murmured:—"Didn't she do it cleverly," and all the heads turning like one watched with sardonic grins the foiled wave go roaring to leeward, white with the foam of a monstrous rage. But when she had not been quick enough and, struck heavily, lay over trembling under the blow, we clutched at ropes, and looking up at the narrow bands of drenched and strained sails waving desperately aloft, we thought in our hearts:—"No wonder. Poor thing!"

The thirty-second day out of Bombay began inauspiciously. In the morning a sea smashed one of the galley doors. We dashed in through lots of steam and found the cook very wet and indignant with the ship:—"She's getting worse every day. She's trying to drown me in front of my own stove!" He was very angry. We pacified him, and the carpenter, though washed away twice from there, managed to repair the door. Through that accident our dinner was not ready till late, but it didn't matter in the end because Knowles, who went to fetch it, got knocked down by a sea and the dinner went over the side. Captain Allistoun, looking more hard and thin-lipped than ever, hung on to full topsails and foresail, and would not notice that the ship, asked to do too much, appeared to lose heart altogether for the first time since we knew her. She refused to rise, and bored her way sullenly through the seas. Twice running, as though she had been blind or weary of life, she put her nose deliberately into a big wave and swept the decks from end to end. As the boatswain observed with marked annoyance, while we were splashing about in a body to try and save a worthless wash-tub:—"Every blooming thing in the ship is going overboard this afternoon." Venerable Singleton broke his habitual silence and said with a glance aloft:—"The old man's in a temper with the weather, but it's no good bein' angry with the winds of heaven." Jimmy had shut his door, of course. We knew he was dry and comfortable within his little cabin, and in our absurd way were pleased one moment, exasperated the next, by that certitude. Donkin skulked shamelessly, uneasy and miserable. He grumbled:—"I'm perishin' with cold houtside in bloomin' wet rags, an' that 'ere black sojer[1] sits dry on a blamed chest full of bloomin' clothes; blank his black soul!" We took no notice of him; we hardly gave a thought to Jimmy and his bosom friend. There was no leisure for idle probing of hearts. Sails blew adrift. Things broke loose. Cold and wet, we were washed about the

1. Conrad's rendition of Donkin's pronunciation of *soldier*.

deck while trying to repair damages. The ship tossed about, shaken furiously, like a toy in the hand of a lunatic. Just at sunset there was a rush to shorten sail before the menace of a sombre hail cloud. The hard gust of wind came brutal like the blow of a fist. The ship relieved of her canvas in time received it pluckily: she yielded reluctantly to the violent onset; then, coming up with a stately and irresistible motion, brought her spars to windward in the teeth of the screeching squall. Out of the abysmal darkness of the black cloud overhead white hail streamed on her, rattled on the rigging, leaped in handfuls off the yards, rebounded on the deck—round and gleaming in the murky turmoil like a shower of pearls. It passed away. For a moment a livid[2] sun shot horizontally the last rays of sinister light between the hills of steep, rolling waves. Then a wild night rushed in—stamped out in a great howl that dismal remnant of a stormy day.

There was no sleep on board that night. Most seamen remember in their life one or two such nights of a culminating gale. Nothing seems left of the whole universe but darkness, clamour, fury—and the ship. And like the last vestige of a shattered creation she drifts, bearing an anguished remnant of sinful mankind, through the distress, tumult, and pain of an avenging terror. No one slept in the forecastle. The tin oil-lamp suspended on a long string, smoking, described wide circles; wet clothing made dark heaps on the glistening floor; a thin layer of water rushed to and fro. In the bed-places men lay booted, resting on elbows and with open eyes. Hung-up suits of oilskin swung out and in, lively and disquieting like reckless ghosts of decapitated seamen dancing in a tempest. No one spoke and all listened. Outside the night moaned and sobbed to the accompaniment of a continuous loud tremor as of innumerable drums beating far off. Shrieks passed through the air. Tremendous dull blows made the ship tremble while she rolled under the weight of the seas toppling on her deck. At times she soared up swiftly as if to leave this earth for ever, then during interminable moments fell through a void with all the hearts on board of her standing still, till a frightful shock, expected and sudden, started them off again with a big thump. After every dislocating jerk of the ship, Wamibo, stretched full length, his face on the pillow, groaned slightly with the pain of his tormented universe. Now and then, for the fraction of an intolerable second, the ship, in the fiercer burst of a terrible uproar, remained on her side, vibrating and still, with a stillness more appalling than the wildest motion. Then upon all those prone bodies a stir would pass, a shiver of suspense. A man would protrude his anxious head and a pair of eyes glistened in the sway of light glaring wildly. Some

2. See p. 12, n. 4.

moved their legs a little as if making ready to jump out. But several, motionless on their backs and with one hand gripping hard the edge of the bunk, smoked nervously with quick puffs, staring upwards; immobilised in a great craving for peace.

At midnight, orders were given to furl the fore and mizzen topsails. With immense efforts men crawled aloft through a merciless buffeting, saved the canvas, and crawled down almost exhausted, to bear in panting silence the cruel battering of the seas. Perhaps for the first time in the history of the merchant service the watch, told to go below, did not leave the deck, as if compelled to remain there by the fascination of a venomous violence. At every heavy gust men, huddled together, whispered to one another:—"It can blow no harder"— and presently the gale would give them the lie with a piercing shriek, and drive their breath back into their throats. A fierce squall seemed to burst asunder the thick mass of sooty vapours; and above the wrack of torn clouds glimpses could be caught of the high moon rushing backwards with frightful speed over the sky, right into the wind's eye. Many hung their heads, muttering that it "turned their inwards out" to look at it. Soon the clouds closed up, and the world again became a raging, blind darkness that howled, flinging at the lonely ship salt sprays and sleet.

About half-past seven the pitchy obscurity round us turned a ghastly grey, and we knew that the sun had risen. This unnatural and threatening daylight, in which we could see one another's wild eyes and drawn faces, was only an added tax on our endurance. The horizon seemed to have come on all sides within arm's length of the ship. Into that narrowed circle furious seas leaped in, struck, and leaped out. A rain of salt, heavy drops flew aslant like mist. The main-topsail had to be goose-winged, and with stolid resignation every one prepared to go aloft once more; but the officers yelled, pushed back, and at last we understood that no more men would be allowed to go on the yard than were absolutely necessary for the work. As at any moment the masts were likely to be jumped out or blown overboard, we concluded that the captain didn't want to see all his crowd go over the side at once. That was reasonable. The watch then on duty, led by Mr. Creighton, began to struggle up the rigging. The wind flattened them against the ratlines; then, easing a little, would let them ascend a couple of steps; and again, with a sudden gust, pin all up the shrouds the whole crawling line in attitudes of crucifixion. The other watch plunged down on the main deck to haul up the sail. Men's heads bobbed up as the watch flung them irresistibly from side to side. Mr. Baker grunted encouragingly in our midst, spluttering and blowing amongst the tangled ropes like an energetic porpoise. Favoured by an ominous and untrustworthy lull, the work was done without any one being lost either off the deck or from the yard. For the

moment the gale seemed to take off, and the ship, as if grateful for
our efforts, plucked up heart and made better weather of it.

At eight the men off duty, watching their chance, ran forward over
the flooded deck to get some rest. The other half of the crew remained
aft for their turn of "seeing her through her trouble," as they expressed
it. The two mates urged the master to go below. Mr. Baker grunted in
his ear:—"Ough! surely now. . . . Ough! . . . confidence in us. . . .
nothing more to do. . . . she must lay it out or go. Ough! Ough!" Tall
young Mr. Creighton smiled down at him cheerfully:—". . . . She's
right as a trivet![3] Take a spell, sir." He looked at them stonily with
bloodshot, sleepless eyes. The rims of his eyelids were scarlet, and
he moved his jaw unceasingly with a slow effort, as though he had
been masticating a lump of india-rubber.[4] He shook his head. He
repeated:—"Never mind me. I must see it out—I must see it out," but
he consented to sit down for a moment on the skylight, with his hard
face turned unflinchingly to windward. The sea spat at it—and, stoi-
cal, it streamed with water as though he had been weeping. On the
weather side of the poop the watch, hanging on to the mizzen-rigging
and to one another, tried to exchange encouraging words. Singleton,
at the wheel, yelled out:—"Look out for yourselves!" His voice reached
them in a warning whisper. They were startled.

A big, foaming sea came out of the mist; it made for the ship,
roaring wildly, and in its rush it looked as mischievous and discom-
posing as a madman with an axe. One or two, shouting, scrambled
up the rigging; most, with a convulsive catch of the breath, held
on where they stood. Singleton dug his knees under the wheel-box,
and carefully eased the helm to the headlong pitch of the ship, but
without taking his eyes off the coming wave. It towered close-to
and high, like a wall of green glass topped with snow. The ship rose
to it as though she had soared on wings, and for a moment rested
poised upon the foaming crest, as if she had been a great sea-bird.
Before we could draw breath a heavy gust struck her, another roller
took her unfairly under the weather bow, she gave a toppling lurch,
and filled her decks. Captain Allistoun leaped up, and fell; Archie
rolled over him, screaming:—"She will rise!" She gave another
lurch to leeward; the lower dead-eyes dipped heavily; the men's feet
flew from under them, and they hung kicking above the slanting
poop. They could see the ship putting her side in the water, and
shouted all together:—"She's going!" Forward the forecastle doors
flew open, and the watch below were seen leaping out one after
another, throwing their arms up; and, falling on hands and knees,
scrambled aft on all fours along the high side of the deck, sloping

3. An iron tripod for holding a pot over a fire. The phrase means that something is in
   perfect working order, referring to a trivet's stability.
4. See p. 22, n. 1. "Masticating": chewing.

more than the roof of a house. From leeward the seas rose, pursuing them; they looked wretched in a hopeless struggle, like vermin fleeing before a flood; they fought up the weather ladder of the poop one after another, half naked and staring wildly; and as soon as they got up they shot to leeward in clusters, with closed eyes, till they brought up heavily with their ribs against the iron stanchions of the rail; then, groaning, they rolled in a confused mass. The immense volume of water thrown forward by the last scend of the ship had burst the lee door of the forecastle. They could see their chests, pillows, blankets, clothing, come out floating upon the sea. While they struggled back to windward they looked in dismay. The straw beds swam high, the blankets, spread out, undulated; while the chests, waterlogged and with a heavy list, pitched heavily, like dismasted hulks, before they sank; Archie's big coat passed with outspread arms, resembling a drowned seaman floating with his head under water. Men were slipping down while trying to dig their fingers into the planks; others, jammed in corners, rolled enormous eyes. They all yelled unceasingly:—"The masts! Cut! Cut![5] . . ." A black squall howled !ow over the ship, that lay on her side with the weather yard-arms pointing to the clouds; while the tall masts, inclined nearly to the horizon, seemed to be of an unmeasurable length. The carpenter let go his hold, rolled against the skylight, and began to crawl to the cabin entrance, where a big axe was kept ready for just such an emergency. At that moment the topsail sheet parted, the end of the heavy chain racketed[6] aloft, and sparks of red fire streamed down through the flying sprays. The sail flapped once with a jerk that seemed to tear our hearts out through our teeth, and instantly changed into a bunch of fluttering narrow ribbons that tied themselves into knots and became quiet along the yard. Captain Allistoun struggled, managed to stand up with his face near the deck, upon which men swung on the ends of ropes, like nest robbers upon a cliff. One of his feet was on somebody's chest; his face was purple; his lips moved. He yelled also; he yelled, bending down:—"No! No!" Mr. Baker, one leg over the binnacle-stand, roared out:—"Did you say no? Not cut?" He shook his head madly. "No! No!" Between his legs the crawling carpenter heard, collapsed at once, and lay full length in the angle of the skylight. Voices took up the shout—"No! No!" Then all became still. They waited for the ship to turn over altogether, and shake them out into the sea; and upon the terrific noise of wind and sea not a murmur of remonstrance came out from those men, who each would have given ever so many years of life to see "them damned sticks go overboard!" They all

5. The crew want to cut the masts to right the ship.
6. Struck as if with a racket.

believed it their only chance; but a little hard-faced man shook his grey head and shouted "No!" without giving them as much as a glance. They were silent, and gasped. They gripped rails, they had wound ropes'-ends under their arms; they clutched ringbolts, they crawled in heaps where there was foothold; they held on with both arms, hooked themselves to anything to windward with elbows, with chins, almost with their teeth: and some, unable to crawl away from where they had been flung, felt the sea leap up, striking against their backs as they struggled upwards. Singleton had stuck to the wheel. His hair flew out in the wind; the gale seemed to take its life-long adversary by the beard and shake his old head. He wouldn't let go, and, with his knees forced between the spokes, flew up and down like a man on a bough. As Death appeared unready, they began to look about. Donkin, caught by one foot in a loop of some rope, hung, head down, below us, and yelled, with his face to the deck:—"Cut! Cut!" Two men lowered themselves cautiously to him; others hauled on the rope. They caught him up, shoved him into a safer place, held him. He shouted curses at the master, shook his fist at him with horrible blasphemies, called upon us in filthy words to "Cut! Don't mind that murdering fool! Cut, some of you!" One of his rescuers struck him a back-handed blow over the mouth; his head banged on the deck, and he became suddenly very quiet, with a white face, breathing hard, and with a few drops of blood trickling from his cut lip. On the lee side another man could be seen stretched out as if stunned; only the washboard prevented him from going over the side. It was the steward. We had to sling him up like a bale, for he was paralysed with fright. He had rushed up out of the pantry when he felt the ship go over, and had rolled down helplessly, clutching a china mug. It was not broken. With difficulty we tore it from him, and when he saw it in our hands he was amazed. "Where did you get that thing?" he kept on asking, in a trembling voice. His shirt was blown to shreds; the ripped sleeves flapped like wings. Two men made him fast, and, doubled over the rope that held him, he resembled a bundle of wet rags. Mr. Baker crawled along the line of men, asking:—"Are you all there?" and looking them over. Some blinked vacantly, others shook convulsively; Wamibo's head hung over his breast; and in painful attitudes, cut by lashings, exhausted with clutching, screwed up in corners, they breathed heavily. Their lips twitched, and at every sickening heave of the overturned ship they opened them wide as if to shout. The cook, embracing a wooden stanchion, unconsciously repeated a prayer. In every short interval of the fiendish noises around he could be heard there, without cap or slippers, imploring in that storm the Master of our lives not to lead him into temptation. Soon he also became silent. In all that crowd of cold and hungry men, waiting wearily for a violent death, not a voice was heard; they were mute, and in sombre thoughtfulness listened to the horrible imprecations of the gale.

Hours passed. They were sheltered by the heavy inclination of the ship from the wind that rushed in one long unbroken moan above their heads, but cold rain showers fell at times into the uneasy calm of their refuge. Under the torment of that new infliction a pair of shoulders would writhe a little. Teeth chattered. The sky was clearing, and bright sunshine gleamed over the ship. After every burst of battering seas, vivid and fleeting rainbows arched over the drifting hull in the flick of sprays. The gale was ending in a clear blow, which gleamed and cut like a knife. Between two bearded shellbacks Charley, fastened with somebody's long muffler to a deck ringbolt, wept quietly, with rare tears wrung out by bewilderment, cold, hunger, and general misery. One of his neighbours punched him in the ribs, asking roughly:—"What's the matter with your cheek? In fine weather there's no holding you, youngster." Turning about with prudence he worked himself out of his coat and threw it over the boy. The other man closed up, muttering:—" 'Twill make a bloomin' man of you, sonny." They flung their arms over and pressed against him. Charley drew his feet up and his eye-lids dropped. Sighs were heard, as men, perceiving that they were not to be "drowned in a hurry," tried easier positions. Mr. Creighton, who had hurt his leg, lay amongst us with compressed lips. Some fellows belonging to his watch set about securing him better. Without a word or a glance he lifted his arms one after another to facilitate the operation, and not a muscle moved in his stern, young face. They asked him with solicitude:—"Easier now, sir?" He answered with a curt:—"That'll do." He was a hard young officer, but many of his watch used to say they liked him well enough because he had "such a gentlemanly way of damning us up and down the deck." Others, unable to discern such fine shades of refinement, respected him for his smartness. For the first time since the ship had gone on her beam ends Captain Allistoun gave a short glance down at his men. He was almost upright—one foot against the side of the skylight, one knee on the deck; and with the end of the vang round his waist swung back and forth with his gaze fixed ahead, watchful, like a man looking out for a sign. Before his eyes the ship, with half her deck below water, rose and fell on heavy seas that rushed from under her flashing in the cold sunshine. We began to think she was wonderfully buoyant—considering. Confident voices were heard shouting:—"She'll do, boys!" Belfast exclaimed with fervour:—"I would giv' a month's pay for a draw at a pipe!" One or two, passing dry tongues on their salt lips, muttered something about a "drink of water." The cook, as if inspired, scrambled up with his breast against the poop water-cask and looked in. There was a little at the bottom. He yelled, waving his arms, and two men began to crawl backwards and forwards with the mug. We had a good mouthful all round. The master shook his head impatiently, refusing. When it came to Charley one of his neighbours shouted:— "That bloomin' boy's asleep." He slept as though he had been dosed with narcotics. They let him be. Singleton held to the wheel with one hand while he drank, bending down to shelter his lips from the wind. Wamibo had to be poked and yelled at before he saw the mug held before his eyes. Knowles said sagaciously:—"It's better'n a tot o' rum." Mr. Baker grunted:—"Thank ye." Mr. Creighton drank and nodded. Donkin gulped greedily, glaring over the rim. Belfast made us laugh when with grimacing mouth he shouted:—"Pass it this way. We're all taytottlers here." The master, presented with the mug again by a crouching man, who screamed up at him:—"We all had a drink, captain," groped for it without ceasing to look ahead, and handed it back stiffly as though he could not spare half a glance away from the ship. Faces brightened. We shouted to the cook:—"Well done, doctor!" He sat to leeward, propped by the water-cask and yelled back abundantly, but the seas were breaking in thunder just then, and we only caught snatches that sounded like: "Providence" and "born again." He was at his old game of preaching. We made friendly but derisive gestures at him, and from below he lifted one arm, holding on with the other, moved his lips; he beamed up to us, straining his voice—earnest, and ducking his head before the sprays.

Suddenly some one cried:—"Where's Jimmy?" and we were appalled once more. On the end of the row the boatswain shouted hoarsely:— "Has any one seed him come out?" Voices exclaimed dismally:— "Drowned—is he? . . . No! In his cabin! . . . Good Lord! . . . Caught like a bloomin' rat in a trap. . . . Couldn't open his door. . . . Aye! She went over too quick and the water jammed it. . . . Poor beggar! . . . No help for 'im. . . . Let's go and see. . . ." "Damn him, who could go?" screamed Donkin.—"Nobody expects you to," growled the man next to him; "you're only a thing."—"Is there half a chance to get at 'im?" inquired two or three men together. Belfast untied himself with blind impetuosity, and all at once shot down to leeward quicker than a flash of lightning. We shouted all together with dismay; but with his legs overboard he held and yelled for a rope. In our extremity nothing could be terrible; so we judged him funny kicking there, and with his scared face. Some one began to laugh, and, as if hysterically infected with screaming merriment, all those haggard men went off laughing, wild-eyed, like a lot of maniacs tied up on a wall. Mr. Baker swung off the binnacle-stand and tendered him one leg. He scrambled up rather scared, and consigning us with abominable words to the "divvle." "You are . . . Ough! You're a foul-mouthed beggar, Craik," grunted Mr. Baker. He answered, stuttering with indignation:—"Look at 'em, sorr. The bloomin' dirty images, laughing at a chum going over-board. Call themselves men, too." But from the break of the poop the boatswain called out:—"Come along," and Belfast crawled away in a hurry to join him. The five men, poised and gazing over the edge of the poop, looked for the best way to get forward. They seemed to hesitate. The others, twisting in their lashings, turning painfully, stared with open lips. Captain Allistoun saw nothing; he seemed with his eyes to hold the ship up in a superhuman concentration of effort. The wind screamed loud in sunshine; columns of spray rose straight up; and in the glitter of rainbows bursting over the trembling hull the men went over cautiously, disappearing from sight with deliberate movements.

They went swinging from belaying-pin to cleat above the seas that beat the half-submerged deck. Their toes scraped the planks. Lumps of green cold water toppled over the bulwark and on their heads. They hung for a moment on strained arms, with the breath knocked out of them, and with closed eyes—then, letting go with one hand, balanced with lolling heads, trying to grab some rope or stanchion further forward. The long-armed and athletic boatswain swung quickly, gripping things with a fist hard as iron, and remembering suddenly snatches of the last letter from his "old woman." Little Belfast scrambled rageously, muttering "cursed nigger." Wamibo's tongue hung out with excitement; and Archie, intrepid and calm, watched his chance to move with intelligent coolness.

When above the side of the house, they let go one after another, and falling heavily, sprawled, pressing their palms to the smooth teak wood. Round them the backwash of waves seethed white and hissing. All the doors had become trap-doors, of course. The first was the galley door. The galley extended from side to side, and they could hear the sea splashing with hollow noises in there. The next door was that of the carpenter's shop. They lifted it, and looked down. The room seemed to have been devastated by an earthquake. Everything in it had tumbled on the bulkhead facing the door, and on the other side of that bulkhead there was Jimmy, dead or alive. The bench, a half-finished meat-safe,[7] saws, chisels, wire rods, axes, crowbars, lay in a heap besprinkled with loose nails. A sharp adze stuck up with a shining edge that gleamed dangerously down there like a wicked smile. The men clung to one another peering. A sickening, sly lurch of the ship nearly sent them overboard in a body. Belfast howled "Here goes!" and leaped down. Archie followed cannily,

7. A ventilated cabinet for storing meat.

catching at shelves that gave way with him, and eased himself in
a great crash of ripped wood. There was hardly room for three men
to move. And in the sunshiny blue square of the door, the boatswain's face, bearded and dark, Wamibo's face, wild and pale,
hung over—watching.

Together they shouted: "Jimmy! Jim!" From above the boatswain
contributed a deep growl: "You . . . Wait!" In a pause, Belfast
entreated: "Jimmy, darlin', are ye aloive?" The boatswain said: "Again!
All together, boys!" All yelled excitedly. Wamibo made noises resembling loud barks. Belfast drummed on the side of the bulkhead with
a piece of iron. All ceased suddenly. The sound of screaming and
hammering went on thin and distinct—like a solo after a chorus. He
was alive. He was screaming and knocking below us with the hurry of
a man prematurely shut up in a coffin. We went to work. We attacked
with desperation the abominable heap of things heavy, of things
sharp, of things clumsy to handle. The boatswain crawled away to
find somewhere a flying end of a rope; and Wamibo, held back by
shouts:—"Don't jump! . . . Don't come in here, muddle-head!"—
remained glaring above us—all shining eyes, gleaming fangs, tumbled hair; resembling an amazed and half-witted fiend gloating over
the extraordinary agitation of the damned. The boatswain adjured us
to "bear a hand,"[8] and a rope descended. We made things fast to it
and they went up spinning, never to be seen by man again. A rage
to fling things overboard possessed us. We worked fiercely, cutting
our hands, and speaking brutally to one another. Jimmy kept up a
distracting row; he screamed piercingly, without drawing breath,
like a tortured woman; he banged with hands and feet. The agony of
his fear wrung our hearts so terribly that we longed to abandon him,
to get out of that place deep as a well and swaying like a tree, to get
out of his hearing, back on the poop where we could wait passively
for death in incomparable repose. We shouted to him to "shut up,
for God's sake." He redoubled his cries. He must have fancied we
could not hear him. Probably he heard his own clamour but faintly.
We could picture him crouching on the edge of the upper berth, letting out with both fists at the wood, in the dark, and with his mouth
wide open for that unceasing cry. Those were loathsome moments.
A cloud driving across the sun would darken the doorway menacingly. Every movement of the ship was pain. We scrambled about
with no room to breathe, and felt frightfully sick. The boatswain
yelled down at us:—"Bear a hand! Bear a hand! We two will be
washed away from here directly if you ain't quick!" Three times a

8. Lend a hand.

sea leaped over the high side and flung bucketfuls of water on our heads. Then Jimmy, startled by the shock, would stop his noise for a moment—waiting for the ship to sink, perhaps—and began again, distressingly loud, as if invigorated by the gust of fear. At the bottom the nails lay in a layer several inches thick. It was ghastly. Every nail in the world, not driven in firmly somewhere, seemed to have found its way into that carpenter's shop. There they were, of all kinds, the remnants of stores from seven voyages. Tin-tacks, copper tacks (sharp as needles), pump nails, with big heads, like tiny iron mushrooms; nails without any heads (horrible); French nails polished and slim. They lay in a solid mass more inabordable[9] than a hedgehog. We hesitated, yearning for a shovel, while Jimmy below us yelled as though he had been flayed. Groaning, we dug our fingers in, and very much hurt, shook our hands, scattering nails and drops of blood. We passed up our hats full of assorted nails to the boatswain, who, as if performing a mysterious and appeasing rite, cast them wide upon a raging sea.

We got to the bulkhead at last. Those were stout planks. She was a ship, well finished in every detail—the *Narcissus* was. They were the stoutest planks ever put into a ship's bulkhead—we thought— and then we perceived that, in our hurry, we had sent all the tools overboard. Absurd little Belfast wanted to break it down with his own weight, and with both feet leaped straight up like a springbok,[1] cursing the Clyde shipwrights for not scamping their work. Incidentally he reviled all North Britain, the rest of the earth, the sea—and all his companions. He swore, as he alighted heavily on his heels, that he would never, never any more associate with any fool that "hadn't savee[2] enough to know his knee from his elbow." He managed by his thumping to scare the last remnant of wits out of Jimmy. We could hear the object of our exasperated solicitude darting to and fro under the planks. He had cracked his voice at last, and could only squeak miserably. His back or else his head rubbed the planks, now here, now there, in a puzzling manner. He squeaked as he dodged the invisible blows. It was more heartrending even than his yells. Suddenly Archie produced a crowbar. He had kept it back; also a small hatchet. We howled with satisfaction. He struck a mighty blow and small chips flew at our eyes. The boatswain above shouted:—"Look out! Look out there. Don't kill the man. Easy does it!' Wamibo, maddened with excitement, hung head down and insanely urged us:—"Hoo! Strook 'im! Hoo! Hoo!" We

9. Inaccessible or unapproachable. Conrad appears to be borrowing the word from French (probably unconsciously).
1. An antelope from South Africa that leaps nearly straight up when startled.
2. Or savvy; intelligence or know how (colloquial).

were afraid he would fall in and kill one of us and, hurriedly, we
entreated the boatswain to "shove the blamed Finn overboard." Then,
all together, we yelled down at the planks:—"Stand from under! Get
forward," and listened. We only heard the deep hum and moan of the
wind above us, the mingled roar and hiss of the seas. The ship, as if
overcome with despair, wallowed lifelessly, and our heads swam with
that unnatural motion. Belfast clamoured:—"For the love of God,
Jimmy, where are ye? . . . Knock! Jimmy darlint![3] . . . Knock! You
bloody black beast! Knock!" He was as quiet as a dead man inside a
grave; and, like men standing above a grave, we were on the verge
of tears—but with vexation, the strain, the fatigue; with the great
longing to be done with it, to get away, and lay down to rest somewhere where we could see our danger and breathe. Archie shouted:—
"Gi'e me room!" We crouched behind him, guarding our heads, and
he struck time after time in the joint of planks. They cracked. Suddenly the crowbar went half-way in through a splintered oblong hole.
It must have missed Jimmy's head by less than an inch. Archie withdrew it quickly, and that infamous nigger rushed at the hole, put his
lips to it, and whispered "Help" in an almost extinct voice; he pressed
his head to it, trying madly to get out through that opening one inch
wide and three inches long. In our disturbed state we were absolutely paralysed by his incredible action. It seemed impossible to
drive him away. Even Archie at last lost his composure. "If ye don't
clear oot I'll drive the crowbar thro' your head," he shouted in a
determined voice. He meant what he said, and his earnestness
seemed to make an impression on Jimmy. He disappeared suddenly,
and we set to prising and tearing at the planks with the eagerness
of men trying to get at a mortal enemy, and spurred by the desire to
tear him limb from limb. The wood split, cracked, gave way. Belfast
plunged in head and shoulders and groped viciously. "I've got' 'im!
Got 'im," he shouted. "Oh! There! . . . He's gone; I've got 'im! . . . Pull
at my legs! . . . Pull!" Wamibo hooted unceasingly. The boatswain
shouted directions:—"Catch hold of his hair, Belfast; pull straight
up, you two! . . . Pull fair!" We pulled fair. We pulled Belfast out with
a jerk, and dropped him with disgust. In a sitting posture, purple-
faced, he sobbed despairingly:—"How can I hold on to 'is blooming
short wool?" Suddenly Jimmy's head and shoulders appeared. He
stuck half-way, and with rolling eyes foamed at our feet. We flew at
him with brutal impatience, we tore the shirt off his back, we tugged
at his ears, we panted over him; and all at once he came away in our
hands as though somebody had let go his legs. With the same movement, without a pause, we swung him up. His breath whistled, he

---

3. Conrad's rendition of Irish dialect for *darling*.

kicked our upturned faces, he grasped two pairs of arms above his head, and he squirmed up with such precipitation that he seemed positively to escape from our hands like a bladder[4] full of gas. Streaming with perspiration, we swarmed up the rope, and, coming into the blast of cold wind, gasped like men plunged into icy water. With burning faces we shivered to the very marrow of our bones. Never before had the gale seemed to us more furious, the sea more mad, the sunshine more merciless and mocking, and the position of the ship more hopeless and appalling. Every movement of her was ominous of the end of her agony and of the beginning of ours. We staggered away from the door, and, alarmed by a sudden roll, fell down in a bunch. It appeared to us that the side of the house was more smooth than glass and more slippery than ice. There was nothing to hang on to but a long brass hook used sometimes to keep back an open door. Wamibo held on to it and we held on to Wamibo, clutching our Jimmy. He had completely collapsed now. He did not seem to have the strength to close his hand. We stuck to him blindly in our fear. We were not afraid of Wamibo letting go (we remembered that the brute was stronger than any three men in the ship), but we were afraid of the hook giving way, and we also believed that the ship had made up her mind to turn over at last. But she didn't. A sea swept over us. The boatswain spluttered:—"Up and away. There's a lull. Away aft with you, or we will all go to the devil here." We stood up surrounding Jimmy. We begged him to hold up, to hold on, at least. He glared with his bulging eyes, mute as a fish, and with all the stiffening knocked out of him. He wouldn't stand; he wouldn't even as much as clutch at our necks; he was only a cold black skin loosely stuffed with soft cotton wool; his arms and legs swung jointless and pliable; his head rolled about; the lower lip hung down, enormous and heavy. We pressed round him, bothered and dismayed; sheltering him we swung here and there in a body; and on the very brink of eternity we tottered all together with concealing and absurd gestures, like a lot of drunken men embarrassed with a stolen corpse.

Something had to be done. We had to get him aft. A rope was tied slack under his armpits, and, reaching up at the risk of our lives, we hung him on the fore sheet cleat. He emitted no sound; he looked as ridiculously lamentable as a doll that had lost half its sawdust, and we started on our perilous journey over the main deck, dragging along with care that pitiful, that limp, that hateful burden. He was not very heavy, but had he weighed a ton he could not have been more awkward to handle. We literally passed him from hand to hand. Now and then we had to hang him up on a handy belaying-pin, to

4. A balloon.

draw a breath and reform the line. Had the pin broken he would
have irretrievably gone into the Southern Ocean, but he had to take
his chance of that; and after a little while, becoming apparently
aware of it, he groaned slightly, and with a great effort whispered a
few words. We listened eagerly. He was reproaching us with our
carelessness in letting him run such risks: "Now, after I got myself
out from there," he breathed out weakly. "There" was his cabin.
And he got himself out. We had nothing to do with it apparently! . . .
No matter. . . . We went on and let him take his chances, simply
because we could not help it; for though at that time we hated him
more than ever—more than anything under heaven—we did not
want to lose him. We had so far saved him; and it had become a
personal matter between us and the sea. We meant to stick to him.
Had we (by an incredible hypothesis) undergone similar toil and
trouble for an empty cask, that cask would have become as precious
to us as Jimmy was. More precious, in fact, because we would have
had no reason to hate the cask. And we hated James Wait. We
could not get rid of the monstrous suspicion that this astounding
black-man was shamming sick, had been malingering heartlessly in
the face of our toil, of our scorn, of our patience—and now was
malingering in the face of our devotion—in the face of death. Our
vague and imperfect morality rose with disgust at his unmanly lie.
But he stuck to it manfully—amazingly. No! It couldn't be. He was
at all extremity. His cantankerous temper was only the result of the
provoking invincibleness of that death he felt by his side. Any man
may be angry with such a masterful chum. But, then, what kind of
men were we—with our thoughts! Indignation and doubt grappled
within us in a scuffle that trampled upon the finest of our feelings.
And we hated him because of the suspicion; we detested him because
of the doubt. We could not scorn him safely—neither could we pity
him without risk to our dignity. So we hated him, and passed him
carefully from hand to hand. We cried, "Got him?"—"Yes. All right.
Let go." And he swung from one enemy to another, showing about
as much life as an old bolster would do. His eyes made two narrow
white slits in the black face. He breathed slowly, and the air escaped
through his lips with a noise like the sound of bellows. We reached
the poop ladder at last, and it being a comparatively safe place, we lay
for a moment in an exhausted heap to rest a little. He began to mutter. We were always incurably anxious to hear what he had to say.
This time he mumbled peevishly, "It took you some time to come. I
began to think the whole smart lot of you had been washed overboard. What kept you back? Hey? Funk?"[5] We said nothing. With
sighs we started again to drag him up. The secret and ardent desire

5. See p. 15, n. 3.

of our hearts was the desire to beat him viciously with our fists about the head: and we handled him as tenderly as though he had been made of glass. . . .

The return on the poop was like the return of wanderers after many years amongst people marked by the desolation of time. Eyes were turned slowly in their sockets glancing at us. Faint murmurs were heard, "Have you got 'im after all?" The well-known faces looked strange and familiar; they seemed faded and grimy; they had a mingled expression of fatigue and eagerness. They seemed to have become much thinner during our absence, as if all these men had been starving for a long time in their abandoned attitudes. The captain, with a round turn of a rope on his wrist, and kneeling on one knee, swung with a face cold and stiff; but with living eyes he was still holding the ship up, heeding no one, as if lost in the unearthly effort of that endeavour. We fastened up James Wait in a safe place. Mr. Baker scrambled along to lend a hand. Mr. Creighton, on his back, and very pale, muttered, "Well done," and gave us, Jimmy and the sky, a scornful glance, then closed his eyes slowly. Here and there a man stirred a little, but most remained apathetic, in cramped positions, muttering between shivers. The sun was setting. A sun enormous, unclouded and red, declining low as if bending down to look into their faces. The wind whistled across long sunbeams that, resplendent and cold, struck full on the dilated pupils of staring eyes without making them wink. The wisps of hair and the tangled beards were grey with the salt of the sea. The faces were earthy, and the dark patches under the eyes extended to the ears, smudged into the hollows of sunken cheeks. The lips were livid and thin, and when they moved it was with difficulty, as though they had been glued to the teeth. Some grinned sadly in the sunlight, shaking with cold. Others were sad and still. Charley, subdued by the sudden disclosure of the insignificance of his youth, darted fearful glances. The two smooth-faced Norwegians resembled decrepid children, staring stupidly. To leeward, on the edge of the horizon, black seas leaped up towards the glowing sun. It sank slowly, round and blazing, and the crests of waves splashed on the edge of the luminous circle. One of the Norwegians appeared to catch sight of it, and, after giving a violent start, began to speak. His voice, startling the others, made them stir. They moved their heads stiffly, or turning with difficulty, looked at him with surprise, with fear, or in grave silence. He chattered at the setting sun, nodding his head, while the big seas began to roll across the crimson disc; and over miles of turbulent waters the shadows of high waves swept with a running darkness the faces of men. A crested roller broke with a loud hissing roar, and the sun, as if put out, disappeared. The chattering voice faltered, went out together with the light. There were sighs.

In the sudden lull that follows the crash of a broken sea a man said wearily, "Here's that blooming Dutchman gone off his chump."[6] A seaman, lashed by the middle, tapped the deck with his open hand with unceasing quick flaps. In the gathering greyness of twilight a bulky form was seen rising aft, and began marching on all fours with the movements of some big cautious beast. It was Mr. Baker passing along the line of men. He grunted encouragingly over every one, felt their fastenings. Some, with half-open eyes, puffed like men oppressed by heat; others mechanically and in dreamy voices answered him, "Aye! aye! sir!" He went from one to another grunting, "Ough! . . . See her through it yet"; and unexpectedly, with loud angry outbursts, blew up Knowles for cutting off a long piece from the fall of the relieving tackle. "Ough!—Ashamed of yourself— Relieving tackle—Don't you know better!—Ough!—Able seaman! Ough!" The lame man was crushed. He muttered, "Get som'think for a lashing for myself, sir."—"Ough! Lashing—yourself. Are you a tin- ker or a sailor—What? Ough!—May want that tackle directly— Ough!—More use to the ship than your lame carcass. Ough!—Keep it!—Keep it, now you've done it." He crawled away slowly, muttering to himself about some men being "worse than children." It had been a comforting row. Low exclamations were heard: "Hallo . . . Hallo." . . . Those who had been painfully dozing asked with convulsive starts, "What's up? . . . What is it?" The answers came with unexpected cheerfulness: "The mate is going bald-headed[7] for lame Jack about something or other." "No!" . . . "What 'as he done?" Some one even chuckled. It was like a whiff of hope, like a reminder of safe days. Donkin, who had been stupefied with fear, revived suddenly and began to shout:—"'Ear 'im; that's the way they tawlk to hus. Vy donch'ee 'it 'im—one ov yer?[8] 'It 'im. 'It 'im! Comin' the mate hover hus. We are as good men as 'ee! We're hall goin' to 'ell now. We 'ave been starved in this rotten ship, an' now we're goin' to be drowned for them black-'earted bullies! 'It 'im!" He shrieked in the deepening gloom, he blubbered and sobbed, screaming:—"'It 'im! 'It 'im!" The rage and fear of his disregarded right to live tried the steadfastness of hearts more than the menacing shadows of the night that advanced through the unceasing clamour of the gale. From aft Mr. Baker was heard:—"Is one of you men going to stop him—must I come along?" "Shut up!" . . . "Keep quiet!" cried various voices, exasperated, trem- bling with cold.—"You'll get one across the mug from me directly," said an invisible seaman, in a weary tone, "I won't let the mate have the trouble." He ceased and lay still with the silence of despair. On

6. Gone insane (slang).
7. See p. 72, n. 6.
8. Why don't you hit him—one of you?

the black sky the stars, coming out, gleamed over an inky sea that, speckled with foam, flashed back at them the evanescent and pale light of a dazzling whiteness born from the black turmoil of the waves. Remote in the eternal calm they glittered hard and cold above the uproar of the earth; they surrounded the vanquished and tormented ship on all sides: more pitiless than the eyes of a triumphant mob, and as unapproachable as the hearts of men.

The icy south wind howled exultingly under the sombre splendour of the sky. The cold shook the men with a resistless violence as though it had tried to shake them to pieces. Short moans were swept unheard off the stiff lips. Some complained in mutters of "not feeling themselves below the waist"; while those who had closed their eyes, imagined they had a block of ice on their chests. Others, alarmed at not feeling any pain in their fingers, beat the deck feebly with their hands—obstinate and exhausted. Wamibo stared vacant and dreamy. The Scandinavians kept on a meaningless mutter through chattering teeth. The spare Scotchmen, with determined efforts, kept their lower jaws still. The West-country men lay big and stolid in an invulnerable surliness. A man yawned and swore in turns. Another breathed with a rattle in his throat. Two elderly hard-weather shellbacks, fast side by side, whispered dismally to one another about the landlady of a boarding-house in Sunderland,[9] whom they both knew. They extolled her motherliness and her liberality; they tried to talk about the joint of beef and the big fire in the downstairs kitchen. The words dying faintly on their lips, ended in light sighs. A sudden voice cried into the cold night, "Oh Lord!" No one changed his position or took any notice of the cry. One or two passed, with a repeated and vague gesture, their hand over their faces, but most of them kept very still. In the benumbed immobility of their bodies they were excessively wearied by their thoughts, that rushed with the rapidity and vividness of dreams. Now and then, by an abrupt and startling exclamation, they answered the weird hail of some illusion; then, again, in silence contemplated the vision of known faces and familiar things. They recalled the aspect of forgotten shipmates and heard the voice of dead and gone skippers. They remembered the noise of gaslit streets, the steamy heat of tap-rooms, or the scorching sunshine of calm days at sea.

Mr. Baker left his insecure place, and crawled, with stoppages, along the poop. In the dark and on all fours he resembled some carnivorous animal prowling amongst corpses. At the break, propped to windward of a stanchion, he looked down on the main deck. It seemed to him that the ship had a tendency to stand up a little more. The wind had eased a little, he thought, but the sea ran as high as

---

9. A port in northeast England.

ever. The waves foamed viciously, and the lee side of the deck disappeared under a hissing whiteness as of boiling milk, while the rigging sang steadily with a deep vibrating note, and, at every upward
swing of the ship, the wind rushed with a long-drawn clamour
amongst the spars. Mr. Baker watched very still. A man near him
began to make a blabbing noise with his lips, all at once and very
loud, as though the cold had broken brutally through him. He went
on:—"Ba—ba—ba—brrr—brr—ba—ba."—"Stop that!" cried Mr.
Baker, groping in the dark. "Stop it!" He went on shaking the leg
he found under his hand.—"What is it, sir?" called out Belfast, in the
tone of a man awakened suddenly; "we are looking after that 'ere
Jimmy."—"Are you? Ough! Don't make that row then. Who's that
near you?"—"It's me—the boatswain, sir," growled the West-country
man; "we are trying to keep life in that poor devil."—"Aye, aye!" said
Mr. Baker, "Do it quietly, can't you."—"He wants us to hold him up
above the rail," went on the boatswain, with irritation, "says he can't
breathe here under our jackets."—"If we lift 'im, we drop 'im overboard," said another voice, "we can't feel our hands with cold."—"I
don't care. I am choking!" exclaimed James Wait in a clear tone.—
"Oh, no, my son," said the boatswain, desperately, "you don't go till
we all go on this fine night."—"You will see yet many a worse," said
Mr. Baker, cheerfully.—"It's no child's play, sir!" answered the
boatswain. "Some of us further aft, here, are in a pretty bad way."—
"If the blamed sticks had been cut out of her she would be running
along on her bottom now like any decent ship, an' giv' us all a
chance," said some one, with a sigh.—"The old man wouldn't have
it . . . much he cares for us," whispered another.—"Care for you!"
exclaimed Mr. Baker, angrily. "Why should he care for you? Are you
a lot of women passengers to be taken care of? We are here to take
care of the ship—and some of you ain't up to that. Ough! . . . What
have you done so very smart to be taken care of? Ough! . . . Some of
you can't stand a bit of a breeze without crying over it."—"Come,
sorr. We ain't so bad," protested Belfast, in a voice shaken by shivers;
"we ain't . . . brrr . . ."—"Again," shouted the mate, grabbing at the
shadowy form; "again! . . . Why, you're in your shirt! What have you
done?"—"I've put my oilskin and jacket over that half-dead nayggur—
and he says he chokes," said Belfast, complainingly.—"You wouldn't
call me nigger if I wasn't half dead, you Irish beggar!" boomed James
Wait, vigorously.—"You . . . brrr . . . You wouldn't be white if you
were ever so well . . . I will fight you . . . brrrr . . . in fine weather . . .
brrr . . . with one hand tied behind my back . . . brrrrrr . . ."—"I
don't want your rags—I want air," gasped out the other faintly, as if
suddenly exhausted.

The sprays swept over whistling and pattering. Men disturbed in
their peaceful torpor by the pain of quarrelsome shouts, moaned,

muttering curses. Mr. Baker crawled off a little way to leeward where a water-cask loomed up big, with something white against it. "Is it you, Podmore?" asked Mr. Baker. He had to repeat the question twice before the cook turned, coughing feebly.—"Yes, sir. I've been praying in my mind for a quick deliverance; for I am prepared for any call. . . . I—"—"Look here, cook," interrupted Mr. Baker, "the men are perishing with cold."—"Cold!" said the cook, mournfully; "they will be warm enough before long."—"What?" asked Mr. Baker, looking along the deck into the faint sheen of frothing water.—"They are a wicked lot," continued the cook solemnly, but in an unsteady voice, "about as wicked as any ship's company in this sinful world! Now, I"—he trembled so that he could hardly speak; his was an exposed place, and in a cotton shirt, a thin pair of trousers, and with his knees under his nose, he received, quaking, the flicks of stinging, salt drops; his voice sounded exhausted—"now, I—any time . . . My eldest youngster, Mr. Baker . . . a clever boy . . . last Sunday on shore before this voyage he wouldn't go to church, sir. Says I, 'You go and clean yourself or I'll know the reason why!' What does he do? . . . Pond, Mr. Baker—fell into the pond in his best rig,[1] sir! . . . Accident? . . . 'Nothing will save you, fine scholar though you are!' says I . . . Accident? . . . I whopped him, sir, till I couldn't lift my arm. . . ." His voice faltered. "I whopped 'im!" he repeated, rattling his teeth; then, after a while, let out a mournful sound that was half a groan, half a snore. Mr. Baker shook him by the shoulders. "Hey! Cook! Hold up, Podmore! Tell me—is there any fresh water in the galley tank? The ship is lying along less, I think; I would try to get forward. A little water would do them good. Hallo! Look out! Look out!" The cook struggled.—"Not you, sir—not you!" He began to scramble to windward. "Galley! . . . my business!" he shouted.— "Cook's going crazy now," said several voices. He yelled:—"Crazy, am I? I am more ready to die than any of you, officers incloosive—there! As long as she swims I will cook! I will get you coffee."—"Cook, ye are a gentleman!" cried Belfast. But the cook was already going over the weather ladder. He stopped for a moment to shout back on the poop:—"As long as she swims I will cook!" and disappeared as though he had gone overboard. The men who had heard sent after him a cheer that sounded like a wail of sick children. An hour or more afterwards some one said distinctly: 'He's gone for good.'—"Very likely," assented the boatswain; "even in fine weather he was as smart about the deck as a milch-cow[2] on her first voyage. We ought to go and see." Nobody moved. As the hours dragged slowly through the darkness Mr. Baker crawled back and forth along the poop several

---

1. See p. 52, n. 4.
2. A milk cow; brought aboard to provide fresh milk for the crew.

times. Some men fancied they had heard him exchange murmurs with the master, but at that time the memories were incomparably more vivid than anything actual, and they were not certain whether the murmurs were heard now or many years ago. They did not try to find out. A mutter more or less did not matter. It was too cold for curiosity, and almost for hope. They could not spare a moment or a thought from the great mental occupation of wishing to live. And the desire of life kept them alive, apathetic and enduring, under the cruel persistence of wind and cold; while the bestarred black dome of the sky revolved slowly above the ship, that drifted, bearing their patience and their suffering, through the stormy solitude of the sea.

Huddled close to one another, they fancied themselves utterly alone. They heard sustained loud noises, and again bore the pain of existence through long hours of profound silence. In the night they saw sunshine, felt warmth, and suddenly, with a start, thought that the sun would never rise upon a freezing world. Some heard laughter, listened to songs; others, near the end of the poop, could hear loud human shrieks, and, opening their eyes, were surprised to hear them still, though very faint, and far away. The boatswain said:—"Why, it's the cook, hailing from forward, I think." He hardly believed his own words or recognised his own voice. It was a long time before the man next to him gave a sign of life. He punched hard his other neighbour and said:—"The cook's shouting!" Many did not understand, others did not care; the majority further aft did not believe. But the boatswain and another man had the pluck to crawl away forward to see. They seemed to have been gone for hours, and were very soon forgotten. Then suddenly men that had been plunged in a hopeless resignation became as if possessed with a desire to hurt. They belaboured one another with fists. In the darkness they struck persistently anything soft they could feel near, and, with a greater effort than for a shout, whispered excitedly:—"They've got some hot coffee.... Boss'n got it...." "No! ... Where?" ... "It's coming! Cook made it." James Wait moaned. Donkin scrambled viciously, caring not where he kicked, and anxious that the officers should have none of it. It came in a pot, and they drank in turns. It was hot, and while it blistered the greedy palates, it seemed incredible. The men sighed out parting with the mug:—"How 'as he done it?" Some cried weakly:—"Bully for you, doctor!"

He had done it somehow. Afterwards Archie declared that the thing was "meeraculous." For many days we wondered, and it was the one ever-interesting subject of conversation to the end of the voyage. We asked the cook, in fine weather, how he felt when he saw his stove "reared up on end." We inquired, in the north-east trade[3] and

3. The Atlantic trade wind north of the equator.

on serene evenings, whether he had to stand on his head to put things right somewhat. We suggested he had used his bread-board for a raft, and from there comfortably had stoked his grate; and we did our best to conceal our admiration under the wit of fine irony. He affirmed not to know anything about it, rebuked our levity, declared himself, with solemn animation, to have been the object of a special mercy for the saving of our unholy lives. Fundamentally he was right, no doubt; but he need not have been so offensively positive about it—he need not have hinted so often that it would have gone hard with us had he not been there, meritorious and pure, to receive the inspiration and the strength for the work of grace. Had we been saved by his recklessness or his agility, we could have at length become reconciled to the fact; but to admit our obligation to anybody's virtue and holiness alone was as difficult for us as for any other handful of mankind. Like many benefactors of humanity, the cook took himself too seriously, and reaped the reward of irreverence. We were not ungrateful, however. He remained heroic. His saying—*the* saying of his life—became proverbial in the mouths of men as are the sayings of conquerors or sages. Later on, whenever one of us was puzzled by a task and advised to relinquish it, he would express his determination to persevere and to succeed by the words:—"As long as she swims I will cook!"

The hot drink helped us through the bleak hours that precede the dawn. The sky low by the horizon took on the delicate tints of pink and yellow like the inside of a rare shell. And higher, where it glowed with a pearly sheen, a small black cloud appeared, like a forgotten fragment of the night set in a border of dazzling gold. The beams of light skipped on the crests of waves. The eyes of men turned to the eastward. The sunlight flooded their weary faces. They were giving themselves up to fatigue as though they had done for ever with their work. On Singleton's black oilskin coat the dried salt glistened like hoar frost. He hung on by the wheel, with open and lifeless eyes. Captain Allistoun, unblinking, faced the rising sun. His lips stirred, opened for the first time in twenty-four hours, and with a fresh firm voice he cried, "Wear ship!"

The commanding sharp tones made all these torpid men start like a sudden flick of a whip. Then again, motionless where they lay, the force of habit made some of them repeat the order in hardly audible murmurs. Captain Allistoun glanced down at his crew, and several, with fumbling fingers and hopeless movements, tried to cast themselves adrift. He repeated impatiently, "Wear ship. Now then, Mr. Baker, get the men along. What's the matter with them?"— "Wear ship. Do you hear there?—Wear ship!" thundered out the boatswain suddenly. His voice seemed to break through a deadly spell.

Men began to stir and crawl.—"I want the fore-topmast staysail run up smartly," said the master, very loudly; "if you can't manage it standing up you must do it lying down—that's all. Bear a hand!"— "Come along! Let's give the old girl a chance," urged the boatswain.—"Aye! aye! Wear ship!" exclaimed quavering voices. The forecastle men, with reluctant faces, prepared to go forward. Mr. Baker pushed ahead grunting on all fours to show the way, and they followed him over the break. The others lay still with a vile hope in their hearts of not being required to move till they got saved or drowned in peace.

After some time they could be seen forward appearing on the forecastle-head, one by one in unsafe attitudes; hanging on to the rails; clambering over the anchors; embracing the cross-head of the windlass or hugging the fore-capstan. They were restless with strange exertions, waved their arms, knelt, lay flat down, staggered up, seemed to strive their hardest to go overboard. Suddenly a small white piece of canvas fluttered amongst them, grew larger, beating. Its narrow head rose in jerks—and at last it stood distended and triangular in the sunshine.—"They have done it!" cried the voices aft. Captain Allistoun let go the rope he had round his wrist and rolled to leeward headlong. He could be seen casting the lee main-braces off the pins while the backwash of waves splashed over him.— "Square the main yard!" he shouted up to us—who stared at him in wonder. We hesitated to stir. "The main-brace, men. Haul! haul anyhow! Lay on your backs and haul!" he screeched, half-drowned down there. We did not believe we could move the main yard, but the strongest and the less discouraged tried to execute the order. Others assisted half-heartedly. Singleton's eyes blazed suddenly as he took a fresh grip of the spokes. Captain Allistoun fought his way up to windward.—"Haul men! Try to move it! Haul, and help the ship." His hard face worked suffused and furious. "Is she going off,[4] Singleton?" he cried.—"Not a move yet, sir," croaked the old seaman in a horribly hoarse voice.—"Watch the helm, Singleton," spluttered the master. "Haul men! Have you no more strength than rats? Haul, and earn your salt." Mr. Creighton, on his back, with a swollen leg and a face as white as a piece of paper, blinked his eyes; his bluish lips twitched. In the wild scramble men grabbed at him, crawled over his hurt leg, knelt on his chest. He kept perfectly still, setting his teeth without a moan, without a sigh. The master's ardour, the cries of that silent man inspired us. We hauled and hung in bunches on the rope. We heard him say with violence to Donkin, who sprawled abjectly on his stomach,—"I will brain you with this

4. Starting or commencing.

belaying-pin if you don't catch hold of the brace," and that victim of men's injustice, cowardly and cheeky, whimpered:—"Are you goin' ter murder hus now?" while with sudden desperation he gripped the rope. Men sighed, shouted, hissed meaningless words, groaned. The yards moved, came slowly square against the wind, that hummed loudly on the yard-arms.—"Going off, sir," shouted Singleton, "she's just started."—"Catch a turn with that brace. Catch a turn!" clamoured the master. Mr. Creighton, nearly suffocated and unable to move, made a mighty effort, and with his left hand managed to nip the rope.—"All fast!" cried some one. He closed his eyes as if going off into a swoon, while huddled together about the brace we watched with scared looks what the ship would do now.

She went off slowly as though she had been weary and disheartened like the men she carried. She paid off very gradually, making us hold our breath till we choked, and as soon as she had brought the wind abaft the beam she started to move, and fluttered our hearts. It was awful to see her, nearly overturned, begin to gather way and drag her submerged side through the water. The dead-eyes of the rigging churned the breaking seas. The lower half of the deck was full of mad whirlpools and eddies; and the long line of the lee rail could be seen showing black now and then in the swirls of a field of foam as dazzling and white as a field of snow. The wind sang shrilly amongst the spars; and at every slight lurch we expected her to slip to the bottom sideways from under our backs. When dead before it she made the first distinct attempt to stand up, and we encouraged her with a feeble and discordant howl. A great sea came running up aft and hung for a moment over us with a curling top; then crashed down under the counter and spread out on both sides into a great sheet of bursting froth. Above its fierce hiss we heard Singleton's croak:—"She is steering!" He had both his feet now planted firmly on the grating, and the wheel spun fast as he eased the helm.— "Bring the wind on the port quarter and steady her!" called out the master, staggering to his feet, the first man up from amongst our prostrate heap. One or two screamed with excitement:—"She rises!" Far away forward, Mr. Baker and three others were seen erect and black on the clear sky, lifting their arms, and with open mouths as though they had been shouting all together. The ship trembled, try-ing to lift her side, lurched back, seemed to give up with a nerveless dip, and suddenly with an unexpected jerk swung violently to wind-ward, as though she had torn herself out from a deadly grasp. The whole immense volume of water, lifted by her deck, was thrown bodily across to starboard. Loud cracks were heard. Iron ports breaking open thundered with ringing blows. The water topped over the starboard rail with the rush of a river falling over a dam. The sea on deck, and the seas on every side of her, mingled together

in a deafening roar. She rolled violently. We got up and were helplessly run or flung about from side to side. Men, rolling over and
over, yelled—"The house will go!"—"She clears herself!" Lifted by
a towering sea she ran along with it for a moment, spouting thick
streams of water through every opening of her wounded sides. The
lee braces having been carried away or washed off the pins, all the
ponderous yards on the fore swung from side to side and with
appalling rapidity at every roll. The men forward were seen crouching here and there with fearful glances upwards at the enormous
spars that whirled about over their heads. The torn canvas and the
ends of broken gear streamed in the wind like wisps of hair. Through
the clear[5] sunshine, over the flashing turmoil and uproar of the
seas, the ship ran blindly, dishevelled and headlong, as if fleeing for
her life; and on the poop we spun, we tottered about, distracted and
noisy. We all spoke at once in a thin babble; we had the aspect of
invalids and the gestures of maniacs. Eyes shone, large and haggard, in smiling, meagre faces that seemed to have been dusted
over with powdered chalk. We stamped, clapped our hands, feeling
ready to jump and do anything; but in reality hardly able to keep on
our feet. Captain Allistoun, hard and slim, gesticulated madly from
the poop at Mr. Baker: "Steady these foreyards! Steady them the
best you can!" On the main deck, men excited by his cries, splashed,
dashing aimlessly here and there with the foam swirling up to their
waists. Apart, far aft, and alone by the helm, old Singleton had
deliberately tucked his white beard under the top button of his
glistening coat. Swaying upon the din and tumult of the seas, with
the whole battered length of the ship launched forward in a rolling
rush before his steady old eyes, he stood rigidly still, forgotten by
all, and with an attentive face. In front of his erect figure only the
two arms moved cross-wise with a swift and sudden readiness, to
check or urge again the rapid stir of circling spokes. He steered
with care.

IV

On men reprieved by its disdainful mercy, the immortal sea confers
in its justice the full privilege of desired unrest. Through the perfect
wisdom of its grace they are not permitted to meditate at ease upon
the complicated and acrid savour of existence, lest they should
remember and, perchance, regret the reward of a cup of inspiring
bitterness, tasted so often, and so often withdrawn from before their
stiffening but reluctant lips. They must without pause justify their
life to the eternal pity that commands toil to be hard and unceasing,

5. Bright (archaic).

from sunrise to sunset, from sunset to sunrise: till the weary succession of nights and days tainted by the obstinate clamour of sages,
demanding bliss and an empty heaven, is redeemed at last by the vast
silence of pain and labour, by the dumb fear and the dumb courage
of men obscure, forgetful, and enduring.

The master and Mr. Baker coming face to face stared for a moment,
with the intense and amazed looks of men meeting unexpectedly
after years of trouble. Their voices were gone, and they whispered
desperately at one another.—"Any one missing?" asked Captain
Allistoun.—"No. All there."—"Anybody hurt?"—"Only the second
mate."—"I will look after him directly. We're lucky."—"Very," articulated Mr. Baker, faintly. He gripped the rail and rolled bloodshot
eyes. The little grey man made an effort to raise his voice above a
dull mutter, and fixed his chief mate with a cold gaze, piercing like
a dart.—"Get sail on the ship," he said, speaking authoritatively, and
with an inflexible snap of his thin lips. "Get sail on her as soon as you
can. This is a fair wind. At once, sir—Don't give the men time to feel
themselves. They will get done up and stiff, and we will never . . . We
must get her along now." . . . He reeled to a long heavy roll; the rail
dipped into the glancing hissing water. He caught a shroud, swung
helplessly against the mate . . . "now we have a fair wind at last.—
Make—sail." His head rolled from shoulder to shoulder. His eyelids
began to beat rapidly. "And the pumps—pumps, Mr. Baker." He
peered as though the face within a foot of his eyes had been half a
mile off. "Keep the men on the move to—to get her along," he mumbled in a drowsy tone, like a man going off into a doze. He pulled
himself together suddenly. "Mustn't stand. Won't do," he said with a
painful attempt at a smile. He let go his hold, and, propelled by the
dip of the ship, ran aft unwillingly, with small steps, till he brought
up against the binnacle-stand. Hanging on there he looked up in an
objectless manner at Singleton, who, unheeding him, watched anxiously the end of the jib-boom—"Steering-gear works all right?" he
asked. There was a noise in the old seaman's throat, as though the
words had been rattling there together before they could come out.—
"Steers . . . like a little boat," he said, at last, with hoarse tenderness,
without giving the master as much as half a glance—then, watchfully, spun the wheel down, steadied, flung it back again. Captain
Allistoun tore himself away from the delight of leaning against the
binnacle, and began to walk the poop, swaying and reeling to preserve his balance. . . .

The pump-rods, clanking, stamped in short jumps, while the fly-
wheels turned smoothly, with great speed, at the foot of the mainmast, flinging back and forth with a regular impetuosity two limp
clusters of men clinging to the handles. They abandoned themselves,

swaying from the hip with twitching faces and stony eyes. The carpenter, sounding from time to time, exclaimed mechanically: "Shake her up! Keep her going!" Mr. Baker could not speak, but found his voice to shout; and under the goad of his objurgations, men looked to the lashings, dragged out new sails; and thinking themselves unable to move, carried heavy blocks aloft—overhauled the gear. They went up the rigging with faltering and desperate efforts. Their heads swam as they shifted their hold, stepped blindly on the yards like men in the dark; or trusted themselves to the first rope to hand with the negligence of exhausted strength. The narrow escapes from falls did not disturb the languid beat of their hearts; the roar of the seas seething far below them sounded continuous and faint like an indistinct noise from another world: the wind filled their eyes with tears, and with heavy gusts tried to push them off from where they swayed in insecure positions. With streaming faces and blowing hair they flew up and down between sky and water, bestriding the ends of yard-arms, crouching on foot-ropes, embracing lifts to have their hands free, or standing up against chain ties. Their thoughts floated vaguely between the desire of rest and the desire of life, while their stiffened fingers cast off head-earrings, fumbled for knives, or held with tenacious grip against the violent shocks of beating canvas. They glared savagely at one another, made frantic signs with one hand while they held their life in the other, looked down on the narrow strip of flooded deck, shouted along to leeward: "Light-to!" . . . "Haul out!" . . . "Make fast!" Their lips moved, their eyes started, furious and eager with the desire to be understood, but the wind tossed their words unheard upon the disturbed sea. In an unendurable and unending strain they worked like men driven by a merciless dream to toil in an atmosphere of ice or flame. They burnt and shivered in turns. Their eyeballs smarted as if in the smoke of a conflagration; their heads were ready to burst with every shout. Hard fingers seemed to grip their throats. At every roll they thought: "Now I must let go. It will shake us all off"—and thrown about aloft they cried wildly: "Look out there—catch the end." . . . "Reeve clear" . . . "Turn this block. . . ." They nodded desperately; shook infuriated faces, "No! No! From down up." They seemed to hate one another with a deadly hate. The longing to be done with it all gnawed their breasts, and the wish to do things well was a burning pain. They cursed their fate, contemned their life, and wasted their breath in deadly imprecations upon one another. The sailmaker, with his bald head bared, worked feverishly, forgetting his intimacy with so many admirals. The boatswain, climbing up with marlinspikes and bunches of spunyarn rovings, or kneeling on the yard and ready to take a turn with the midship-stop, had acute and fleeting visions of his old woman and the youngsters in a moorland village. Mr. Baker, feeling very weak, tottered here and there, grunting and inflexible, like a man of iron. He waylaid those who, coming from aloft, stood gasping for breath. He ordered, encouraged, scolded. "Now then—to the main-topsail now! Tally on to that gantline. Don't stand about there!"—"Is there no rest for us?" muttered voices. He spun round fiercely, with a sinking heart.—"No! No rest till the work is done. Work till you drop. That's what you're here for." A bowed seaman at his elbow gave a short laugh.—"Do or die,"[6] he croaked bitterly, then spat into his broad palms, swung up his long arms, and grasping the rope high above his head sent out a mournful, wailing cry for a pull all together. A sea boarded the quarter-deck and sent the whole lot sprawling to leeward. Caps, handspikes floated. Clenched hands, kicking legs, with here and there a spluttering face, stuck out of the white hiss of foaming water. Mr. Baker, knocked down with the rest, screamed—"Don't let go that rope! Hold on to it! Hold!" And sorely bruised by the brutal fling, they held on to it, as though it had been the fortune of their life. The ship ran, rolling heavily, and the topping crests glanced past port and starboard flashing their white heads. Pumps were freed. Braces were rove. The three topsails and foresail were set. She spurted faster over the water, outpacing the swift rush of waves. The menacing thunder of distanced seas rose behind her—filled the air with the tremendous vibrations of its voice. And devastated, battered, and wounded she drove foaming to the northward, as though inspired by the courage of a high endeavour. . . .

The forecastle was a place of damp desolation. They looked at their dwelling with dismay. It was slimy, dripping; it hummed hollow with the wind, and was strewn with shapeless wreckage like a half-tide cavern in a rocky and exposed coast. Many had lost all they had in the world, but most of the starboard-watch had preserved their chests; thin streams of water trickled out of them, however. The beds were soaked; the blankets spread out and saved by some nail squashed under foot. They dragged wet rags from evil-smelling corners, and, wringing the water out, recognised their property. Some smiled stiffly. Others looked round blank and mute. There were cries of joy over old waistcoats, and groans of sorrow over shapeless things found amongst the black splinters of smashed bed boards. One lamp was discovered jammed under the bowsprit. Charley whimpered a little. Knowles stumped here and there, sniffing, examining dark places for salvage. He poured dirty water out of a boot, and was concerned to find the owner. Those who,

---

6. The motto on the the the stern of the *Judea* in Conrad's "Youth" (Y 13).

overwhelmed by their losses, sat on the forepeak hatch, remained
elbows on knees, and, with a fist against each cheek, disdained to
look up. He pushed it under their noses. "Here's a good boot. Yours?"
They snarled, "No—get out." One snapped at him, "Take it to hell out
of this." He seemed surprised. "Why? It's a good boot," but remembering suddenly that he had lost every stitch of his clothing, he dropped
his find and began to swear. In the dim light cursing voices clashed.
A man came in and, dropping his arms, stood still, repeating from
the doorstep, "Here's a bloomin' old go?[7] Here's a bloomin' old go!"
A few rooted anxiously in flooded chests for tobacco. They breathed
hard, clamoured with heads down. "Look at that, Jack!" . . . "Here!
Sam! Here's my shore-going rig spoilt for ever." One blasphemed
tearfully holding up a pair of dripping trousers. No one looked at
him. The cat came out from somewhere. He had an ovation. They
snatched him from hand to hand, caressed him in a murmur of pet
names. They wondered where he had "weathered it out"; disputed
about it. A squabbling argument began. Two men came in with a
bucket of fresh water, and all crowded round it; but Tom, lean and
mewing, came up with every hair astir and had the first drink. A
couple of men went aft for oil and biscuits.

Then in the yellow light and in the intervals of mopping the deck
they crunched hard bread, arranging to "worry through somehow."
Men chummed as to beds. Turns were settled for wearing boots and
having the use of oilskin coats. They called one another "old man"
and "sonny" in cheery voices. Friendly slaps resounded. Jokes were
shouted. One or two stretched on the wet deck, slept with heads pil-
lowed on their bent arms, and several, sitting on the hatch, smoked.
Their weary faces appeared through a thin blue haze, pacified and
with sparkling eyes. The boatswain put his head through the door.
"Relieve the wheel, one of you"—he shouted inside—"it's six.
Blamme if that old Singleton hasn't been there more'n thirty hours.
You are a fine lot." He slammed the door again. "Mate's watch on
deck," said some one. "Hey, Donkin, it's your relief!" shouted three or
four together. He had crawled into an empty bunk and on wet planks
lay still. "Donkin, your wheel." He made no sound. "Donkins dead,"
guffawed some one. "Sell 'is bloomin' clothes," shouted another.
"Donkin, if ye don't go to the bloomin' wheel they will sell your
clothes—d'ye hear?" jeered a third. He groaned from his dark hole. He
complained about pains in all his bones, he whimpered pitifully.
"He won't go," exclaimed a contemptuous voice, "your turn, Davies."
The young seaman rose painfully squaring his shoulders. Donkin

---

7. Obscure meaning, possibly a bad turn of affairs.

stuck his head out, and it appeared in the yellow light, fragile and ghastly. "I will giv' yer a pound of tobaccer," he whined in a conciliating voice, "so soon as I draw it from haft. I will—s'elp me. . . ." Davies swung his arm backhanded and the head vanished. "I'll go," he said, "but you will pay for it." He walked unsteady but resolute to the door. "So I will," yelped Donkin, popping out behind him. "So I will—s'elp me . . . a pound . . . three bob[8] they chawrge." Davies flung the door open. "You will pay my price . . . in fine weather," he shouted over his shoulder. One of the men unbuttoned his wet coat rapidly, threw it at his head. "Here, Taffy[9]—take that, you thief!" "Thank you!" he cried from the darkness above the swish of rolling water. He could be heard splashing; a sea came on board with a thump. "He's got his bath already," remarked a grim shellback. "Aye, aye!" grunted others. Then, after a long silence, Wamibo made strange noises. "Hallo, what's up with you?" said some one grumpily. "He says he would have gone for Davy," explained Archie, who was the Finn's interpreter generally. "I believe him!" cried voices. . . . "Never mind, Dutchy . . . You'll do, muddle-head . . . Your turn will come soon enough . . . You don't know when ye're well off." They ceased, and all together turned their faces to the door. Singleton stepped in, made two paces, and stood swaying slightly. The sea hissed, flowed roaring past the bows, and the forecastle trembled, full of a deep rumour; the lamp flared, swinging like a pendulum. He looked with a dreamy and puzzled stare, as though he could not distinguish the still men from their restless shadows. There were awestruck murmurs:—"Hallo, hallo" . . . "How does it look outside now, Singleton?" Those who sat on the hatch lifted their eyes in silence, and the next oldest seaman in the ship (those two understood one another, though they hardly exchanged three words in a day) gazed up at his friend attentively for a moment, then taking a short clay pipe out of his mouth, offered it without a word. Singleton put out his arm towards it, missed, staggered, and suddenly fell forward, crashing down, stiff and headlong like an uprooted tree. There was a swift rush. Men pushed, crying:—"He's done!" . . . "Turn him over!" . . . "Stand clear there!" Under a crowd of startled faces bending over him he lay on his back, staring upwards in a continuous and intolerable manner. In the breathless silence of a general consternation, he said in a grating murmur:—"I am all right," and clutched with his hands. They helped him up. He mumbled despondently:—"I am getting old . . . old."—"Not you," cried Belfast, with ready tact. Supported on all sides, he hung his head.—"Are you better?" they asked. He glared at them from under his eyebrows with large black eyes, spreading over his chest the

8. Three shillings (3/20 of one pound sterling) in the former British monetary system.
9. A nickname for a Welshman. An allusion to the nursery rhyme "Taffy was a Welshman, / Taffy was a thief."

bushy whiteness of a beard long and thick.—"Old! old!" he repeated
sternly. Helped along, he reached his bunk. There was in it a slimy
soft heap of something that smelt, as does at dead low water a
muddy foreshore. It was his soaked straw bed. With a convulsive
effort he pitched himself on it, and in the darkness of the narrow
place could be heard growling angrily, like an irritated and savage
animal uneasy in its den:—"Bit of breeze . . . small thing . . . can't
stand up . . . old!" He slept at last. He breathed heavily, high-
booted, sou'wester[1] on head, and his oilskin clothes rustled, when
with a deep sighing groan he turned over. Men conversed about
him in quiet concerned whispers. "This will break 'im up." . . .
"Strong as a horse." . . . "Aye. But he ain't what he used to be." . . . In
sad murmurs they gave him up. Yet at midnight he turned out to
duty as if nothing had been the matter, and answered to his name
with a mournful "Here!" He brooded alone more than ever, in an
impenetrable silence and with a saddened face. For many years he
had heard himself called "Old Singleton," and had serenely accepted
the qualification, taking it as a tribute of respect due to a man who
through half a century had measured his strength against the
favours and the rages of the sea. He had never given a thought to
his mortal self. He lived unscathed, as though he had been indestructible, surrendering to all the temptations, weathering many
gales. He had panted in sunshine, shivered in the cold; suffered
hunger, thirst, debauch; passed through many trials—known all
the furies. Old! It seemed to him he was broken at last. And like a
man bound treacherously while he sleeps, he woke up fettered by
the long chain of disregarded years. He had to take up at once the
burden of all his existence, and found it almost too heavy for his
strength. Old! He moved his arms, shook his head, felt his limbs.
Getting old . . . and then? He looked upon the immortal sea with
the awakened and groping perception of its heartless might; he saw
it unchanged, black and foaming under the eternal scrutiny of the
stars; he heard its impatient voice calling for him out of a pitiless
vastness full of unrest, of turmoil, and of terror. He looked afar
upon it, and he saw an immensity tormented and blind, moaning
and furious, that claimed all the days of his tenacious life, and,
when life was over, would claim the worn-out body of its slave.

This was the last of the breeze. It veered quickly, changed to a
black south-easter, and blew itself out, giving the ship a famous
shove to the northward into the joyous sunshine of the trade.[2]
Rapid and white she ran homewards in a straight path, under a blue

1. See p. 15, n. 6.
2. I.e., trade wind; in this instance, the trade wind that blows constantly in the Southern
   Hemisphere from southeast toward the equator from about the thirtieth parallel.
   "Black south-easter": a strong wind from the southeast.

sky and upon the plain of a blue sea. She carried Singleton's completed wisdom, Donkin's delicate susceptibilities, and the conceited
folly of us all. The hours of ineffective turmoil were forgotten; the
fear and anguish of these dark moments were never mentioned in
the glowing peace of fine days. Yet from that time our life seemed
to start afresh as though we had died and had been resuscitated.
All the first part of the voyage, the Indian Ocean on the other side
of the Cape, all that was lost in a haze, like an ineradicable suspicion of some previous existence. It had ended—then there were
blank hours: a livid blurr—and again we lived! Singleton was possessed of sinister truth; Mr. Creighton of a damaged leg; the cook
of fame—and shamefully abused the opportunities of his distinction. Donkin had an added grievance. He went about repeating
with insistence:—"'E said 'e would brain me—did yer 'ear? They
hare goin' to murder hus now for the least little thing." We began at
last to think it was rather awful. And we were conceited! We boasted
of our pluck, of our capacity for work, of our energy. We remembered
honourable episodes: our devotion, our indomitable perseverance—
and were proud of them as though they had been the outcome of
our unaided impulses. We remembered our danger, our toil—and
conveniently forgot our horrible scare. We decried our officers—
who had done nothing—and listened to the fascinating Donkin.
His care for our rights, his disinterested concern for our dignity,
were not discouraged by the invariable contumely of our words, by
the disdain of our looks. Our contempt for him was unbounded—
and we could not but listen with interest to that consummate artist.
He told us we were good men—a "bloomin' condemned[3] lot of good
men." Who thanked us? Who took any notice of our wrongs? Didn't
we lead a "dorg's loife for two poun' ten a month?"[4] Did we think
that miserable pay enough to compensate us for the risk to our lives
and for the loss of our clothes? "We've lost hevery rag!" he cried. He
made us forget that he, at any rate, had lost nothing of his own. The
younger men listened, thinking—this 'ere Donkin's a long-headed[5]
chap, though no kind of man, anyhow. The Scandinavians were
frightened at his audacities; Wamibo did not understand; and the
older seamen thoughtfully nodded their heads making the thin gold
earrings glitter in the fleshy lobes of hairy ears. Severe, sunburnt
faces were propped meditatively on tattooed fore-arms. Veined,
brown fists held in their knotted grip the dirty white clay of smouldering pipes. They listened, impenetrable, broad-backed, with bent

---

3. Another euphemism for *damned*.
4. The actual pay for able seamen aboard the *Narcissus* was £3 per month.
5. Far-seeing, discerning, shrewd.

shoulders, and in grim silence. He talked with ardour, despised and irrefutable. His picturesque and filthy loquacity flowed like a troubled stream from a poisoned source. His beady little eyes danced, glancing right and left, ever on the watch for the approach of an officer. Sometimes Mr. Baker going forward to take a look at the head sheets would roll with his uncouth gait through the sudden stillness of the men; or Mr. Creighton limped along, smooth-faced, youthful, and more stern than ever, piercing our short silence with a keen glance of his clear eyes. Behind his back Donkin would begin again darting stealthy, sidelong looks.—"'Ere's one of 'em. Some of yer 'as made 'im fast that day. Much thanks yer got for hit. Ain't 'ee a-drivin' yer wusse'n hever?[6] . . . Let 'im slip hoverboard. . . . Vy not? It would 'ave been less trouble. Vy not?" He advanced confidentially, backed away with great effect; he whispered, he screamed, waved his miserable arms no thicker than pipe-stems—stretched his lean neck—spluttered—squinted. In the pauses of his impassioned orations the wind sighed quietly aloft, the calm sea unheeded murmured in a warning whisper along the ship's side. We abominated the creature and could not deny the luminous truth of his contentions. It was all so obvious. We were indubitably good men; our deserts were great and our pay small. Through our exertions we had saved the ship and the skipper would get the credit of it. What had he done? we wanted to know. Donkin asked:—"What 'ee could do without hus?" and we could not answer. We were oppressed by the injustice of the world, surprised to perceive how long we had lived under its burden without realising our unfortunate state, annoyed by the uneasy suspicion of our undiscerning stupidity. Donkin assured us it was all our "good 'eartedness," but we would not be consoled by such shallow sophistry. We were men enough to courageously admit to ourselves our intellectual shortcomings; though from that time we refrained from kicking him, tweaking his nose, or from accidentally knocking him about, which last, after we had weathered the Cape, had been rather a popular amusement. Davies ceased to talk at him provokingly about black eyes and flattened noses. Charley, much subdued since the gale, did not jeer at him. Knowles deferentially and with a crafty air propounded questions such as:—"Could we all have the same grub as the mates? Could we all stop ashore till we got it? What would be the next thing to try for if we got that?" He answered readily with contemptuous certitude; he strutted with assurance in clothes that were much too big for him as though he had tried to disguise himself. These were Jimmy's clothes mostly—though he would accept anything from anybody; but

6. Ain't he driving you worse than ever?

nobody, except Jimmy, had anything to spare. His devotion to Jimmy was unbounded. He was for ever dodging in the little cabin, ministering to Jimmy's wants, humoring his whims, submitting to his exacting peevishness, often laughing with him. Nothing could keep him away from the pious work of visiting the sick, especially when there was some heavy hauling to be done on deck. Mr. Baker had on two occasions jerked him out from there by the scruff of the neck to our inexpressible scandal. Was a sick chap to be left without attendance? Were we to be ill-used for attending a shipmate?— "What?" growled Mr. Baker, turning menacingly at the mutter, and the whole half-circle like one man stepped back a pace. "Set the topmast stun-sail. Away aloft, Donkin, overhaul the gear," ordered the mate inflexibly. "Fetch the sail along; bend the down-haul clear. Bear a hand." Then, the sail set, he would go slowly aft and stand looking at the compass for a long time, careworn, pensive, and breathing hard as if stifled by the taint of unaccountable ill-will that pervaded the ship. "What's up amongst them?" he thought. "Can't make out this hanging back and growling. A good crowd, too, as they go nowadays." On deck the men exchanged bitter words, suggested by a silly exasperation against something unjust and irremediable that would not be denied, and would whisper into their ears long after Donkin had ceased speaking. Our little world went on its curved and unswerving path carrying a discontented and aspiring population. They found comfort of a gloomy kind in an interminable and conscientious analysis of their unappreciated worth; and inspired by Donkin's hopeful doctrines they dreamed enthusiastically of the time when every lonely ship would travel over a serene sea, manned by a wealthy and well-fed crew of satisfied skippers.

It looked as if it would be a long passage. The south-east trades,[7] light and unsteady, were left behind; and then, on the equator and under a low grey sky, the ship, in close heat, floated upon a smooth sea that resembled a sheet of ground glass. Thunder squalls hung on the horizon, circled round the ship, far off and growling angrily, like a troop of wild beasts afraid to charge home. The invisible sun, sweeping above the upright masts, made on the clouds a blurred stain of rayless light, and a similar patch of faded radiance kept pace with it from east to west over the unglittering level of the waters. At night, through the impenetrable darkness of earth and heaven, broad sheets of flame[8] waved noiselessly; and for half a second the becalmed craft stood out with its masts and rigging, with every sail and every rope distinct and black in the centre of a fiery outburst,

7. See p. 205, n. 2.
8. See p. 12, n. 3.

like a charred ship enclosed in a globe of fire. And, again, for long hours she remained lost in a vast universe of night and silence where gentle sighs wandering here and there like forlorn souls, made the still sails flutter as in sudden fear, and the ripple of a beshrouded ocean whisper its compassion afar—in a voice mournful, immense, and faint. . . .

When the lamp was put out, and through the door thrown wide open, Jimmy, turning on his pillow, could see vanishing beyond the straight line of top-gallant rail, the quick, repeated visions of a fabulous world made up of leaping fire and sleeping water. The lightning gleamed in his big sad eyes that seemed in a red flicker to burn themselves out in his black face, and then he would lay blinded and invisible in the midst of an intense darkness. He could hear on the quiet deck soft footfalls, the breathing of some man lounging on the doorstep; the low creak of swaying masts; or the calm voice of the watch-officer reverberating aloft, hard and loud, amongst the unstirring sails. He listened with avidity, taking a rest in the attentive perception of the slightest sound from the fatiguing wanderings of his sleeplessness. He was cheered by the rattling of blocks, reassured by the stir and murmur of the watch, soothed by the slow yawn of some sleepy and weary seaman settling himself deliberately for a snooze on the planks. Life seemed an indestructible thing. It went on in darkness, in sunshine, in sleep; tireless, it hovered affectionately round the imposture of his ready death. It was bright, like the twisted flare of lightning, and more full of surprises than the dark night. It made him safe, and the calm of its overpowering darkness was as precious as its restless and dangerous light.

But in the evening, in the dog-watches, and even far into the first night-watch, a knot of men could always be seen congregated before Jimmy's cabin. They leaned on each side of the door, peacefully interested and with crossed legs; they stood astride the doorstep discoursing, or sat in silent couples on his sea-chest; while against the bulwark along the spare topmast, three or four in a row stared meditatively, with their simple faces lit up by the projected glare of Jimmy's lamp. The little place, repainted white, had, in the night, the brilliance of a silver shrine where a black idol, reclining stiffly under a blanket, blinked its weary eyes and received our homage. Donkin officiated. He had the air of a demonstrator showing a phenomenon, a manifestation bizarre, simple, and meritorious, that, to the beholders, should be a profound and an everlasting lesson. "Just look at 'im, 'ee knows what's what—never fear!" he exclaimed now and then, flourishing a hand hard and fleshless like the claw of a snipe. Jimmy, on his back, smiled with reserve and without moving a limb. He affected the languor of extreme weakness, so as to make it manifest to us that our delay in hauling him out from his horrible confinement, and then that night spent on the poop among our selfish neglect of his needs, had "done for him." He rather liked to talk about it, and of course we were always interested. He spoke spasmodically, in fast rushes with long pauses between, as a tipsy man walks. . . . "Cook had just given me a pannikin of hot coffee. . . . Slapped it down there, on my chest—banged the door to. . . . I felt a heavy roll coming; tried to save my coffee, burnt my fingers . . . and fell out of my bunk. . . . She went over so quick. . . . Water came in through the ventilator. . . . I couldn't move the door . . . dark as a grave . . . tried to scramble up into the upper berth. . . . Rats . . . a rat bit my finger as I got up. . . . I could hear him swimming below me. . . . I thought you would never come. . . . I thought you were all gone overboard . . . of course . . . Could hear nothing but the wind. . . . Then you came . . . to look for the corpse, I suppose. A little more and . . ."

"Man! But ye made a rare lot of noise in here," observed Archie, thoughtfully.

"You chaps kicked up such a confounded row above. . . . Enough to scare any one. . . . I didn't know what you were up to. . . . Bash in the blamed planks . . . my head. . . . Just what a silly, scary gang of fools would do. . . . Not much good to me anyhow. . . . Just as well . . . drown. . . . Pah."

He groaned, snapped his big white teeth, and gazed with scorn. Belfast lifted a pair of dolorous eyes, with a broken-hearted smile, clenched his fists stealthily; blue-eyed Archie caressed his red whiskers with a hesitating hand; the boatswain at the door stared a moment, and brusquely went away with a loud guffaw. Wamibo dreamed. . . . Donkin felt all over his sterile chin for the few rare hairs, and said, triumphantly, with a sidelong glance at Jimmy:— "Look at 'im! Wish I was 'arf has 'ealthy has 'e his—I do." He jerked a short thumb over his shoulder towards the after-end of the ship. "That's the blooming way to do 'em!" he yelped, with forced heartiness. Jimmy said:—"Don't be a dam' fool," in a pleasant voice. Knowles, rubbing his shoulder against the doorpost, remarked shrewdly:—"We can't all go an' be took sick—it would be mutiny."— "Mutiny—gawn!" jeered Donkin; "there's no bloomin' law against bein' sick."—"There's six weeks' hard for refoosing dooty," argued Knowles, "I mind I once seed in Cardiff[9] the crew of an overloaded ship—leastways she weren't overloaded, only a fatherly old gentleman with a white beard and an umbreller came along the quay and

9. See p. 9, n. 8. "Six weeks' hard": a sentence of six weeks' hard labor.

talked to the hands. Said as how it was crool hard to be drownded in winter just for the sake of a few pounds more for the owner—he said. Nearly cried over them—he did; and he had a square mainsail coat, and a gaff-topsail hat[1] too—all proper. So they chaps they said they wouldn't go to be drownded in winter—depending upon that 'ere Plimsoll man[2] to see 'em through the court. They thought to have a bloomin' lark and two or three days' spree. And the beak[3] giv' 'em six weeks—coss the ship warn't overloaded. Anyways they made it out in court that she wasn't. There wasn't one overloaded ship in Penarth Dock at all. 'Pears that old coon[4] he was only on pay and allowance from some kind people, under orders to look for overloaded ships, and he couldn't see no further than the length of his umbreller. Some of us in the boarding-house, where I live when I'm looking for a ship in Cardiff, stood by to duck that old weeping spunger in the dock. We kept a good look out, too—but he topped his boom[5] directly he was outside the court. . . . Yes. They got six weeks' hard. . . ."

They listened, full of curiosity, nodding in the pauses their rough pensive faces. Donkin opened his mouth once or twice, but restrained himself. Jimmy lay still with open eyes and not at all interested. A seaman emitted the opinion that after a verdict of atrocious partiality "the bloomin' beaks go an' drink at the skipper's expense." Others assented. It was clear, of course. Donkin said:— "Well, six weeks hain't much trouble. You sleep hall night in, reg'lar, in chokey.[6] Do it hon my 'ead." "You are used to it ainch 'ee, Donkin?" asked somebody. Jimmy condescended to laugh. It cheered up every one wonderfully. Knowles, with surprising mental agility, shifted his ground. "If we all went sick what would become of the ship? Eh?" He posed the problem and grinned all round.—"Let 'er go to 'ell," sneered Donkin. "Damn 'er. She ain't yourn."—"What? Just let her drift?" insisted Knowles in a tone of unbelief.—"Aye! Drift, an' be blowed," affirmed Donkin with fine recklessness. The other did not see it—meditated.—"The stores would run out," he muttered, "and . . . never get anywhere . . . and what about pay-day?" he added with greater assurance.—"Jack likes a good pay-day," exclaimed a listener on the doorstep. "Aye, because then the girls put one arm round his neck an' t'other in his pocket, an' call him

---

1. Frock coat and top hat (slang).
2. A supporter of Samuel Plimsoll (1824–1898), a radical member of Parliament from 1868 to 1890. Plimsoll championed the rights of common sailors.
3. A magistrate or justice of the peace (slang). "Lark": playful adventure.
4. A sly, knowing fellow. "Penarth Dock": a seaport in southeast Wales on the Bristol Channel. The actual ship *Narcissus* left from Penarth on its voyage to the East.
5. To leave (slang). "Spunger": a sponger or parasite; one who lives at the expense of others. "Duck": dunk (slang).
6. Jail or prison (Hindi).

ducky. Don't they, Jack?"—"Jack, you're a terror with the gals."—
"He takes three of 'em in tow to once, like one of 'em Watkinses
two-funnel tugs[7] waddling away with three schooners behind."—
"Jack, you're a lame scamp.—"Jack, tell us about that one with a blue
eye and a black eye. Do."—"There's plenty of girls with one black eye
along the Highway by . . ."—"No, that's a speshul one—come Jack."
Donkin looked severe and disgusted; Jimmy very bored; a grey-haired
sea-dog shook his head slightly, smiling at the bowl of his pipe, dis-
creetly amused. Knowles turned about bewildered; stammered first
at one, then at another.—"No! . . . I never! . . . can't talk sensible
sense midst you. . . . Always on the kid."[8] He retired bashfully—
muttering and pleased. They laughed, hooting in the crude light,
around Jimmy's bed, where on a white pillow his hollowed black
face moved to and fro restlessly. A puff of wind came, made the
flame of the lamp leap, and outside, high up, the sails fluttered,
while near by the block of the foresheet struck a ringing blow on
the iron bulwark. A voice far off cried, "Helm up!" another, more
faint, answered, "Hard-up, sir!" They became silent—waited expec-
tantly. The grey-haired seaman knocked his pipe on the doorstep
and stood up. The ship leaned over gently and the sea seemed to
wake up, murmuring drowsily. "Here's a little wind comin'," said
some one very low. Jimmy turned over slowly to face the breeze.
The voice in the night cried loud and commanding:—"Haul the
spanker out." The group before the door vanished out of the light.
They could be heard tramping aft while they repeated with varied
intonations:—"Spanker   out!" . . . "Out   spanker,   sir!" Donkin
remained alone with Jimmy. There was a silence. Jimmy opened
and shut his lips several times as if swallowing draughts of fresher
air; Donkin moved the toes of his bare feet and looked at them
thoughtfully.

"Ain't you going to give them a hand with the sail?" asked Jimmy.

"No. Hif six ov 'em hain't 'nough beef[9] to set that blamed, rotten
spanker, they hain't fit to live," answered Donkin in a bored, far-
away voice, as though he had been talking from the bottom of a
hole. Jimmy considered the conical, fowl-like profile with a queer
kind of interest; he was leaning out of his bunk with the calculat-
ing, uncertain expression of a man who reflects how best to lay hold
of some strange creature that looks as though it could sting or bite.
But he said only:—"The mate will miss you—and there will be
ructions."

---

7. William Watkins Ltd. was one of the first tugboat companies. It was founded in 1833
   by John Roger Watkins (b. 1790) with his son William (1819–1900).
8. Always kidding.
9. Don't have enough muscle.

Donkin got up to go. "I will do for 'im hon some dark night, see hif I don't," he said over his shoulder.

Jimmy went on quickly:—"You're like a poll-parrot, like a screechin' poll-parrot." Donkin stopped and cocked his head attentively on one side. His big ears stood out, transparent and veined, resembling the thin wings of a bat.

"Yuss?" he said, with his back towards Jimmy.

"Yes! Chatter out all you know—like . . . like a dirty white cockatoo."

Donkin waited. He could hear the other's breathing, long and slow; the breathing of a man with a hundredweight or so on the breastbone. Then he asked calmly:—"What do I know?"

"What? . . . What I tell you . . . not much. What do you want . . . to talk about my health so . . ."

"Hit's a blooming himposyshun.[1] A bloomin', stinkin' first-class himposyshun—but hit don't tyke me hin. Not hit."

Jimmy kept still. Donkin put his hands in his pockets, and in one slouching stride came up to the bunk.

"I talk—what's the hodds. They hain't men here—sheep they hare. A driven lot of sheep. I 'old you hup . . . Vy not? You're well hoff."

"I am. . . . I don't say anything about that. . . ."

"Well. Let 'em see hit. Let 'em larn what a man can do. I ham a man, I know hall about yer. . . ." Jimmy threw himself further away on the pillow; the other stretched out his skinny neck, jerked his bird face down at him as though pecking at the eyes. "I ham a man. I've seen the hinside of every chokey in the Colonies rather'n give hup my rights. . . ."

"You are a jail-prop,"[2] said Jimmy weakly.

"I ham . . . an' proud of it too. You! You 'aven't the bloomin' nerve—so you hinventyd this 'ere dodge. . . ." He paused; then with marked afterthought accentuated slowly:—"Yer ain't sick—hare yer?"

"No," said Jimmy firmly. "Been out of sorts now and again this year," he mumbled with a sudden drop in his voice.

Donkin closed one eye, amicable and confidential. He whispered:—"Ye 'ave done hit afore—'aven't chee?"[3] Jimmy smiled—then as if unable to hold back he let himself go:—"Last ship—yes. I was out of sorts on the passage. See? It was easy. They paid me off in Calcutta,[4] and the skipper made no bones about it either. . . . I got my money all right. Laid up fifty-eight days! The fools! O Lord! The fools! Paid

---

1. Imposition.
2. Literally, someone who props up a jail; but meaning a person who is regularly in jail.
3. Haven't ye?
4. Or Kolkata; a seaport in northeastern India on the Bay of Bengal. See p. 336.

right off." He laughed spasmodically. Donkin chummed,[5] giggling. Then Jimmy coughed violently. "I am as well as ever," he said, as soon as he could draw breath.

Donkin made a derisive gesture. "In course," he said profoundly, "hany one can see that."—"They don't," said Jimmy, gasping like a fish.—"They would swallow any yarn," affirmed Donkin.—"Don't you let on too much," admonished Jimmy in an exhausted voice.— "Your little gyme? Eh?" commented Donkin jovially. Then with sudden disgust: "Yer hall for yerself, s'long has ye're right. . . ."

So charged with egoism James Wait pulled the blanket up to his chin and lay still for awhile. His heavy lips protruded in an everlasting black pout. "Why are you so hot on making trouble?" he asked without much interest.

" 'Cos hit's a bloomin' shayme. We hare put hon . . . bad food, bad pay . . . I want hus to kick up a bloomin' row; a blamed 'owling row that would make 'em remember! Knocking people habout . . . brain hus . . . hindeed! Ain't we men?" His altruistic indignation blazed. Then he said calmly:—"I've been a-hairing ov yer clothes."—"All right," said Jimmy languidly, "bring them in."—"Giv' us the key of your chest, I'll put 'em away for yer," said Donkin with friendly eagerness.—"Bring 'em in, I will put them away myself," answered James Wait with severity. Donkin looked down, muttering. . . . "What d'you say? What d'you say?" inquired Wait anxiously.— "Nothink. The night's dry; let 'em 'ang out till the morning," said Donkin, in a strangely trembling voice, as though restraining laughter or rage. Jimmy seemed satisfied.—"Give me a little water for the night in my mug—there," he said. Donkin took a stride over the doorstep.— "Git it yerself," he replied in a surly tone. "You can do it, hunless you *hare* sick."—"Of course I can do it," said Wait, "only . . ."—"Well, then, do it," said Donkin viciously, "if yer can look hafter yer clothes, yer can look hafter yerself." He went on deck without a look back.

Jimmy reached out for the mug. Not a drop. He put it back gently with a faint sigh—and closed his eyes. He thought:—That lunatic Belfast will bring me some water if I ask. Fool. I am very thirsty. . . . It was very hot in the cabin, and it seemed to turn slowly round, detach itself from the ship, and swing out smoothly into a luminous, arid space where a black sun shone, spinning very fast. A place without any water! No water! A policeman with the face of Donkin drank a glass of beer by the side of an empty well, and flew away flapping vigorously. A ship whose mastheads protruded through the sky and could not be seen, was discharging grain, and the wind whirled the dry husks in spirals along the quay of a dock with no

5. Was friendly or intimate.

water in it. He whirled along with the husks—very tired and light. All his inside was gone. He felt lighter than the husks—and more dry. He expanded his hollow chest. The air streamed in carrying away in its rush a lot of strange things that resembled houses, trees, people, lamp-posts. . . . No more! There was no more air—and he had not finished drawing his long breath. But he was in gaol! They were locking him up. A door slammed. They turned the key twice, flung a bucket of water over him—Phoo! What for?

He opened his eyes, thinking the fall had been very heavy for an empty man—empty—empty. He was in his cabin. Ah! All right! His face was streaming with perspiration, his arms heavier than lead. He saw the cook standing in the doorway, a brass key in one hand and a bright tin hook-pot in the other.

"I have been locking up for the night," said the cook, beaming benevolently. "Eight bells just gone. I brought you a pot of cold tea for your night's drinking, Jimmy. I sweetened it with some white cabin sugar, too. Well—it won't break the ship."

He came in, hung the pot on the edge of the bunk, asked perfunctorily, "How goes it?" and sat down on the box.—"H'm," grunted Wait inhospitably. The cook wiped his face with a dirty cotton rag, which, afterwards, he tied round his neck.—"That's how them firemen do in steamboats," he said serenely, and much pleased with himself. "My work is as heavy as theirs—I'm thinking—and longer hours. Did you ever see them down the stokehold? Like fiends they look—firing—firing—firing—down there."

He pointed his forefinger at the deck. Some gloomy thought darkened his shining face, fleeting, like the shadow of a travelling cloud over the light of a peaceful sea. The relieved watch tramped noisily forward, passing in a body across the sheen of the doorway. Some one cried, "Good night!" Belfast stopped for a moment and looked in at Jimmy, quivering and speechless as if with repressed emotion. He gave the cook a glance charged with dismal foreboding, and vanished. The cook cleared his throat. Jimmy stared upwards and kept as still as a man in hiding.

The night was clear, with a gentle breeze. The ship heeled over a little, slipping quietly over a sombre sea towards the inaccessible and festal splendour of a black horizon pierced by points of flickering fire. Above the mastheads the resplendent curve of the Milky Way[6] spanned the sky like a triumphal arch of eternal light, thrown over the dark pathway of the earth. On the forecastle-head a man whistled with loud precision a lively jig, while another could be heard faintly, shuffling and stamping in time. There came from

6. The faintly luminous band in the night sky composed of billions of stars.

forward a confused murmur of voices, laughter—snatches of song. The cook shook his head, glanced obliquely at Jimmy, and began to mutter. "Aye. Dance and sing. That's all they think of. I am surprised the Providence don't get tired. . . . They forget the day that's sure to come . . . but you. . . ."

Jimmy drank a gulp of tea, hurriedly, as though he had stolen it, and shrank under his blanket, edging away towards the bulkhead. The cook got up, closed the door, then sat down again and said distinctly:—

"Whenever I poke my galley fire I think of you chaps—swearing, stealing, lying, and worse—as if there was no such thing as another world. . . . Not bad fellows, either, in a way," he conceded slowly; then, after a pause of regretful musing, he went on in a resigned tone:—"Well, well. They will have a hot time of it. Hot! Did I say? The furnaces of one of them White Star boats[7] ain't nothing to it."

He kept very quiet for a while. There was a great stir in his brain; an addled vision of bright outlines; an exciting row of rousing songs and groans of pain. He suffered, enjoyed, admired, approved. He was delighted, frightened, exalted—as on that evening (the only time in his life—twenty-seven years ago; he loved to recall the number of years) when as a young man he had—through keeping bad company—become intoxicated in an East-end music-hall. A tide of sudden feeling swept him clean out of his body. He soared. He contemplated the secret of the hereafter. It commended itself to him. It was excellent; he loved it, himself, all hands, and Jimmy. His heart overflowed with tenderness, with comprehension, with the desire to meddle, with anxiety for the soul of that black man, with the pride of possessed eternity, with the feeling of might. Snatch him up in his arms and pitch him right into the middle of salvation . . . the black soul—blacker—body—rot—Devil. No! Talk—strength—Samson.[8] . . . There was a great din as of cymbals in his ears; he flashed through an ecstatic jumble of shining faces, lilies, prayerbooks, unearthly joy, white shirts, gold harps, black coats, wings. He saw flowing garments, clean shaved faces, a sea of light—a lake of pitch. There were sweet scents, a smell of sulphur—red tongues of flame licking a white mist. An awesome voice thundered! . . . It lasted three seconds.

"Jimmy!" he cried in an inspired tone. Then he hesitated. A spark of human pity glimmered yet through the infernal fog of his supreme conceit.

---

7. The White Star Line was founded in 1845 in Liverpool. Initially, it was involved with Australia/United Kingdom trade, but in 1871 it began to focus on the passenger trade between Liverpool and New York. The company merged with the Cunard Line in 1933.
8. A reference to the biblical strong man; see Judges 13:24–16:30.

"What?" said James Wait, unwillingly. There was a silence. He turned his head just the least bit, and stole a cautious glance. The cook's lips moved inaudibly; his face was rapt, his eyes turned up. He seemed to be mentally imploring deck beams, the brass hook of the lamp, two cockroaches.

"Look here," said Wait, "I want to go to sleep. I think I could."

"This is no time for sleep!" exclaimed the cook, very loud. He had prayerfully divested himself of the last vestige of his humanity. He was a voice—a fleshless and sublime thing, as on that memorable night—the night when he went over the sea to make coffee for perishing sinners. "This is no time for sleeping," he repeated with exaltation. "*I* can't sleep."

"Don't care damn," said Wait, with factitious energy. "I can. Go an' turn in."

"Swear . . . in the very jaws!⁹ . . . In the very jaws! Don't you see the fire . . . don't you feel it? Blind, chockfull of sin! I can see it for you. I can't bear it. I hear the call to save you. Night and day. Jimmy let me save you!" The words of entreaty and menace broke out of him in a roaring torrent. The cockroaches ran away. Jimmy perspired, wriggling stealthily under his blanket. The cook yelled. . . . "Your days are numbered! . . ."—"Get out of this," boomed Wait, courageously.—"Pray with me! . . ."—"I won't! . . ." The little cabin was as hot as an oven. It contained an immensity of fear and pain; an atmosphere of shrieks and moans; prayers vociferated like blasphemies and whispered curses. Outside, the men called by Charley, who informed them in tones of delight that there was a row going on in Jimmy's place, pushed before the closed door, too startled to open it. All hands were there. The watch below had jumped out on deck in their shirts, as after a collision. Men running up, asked:— "What is it?" Others said:—"Listen!" The muffled screaming went on:—"On your knees! On your knees!"—"Shut up!"—"Never! You are delivered into my hands. . . . Your life has been saved. . . . Purpose. . . . Mercy. . . . Repent."—"You are a crazy fool! . . ."—"Account of you . . . you . . . Never sleep in this world, if I . . ."—"Leave off"— "No! . . . stokehold . . . only think! . . ." Then an impassioned screeching babble where words pattered like hail.—"No!" shouted Jim.—"Yes. You are! . . . No help. . . . Everybody says so."—"You lie!"—"I see you dying this minnyt . . . before my eyes . . . as good as dead now."—"Help!" shouted Jimmy, piercingly.—"Not in this valley.¹ . . . look upwards," howled the other.—"Go away! Murder!

9. I.e., the very jaws of hell.
1. Possibly an allusion to Psalms 23:4: "Yea, though I walk through the valley of the shadow of death."

Help!" clamoured Jimmy. His voice broke. There were moanings, low mutters, a few sobs.

"What's the matter now?" said a seldom-heard voice.—"Fall back, men! Fall back, there!" repeated Mr. Creighton sternly, pushing through.—"Here's the old man," whispered some.—"The cook's in there, sir," exclaimed several, backing away. The door clattered open; a broad stream of light darted out on wondering faces; a warm whiff of vitiated air passed. The two mates towered head and shoulders above the spare, grey-headed man who stood revealed between them, in shabby clothes, stiff and angular, like a small carved figure, and with a thin, composed face. The cook got up from his knees. Jimmy sat high in the bunk, clasping his drawn-up legs. The tassel of the blue nightcap almost imperceptibly trembled over his knees. They gazed astonished at his long, curved back, while the white corner of one eye gleamed blindly at them. He was afraid to turn his head, he shrank within himself; and there was an aspect astounding and animal-like in the perfection of his expectant immobility. A thing of instinct—the unthinking stillness of a scared brute.

"What are you doing here?" asked Mr. Baker, sharply.—"My duty," said the cook, with ardour.—"Your . . . what?" began the mate. Captain Allistoun touched his arm lightly.—"I know his caper," he said, in a low voice. "Come out of that, Podmore," he ordered, aloud.

The cook wrung his hands, shook his fists above his head, and his arms dropped as if too heavy. For a moment he stood distracted and speechless.—"Never," he stammered, "I . . . he . . . I."—"What—do—you—say?" pronounced Captain Allistoun. "Come out at once—or . . ."—"I am going," said the cook, with a hasty and sombre resignation. He strode over the doorstep firmly—hesitated—made a few steps.[2] They looked at him in silence.—"I make you responsible!" he cried desperately, turning half round. "That man is dying. I make you . . ."—"You there yet?" called the master in a threatening tone.—"No, sir," he exclaimed hurriedly in a startled voice. The boatswain led him away by the arm; some one laughed; Jimmy lifted his head for a stealthy glance, and in one unexpected leap sprang out of his bunk; Mr. Baker made a clever catch and felt him very limp in his arms; the group at the door grunted with surprise.— "He lies," gasped Wait, "he talked about black devils—he is a devil—a white devil—I am all right." He stiffened himself, and Mr. Baker, experimentally, let him go. He staggered a pace or two; Captain Allistoun watched him with a quiet and penetrating gaze; Belfast ran to his support. He did not appear to be aware of any one

2. Took a few steps.

near him; he stood silent for a moment, battling single-handed with a legion of nameless terrors, amidst the eager looks of excited men who watched him far off, utterly alone in the impenetrable solitude of his fear. Heavy breathings stirred the darkness. The sea gurgled through the scuppers as the ship heeled over to a short puff of wind.

"Keep him away from me," said James Wait at last in his fine baritone voice, and leaning with all his weight on Belfast's neck. "I've been better this last week . . . I am well . . . I was going back to duty . . . to-morrow—now if you like—Captain." Belfast hitched his shoulders to keep him upright.

"No," said the master, looking at him fixedly.

Under Jimmy's armpit Belfast's red face moved uneasily. A row of eyes gleaming stared on the edge of light. They pushed one another with elbows, turned their heads, whispered. Wait let his chin fall on his breast and, with lowered eyelids, looked round in a suspicious manner.

"Why not?" cried a voice from the shadows, "the man's all right, sir."

"I am all right," said Wait with eagerness. "Been sick . . . better . . . turn-to[3] now." He sighed.—"Howly Mother!" exclaimed Belfast with a heave of the shoulders, "stand up, Jimmy."—"Keep away from me then," said Wait, giving Belfast a petulant push, and reeling fetched against the door-post. His cheekbones glistened as though they had been varnished. He snatched off his night-cap, wiped his perspiring face with it, flung it on the deck. "I am coming out," he said without stirring.

"No. You don't," said the master curtly. Bare feet shuffled, disapproving voices murmured all round; he went on as if he had not heard:—"You have been skulking nearly all the passage and now you want to come out. You think you are near enough to the pay-table now. Smell the shore, hey?"

"I've been sick . . . now—better," mumbled Wait glaring in the light.—"You have been shamming sick," retorted Captain Allistoun with severity; "Why . . ." he hesitated for less than half a second. "Why, anybody can see that. There's nothing the matter with you, but you choose to lie-up to please yourself— and now you shall lie-up to please me. Mr. Baker, my orders are that this man is not to be allowed on deck to the end of the passage."

There were exclamations of surprise, triumph, indignation. The dark group of men swung across the light. "What for?" "Told you so . . ." "Bloomin' shame . . ."—"We've got to say something habout that," screeched Donkin from the rear.—"Never mind, Jim—we will

3. To set to work on a task.

see you righted," cried several together. An elderly seaman stepped to the front. "D'ye mean to say, sir," he asked ominously, "that a sick chap ain't allowed to get well in this 'ere hooker?" Behind him Donkin whispered excitedly amongst a staring crowd where no one spared him a glance, but Captain Allistoun shook a forefinger at the angry bronzed face of the speaker.—"You—you hold your tongue," he said warningly— "This isn't the way," clamoured two or three younger men.—"Hare we bloomin' masheens?" inquired Donkin in a piercing tone, and dived under the elbows of the front rank.—"Soon show 'im we ain't boys . . ."—"The man's a man if he is black."—"We ain't goin' to work this bloomin' ship shorthanded if Snowball's[4] all right . . ."—"He says he is."—"Well then, strike, boys, strike!"—"That's the bloomin' ticket." Captain Allistoun said sharply to the second mate: "Keep quiet, Mr. Creighton," and stood composed in the tumult, listening with profound attention to mixed growls and screeches, to every exclamation and every curse of the sudden outbreak. Somebody slammed the cabin door to with a kick; the darkness full of menacing mutters leaped with a short clatter over the streak of light, and the men became gesticulating shadows that growled, hissed, laughed excitedly. Mr. Baker whispered:— "Get away from them, sir." The big shape of Mr. Creighton hovered silently about the slight figure of the master.—"We have been hymposed upon all this voyage," said a gruff voice, "but this 'ere fancy takes the cake."—"That man is a shipmate."—"Are we bloomin' kids?"—"The port-watch will refuse duty." Charley carried away by his feelings whistled shrilly, then yelped:—"Giv' us our Jimmy!" This seemed to cause a variation in the disturbance. There was a fresh burst of squabbling uproar. A lot of quarrels were set going at once.—"Yes"—"No."—"Never been sick."—"Go for them at once."—"Shut yer mouth, youngster—this is men's work."—"Is it?" muttered Captain Allistoun bitterly. Mr. Baker grunted: "Ough! They're gone silly. They've been simmering for the last month."— "I did notice," said the master.—"They have started a row amongst themselves now," said Mr. Creighton with disdain, "better get aft, sir. We will soothe them."—"Keep your temper, Creighton," said the master. And the three men began to move slowly towards the cabin door.

In the shadows of the fore-rigging a dark mass stamped, eddied, advanced, retreated. There were words of reproach, encouragement, unbelief, execration. The elder seamen, bewildered and angry, growled their determination to go through with something or other; but the younger school of advanced thought exposed their and Jimmy's wrongs with confused shouts, arguing amongst themselves.

4. Ironic reference to James Wait.

They clustered round that moribund carcass, the fit emblem of their aspirations, and encouraging one another they swayed, they tramped on one spot, shouting that they would not be "put upon." Inside the cabin, Belfast, helping Jimmy into his bunk, twitched all over in his desire not to miss all the row, and with difficulty restrained the tears of his facile emotion. James Wait, flat on his back under the blanket, gasped complaints.—"We will back you up, never fear," assured Belfast, busy about his feet.—"I'll come out to-morrow morning—take my chance—you fellows must—" mumbled Wait, "I come out to-morrow—skipper or no skipper." He lifted one arm with great difficulty, passed the hand over his face; "Don't you let that cook . . ." he breathed out.—"No, no," said Belfast, turning his back on the bunk, "I will put a head on him[5] if he comes near you."—"I will smash his mug!" exclaimed faintly Wait, enraged and weak; "I don't want to kill a man, but . . ." He panted fast like a dog after a run in sunshine. Some one just outside the door shouted, "He's as fit as any ov us!" Belfast put his hand on the door-handle.— "Here!" called James Wait hurriedly and in such a clear voice that the other spun round with a start. James Wait, stretched out black and deathlike in the dazzling light, turned his head on the pillow. His eyes stared at Belfast, appealing and impudent. "I am rather weak from lying-up so long," he said distinctly. Belfast nodded. "Getting quite well now," insisted Wait.—"Yes. I noticed you getting better this . . . last month," said Belfast looking down. "Hallo! What's this?" he shouted and ran out.

He was flattened directly against the side of the house by two men who lurched against him. A lot of disputes seemed to be going on all round. He got clear and saw three indistinct figures standing alone in the fainter darkness under the arched foot of the mainsail, that rose above their heads like a convex wall of a high edifice. Donkin hissed:—"Go for them . . . it's dark!" The crowd took a short run aft in a body—then there was a check. Donkin, agile and thin, flitted past with his right arm going like a windmill—and then stood still suddenly with his arm pointing rigidly above his head. The hurtling flight of some small heavy object was heard; it passed between the heads of the two mates, bounded heavily along the deck, struck the after-hatch with a ponderous and deadened blow. The bulky shape of Mr. Baker grew distinct. "Come to your senses, men!" he cried, advancing at the arrested crowd. "Come back, Mr. Baker!" called the master's quiet voice. He obeyed unwillingly. There was a minute of silence, then a deafening hubbub arose. Above it Archie was heard energetically:—"If ye do oot ageen

5. Punch or assault him.

I wull tell!" There were shouts. "Don't!" "Drop it!"—"We ain't that kind!" The black cluster of human forms reeled against the bulwark, back again towards the house. Shadowy figures could be seen tottering, falling, leaping up. Ringbolts rang under stumbling feet.—"Drop it!" "Let me!"—"No!"—"Curse you . . . hah!" Then sounds as of some one's face being slapped; a piece of iron fell on the deck; a short scuffle, and some one's shadowy body scuttled rapidly across the main-hatch before the shadow of a kick. A raging voice sobbed out a torrent of filthy language . . . —"Throwing things—good God!" grunted Mr. Baker in dismay.—"That was meant for me," said the master quietly; "I felt the wind of that thing; what was it—an iron belaying-pin?"—"By jove!" muttered Mr. Creighton. The confused voices of men talking amidships mingled with the wash of the sea, ascended between the silent and distended sails—seemed to flow away into the night, further than the horizon, higher than the sky. The stars burned steadily over the inclined mastheads. Trails of light lay on the water, broke before the advancing hull, and, after she had passed, trembled for a long time as if in awe of the murmuring sea.

Meantime the helmsman, anxious to know what the row was about, had let go the wheel, and, bent double, ran with long stealthy footsteps to the break of the poop. The *Narcissus*, left to herself, came up gently to the wind without any one being aware of it. She gave a slight roll, and the sleeping sails woke suddenly, coming all together with a mighty flap against the masts, then filled again one after another in a quick succession of loud reports that ran down the lofty spars, till the collapsed mainsail flew out last with a violent jerk. The ship trembled from trucks to keel; the sails kept on rattling like a discharge of musketry; the chain sheets and loose shackles jingled aloft in a thin peal; the gin blocks groaned. It was as if an invisible hand had given the ship an angry shake to recall the men that peopled her decks to the sense of reality, vigilance, and duty.—"Helm up!" cried the master sharply. "Run aft, Mr. Creighton, and see what that fool there is up to."—"Flatten in the head sheets. Stand by the weather forebraces," growled Mr. Baker. Startled men ran swiftly repeating the orders. The watch below, abandoned all at once by the watch on deck, drifted towards the forecastle in twos and threes, arguing noisily as they went.—"We shall see tomorrow!" cried a loud voice, as if to cover with a menacing hint an inglorious retreat. And then only orders were heard, the falling of heavy coils of rope, the rattling of blocks. Singleton's white head flitted here and there in the night, high above the deck, like the ghost of a bird.—"Going off, sir!" shouted Mr. Creighton from aft.—"Full again."—"All right . . ."—"Ease off the head sheets. That will do the braces. Coil the ropes," grunted Mr. Baker, bustling about.

Gradually the tramping noises, the confused sound of voices, died out, and the officers, coming together on the poop, discussed the events. Mr. Baker was bewildered and grunted; Mr. Creighton was calmly furious; but Captain Allistoun was composed and thoughtful. He listened to Mr. Baker's growling argumentation, to Creighton's interjected and severe remarks, while looking down on the deck he weighed in his hand the iron belaying-pin—that a moment ago had just missed his head—as if it had been the only tangible fact of the whole transaction. He was one of those commanders who speak little, seem to hear nothing, look at no one—and know everything, hear every whisper, see every fleeting shadow of their ship's life. His two big officers towered above his lean, short figure; they talked over his head; they were dismayed, surprised, and angry, while between them the little quiet man seemed to have found his taciturn serenity in the profound depths of a larger experience. Lights were burning in the forecastle; now and then a loud gust of babbling chatter came from forward, swept over the decks, and became faint, as if the unconscious ship, gliding gently through the great peace of the sea, had left behind and for ever the foolish noise of turbulent mankind. But it was renewed again and again. Gesticulating arms, profiles of heads with open mouths appeared for a moment in the illuminated squares of doorways; black fists darted—withdrew. . . . "Yes. It was most damnable to have such an unprovoked row sprung on one," assented the master. . . . A tumult of yells rose in the light, abruptly ceased. . . . He didn't think there would be any further trouble just then. . . . A bell was struck aft, another, forward, answered in a deeper tone, and the clamour of ringing metal spread round the ship in a circle of wide vibrations that ebbed away into the immeasurable night of an empty sea. . . . Didn't he know them! Didn't he! In past years. Better men, too. Real men to stand by one in a tight place. Worse than devils too sometimes—downright, horned devils. Pah! This—nothing. A miss as good as a mile. . . . The wheel was being relieved in the usual way.—"Full and by," said, very loud, the man going off.—"Full and by," repeated the other, catching hold of the spokes.—"This head wind is my trouble," exclaimed the master, stamping his foot in sudden anger; "head wind! all the rest is nothing." He was calm again in a moment. "Keep them on the move to-night, gentlemen; just to let them feel we've got hold all the time—quietly, you know. Mind you keep your hands off them, Creighton. To-morrow I will talk to them like a Dutch Uncle.[6] A crazy crowd of tinkers! Yes, tinkers! I could count the real sailors amongst them on the fingers of one hand.

6. A severe and moralizing individual.

Nothing will do but a row—if—you—please." He paused. "Did you think I had gone wrong there, Mr. Baker?" He tapped his forehead, laughed short. "When I saw him standing there, three parts dead and so scared—black amongst that gaping lot—no grit to face what's coming to us all—the notion came to me all at once, before I could think. Sorry for him—like you would be for a sick brute. If ever creature was in a mortal funk to die! . . . I thought I would let him go out in his own way. Kind of impulse. It never came into my head, those fools. . . . H'm! Stand to it now—of course. He stuck the belaying-pin in his pocket, seemed ashamed of himself, then sharply:—"If you see Podmore at his tricks again tell him I will have him put under the pump.[7] Had to do it once before. The fellow breaks out like that now and then. Good cook tho'." He walked away quickly, came back to the companion. The two mates followed him through the starlight with amazed eyes. He went down three steps, and changing his tone, spoke with his head near the deck:— "I shan't turn in to-night, in case of anything; just call out if . . . Did you see the eyes of that sick nigger, Mr. Baker? I fancied he begged me for something. What? Past all help. One lone black beggar amongst the lot of us, and he seemed to look through me into the very hell. Fancy, this wretched Podmore! Well, let him die in peace. I am master here after all. Say what I like. Let him be. He might have been half a man once . . . Keep a good look-out." He disappeared down below, leaving his mates facing one another, and more impressed than if they had seen a stone image shed a miraculous tear of compassion over the incertitudes of life and death. . . .

In the blue mist spreading from twisted threads that stood upright in the bowls of pipes, the forecastle appeared as vast as a hall. Between the beams a heavy cloud stagnated; and the lamps surrounded by halos burned each at the core of a purple glow in two lifeless flames without rays. Wreaths drifted in denser wisps. Men sprawled about on the deck, sat in negligent poses, or, bending a knee, drooped with one shoulder against a bulkhead. Lips moved, eyes flashed, waving arms made sudden eddies in the smoke. The murmur of voices seemed to pile itself higher and higher as if unable to run out quick enough through the narrow doors. The watch below in their shirts, and striding on long white legs, resembled raving somnambulists; while now and then one of the watch on deck would rush in, looking strangely over-dressed, listen a moment, fling a rapid sentence into the noise and run out again; but a few remained near the door, fascinated, and with one ear turned to the deck.— "Stick together, boys," roared Davies. Belfast tried to make himself heard. Knowles grinned in a slow, dazed way. A short fellow with a

7. The threat of dire punishment.

thick clipped beard kept on yelling periodically:—"Who's afeard? Who's afeard?" Another one jumped up, excited, with blazing eyes, sent out a string of unattached curses and sat down quietly. Two men discussed familiarly, striking one another's breast in turn, to clinch arguments. Three others, with their heads in a bunch, spoke all together with a confidential air, and at the top of their voices. It was a stormy chaos of speech where intelligible fragments tossing, struck the ear. One could hear:—"In the last ship"—"Who cares? Try it on any one of us if—." "Knock under"[8]—"Not a hand's turn"[9]—"He says he is all right"—"I always thought"—"Never mind. . . ." Donkin, crouching all in a heap against the bowsprit, hunched his shoulder-blades as high as his ears, and hanging a peaked nose, resembled a sick vulture with ruffled plumes. Belfast, straddling his legs, had a face red with yelling, and with arms thrown up, figured a Maltese cross.[1] The two Scandinavians, in a corner, had the dumbfounded and distracted aspect of men gazing at a cataclysm. And, beyond the light, Singleton stood in the smoke, monumental, indistinct, with his head touching the beam; like a statue of heroic size in the gloom of a crypt.

He stepped forward, impassive and big. The noise subsided like a broken wave: but Belfast cried once more with uplifted arms:—"The man is dying I tell ye!" then sat down suddenly on the hatch and took his head between his hands. All looked at Singleton, gazing upwards from the deck, staring out of dark corners, or turning their heads with curious glances. They were expectant and appeased as if that old man, who looked at no one, had possessed the secret of their uneasy indignations and desires, a sharper vision, a clearer knowledge. And indeed standing there amongst them, he had the uninterested appearance of one who had seen multitudes of ships, had listened many times to voices such as theirs, had already seen all that could happen on the wide seas. They heard his voice rumble in his broad chest as though the words had been rolling towards them out of a rugged past. "What do you want to do?" he asked. No one answered. Only Knowles muttered—"Aye, aye," and somebody said low:—"It's a bloomin' shame." He waited, made a contemptuous gesture.—"I have seen rows aboard ship before some of you were born," he said slowly, "for something or nothing; but never for such a thing."—"The man is dying, I tell ye," repeated Belfast woefully, sitting at Singleton's feet.—"And a black fellow, too," went on the old seaman, "I have seen them die like flies." He stopped, thoughtful, as if trying to recollect gruesome things, details

8. To submit, to knuckle under.
9. A slight helping hand.
1. A cross that has four V-shaped arms joined at their points, making the shape of a cross.

of horrors, hecatombs of niggers. They looked at him fascinated.
He was old enough to remember slavers, bloody mutinies, pirates
perhaps; who could tell through what violences and terrors he had
lived! What would he say? He said:—"You can't help him; die he
must." He made another pause. His moustache and beard stirred.
He chewed words, mumbled behind tangled white hairs; incomprehensible and exciting, like an oracle behind a veil. . . . —"Stop
ashore—sick.—Instead—bringing all this head wind. Afraid. The
sea will have her own.—Die in sight of land. Always so. They know
it—long passage—more days, more dollars.—You keep quiet. What
do you want? Can't help him." He seemed to wake up from a dream.
"You can't help yourselves," he said austerely, "Skipper's no fool. He
has something in his mind. Look out—I say! I know 'em!" With eyes
fixed in front he turned his head from right to left, from left to
right, as if inspecting a long row of astute skippers.—"He said 'e
would brain me!" cried Donkin in a heartrending tone. Singleton
peered downwards with puzzled attention, as though he couldn't
find him.—"Damn you!" he said vaguely, giving it up. He radiated
unspeakable wisdom, hard unconcern, the chilling air of resignation. Round him all the listeners felt themselves somehow completely enlightened by their disappointment, and, mute, they lolled
about with the careless ease of men who can discern perfectly the
irremediable aspect of their existence. He, profound and unconscious, waved his arm once, and strode out on deck without another
word.

Belfast was lost in a round-eyed meditation. One or two vaulted
heavily into upper berths, and, once there, sighed; others dived head
first inside lower bunks—swift, and turning round instantly upon
themselves, like animals going into lairs. The grating of a knife scraping burnt clay was heard. Knowles grinned no more. Davies said, in a
tone of ardent conviction:—"Then our skipper's looney." Archie
muttered:—"My faith! we haven't heard the last of it yet!" Four bells
were struck.—"Half our watch below is gone!" cried Knowles in
alarm, then reflected. "Well, two hours' sleep is something towards
a rest," he observed consolingly. Some already pretended to slumber; and Charley, sound asleep, suddenly said a few slurred words in
an arbitrary, blank voice.—"This blamed boy has worrums!" commented Knowles from under a blanket, and in a learned manner. Belfast got up and approached Archie's berth.—"We pulled him out," he
whispered sadly.—"What?" said the other, with sleepy discontent.—
"And now we will have to chuck him overboard," went on Belfast,
whose lower lip trembled.—"Chuck what?" asked Archie.—"Poor
Jimmy," breathed out Belfast.—"He be blowed!" said Archie with
untruthful brutality, and sat up in his bunk; "It's all through him. If

it hadn't been for me, there would have been murder on board this ship!"—"'Tain't his fault, is it?" argued Belfast, in a murmur; "I've put him to bed . . . an' he ain't no heavier than an empty beef-cask," he added, with tears in his eyes. Archie looked at him steadily, then turned his nose to the ship's side with determination. Belfast wandered about as though he had lost his way in the dim forecastle, and nearly fell over Donkin. He contemplated him from on high for awhile. "Ain't ye going to turn in?" he asked. Donkin looked up hopelessly.—"That black-'earted Scotch son of a thief kicked me!" he whispered from the floor, in a tone of utter desolation.—"And a good job, too!" said Belfast, still very depressed; "You were as near hanging as damn-it to-night, sonny. Don't you play any of your murthering games around my Jimmy! You haven't pulled him out. You just mind! 'Cos if I start to kick you"—he brightened up a bit—"if I start to kick you, it will be Yankee fashion[2]—to break something!" He tapped lightly with his knuckles the top of the bowed head. "You moind, me bhoy!" he concluded, cheerily. Donkin let it pass.— "Will they split on me?"[3] he asked, with pained anxiety.—"Who— split?" hissed Belfast, coming back a step. "I would split your nose this minyt if I hadn't Jimmy to look after! Who d'ye think we are?" Donkin rose and watched Belfast's back lurch through the doorway. On all sides invisible men slept, breathing calmly. He seemed to draw courage and fury from the peace around him. Venomous and thin-faced, he glared from the ample misfit of borrowed clothes as if looking for something he could smash. His heart leaped wildly in his narrow chest. They slept! He wanted to wring necks, gouge eyes, spit on faces. He shook a dirty pair of meagre fists at the smoking lights. "Ye're no men!" he cried, in a deadened tone. No one moved. "Yer 'aven't the pluck of a mouse!" His voice rose to a husky screech. Wamibo darted out a dishevelled head, and looked at him wildly. "Ye're sweepings ov ships! I 'ope you will hall rot before you die!" Wamibo blinked, uncomprehending but interested. Donkin sat down heavily; he blew with force through quivering nostrils, he ground and snapped his teeth, and, with the chin pressed hard against the breast, he seemed busy gnawing his way through it, as if to get at the heart within. . . .

In the morning the ship, beginning another day of her wandering life, had an aspect of sumptuous freshness, like the spring-time of the earth. The washed decks glistened in a long clear stretch; the oblique sunlight struck the yellow brasses in dazzling splashes,

---

2. See p. 29, n. 4.
3. Inform on me (slang).

darted over the polished rods in lines of gold, and the single drops of salt water forgotten here and there along the rail were as limpid as drops of dew, and sparkled more than scattered diamonds. The sails slept, hushed by a gentle breeze. The sun, rising lonely and splendid in the blue sky, saw a solitary ship gliding close-hauled on the blue sea.

The men pressed three deep abreast of the mainmast and opposite the cabin-door. They shuffled, pushed, had an irresolute mien and stolid faces. At every slight movement Knowles lurched heavily on his short leg. Donkin glided behind backs, restless and anxious, like a man looking for an ambush. Captain Allistoun came out suddenly. He walked to and fro before the front. He was grey, slight, alert, shabby in the sunshine, and as hard as adamant. He had his right hand in the side-pocket of his jacket, and also something heavy in there that made folds all down that side. One of the seamen cleared his throat ominously.—"I haven't till now found fault with you men," said the master, stopping short. He faced them with his worn, steely gaze, that by an universal illusion looked straight into every individual pair of the twenty pairs of eyes before his face. At his back Mr. Baker, gloomy and bull-necked, grunted low; Mr. Creighton, fresh as paint, had rosy cheeks and a ready, resolute bearing. "And I don't now," continued the master; "but I am here to drive this ship and keep every man-jack aboard of her up to the mark. If you knew your work as well as I do mine, there would be no trouble. You've been braying in the dark about 'See to-morrow morning!' Well, you see me now. What do you want?" He waited, stepping quickly to and fro, giving them searching glances. What did they want? They shifted from foot to foot, they balanced their bodies; some, pushing back their caps, scratched their heads. What did they want? Jimmy was forgotten; no one thought of him, alone forward in his cabin, fighting great shadows, clinging to brazen lies, chuckling painfully over his transparent deceptions. No, not Jimmy; he was more forgotten than if he had been dead. They wanted great things. And suddenly all the simple words they knew seemed to be lost for ever in the immensity of their vague and burning desire. They knew what they wanted, but they could not find anything worth saying. They stirred on one spot, swinging, at the end of muscular arms, big tarry hands with crooked fingers. A murmur died out.—"What is it—food?" asked the master, "You know the stores had been spoiled off the Cape."—"We know that, sir," said a bearded shell-back in the front rank.—"Work too hard—eh? Too much for your strength?" he asked again. There was an offended silence.—"We don't want to go shorthanded, sir," began at last Davies in a wavering voice, "and this 'ere black . . ."—"Enough!" cried the master. He stood scanning them for a moment, then walking a few steps this way and that began to storm at them coldly, in gusts violent and cutting like the gales of those icy seas that had known his youth.—"Tell you what's the matter? Too big for your boots. Think yourselves damn good men. Know half your work. Do half your duty. Think it too much. If you did ten times as much it wouldn't be enough."—"We did our best by her, sir," cried some one with shaky exasperation.— "Your best," stormed on the master; "You hear a lot on shore, don't you? They don't tell you there your best isn't much to boast of. I tell you—your best is no better than bad. You can do no more? No, I know, and say nothing. But you stop your caper or I will stop it for you. I am ready for you! Stop it!" He shook a finger at the crowd. "As to that man," he raised his voice very much; "as to that man, if he puts his nose out on deck without my leave I will clap him in irons.[4] There!" The cook heard him forward, ran out of the galley lifting his arms, horrified, unbelieving, amazed, and ran in again. There was a moment of profound silence during which a bow-legged sea-man, stepping aside, expectorated decorously into the scupper. "There is another thing," said the master calmly. He made a quick stride and with a swing took an iron belaying-pin out of his pocket. "This!" His movement was so unexpected and sudden that the crowd stepped back. He gazed fixedly at their faces, and some at once put on a surprised air as though they had never seen a belaying-pin before. He held it up. "This is my affair. I don't ask you any questions, but you all know it; it has got to go where it came from." His eyes became angry. The crowd stirred uneasily. They looked away from the piece of iron, they appeared shy, they were embarrassed and shocked as though it had been something hor-rid, scandalous, or indelicate, that in common decency should not have been flourished like this in broad daylight. The master watched them attentively. "Donkin," he called out in a short, sharp tone.

Donkin dodged behind one, then behind another, but they looked over their shoulders and moved aside. The ranks kept on opening before him, closing behind, till at last he appeared alone before the master as though he had come up through the deck. Captain Allis-toun moved close to him. They were much of a size, and at short range the master exchanged a deadly glance with the beady eyes. They wavered.—"You know this?" asked the master.—"No, I don't," answered the other with cheeky trepidation.—"You are a cur. Take it," ordered the master. Donkin's arms seemed glued to his thighs;

---

4. Bind him in iron shackles or fetters.

he stood, eyes front, as if drawn on parade.[5] "Take it," repeated the master, and stepped closer; they breathed on one another. "Take it," said Captain Allistoun again, making a menacing gesture. Donkin tore away one arm from his side.—"Vy hare yer down hon me?" he mumbled with effort and as if his mouth had been full of dough.— "If you don't . . ." began the master. Donkin snatched at the pin as though his intention had been to run away with it, and remained stock still holding it like a candle. "Put it back where you took it from," said Captain Allistoun, looking, at him fiercely. Donkin stepped back opening wide eyes. "Go, you blackguard, or I will make you," cried the master, driving him slowly backwards by a menacing advance. He dodged, and with the dangerous iron tried to guard his head from a threatening fist. Mr. Baker ceased grunting for a moment.—"Good! By Jove," murmured appreciatively Mr. Creighton in the tone of a connoisseur.—"Don't tech me," snarled Donkin, backing away.— "Then go. Go faster."—"Don't yer 'it me. . . . I will pull yer hup afore the magistryt. . . . I'll show yer hup." Captain Allistoun made a long stride, and Donkin, turning his back fairly, ran off a little, then stopped and over his shoulder showed yellow teeth.—"Further on, fore-rigging," urged the master, pointing with his arm.—"Hare yer goin' to stand by and see me bullied?" screamed Donkin at the silent crowd that watched him. Captain Allistoun walked at him smartly. He started off again with a leap, dashed at the fore-rigging, rammed the pin into its hole violently. "I will be heven with yer yet," he screamed at the ship at large and vanished beyond the foremast. Captain Allistoun spun round and walked back aft with a composed face, as though he had already forgotten the scene. Men moved out of his way. He looked at no one.—"That will do, Mr. Baker. Send the watch below," he said quietly. "And you men try to walk straight for the future," he added in a calm voice. He looked pensively for a while at the backs of the impressed and retreating crowd. "Breakfast, steward," he called in a tone of relief through the cabin door.—"I didn't like to see you—Ough!—give that pin to that chap, sir," observed Mr. Baker; "he could have bust—Ough!—bust your head like an eggshell with it.—"O! he!" muttered the master absently. "Queer lot," he went on in a low voice. "I suppose it's all right now. Can never tell tho', nowadays, with such a . . . Years ago; I was a young master then— one China voyage I had a mutiny; real mutiny, Baker. Different men tho'. I knew what they wanted: they wanted to broach cargo and get at the liquor. Very simple. . . . We knocked them about for two days, and when they had enough—gentle as lambs. Good crew. And a smart trip I made." He glanced aloft at the yards braced sharp up. "Head wind day after day," he exclaimed bitterly. "Will we never get a

5. Standing at attention.

decent slant this passage?"—"Ready, sir," said the steward, appearing before them as if by magic and with a stained napkin in his hand.—"Ah! All right. Come along, Mr. Baker—it's late—with all this nonsense."

V

A heavy atmosphere of oppressive quietude pervaded the ship. In the afternoon men went about washing clothes and hanging them out to dry in the unprosperous breeze with the meditative languor of disenchanted philosophers. Very little was said. The problem of life seemed too voluminous for the narrow limits of human speech, and by common consent it was abandoned to the great sea that had from the beginning enfolded it in its immense grip; to the sea that knew all, and would in time infallibly unveil to each the wisdom hidden in all the errors, the certitude that lurks in doubts, the realm of safety and peace beyond the frontiers of sorrow and fear. And in the confused current of impotent thoughts that set unceasingly this way and that through bodies of men, Jimmy bobbed up upon the surface, compelling attention, like a black buoy chained to the bottom of a muddy stream. Falsehood triumphed. It triumphed through doubt, through stupidity, through pity, through sentimentalism. We set ourselves to bolster it up, from compassion, from recklessness, from a sense of fun. Jimmy's steadfastness to his untruthful attitude in the face of the inevitable truth had the proportions of a colossal enigma—of a manifestation grand and incomprehensible that at times inspired a wondering awe; and there was also, to many, something exquisitely droll in fooling him thus to the top of his bent.[6] The latent egoism of tenderness to suffering appeared in the developing anxiety not to see him die. His obstinate non-recognition of the only certitude whose approach we could watch from day to day was as disquieting as the failure of some law of nature. He was so utterly wrong about himself that one could not but suspect him of having access to some source of supernatural knowledge. He was absurd to the point of inspiration. He was unique, and as fascinating as only something inhuman could be; he seemed to shout his denials already from beyond the awful border. He was becoming immaterial like an apparition; his cheekbones rose, the forehead slanted more; the face was all hollows, patches of shade; and the fleshless head resembled a disinterred black skull, fitted with two restless globes of silver in the sockets of eyes. He was demoralising. Through him we were becoming highly humanised, tender, complex, excessively decadent: we understood the

---

6. Endurance or capacity. Cf. *Hamlet* 3.2.353: "They fool me to the top of my bent."

subtlety of his fear, sympathised with all his repulsions, shrinkings, evasions, delusions—as though we had been over-civilised, and rotten, and without any knowledge of the meaning of life. We had the air of being initiated in some infamous mysteries; we had the profound grimaces of conspirators, exchanged meaning glances, significant short words. We were inexpressibly vile and very much pleased with ourselves. We lied to him with gravity, with emotion, with unction, as if performing some moral trick with a view to an eternal reward. We made a chorus of affirmation to his wildest assertions, as though he had been a millionaire, a politician, or a reformer—and we a crowd of ambitious lubbers. When we ventured to question his statements we did it after the manner of obsequious sycophants, to the end that his glory should be augmented by the flattery of our dissent. He influenced the moral tone of our world as though he had it in his power to distribute honours, treasures, or pain; and he could give us nothing but his contempt. It was immense; it seemed to grow gradually larger, as his body day by day shrank a little more, while we looked. It was the only thing about him—of him—that gave the impression of durability and vigour. It lived within him with an unquenchable life. It spoke through the eternal pout of his black lips; it looked at us through the profound impertinence of his large eyes, that stood far out of his head like the eyes of crabs. We watched them intently. Nothing else of him stirred. He seemed unwilling to move, as if distrustful of his own solidity. The slightest gesture must have disclosed to him (it could not surely be otherwise) his bodily weakness, and caused a pang of mental suffering. He was chary of movements. He lay stretched out, chin on blanket, in a kind of sly, cautious immobility. Only his eyes roamed over faces: his eyes disdainful, penetrating and sad.

It was at that time that Belfast's devotion—and also his pugnacity—secured universal respect. He spent every moment of his spare time in Jimmy's cabin. He tended him, talked to him; was as gentle as a woman, as tenderly gay as an old philanthropist, as sentimentally careful of his nigger as a model slave-owner. But outside he was irritable, explosive as gunpowder, sombre, suspicious, and never more brutal than when most sorrowful. With him it was a tear and a blow: a tear for Jimmy, a blow for any one who did not seem to take a scrupulously orthodox view of Jimmy's case. We talked about nothing else. The two Scandinavians, even, discussed the situation—but it was impossible to know in what spirit, because they quarrelled in their own language. Belfast suspected one of them of irreverence, and in this incertitude thought that there was no option but to fight them both. They became very much terrified by his truculence, and henceforth lived amongst us, dejected, like a pair of mutes. Wamibo never spoke intelligibly, but he was as smileless as an animal—seemed to know much less about it all than the cat—and consequently was safe. Moreover he had belonged to the chosen band of Jimmy's rescuers, and was above suspicion. Archie was silent generally, but often spent an hour or so talking to Jimmy quietly with an air of proprietorship. At any time of the day and often through the night some man could be seen sitting on Jimmy's box. In the evening, between six and eight, the cabin was crowded, and there was an interested group at the door. Every one stared at the nigger.

He basked in the warmth of our interest. His eyes gleamed ironically, and in a weak voice he reproached us with our cowardice. He would say, "If you fellows had stuck out for me I would be now on deck." We hung our heads. "Yes, but if you think I am going to let them put me in irons just to show you sport . . . Well, no . . . It ruins my health, this lying up, it does. You don't care." We were as abashed as if it had been true. His superb impudence carried all before it. We would not have dared to revolt. We didn't want to really. We wanted to keep him alive till home—to the end of the voyage.

Singleton as usual held aloof, appearing to scorn the insignificant events of an ended life. Once only he came along, and unexpectedly stopped in the doorway. He peered at Jimmy in profound silence, as if desirous to add that black image to the crowd of Shades that peopled his old memory. We kept very quiet, and for a long time Singleton stood there as though he had come by appointment to call for some one, or to see some important event. James Wait lay perfectly still, and apparently not aware of the gaze scrutinising him with a steadiness full of expectation. There was a sense of tussle in the air. We felt the inward strain of men watching a wrestling bout. At last Jimmy with perceptible apprehension turned his head on the pillow.— "Good evening," he said in a conciliating tone.—"H'm," answered the old seaman, grumpily. For a moment longer he looked at Jimmy with severe fixity, then suddenly went away. It was a long time before any one spoke in the little cabin, though we all breathed more freely as men do after an escape from some dangerous situation. We all knew the old man's ideas about Jimmy, and nobody dared to combat them. They were unsettling, they caused pain; and, what was worse, they might have been true for all we knew. Only once did he condescend to explain them fully, but the impression was lasting. He said that Jimmy was the cause of head winds. Mortally sick men—he maintained— linger till the first sight of land, and then die; and Jimmy knew that the land would draw his life from him. It is so in every ship. Didn't we know it? He asked us with austere contempt: what did we know?

What would we doubt next? Jimmy's desire encouraged by us and aided by Wamibo's (he was a Finn—wasn't he? Very well!) by Wamibo's spells[7] delayed the ship in the open sea. Only lubberly fools couldn't see it. Whoever heard of such a run of calms and head winds? It wasn't natural . . . We could not deny that it was strange. We felt uneasy. The common saying, "more days, more dollars," did not give the usual comfort because the stores were running short. Much had been spoiled off the Cape, and we were on half allowance of biscuit. Peas, sugar and tea had been finished long ago. Salt meat was giving out. We had plenty of coffee but very little water to make it with. We took up another hole in our belts and went on scraping, polishing, painting the ship from morning to night. And soon she looked as though she had come out of a band-box;[8] but hunger lived on board of her. Not dead starvation, but steady, living hunger that stalked about the decks, slept in the forecastle; the tormentor of waking moments, the disturber of dreams. We looked to windward for signs of change. Every few hours of night and day we put her round with the hope that she would come up on that tack at last! She didn't. She seemed to have forgotten the way home; she rushed to and fro, heading northwest, heading east; she ran backwards and forwards, distracted, like a timid creature at the foot of a wall. Sometimes, as if tired to death, she would wallow languidly for a day in the smooth swell of an unruffled sea. All up the swinging masts the sails thrashed furiously through the hot stillness of the calm. We were weary, hungry, thirsty; we commenced to believe Singleton, but with unshaken fidelity dissembled to Jimmy. We spoke to him with jocose allusiveness, like cheerful accomplices in a clever plot; but we looked to the westward over the rail with mournful eyes for a sign of hope, for a sign of fair wind; even if its first breath should bring death to our reluctant Jimmy. In vain! The universe conspired with James Wait. Light airs from the northward sprang up again; the sky remained clear; and round our weariness the glittering sea, touched by the breeze, basked voluptuously in the great sunshine, as though it had forgotten our life and trouble.

Donkin looked out for a fair wind along with the rest. No one knew the venom of his thoughts now. He was silent, and appeared thinner, as if consumed slowly by an inward rage at the injustice of men and of fate. He was ignored by all and spoke to no one, but his hate for every man looked out through his eyes. He talked with the cook

---

7. See p. 150, n. 3.
8. A box constructed of thin materials, originally used for bands or ruffs.

only, having somehow persuaded the good man that he—Donkin—
was a much calumniated and persecuted person. Together they
bewailed the immorality of the ship's company. There could be no
greater criminals than we, who by our lies conspired to send the
soul of a poor ignorant black man to everlasting perdition. Podmore cooked what there was to cook, remorsefully, and felt all the
time that by preparing the food of such sinners he imperilled his
own salvation. As to the Captain—he had lived with him for seven
years, he said, and would not have believed it possible that such a
man . . . "Well. Well . . . There it is. . . . Can't get out of it. Judgment
capsized all in a minute . . . Struck in all his pride . . . More like a
sudden visitation than anything else." Donkin, perched sullenly on
the coal-locker, swung his legs and concurred. He paid in the coin of
spurious assent for the privilege to sit in the galley; he was disheartened and scandalised; he agreed with the cook; could find no words
severe enough to criticise our conduct; and when in the heat of rep-
robation he swore at us, Podmore, who would have liked to swear
also if it hadn't been for his principles, pretended not to hear. So
Donkin, unrebuked, cursed enough for two, cadged for matches,
borrowed tobacco, and loafed for hours, very much at home before the
stove. From there he could hear us on the other side of the bulkhead,
talking to Jimmy. The cook knocked the pots about, slammed the oven
door, muttered prophesies of damnation for all the ship's company;
and Donkin, who did not admit of any hereafter, except for purposes
of blasphemy, listened, concentrated and angry, gloating fiercely
over a called-up image of infinite torment—as men gloat over the
accursed images of cruelty and revenge, of greed, and of power. . . .

On clear evenings the silent ship, under the cold sheen of the dead
moon, took on the false aspect of passionless repose resembling the
winter of the earth. Under her a long band of gold barred the black
disc of the sea. Footsteps echoed on her quiet decks. The moonlight
clung to her like a frosted mist, and the white sails stood out in dazzling cones as of stainless snow. In the magnificence of the phantom
rays the ship appeared pure like a vision of ideal beauty, illusive like
a tender dream of serene peace. And nothing in her was real, nothing
was distinct and solid but the heavy shadows that filled her decks
with their unceasing and noiseless stir; the shadows blacker than the
night and more restless than the thoughts of men.

Donkin prowled spiteful and alone amongst the shadows, thinking that Jimmy too long delayed to die. That evening, just before
dark, land had been reported from aloft, and the master, while
adjusting the tubes of the long glass,[9] had observed with quiet

9. A telescope.

bitterness to Mr. Baker that, after fighting our way inch by inch to the Western Islands,[1] there was nothing to expect now but a spell of calm. The sky was clear and the barometer high. The light breeze dropped with the sun, and an enormous stillness, forerunner of a night without wind, descended upon the heated waters of the ocean. As long as daylight lasted, the hands collected on the forecastle-head watched on the eastern sky the island of Flores,[2] that rose above the level expanse of the sea with irregular and broken outlines like a sombre ruin upon a vast and deserted plain. It was the first land seen for nearly four months. Charley was excited, and in the midst of general indulgence took liberties with his betters. Men strangely elated without knowing why, talked in groups, and pointed with bared arms. For the first time that voyage Jimmy's sham existence seemed for a moment forgotten in the face of a solid reality. We had got so far anyhow. Belfast discoursed, quoting imaginary examples of short homeward passages from the Islands. "Them smart fruit schooners do it in five days," he affirmed. "What do you want?—only a good little breeze." Archie maintained that seven days was the shortest passage, and they disputed amicably with insulting words. Knowles declared he could already smell home from there, and with a heavy list on his short leg laughed fit to split his sides. A group of grizzled sea-dogs looked out for a time in silence and with grim absorbed faces. One said suddenly—"'Tain't far to London now."—"My first night ashore, blamme if I haven't steak and onions for supper . . . and a pint of bitter,"[3] said another.—"A barrel ye mean," shouted some one.— "Ham an' eggs three times a day. That's the way I live!" cried an excited voice. There was a stir, appreciative murmurs; eyes began to shine; jaws champed; short nervous laughs were heard. Archie smiled with reserve all to himself. Singleton came up, gave a negligent glance, and went down again without saying a word, indifferent, like a man who had seen Flores an incalculable number of times. The night travelling from the East blotted out of the limpid sky the purple stain of the high land. "Dead calm," said somebody quietly. The murmur of lively talk suddenly wavered, died out; the clusters broke up; men began to drift away one by one, descending the ladders slowly and with serious faces as if sobered by that reminder of their dependence upon the invisible. And when the big yellow moon ascended gently above the sharp rim of the clear horizon it found

1. The Azores, an archipelago in the North Atlantic Ocean, approximately eight hundred miles west of Portugal. In 1976, the Azores became an autonomous region of Portugal. See p. 336.
2. One of the western group of islands in the Azores, lying in the northwest part of the archipelago.
3. I.e., bitter beer.

the ship wrapped up in a breathless silence; a fearless ship that seemed to sleep profoundly, dreamlessly, on the bosom of the sleeping and terrible sea.

Donkin chafed at the peace—at the ship—at the sea that stretching away on all sides merged into the illimitable silence of all creation. He felt himself pulled up sharp by unrecognised grievances. He had been physically cowed, but his injured dignity remained indomitable, and nothing could heal his lacerated feelings. Here was land already—home very soon—a bad pay-day—no clothes—more hard work. How offensive all this was. Land. The land that draws away life from sick sailors. That nigger there had money—clothes— easy times; and would not die. Land draws life away . . . He felt tempted to go and see whether it did. Perhaps already . . . It would be a bit of luck. There was money in the beggar's chest. He stepped briskly out of the shadows into the moonlight, and, instantly, his craving, hungry face from sallow became livid. He opened the door of the cabin and had a shock. Sure enough, Jimmy was dead! He moved no more than a recumbent figure with clasped hands, carved on the lid of a stone coffin. Donkin glared with avidity. Then Jimmy, without stirring, blinked his eyelids, and Donkin had another shock. Those eyes were rather startling. He shut the door behind his back with gentle care, looking intently the while at James Wait as though he had come in there at a great risk to tell some secret of startling importance. Jimmy did not move but glanced languidly out of the corners of his eyes.—"Calm?" he asked.—"Yuss," said Donkin, very disappointed, and sat down on the box.

Jimmy breathed with composure. He was used to such visits at all times of night or day. Men succeeded one another. They spoke in clear voices, pronounced cheerful words, repeated old jokes, listened to him; and each, going out, seemed to leave behind a little of his own vitality, surrender some of his own strength, renew the assurance of life—the indestructible thing! He did not like to be alone in his cabin, because, when he was alone, it seemed to him as if he hadn't been there at all. There was nothing. No pain. Not now. Perfectly right— but he couldn't enjoy his healthful repose unless some one was by to see it. This man would do as well as anybody. Donkin watched him stealthily.—"Soon home now," observed Wait.—"Why d'yer whisper?" asked Donkin with interest, "can't yer speak hup?" Jimmy looked annoyed and said nothing for a while; then in a lifeless unringing voice:—"Why should I shout? You ain't deaf that I know."—"Oh! I can 'ear right enough," answered Donkin in a low tone, and looked down. He was thinking sadly of going out when Jimmy spoke again.— "Time we did get home . . . to get something decent to eat . . . I am always hungry." Donkin felt angry all of a sudden.—"What habout me," he hissed, "I am 'ungry too an' got ter work. You 'ungry!"—"Your

work won't kill you," commented Wait, feebly; "there's a couple of biscuits in the lower bunk there—you may have one. I can't eat them."
Donkin dived in, groped in the corner, and when he came up again
his mouth was full. He munched with ardour. Jimmy seemed to doze
with open eyes. Donkin finished his hard bread and got up.—"You're
not going?" asked Jimmy, staring at the ceiling.—"No," said Donkin
impulsively, and instead of going out leaned his back against the
closed door. He looked at James Wait, and saw him long, lean, dried
up, as though all his flesh had shrivelled on his bones in the heat of
a white furnace; the meagre fingers of one hand moved lightly upon
the edge of the bunk playing an endless tune. To look at him was
irritating and fatiguing; he could last like this for days; he was
outrageous—belonging wholly neither to death nor life, and perfectly invulnerable in his apparent ignorance of both. Donkin felt
tempted to enlighten him.—"What hare yer thinkin' of?" he asked
surlily. James Wait had a grimacing smile that passed over the
deathlike impassiveness of his bony face, incredible and frightful as
would, in a dream, have been the sudden smile of a corpse.

"There is a girl," whispered Wait . . . "Canton Street girl[4]—She
chucked a third engineer of a Rennie boat[5]—for me. Cooks oysters
just as I like . . . She says—she would chuck—any toff—for a coloured
gentleman . . . That's me. I am kind to wimmen," he added a shade
louder.

Donkin could hardly believe his ears. He was scandalised.—
"Would she? Yer wouldn't be hany good to 'er," he said with unrestrained disgust. Wait was not there to hear him. He was swaggering
up the East India Dock Road;[6] saying kindly, "Come along for a
treat," pushing glass swing-doors, posing with superb assurance in
the gaslight above a mahogany counter.—"D'yer think yer will hever
get ashore?" asked Donkin angrily. Wait came back with a start.—
"Ten days," he said promptly, and returned at once to the regions of
memory that know nothing of time. He felt untired, calm, and as if
safely withdrawn within himself beyond the reach of every grave
incertitude. There was something of the immutable quality of eternity in the slow moments of his complete restfulness. He was very
quiet and easy amongst his vivid reminiscences which he mistook
joyfully for images of an undoubted future. He cared for no one.
Donkin felt this vaguely like a blind man may feel in his darkness
the fatal antagonism of all the surrounding existences, that to him

4. A girl from a street near the East India Docks, located in Blackwall in east London,
  which was well known for the prostitutes who worked it, although Wait seems to imply
  (perhaps erroneously) that his "Canton Street girl" was not a prostitute.
5. A boat built by J. & G. Rennie, a firm established in 1821 by brothers John (1791–1874)
  and George Rennie (1791–1866) upon the death of their father, John Rennie (1761–1821).
6. A road constructed between 1806 and 1812 that connects the East India Docks to central
  London.

shall for ever remain irrealisable, unseen and enviable. He had a desire to assert his importance, to break, to crush; to be even with everybody for everything; to tear the veil, unmask, expose, leave no refuge—a perfidious desire of truthfulness! He laughed in a mocking splutter and said:

"Ten days. Strike me blind if I hever! . . . You will be dead by this time to-morrow p'r'aps. Ten days!" He waited for a while. "D'ye 'ear me? Blamme if yer don't look dead halready."

Jimmy must have been collecting his strength for he said almost aloud—"You're a stinking, cadging liar. Every one knows you." And sitting up, against all probability, startled his visitor horribly. But very soon Donkin recovered himself. He blustered,

"What? What? Who's a liar? You hare—the crowd hare—the skipper—heverybody. I haint! Putting on hairs! Who's yer?" He nearly choked himself with indignation. "Who's yer to put on hairs," he repeated trembling. "'Ave one—'ave one, says 'ee—an' cawn't heat 'em 'isself. Now I'll 'ave both. By Gawd—I will! Yer nobody!"

He plunged into the lower bunk, rooted in there and brought to light another dusty biscuit. He held it up before Jimmy—then took a bite defiantly.

"What now?" he asked with feverish impudence. "Yer may take one—says yer. Why not giv' me both? No. I'm a mangy dorg. One fur a mangy dorg. I'll tyke both. Can yer stop me? Try. Come on. Try."

Jimmy was clasping his legs and hiding his face on the knees. His shirt clung to him. Every rib was visible. His emaciated back was shaken in repeated jerks by the panting catches of his breath.

"Yer won't? Yer can't! What did I say?" went on Donkin fiercely. He swallowed another dry mouthful with a hasty effort. The other's silent helplessness, his weakness, his shrinking attitude exasperated him. "Ye're done!" he cried. "Who's yer to be lied to; to be waited on 'and an' foot like a bloomin' hymperor. Yer nobody. Yer no one at all!" he spluttered with such a strength of unerring conviction that it shook him from head to foot in coming out, and left him vibrating like a released string.

Jimmy rallied again. He lifted his head and turned bravely at Donkin, who saw a strange face, an unknown face, a fantastic and grimacing mask of despair and fury. Its lips moved rapidly; and hollow, moaning, whistling sounds filled the cabin with a vague mutter full of menace, complaint and desolation, like the far-off murmur of a rising wind. Wait shook his head; rolled his eyes; he denied, cursed, menaced—and not a word had the strength to pass beyond the sorrowful pout of those black lips. It was incomprehensible and disturbing; a gibberish of emotions, a frantic dumb show of speech pleading for impossible things, threatening a shadowy vengeance. It sobered Donkin into a scrutinising watchfulness.

"Yer can't holler. See? What did I tell yer?" he said slowly after a moment of attentive examination. The other kept on headlong and unheard, nodding passionately, grinning with grotesque and appalling flashes of big white teeth. Donkin, as if fascinated by the dumb eloquence and anger of that black phantom, approached, stretching his neck out with distrustful curiosity; and it seemed to him suddenly that he was looking only at the shadow of a man crouching high in the bunk on the level with his eyes.—"What? What?" he said. He seemed to catch the shape of some words in the continuous panting hiss. "Yer will tell Belfast! Will yer? Hare yer a bloomin' kid?" He trembled with alarm and rage. "Tell yer gran'mother! Yer afeard! Who's yer ter be afeard more'n hanyone?" His passionate sense of his own importance ran away with a last remnant of caution. "Tell an' be damned! Tell, if yer can!" he cried. "I've been treated worser'n a dorg by your blooming back-lickers. They 'as set me on, honly to turn aginst me. I ham the honly man 'ere. They clouted me, kicked me—an' yer laffed—yer black, rotten hincumbrance, you! You will pay fur it. They giv' yer their grub, their water—yer will pay fur hit to me, by Gawd! Who haxed me ter 'ave a drink of water? They put their bloomin' rags on yer that night, an' what did they giv' ter me—a clout on the bloomin' mouth—blast their . . . S'elp me! . . . Yer will pay fur hit with yer money. Hi'm goin' ter 'ave it in a minyte; has soon has ye're dead, yer bloomin' useless fraud. That's the man I ham. An' ye're a thing—a bloody thing. Yah—you corpse!"

He flung at Jimmy's head the biscuit he had been all the time clutching hard, but it only grazed, and striking with a loud crack the bulkhead beyond burst like a hand-grenade into flying pieces. James Wait, as though wounded mortally, fell back on the pillow. His lips ceased to move and the rolling eyes became quiet and stared upwards with an intense and steady persistence. Donkin was surprised; he sat suddenly on the chest, and looked down, exhausted and gloomy. After a moment he began to mutter to himself, "Die, you beggar— die. Somebody'll come in . . . I wish I was drunk . . . Ten days . . . Hoysters . . ." He looked up and spoke louder. "No . . . No more for yer . . . No more bloomin' gals that cook hoysters . . . Who's yer? Hit's my turn now . . . I wish I was drunk; I would soon giv' you a leg up haloft. That's where yer will go. Feet fust, through a port . . . Splash! Never see yer hany more. Hoverboard! Good 'nuff fur yer."

Jimmy's head moved slightly and he turned his eyes to Donkin's face; a gaze unbelieving, desolated and appealing, of a child frightened by the menace of being shut up alone in the dark. Donkin observed him from the chest with hopeful eyes; then without rising he tried the lid. Locked. "I wish I was drunk," he muttered and getting up listened anxiously to the distant sound of footsteps on the deck. They approached—ceased. Some one yawned interminably just outside the door, and the footsteps went away shuffling lazily. Donkin's fluttering heart eased its pace, and when he looked towards the bunk again Jimmy was staring as before at the white beam.—"'Ow d'yer feel now?" he asked.—"Bad," breathed out Jimmy.

Donkin sat down patient and purposeful. Every half-hour the bells spoke to one another ringing along the whole length of the ship. Jimmy's respiration was so rapid that it couldn't be counted, so faint that it couldn't be heard. His eyes were terrified as though he had been looking at unspeakable horrors; and by his face one could see that he was thinking of abominable things. Suddenly with an incredibly strong and heart-breaking voice he sobbed out:

"Overboard! . . . I! . . . My God!"

Donkin writhed a little on the box. He looked unwillingly. Jimmy was mute. His two long bony hands smoothed the blanket upwards, as though he had wished to gather it all up under his chin. A tear, a big solitary tear, escaped from the corner of his eye and, without touching the hollow cheek, fell on the pillow. His throat rattled faintly.[7]

And Donkin, watching the end of that hateful nigger, felt the anguishing grasp of a great sorrow on his heart at the thought that he himself, some day, would have to go through it all—just like this—perhaps! His eyes became moist. "Poor beggar," he murmured. The night seemed to go by in a flash; it seemed to him he could hear the irremediable rush of precious minutes. How long would this blooming affair last? Too long surely. No luck. He could not restrain himself. He got up and approached the bunk. Wait did not stir. Only his eyes appeared alive and his hands continued their smoothing movement with a horrible and tireless industry. Donkin bent over.

"Jimmy," he called low. There was no answer, but the rattle stopped. "D'yer see me?" he asked trembling. Jimmy's chest heaved. Donkin, looking away, bent his ear to Jimmy's lips, and heard a sound like the rustle of a single dry leaf driven along the smooth sand of a beach. It shaped itself.

"Light . . . the lamp . . . and . . . go," breathed out Wait.

Donkin, instinctively, glanced over his shoulder at the blazing flame; then, still looking away, felt under the pillow for a key. He got it at once and for the next few minutes was shakily but swiftly busy about the box. When he got up, his face—for the first time in his life—had a pink flush—perhaps of triumph.

He slipped the key under the pillow again, avoiding to glance at Jimmy, who had not moved. He turned his back squarely from the bunk, and started to the door as though he were going to walk a

---

7. Paul Kirschner, in *Conrad: The Psychologist as Artist* (Edinburgh: Oliver & Boyd, 1968, 200–4), argues that Conrad borrows Wait's death scene from Charles Forestier's death in Maupassant's *Bel-Ami* (1885).

mile. At his second stride he had his nose against it. He clutched the handle cautiously, but at that moment he received the irresistible impression of something happening behind his back. He spun round as though he had been tapped on the shoulder. He was just in time to see Jimmy's eyes blaze up and go out at once, like two lamps overturned together by a sweeping blow. Something resembling a scarlet thread hung down his chin out of the corner of his lips—and he had ceased to breathe.[8]

Donkin closed the door behind him gently but firmly. Sleeping men, huddled under jackets, made on the lighted deck shapeless dark mounds that had the appearance of neglected graves. Nothing had been done all through the night and he hadn't been missed. He stood motionless and perfectly astounded to find the world outside as he had left it; there was the sea, the ship—sleeping men; and he wondered absurdly at it, as though he had expected to find the men dead, familiar things gone for ever: as though, like a wanderer returning after many years, he had expected to see bewildering changes. He shuddered a little in the penetrating freshness of the air, and hugged himself forlornly. The declining moon drooped sadly in the western board as if withered by the cold touch of a pale dawn. The ship slept. And the immortal sea stretched away, immense and hazy, like the image of life, with a glittering surface and lightless depths; promising, empty, inspiring—terrible. Donkin gave it a defiant glance and slunk off noiselessly as if judged and cast out by the august silence of its might.

Jimmy's death, after all, came as a tremendous surprise. We did not know till then how much faith we had put in his delusions. We had taken his chances of life so much at his own valuation that his death, like the death of an old belief, shook the foundations of our society. A common bond was gone; the strong, effective and respectable bond of a sentimental lie. All that day we mooned at our work, with suspicious looks and a disabused air. In our hearts we thought that in the matter of his departure Jimmy had acted in a perverse and unfriendly manner. He didn't back us up, as a shipmate should. In going he took away with himself the gloomy and solemn shadow in which our folly had posed, with humane satisfaction, as a tender arbiter of fate. And now we saw it was no such thing. It was just common foolishness; a silly and ineffectual meddling with issues of majestic import—that is, if Podmore was right. Perhaps he was? Doubt survived Jimmy; and, like a community of banded criminals disintegrated by a touch of grace, we were profoundly scandalised

---

8. During the actual voyage of the *Narcissus*, Joseph Barron (c. 1859–1884) died and was buried at sea, but it is unknown whether he was of African heritage.

with each other. Men spoke unkindly to their best chums. Others refused to speak at all. Singleton only was not surprised. "Dead—is he? Of course," he said, pointing at the island right abeam: for the calm still held the ship spell-bound within sight of Flores. Dead—of course. *He* wasn't surprised. Here was the land, and there, on the forehatch and waiting for the sailmaker[9]—there was that corpse. Cause and effect. And for the first time that voyage, the old seaman became quite cheery and garrulous, explaining and illustrating from the stores of experience how, in sickness, the sight of an island (even a very small one) is generally more fatal than the view of a continent. But he couldn't explain why.

Jimmy was to be buried at five, and it was a long day till then—a day of mental disquiet and even of physical disturbance. We took no interest in our work and, very properly, were rebuked for it. This, in our constant state of hungry irritation, was exasperating. Donkin worked with his brow bound in a dirty rag, and looked so ghastly that Mr. Baker was touched with compassion at the sight of this plucky suffering.—"Ough! You, Donkin! Put down your work and go lay-up this watch. You look ill."—"Hi ham, sir—in my 'ead," he said in a subdued voice, and vanished speedily. This annoyed many, and they thought the mate "bloomin' soft to-day." Captain Allistoun could be seen on the poop watching the sky cloud over from the south-west, and it soon got to be known about the decks that the barometer had begun to fall in the night, and that a breeze might be expected before long. This, by a subtle association of ideas, led to violent quarrelling as to the exact moment of Jimmy's death. Was it before or after "that 'ere glass started down"? It was impossible to know, and it caused much contemptuous growling at one another. All of a sudden there was a great tumult forward. Pacific Knowles and good-tempered Davies had come to blows over it. The watch below interfered with spirit, and for ten minutes there was a noisy scrimmage round the hatch, where, in the balancing shade of the sails, Jimmy's body, wrapped up in a white blanket, was watched over by the sorrowful Belfast, who, in his desolation, disdained the fray. When the noise had ceased, and the passions had calmed into surly silence, he stood up at the head of the swathed body, and lifting both arms on high, cried with pained indignation:—"You ought to be ashamed of yourselves! . . ." We were.

Belfast took his bereavement very hard. He gave proofs of unextinguishable devotion. It was he, and no other man, who would help the sailmaker to prepare what was left of Jimmy for a solemn surrender to the insatiable sea. He arranged the weights carefully at the feet: two holystones, an old anchor-shackle without its pin, some

9. To make Wait's burial shroud.

broken links of a worn-out stream cable. He arranged them this way, then that. "Bless my soul! you aren't afraid he will chafe his heel?" said the sailmaker, who hated the job. He pushed the needle, puffing furiously, with his head in a cloud of tobacco smoke; he turned the flaps over, pulled at the stitches, stretched at the canvas.—"Lift his shoulders . . . Pull to you a bit . . . So—o—o. Steady." Belfast obeyed, pulled, lifted, overcome with sorrow, dropping tears on the tarred twine.—"Don't you drag the canvas too taut over his poor face, Sails,"[1] he entreated tearfully.—"What are you fashing[2] yourself for? He will be comfortable enough," assured the sailmaker, cutting the thread after the last stitch, that came about the middle of Jimmy's forehead. He rolled up the remaining canvas, put away the needles. "What makes you take on so?" he asked. Belfast looked down at the long package of grey sailcloth.—"I pulled him out," he whispered, "and he did not want to go. If I had sat up with him last night he would have kept alive for me . . . but something made me tired." The sailmaker took vigorous draws at his pipe and mumbled:— "When I . . . West India Station . . . In the *Blanche* frigate . . . Yellow Jack . . . sewed in twenty men a day . . . Portsmouth—Devonport men—townies—knew their fathers, mothers—sisters—the whole boiling of 'em.[3] Thought nothing of it. And these niggers like this one—you don't know where it comes from. Got nobody. No use to nobody. Who will miss him?"—"I do—I pulled him out," mourned Belfast dismally.

On two planks nailed together, and apparently resigned and still under the folds of the Union Jack with a white border,[4] James Wait, carried aft by four men, was deposited slowly, with his feet pointing at an open port. A swell had set in from the westward, and following on the roll of the ship, the Red Ensign,[5] at halfmast, darted out and collapsed again on the grey sky, like a tongue of flickering fire; Charley tolled the bell; and at every swing to starboard the whole vast semi-circle of steely waters visible on that side seemed to come up with a rush to the edge of the port, as if impatient to get at our

1. Short for *sailmaker*.
2. To vex, annoy, trouble (Scottish).
3. The whole lot of them. "West India Station": the British navy stationed in the West Indies. The HMS *Blanche* was a six-gun screw sloop, first launched in 1867. "Yellow Jack": a signal flag indicating quarantine. "sewed in twenty men a day": twenty men per day dying and being sewn into burial shrouds. Portsmouth was the chief naval station, located in central southern England on the English Channel. Devonport is a port city in the district of Plymouth in southwestern England. "Townies": town dwellers.
4. In 1801, the Union Flag (or Union Jack) was adopted as the national flag of the United Kingdom. In 1824, the Union Jack with a white border was officially allowed to be flown on merchant vessels. Originally, it was meant to designate a vessel in need of a pilot; it also came to be used less discriminatingly, as simply the civil version of the Union Flag. The latter appears to be the case here.
5. See p. 48, n. 8.

Jimmy. Every one was there but Donkin, who was too ill to come; the Captain and Mr. Creighton stood bareheaded on the break of the poop; Mr. Baker, directed by the master, who had said to him gravely:—"You know more about the prayer book than I do," came out of the cabin door quickly and a little embarrassed. All the caps went off. He began to read in a low tone, and with his usual harmlessly menacing utterance, as though he had been for the last time reproving confidentially that dead seaman at his feet. The men listened in scattered groups; they leaned on the fife rail, gazing on the deck; they held their chins in their hands thoughtfully, or, with crossed arms and one knee slightly bent, hung their heads in an attitude of upright meditation. Wamibo dreamed. Mr. Baker read on, grunting reverently at the turn of every page. The words, missing the unsteady hearts of men, rolled out to wander without a home upon the heartless sea; and James Wait, silenced for ever, lay uncritical and passive under the hoarse murmur of despair and hopes.

Two men made ready and waited for those words that send so many of our brothers to their last plunge. Mr. Baker began the passage. "Stand by," muttered the boatswain. Mr. Baker read out: "To the deep,"[6] and paused. The men lifted the inboard end of the planks, the boatswain snatched off the Union Jack, and James Wait did not move.—"Higher," muttered the boatswain angrily. All the heads were raised; every man stirred uneasily, but James Wait gave no sign of going. In death and swathed up for all eternity, he yet seemed to hang on to the ship with the grip of an undying fear. "Higher! Lift!" whispered the boatswain fiercely.—"He won't go," stammered one of the men shakily, and both appeared ready to drop everything. Mr. Baker waited, burying his face in the book, and shuffling his feet nervously. All the men looked profoundly disturbed; from their midst a faint humming noise spread out—growing louder. . . . "Jimmy!" cried Belfast in a wailing tone, and there was a second of shuddering dismay.

"Jimmy, be a man!" he shrieked passionately. Every mouth was wide open, not an eyelid winked. He stared wildly, twitching all over; he bent his body forward like a man peering at an horror. "Go!" he shouted, and leaped off with his arm thrown out. "Go, Jimmy!—Jimmy, go! Go!" His fingers touched the head of the body, and the grey package started reluctantly to, all at once, whizz off the lifted planks with the suddenness of a flash of lightning. The crowd stepped forward like one man; a deep Ah—h—h! came out vibrating from the broad chests. The ship rolled as if relieved of an unfair burden; the sails flapped. Belfast, supported by Archie, gasped hysterically;

6. From "We therefore commit his body to the deep," a line from "The Order of the Burial of the Dead at Sea" in the Anglican *Book of Common Prayer* (1623).

and Charley, who, anxious to see Jimmy's last dive, leaped headlong on the rail, was too late to see anything but the faint circle of a vanishing ripple.

Mr. Baker, perspiring abundantly, read out the last prayer in a deep rumour of excited men and fluttering sails. "Amen!" he said in an unsteady growl, and closed the book.

"Square the yards!" thundered a voice above his head. All hands gave a jump; one or two dropped their caps; Mr. Baker looked up surprised. The master, standing on the break of the poop, pointed to the westward. "Breeze coming," he said, "square the yards. Look alive, men!" Mr. Baker crammed the book hurriedly into his pocket.— "Forward, there—let go the foretack!" he hailed joyfully, bareheaded and brisk; "Square the foreyard, you port-watch!"—"Fair wind—fair wind," muttered the men going to the braces.—"What did I tell you?" mumbled old Singleton, flinging down coil after coil with hasty energy; "I knowed it—he's gone, and here it comes."

It came with the sound of a lofty and powerful sigh. The sails filled, the ship gathered way, and the waking sea began to murmur sleepily of home to the ears of men.

That night, while the ship rushed foaming to the Northward before a freshening gale, the boatswain unbosomed himself to the petty officers' berth:—"The chap was nothing but trouble," he said, "from the moment he came aboard—d'ye remember—that night in Bombay? Been bullying all that softy crowd—cheeked the old man—we had to go fooling all over a half-drowned ship to save him. Dam' nigh a mutiny all for him—and now the mate abused me like a pickpocket for forgetting to dab a lump of grease on them planks. So I did, but you ought to have known better, too, than to leave a nail sticking up—hey, Chips?"[7] "And you ought to have known better than to chuck all my tools overboard for 'im, like a skeary greenhorn,"[8] retorted the morose carpenter. "Well—he's gone after 'em now," he added in an unforgiving tone. "On the China Station,[9] I remember once, the Admiral he says to me . . ." began the sailmaker.

A week afterwards the *Narcissus* entered the chops of the Channel.[1]

Under white wings[2] she skimmed low over the blue sea like a great tired bird speeding to its nest. The clouds raced with her mastheads; they rose astern enormous and white, soared to the zenith, flew past, and falling down the wide curve of the sky seemed to dash headlong into the sea—the clouds swifter than the ship, more

---

7. Nickname for the ship's carpenter.
8. A frightened novice (colloquial).
9. The British navy stationed in the China Seas.
1. The opening of the English Channel from the Atlantic Ocean.
2. See p. 67, n. 5.

free, but without a home. The coast to welcome her stepped out of space into the sunshine. The lofty headlands trod masterfully into the sea; the wide bays smiled in the light; the shadows of home-less clouds ran along the sunny plains, leaped over valleys, without a check darted up the hills, rolled down the slopes; and the sunshine pursued them with patches of running brightness. On the brows of dark cliffs white lighthouses shone in pillars of light. The Channel glittered like a blue mantle[3] shot with gold and starred by the silver of the capping seas. The *Narcissus* rushed past the headlands and the bays. Outward-bound vessels crossed her track, lying over, and with their masts stripped for a slogging fight with the hard sou'wester.[4] And, inshore, a string of smoking steamboats waddled, hugging the coast, like migrating and amphibious monsters, distrustful of the restless waves.

At night the headlands retreated, the bays advanced into one unbroken line of gloom. The lights of the earth mingled with the lights of heaven; and above the tossing lanterns of a trawling fleet a great lighthouse shone steadily, such as an enormous riding-light burning above a vessel of fabulous dimensions. Below its steady glow, the coast, stretching away straight and black, resembled the high side of an indestructible craft riding motionless upon the immortal and unresting sea. The dark land lay alone in the midst of waters, like a mighty ship bestarred with vigilant lights—a ship carrying the burden of millions of lives—a ship freighted with dross and with jewels, with gold and with steel. She towered up immense and strong, guarding priceless traditions and untold suffering, sheltering glorious memories and base forgetfulness, ignoble virtues and splen-did transgressions. A great ship! For ages had the ocean battered in vain her enduring sides; she was there when the world was vaster and darker, when the sea was great and mysterious, and ready to surrender the prize of fame to audacious men. A ship mother of fleets and nations! The great flagship of the race; stronger than the storms! and anchored in the open sea.

The *Narcissus*, heeling over to off-shore gusts, rounded the South Foreland, passed through the Downs, and, in tow, entered the river.[5] Shorn of the glory of her white wings, she wound obediently after the tug through the maze of invisible channels. As she passed them the red-painted light-vessels, swung at their moorings, seemed for an instant to sail with great speed in the rush of tide, and the

3. A blanket or covering cloth.
4. A strong wind from the southwest.
5. The River Thames. South Foreland is the headland on the Kent coast in southeastern England. The Downs is the roadstead between North and South Foreland, off the Kent coast.

next moment were left hopelessly behind. The big buoys on the tails of banks slipped past her sides very low, and, dropping in her wake, tugged at their chains like fierce watch-dogs. The reach narrowed; from both sides the land approached the ship. She went steadily up the river. On the riverside slopes the houses appeared in groups— seemed to stream down the declivities at a run to see her pass, and, checked by the mud of the foreshore, crowded on the banks. Further on, the tall factory chimneys appeared in insolent bands and watched her go by, like a straggling crowd of slim giants, swaggering and upright under the black plumets[6] of smoke, cavalierly aslant. She swept round the bends; an impure breeze shrieked a welcome between her stripped spars; and the land, closing in, stepped between the ship and the sea.

A low cloud hung before her—a great opalescent and tremulous cloud, that seemed to rise from the steaming brows of millions of men. Long drifts of smoky vapours soiled it with livid trails; it throbbed to the beat of millions of hearts, and from it came an immense and lamentable murmur—the murmur of millions of lips praying, cursing, sighing, jeering—the undying murmur of folly, regret, and hope exhaled by the crowds of the anxious earth. The *Narcissus* entered the cloud; the shadows deepened; on all sides there was the clang of iron, the sound of mighty blows, shrieks, yells. Black barges drifted stealthily on the murky stream. A mad jumble of begrimed walls loomed up vaguely in the smoke, bewildering and mournful, like a vision of disaster. The tugs, panting furiously, backed and filled in the stream, to hold the ship steady at the dock-gates; from her bows two lines went through the air whistling, and struck at the land viciously, like a pair of snakes. A bridge broke in two[7] before her, as if by enchantment; big hydraulic capstans began to turn all by themselves, as though animated by a mysterious and unholy spell. She moved through a narrow lane of water between two low walls of granite, and men with check-ropes in their hands kept pace with her, walking on the broad flagstones. A group waited impatiently on each side of the vanished bridge: rough heavy men in caps; sallow-faced men in high hats; two bareheaded women; ragged children, fascinated, and with wide eyes. A cart coming at a jerky trot pulled up sharply. One of the women screamed at the silent ship—"Hallo, Jack!" without looking at any one in particular, and all hands looked at her from the forecastle-head.—"Stand clear! Stand clear of that rope!" cried the dockmen, bending over stone posts. The crowd murmured, stamped where they stood.—"Let go

6. Small plumes (French).
7. Tower Bridge, constructed between 1886 and 1894, is a bascule bridge that allows ships up the Thames.

your quarter-checks! Let go!" sang out a ruddy-faced old man on the quay. The ropes splashed heavily falling in the water, and the *Narcissus* entered the dock.

The stony shores ran away right and left in straight lines, enclosing a sombre and rectangular pool.[8] Brick walls rose high above the water—soulless walls, staring through hundreds of windows as troubled and dull as the eyes of over-fed brutes. At their base monstrous iron cranes crouched, with chains hanging from their long necks, balancing cruel-looking hooks over the decks of lifeless ships. A noise of wheels rolling over stones, the thump of heavy things falling, the racket of feverish winches, the grinding of strained chains, floated on the air. Between high buildings the dust of all the continents soared in short flights; and a penetrating smell of perfumes and dirt, of spices and hides, of things costly and of things filthy, pervaded the space, made for it an atmosphere precious and disgusting. The *Narcissus* came gently into her berth; the shadows of soulless walls fell upon her, the dust of all the continents leaped upon her deck, and a swarm of strange men, clambering up her sides, took possession of her in the name of the sordid earth. She had ceased to live.

A toff in a black coat and high hat scrambled with agility, came up to the second mate, shook hands, and said:—"Hallo, Herbert." It was his brother. A lady appeared suddenly. A real lady, in a black dress and with a parasol. She looked extremely elegant in the midst of us, and as strange as if she had fallen there from the sky. Mr. Baker touched his cap to her. It was the master's wife. And very soon the Captain, dressed very smartly and in a white shirt, went with her over the side. We didn't recognise him at all till, turning on the quay, he called to Mr. Baker:—"Remember to wind up the chronometers to-morrow morning." An underhand lot of seedy-looking chaps with shifty eyes wandered in and out of the forecastle looking for a job—they said.—"More likely for something to steal," commented Knowles cheerfully. Poor beggars. Who cared? Weren't we home! But Mr. Baker went for one of them who had given him some cheek, and we were delighted. Everything was delightful.— "I've finished aft, sir," called out Mr. Creighton.—"No water in the well, sir," reported for the last time the carpenter, sounding-rod in hand. Mr. Baker glanced along the decks at the expectant groups of men, glanced aloft at the yards.—"Ough! That will do, men," he grunted. The groups broke up. The voyage was ended.

---

8. Berthoud (*BNN*) identifies this as a part of the Thames just below London Bridge, but Stape and Simmons (*NNOS*) suggest that it is probably St. Katherine's Dock near Tower Bridge.

Rolled-up beds went flying over the rail; lashed chests went slid-ing down the gangway—mighty few of both at that. "The rest is hav-ing a cruise off the Cape," explained Knowles enigmatically to a dock-loafer with whom he had struck a sudden friendship. Men ran, calling to one another, hailing utter strangers to "lend a hand with the dunnage," then with sudden decorum approached the mate to shake hands before going ashore.—"Good-bye, sir," they repeated in various tones. Mr. Baker grasped hard palms, grunted in a friendly manner at every one, his eyes twinkled.—"Take care of your money, Knowles. Ough! Soon get a nice wife if you do." The lame man was delighted.—"Good-bye, sir," said Belfast with emotion, wringing the mate's hand, and looked up with swimming eyes. "I thought I would take 'im ashore with me," he went on plaintively. Mr. Baker did not understand, but said kindly:—"Take care of yourself, Craik," and the bereaved Belfast went over the rail mourning and alone.

Mr. Baker in the sudden peace of the ship moved about solitary and grunting, trying door-handles, peering into dark places, never done—a model chief mate! No one waited for him ashore. Mother dead; father and two brothers, Yarmouth fishermen, drowned together on the Dogger Bank;[9] sister married and unfriendly. Quite a lady. Married to the leading tailor of a little town, and its leading politician, who did not think his sailor brother-in-law quite respect-able enough for him. "Quite a lady, quite a lady," he thought, sitting down for a moment's rest on the quarter-hatch. Time enough to go ashore and get a bite, and sup, and a bed somewhere. He didn't like to part with a ship. No one to think about then. The darkness of a misty evening fell, cold and damp, upon the deserted deck; and Mr. Baker sat smoking, thinking of all the successive ships to whom through many long years he had given the best of a sea-man's care. And never a command in sight. Not once!—"I haven't somehow the cut of a skipper about me," he meditated placidly, while the shipkeeper (who had taken possession of the galley), a wizened old man with bleared eyes, cursed him in whispers for "hanging about so."—"Now, Creighton," he pursued the unenvious train of thought, "quite a gentleman . . . swell friends . . . will get on. Fine young fellow . . . a little more experience." He got up and shook himself. "I'll be back first thing to-morrow morning for the hatches.[1] Don't you let them touch anything before I come, ship-keeper," he called out. Then, at last, he also went ashore—a model chief mate!

9. A large, submerged sand bank in the North Sea, approximately sixty miles off the east-ern coast of England. Yarmouth is a port city in eastern England. It lies at the conflu-ence of the Yare River and the North Sea.
1. To open the hatches for unloading.

The men scattered by the dissolving contact of the land came together once more in the shipping office.—"The *Narcissus* pays off," shouted outside a glazed door a brass-bound old fellow with a crown, and the capitals B. T.[2] on his cap. A lot trooped in at once but many were late. The room was large, white-washed, and bare; a counter surmounted by a brass-wire grating fenced off a third of the dusty space, and behind the grating a pasty-faced clerk, with his hair parted in the middle, had the quick, glittering eyes and the vivacious, jerky movements of a caged bird. Poor Captain Allistoun also in there, and sitting before a little table with piles of gold and notes on it, appeared subdued by his captivity. Another Board of Trade bird was perching on a high stool near the door: an old bird that did not mind the chaff of elated sailors. The crew of the *Narcissus*, broken up into knots, pushed in the corners. They had new shore togs, smart jackets that looked as if they had been shaped with an axe, glossy trousers that seemed made of crumpled sheet-iron, collarless flannel shirts, shiny new boots. They tapped on shoulders, button-holed one another, asked:—"Where did you sleep last night?" whispered gaily, slapped their thighs, stamped, with bursts of subdued laughter. Most had clean radiant faces; only one or two were dishevelled and sad; the two young Norwegians looked tidy, meek, and altogether of a promising material for the kind ladies that patronise the Scandinavian Home.[3] Wamibo, still in his working clothes, dreamed, upright and burly in the middle of the room, and, when Archie came in, woke up for a smile. But the wide-awake clerk called out a name, and the paying-off business began.

One by one they came up to the pay-table to get the wages of their glorious and obscure toil. They swept the money with care into broad palms, rammed it trustfully into trousers' pockets, or, turning their backs on the table, reckoned with difficulty in the hollow of their stiff hands.—"Money right? Sign the release. There—there," repeated the clerk, impatiently. "How stupid those sailors are!" he thought. Singleton came up, venerable—and uncertain as to daylight; brown drops of tobacco juice maculated his white beard; his hands, that never hesitated in the great light of the open sea, could hardly find the small pile of gold in the profound darkness of the shore. "Can't write?" said the clerk, shocked. "Make a mark, then." Singleton painfully sketched in a heavy cross, blotted the page. "What a disgusting old brute," muttered the clerk. Somebody opened the door for him, and the patriarchal seaman passed through unsteadily, without as much as a glance at any of us.

2. Board of Trade; see p. 147, n. 6. "Brass-bound": tradition-bound; inflexible.
3. Scandinavian Sailor's Temperance Home, founded in 1880, near West India Quay.

Archie had a pocket-book.[4] He was chaffed. Belfast, who looked wild, as though he had already luffed up through a public-house[5] or two, gave signs of emotion and wanted to speak to the Captain privately. The master was surprised. They spoke through the wires, and we could hear the Captain saying:—"I've given it up to the Board of Trade." "I should've liked to get something of his," mumbled Belfast. "But you can't, my man. It's given up, locked and sealed, to the Marine Office," expostulated the master; and Belfast stood back, with drooping mouth and troubled eyes. In a pause of the business we heard the master and the clerk talking. We caught "James Wait—deceased—found no papers of any kind—no relations—no trace—the Office must hold his wages then." Donkin entered. He seemed out of breath, was grave, full of business. He went straight to the desk, talked with animation to the clerk, who thought him an intelligent man. They discussed the account, dropping h's against one another as if for a wager—very friendly. Captain Allistoun paid. "I give you a bad discharge,"[6] he said, quietly. Donkin raised his voice:—"I don't want your bloomin' discharge—keep it. I'm goin' ter 'ave a job hashore." He turned to us. "No more bloomin' sea fur me," he said, aloud. All looked at him. He had better clothes, had an easy air, appeared more at home than any of us; he stared with assurance, enjoying the effect of his declaration. "Yuss. I 'ave friends well hoff. That's more'n yer got. But I ham a man. Yer shipmates for all that. Who's comin' fur a drink?"

No one moved. There was a silence; a silence of blank faces and stony looks. He waited a moment, smiled bitterly, and went to the door. There he faced round once more. "Yer won't? Yer bloomin' lot of 'yrpocrits. No? What 'ave I done to yer? Did I bully yer? Did I hurt yer? Did I? . . . Yer won't drink? . . . No! . . . Then may yer die of thirst, hevery mother's son of yer! Not one of yer 'as the sperrit of a bug. Ye're the scum of the world. Work and starve!"

He went out, and slammed the door with such violence that the old Board of Trade bird nearly fell off his perch.

"He's mad," said Archie. "No! No! He's drunk," insisted Belfast, lurching about, and in a maudlin tone. Captain Allistoun sat smiling thoughtfully at the cleared pay-table.

Outside, on Tower Hill,[7] they blinked, hesitated clumsily, as if blinded by the strange quality of the hazy light, as if discomposed

---

4. The word had several meanings at the time. Here it almost certainly refers to a small book used for appointments or notes.
5. A tavern or pub. "Luffed up": literally, to steer at too close an angle to the wind such that sails lose the wind and start flapping. Here Conrad seems to be using the term metaphorically to suggest that Belfast has too much to drink and is staggering like the flapping of a sail that is luffed up.
6. A bad report or recommendation.
7. The hill behind the Tower of London, a castle built by William I (1027/28–1087) in the late 11th century that later also served as a prison, particularly for political prisoners.

by the view of so many men; and they who could hear one another in the howl of gales seemed deafened and distracted by the dull roar of the busy earth.—"To the Black Horse![8] To the Black Horse!" cried some. "Let us have a drink together before we part." They crossed the road, clinging to one another. Only Charley and Belfast wandered off alone. As I came up I saw a red-faced, blowsy woman, in a grey shawl, and with dusty, fluffy hair, fall on Charley's neck. It was his mother. She slobbered over him:—"O, my boy! My boy!"—"Leggo of me," said Charley, "Leggo, mother!" I was passing him at the time, and over the untidy head of the blubbering woman he gave me a humorous smile and a glance ironic, courageous, and profound, that seemed to put all my knowledge of life to shame. I nodded and passed on, but heard him say again, good-naturedly:—"If you leggo of me this minyt—ye shall 'ave a bob for a drink out of my pay." In the next few steps I came upon Belfast. He caught my arm with tremulous enthusiasm.—"I couldn't go wi' 'em," he stammered, indicating by a nod our noisy crowd, that drifted slowly along the other sidewalk. "When I think of Jimmy. . . . Poor Jim! When I think of him I have no heart for drink. You were his chum, too . . . but I pulled him out . . . didn't I? Short wool he had. . . . Yes. And I stole the blooming pie. . . . He wouldn't go. . . . He wouldn't go for nobody." He burst into tears. "I never touched him—never—never!" he sobbed. "He went for me like . . . like . . . a lamb."

I disengaged myself gently. Belfast's crying fits generally ended in a fight with some one, and I wasn't anxious to stand the brunt of his inconsolable sorrow. Moreover, two bulky policemen stood near by, looking at us with a disapproving and incorruptible gaze.—"So long!" I said, and went off.

But at the corner I stopped to take my last look at the crew of the *Narcissus*. They were swaying irresolute and noisy on the broad flag-stones before the Mint.[9] They were bound for the Black Horse, where men, in fur caps with brutal faces and in shirt sleeves, dispense out of varnished barrels the illusions of strength, mirth, happiness; the illusion of splendour and poetry of life, to the paid-off crews of southern-going ships. From afar I saw them discoursing, with jovial eyes and clumsy gestures, while the sea of life thundered into their ears ceaseless and unheeded. And swaying about there on the white stones, surrounded by the hurry and clamour of men, they appeared to be creatures of another kind—lost, alone, forgetful, and doomed; they were like castaways, like reckless and joyous castaways, like

---

8. According to Kimbrough, it was a pub that faced the Board of Trade.
9. The Royal Mint, established in the Tower of London in 1279, remained there until the early 19th century, when it moved to a separate building nearby and remained there until 1975.

mad castaways making merry in the storm and upon an insecure ledge of a treacherous rock. The roar of the town resembled the roar of topping breakers, merciless and strong, with a loud voice and cruel purpose; but overhead the clouds broke; a flood of sunshine streamed down the walls of grimy houses. The dark knot of seamen drifted in sunshine. To the left of them the trees in Tower Gardens sighed, the stones of the Tower gleaming, seemed to stir in the play of light, as if remembering suddenly all the great joys and sorrows of the past, the fighting prototypes of these men; press-gangs;[1] mutinous cries; the wailing of women by the riverside, and the shouts of men welcoming victories. The sunshine of heaven fell like a gift of grace on the mud of the earth, on the remembering and mute stones, on greed, selfishness; on the anxious faces of forgetful men. And to the right of the dark group the stained front of the Mint, cleansed by the flood of light, stood out for a moment, dazzling and white, like a marble palace in a fairy tale. The crew of the *Narcissus* drifted out of sight.

I never saw them again. The sea took some, the steamers took others, the graveyards of the earth will account for the rest. Singleton has no doubt taken with him the long record of his faithful work into the peaceful depths of an hospitable sea. And Donkin, who never did a decent day's work in his life, no doubt earns his living by discoursing with filthy eloquence upon the right of labour to live. So be it! Let the earth and the sea each have its own.

A gone shipmate, like any other man, is gone for ever; and I never saw one of them again. But at times the spring-flood of memory sets with force up the dark River of the Nine Bends.[2] Then on the waters of the forlorn stream drifts a ship—a shadowy ship manned by a crew of Shades. They pass and make a sign, in a shadowy hail. Haven't we, together and upon the immortal sea, wrung out a meaning from our sinful lives? Good-bye, brothers! You were a good crowd. As good a crowd as ever fisted with wild cries the beating canvas of a heavy foresail; or tossing aloft, invisible in the night, gave back yell for yell to a westerly gale.

1. Groups of men officially employed to draft civilians forcibly into military service. Tower Gardens is a public garden between Tower Hill and the Tower of London.
2. An allusion to the River Styx of classical mythology over which the dead are ferried. Watts (*WNN*) suggests that Conrad actually has in mind the Lethe, another river of the classical Underworld, the river of oblivion, hence the reference to "the spring-flood of memory."

Author's Note [to *Typhoon and Other Stories*]†

The main characteristic of this volume consists in this, that all the stories composing it belong not only to the same period but have been written one after another in the order in which they appear in the book.

The period is that which follows on my connection with *Blackwood's Magazine*.¹ I had just finished writing "The End of the Tether" [1902] and was casting about for some subject which could be developed in a shorter form than the tales in the volume of *Youth* [1902] when the instance of a steamship full of returning coolies from Singapore to some port in northern China² occurred to my recollection. Years before I had heard it being talked about in the East as a recent occurrence. It was for us merely one subject of conversation amongst many others of the kind. Men earning their bread in any very specialized occupation will talk shop, not only because it is the most vital interest of their lives but also because they have not much knowledge of other subjects. They have never had the time to get acquainted with them. Life, for most of us, is not so much a hard as an exacting taskmaster.

I never met anybody personally concerned in this affair, the interest of which for us was, of course, not the bad weather but the extraordinary complication brought into the ship's life at a moment of exceptional stress by the human element below her deck. Neither was the story itself ever enlarged upon in my hearing. In that company each of us could imagine easily what the whole thing was like. The financial difficulty of it, presenting also a human problem, was solved by a mind much too simple to be perplexed by anything in the world except men's idle talk for which it was not adapted.

From the first the mere anecdote, the mere statement I might say, that such a thing had happened on the high seas, appeared to me a sufficient subject for meditation. Yet it was but a bit of a sea yarn after

---

† "Author's Note": written in 1919 for the Doubleday, Page & Co. collected edition, *The Works of Joseph Conrad*. *Typhoon and Other Stories* was originally published in 1903 and included "Typhoon" (1902), "Amy Foster" (1901), "Falk" (1903), and "To-morrow" (1902).

1. A prominent conservative British magazine established in 1817 by William Blackwood (1776–1834) that ran until 1980. Conrad published several works in *Blackwood's*, including "Karain" (1897), "Youth" (1898), "Heart of Darkness" (1899), and the serialized *Lord Jim* (1899–1900).

2. In "Typhoon," the trip is to southern China. See p. 335. "*Youth*": *Youth: A Narrative and Two Other Stories* contains "Youth," "Heart of Darkness," and "The End of the Tether." "Steamship full of returning coolies": according to Sherry, on both September 30, and October 28, 1887, the *Vidar* was in Singapore when the *Nan-shan*, commanded by a Captain Blackburn, was in port with a large contingent of Chinese passengers. Sherry speculates that it was on one of these occasions that Conrad heard the story about the Chinese and their money (*NNTF*, 289). Richard Curle, however, says that Conrad told him that the *Nan-Shan* is based on the S. S. *John P. Best* (*Joseph Conrad: A Study* [Doubleday, Page 1914], 18).

all. I felt that to bring out its deeper significance which was quite apparent to me, something other, something more was required; a leading motive that would harmonize all these violent noises, and a point of view that would put all that elemental fury into its proper place.

What was needed of course was Captain MacWhirr.[3] Directly I perceived him I could see that he was the man for the situation. I don't mean to say that I ever saw Captain MacWhirr in the flesh, or had ever come in contact with his literal mind and his dauntless temperament. MacWhirr is not an acquaintance of a few hours, or a few weeks, or a few months. He is the product of twenty years of life. My own life. Conscious invention had little to do with him. If it is true that Captain MacWhirr never walked and breathed on this earth (which I find for my part extremely difficult to believe) I can also assure my readers that he is perfectly authentic. I may venture to assert the same of every aspect of the story, while I confess that the particular typhoon of the tale was not a typhoon of my actual experience.

At its first appearance "Typhoon," the story, was classed by some critics as a definitely intended storm-piece. Others picked out Mac-Whirr, in whom they perceived a definite symbolic intention. Neither was exclusively my intention. Both the typhoon and Captain MacWhirr presented themselves to me as the necessities of the deep conviction with which I approached the subject of the story. It was their opportunity. It was also my opportunity; and it would be vain to discourse about what I made of it in a handful of pages, since the pages themselves are here, between the covers of this volume, to speak for themselves.

This is a belated reflection. If it had occurred to me before it would have perhaps done away with the existence of this Author's Note; for, indeed, the same remark applies to every story in this volume. None of them are stories of experience in the absolute sense of the word. Experience in them is but the canvas of the attempted picture. Each of them has its more than one intention. With each the question is what the writer has done with his opportunity; and each answers the question for itself in words which, if I may say so without undue solemnity, were written with a conscientious regard for the truth of my own sensations. And each of those stories, to mean something, must justify itself in its own way to the conscience of each successive reader. * * *

The "Typhoon" appeared in the early numbers of the *Pall Mall Magazine*, then under the direction of the late Mr. Halkett.[4] It was

---

3. Conrad borrowed the name from John McWhir (1858–1895), captain of the *Highland Forest,* aboard which Conrad served in 1887.
4. George Halkett (1855–1918) edited the *Pall Mall Magazine* from 1900 to 1905. This British magazine, which ran from 1893 to 1914, was particularly noted for its illustrations. "Typhoon" appeared in the January, February, and March 1902 issues.

on that occasion, too, that I saw for the first time my conceptions rendered by an artist in another medium. Mr. Maurice Greiffen-hagen[5] knew how to combine in his illustrations the effect of his own most distinguished personal vision with an absolute fidelity to the inspiration of the writer. * * * I may also add that each of the four stories on their appearance in book form was picked out on various grounds as the "best of the lot" by different critics, who reviewed the volume with a warmth of appreciation and understanding, a sympathetic insight and a friendliness of expression for which I cannot be sufficiently grateful.

1919.
J. C.

---

5. Greiffenhagen (1862–1931), British artist and member of the Royal Academy. Along with "Typhoon," he illustrated such well-known works as *She* (1887) and *Montezuma's Daughter* (1894) by H. Rider Haggard (1856–1925). Conrad was particularly pleased with the illustrations and in a letter to S. Nevile Foster (December 12, 1918) wrote: "I don't suppose that Mr Grieffenhagen for instance had ever seen the appearances of a typhoon, but he had imagination enough to understand the words I had written. * * * He displayed a fidelity to my vision by which I was deeply touched. McWhirr, Jukes, the engineer, the very Chinamen, were treated in a way to bring their individualities out in accord with my vision & with a scrupulous care" (*CL* 6:328).

Typhoon

I

Captain MacWhirr, of the steamer *Nan-Shan*, had a physiognomy[1] that, in the order of material appearances, was the exact counterpart of his mind: it presented no marked characteristics of firmness or stupidity; it had no pronounced characteristics whatever; it was simply ordinary, irresponsive, and unruffled.

The only thing his aspect might have been said to suggest, at times, was bashfulness; because he would sit, in business offices ashore, sunburnt and smiling faintly, with downcast eyes. When he raised them, they were perceived to be direct in their glance and of blue colour. His hair was fair and extremely fine, clasping from temple to temple the bald dome of his skull in a clamp as of fluffy silk. The hair of his face, on the contrary, carroty and flaming, resembled a growth of copper wire clipped short to the line of the lip; while, no matter how close he shaved, fiery metallic gleams passed, when he moved his head, over the surface of his cheeks. He was rather below the medium height, a bit round-shouldered, and so sturdy of limb that his clothes always looked a shade too tight for his arms and legs. As if unable to grasp what is due to the difference of latitudes, he wore a brown bowler hat, a complete suit of a brownish hue, and clumsy black boots. These harbour togs[2] gave to his thick figure an air of stiff and uncouth smartness. A thin silver watch-chain looped his waistcoat, and he never left his ship for the shore without clutching in his powerful, hairy fist an elegant umbrella of the very best quality, but generally unrolled. Young Jukes, the chief mate, attending his commander to the gangway, would sometimes venture to say, with the greatest gentleness, "Allow me, sir"— and possessing himself of the umbrella deferentially, would elevate the ferule,[3] shake the folds, twirl a neat furl in a jiffy, and hand it back;

---

1. See p. 82, n. 5. "*Nan-Shan*": Sherry suggests that Conrad took the name from an actual ship (*CEW* 270–271).
2. See p. 157, n. 4. "Bowler hat": a stiff felt hat with a dome-shaped crown and a narrow, somewhat rolled, brim; also called a derby hat.
3. Usually, a rod or similar instrument used to punish schoolchildren; in this case, simply an object of similar shape.

going through the performance with a face of such portentous gravity, that Mr. Solomon Rout, the chief engineer, smoking his morning cigar over the skylight, would turn away his head in order to hide
a smile. "Oh! aye! The blessed gamp. . . . Thank 'ee, Jukes, thank
'ee," would mutter Captain MacWhirr heartily, without looking up.

Having just enough imagination to carry him through each successive day, and no more, he was tranquilly sure of himself; and from
the very same cause he was not in the least conceited. It is your imaginative superior who is touchy, overbearing, and difficult to please;
but every ship Captain MacWhirr commanded was the floating
abode of harmony and peace. It was, in truth, as impossible for
him to take a flight of fancy as it would be for a watchmaker to put
together a chronometer with nothing except a two-pound hammer
and a whip-saw in the way of tools. Yet the uninteresting lives of
men so entirely given to the actuality of the bare existence have
their mysterious side. It was impossible in Captain MacWhirr's
case, for instance, to understand what under heaven could have
induced that perfectly satisfactory son of a petty grocer in Belfast[4]
to run away to sea. And yet he had done that very thing at the age
of fifteen. It was enough, when you thought it over, to give you the
idea of an immense, potent, and invisible hand[5] thrust into the antheap of the earth, laying hold of shoulders, knocking heads together,
and setting the unconscious faces of the multitude towards inconceivable goals and in undreamt-of directions.

His father never really forgave him for this undutiful stupidity.
"We could have got on without him," he used to say later on, "but
there's the business. And he an only son too!" His mother wept very
much after his disappearance. As it had never occurred to him to
leave word behind, he was mourned over for dead till, after eight
months, his first letter arrived from Talcahuano.[6] It was short, and
contained the statement: "We had very fine weather on our passage
out." But evidently, in the writer's mind, the only important intelligence was to the effect that his captain had, on the very day of writing, entered him regularly on the ship's articles as Ordinary Seaman.
"Because I can do the work," he explained. The mother again wept
copiously, while the remark, "Tom's an ass," expressed the emotions
of the father. He was a corpulent man, with a gift for sly chaffing,
which to the end of his life he exercised in his intercourse with his
son, a little pityingly, as if upon a half-witted person.

---

4. A city in northern Ireland.
5. Pearson suggests an allusion to Adam Smith's idea in *The Wealth of Nations* (1776) of
   the "invisible hand that drives a human instinct to obtain wealth."
6. A port in central Chile.

MacWhirr's visits to his home were necessarily rare, and in the course of years he despatched other letters to his parents, informing them of his successive promotions and of his movements upon the vast earth. In these missives could be found sentences like this: "The heat here is very great." Or: "On Christmas day at 4 P.M. we fell in with some icebergs." The old people ultimately became acquainted with a good many names of ships, and with the names of the skippers who commanded them—with the names of Scots and English shipowners—with the names of seas, oceans, straits, promontories—with outlandish names of lumber-ports, of rice-ports, of cotton-ports—with the names of islands—with the name of their son's young woman. She was called Lucy. It did not suggest itself to him to mention whether he thought the name pretty. And then they died.

The great day of MacWhirr's marriage came in due course, following shortly upon the great day when he got his first command.

All these events had taken place many years before the morning when, in the chart-room of the steamer *Nan-Shan*, he stood confronted by the fall of a barometer he had no reason to distrust. The fall—taking into account the excellence of the instrument, the time of the year, and the ship's position on the terrestrial globe—was of a nature ominously prophetic; but the red face of the man betrayed no sort of inward disturbance. Omens were as nothing to him, and he was unable to discover the message of a prophecy till the fulfilment had brought it home to his very door. "That's a fall, and no mistake," he thought. "There must be some uncommonly dirty weather knocking about."

The *Nan-Shan* was on her way from the southward to the treaty port of Fu-chau, with some cargo in her lower holds, and two hundred Chinese coolies returning to their village homes in the province of Fo-kien,[7] after a few years of work in various tropical colonies. The morning was fine, the oily sea heaved without a sparkle, and there was a queer white misty patch in the sky like a halo of the sun. The foredeck, packed with Chinamen, was full of sombre clothing, yellow faces, and pigtails, sprinkled over with a good many naked shoulders, for there was no wind, and the heat was close. The coolies lounged, talked, smoked, or stared over the rail; some, drawing water over the side, sluiced each other; a few slept on hatches, while several small parties of six sat on their heels surrounding iron trays with plates of rice and tiny teacups; and every single Celestial[8] of them was carrying with him all he had in the world—a wooden chest with a ringing lock and brass on the corners, containing the savings

---

7. Now Fujian, a province in southeastern China. Fu-chau is a city in southeastern China (now Fuzhou). See p. 335. "Coolies": see p. 74, n. 8.
8. A native of China. "Sluice": to pour or throw water over.

of his labours: some clothes of ceremony, sticks of incense,[9] a little opium maybe, bits of nameless rubbish of conventional value, and a small hoard of silver dollars, toiled for in coal-lighters, won in gambling-houses or in petty trading, grubbed out of earth, sweated out in mines, on railway lines, in deadly jungle, under heavy burdens—amassed patiently, guarded with care, cherished fiercely.

A cross swell had set in from the direction of Formosa Channel[1] about ten o'clock, without disturbing these passengers much, because the *Nan-Shan*, with her flat bottom, rolling chocks on bilges, and great breadth of beam, had the reputation of an exceptionally steady ship in a sea-way. Mr. Jukes, in moments of expansion on shore, would proclaim loudly that the "old girl was as good as she was pretty." It would never have occurred to Captain MacWhirr to express his favourable opinion so loud or in terms so fanciful.

She was a good ship, undoubtedly, and not old either. She had been built in Dumbarton less than three years before, to the order of a firm of merchants in Siam—Messrs. Sigg and Son.[2] When she lay afloat, finished in every detail and ready to take up the work of her life, the builders contemplated her with pride.

"Sigg has asked us for a reliable skipper to take her out," remarked one of the partners; and the other, after reflecting for a while, said: "I think MacWhirr is ashore just at present." "Is he? Then wire him at once. He's the very man," declared the senior, without a moment's hesitation.

Next morning MacWhirr stood before them unperturbed, having travelled from London by the midnight express after a sudden but undemonstrative parting with his wife. She was the daughter of a superior couple who had seen better days.

"We had better be going together over the ship, Captain," said the senior partner; and the three men started to view the perfections of the *Nan-Shan* from stem to stern, and from her keelson to the trucks of her two stumpy pole-masts.

Captain MacWhirr had begun by taking off his coat, which he hung on the end of a steam windlass embodying all the latest improvements.

"My uncle wrote of you favourably by yesterday's mail to our good friends—Messrs. Sigg, you know—and doubtless they'll continue you out there in command," said the junior partner. "You'll be able to boast of being in charge of the handiest boat of her size on the coast of China, Captain," he added.

---

9. For use in Buddhist ceremonies.
1. Now the Straits of Taiwan, the body of water between Taiwan and mainland China. See p. 335.
2. Sherry suggests that Conrad bases this company on the Swiss firm of Jucker & Sigg & Co. of Bangkok (*CEW* 238). Dumbarton was a shipbuilding town on the Clyde River in Scotland. For Siam, see p. 3, n. 1.

"Have you? Thank 'ee," mumbled vaguely MacWhirr, to whom the view of a distant eventuality could appeal no more than the beauty of a wide landscape to a purblind tourist; and his eyes happening at the moment to be at rest upon the lock of the cabin door, he walked up to it, full of purpose, and began to rattle the handle vigorously, while he observed, in his low, earnest voice, "You can't trust the workmen nowadays. A brand-new lock, and it won't act at all. Stuck fast. See? See?"

As soon as they found themselves alone in their office across the yard: "You praised that fellow up to Sigg. What is it you see in him?" asked the nephew, with faint contempt.

"I admit he has nothing of your fancy skipper about him, if that's what you mean," said the elder man curtly. "Is the foreman of the joiners on the *Nan-Shan* outside? . . . Come in, Bates. How is it that you let Tait's people put us off with a defective lock on the cabin door? The Captain could see directly he set eye on it. Have it replaced at once. The little straws,[3] Bates . . . the little straws. . . ."

The lock was replaced accordingly, and a few days afterwards the *Nan-Shan* steamed out to the East, without MacWhirr having offered any further remark as to her fittings, or having been heard to utter a single word hinting at pride in his ship, gratitude for his appointment, or satisfaction at his prospects.

With a temperament neither loquacious nor taciturn, he found very little occasion to talk. There were matters of duty, of course— directions, orders, and so on; but the past being to his mind done with, and the future not there yet, the more general actualities of the day required no comment—because facts can speak for themselves with overwhelming precision.

Old Mr. Sigg liked a man of few words, and one that "you could be sure would not try to improve upon his instructions." MacWhirr satisfying these requirements, was continued in command of the *Nan-Shan*, and applied himself to the careful navigation of his ship in the China seas.[4] She had come out on a British register, but after some time Messrs. Sigg judged it expedient to transfer her to the Siamese flag.[5]

At the news of the contemplated transfer Jukes grew restless, as if under a sense of personal affront. He went about grumbling to himself, and uttering short scornful laughs. "Fancy having a ridiculous

---

3. Probably short for the saying "little straws show which way the wind blows," that is, the little straws point to the direction of larger things.
4. The South China Sea (see p. 109, n. 7) and the East China Sea, a marginal sea of the Pacific Ocean, bordered on the west by China, on the north by Korea, on the east by Japan, and on the south by Taiwan. See p. 335.
5. The *Nan-Shan* was originally registered as a British ship, but the owners transferred its register to Siam, presumably to save money on port dues as a local ship. From 1855 to 1916, the Siamese flag consisted of a white elephant on a red background.

Noah's Ark elephant in the ensign of one's ship," he said once at the engine-room door. "Dash me[6] if I can stand it: I'll throw up the billet. Don't it make *you* sick, Mr. Rout?" The chief engineer only cleared his throat with the air of a man who knows the value of a good billet.

The first morning the new flag floated over the stern of the *Nan-Shan* Jukes stood looking at it bitterly from the bridge. He struggled with his feelings for a while, and then remarked, "Queer flag for a man to sail under, sir."

"What's the matter with the flag?" inquired Captain MacWhirr. "Seems all right to me." And he walked across to the end of the bridge to have a good look.

"Well, it looks queer to me," burst out Jukes, greatly exasperated, and flung off the bridge.

Captain MacWhirr was amazed at these manners. After a while he stepped quietly into the chart-room, and opened his International Signal Code-book at the plate where the flags of all the nations are correctly figured in gaudy rows. He ran his finger over them, and when he came to Siam he contemplated with great attention the red field and the white elephant. Nothing could be more simple; but to make sure he brought the book out on the bridge for the purpose of comparing the coloured drawing with the real thing at the flag-staff astern. When next Jukes, who was carrying on the duty that day with a sort of suppressed fierceness, happened on the bridge, his commander observed:

"There's nothing amiss with that flag."

"Isn't there?" mumbled Jukes, falling on his knees before a deck-locker and jerking therefrom viciously a spare lead-line.

"No. I looked up the book. Length twice the breadth and the elephant exactly in the middle. I thought the people ashore would know how to make the local flag. Stands to reason. You were wrong, Jukes. . . ."

"Well, sir," began Jukes, getting up excitedly, "all I can say—" He fumbled for the end of the coil of line with trembling hands.

"That's all right." Captain MacWhirr soothed him, sitting heavily on a little canvas folding-stool he greatly affected. "All you have to do is to take care they don't hoist the elephant upside-down[7] before they get quite used to it."

Jukes flung the new lead-line over on the fore-deck with a loud "Here you are, boss'n—don't forget to wet it thoroughly," and turned with immense resolution towards his commander; but Captain MacWhirr spread his elbows on the bridge-rail comfortably.

6. A euphemism for *damn me*; see p. 53, n. 7.
7. A signal of distress.

"Because it would be, I suppose, understood as a signal of distress," he went on. "What do you think? That elephant there, I take it, stands for something in the nature of the Union Jack[8] in the flag. . . ."

"Does it!" yelled Jukes, so that every head on the *Nan-Shan's* decks looked towards the bridge. Then he sighed, and with sudden resignation: "It would certainly be a dam' distressful sight," he said meekly.

Later in the day he accosted the chief engineer with a confidential "Here, let me tell you the old man's latest."

Mr. Solomon Rout (frequently alluded to as Long Sol, Old Sol, or Father Rout), from finding himself almost invariably the tallest man on board every ship he joined, had acquired the habit of a stooping, leisurely condescension. His hair was scant and sandy, his flat cheeks were pale, his bony wrists and long scholarly hands were pale too, as though he had lived all his life in the shade.

He smiled from on high at Jukes, and went on smoking and glancing about quietly, in the manner of a kind uncle lending an ear to the tale of an excited schoolboy. Then, greatly amused but impassive, he asked:

"And did you throw up the billet?"

"No," cried Jukes, raising a weary, discouraged voice above the harsh buzz of the *Nan-Shan's* friction winches. All of them were hard at work, snatching slings of cargo, high up, to the end of long derricks, only, as it seemed, to let them rip down recklessly by the run. The cargo chains groaned in the gins, clinked on coamings, rattled over the side; and the whole ship quivered, with her long grey flanks smoking in wreaths of steam. "No," cried Jukes, "I didn't. What's the good? I might just as well fling my resignation at this bulkhead. I don't believe you can make a man like that understand anything. He simply knocks me over."

At that moment Captain MacWhirr, back from the shore, crossed the deck, umbrella in hand, escorted by a mournful, self-possessed Chinaman, walking behind in paper-soled silk shoes, and who also carried an umbrella.

The master of the *Nan-Shan*, speaking just audibly and gazing at his boots as his manner was, remarked that it would be necessary to call at Fu-chau this trip, and desired Mr. Rout to have steam up to-morrow afternoon at one o'clock sharp. He pushed back his hat to wipe his forehead, observing at the same time that he hated going ashore anyhow; while overtopping him Mr. Rout, without deigning a word, smoked austerely, nursing his right elbow in the palm of his left hand. Then Jukes was directed in the same subdued voice to keep the forward 'tween-deck clear of cargo. Two hundred coolies were going

8. See p. 244, n. 4.

to be put down there. The Bun Hin Company[9] were sending that lot home. Twenty-five bags of rice would be coming off in a sampan directly, for stores. All seven-years'-men they were, said Captain MacWhirr, with a camphor-wood chest[1] to every man. The carpenter should be set to work nailing three-inch battens along the deck below, fore and aft, to keep these boxes from shifting in a sea-way. Jukes had better look to it at once. "D'ye hear, Jukes?" This Chinaman here was coming with the ship as far as Fu-chau—a sort of interpreter he would be. Bun Hin's clerk he was, and wanted to have a look at the space. Jukes had better take him forward. "D'ye hear, Jukes?"

Jukes took care to punctuate these instructions in proper places with the obligatory "Yes, sir," ejaculated without enthusiasm. His brusque "Come along John;[2] make look see" set the Chinaman in motion at his heels.

"Wanchee look see, all same look see can do," said Jukes, who having no talent for foreign languages mangled the very pidgin-English cruelly. He pointed at the open hatch. "Catchee number one piecie place to sleep in. Eh?"

He was gruff, as became his racial superiority, but not unfriendly. The Chinaman, gazing sad and speechless into the darkness of the hatchway, seemed to stand at the head of a yawning grave.

"No catchee rain down there—savee?"[3] pointed out Jukes. "Suppose all 'ee same fine weather, one piecie coolie-man come topside," he pursued, warming up imaginatively. "Make so—Phooooo!" He expanded his chest and blew out his cheeks. "Savee, John? Breathe—fresh air. Good. Eh? Washee him piecie pants, chow-chow[4] topside—see, John?"

With his mouth and hands he made exuberant motions of eating rice and washing clothes; and the Chinaman, who concealed his distrust of this pantomime under a collected demeanour tinged by a gentle and refined melancholy, glanced out of his almond eyes from Jukes to the hatch and back again. "Velly good," he murmured, in a disconsolate undertone, and hastened smoothly along the decks, dodging obstacles in his course. He disappeared, ducking low under a sling of ten dirty gunny-bags full of some costly merchandise and exhaling a repulsive smell.

---

9. An important Chinese shipping company in Singapore.
1. A chest coated with camphor to protect against moths. "Seven-years'-men": men working on seven-year contracts.
2. An abbreviation of *John Chinaman*, a humorous or derogatory label for a Chinese man, roughly equivalent to guys, fellows, or chaps.
3. I.e., savvy; understand.
4. A mixture or assortment of any kind, especially concerning food or eating, as in this case.

Captain MacWhirr meantime had gone on the bridge, and into the chart-room, where a letter, commenced two days before, awaited termination. These long letters began with the words, "My darling wife," and the steward, between the scrubbing of the floors and the dusting of chronometer-boxes, snatched at every opportunity to read them. They interested him much more than they possibly could the woman for whose eye they were intended; and this for the reason that they related in minute detail each successive trip of the *Nan-Shan*.

Her master, faithful to facts, which alone his consciousness reflected, would set them down with painstaking care upon many pages. The house in a northern suburb to which these pages were addressed had a bit of garden before the bow-windows, a deep porch of good appearance, coloured glass with imitation lead frame in the front door. He paid five-and-forty pounds a year for it, and did not think the rent too high, because Mrs. MacWhirr (a pretentious person with a scraggy neck and a disdainful manner) was admittedly ladylike, and in the neighbourhood considered as "quite superior." The only secret of her life was her abject terror of the time when her husband would come home to stay for good. Under the same roof there dwelt also a daughter called Lydia and a son, Tom. These two were but slightly acquainted with their father. Mainly, they knew him as a rare but privileged visitor, who of an evening smoked his pipe in the dining-room and slept in the house. The lanky girl, upon the whole, was rather ashamed of him; the boy was frankly and utterly indifferent in a straightforward, delightful, unaffected way manly boys have.

And Captain MacWhirr wrote home from the coast of China twelve times every year, desiring quaintly to be "remembered to the children," and subscribing himself "your loving husband," as calmly as if the words so long used by so many men were, apart from their shape, worn-out things, and of a faded meaning.

The China seas north and south[5] are narrow seas. They are seas full of every-day, eloquent facts, such as islands, sand-banks, reefs, swift and changeable currents—tangled facts that nevertheless speak to a seaman in clear and definite language. Their speech appealed to Captain MacWhirr's sense of realities so forcibly that he had given up his state-room below and practically lived all his days on the bridge of his ship, often having his meals sent up, and sleeping at night in the chart-room. And he indited there his home letters. Each of them, without exception, contained the phrase, "The weather has been very fine this trip," or some other form of a

5. The East China Sea and South China Sea, respectively.

statement to that effect. And this statement, too, in its wonderful persistence, was of the same perfect accuracy as all the others they contained.

Mr. Rout likewise wrote letters; only no one on board knew how chatty he could be pen in hand, because the chief engineer had enough imagination to keep his desk locked. His wife relished his style greatly. They were a childless couple, and Mrs. Rout, a big, high-bosomed, jolly woman of forty, shared with Mr. Rout's toothless and venerable mother a little cottage near Teddington.[6] She would run over her correspondence, at breakfast, with lively eyes, and scream out interesting passages in a joyous voice at the deaf old lady, prefacing each extract by the warning shout, "Solomon says!" She had the trick of firing off Solomon's utterances also upon strangers, astonishing them easily by the unfamiliar text and the unexpectedly jocular vein of these quotations. On the day the new curate called for the first time at the cottage, she found occasion to remark, "As Solomon says: 'the engineers that go down to the sea in ships behold the wonders of sailor nature,'"[7] when a change in the visitor's countenance made her stop and stare.

"Solomon . . . Oh! . . . Mrs. Rout," stuttered the young man, very red in the face, "I must say . . . I don't . . ."

"He's my husband," she announced in a great shout, throwing herself back in the chair. Perceiving the joke, she laughed immoderately with a handkerchief to her eyes, while he sat wearing a forced smile, and, from his inexperience of jolly women, fully persuaded that she must be deplorably insane. They were excellent friends afterwards; for, absolving her from irreverent intention, he came to think she was a very worthy person indeed; and he learned in time to receive without flinching other scraps of Solomon's wisdom.[8]

"For my part," Solomon was reported by his wife to have said once, "give me the dullest ass for a skipper before a rogue. There is a way to take a fool; but a rogue is smart and slippery." This was an airy generalisation drawn from the particular case of Captain Mac-Whirr's honesty, which, in itself, had the heavy obviousness of a lump of clay. On the other hand, Mr. Jukes, unable to generalise, unmarried, and unengaged, was in the habit of opening his heart after another fashion to an old chum and former shipmate, actually serving as second officer on board an Atlantic liner.

First of all he would insist upon the advantages of the Eastern trade, hinting at its superiority to the Western Ocean[9] service. He

6. A village in southwest London on the north bank of the Thames.
7. An allusion to Psalms 107:23–24: "They that go down to the sea in ships, that do business in great waters; These see the works of the Lord, and his wonders in the deep."
8. A play on the Israeli king Solomon, son of David, who was known for his wisdom.
9. See p. 156, n. 8.

extolled the sky, the seas, the ships, and the easy life of the Far East.[1]
The *Nan-Shan*, he affirmed, was second to none as a sea-boat.

"We have no brass-bound uniforms,[2] but then we are like brothers here," he wrote. "We all mess together and live like fighting-
cocks. . . . All the chaps of the black-squad are as decent as they
make that kind, and old Sol, the chief, is a dry stick.[3] We are good
friends. As to our old man, you could not find a quieter skipper.
Sometimes you would think he hadn't sense enough to see anything
wrong. And yet it isn't that. Can't be. He has been in command for
a good few years now. He doesn't do anything actually foolish, and
gets his ship along all right without worrying anybody. I believe he
hasn't brains enough to enjoy kicking up a row. I don't take advantage of him. I would scorn it. Outside the routine of duty he doesn't
seem to understand more than half of what you tell him. We get a
laugh out of this at times; but it is dull, too, to be with a man like
this—in the long-run. Old Sol says he hasn't much conversation.
Conversation! O Lord! He never talks. The other day I had been
yarning under the bridge with one of the engineers, and he must
have heard us. When I came up to take my watch, he steps out of the
chart-room and has a good look all round, peeps over at the sidelights, glances at the compass, squints upwards at the stars. That's
his regular performance. By-and-by he says: 'Was that you talking
just now in the port alleyway?' 'Yes, sir.' 'With the third engineer?'
'Yes, sir.' He walks off to starboard, and sits under the dodger on a
little campstool of his, and for half an hour perhaps he makes no
sound, except that I heard him sneeze once. Then after a while I
hear him getting up over there, and he strolls across to port, where
I was. 'I can't understand what you can find to talk about,' says he.
'Two solid hours. I am not blaming you. I see people ashore at it all
day long, and then in the evening they sit down and keep at it over
the drinks. Must be saying the same things over and over again. I
can't understand.'

"Did you ever hear anything like that? And he was so patient
about it. It made me quite sorry for him. But he is exasperating too
sometimes. Of course one would not do anything to vex him even if
it were worth while. But it isn't. He's so jolly innocent that if you

---

1. See similar comments in *The Shadow-Line*; "Afraid of the sails. Afraid of a white crew.
   Too much trouble. Too much work. Too long out here. Easy life and deck-chairs more
   their mark" (p. 67); and also in *Lord Jim*: "They were attuned to the eternal peace of
   Eastern sky and sea. They loved short passages, good deck-chairs, large native crews,
   and the distinction of being white. They shuddered at the thought of hard work, and
   led precariously easy lives" (*LJ* 13).
2. See p. 251, n. 2.
3. A humorless person. "Black-squad": the crew assigned to the engine room, also called
   the "black gang," who were black from the coal used to fuel steamships.

270 JOSEPH CONRAD

were to put your thumb to your nose and wave your fingers at him he would only wonder gravely to himself what got into you. He told me once quite simply that he found it very difficult to make out what made people always act so queerly. He's too dense to trouble about, and that's the truth."

Thus wrote Mr. Jukes to his chum in the Western Ocean trade, out of the fulness of his heart and the liveliness of his fancy.

He had expressed his honest opinion. It was not worth while trying to impress a man of that sort. If the world had been full of such men, life would have probably appeared to Jukes an unentertaining and unprofitable business. He was not alone in his opinion. The sea itself, as if sharing Mr. Jukes' good-natured forbearance, had never put itself out to startle the silent man, who seldom looked up, and wandered innocently over the waters with the only visible purpose of getting food, raiment,[4] and house-room for three people ashore. Dirty weather he had known, of course. He had been made wet, uncomfortable, tired in the usual way, felt at the time and presently forgotten. So that upon the whole he had been justified in reporting fine weather at home. But he had never been given a glimpse of immeasurable strength and of immoderate wrath, the wrath that passes exhausted but never appeased—the wrath and fury of the passionate sea. He knew it existed, as we know that crime and abominations exist; he had heard of it as a peaceable citizen in a town hears of battles, famines, and floods,[5] and yet knows nothing of what these things mean—though, indeed, he may have been mixed up in a street row, have gone without his dinner once, or been soaked to the skin in a shower. Captain MacWhirr had sailed over the surface of the oceans as some men go skimming over the years of existence to sink gently into a placid grave, ignorant of life to the last, without ever having been made to see all it may contain of perfidy, of violence, and of terror. There are on sea and land such men thus fortunate—or thus disdained by destiny or by the sea.

II

Observing the steady fall of the barometer, Captain MacWhirr thought, "There's some dirty weather knocking about." This is precisely what he thought. He had had an experience of moderately dirty weather—the term dirty as applied to the weather implying only moderate discomfort to the seaman. Had he been informed by an indisputable authority that the end of the world was to be finally

4. An echo of 1 Timothy 6:8: "And having food and raiment let us be therewith content."
5. Stape suggests an echo of "The Litany of the Saints": "A peste, fame et bello" ("from pestilence, famine, and battle").

accomplished by a catastrophic disturbance of the atmosphere, he would have assimilated the information under the simple idea of dirty weather, and no other, because he had no experience of cataclysms, and belief does not necessarily imply comprehension. The wisdom of his country had pronounced by means of an Act of Parliament[6] that before he could be considered as fit to take charge of a ship he should be able to answer certain simple questions on the subject of circular storms such as hurricanes, cyclones, typhoons; and apparently he had answered them, since he was now in command of the *Nan-Shan* in the China seas during the season of typhoons.[7] But if he had answered he remembered nothing of it. He was, however, conscious of being made uncomfortable by the clammy heat. He came out on the bridge, and found no relief to this oppression. The air seemed thick. He gasped like a fish, and began to believe himself greatly out of sorts.

The *Nan-Shan* was ploughing a vanishing furrow upon the circle of the sea that had the surface and the shimmer of an undulating piece of grey silk. The sun, pale and without rays, poured down leaden heat in a strangely indecisive light, and the Chinamen were lying prostrate about the decks. Their bloodless, pinched, yellow faces were like the faces of bilious invalids. Captain MacWhirr noticed two of them especially, stretched out on their backs below the bridge. As soon as they had closed their eyes they seemed dead. Three others, however, were quarrelling barbarously away forward; and one big fellow, half naked, with Herculean shoulders,[8] was hanging limply over a winch; another, sitting on the deck, his knees up and his head drooping sideways in a girlish attitude, was plaiting his pigtail with infinite languor depicted in his whole person and in the very movement of his fingers. The smoke struggled with difficulty out of the funnel, and instead of streaming away spread itself out like an infernal sort of cloud, smelling of sulphur and raining soot all over the decks.

"What the devil are you doing there, Mr. Jukes?" asked Captain MacWhirr.

This unusual form of address, though mumbled rather than spoken, caused the body of Mr. Jukes to start as though it had been prodded under the fifth rib.[9] He had had a low bench brought on the bridge, and sitting on it, with a length of rope curled about his feet and a piece of canvas stretched over his knees, was pushing a

---

6. A reference to the Merchant Shipping Act of 1854, which regulated the merchant marine service, including the examinations for the various officer ranks.
7. From May through December.
8. A reference to Hercules (or Heracles), son of Zeus, known particularly for his strength.
9. There are several references in 2 Samuel to someone being stabbed under the fifth rib, resulting in death from a wound, presumably to the heart.

sail-needle vigorously. He looked up, and his surprise gave to his eyes an expression of innocence and candour.

"I am only roping some of that new set of bags we made last trip for whipping up coals," he remonstrated gently. "We shall want them for the next coaling, sir."

"What became of the others?"

"Why, worn out of course, sir."

Captain MacWhirr, after glaring down irresolutely at his chief mate, disclosed the gloomy and cynical conviction that more than half of them had been lost overboard, "if only the truth was known," and retired to the other end of the bridge. Jukes, exasperated by this unprovoked attack, broke the needle at the second stitch, and dropping his work got up and cursed the heat in a violent undertone.

The propeller thumped, the three Chinamen forward had given up squabbling very suddenly, and the one who had been plaiting his tail clasped his legs and stared dejectedly over his knees. The lurid sunshine cast faint and sickly shadows. The swell ran higher and swifter every moment, and the ship lurched heavily in the smooth, deep hollows of the sea.

"I wonder where that beastly swell comes from," said Jukes aloud, recovering himself after a stagger.

"North-east," grunted the literal MacWhirr, from his side of the bridge. "There's some dirty weather knocking about. Go and look at the glass."[1]

When Jukes came out of the chart-room, the cast of his countenance had changed to thoughtfulness and concern. He caught hold of the bridge-rail and stared ahead.

The temperature in the engine-room had gone up to a hundred and seventeen degrees. Irritated voices were ascending through the skylight and through the fiddle of the stokehold in a harsh and resonant uproar, mingled with angry clangs and scrapes of metal, as if men with limbs of iron and throats of bronze had been quarrelling down there. The second engineer was falling foul of the stokers for letting the steam go down. He was a man with arms like a blacksmith, and generally feared; but that afternoon the stokers were answering him back recklessly, and slammed the furnace doors with the fury of despair. Then the noise ceased suddenly, and the second engineer appeared, emerging out of the stokehold streaked with grime and soaking wet like a chimney-sweep coming out of a well. As soon as his head was clear of the fiddle he began to scold Jukes for not trimming properly the stokehold ventilators; and in answer Jukes made with his hands deprecatory soothing signs meaning: No wind—can't be helped—you can see for yourself. But

---

1. The barometer.

the other wouldn't hear reason. His teeth flashed angrily in his dirty face. He didn't mind, he said, the trouble of punching their blanked heads down there, blank his soul, but did the condemned sailors think you could keep steam up in the God-forsaken boilers simply by knocking the blanked[2] stokers about? No, by George![3] You had to get some draught too—may he be everlastingly blanked for a swab-headed deck-hand if you didn't! And the chief, too, rampaging before the steam-gauge and carrying on like a lunatic up and down the engine-room ever since noon. What did Jukes think he was stuck up there for, if he couldn't get one of his decayed,[4] good-for-nothing deck-cripples to turn the ventilators to the wind?

The relations of the "engine-room" and the "deck" of the *Nan-Shan* were, as is known, of a brotherly nature; therefore Jukes leaned over and begged the other in a restrained tone not to make a disgusting ass of himself; the skipper was on the other side of the bridge. But the second declared mutinously that he didn't care a rap[5] who was on the other side of the bridge, and Jukes, passing in a flash from lofty disapproval into a state of exaltation, invited him in unflattering terms to come up and twist the beastly things to please himself, and catch such wind as a donkey[6] of his sort could find. The second rushed up to the fray. He flung himself at the port ventilator as though he meant to tear it out bodily and toss it overboard. All he did was to move the cowl round a few inches, with an enormous expenditure of force, and seemed spent in the effort. He leaned against the back of the wheelhouse, and Jukes walked up to him.

"Oh, Heavens!" ejaculated the engineer in a feeble voice. He lifted his eyes to the sky, and then let his glassy stare descend to meet the horizon that, tilting up to an angle of forty degrees, seemed to hang on a slant for a while and settled down slowly. "Heavens! Phew! What's up, anyhow?"

Jukes, straddling his long legs like a pair of compasses, put on an air of superiority. "We're going to catch it this time," he said. "The barometer is tumbling down like anything, Harry. And you trying to kick up that silly row . . ."

The word "barometer" seemed to revive the second engineer's mad animosity. Collecting afresh all his energies, he directed Jukes in a low and brutal tone to shove the unmentionable instrument down his gory throat. Who cared for his crimson[7] barometer? It was the

---

2. Substitutions for profanity.
3. A mild oath, originally referring to St. George (d. 303?).
4. Probably a euphemism for *rotten*.
5. A coin worth half a farthing in 18th-century Ireland, hence a coin of the least possible value.
6. Euphemism for *ass*.
7. Euphemism for *bloody*. "Gory": another euphemism for *bloody*.

steam—the steam—that was going down; and what between the firemen going faint and the chief going silly, it was worse than a dog's life for him; he didn't care a tinker's curse[8] how soon the whole show was blown out of the water. He seemed on the point of having a cry, but after regaining his breath he muttered darkly, "I'll faint them,"[9] and dashed off. He stopped upon the fiddle long enough to shake his fist at the unnatural daylight, and dropped into the dark hole with a whoop.

When Jukes turned, his eyes fell upon the rounded back and the big red ears of Captain MacWhirr, who had come across. He did not look at his chief officer, but said at once, "That's a very violent man, that second engineer."

"Jolly good second, anyhow," grunted Jukes. "They can't keep up steam," he added rapidly, and made a grab at the rail against the coming lurch.

Captain MacWhirr, unprepared, took a run and brought himself up with a jerk by an awning stanchion.

"A profane man," he said obstinately. "If this goes on, I'll have to get rid of him the first chance."

"It's the heat," said Jukes. "The weather's awful. It would make a saint swear. Even up here I feel exactly as if I had my head tied up in a woollen blanket."

Captain MacWhirr looked up. "D'ye mean to say, Mr. Jukes, you ever had your head tied up in a blanket? What was that for?"

"It's a manner of speaking, sir," said Jukes stolidly.

"Some of you fellows do go on! What's that about saints swearing? I wish you wouldn't talk so wild. What sort of saint would that be that would swear? No more saint than yourself, I expect. And what's a blanket got to do with it—or the weather either . . . The heat does not make me swear—does it? It's filthy bad temper. That's what it is. And what's the good of your talking like this?"

Thus Captain MacWhirr expostulated against the use of images in speech, and at the end electrified Jukes by a contemptuous snort, followed by words of passion and resentment: "Damme! I'll fire him out of the ship if he don't look out."

And Jukes, incorrigible, thought: "Goodness me! Somebody's put a new inside to my old man. Here's temper, if you like. Of course it's the weather; what else? It would make an angel quarrelsome—let alone a saint."

All the Chinamen on deck appeared at their last gasp.

At its setting the sun had a diminished diameter and an expiring brown, rayless glow, as if millions of centuries elapsing since the

8. A phrase meaning *absolutely worthless.*
9. I'll make them faint.

morning had brought it near its end. A dense bank of cloud became visible to the northward; it had a sinister dark olive tint, and lay low and motionless upon the sea, resembling a solid obstacle in the path of the ship. She went floundering towards it like an exhausted creature driven to its death. The coppery twilight retired slowly, and the darkness brought out overhead a swarm of unsteady, big stars, that, as if blown upon, flickered exceedingly and seemed to hang very near the earth. At eight o'clock Jukes went into the chart-room to write up the ship's log.

He copied neatly out of the rough-book the number of miles, the course of the ship, and in the column for "wind" scrawled the word "calm" from top to bottom of the eight hours since noon. He was exasperated by the continuous, monotonous rolling of the ship. The heavy inkstand would slide away in a manner that suggested perverse intelligence in dodging the pen. Having written in the large space under the head of "Remarks" "Heat very oppressive," he stuck the end of the penholder in his teeth, pipe fashion, and mopped his face carefully.

"Ship rolling heavily in a high cross swell," he began again, and commented to himself, "Heavily is no word for it." Then he wrote: "Sunset threatening, with a low bank of clouds to N. and E. Sky clear overhead."

Sprawling over the table with arrested pen, he glanced out of the door, and in that frame of his vision he saw all the stars flying upwards between the teakwood jambs[1] on a black sky. The whole lot took flight together and disappeared, leaving only a blackness flecked with white flashes, for the sea was as black as the sky and speckled with foam afar. The stars that had flown to the roll came back on the return swing of the ship, rushing downwards in their glittering multitude, not of fiery points, but enlarged to tiny discs brilliant with a clear wet sheen.

Jukes watched the flying big stars for a moment, and then wrote: "8 P.M. Swell increasing. Ship labouring and taking water on her decks. Battened down the coolies for the night. Barometer still falling." He paused, and thought to himself, "Perhaps nothing whatever'll come of it." And then he closed resolutely his entries: "Every appearance of a typhoon coming on."

On going out he had to stand aside, and Captain MacWhirr strode over the doorstep without saying a word or making a sign.

"Shut the door, Mr. Jukes, will you?" he cried from within.

Jukes turned back to do so, muttering ironically: "Afraid to catch cold, I suppose." It was his watch below, but he yearned for

---

1. The posts on either side of the doorway.

communion with his kind; and he remarked cheerily to the second mate: "Doesn't look so bad, after all—does it?"

The second mate was marching to and fro on the bridge, tripping down with small steps one moment, and the next climbing with difficulty the shifting slope of the deck. At the sound of Jukes' voice he stood still, facing forward, but made no reply.

"Hallo! That's a heavy one," said Jukes, swaying to meet the long roll till his lowered hand touched the planks. This time the second mate made in his throat a noise of an unfriendly nature.

He was an oldish, shabby little fellow, with bad teeth and no hair on his face. He had been shipped in a hurry in Shanghai,[2] that trip when the second officer brought from home had delayed the ship three hours in port by contriving (in some manner Captain Mac-Whirr could never understand) to fall overboard into an empty coal-lighter lying alongside, and had to be sent ashore to the hospital with concussion of the brain and a broken limb or two.

Jukes was not discouraged by the unsympathetic sound. "The Chinamen must be having a lovely time of it down there," he said. "It's lucky for them the old girl has the easiest roll of any ship I've ever been in. There now! This one wasn't so bad."

"You wait," snarled the second mate.

With his sharp nose, red at the tip, and his thin pinched lips, he always looked as though he were raging inwardly; and he was concise in his speech to the point of rudeness. All his time off duty he spent in his cabin with the door shut, keeping so still in there that he was supposed to fall asleep as soon as he had disappeared; but the man who came in to wake him for his watch on deck would invariably find him with his eyes wide open, flat on his back in the bunk, and glaring irritably from a soiled pillow. He never wrote any letters, did not seem to hope for news from anywhere; and though he had been heard once to mention West Hartlepool,[3] it was with extreme bitterness, and only in connection with the extortionate charges of a boarding-house. He was one of those men who are picked up at need in the ports of the world. They are competent enough, appear hopelessly hard up, show no evidence of any sort of vice, and carry about them all the signs of manifest failure. They come aboard on an emergency, care for no ship afloat, live in their own atmosphere of casual connection amongst their shipmates who know nothing of them, and make up their minds to leave at inconvenient times. They clear out with no words of leave-taking in some God-forsaken

2. A city on the east coast of China, located on the Huangpu River (a tributary of the Yangtze River) at the confluence of the Yangtze and the East China Sea. See p. 335.
3. A port town in northeast England, important for shipping and rail trade in the 19th century.

port other men would fear to be stranded in, and go ashore in company of a shabby sea-chest, corded like a treasure-box, and with an air of shaking the ship's dust off their feet.[4]

"You wait," he repeated, balanced in great swings with his back to Jukes, motionless and implacable.

"Do you mean to say we are going to catch it hot?" asked Jukes with boyish interest.

"Say? . . . I say nothing. You don't catch me," snapped the little second mate, with a mixture of pride, scorn, and cunning, as if Jukes' question had been a trap cleverly detected. "Oh no! None of you here shall make a fool of me if I know it," he mumbled to himself.

Jukes reflected rapidly that this second mate was a mean little beast, and in his heart he wished poor Jack Allen had never smashed himself up in the coal-lighter. The far-off blackness ahead of the ship was like another night seen through the starry night of the earth—the starless night of the immensities beyond the created universe, revealed in its appalling stillness through a low fissure in the glittering sphere of which the earth is the kernel.

"Whatever there might be about," said Jukes, "we are steaming straight into it."

"*You've* said it," caught up the second mate, always with his back to Jukes. "You've said it, mind—not I."

"Oh, go to Jericho!"[5] said Jukes frankly; and the other emitted a triumphant little chuckle.

"You've said it," he repeated.

"And what of that?"

"I've known some real good men get into trouble with their skippers for saying a dam' sight less," answered the second mate feverishly. "Oh no! You don't catch me."

"You seem deucedly anxious not to give yourself away," said Jukes, completely soured by such absurdity. "I wouldn't be afraid to say what I think."

"Aye, to me! That's no great trick. I am nobody, and well I know it."

The ship, after a pause of comparative steadiness, started upon a series of rolls, one worse than the other, and for a time Jukes, preserving his equilibrium, was too busy to open his mouth. As soon as the violent swinging had quieted down somewhat, he said: "This is a bit too much of a good thing. Whether anything is coming or not I think she ought to be put head on to that swell. The old man is just gone in to lie down. Hang me if I don't speak to him."

4. An allusion to Christ's injunction to his disciples in Luke 9:5 when he sends them out as missionaries: "And whosoever will not receive you, when ye go out of that city, shake off the very dust from your feet for a testimony against them" (see also Matthew 10:14 and Mark 6:11).
5. Roughly equivalent to *Oh, go to hell!*

But when he opened the door of the chart-room he saw his captain reading a book. Captain MacWhirr was not lying down: he was standing up with one hand grasping the edge of the bookshelf and the other holding open before his face a thick volume. The lamp wriggled in the gimbals, the loosened books toppled from side to side on the shelf, the long barometer swung in jerky circles, the table altered its slant every moment. In the midst of all this stir and movement Captain MacWhirr, holding on, showed his eyes above the upper edge, and asked, "What's the matter?"

"Swell getting worse, sir."

"Noticed that in here," muttered Captain MacWhirr. "Anything wrong?"

Jukes, inwardly disconcerted by the seriousness of the eyes looking at him over the top of the book, produced an embarrassed grin.

"Rolling like old boots," he said sheepishly.

"Aye! Very heavy—very heavy. What do you want?"

At this Jukes lost his footing and began to flounder.

"I was thinking of our passengers," he said, in the manner of a man clutching at a straw.

"Passengers?" wondered the Captain gravely. "What passengers?"

"Why, the Chinamen, sir," explained Jukes, very sick of this conversation.

"The Chinamen! Why don't you speak plainly? Couldn't tell what you meant. Never heard a lot of coolies spoken of as passengers before. Passengers, indeed! What's come to you?"

Captain MacWhirr, closing the book on his forefinger, lowered his arm and looked completely mystified. "Why are you thinking of the Chinamen, Mr. Jukes?" he inquired.

Jukes took a plunge, like a man driven to it. "She's rolling her decks full of water, sir. Thought you might put her head on perhaps—for a while. Till this goes down a bit—very soon, I dare say. Head to the eastward. I never knew a ship roll like this."

He held on in the doorway, and Captain MacWhirr, feeling his grip on the shelf inadequate, made up his mind to let go in a hurry, and fell heavily on the couch.

"Head to the eastward?" he said, struggling to sit up. "That's more than four points[6] off her course."

"Yes, sir. Fifty degrees . . . Would just bring her head far enough round to meet this . . ."

Captain MacWhirr was now sitting up. He had not dropped the book, and he had not lost his place.

"To the eastward?" he repeated, with dawning astonishment. "To the . . . Where do you think we are bound to? You want me to haul

---

6. Four points on a compass.

a full-powered steamship four points off her course to make the Chinamen comfortable! Now, I've heard more than enough of mad things done in the world—but this . . . If I didn't know you, Jukes, I would think you were in liquor. Steer four points off . . . And what afterwards? Steer four points over the other way, I suppose, to make the course good. What put it into your head that I would start to tack a steamer as if she were a sailing-ship?"

"Jolly good thing she isn't," threw in Jukes, with bitter readiness. "She would have rolled every blessed stick out of her this afternoon."

"Aye! And you just would have had to stand and see them go," said Captain MacWhirr, showing a certain animation. "It's a dead calm, isn't it?"

"It is, sir. But there's something out of the common coming, for sure."

"Maybe. I suppose you have a notion I should be getting out of the way of that dirt," said Captain MacWhirr, speaking with the utmost simplicity of manner and tone, and fixing the oilcloth[7] on the floor with a heavy stare. Thus he noticed neither Jukes' discomfiture nor the mixture of vexation and astonished respect on his face.

"Now, here's this book," he continued with deliberation, slapping his thigh with the closed volume. "I've been reading the chapter on the storms there."

This was true. He had been reading the chapter on the storms. When he had entered the chart-room, it was with no intention of taking the book down. Some influence in the air—the same influence, probably, that caused the steward to bring without orders the Captain's sea-boots and oilskin[8] coat up to the chart-room—had as it were guided his hand to the shelf; and without taking the time to sit down he had waded with a conscious effort into the terminology of the subject. He lost himself amongst advancing semi-circles, left- and right-hand quadrants, the curves of the tracks, the probable bearing of the centre, the shifts of wind, and the readings of barometer. He tried to bring all these things into a definite relation to himself, and ended by becoming contemptuously angry with such a lot of words and with so much advice, all head-work and supposition, without a glimmer of certitude.

"It's the damnedest thing, Jukes," he said. "If a fellow was to believe all that's in there, he would be running most of his time all over the sea trying to get behind the weather."

Again he slapped his leg with the book; and Jukes opened his mouth, but said nothing.

7. Fabric made waterproof by applying oil to it.
8. See p. 17, n. 8.

"Running to get behind the weather! Do you understand that, Mr. Jukes? It's the maddest thing!" ejaculated Captain MacWhirr, with pauses, gazing at the floor profoundly. "You would think an old woman had been writing this. It passes me. If that thing means anything useful, then it means that I should at once alter the course away, away to the devil somewhere, and come booming down on Fu-chau from the northward at the tail of this dirty weather that's supposed to be knocking about in our way. From the north! Do you understand, Mr. Jukes? Three hundred extra miles to the distance, and a pretty coal bill to show. I couldn't bring myself to do that if every word in there was gospel truth, Mr. Jukes. Don't you expect me . . ."

And Jukes, silent, marvelled at this display of feeling and loquacity.

"But the truth is that you don't know if the fellow is right anyhow. How can you tell what a gale is made of till you get it? He isn't aboard here, is he? Very well. Here he says that the centre of them things bears eight points off the wind; but we haven't got any wind, for all the barometer falling. Where's his centre now?"

"We will get the wind presently," mumbled Jukes.

"Let it come, then," said Captain MacWhirr, with dignified indignation. "It's only to let you see, Mr. Jukes, that you don't find everything in books. All these rules for dodging breezes and circumventing the winds of heaven, Mr. Jukes, seem to me the maddest thing, when you come to look at it sensibly."

He raised his eyes, saw Jukes gazing at him dubiously, and tried to illustrate his meaning.

"About as queer as your extraordinary notion of dodging the ship head to sea, for I don't know how long, to make the Chinamen comfortable; whereas all we've got to do is to take them to Fu-chau, being timed to get there before noon on Friday. If the weather delays me— very well. There's your log-book to talk straight about the weather. But suppose I went swinging off my course and came in two days late, and they asked me: 'Where have you been all that time, Captain?' What could I say to that? 'Went around to dodge the bad weather,' I would say. 'It must've been dam' bad,' they would say. 'Don't know,' I would have to say; 'I've dodged clear of it.' See that, Jukes? I have been thinking it all out this afternoon."

He looked up again in his unseeing, unimaginative way. No one had ever heard him say so much at one time. Jukes, with his arms open in the doorway, was like a man invited to behold a miracle. Unbounded wonder was the intellectual meaning of his eye, while incredulity was seated in his whole countenance.

"A gale is a gale, Mr. Jukes," resumed the Captain, "and a full-powered steamship has got to face it. There's just so much dirty weather knocking about the world, and the proper thing is to go through it with none of what old Captain Wilson of the *Melita*[9] calls 'storm strategy.' The other day ashore I heard him hold forth about it to a lot of shipmasters who came in and sat at a table next to mine. It seemed to me the greatest nonsense. He was telling them how he—outmanœuvred, I think he said, a terrific gale, so that it never came nearer than fifty miles to him. A neat piece of head-work he called it. How he knew there was a terrific gale fifty miles off beats me altogether. It was like listening to a crazy man. I would have thought Captain Wilson was old enough to know better."

Captain MacWhirr ceased for a moment, then said, "It's your watch below, Mr. Jukes?"

Jukes came to himself with a start. "Yes, sir."

"Leave orders to call me at the slightest change," said the Captain. He reached up to put the book away, and tucked his legs upon the couch. "Shut the door so that it don't fly open, will you? I can't stand a door banging. They've put a lot of rubbishy locks into this ship, I must say."

Captain MacWhirr closed his eyes.

He did so to rest himself. He was tired, and he experienced that state of mental vacuity which comes at the end of an exhaustive discussion that has liberated some belief matured in the course of meditative years. He had indeed been making his confession of faith, had he only known it; and its effect was to make Jukes, on the other side of the door, stand scratching his head for a good while.

Captain MacWhirr opened his eyes.

He thought he must have been asleep. What was that loud noise? Wind? Why had he not been called? The lamp wriggled in its gimbals, the barometer swung in circles, the table altered its slant every moment; a pair of limp sea-boots with collapsed tops went sliding past the couch. He put out his hand instantly, and captured one.

Jukes' face appeared in a crack of the door: only his face, very red, with staring eyes. The flame of the lamp leaped, a piece of paper flew up, a rush of air enveloped Captain MacWhirr. Beginning to draw on the boot, he directed an expectant gaze at Jukes' swollen, excited features.

"Came on like this," shouted Jukes, "five minutes ago . . . all of a sudden."

The head disappeared with a bang, and a heavy splash and patter of drops swept past the closed door as if a pailful of melted lead had been flung against the house. A whistling could be heard now upon the deep vibrating noise outside. The stuffy chart-room seemed as full of draughts as a shed. Captain MacWhirr collared the other sea-boot on its violent passage along the floor. He was not flustered,

9. See p. 68, n. 2.

but he could not find at once the opening for inserting his foot. The shoes he had flung off were scurrying from end to end of the cabin, gambolling playfully over each other like puppies. As soon as he stood up he kicked at them viciously, but without effect.

He threw himself into the attitude of a lunging fencer, to reach after his oilskin coat; and afterwards he staggered all over the confined space while he jerked himself into it. Very grave, straddling his legs far apart, and stretching his neck, he started to tie deliberately the strings of his sou'-wester[1] under his chin, with thick fingers that trembled slightly. He went through all the movements of a woman putting on her bonnet before a glass, with a strained, listening attention, as though he had expected every moment to hear the shout of his name in the confused clamour that had suddenly beset his ship. Its increase filled his ears while he was getting ready to go out and confront whatever it might mean. It was tumultuous and very loud—made up of the rush of the wind, the crashes of the sea, with that prolonged deep vibration of the air, like the roll of an immense and remote drum beating the charge of the gale.

He stood for a moment in the light of the lamp, thick, clumsy, shapeless in his panoply of combat, vigilant and red-faced.

"There's a lot of weight in this," he muttered.

As soon as he attempted to open the door the wind caught it. Clinging to the handle, he was dragged out over the doorstep, and at once found himself engaged with the wind in a sort of personal scuffle whose object was the shutting of that door. At the last moment a tongue of air scurried in and licked out the flame of the lamp.

Ahead of the ship he perceived a great darkness lying upon a multitude of white flashes; on the starboard beam a few amazing stars drooped, dim and fitful, above an immense waste of broken seas, as if seen through a mad drift of smoke.

On the bridge a knot of men, indistinct and toiling, were making great efforts in the light of the wheelhouse windows that shone mistily on their heads and backs. Suddenly darkness closed upon one pane, then on another. The voices of the lost group reached him after the manner of men's voices in a gale, in shreds and fragments of forlorn shouting snatched past the ear. All at once Jukes appeared at his side, yelling, with his head down.

"Watch—put in—wheelhouse shutters—glass—afraid—blow in."

Jukes heard his commander upbraiding.

"This—come—anything—warning—call me."

He tried to explain, with the uproar pressing on his lips.

---

1. See p. 15, n. 6.

"Light air—remained—bridge—sudden—north-east—could turn—thought—you—sure—hear."

They had gained the shelter of the weather-cloth, and could converse with raised voices, as people quarrel.

"I got the hands along to cover up all the ventilators. Good job I had remained on deck I didn't think you would be asleep, and so . . . What did you say, sir? What?"

"Nothing," cried Captain MacWhirr. "I said—all right."

"By all the powers! We've got it this time," observed Jukes in a howl.

"You haven't altered her course?" inquired Captain MacWhirr, straining his voice.

"No, sir. Certainly not. Wind came out right ahead. And here comes the head sea."

A plunge of the ship ended in a shock as if she had landed her forefoot upon something solid. After a moment of stillness a lofty flight of sprays drove hard with the wind upon their faces.

"Keep her at it as long as we can," shouted Captain MacWhirr.

Before Jukes had squeezed the salt water out of his eyes all the stars had disappeared.

III

Jukes was as ready a man as any half-dozen young mates that may be caught by casting a net upon the waters; and though he had been somewhat taken aback by the startling viciousness of the first squall, he had pulled himself together on the instant, had called out the hands and had rushed them along to secure such openings about the deck as had not been already battened down earlier in the evening. Shouting in his fresh, stentorian voice, "Jump, boys, and bear a hand!"[2] he led in the work, telling himself the while that he had "just expected this."

But at the same time he was growing aware that this was rather more than he had expected. From the first stir of the air felt on his cheek the gale seemed to take upon itself the accumulated impetus of an avalanche. Heavy sprays enveloped the *Nan-Shan* from stem to stern, and instantly in the midst of her regular rolling she began to jerk and plunge as though she had gone mad with fright.

Jukes thought, "This is no joke." While he was exchanging explanatory yells with his captain, a sudden lowering of the darkness came upon the night, falling before their vision like something palpable. It was as if the masked lights of the world had been turned down. Jukes was uncritically glad to have his captain at hand. It relieved

2. See p. 185, n. 8.

him as though that man had, by simply coming on deck, taken most of the gale's weight upon his shoulders. Such is the prestige, the privilege, and the burden of command.

Captain MacWhirr could expect no relief of that sort from any one on earth. Such is the loneliness of command. He was trying to see, with that watchful manner of a seaman who stares into the wind's eye as if into the eye of an adversary, to penetrate the hidden intention and guess the aim and force of the thrust. The strong wind swept at him out of a vast obscurity; he felt under his feet the uneasiness of his ship, and he could not even discern the shadow of her shape. He wished it were not so; and very still he waited, feeling stricken by a blind man's helplessness.

To be silent was natural to him, dark or shine. Jukes, at his elbow, made himself heard yelling cheerily in the gusts, "We must have got the worst of it at once, sir." A faint burst of lightning quivered all round, as if flashed into a cavern—into a black and secret chamber of the sea, with a floor of foaming crests.

It unveiled for a sinister, fluttering moment a ragged mass of clouds hanging low, the lurch of the long outlines of the ship, the black figures of men caught on the bridge, heads forward, as if petrified in the act of butting. The darkness palpitated down upon all this, and then the real thing came at last.

It was something formidable and swift, like the sudden smashing of a vial of wrath.[3] It seemed to explode all round the ship with an overpowering concussion and a rush of great waters, as if an immense dam had been blown up to windward. In an instant the men lost touch of each other. This is the disintegrating power of a great wind: it isolates one from one's kind. An earthquake, a landslip, an avalanche, overtake a man incidentally, as it were—without passion. A furious gale attacks him like a personal enemy, tries to grasp his limbs, fastens upon his mind, seeks to rout his very spirit out of him.

Jukes was driven away from his commander. He fancied himself whirled a great distance through the air. Everything disappeared—even, for a moment, his power of thinking; but his hand had found one of the rail-stanchions. His distress was by no means alleviated by an inclination to disbelieve the reality of this experience. Though young, he had seen some bad weather, and had never doubted his ability to imagine the worst; but this was so much beyond his powers of fancy that it appeared incompatible with the existence of any ship whatever. He would have been incredulous about himself in

---

3. An allusion to Revelation 15:7: "And one of the four beasts gave unto the seven angels seven golden vials full of the wrath of God, who liveth for ever and ever"; or Revelation 16:1: "And I heard a great voice out of the temple saying to the seven angels, Go your ways, and pour out the vials of the wrath of God upon the earth."

the same way, perhaps, had he not been so harassed by the necessity of exerting a wrestling effort against a force trying to tear him away from his hold. Moreover, the conviction of not being utterly destroyed returned to him through the sensations of being half-drowned, bestially shaken, and partly choked.

It seemed to him he remained there precariously alone with the stanchion for a long, long time. The rain poured on him, flowed, drove in sheets. He breathed in gasps; and sometimes the water he swallowed was fresh and sometimes it was salt. For the most part he kept his eyes shut tight, as if suspecting his sight might be destroyed in the immense flurry of the elements. When he ventured to blink hastily, he derived some moral support from the green gleam of the starboard light shining feebly upon the flight of rain and sprays. He was actually looking at it when its ray fell upon the uprearing sea which put it out. He saw the head of the wave topple over, adding the mite[4] of its crash to the tremendous uproar raging around him, and almost at the same instant the stanchion was wrenched away from his embracing arms. After a crushing thump on his back he found himself suddenly afloat and borne upwards. His first irresistible notion was that the whole China Sea had climbed on the bridge. Then, more sanely, he concluded himself gone overboard. All the time he was being tossed, flung, and rolled in great volumes of water, he kept on repeating mentally, with the utmost precipitation, the words: "My God! My God! My God! My God!"

All at once, in a revolt of misery and despair, he formed the crazy resolution to get out of that. And he began to thresh about with his arms and legs. But as soon as he commenced his wretched struggles he discovered that he had become somehow mixed up with a face, an oilskin coat, somebody's boots. He clawed ferociously all these things in turn, lost them, found them again, lost them once more, and finally was himself caught in the firm clasp of a pair of stout arms. He returned the embrace closely round a thick solid body. He had found his captain.

They tumbled over and over, tightening their hug. Suddenly the water let them down with a brutal bang; and, stranded against the side of the wheelhouse, out of breath and bruised, they were left to stagger up in the wind and hold on where they could.

Jukes came out of it rather horrified, as though he had escaped some unparalleled outrage directed at his feelings. It weakened his faith in himself. He started shouting aimlessly to the man he could feel near him in that fiendish blackness, "Is it you, sir? Is it you, sir?" till his temples seemed ready to burst. And he heard in answer

---

4. A coin of very small denomination, used here metaphorically to indicate a very small amount.

a voice, as if crying far away, as if screaming to him fretfully from a very great distance, the one word "Yes!" Other seas swept again over the bridge. He received them defencelessly right over his bare head, with both his hands engaged in holding.

The motion of the ship was extravagant. Her lurches had an appalling helplessness: she pitched as if taking a header into a void, and seemed to find a wall to hit every time. When she rolled she fell on her side headlong, and she would be righted back by such a demolishing blow that Jukes felt her reeling as a clubbed man reels before he collapses. The gale howled and scuffled about gigantically in the darkness, as though the entire world were one black gully. At certain moments the air streamed against the ship as if sucked through a tunnel with a concentrated solid force of impact that seemed to lift her clean out of the water and keep her up for an instant with only a quiver running through her from end to end. And then she would begin her tumbling again as if dropped back into a boiling cauldron. Jukes tried hard to compose his mind and judge things coolly.

The sea, flattened down in the heavier gusts, would uprise and overwhelm both ends of the *Nan-Shan* in snowy rushes of foam, expanding wide, beyond both rails, into the night. And on this dazzling sheet, spread under the blackness of the clouds and emitting a bluish glow, Captain MacWhirr could catch a desolate glimpse of a few tiny specks black as ebony, the tops of the hatches, the battened companions, the heads of the covered winches, the foot of a mast. This was all he could see of his ship. Her middle structure, covered by the bridge which bore him, his mate, the closed wheelhouse where a man was steering shut up with the fear of being swept overboard together with the whole thing in one great crash—her middle structure was like a half-tide rock awash upon a coast. It was like an outlying rock with the water boiling up, streaming over, pouring off, beating round—like a rock in the surf to which shipwrecked people cling before they let go—only it rose, it sank, it rolled continuously, without respite and rest, like a rock that should have miraculously struck adrift from a coast and gone wallowing upon the sea.

The *Nan-Shan* was being looted by the storm with a senseless, destructive fury: trysails torn out of the extra gaskets, double-lashed awnings blown away, bridge swept clean, weather-cloths burst, rails twisted, light-screens smashed—and two of the boats had gone already. They had gone unheard and unseen, melting, as it were, in the shock and smother of the wave. It was only later, when upon the white flash of another high sea hurling itself amidships, Jukes had a vision of two pairs of davits leaping black and empty out of the solid blackness, with one overhauled fall flying and an iron-bound block capering in the air, that he became aware of what had happened within about three yards of his back.

He poked his head forward, groping for the ear of his commander. His lips touched it—big, fleshy, very wet. He cried in an agitated tone, "Our boats are going now, sir."

And again he heard that voice, forced and ringing feebly, but with a penetrating effect of quietness in the enormous discord of noises,[5] as if sent out from some remote spot of peace beyond the black wastes of the gale; again he heard a man's voice—the frail and indomitable sound that can be made to carry an infinity of thought, resolution, and purpose, that shall be pronouncing confident words on the last day, when heavens fall, and justice is done[6]— again he heard it, and it was crying to him, as if from very, very far—"All right."

He thought he had not managed to make himself understood. "Our boats—I say boats—the boats, sir! Two gone!"

The same voice, within a foot of him and yet so remote, yelled sensibly, "Can't be helped."

Captain MacWhirr had never turned his face, but Jukes caught some more words on the wind.

"What can—expect—when hammering through—such— Bound to leave—something behind—stands to reason."

Watchfully Jukes listened for more. No more came. This was all Captain MacWhirr had to say; and Jukes could picture to himself rather than see the broad squat back before him. An impenetrable obscurity pressed down upon the ghostly glimmers of the sea. A dull conviction seized upon Jukes that there was nothing to be done.

If the steering-gear did not give way, if the immense volumes of water did not burst the deck in or smash one of the hatches, if the engines did not give up, if way could be kept on the ship against this terrific wind, and she did not bury herself in one of these awful seas, of whose white crests alone, topping high above her bows, he could now and then get a sickening glimpse—then there was a chance of her coming out of it. Something within him seemed to turn over, bringing uppermost the feeling that the *Nan-Shan* was lost.

"She's done for," he said to himself, with a surprising mental agitation, as though he had discovered an unexpected meaning in this

---

5. Watts suggests an allusion to 1 Kings 19:11–12: "And, behold, the Lord passed by, and a great and strong wind rent the mountains, and brake in pieces the rocks before the Lord; but the Lord was not in the wind: and after the wind an earthquake; but the Lord was not in the earthquake: And after the earthquake a fire; but the Lord was not in the fire: and after the fire a still small voice."
6. Watts suggests a play on the Latin phrase *Fiat iustitia ruat caelum* (Let justice be done though the heavens fall).

thought. One of these things was bound to happen. Nothing could be prevented now, and nothing could be remedied. The men on board did not count, and the ship could not last. This weather was too impossible.

Jukes felt an arm thrown heavily over his shoulders; and to this overture he responded with great intelligence by catching hold of his captain round the waist.

They stood clasped thus in the blind night, bracing each other against the wind, cheek to cheek and lip to ear, in the manner of two hulks lashed stem to stern together.

And Jukes heard the voice of his commander hardly any louder than before, but nearer, as though, starting to march athwart the prodigious rush of the hurricane, it had approached him, bearing that strange effect of quietness like the serene glow of a halo.

"D'ye know where the hands got to?" it asked, vigorous and eva-nescent at the same time, overcoming the strength of the wind, and swept away from Jukes instantly.

Jukes didn't know. They were all on the bridge when the real force of the hurricane struck the ship. He had no idea where they had crawled to. Under the circumstances they were nowhere, for all the use that could be made of them. Somehow the Captain's wish to know distressed Jukes.

"Want the hands, sir?" he cried apprehensively.

"Ought to know," asserted Captain MacWhirr. "Hold hard."

They held hard. An outburst of unchained fury, a vicious rush of the wind absolutely steadied the ship; she rocked only, quick and light like a child's cradle, for a terrific moment of suspense, while the whole atmosphere, as it seemed, streamed furiously past her, roaring away from the tenebrous earth.

It suffocated them, and with eyes shut they tightened their grasp. What from the magnitude of the shock might have been a column of water running upright in the dark, butted against the ship, broke short, and fell on her bridge, crushingly, from on high, with a dead burying weight.

A flying fragment of that collapse, a mere splash, enveloped them in one swirl from their feet over their heads, filling violently their ears, mouths, and nostrils with salt water. It knocked out their legs, wrenched in haste at their arms, seethed away swiftly under their chins; and opening their eyes, they saw the piled-up masses of foam dashing to and fro amongst what looked like the fragments of a ship. She had given way as if driven straight in. Their panting hearts yielded too before the tremendous blow; and all at once she sprang up again to her desperate plunging, as if trying to scramble out from under the ruins.

The seas in the dark seemed to rush from all sides to keep her back where she might perish. There was hate in the way she was handled, and a ferocity in the blows that fell. She was like a living creature thrown to the rage of a mob: hustled terribly, struck at, borne up, flung down, leaped upon. Captain MacWhirr and Jukes kept hold of each other, deafened by the noise, gagged by the wind; and the great physical tumult beating about their bodies, brought, like an unbridled display of passion, a profound trouble to their souls. One of these wild and appalling shrieks that are heard at times passing mysteriously overhead in the steady roar of a hurricane, swooped, as if borne on wings, upon the ship, and Jukes tried to outscream it.

"Will she live through this?"

The cry was wrenched out of his breast. It was as unintentional as the birth of a thought in the head, and he heard nothing of it himself. It all became extinct at once—thought, intention, effort—and of his cry the inaudible vibration added to the tempest waves of the air.

He expected nothing from it. Nothing at all. For indeed what answer could be made? But after a while he heard with amazement the frail and resisting voice in his ear, the dwarf sound, unconquered in the giant tumult.

"She may!"

It was a dull yell, more difficult to seize than a whisper. And presently the voice returned again, half submerged in the vast crashes, like a ship battling against the waves of an ocean.

"Let's hope so!" it cried—small, lonely, and unmoved, a stranger to the visions of hope or fear; and it flickered into disconnected words: "Ship . . . This . . . Never—Anyhow . . . for the best." Jukes gave it up.

Then, as if it had come suddenly upon the one thing fit to withstand the power of a storm, it seemed to gain force and firmness for the last broken shouts:

"Keep on hammering . . . builders . . . good men . . . And chance it . . . engines . . . Rout . . . good man."

Captain MacWhirr removed his arm from Jukes' shoulders, and thereby ceased to exist for his mate, so dark it was; Jukes, after a tense stiffening of every muscle, would let himself go limp all over. The gnawing of profound discomfort existed side by side with an incredible disposition to somnolence, as though he had been buffeted and worried into drowsiness. The wind would get hold of his head and try to shake it off his shoulders; his clothes, full of water, were as heavy as lead, cold and dripping like an armour of melting ice: he shivered—it lasted a long time; and with his hands closed hard on his hold, he was letting himself sink slowly into the depths of bodily misery. His mind became concentrated upon himself in an aimless, idle way, and when something pushed lightly at the back of his knees he nearly, as the saying is, jumped out of his skin.

In the start forward he bumped the back of Captain MacWhirr, who didn't move; and then a hand gripped his thigh. A lull had come, a menacing lull of the wind, the holding of a stormy breath—and he felt himself pawed all over. It was the boatswain. Jukes recognised these hands, so thick and enormous that they seemed to belong to some new species of man.

The boatswain had arrived on the bridge, crawling on all fours against the wind, and had found the chief mate's legs with the top of his head. Immediately he crouched and began to explore Jukes' person upwards, with prudent, apologetic touches, as became an inferior.

He was an ill-favoured, undersized, gruff sailor of fifty, coarsely hairy, short-legged, long-armed, resembling an elderly ape. His strength was immense; and in his great lumpy paws, bulging like brown boxing-gloves on the end of furry fore-arms, the heaviest objects were handled like playthings. Apart from the grizzled pelt on his chest, the menacing demeanour, and the hoarse voice, he had none of the classical attributes of his rating. His good nature almost amounted to imbecility: the men did what they liked with him, and he had not an ounce of initiative in his character, which was easy-going and talkative. For these reasons Jukes disliked him; but Captain MacWhirr, to Jukes' scornful disgust, seemed to regard him as a first-rate petty officer.

He pulled himself up by Jukes' coat, taking that liberty with the greatest moderation, and only so far as it was forced upon him by the hurricane.

"What is it, boss'n, what is it?" yelled Jukes, impatiently. What could that fraud of a boss'n want on the bridge? The typhoon had got on Jukes' nerves. The husky bellowings of the other, though unintelligible, seemed to suggest a state of lively satisfaction. There could be no mistake. The old fool was pleased with something.

The boatswain's other hand had found some other body, for in a changed tone he began to inquire: "Is it you, sir? Is it you, sir?" The wind strangled his howls.

"Yes!" cried Captain MacWhirr.

IV

All that the boatswain, out of a superabundance of yells, could make clear to Captain MacWhirr was the bizarre intelligence that "All them Chinamen in the fore 'tween-deck have fetched away, sir."

Jukes to leeward could hear these two shouting within six inches of his face, as you may hear on a still night half a mile away two men conversing across a field. He heard Captain MacWhirr's exasperated "What? What?" and the strained pitch of the other's hoarseness. "In a lump . . . seen them myself . . . Awful sight, sir . . . thought . . . tell you."

Jukes remained indifferent, as if rendered irresponsible by the force of the hurricane, which made the very thought of action utterly vain. Besides, being very young, he had found the occupation of keeping his heart completely steeled against the worst so engrossing that he had come to feel an overpowering dislike towards any other form of activity whatever. He was not scared; he knew this because, firmly believing he would never see another sunrise, he remained calm in that belief.

These are the moments of do-nothing heroics to which even good men surrender at times. Many officers of ships can no doubt recall a case in their experience when just such a trance of confounded stoicism would come all at once over a whole ship's company. Jukes, however, had no wide experience of men or storms. He conceived himself to be calm—inexorably calm; but as a matter of fact he was daunted; not abjectly, but only so far as a decent man may, without becoming loathsome to himself.

It was rather like a forced-on numbness of spirit. The long, long stress of a gale does it; the suspense of the interminably culminating catastrophe; and there is a bodily fatigue in the mere holding on to existence within the excessive tumult; a searching and insidious fatigue that penetrates deep into a man's breast to cast down and sadden his heart, which is incorrigible, and of all the gifts of the earth—even before life itself—aspires to peace.

Jukes was benumbed much more than he supposed. He held on—very wet, very cold, stiff in every limb; and in a momentary hallucination of swift visions (it is said that a drowning man thus reviews all his life) he beheld all sorts of memories altogether unconnected with his present situation. He remembered his father, for instance: a worthy business man, who at an unfortunate crisis in his affairs went quietly to bed and died forthwith in a state of resignation. Jukes did not recall these circumstances, of course, but remaining otherwise unconcerned he seemed to see distinctly the poor man's face; a certain game of nap played when quite a boy in Table Bay[7] on board a ship, since lost with all hands; the thick eyebrows of his first skipper; and without any emotion, as he might years ago have walked listlessly into her room and found her sitting there with a book, he remembered his mother—dead, too, now—the

---

7. A bay on the Atlantic Ocean near Cape Town, South Africa. See p. 336. "Game of nap": a card game named after Napoleon I, involving the taking of tricks and bearing a slight resemblance to bridge.

resolute woman, left badly off, who had been very firm in his bringing up.

It could not have lasted more than a second, perhaps not so
much. A heavy arm had fallen about his shoulders; Captain Mac-
Whirr's voice was speaking his name into his ear.

"Jukes! Jukes!"

He detected the tone of deep concern. The wind had thrown its
weight on the ship, trying to pin her down amongst the seas. They
made a clean breach over her, as over a deep-swimming log; and the
gathered weight of crashes menaced monstrously from afar. The
breakers flung out of the night with a ghostly light on their crests—
the light of sea-foam that in a ferocious, boiling-up pale flash showed
upon the slender body of the ship the toppling rush, the downfall,
and the seething mad scurry of each wave. Never for a moment could
she shake herself clear of the water; Jukes, rigid, perceived in her
motion the ominous sign of haphazard floundering. She was no longer struggling intelligently. It was the beginning of the end; and the
note of busy concern in Captain MacWhirr's voice sickened him
like an exhibition of blind and pernicious folly.

The spell of the storm had fallen upon Jukes. He was penetrated
by it, absorbed by it; he was rooted in it with a rigour of dumb attention. Captain MacWhirr persisted in his cries, but the wind got
between them like a solid wedge. He hung round Jukes' neck as
heavy as a millstone,[8] and suddenly the sides of their heads knocked
together.

"Jukes! Mr. Jukes, I say!"

He had to answer that voice that would not be silenced. He
answered in the customary manner: ". . . Yes, sir."

And directly, his heart, corrupted by the storm that breeds a craving for peace, rebelled against the tyranny of training and command.

Captain MacWhirr had his mate's head fixed firm in the crook of
his elbow, and pressed it to his yelling lips mysteriously. Sometimes
Jukes would break in, admonishing hastily: "Look out, sir!" or Captain MacWhirr would bawl an earnest exhortation to "Hold hard,
there!" and the whole black universe seemed to reel together with
the ship. They paused. She floated yet. And Captain MacWhirr would
resume his shouts. ". . . Says . . . whole lot . . . fetched away . . .
Ought to see . . . what's the matter."

Directly the full force of the hurricane had struck the ship, every
part of her deck became untenable; and the sailors, dazed and dismayed, took shelter in the port alleyway under the bridge. It had a

8. An oblique allusion to Luke 17:2: "It were better for him that a millstone were hanged
about his neck, and he cast into the sea, than that he should offend one of these little
ones" (see also Matthew 18:6 and Mark 9:42).

door aft, which they shut; it was very black, cold, and dismal. At each heavy fling of the ship they would groan all together in the dark, and tons of water could be heard scuttling about as if trying to get at them from above. The boatswain had been keeping up a gruff talk, but a more unreasonable lot of men, he said afterwards, he had never been with. They were snug enough there, out of harm's way, and not wanted to do anything, either; and yet they did nothing but grumble and complain peevishly like so many sick kids. Finally, one of them said that if there had been at least some light to see each other's noses by, it wouldn't be so bad. It was making him crazy, he declared, to lie there in the dark waiting for the blamed[9] hooker to sink.

"Why don't you step outside, then, and be done with it at once?" the boatswain turned on him.

This called up a shout of execration. The boatswain found himself overwhelmed with reproaches of all sorts. They seemed to take it ill that a lamp was not instantly created for them out of nothing.[1] They would whine after a light to get drowned by—anyhow! And though the unreason of their revilings was patent—since no one could hope to reach the lamp-room, which was forward—he became greatly distressed. He did not think it was decent of them to be nagging at him like this. He told them so, and was met by general contumely. He sought refuge, therefore, in an embittered silence. At the same time their grumbling and sighing and muttering worried him greatly, but by-and-by it occurred to him that there were six globe lamps[2] hung in the 'tween-deck, and that there could be no harm in depriving the coolies of one of them.

The *Nan-Shan* had an athwartship coal-bunker, which, being at times used as cargo space, communicated by an iron door with the fore 'tween-deck. It was empty then, and its manhole was the foremost one in the alleyway. The boatswain could get in, therefore, without coming out on deck at all; but to his great surprise he found he could induce no one to help him in taking off the manhole cover. He groped for it all the same, but one of the crew lying in his way refused to budge.

"Why, I only want to get you that blamed light you are crying for," he expostulated, almost pitifully.

Somebody told him to go and put his head in a bag. He regretted he could not recognise the voice, and that it was too dark to see, otherwise, as he said, he would have put a head on[3] *that* son of a sea-cook,

9. See p. 111, n. 8.
1. An allusion to the theological principle of creation ex nihilo (out of nothing), which posits that God created the universe out of nothing.
2. Lamps with their light protected by a glass globe.
3. See p. 221, n. 5.

anyway, sink or swim. Nevertheless, he had made up his mind to
show them he could get a light, if he were to die for it.

Through the violence of the ship's rolling, every movement was
dangerous. To be lying down seemed labour enough. He nearly
broke his neck dropping into the bunker. He fell on his back, and
was sent shooting helplessly from side to side in the dangerous
company of a heavy iron bar—a coal-trimmer's slice probably—left
down there by somebody. This thing made him as nervous as though
it had been a wild beast. He could not see it, the inside of the bunker coated with coal-dust being perfectly and impenetrably black;
but he heard it sliding and clattering, and striking here and there,
always in the neighbourhood of his head. It seemed to make an
extraordinary noise, too—to give heavy thumps as though it had
been as big as a bridge girder. This was remarkable enough for him
to notice while he was flung from port to starboard and back again,
and clawing desperately the smooth sides of the bunker in the
endeavour to stop himself. The door into the 'tween-deck not fitting
quite true, he saw a thread of dim light at the bottom.

Being a sailor, and a still active man, he did not want much of a
chance to regain his feet; and as luck would have it, in scrambling
up he put his hand on the iron slice, picking it up as he rose. Otherwise he would have been afraid of the thing breaking his legs, or at
least knocking him down again. At first he stood still. He felt unsafe
in this darkness that seemed to make the ship's motion unfamiliar,
unforeseen, and difficult to counteract. He felt so much shaken for
a moment that he dared not move for fear of "taking charge again."
He had no mind to get battered to pieces in that bunker.

He had struck his head twice; he was dazed a little. He seemed
to hear yet so plainly the clatter and bangs of the iron slice flying
about his ears that he tightened his grip to prove to himself he had
it there safely in his hand. He was vaguely amazed at the plainness
with which down there he could hear the gale raging. Its howls
and shrieks seemed to take on, in the emptiness of the bunker,
something of the human character, of human rage and pain—being
not vast but infinitely poignant. And there were, with every roll,
thumps too—profound, ponderous thumps, as if a bulky object of
five-ton weight or so had got play in the hold. But there was no such
thing in the cargo. Something on deck? Impossible. Or alongside?
Couldn't be.

He thought all this quickly, clearly, competently, like a seaman,
and in the end remained puzzled. This noise, though, came deadened from outside, together with the washing and pouring of water
on deck above his head. Was it the wind? Must be. It made down
there a row like the shouting of a big lot of crazed men. And he
discovered in himself a desire for a light too—if only to get drowned

by—and a nervous anxiety to get out of that bunker as quickly as possible.

He pulled back the bolt: the heavy iron plate turned on its hinges; and it was as though he had opened the door to the sounds of the tempest. A gust of hoarse yelling met him: the air was still; and the rushing of water overhead was covered by a tumult of strangled, throaty shrieks that produced an effect of desperate confusion. He straddled his legs the whole width of the doorway and stretched his neck. And at first he perceived only what he had come to seek: six small yellow flames swinging violently on the great body of the dusk.

It was stayed[4] like the gallery of a mine, with a row of stanchions in the middle, and cross-beams overhead, penetrating into the gloom ahead—indefinitely. And to port there loomed, like the caving in of one of the sides, a bulky mass with a slanting outline. The whole place, with the shadows and the shapes, moved all the time. The boatswain glared: the ship lurched to starboard, and a great howl came from that mass that had the slant of fallen earth.

Pieces of wood whizzed past. Planks, he thought, inexpressibly startled, and flinging back his head. At his feet a man went sliding over, open-eyed, on his back, straining with uplifted arms for nothing: and another came bounding like a detached stone with his head between his legs and his hands clenched. His pigtail whipped in the air; he made a grab at the boatswain's legs, and from his opened hand a bright white disc rolled against the boatswain's foot. He recognised a silver dollar, and yelled at it with astonishment. With a precipitated sound of trampling and shuffling of bare feet, and with guttural cries, the mound of writhing bodies piled up to port detached itself from the ship's side and shifted to starboard, sliding, inert and struggling, to a dull, brutal thump. The cries ceased. The boatswain heard a long moan through the roar and whistling of the wind; he saw an inextricable confusion of heads and shoulders, naked soles kicking upwards, fists raised, tumbling backs, legs, pigtails, faces.

"Good Lord!" he cried, horrified, and banged-to[5] the iron door upon this vision.

This was what he had come on the bridge to tell. He could not keep it to himself; and on board ship there is only one man to whom it is worth while to unburden yourself. On his passage back the hands in the alleyway swore at him for a fool. Why didn't he bring that lamp? What the devil did the coolies matter to anybody? And when he came out, the extremity of the ship made what went on inside of her appear of little moment.

4. Steadied or secured with supports.
5. Slammed with a loud noise.

At first he thought he had left the alleyway in the very moment of her sinking. The bridge ladders had been washed away, but an enormous sea filling the after-deck floated him up. After that he had to lie on his stomach for some time, holding to a ringbolt, getting his breath now and then, and swallowing salt water. He struggled farther on his hands and knees, too frightened and distracted to turn back. In this way he reached the after-part of the wheelhouse. In that comparatively sheltered spot he found the second mate. The boatswain was pleasantly surprised—his impression being that everybody on deck must have been washed away a long time ago. He asked eagerly where the captain was.

The second mate was lying low, like a malignant little animal under a hedge.

"Captain? Gone overboard, after getting us into this mess." The mate, too, for all he knew or cared. Another fool. Didn't matter. Everybody was going by-and-by.

The boatswain crawled out again into the strength of the wind; not because he much expected to find anybody, he said, but just to get away from "that man." He crawled out as outcasts go to face an inclement world. Hence his great joy at finding Jukes and the Captain. But what was going on in the 'tween-deck was to him a minor matter by that time. Besides, it was difficult to make yourself heard. But he managed to convey the idea that the Chinamen had broken adrift together with their boxes, and that he had come up on purpose to report this. As to the hands, they were all right. Then, appeased, he subsided on the deck in a sitting posture, hugging with his arms and legs the stand of the engine-room telegraph—an iron casting as thick as a post. When that went, why, he expected he would go too. He gave no more thought to the coolies.

Captain MacWhirr had made Jukes understand that he wanted him to go down below—to see.

"What am I to do then, sir?" And the trembling of his whole wet body caused Jukes' voice to sound like bleating.

"See first . . . Boss'n . . . says . . . adrift."

"That boss'n is a confounded fool," howled Jukes shakily.

The absurdity of the demand made upon him revolted Jukes. He was as unwilling to go as if the moment he had left the deck the ship were sure to sink.

"I must know . . . can't leave . . ."

"They'll settle, sir."

"Fight . . . boss'n says they fight. . . . Why? Can't have . . . fighting . . . board ship. . . . Much rather keep you here . . . case . . . I should . . . washed overboard myself. . . . Stop it . . . some way. You

see and tell me . . . through engine-room tube. Don't want you . . .
come up here . . . too often. Dangerous . . . moving about . . . deck."

Jukes, held with his head in chancery,[6] had to listen to what
seemed horrible suggestions.

"Don't want . . . you get lost . . . so long . . . ship isn't. . . . Rout . . .
Good man . . . Ship . . . may . . . through this . . . all right yet."

All at once Jukes understood he would have to go.

"Do you think she may?" he screamed.

But the wind devoured the reply, out of which Jukes heard only
the one word, pronounced with great energy: ". . . Always . . ."

Captain MacWhirr released Jukes, and bending over the boatswain, yelled "Get back with the mate." Jukes only knew that the
arm was gone off his shoulders. He was dismissed with his
orders—to do what? He was exasperated into letting go his hold
carelessly, and on the instant was blown away. It seemed to him
that nothing could stop him from being blown right over the stern.
He flung himself down hastily, and the boatswain, who was following, fell on him.

"Don't you get up yet, sir," cried the boatswain. "No hurry!"

A sea swept over. Jukes understood the boatswain to splutter that
the bridge ladders were gone. "I'll lower you down, sir, by your
hands," he screamed. He shouted also something about the smokestack being as likely to go overboard as not. Jukes thought it very
possible, and imagined the fires out, the ship helpless. . . . The boatswain by his side kept on yelling. "What? What is it?" Jukes cried
distressfully; and the other repeated, "What would my old woman
say if she saw me now?"

In the alleyway, where a lot of water had got in and splashed in
the dark, the men were still as death, till Jukes stumbled against
one of them and cursed him savagely for being in the way. Two or
three voices then asked, eager and weak, "Any chance for us, sir?"

"What's the matter with you fools?" he said brutally. He felt as
though he could throw himself down amongst them and never
move any more. But they seemed cheered; and in the midst of obsequious warnings, "Look out! Mind that manhole lid, sir," they lowered him into the bunker. The boatswain tumbled down after him,
and as soon as he had picked himself up he remarked, "She would
say, 'Serve you right, you old fool, for going to sea.'"

The boatswain had some means, and made a point of alluding to
them frequently. His wife—a fat woman—and two grown-up daughters kept a greengrocer's shop in the East-end of London.[7]

---

6. A position in which one holds an opponent's head under one arm, leaving the other at
   liberty to hit the opponent freely without retaliation.
7. See p. 52, n. 5.

In the dark, Jukes, unsteady on his legs, listened to a faint thunderous patter. A deadened screaming went on steadily at his elbow, as it were; and from above the louder tumult of the storm descended upon these near sounds. His head swam. To him, too, in that bunker, the motion of the ship seemed novel and menacing, sapping his resolution as though he had never been afloat before.

He had half a mind to scramble out again; but the remembrance of Captain MacWhirr's voice made this impossible. His orders were to go and see. What was the good of it, he wanted to know. Enraged, he told himself he would see—of course. But the boatswain, staggering clumsily, warned him to be careful how he opened that door; there was a blamed fight going on. And Jukes, as if in great bodily pain, desired irritably to know what the devil they were fighting for.

"Dollars! Dollars, sir. All their rotten chests got burst open. Blamed money skipping all over the place, and they are tumbling after it head over heels—tearing and biting like anything. A regular little hell in there."

Jukes convulsively opened the door. The short boatswain peered under his arm.

One of the lamps had gone out, broken perhaps. Rancorous, guttural cries burst out loudly on their ears, and a strange panting sound, the working of all these straining breasts. A hard blow hit the side of the ship: water fell above with a stunning shock, and in the forefront of the gloom, where the air was reddish and thick, Jukes saw a head bang the deck violently, two thick calves waving on high, muscular arms twined round a naked body, a yellow-face, open-mouthed and with a set wild stare, look up and slide away. An empty chest clattered turning over; a man fell head first with a jump, as if lifted by a kick; and farther off, indistinct, others streamed like a mass of rolling stones down a bank, thumping the deck with their feet and flourishing their arms wildly. The hatchway ladder was loaded with coolies swarming on it like bees on a branch. They hung on the steps in a crawling, stirring cluster, beating madly with their fists the underside of the battened hatch, and the headlong rush of the water above was heard in the intervals of their yelling. The ship heeled over more, and they began to drop off: first one, then two, then all the rest went away together, falling straight off with a great cry.

Jukes was confounded. The boatswain, with gruff anxiety, begged him, "Don't you go in there, sir."

The whole place seemed to twist upon itself, jumping incessantly the while; and when the ship rose to a sea Jukes fancied that all these men would be shot upon him in a body. He backed out, swung the door to,[8] and with trembling hands pushed at the bolt. . . .

8. Swung the door closed.

As soon as his mate had gone Captain MacWhirr, left alone on the bridge, sidled and staggered as far as the wheelhouse. Its door being hinged forward, he had to fight the gale for admittance, and when at last he managed to enter, it was with an instantaneous clatter and a bang, as though he had been fired through the wood. He stood within, holding on to the handle.

The steering-gear leaked steam, and in the confined space the glass of the binnacle made a shiny oval of light in a thin white fog. The wind howled, hummed, whistled, with sudden booming gusts that rattled the doors and shutters in the vicious patter of sprays. Two coils of lead-line and a small canvas bag, hung on a long lanyard, swung wide off, and came back clinging to the bulkheads. The gratings underfoot were nearly afloat; with every sweeping blow of a sea, water squirted violently through the cracks all round the door, and the man at the helm had flung down his cap, his coat, and stood propped against the gear-casing in a striped cotton shirt open on his breast. The little brass wheel in his hands had the appearance of a bright and fragile toy. The cords of his neck stood hard and lean, a dark patch lay in the hollow of his throat, and his face was still and sunken as in death.

Captain MacWhirr wiped his eyes. The sea that had nearly taken him overboard had, to his great annoyance, washed his sou'-wester hat off his bald head. The fluffy, fair hair, soaked and darkened, resembled a mean skein of cotton threads festooned round his bare skull. His face, glistening with sea-water, had been made crimson with the wind, with the sting of sprays. He looked as though he had come off sweating from before a furnace.

"You here?" he muttered heavily.

The second mate had found his way into the wheelhouse some time before. He had fixed himself in a corner with his knees up, a fist pressed against each temple; and this attitude suggested rage, sorrow, resignation, surrender, with a sort of concentrated unforgiveness. He said mournfully and defiantly, "Well, it's my watch below now: ain't it?"

The steam gear clattered, stopped, clattered again; and the helmsman's eyeballs seemed to project out of a hungry face as if the compass-card behind the binnacle glass had been meat. God knows how long he had been left there to steer, as if forgotten by all his shipmates. The bells had not been struck; there had been no reliefs; the ship's routine had gone down wind; but he was trying to keep her head north-north-east. The rudder might have been gone for all he knew, the fires out, the engines broken down, the ship ready to roll over like a corpse. He was anxious not to get muddled and lose control of her head, because the compass-card swung far both ways, wriggling on the pivot, and sometimes seemed to whirl right round.

He suffered from mental stress. He was horribly afraid, also, of the wheelhouse going. Mountains of water kept on tumbling against it. When the ship took one of her desperate dives the corners of his lips twitched.

Captain MacWhirr looked up at the wheelhouse clock. Screwed to the bulkhead, it had a white face on which the black hands appeared to stand quite still. It was half-past one in the morning.

"Another day," he muttered to himself.

The second mate heard him, and lifting his head as one grieving amongst ruins, "You won't see it break," he exclaimed. His wrists and his knees could be seen to shake violently. "No, by God! You won't . . ."

He took his face again between his fists.

The body of the helmsman had moved slightly, but his head didn't budge on his neck—like a stone head fixed to look one way from a column. During a roll that all but took his booted legs from under him, and in the very stagger to save himself, Captain Mac-Whirr said austerely, "Don't you pay any attention to what that man says." And then, with an indefinable change of tone, very grave, he added, "He isn't on duty."

The sailor said nothing.

The hurricane boomed, shaking the little place, which seemed air-tight; and the light of the binnacle flickered all the time.

"You haven't been relieved," Captain MacWhirr went on, looking down. "I want you to stick to the helm, though, as long as you can. You've got the hang of her. Another man coming here might make a mess of it. Wouldn't do. No child's play. And the hands are probably busy with a job down below. . . . Think you can?"

The steering-gear leaped into an abrupt short clatter, stopped smouldering like an ember; and the still man, with a motionless gaze, burst out, as if all the passion in him had gone into his lips: "By Heavens, sir! I can steer for ever if nobody talks to me."

"Oh! aye! All right. . . ." The Captain lifted his eyes for the first time to the man, ". . . Hackett."

And he seemed to dismiss this matter from his mind. He stooped to the engine-room speaking-tube, blew in, and bent his head. Mr. Rout below answered, and at once Captain MacWhirr put his lips to the mouthpiece.

With the uproar of the gale around him he applied alternately his lips and his ear, and the engineer's voice mounted to him, harsh and as if out of the heat of an engagement. One of the stokers was disabled, the others had given in, the second engineer and the donkey-man were firing-up. The third engineer was standing by the steam-valve. The engines were being tended by hand. How was it above?

"Bad enough. It mostly rests with you," said Captain MacWhirr. Was the mate down there yet? No? Well, he would be presently. Would Mr. Rout let him talk through the speaking-tube?—through the deck speaking-tube, because he—the Captain—was going out again on the bridge directly. There was some trouble amongst the Chinamen. They were fighting, it seemed. Couldn't allow fighting anyhow. . . .

Mr. Rout had gone away, and Captain MacWhirr could feel against his ear the pulsation of the engines, like the beat of the ship's heart. Mr. Rout's voice down there shouted something distantly. The ship pitched headlong, the pulsation leaped with a hissing tumult, and stopped dead. Captain MacWhirr's face was impassive, and his eyes were fixed aimlessly on the crouching shape of the second mate. Again Mr. Rout's voice cried out in the depths, and the pulsating beats recommenced, with slow strokes—growing swifter.

Mr. Rout had returned to the tube. "It don't matter much what they do," he said hastily; and then, with irritation, "She takes these dives as if she never meant to come up again."

"Awful sea," said the Captain's voice from above.

"Don't let me drive her under," barked Solomon Rout up the pipe.

"Dark and rain. Can't see what's coming," uttered the voice. "Must—keep—her—moving—enough to steer—and chance it," it went on to state distinctly.

"I am doing as much as I dare."

"We are—getting—smashed up—a good deal up here," proceeded the voice mildly. "Doing—fairly well—though. Of course, if the wheelhouse should go . . ."

Mr. Rout, bending an attentive ear, muttered peevishly something under his breath.

But the deliberate voice up there became animated to ask: "Jukes turned up yet?" Then, after a short wait, "I wish he would bear a hand. I want him to be done and come up here in case of anything. To look after the ship. I am all alone. The second mate's lost . . ."

"What?" shouted Mr. Rout into the engine-room, taking his head away. Then up the tube he cried, "Gone overboard?" and clapped his ear to.

"Lost his nerve," the voice from above continued in a matter-of-fact tone. "Damned awkward circumstance."

Mr. Rout, listening with bowed neck, opened his eyes wide at this. However, he heard something like the sounds of a scuffle and broken exclamations coming down to him. He strained his hearing; and all the time Beale, the third engineer, with his arms uplifted, held between the palms of his hands the rim of a little black wheel projecting at the side of a big copper pipe. He seemed to be poising it above his head, as though it were a correct attitude in some sort of game.

To steady himself, he pressed his shoulder against the white bulk-head, one knee bent, and a sweat-rag tucked in his belt hanging on his hip. His smooth cheek was begrimed and flushed, and the coal-dust on his eyelids, like the black pencilling of a make-up, enhanced the liquid brilliance of the whites, giving to his youthful face some-thing of a feminine, exotic, and fascinating aspect. When the ship pitched he would with hasty movements of his hands screw hard at the little wheel.

"Gone crazy," began the Captain's voice suddenly in the tube. "Rushed at me. . . . Just now. Had to knock him down. . . . This minute. You heard, Mr. Rout?"

"The devil!" muttered Mr. Rout. "Look out, Beale!"

His shout rang out like the blast of a warning trumpet,[9] between the iron walls of the engine-room. Painted white, they rose high into the dusk of the skylight, sloping like a roof; and the whole lofty space resembled the interior of a monument, divided by floors of iron grating, with lights flickering at different levels, and a mass of gloom lingering in the middle, within the columnar stir of machin-ery under the motionless swelling of the cylinders. A loud and wild resonance, made up of all the noises of the hurricane, dwelt in the still warmth of the air. There was in it the smell of hot metal, of oil, and a slight mist of steam. The blows of the sea seemed to traverse it in an unringing, stunning shock, from side to side.

Gleams, like pale long flames, trembled upon the polish of metal; from the flooring below the enormous crank-heads emerged in their turns with a flash of brass and steel—going over; while the connecting-rods, big-jointed like skeleton limbs, seemed to thrust them down and pull them up again with an irresistible precision. And deep in the half-light other rods dodged deliberately to and fro, cross-heads nodded, discs of metal rubbed smoothly against each other, slow and gentle, in a commingling of shadows and gleams.

Sometimes all those powerful and unerring movements would slow down simultaneously, as if they had been the functions of a living organism, stricken suddenly by the blight of languor; and Mr. Rout's eyes would blaze darker in his long sallow face. He was fight-ing this fight in a pair of carpet slippers.[1] A short shiny jacket barely covered his loins, and his white wrists protruded far out of the tight

9. An oblique allusion to Ezekiel 33:4–5: "Then whosoever heareth the sound of the trumpet, and taketh not warning; if the sword come, and take him away, his blood shall be upon his own head. He heard the sound of the trumpet, and took not warning; his blood shall be upon him. But he that taketh warning shall deliver his soul."
1. Slippers whose upper parts were originally made of a carpetlike material.

sleeves, as though the emergency had added to his stature, had lengthened his limbs, augmented his pallor, hollowed his eyes.

He moved, climbing high up, disappearing low down, with a restless, purposeful industry, and when he stood still, holding the guard-rail in front of the starting-gear, he would keep glancing to the right at the steam-gauge, at the water-gauge, fixed upon the white wall in the light of a swaying lamp. The mouths of two speaking-tubes gaped stupidly at his elbow, and the dial of the engine-room telegraph resembled a clock of large diameter, bearing on its face curt words instead of figures. The grouped letters stood out heavily black, around the pivot-head of the indicator, emphatically symbolic of loud exclamations: AHEAD, ASTERN, SLOW, HALF, STAND BY; and the fat black hand pointed downwards to the word FULL, which, thus singled out, captured the eye as a sharp cry secures attention.

The wood-encased bulk of the low-pressure cylinder, frowning portly from above, emitted a faint wheeze at every thrust, and except for that low hiss the engines worked their steel limbs headlong or slow with a silent, determined smoothness. And all this, the white walls, the moving steel, the floor plates under Solomon Rout's feet, the floors of iron grating above his head, the dusk and the gleams, uprose and sank continuously, with one accord, upon the harsh wash of the waves against the ship's side. The whole loftiness of the place, booming hollow to the great voice of the wind, swayed at the top like a tree, would go over bodily, as if borne down this way and that by the tremendous blasts.

"You've got to hurry up," shouted Mr. Rout, as soon as he saw Jukes appear in the stokehold doorway.

Jukes' glance was wandering and tipsy; his red face was puffy, as though he had overslept himself. He had had an arduous road, and had travelled over it with immense vivacity, the agitation of his mind corresponding to the exertions of his body. He had rushed up out of the bunker, stumbling in the dark alleyway amongst a lot of bewildered men who, trod upon, asked "What's up, sir?" in awed mutters all round him—down the stokehold ladder, missing many iron rungs in his hurry, down into a place deep as a well, black as Tophet,[2] tipping over back and forth like a see-saw. The water in the bilges thundered at each roll, and lumps of coal skipped to and fro, from end to end, rattling like an avalanche of pebbles on a slope of iron.

Somebody in there moaned with pain, and somebody else could be seen crouching over what seemed the prone body of a dead man; a lusty voice blasphemed; and the glow under each fire-door was like a pool of flaming blood radiating quietly in a velvety blackness.

---

2. A figurative association for hell.

A gust of wind struck upon the nape of Jukes' neck, and next moment he felt it streaming about his wet ankles. The stokehold ventilators hummed: in front of the six fire-doors two wild figures, stripped to the waist, staggered and stooped, wrestling with two shovels.

"Hallo! Plenty of draught now," yelled the second engineer at once, as though he had been all the time looking out for Jukes. The donkey-man, a dapper little chap with a dazzling fair skin and a tiny, gingery moustache, worked in a sort of mute transport. They were keeping a full head of steam, and a profound rumbling, as of an empty furniture van trotting over a bridge, made a sustained bass to all the other noises of the place.

"Blowing off all the time," went on yelling the second. With a sound as of a hundred scoured sauce-pans, the orifice of a ventilator spat upon his shoulder a sudden gush of salt water, and he volleyed a stream of curses upon all things on earth including his own soul, ripping and raving, and all the time attending to his business. With a sharp clash of metal the ardent pale glare of the fire opened upon his bullet head, showing his spluttering lips, his insolent face, and with another clang closed like the white-hot wink of an iron eye.

"Where's the blooming ship? Can you tell me? blast my eyes! Under water—or what? It's coming down here in tons. Are the condemned[3] cowls gone to Hades? Hey? Don't you know anything—you jolly sailor-man you . . . ?"

Jukes, after a bewildered moment, had been helped by a roll to dart through; and as soon as his eyes took in the comparative vastness, peace, and brilliance of the engine-room, the ship, setting her stern heavily in the water, sent him charging head down upon Mr. Rout.

The chief's arm, long like a tentacle, and straightening as if worked by a spring, went out to meet him, and deflected his rush into a spin towards the speaking-tubes. At the same time Mr. Rout repeated earnestly: "You've got to hurry up, whatever it is."

Jukes yelled "Are you there, sir?" and listened. Nothing. Suddenly the roar of the wind fell straight into his ear, but presently a small voice shoved aside the shouting hurricane quietly.

"You, Jukes?—Well?"

Jukes was ready to talk: it was only time that seemed to be wanting. It was easy enough to account for everything. He could perfectly imagine the coolies battened down in the reeking 'tween-deck, lying sick and scared between the rows of chests. Then one of these

3. See p. 206, n. 3.

chests—or perhaps several at once—breaking loose in a roll, knocking out others, sides splitting, lids flying open, and all these clumsy Chinamen rising up in a body to save their property. Afterwards every fling of the ship would hurl that tramping, yelling mob here and there, from side to side, in a whirl of smashed wood, torn clothing, rolling dollars. A struggle once started, they would be unable to stop themselves. Nothing could stop them now except main force. It was a disaster. He had seen it, and that was all he could say. Some of them must be dead, he believed. The rest would go on fighting. . . .

He sent up his words, tripping over each other, crowding the narrow tube. They mounted as if into a silence of an enlightened comprehension dwelling alone up there with a storm.[4] And Jukes wanted to be dismissed from the face of that odious trouble intruding on the great need of the ship.

V

He waited. Before his eyes the engines turned with slow labour, that in the moment of going off into a mad fling would stop dead at Mr. Rout's shout, "Look out, Beale!" They paused in an intelligent immobility, stilled in mid-stroke, a heavy crank arrested on the cant, as if conscious of danger and the passage of time. Then, with a "Now, then!" from the chief, and the sound of a breath expelled through clenched teeth, they would accomplish the interrupted revolution and begin another.

There was the prudent sagacity of wisdom and the deliberation of enormous strength in their movements. This was their work—this patient coaxing of a distracted ship over the fury of the waves and into the very eye of the wind. At times Mr. Rout's chin would sink on his breast, and he watched them with knitted eyebrows as if lost in thought.

The voice that kept the hurricane out of Jukes' ear began: "Take the hands with you . . ." and left off unexpectedly.

"What could I do with them, sir?"

A harsh, abrupt, imperious clang exploded suddenly. The three pairs of eyes flew up to the telegraph dial to see the hand jump from FULL to STOP, as if snatched by a devil. And then these three men in the engine-room had the intimate sensation of a check upon the ship, of a strange shrinking, as if she had gathered herself for a desperate leap.

"Stop her!" bellowed Mr. Rout.

---

4. Pearson suggests an allusion to *Hamlet* 3.3.97–98: "My words fly up, my thoughts remain below. / Words without thoughts never to heaven go."

Nobody—not even Captain MacWhirr, who alone on deck had caught sight of a white line of foam coming on at such a height that he couldn't believe his eyes—nobody was to know the steepness of that sea and the awful depth of the hollow the hurricane had scooped out behind the running wall of water.

It raced to meet the ship, and, with a pause, as of girding the loins,[5] the *Nan-Shan* lifted her bows and leaped. The flames in all the lamps sank, darkening the engine-room. One went out. With a tearing crash and a swirling, raving tumult, tons of water fell upon the deck, as though the ship had darted under the foot of a cataract.

Down there they looked at each other, stunned.

"Swept from end to end, by God!" bawled Jukes.

She dipped into the hollow straight down, as if going over the edge of the world. The engine-room toppled forward menacingly, like the inside of a tower nodding in an earthquake. An awful racket, of iron things falling, came from the stokehold. She hung on this appalling slant long enough for Beale to drop on his hands and knees and begin to crawl as if he meant to fly on all fours out of the engine-room, and for Mr. Rout to turn his head slowly, rigid, cavernous, with the lower jaw dropping. Jukes had shut his eyes, and his face in a moment became hopelessly blank and gentle, like the face of a blind man.

At last she rose slowly, staggering, as if she had to lift a mountain with her bows.

Mr. Rout shut his mouth; Jukes blinked; and little Beale stood up hastily.

"Another one like this, and that's the last of her," cried the chief.

He and Jukes looked at each other, and the same thought came into their heads. The Captain! Everything must have been swept away. Steering-gear gone—ship like a log. All over directly.

"Rush!" ejaculated Mr. Rout thickly, glaring with enlarged, doubtful eyes at Jukes, who answered him by an irresolute glance.

The clang of the telegraph gong soothed them instantly. The black hand dropped in a flash from STOP to FULL.

"Now then, Beale!" cried Mr. Rout.

The steam hissed low. The piston-rods slid in and out. Jukes put his ear to the tube. The voice was ready for him. It said: "Pick up all the money. Bear a hand now. I'll want you up here." And that was all.

"Sir?" called up Jukes. There was no answer.

He staggered away like a defeated man from the field of battle. He had got, in some way or other, a cut above his left eyebrow—a

---

5. A phrase derived from numerous biblical passages denoting preparing oneself for a difficult task.

cut to the bone. He was not aware of it in the least: quantities of the China Sea, large enough to break his neck for him, had gone over his head, had cleaned, washed, and salted that wound. It did not bleed, but only gaped red; and this gash over the eye, his dishevelled hair, the disorder of his clothes, gave him the aspect of a man worsted in a fight with fists.

"Got to pick up the dollars." He appealed to Mr. Rout, smiling pitifully at random.

"What's that?" asked Mr. Rout wildly. "Pick up . . . ? I don't care. . . ." Then, quivering in every muscle, but with an exaggeration of paternal tone, "Go away now, for God's sake. You deck people'll drive me silly. There's that second mate been going for the old man. Don't you know? You fellows are going wrong for want of something to do. . . ."

At these words Jukes discovered in himself the beginnings of anger. Want of something to do—indeed. . . . Full of hot scorn against the chief, he turned to go the way he had come. In the stokehold the plump donkey-man toiled with his shovel mutely, as if his tongue had been cut out; but the second was carrying on like a noisy, undaunted maniac, who had preserved his skill in the art of stoking under a marine boiler.

"Hallo, you wandering officer! Hey! Can't you get some of your slush-slingers[6] to wind up a few of them ashes? I am getting choked with them here. Curse it! Hallo! Hey! Remember the articles: *Sailors and firemen to assist each other.* Hey! D'ye hear?"

Jukes was climbing out frantically, and the other, lifting up his face after him, howled, "Can't you speak? What are you poking about here for? What's your game, anyhow?"

A frenzy possessed Jukes. By the time he was back amongst the men in the darkness of the alleyway, he felt ready to wring all their necks at the slightest sign of hanging back. The very thought of it exasperated him. *He* couldn't hang back. They shouldn't.

The impetuosity with which he came amongst them carried them along. They had already been excited and startled at all his comings and goings—by the fierceness and rapidity of his movements; and more felt than seen in his rushes, he appeared formidable—busied with matters of life and death that brooked[7] no delay. At his first word he heard them drop into the bunker one after another obediently, with heavy thumps.

They were not clear as to what would have to be done. "What is it? What is it?" they were asking each other. The boatswain tried to explain; the sounds of a great scuffle surprised them: and the mighty

6. Slang for the deckmen.
7. Tolerated, bore, endured, put up with.

shocks, reverberating awfully in the black bunker, kept them in mind of their danger. When the boatswain threw open the door it seemed that an eddy of the hurricane,[8] stealing through the iron sides of the ship, had set all these bodies whirling like dust: there came to them a confused uproar, a tempestuous tumult, a fierce mutter, gusts of screams dying away, and the tramping of feet mingling with the blows of the sea.

For a moment they glared amazed, blocking the doorway. Jukes pushed through them brutally. He said nothing, and simply darted in. Another lot of coolies on the ladder, struggling suicidally to break through the battened hatch to a swamped deck, fell off as before, and he disappeared under them like a man overtaken by a landslide.

The boatswain yelled excitedly: "Come along. Get the mate out. He'll be trampled to death. Come on."

They charged in, stamping on breasts, on fingers, on faces, catching their feet in heaps of clothing, kicking broken wood; but before they could get hold of him Jukes emerged waist deep in a multitude of clawing hands. In the instant he had been lost to view, all the buttons of his jacket had gone, its back had got split up to the collar, his waistcoat had been torn open. The central struggling mass of Chinamen went over to the roll, dark, indistinct, helpless, with a wild gleam of many eyes in the dim light of the lamps.

"Leave me alone—damn you. I am all right," screeched Jukes. "Drive them forward. Watch your chance when she pitches. Forward with 'em. Drive them against the bulkhead. Jam 'em up."

The rush of the sailors into the seething 'tween-deck was like a splash of cold water into a boiling cauldron. The commotion sank for a moment.

The bulk of Chinamen were locked in such a compact scrimmage that, linking their arms and aided by an appalling dive of the ship, the seamen sent it forward in one great shove, like a solid block. Behind their backs small clusters and loose bodies tumbled from side to side.

The boatswain performed prodigious feats of strength. With his long arms open, and each great paw clutching at a stanchion, he stopped the rush of seven entwined Chinamen rolling like a boulder. His joints cracked; he said, "Ha!" and they flew apart. But the carpenter showed the greater intelligence. Without saying a word to anybody he went back into the alleyway, to fetch several coils of cargo gear he had seen there—chain and rope. With these life-lines were rigged.

8. A circular motion of the storm's wind.

There was really no resistance. The struggle, however it began, had turned into a scramble of blind panic. If the coolies had started up after their scattered dollars they were by that time fighting only for their footing. They took each other by the throat merely to save themselves from being hurled about. Whoever got a hold anywhere would kick at the others who caught at his legs and hung on, till a roll sent them flying together across the deck.

The coming of the white devils[9] was a terror. Had they come to kill? The individuals torn out of the ruck became very limp in the seamen's hands: some, dragged aside by the heels, were passive, like dead bodies, with open, fixed eyes. Here and there a coolie would fall on his knees as if begging for mercy; several, whom the excess of fear made unruly, were hit with hard fists between the eyes, and cowered; while those who were hurt submitted to rough handling, blinking rapidly without a plaint. Faces streamed with blood; there were raw places on the shaven heads, scratches, bruises, torn wounds, gashes. The broken porcelain out of the chests was mostly responsible for the latter. Here and there a Chinaman, wild-eyed, with his tail unplaited, nursed a bleeding sole.

They had been ranged closely, after having been shaken into submission, cuffed a little to allay excitement, addressed in gruff words of encouragement that sounded like promises of evil. They sat on the deck in ghastly, drooping rows, and at the end the carpenter, with two hands to help him, moved busily from place to place, setting taut and hitching the life-lines. The boatswain, with one leg and one arm embracing a stanchion, struggled with a lamp pressed to his breast, trying to get a light, and growling all the time like an industrious gorilla. The figures of seamen stooped repeatedly, with the movements of gleaners, and everything was being flung into the bunker: clothing, smashed wood, broken china, and the dollars too, gathered up in men's jackets. Now and then a sailor would stagger towards the doorway with his arms full of rubbish; and dolorous, slanting eyes followed his movements.

With every roll of the ship the long rows of sitting Celestials would sway forward brokenly, and her headlong dives knocked together the line of shaven polls from end to end. When the wash of water rolling on the deck died away for a moment, it seemed to Jukes, yet quivering from his exertions, that in his mad struggle down there he had overcome the wind somehow: that a silence had fallen upon the ship, a silence in which the sea struck thunderously at her sides.

9. A Chinese slur against Westerners; literally, *foreign devils*.

Everything had been cleared out of the 'tween-deck—all the wreckage, as the men said. They stood erect and tottering above the level of heads and drooping shoulders. Here and there a coolie sobbed for his breath. Where the high light fell, Jukes could see the salient ribs of one, the yellow, wistful face of another; bowed necks; or would meet a dull stare directed at his face. He was amazed that there had been no corpses; but the lot of them seemed at their last gasp, and they appeared to him more pitiful than if they had been all dead.

Suddenly one of the coolies began to speak. The light came and went on his lean, straining face; he threw his head up like a baying hound. From the bunker came the sounds of knocking and the tinkle of some dollars rolling loose; he stretched out his arm, his mouth yawned black, and the incomprehensible guttural hooting sounds, that did not seem to belong to a human language, penetrated Jukes with a strange emotion as if a brute had tried to be eloquent.

Two more started mouthing what seemed to Jukes fierce denunciations; the others stirred with grunts and growls. Jukes ordered the hands out of the 'tween-decks hurriedly. He left last himself, backing through the door, while the grunts rose to a loud murmur and hands were extended after him as after a malefactor. The boatswain shot the bolt, and remarked uneasily, "Seems as if the wind had dropped, sir."

The seamen were glad to get back into the alleyway. Secretly each of them thought that at the last moment he could rush out on deck—and that was a comfort. There is something horribly repugnant in the idea of being drowned under a deck. Now they had done with the Chinamen, they again became conscious of the ship's position.

Jukes on coming out of the alleyway found himself up to the neck in the noisy water. He gained the bridge, and discovered he could detect obscure shapes as if his sight had become preternaturally acute. He saw faint outlines. They recalled not the familiar aspect of the *Nan-Shan*, but something remembered—an old dismantled steamer he had seen years ago rotting on a mudbank. She recalled that wreck.

There was no wind, not a breath, except the faint currents created by the lurches of the ship. The smoke tossed out of the funnel was settling down upon her deck. He breathed it as he passed forward. He felt the deliberate throb of the engines, and heard small sounds that seemed to have survived the great uproar: the knocking of broken fittings, the rapid tumbling of some piece of wreckage on the bridge. He perceived dimly the squat shape of his captain holding on to a twisted bridge-rail, motionless and swaying as if rooted to the planks. The unexpected stillness of the air oppressed Jukes.

"We have done it, sir," he gasped.

"Thought you would," said Captain MacWhirr.

"Did you?" murmured Jukes to himself.

"Wind fell all at once," went on the Captain.

Jukes burst out: "If you think it was an easy job—"

But his captain, clinging to the rail, paid no attention. "According to the books the worst is not over yet."

"If most of them hadn't been half dead with sea-sickness and fright, not one of us would have come out of that 'tween-deck alive," said Jukes.

"Had to do what's fair by them," mumbled MacWhirr stolidly. "You don't find everything in books."

"Why, I believe they would have risen on us if I hadn't ordered the hands out of that pretty quick," continued Jukes with warmth.

After the whisper of their shouts, their ordinary tones, so distinct, rang out very loud to their ears in the amazing stillness of the air. It seemed to them they were talking in a dark and echoing vault.

Through a jagged aperture in the dome of clouds the light of a few stars fell upon the black sea, rising and falling confusedly. Sometimes the head of a watery cone would topple on board and mingle with the rolling flurry of foam on the swamped deck; and the *Nan-Shan* wallowed heavily at the bottom of a circular cistern of clouds. This ring of dense vapours, gyrating madly round the calm of the centre, encompassed the ship like a motionless and unbroken wall of an aspect inconceivably sinister. Within, the sea, as if agitated by an internal commotion, leaped in peaked mounds that jostled each other, slapping heavily against her sides; and a low moaning sound, the infinite plaint of the storm's fury, came from beyond the limits of the menacing calm. Captain MacWhirr remained silent, and Jukes' ready ear caught suddenly the faint, long-drawn roar of some immense wave rushing unseen under that thick blackness, which made the appalling boundary of his vision.

"Of course," he started resentfully, "they thought we had caught at the chance to plunder them. Of course! You said—pick up the money. Easier said than done. They couldn't tell what was in our heads. We came in, smash—right into the middle of them. Had to do it by a rush."

"As long as it's done . . . ," mumbled the Captain, without attempting to look at Jukes. "Had to do what's fair."

"We shall find yet there's the devil to pay when this is over," said Jukes, feeling very sore. "Let them only recover a bit, and you'll see. They will fly at our throats, sir. Don't forget, sir, she isn't a British ship now. These brutes know it well, too. The damn'd Siamese flag."

"We are on board, all the same," remarked Captain MacWhirr.

"The trouble's not over yet," insisted Jukes prophetically, reeling and catching on. "She's a wreck," he added faintly.

"The trouble's not over yet," assented Captain MacWhirr, half aloud. . . . "Look out for her a minute."

"Are you going off the deck, sir?" asked Jukes hurriedly, as if the storm were sure to pounce upon him as soon as he had been left alone with the ship.

He watched her, battered and solitary, labouring heavily in a wild scene of mountainous black waters lit by the gleams of distant worlds. She moved slowly, breathing into the still core of the hurricane the excess of her strength in a white cloud of steam—and the deep-toned vibration of the escape was like the defiant trumpeting of a living creature of the sea impatient for the renewal of the contest. It ceased suddenly. The still air moaned. Above Jukes' head a few stars shone into the pit of black vapours. The inky edge of the cloud-disc frowned upon the ship under the patch of glittering sky. The stars too seemed to look at her intently, as if for the last time, and the cluster of their splendour sat like a diadem on a lowering brow.

Captain MacWhirr had gone into the chart-room. There was no light there; but he could feel the disorder of that place where he used to live tidily. His armchair was upset. The books had tumbled out on the floor: he scrunched a piece of glass under his boot. He groped for the matches, and found a box on a shelf with a deep ledge. He struck one, and puckering the corners of his eyes, held out the little flame towards the barometer whose glittering top of glass and metals nodded at him continuously.

It stood very low—incredibly low, so low that Captain MacWhirr grunted. The match went out, and hurriedly he extracted another, with thick, stiff fingers.

Again a little flame flared up before the nodding glass and metal of the top. His eyes looked at it, narrowed with attention, as if expecting an imperceptible sign. With his grave face he resembled a booted and misshapen pagan burning incense before the oracle of a Joss.[1] There was no mistake. It was the lowest reading he had ever seen in his life.

Captain MacWhirr emitted a low whistle. He forgot himself till the flame diminished to a blue spark, burnt his fingers, and vanished. Perhaps something had gone wrong with the thing!

There was an aneroid glass[2] screwed above the couch. He turned that way, struck another match, and discovered the white face of the other instrument looking at him from the bulkhead, meaningly,

1. A Chinese deity or idol.
2. An aneroid barometer.

not to be gainsaid, as though the wisdom of men were made unerring by the indifference of matter. There was no room for doubt now. Captain MacWhirr pshawed at it, and threw the match down.

The worst was to come, then—and if the books were right this worst would be very bad. The experience of the last six hours had enlarged his conception of what heavy weather could be like. "It'll be terrific," he pronounced mentally. He had not consciously looked at anything by the light of the matches except at the barometer; and yet somehow he had seen that his water-bottle and the two tumblers had been flung out of their stand. It seemed to give him a more intimate knowledge of the tossing the ship had gone through. "I wouldn't have believed it," he thought. And his table had been cleared too; his rulers, his pencils, the inkstand—all the things that had their safe appointed places—they were gone, as if a mischievous hand had plucked them out one by one and flung them on the wet floor. The hurricane had broken in upon the orderly arrangements of his privacy. This had never happened before, and the feeling of dismay reached the very seat of his composure. And the worst was to come yet! He was glad the trouble in the 'tween-deck had been discovered in time. If the ship had to go after all, then, at least, she wouldn't be going to the bottom with a lot of people in her fighting teeth and claw. That would have been odious. And in that feeling there was a humane intention and a vague sense of the fitness of things.

These instantaneous thoughts were yet in their essence heavy and slow, partaking of the nature of the man. He extended his hand to put back the matchbox in its corner of the shelf. There were always matches there—by his order. The steward had his instructions impressed upon him long before. "A box . . . just there, see? Not so very full . . . where I can put my hand on it, steward. Might want a light in a hurry. Can't tell on board ship *what* you might want in a hurry. Mind, now."

And of course on his side he would be careful to put it back in its place scrupulously. He did so now, but before he removed his hand it occurred to him that perhaps he would never have occasion to use that box any more. The vividness of the thought checked him, and for an infinitesimal fraction of a second his fingers closed again on the small object as though it had been the symbol of all these little habits that chain us to the weary round of life. He released it at last, and letting himself fall on the settee, listened for the first sounds of returning wind.

Not yet. He heard only the wash of water, the heavy splashes, the dull shocks of the confused seas boarding his ship from all sides. She would never have a chance to clear her decks.

But the quietude of the air was startlingly tense and unsafe, like a slender hair holding a sword suspended over his head.[3] By this awful pause the storm penetrated the defences of the man and unsealed his lips. He spoke out in the solitude and the pitch darkness of the cabin, as if addressing another being awakened within his breast.

"I shouldn't like to lose her," he said half aloud.

He sat unseen, apart from the sea, from his ship, isolated, as if withdrawn from the very current of his own existence, where such freaks as talking to himself surely had no place. His palms reposed on his knees, he bowed his short neck and puffed heavily, surrendering to a strange sensation of weariness he was not enlightened enough to recognise for the fatigue of mental stress.

From where he sat he could reach the door of a washstand locker. There should have been a towel there. There was. Good. . . . He took it out, wiped his face, and afterwards went on rubbing his wet head. He towelled himself with energy in the dark, and then remained motionless with the towel on his knees. A moment passed, of a stillness so profound that no one could have guessed there was a man sitting in that cabin. Then a murmur arose.

"She may come out of it yet."

When Captain MacWhirr came out on deck, which he did brusquely, as though he had suddenly become conscious of having stayed away too long, the calm had lasted already more than fifteen minutes—long enough to make itself intolerable even to his imagination. Jukes, motionless on the forepart of the bridge, began to speak at once. His voice, blank and forced as though he were talking through hard-set teeth, seemed to flow away on all sides into the darkness, deepening again upon the sea.

"I had the wheel relieved. Hackett began to sing out that he was done. He's lying in there alongside the steering-gear with a face like death. At first I couldn't get anybody to crawl out and relieve the poor devil. That boss'n's worse than no good, I always said. Thought I would have had to go myself and haul out one of them by the neck."

"Ah, well," muttered the Captain. He stood watchful by Jukes' side.

"The second mate's in there too, holding his head. Is he hurt, sir?"

"No—crazy," said Captain MacWhirr, curtly.

"Looks as if he had a tumble, though."

"I had to give him a push," explained the Captain.

Jukes gave an impatient sigh.

3. See p. 32, n. 6.

"It will come very sudden," said Captain MacWhirr, "and from over there, I fancy. God only knows, though. These books are only good to muddle your head and make you jumpy. It will be bad, and there's an end. If we only can steam her round in time to meet it . . ."

A minute passed. Some of the stars winked rapidly and vanished.

"You left them pretty safe?" began the Captain abruptly, as though the silence were unbearable.

"Are you thinking of the coolies, sir? I rigged life-lines all ways across that 'tween-deck."

"Did you? Good idea, Mr. Jukes."

"I didn't . . . think you cared to . . . know," said Jukes—the lurching of the ship cut his speech as though somebody had been jerking him around while he talked—"how I got on with . . . that infernal job. We did it. And it may not matter in the end."

"Had to do what's fair, for all—they are only Chinamen. Give them the same chance with ourselves—hang it all. She isn't lost yet. Bad enough to be shut up below in a gale—"

"That's what I thought when you gave me the job, sir," interjected Jukes moodily.

"—without being battered to pieces," pursued Captain MacWhirr with rising vehemence. "Couldn't let that go on in my ship, if I knew she hadn't five minutes to live. Couldn't bear it, Mr. Jukes."

A hollow echoing noise, like that of a shout rolling in a rocky chasm, approached the ship and went away again. The last star, blurred, enlarged, as if returning to the fiery mist of its beginning, struggled with the colossal depth of blackness hanging over the ship—and went out.

"Now for it!" muttered Captain MacWhirr. "Mr. Jukes."

"Here, sir."

The two men were growing indistinct to each other.

"We must trust her to go through it and come out on the other side. That's plain and straight. There's no room for Captain Wilson's storm-strategy here."

"No, sir."

"She will be smothered and swept again for hours," mumbled the Captain. "There's not much left by this time above deck for the sea to take away—unless you or me."

"Both, sir," whispered Jukes breathlessly.

"You are always meeting trouble half-way, Jukes," Captain Mac-Whirr remonstrated quaintly. "Though it's a fact that the second mate is no good. D'ye hear, Mr. Jukes? You would be left alone if . . ."

Captain MacWhirr interrupted himself, and Jukes, glancing on all sides, remained silent.

"Don't you be put out by anything," the Captain continued, mumbling rather fast. "Keep her facing it. They may say what they like, but the heaviest seas run with the wind. Facing it—always facing it—that's the way to get through. You are a young sailor. Face it. That's enough for any man. Keep a cool head."

"Yes, sir," said Jukes, with a flutter of the heart.

In the next few seconds the Captain spoke to the engine-room and got an answer.

For some reason Jukes experienced an access[4] of confidence, a sensation that came from outside like a warm breath, and made him feel equal to every demand. The distant muttering of the darkness stole into his ears. He noted it unmoved, out of that sudden belief in himself, as a man safe in a shirt of mail would watch a point.

The ship laboured without intermission amongst the black hills of water, paying with this hard tumbling the price of her life. She rumbled in her depths, shaking a white plumet[5] of steam into the night, and Jukes' thought skimmed like a bird through the engine-room, where Mr. Rout—good man—was ready. When the rumbling ceased it seemed to him that there was a pause of every sound, a dead pause in which Captain MacWhirr's voice rang out startlingly.

"What's that? A puff of wind?"—it spoke much louder than Jukes had ever heard it before—"On the bow. That's right. She may come out of it yet."

The mutter of the winds drew near apace. In the forefront could be distinguished a drowsy waking plaint passing on, and far off the growth of a multiple clamour, marching and expanding. There was the throb as of many drums in it, a vicious rushing note, and like the chant of a tramping multitude.

Jukes could no longer see his captain distinctly. The darkness was absolutely piling itself upon the ship. At most he made out movements, a hint of elbows spread out, of a head thrown up.

Captain MacWhirr was trying to do up the top button of his oil-skin coat with unwonted haste. The hurricane, with its power to madden the seas, to sink ships, to uproot trees, to overturn strong walls and dash the very birds of the air to the ground, had found this taciturn man in its path, and, doing its utmost, had managed to wring out a few words. Before the renewed wrath of winds swooped on his ship, Captain MacWhirr was moved to declare, in a tone of vexation, as it were: "I wouldn't like to lose her."

He was spared that annoyance.

---

4. An outburst or sudden fit of feeling or emotion.
5. See p. 248, n. 6.

VI

On a bright sunshiny day, with the breeze chasing her smoke far ahead, the *Nan-Shan* came into Fu-chau. Her arrival was at once noticed on shore, and the seamen in harbour said: "Look! Look at that steamer. What's that? Siamese—isn't she? Just look at her!"

She seemed, indeed, to have been used as a running target for the secondary batteries of a cruiser. A hail of minor shells could not have given her upper works a more broken, torn, and devastated aspect: and she had about her the worn, weary air of ships coming from the far ends of the world—and indeed with truth, for in her short passage she had been very far; sighting, verily, even the coast of the Great Beyond, whence no ship ever returns to give up her crew to the dust of the earth. She was incrusted and grey with salt to the trucks of her masts and to the top of her funnel; as though (as some facetious seaman said) "the crowd on board had fished her out somewhere from the bottom of the sea and brought her in here for salvage." And further, excited by the felicity of his own wit, he offered to give five pounds for her—"as she stands."

Before she had been quite an hour at rest, a meagre little man, with a red-tipped nose and a face cast in an angry mould, landed from a sampan on the quay of the Foreign Concession,[6] and incontinently turned to shake his fist at her.

A tall individual, with legs much too thin for a rotund stomach, and with watery eyes, strolled up and remarked, "Just left her—eh? Quick work."

He wore a soiled suit of blue flannel with a pair of dirty cricketing shoes;[7] a dingy grey moustache drooped from his lip, and daylight could be seen in two places between the rim and the crown of his hat.

"Hallo! what are you doing here?" asked the ex-second-mate of the *Nan-Shan*, shaking hands hurriedly.

"Standing by for a job—chance worth taking—got a quiet hint," explained the man with the broken hat, in jerky, apathetic wheezes.

The second shook his fist again at the *Nan-Shan*. "There's a fellow there that ain't fit to have the command of a scow," he declared, quivering with passion, while the other looked about listlessly.

"Is there?"

But he caught sight on the quay of a heavy seaman's chest, painted brown under a fringed sailcloth cover, and lashed with new manila line. He eyed it with awakened interest.

6. Fu-chau (Fuzhou) was one of five Chinese ports opened for trade as a consequence of the 1842 Treaty of Nanking. The others were Canton (Guanzhou), Amoy (Xiamen), Ningpo (Ningbo), and Shanghai.
7. Shoes with spiked soles for playing cricket.

"I would talk and raise trouble if it wasn't for that damned Siamese flag. Nobody to go to—or I would make it hot for him. The fraud! Told his chief engineer—that's another fraud for you—I had lost my nerve. The greatest lot of ignorant fools that ever sailed the seas. No! You can't think . . . ."

"Got your money all right?" inquired his seedy acquaintance suddenly.

"Yes. Paid me off on board," raged the second mate. " 'Get your breakfast on shore,' says he."

"Mean skunk!" commented the tall man vaguely, and passed his tongue on his lips. "What about having a drink of some sort?"

"He struck me," hissed the second mate.

"No! Struck! You don't say?" The man in blue began to bustle about sympathetically. "Can't possibly talk here. I want to know all about it. Struck—eh? Let's get a fellow to carry your chest. I know a quiet place where they have some bottled beer. . . ."

Mr. Jukes, who had been scanning the shore through a pair of glasses, informed the chief engineer afterwards that "our late second mate hasn't been long in finding a friend. A chap looking uncommonly like a bummer. I saw them walk away together from the quay."

The hammering and banging of the needful repairs did not disturb Captain MacWhirr. The steward found in the letter he wrote, in a tidy chart-room, passages of such absorbing interest that twice he was nearly caught in the act. But Mrs. MacWhirr, in the drawing-room of the forty-pound house, stifled a yawn—perhaps out of self-respect—for she was alone.

She reclined in a plush-bottomed and gilt hammock-chair near a tiled fireplace, with Japanese fans on the mantel and a glow of coals in the grate. Lifting her hands, she glanced wearily here and there into the many pages. It was not her fault they were so prosy, so completely uninteresting—from "My darling wife" at the beginning, to "Your loving husband" at the end. She couldn't be really expected to understand all these ship affairs. She was glad, of course, to hear from him, but she had never asked herself why, precisely.

". . . They are called typhoons . . . The mate did not seem to like it . . . Not in books . . . Couldn't think of letting it go on. . . ."

The paper rustled sharply. ". . . A calm that lasted over twenty minutes," she read perfunctorily; and the next words her thoughtless eyes caught, on the top of another page, were: "see you and the children again. . . ." She had a movement of impatience. He was always thinking of coming home. He had never had such a good salary before. What was the matter now!

It did not occur to her to turn back overleaf to look. She would have found it recorded there that between 4 and 6 A.M. on December 25th, Captain MacWhirr did actually think that his ship could not possibly live another hour in such a sea, and that he would never see his wife and children again. Nobody was to know this (his letters got mislaid so quickly)—nobody whatever but the steward, who had been greatly impressed by that disclosure. So much so, that he tried to give the cook some idea of the "narrow squeak we all had" by saying solemnly, "The old man himself had a dam' poor opinion of our chance."

"How do you know?" asked contemptuously the cook, an old soldier. "He hasn't told you, maybe?"

"Well, he did give me a hint to that effect," the steward brazened it out.

"Get along with you! He will be coming to tell *me* next," jeered the old cook over his shoulder.

Mrs. MacWhirr glanced farther, on the alert. ". . . Do what's fair. . . . Miserable objects. . . . Only three, with a broken leg each, and one . . . Thought had better keep the matter quiet . . . hope to have done the fair thing. . . ."

She let fall her hands. No: there was nothing more about coming home. Must have been merely expressing a pious wish. Mrs. MacWhirr's mind was set at ease, and a black marble clock, priced by the local jeweller at £3 18s. 6d., had a discreet stealthy tick.

The door flew open, and a girl in the long-legged, short-frocked period of existence,[8] flung into the room. A lot of colourless, rather lanky hair was scattered over her shoulders. Seeing her mother, she stood still, and directed her pale prying eyes upon the letter.

"From father," murmured Mrs. MacWhirr. "What have you done with your ribbon?"

The girl put her hands up to her head and pouted.

"He's well," continued Mrs. MacWhirr languidly. "At least I think so. He never says." She had a little laugh. The girl's face expressed a wandering indifference, and Mrs. MacWhirr surveyed her with fond pride.

"Go and get your hat," she said after a while. "I am going out to do some shopping. There is a sale at Linom's."[9]

"Oh, how jolly!" uttered the child impressively, in unexpectedly grave vibrating tones, and bounded out of the room.

It was a fine afternoon, with a grey sky and dry sidewalks. Outside the draper's Mrs. MacWhirr smiled upon a woman in a black

8. Of an age that wears such clothing.
9. The firm of Lewis, Hyland & Linom.

mantle of generous proportions, armoured in jet[1] and crowned with flowers blooming falsely above a bilious matronly countenance. They broke into a swift little babble of greetings and exclamations both together, very hurried, as if the street were ready to yawn open and swallow all that pleasure before it could be expressed.

Behind them the high glass doors were kept on the swing. People couldn't pass, men stood aside waiting patiently, and Lydia was absorbed in poking the end of her parasol between the stone flags.[2] Mrs. MacWhirr talked rapidly.

"Thank you very much. He's not coming home yet. Of course it's very sad to have him away, but it's such a comfort to know he keeps so well." Mrs. MacWhirr drew breath. "The climate there agrees with him," she added beamingly, as if poor MacWhirr had been away touring in China for the sake of his health.

Neither was the chief engineer coming home yet. Mr. Rout knew too well the value of a good billet.

"Solomon says wonders will never cease," cried Mrs. Rout joyously at the old lady in her armchair by the fire. Mr. Rout's mother moved slightly, her withered hands lying in black half-mittens on her lap.

The eyes of the engineer's wife fairly danced on the paper. "That captain of the ship he is in—a rather simple man, you remember, mother?—has done something rather clever, Solomon says."

"Yes, my dear," said the old woman meekly, sitting with bowed silvery head, and that air of inward stillness characteristic of very old people who seem lost in watching the last flickers of life. "I think I remember."

Solomon Rout, Old Sol, Father Sol, The Chief, "Rout, good man"— Mr. Rout, the condescending and paternal friend of youth, had been the baby of her many children—all dead by this time. And she remembered him best as a boy of ten—long before he went away to serve his apprenticeship in some great engineering works in the North. She had seen so little of him since, she had gone through so many years, that she had now to retrace her steps very far back to recognise him plainly in the mist of time. Sometimes it seemed that her daughter-in-law was talking of some strange man.

Mrs. Rout junior was disappointed. "H'm. H'm." She turned the page. "How provoking! He doesn't say what it is. Says I couldn't understand how much there was in it. Fancy! What could it be so very clever? What a wretched man not to tell us!"

She read on without further remark soberly, and at last sat looking into the fire. The chief wrote just a word or two of the typhoon;

---

1. A fashion, mode, or style.
2. I.e., flagstones; flat stones suitable for paving.

but something had moved him to express an increased longing for the companionship of the jolly woman. "If it hadn't been that mother must be looked after, I would send you your passage-money to-day. You could set up a small house out here. I would have a chance to see you sometimes then. We are not growing younger. . . ."

"He's well, mother," sighed Mrs. Rout, rousing herself.

"He always was a strong healthy boy," said the old woman placidly.

But Mr. Jukes' account was really animated and very full. His friend in the Western Ocean trade imparted it freely to the other officers of his liner. "A chap I know writes to me about an extraordinary affair that happened on board his ship in that typhoon—you know—that we read of in the papers two months ago. It's the funniest thing! Just see for yourself what he says. I'll show you his letter."

There were phrases in it calculated to give the impression of light-hearted, indomitable resolution. Jukes had written them in good faith, for he felt thus when he wrote. He described with lurid effect the scenes in the 'tween-deck. ". . . It struck me in a flash that those confounded Chinamen couldn't tell we weren't a desperate kind of robbers. 'Tisn't good to part the Chinaman from his money if he is the stronger party. We need have been desperate indeed to go thieving in such weather, but what could these beggars[3] know of us? So, without thinking of it twice, I got the hands away in a jiffy. Our work was done—that the old man had set his heart on. We cleared out without staying to inquire how they felt. I am convinced that if they had not been so unmercifully shaken, and afraid—each individual one of them—to stand up, we would have been torn to pieces. Oh! It was pretty complete, I can tell you; and you may run to and fro across the Pond[4] to the end of time before you find yourself with such a job on your hands."

After this he alluded professionally to the damage done to the ship, and went on thus:

"It was when the weather quieted down that the situation became confoundedly delicate. It wasn't made any better by us having been lately transferred to the Siamese flag; though the skipper can't see that it makes any difference—'as long as *we* are on board'—he says. There are feelings that this man simply hasn't got—and there's an end of it. You might just as well try to make a bedpost understand. But apart from this it is an infernally lonely state for a ship to be going about the China seas with no proper Consuls,[5] not even a gunboat of her own anywhere, nor a body to go to in case of some trouble.

3. See p. 63, n. 5.
4. The Atlantic Ocean (slang).
5. See p. 19, n. 7.

JOSEPH CONRAD

"My notion was to keep these Johnnies under hatches for another fifteen hours or so; as we weren't much farther than that from Fuchau. We would find there, most likely, some sort of a man-of-war, and once under her guns we were safe enough; for surely any skipper of a man-of-war—English, French, or Dutch—would see white men through as far as a row on board goes. We could get rid of them and their money afterwards by delivering them to their Mandarin or Taotai, or whatever they call these chaps in goggles you see being carried about in sedan-chairs[6] through their stinking streets.

"The old man wouldn't see it somehow. He wanted to keep the matter quiet. He got that notion into his head, and a steam windlass couldn't drag it out of him. He wanted as little fuss made as possible, for the sake of the ship's name and for the sake of the owners—'for the sake of all concerned,' says he, looking at me very hard. It made me hot.[7] Of course you couldn't keep a thing like that quiet; but the chests had been secured in the usual manner and were safe enough for any earthly gale, while this had been an altogether fiendish business I couldn't give you even an idea of.

"Meantime, I could hardly keep on my feet. None of us had a spell of any sort for nearly thirty hours, and there the old man sat rubbing his chin, rubbing the top of his head, and so bothered he didn't even think of pulling his long boots off.

"'I hope, sir,' says I, 'you won't be letting them out on deck before we make ready for them in some shape or other.' Not, mind you, that I felt very sanguine about controlling these beggars if they meant to take charge. A trouble with a cargo of Chinamen is no child's play. I was dam' tired too. 'I wish,' said I, 'you would let us throw the whole lot of these dollars down to them and leave them to fight it out amongst themselves, while we get a rest.'

"'Now you talk wild, Jukes,' says he, looking up in his slow way that makes you ache all over, somehow. 'We must plan out something that would be fair to all parties.'

"I had no end of work on hand, as you may imagine, so I set the hands going, and then I thought I would turn in a bit. I hadn't been asleep in my bunk ten minutes when in rushes the steward and begins to pull at my leg.

"'For God's sake, Mr. Jukes, come out! Come on deck quick, sir. Oh, do come out!'

---

6. Enclosed vehicles carried by two bearers. "Mandarin or Taotai": a Chinese provincial official who oversees a district's military and civil matters.
7. Stape argues that the first English edition's "angry hot" is almost certainly an error in that Conrad simply failed to cross out "angry" in the typescript and failed to notice the error when reading proofs for the first English edition.

"The fellow scared all the sense out of me. I didn't know what had happened: another hurricane—or what. Could hear no wind.

"'The Captain's letting them out. Oh, he is letting them out! Jump on deck, sir, and save us. The chief engineer has just run below for his revolver.'

"That's what I understood the fool to say. However, Father Rout swears he went in there only to get a clean pocket-handkerchief. Anyhow, I made one jump into my trousers and flew on deck aft. There was certainly a good deal of noise going on forward of the bridge. Four of the hands with the boss'n were at work abaft. I passed up to them some of the rifles all the ships on the China coast carry in the cabin, and led them on the bridge. On the way I ran against Old Sol, looking startled and sucking at an unlighted cigar.

"'Come along,' I shouted to him.

"We charged, the seven of us, up to the chart-room. All was over. There stood the old man with his sea-boots still drawn up to the hips and in shirt-sleeves—got warm thinking it out, I suppose. Bun Hin's dandy clerk at his elbow, as dirty as a sweep, was still green in the face. I could see directly I was in for something.

"'What the devil are these monkey tricks, Mr. Jukes?' asks the old man, as angry as ever he could be. I tell you frankly it made me lose my tongue. 'For God's sake, Mr. Jukes,' says he, 'do take away these rifles from the men. Somebody's sure to get hurt before long if you don't. Damme, if this ship isn't worse than Bedlam![8] Look sharp now. I want you up here to help me and Bun Hin's Chinaman to count that money. You wouldn't mind lending a hand too, Mr. Rout, now you are here. The more of us the better.'

"He had settled it all in his mind while I was having a snooze. Had we been an English ship, or only going to land our cargo of coolies in an English port, like Hong-Kong,[9] for instance, there would have been no end of inquiries and bother, claims for damages and so on. But these Chinamen know their officials better than we do.

"The hatches had been taken off already, and they were all on deck after a night and a day down below. It made you feel queer to see so many gaunt, wild faces together. The beggars stared about at the sky, at the sea, at the ship, as though they had expected the whole thing to have been blown to pieces. And no wonder! They had had a doing that would have shaken the soul out of a white man. But then they say a Chinaman has no soul. He has, though, something about him that is deuced tough. There was a fellow (amongst others of the badly hurt) who had had his eye all but knocked out. It stood out of

8. Originally, the Hospital of St. Mary of Bethlehem in London (founded in 1247 for the mentally ill); but later a generic term for chaos.
9. See p. 87, n. 7.

his head the size of half a hen's egg. This would have laid out a white man on his back for a month: and yet there was that chap elbowing here and there in the crowd and talking to the others as if nothing had been the matter. They made a great hubbub amongst themselves, and whenever the old man showed his bald head on the foreside of the bridge, they would all leave off jawing and look at him from below.

"It seems that after he had done his thinking he made that Bun Hin's fellow go down and explain to them the only way they could get their money back. He told me afterwards that, all the coolies having worked in the same place and for the same length of time, he reckoned he would be doing the fair thing by them as near as possible if he shared all the cash we had picked up equally among the lot. You couldn't tell one man's dollars from another's, he said, and if you asked each man how much money he brought on board he was afraid they would lie, and he would find himself a long way short. I think he was right there. As to giving up the money to any Chinese official he could scare up in Fu-chau, he said he might just as well put the lot in his own pocket at once for all the good it would be to them. I suppose they thought so too.

"We finished the distribution before dark. It was rather a sight: the sea running high, the ship a wreck to look at, these Chinamen staggering up on the bridge one by one for their share, and the old man still booted, and in his shirt-sleeves, busy paying out at the chartroom door, perspiring like anything, and now and then coming down sharp on myself or Father Rout about one thing or another not quite to his mind. He took the share of those who were disabled himself to them on the No. 2 hatch. There were three dollars left over, and these went to the three most damaged coolies, one to each. We turned-to afterwards, and shovelled out on deck heaps of wet rags, all sorts of fragments of things without shape, and that you couldn't give a name to, and let them settle the ownership themselves.

"This certainly is coming as near as can be to keeping the thing quiet for the benefit of all concerned. What's your opinion, you pampered mail-boat swell?[1] The old chief says that this was plainly the only thing that could be done. The skipper remarked to me the other day, 'There are things you find nothing about in books.' I think that he got out of it very well for such a stupid man."

1. Someone who is conceited or puffed up. "Mail-boat": literally, a boat that conveys letters and postal packages. Here, Jukes is using the term to suggest someone who has things easy, like someone assigned to a mailboat.

Textual Emendations

The Secret Sharer

main deck] main-deck (8)
main deck] main-deck (10)
after-end] after end (11)
fore-end] fore end (11)
Conway] Conway (14)
Conway] Conway (14)
heaven— And] heaven—And (14)
'Look out! look out!'] "Look out! look out!" (15)
forecastle-head] forecastle head (15)
'Murder!'] "Murder!" (15)
letter L, the] letter L the (16)
already— I] already—I (18)
Conway] Conway (18)
Consul] consul (19)
time— I] time—I (21)
know— I] know—I (21)
poop ladder] poop-ladder (22)
main deck] main-deck (23)
after-braces] after braces (23)
folding-stool] folding stool (24)
clatter—out] clatter — out (24)
point blank] point-blank (27)
mates' rooms] mate's room (28)
Sephora's] *Sephora*s (28)
Not one] No one (29)
main-topsail] maintopsail (30)
boss'n] bo's'n (30)
pagoda] Pagoda (31)
main deck] maindeck (34)
Cambodge] Cambodje (34)
wondered] wonder (39)
head sheets] head-sheets (41)
main yard] mainyard (41)

The Shadow-Line

First Command] "First Command" (44)
The Shadow-Line] "The Shadow Line" (44)
miroir] mirroir (47)
love;] love, (49)
Harbour Office] harbour office (50)
Harbour Office] harbour office (51)
Esplanade] esplanade (51)
East-end] East End (52)
of Oriental] or Oriental (53)
Sulu] Solo (53)
there was] was there (62)
were] was (66)
Only I] I only (74)
it] they (74)
half-turn] half turn (77)
stern sheets] stern-sheets (77)
port-holes] portholes (77)
main-hatch] main hatch (81)
steering-gear] steering gear (81)
rudder-casing] rudder casing (84)
these] those (88)
half an hour] half-an-hour (91)
complete] completed (94)
bulkhead lamp] bulkhead-lamp (97)
washing the decks] washing decks (99)
Cape Liant] Liant (99)
said.] said, (107)
but was otherwise] but otherwise (108)
be just] just be (109)
North-East] Nord-East (109)
called upon to] called to (111)
exists] exist (111)
belaying-pin] belaying pin (113)
mastheads] mast-heads (117)
main yard] main-yard (120)
fever-wasted] fever - wasted (120)
amazingly] amazing] (127)
sir?"] sir." (127)
mate?"] mate," (128)
halyards] halliards (131)
forecastle-head] forecastle head (131)
main deck] main-deck (131)

"Preface" to *The Nigger of the "Narcissus"*

prejudices] prjudices (139)
justification] justifiation (141)
of);] of,) (142)
times, and] times and (142)
faintly, encouraging] faintly encouraging (142)
arms;] arms, (142)

"To My Readers in America"

Nigger] "Nigger" (136)
The Nigger of the "Narcissus"] "The Nigger of the 'Narcissus'" (137)

The Nigger of the "Narcissus"

half-way] halfway (143)
bedding, made] bedding made (144)
sat] set (145)
Pelham.] "Pelham." (145)
can their rough, inexperienced souls find] their rough, inexperi-
    enced souls can find (146)
Pelham] "Pelham" (146)
boss'n] bo'sen (153)
main-hatch] main hatch (154)
coal-locker] coal locker (154)
fore-topmast] fore topmast (157)
chain-cable] chain cable (159)
black beetle] blackbeetle (160)
water-line] waterline (160)
St. Kitts] St. Kitt's (165)
your] YOUR (167)
main pump-rods] main-pump rods (169)
starboard-watch] starboard watch (172)
Cape of Storms] cape of storms (173)
ship, vibrating] ship vibrating (174)
abysmal] abyssmal (177)
mizzen] mizen (178)
mizzen-rigging] mizen rigging (179)
dead-eyes] deadeyes (179)
ringbolt] ring-bolt (182)
images,] images! (184)
belaying-pin] belaying pin (184)
half-way] halfway (187)
fore sheet] foresheet (188)
cleat] cleet (188)

yet";] yet;" (191)

Boss'n] Boss'en (195)

no] on (196)

mouths] mouth (196)

fore-topmast] fore-top-mast (197)

forecastle-head] forecastle head (197)

main-braces] main braces (197)

main-brace] main brace (197)

half-drowned] half drowned (197)

belaying-pin] belaying pin (198)

now?] now, (198)

yelled—] yelled,— (199)

foreyards] fore-yards (199)

now." . . .] now" . . . (200)

binnacle-stand] binnacle stand (200)

Steering-gear] Steering gear (200)

"Now] Now (201)

off"] off (201)

imprecations] implications (201)

main-topsail] main topsail (202)

seaman] seamen (202)

starboard-watch] starboard watch (202)

out";] out;" (203)

as] like (205)

up."] up" (205)

horse."] horse" (205)

shook his] shook s (205)

bloomin'] blooming' (206)

condemned] condemed (206)

fore-arms] forearms (206)

a-drivin'] a-drivin (207)

after-end] after end (210)

Donkin;] Donkin (210)

Eh?] eh? (211)

laughed,] laughed (212)

'aven't chee] aven'tchee (213)

chummed,] chummed (214)

dry;] dry? (214)

Eight bells] Eight-bells (215)

forecastle-head] forecastle head (215)

as] like (216)

port-watch] port watch (220)

at once] to once (220)

fore-rigging] fore rigging (220)

after-hatch] after hatch (221)

main-hatch] main hatch (222)
forebraces] fore-braces (222)
Davies] Davis (224)
You] you (228)
black . . ."] black— . . . ." (228)
this?] this, (229)
bullied?] bullied, (230)
by Wamibo's] and Wamibo's (234)
thrashed] trashed (234)
for] or (235)
tobacco, and loafed] tobacco, loafed (235)
hours, very] hours and very (235)
as] like (235)
enough] 'enough (237)
rage.] rage, (240)
No more] no more (240)
'ead] ead (243)
Red] red (244)
Ensign] ensign (244)
who,] who (246)
riding-light] riding light (247)
plumets] plummets (248)
forecastle-head] forecastle head (248)
door-handles] door handles (250)
"Quite a lady, quite a lady,"] Quite a lady, quite a lady, (250)
comin'] comin (252)
'yrpocrits] yropocrits (252)
Ye're] Ye'rr (252)

Typhoon

Youth] "Youth" (255)
sir"] sir," (259)
coal-lighters] coal lighters (262)
boss'n] bo'ss'en (264)
Fu-chau—] Fu-chau,— (266)
topside] top-side (266)
quaintly] queerly (267)
nature,'"] nature';" (268)
Western Ocean] Western ocean (268)
chief] Chief (269)
Western Ocean] Western ocean (270)
Herculean] herculean (271)
wheelhouse] wheel-house (273)
contemptuous] contemptous (274)

Jukes'] Jukes's (276)
wind, and] wind and (279)
steamship] steam-ship (280)
has] had (281)
sea-boots] seaboots (281)
wheelhouse] wheel-house (282)
bridge, heads] bridge heads (284)
resolution, and] resolution and (287)
MacWhirr.] MacWhirr (288)
mouths, and] mouths and (288)
lonely, and] lonely and (289)
fore-arms] forearms (290)
demeanour, and] demeanour and (290)
'tween-deck] 'tween deck (290)
was as though] was though (295)
ringbolt] ring-bolt (296)
energy:] energy (297)
lid, sir"] lid, sir (297)
wheelhouse] wheel-house (299)
bag, hung] bag hung (299)
striped] stripped (299)
compass-card] compass card (299)
bulkhead] bulk-head (300)
neck—] neck,— (300)
steering-gear] steering gear (300)
stopped, smouldering] stopped smouldering (300)
right. . . .] right, . . . (300)
coal-dust] coal dust (302)
exotic, and] exotic and (302)
big-jointed] big-jointed, (302)
cross-heads] crossheads (302)
him—] him;— (303)
donkey-man] donkeyman (304)
peace, and] peace and (304)
you . . .] you . . . , (305)
steering-gear] steering gear (306)
donkey-man] donkeyman (307)
done . . .] done . . . , (311)
fingers,] fingers (312)
steering-gear] steering gear (314)
boss'n's] boss'en's (314)
hurt, sir?"] hurt, sir? (314)
half-way] half way (315)
plumet] plummet (316)
startlingly] startingly (316)

VI] V (317)
soldier.] soldier, (319)
Consuls] consuls (321)
French, or] French or (322)
as a row] as row (322)
hot] angry hot (322)
boss'n] boss'en (322)
Bun Hin's] Bun-hin's (323)
Bun Hin's] Bun-hin's (323)
better.'] better. (323)
Bun Hin's] Bun-hin's (324)

BACKGROUNDS AND CONTEXTS

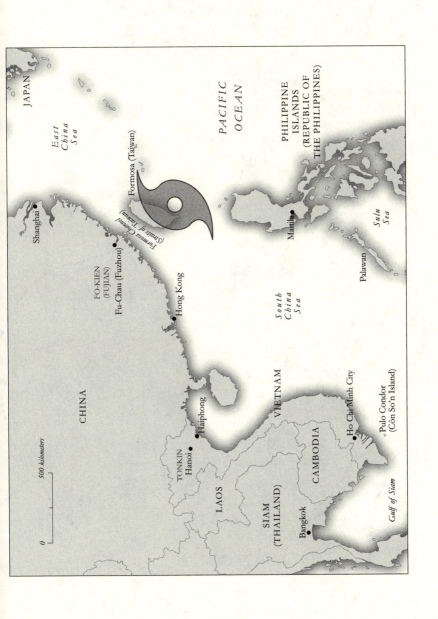

JAPAN

East
China
Sea

Shanghai

CHINA

FO-KIEN
(FUJIAN)
Fu-Chau (Fuzhou)

Hong Kong

Formosa (Taiwan)

Formosa Channel
(Straits of Taiwan)

PACIFIC
OCEAN

PHILIPPINE
ISLANDS
(REPUBLIC OF
THE PHILIPPINES)

Manila

Sulu
Sea

Palawan

South
China
Sea

VIETNAM

Haiphong

TONKIN
Hanoi

LAOS

CHINA

Ho Chi Minh City

Pulo Condor
(Côn Sơ'n Island)

CAMBODIA

SIAM
(THAILAND)

Bangkok

Gulf of Siam

500 kilometers

0

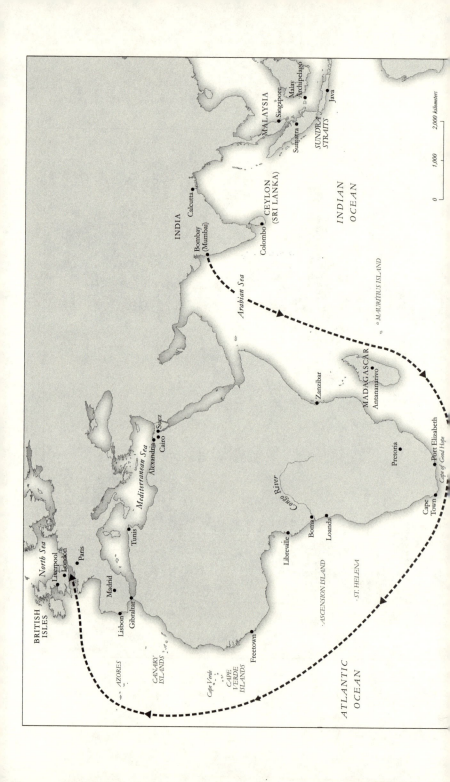

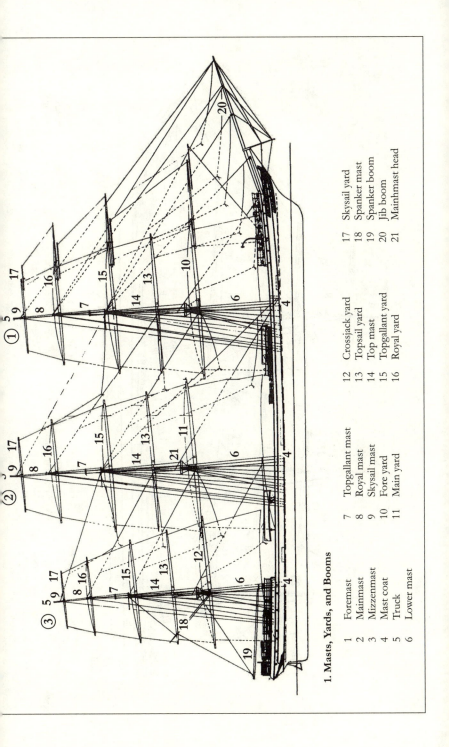

1. Masts, Yards, and Booms

1 Foremast
2 Mainmast
3 Mizzenmast
4 Mast coat
5 Truck
6 Lower mast

7 Topgallant mast
8 Royal mast
9 Skysail mast
10 Fore yard
11 Main yard

12 Crossjack yard
13 Topsail yard
14 Top mast
15 Topgallant yard
16 Royal yard

17 Skysail yard
18 Spanker mast
19 Spanker boom
20 Jib boom
21 Mainmast head

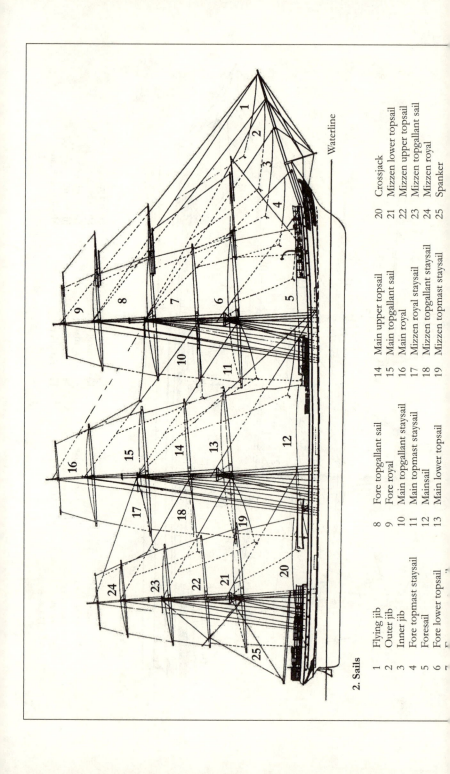

Waterline

2. Sails

1	Flying jib
2	Outer jib
3	Inner jib
4	Fore topmast staysail
5	Foresail
6	Fore lower topsail
7	
8	Fore topgallant sail
9	Fore royal
10	Main topgallant staysail
11	Main topmast staysail
12	Mainsail
13	Main lower topsail
14	Main upper topsail
15	Main topgallant sail
16	Main royal
17	Mizzen royal staysail
18	Mizzen topgallant staysail
19	Mizzen topmast staysail
20	Crossjack
21	Mizzen lower topsail
22	Mizzen upper topsail
23	Mizzen topgallant sail
24	Mizzen royal
25	Spanker

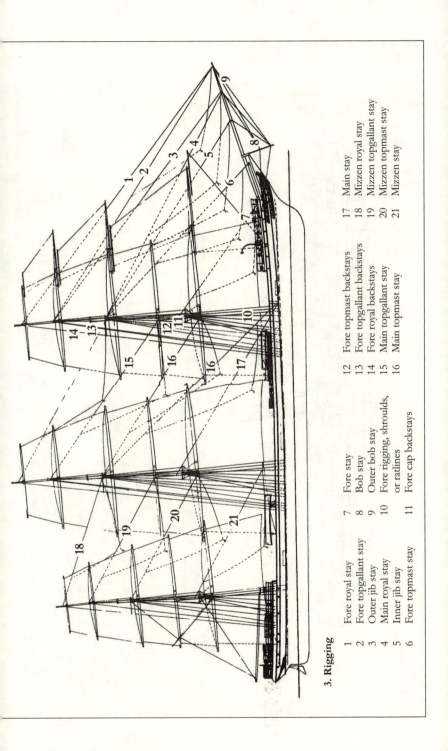

3. Rigging

1	Fore royal stay
2	Fore topgallant stay
3	Outer jib stay
4	Main royal stay
5	Inner jib stay
6	Fore topmast stay
7	Fore stay
8	Bob stay
9	Outer bob stay
10	Fore rigging, shrouds, or ratlines
11	Fore cap backstays
12	Fore topmast backstays
13	Fore topgallant backstays
14	Fore royal backstays
15	Main topgallant stay
16	Main topmast stay
17	Main stay
18	Mizzen royal stay
19	Mizzen topgallant stay
20	Mizzen topmast stay
21	Mizzen stay

4. To Heave To

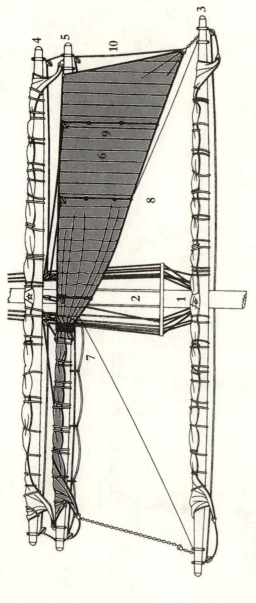

4a

When a sailing ship was in a contrary gale of wind the order to heave to meant that most of the sails were taken in and the helm was put down. This kept the ship's head to the wind, and, with the sea on the bow, she would ride well enough as long as some sail could be carried. This full-rigged ship has the fore topmast staysail, the mizzen staysail, and the goose-winged main lower topsail set. To furl the weather half of a lower topsail was the last resource to shorten sail without having to furl all and drift under bare poles. The large-scale drawing shows a part of the mainmast with the goose-winged lower topsail.

1 Mainmast
2 Heel of topmast
3 Mainyard with
   mainsail furled
4 Upper topsail yard
   with topsail furled
5 Lower topsail yard
6 Goose-winged lower
   topsail

7 Heavy lashing on sail,
   parcelled to protect
   sail from chafe
8 Size of lower topsail
   when set
9 Lower topsail
   buntlines
10 Lower topsail
   clewlines

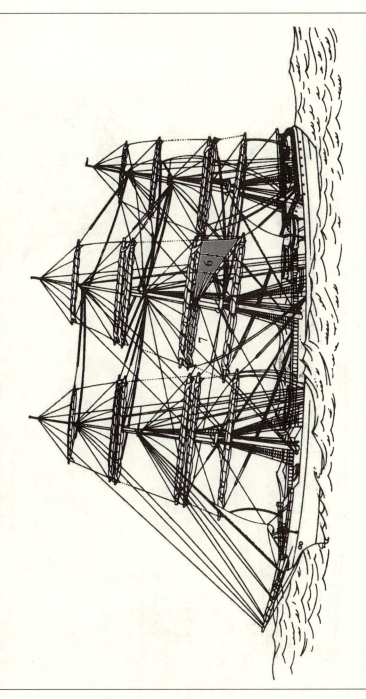

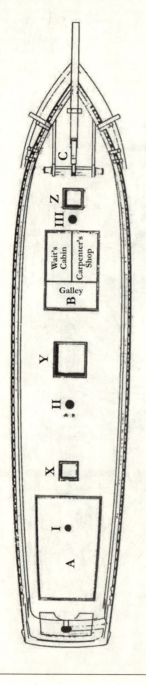

5. Deck Plan and Forecastle Layout

The deck plan, above, of the *Narcissus* shows three masts (I, II, III) coming out of the deck, three hatches (X, Y, Z) in the deck, the cabinhouse (A) for officers on the poop deck at the stern, the deckhouse (B) (with galley, carpenter's shop, and the sail locker converted into a cabin for James Wait) amidships, and the forecastle (C) for the sailors below deck in the bow, from the fore hatch (Z) forward. The detail plan, to the right, shows the below-deck layout of the forecastle:

1   Upper and lower bunks
2   Hawse pipes
3   Bowsprit
4   Cable compressors
5   Fore peak hatch
6   Windlass
7   Hatch to chain locker
Z   Fore hatch

Glossary of Nautical Terms

This glossary briefly defines the various nautical, shipping, and related terms that appear in this volume. In preparing this glossary, I am indebted to *Sailor's Word-Book* by Admiral W. H. Smyth and E. Belcher (1867); *A Dictionary of Sailing* by F. H. Burgess (Penguin, 1961); *Dictionary of Nautical Words and Terms* by C. W. T. Layton and Peter Clissold (Maritime Books, 1981); *International Maritime Dictionary*, 2nd ed., by René Kerchove (Van Nostrand Reinhold, 1961); *The Oxford Companion to Ships & the Sea*, edited by Peter Kemp (Oxford University Press, 1976); *The Mariner's Dictionary* by Gershom Bradford (Barre, 1982); *The Facts on File Dictionary of Nautical Terms* by Thompson Lenfestey and Tom Lenfestey (Facts on File, 1994); *Dictionary of Marine Engineering and Nautical Terms* by G. O. Watson (George Newnes, 1964); and *The Marine Encyclopaedic Dictionary*, 3rd ed., by Eric Sullivan (Lloyd's of London Press, 1992). Italicized words appear elsewhere in the glossary. Special thanks to Mark D. Larabee for his help in compiling this glossary. For illustrations of many terms in this glossary, see pp. 337–42.

aback   The wind filling a *sail* from the opposite direction than intended, causing a ship to move in reverse or to stop.

abaft   See *aft*.

abeam   In line at a right angle to a ship's length; opposite the center of a vessel's side.

able seaman (able-bodied seaman or A. B.)   Experienced seaman, able to perform all duties in boats or on *deck*.

accommodation ladder   A long ladder with railings or ropes, lowered outside a ship to boat level.

adrift   Floating or moving at random.

aft (after)   At the *stern* of a ship or near that area.

after-braces   *Braces* in the *after* end of a ship.

after-capstan   The *capstan* in the *after* end of a ship.

afterdeck   The section of a ship's deck past *amidships* and toward the *stern*.

after-end   The part of a ship *abaft* the center, toward the *stern*.

after grating   Open woodwork made from crosspieces and acting as a covering for the *stern hatchway*.

after-hatch   The *hatch* in the *after* end of a ship.

aftermost   Farthest toward the *aft* of a vessel.

afterpart   The part of a ship near the back or *stern*.

after rail   Railing at the back or *aft* portion of the ship.

after-yards   The *yards* at the *after-end* of a ship.

ahoy   General nautical greeting to call attention.

all aback   Condition of the *sails* all pushed *aback* or *aft* by the wind.

alleyway   A short corridor or passageway below deck.

amidships   The middle (either by length or breadth) of a ship.

anchor   A large heavy instrument used to hold a ship in place.

anchor, to   To lower a ship's *anchor* to keep the vessel from drifting.

anchor cable   A heavy *cable* used to hold a ship at *anchor*.

anchorage   A ground or place that is suitable for safe *anchoring*.

anchor shackle   See *shackle*.

anchor watch(man)   A single man or small number of men on duty to watch for danger while a ship is at *anchor*.

answer the helm   When a ship obeys the *rudder*.

articles   Contract signed by one joining a ship's *crew*, stipulating the requirements of a position.

ashore   On land or aground.

astern   The back or *stern* of a vessel or any distance behind a ship.

athwartship(s) (athwart)   Transversely, from one side to the other, across the ship.

awash   Level with the surface of the sea.

away   Order to depart or a statement indicating that a person or boat has departed.

away aloft   A command to climb to one's station in the *rigging*.

awning   Covering made usually made of *canvas* over a ship's *deck*.

backstays   Wires or ropes attached to the *mastheads* and connecting to the sides of a ship for added support.

backwash   The motion of a receding wave.

ballast, to   To place weighted material in a ship to stabilize it.

bar   Sandbank or accumulation of silt at the entrance of an inlet or harbor.

bare poles   Having no *sails* raised on a ship's *masts*.

bark   Small sailing ship with a square *stern*, usually a three-masted vessel.

barometer   Instrument that measures changes in atmospheric pressures that indicate changing weather conditions.

barque   See *bark*.

batten   Long, narrow metal slats or strips of wood.

batten down, to   To secure *hatches* with tarpaulins or other covers by means of *battens*.

baulk   Square *beam* of timber.

beam   Broadest part of a ship; a wood or steel bar, used to support the *deck*.

beam ends   A ship is on its *beam ends* when it has turned over to one side so far that *beams* are approaching a vertical position.

bearings   The direction from which a point lies from a point of reference, particularly as measured in degrees from one of the *quarters* of the *compass*.

beat, to   To sail against the wind by zigzagging.

before the mast   Working sailors as distinguished from the ship's officers.

before the wind   When a sailing vessel runs directly with the wind.

belaying pin   One of a number or wooden or metal pegs, fixed in racks in various sections of a vessel, around which ropes can be made secure.

bells   A bell is sounded every half hour to indicate how many half-hour periods have elapsed in a four-hour *watch*.

bend, to   To fasten a rope to another rope or object.

bend a sail, to   To extend or make fast a *sail* to its *stay* or *yard*.

bengal light (blue light)   Pyrotechnic flare for signaling at night.

berth   Position as a *crew* member; accommodations for a ship's *crew*.

bight   Loop or bend in a rope.

bilge   Lowest inside part of a ship's *hull*.

billet   Place assigned for sleeping; also used metaphorically to mean a position on a ship.

binnacle   Box or case for holding a ship's *compass*.

binnacle glass   Glass part of the *binnacle*.

binnacle lamp   Light attached to the *binnacle* for reading the *compass* at night.

binnacle light   See *binnacle lamp*.

binnacle stand   Stand that houses the *binnacle*.

bitts   Strong, wooden or metal vertical posts for securing ropes.

block   Metal or wooden casing containing a wheel or sheave, through which ropes are passed; a pulley-like device.

bluejackets   Colloquial term for Royal Navy seamen.

board, to   To come onto a ship.

boatswain   Officer responsible for *rigging*, *sails*, *anchors*, *cables*, and so on and who calls the *crew* to duty.

bolster   Circular or other shaped *canvas* or timber pads to prevent rope or *cable* from chafing.

boom   Long *spar* that goes out from a different part of a ship to extend the foot of a *sail*.

boss'n   See *boatswain*.

bow   Forward section of a ship, beginning at the point at which the ship curves toward its *stem*.

bowsprit   *Spar* extending from the *bow* and to which the *sails* are fastened.

brace   Ropes attached to each of a ship's *yards* for adjusting the *sails*.

brace up the yards   Command to bring the *yards* toward a *fore-and-aft* direction.

breach, to   When the sea breaks over a vessel in bad weather.

break   Sudden rise of a *deck* that is not flush.

breakers   Waves that break over rocks, reefs, or shallows.

break ground, to   To begin pulling an *anchor* in.

break of the poop   Forward section of the *poop deck;* see *break.*

bridge   Raised platform above the *upper deck* with a clear view all around and from which a ship is navigated.

bridge ladder   The ladder leading to the *bridge.*

bridge rail   The railing around the *bridge.*

bring up, to   To come to a stop.

bucket rack   Rack for holding fire-fighting buckets; located on the *poop deck.*

bulkhead   Vertical partition separating sections below *deck;* some bulkheads are built to make a compartment watertight.

bulkhead lamp   A lamp mounted on a *bulkhead* wall.

bulwark   The sides around a ship above *deck* for protection to keep water from easily coming on board and to keep equipment or people from easily falling overboard.

bumboat   A boat carrying vegetables, provisions, and small merchandise for sale to ships.

bunker   Compartment for storing coal or other fuel for a ship.

buntline   Rope that passes from the *footrope* to the *mast* and then to the *deck* to help in *hauling sails.*

buoy   A floating object used to mark navigable areas.

by the run   To let a rope run without hindrance.

cabin   A room or compartment where officers or passengers reside.

cable   See *anchor cable.*

cant   Corner or angle.

canvas   Literally a heavy cloth; also used metaphorically to mean a ship's *sails.*

capping sea   A sea with white caps.

capstan   Mechanical device for lifting heavy weights, such as heavy *cables* or ropes. Capstans may be located in various places on a ship.

capstan bar   A bar used somewhat like a *handspike* but to move the *capstan.*

captain   The commander of a vessel; see *master.*

cargo   Any merchandise, goods, or other materials conveyed in a ship from one destination to another.

cargo gear   The general term for the *gear* located near the *cargo hatches* and used for loading or unloading *cargo.*

cast, to   When getting *under way,* to point in the direction to *tack* properly.

catch a turn   A quick turn of a rope around a *belaying pin* or other object to temporarily hold a weight.

certificate   A license to work aboard a ship.

chain cable   See *anchor cable.*

chain compressor   A mechanism for preventing a chain from running out too quickly.

chain sheet   A chain connected to the bottom lower corner of a *sail* and used for changing a *sail.*

charter party   Contract between a merchant and a shipowner to charter a ship, specifying the terms under which the ship is hired.

chart room   A space or room on or near the *bridge* for housing charts and other materials used for navigating a ship.

check, to   To stop or impede a ship's progress.

check-rope   A rope used *to check* the *way* of a docking ship.

chief engineer   The crew member in charge of the engine room in a *steamship* and responsible for the ship's engine and machinery.

chief mate   The officer responsible for carrying out the *captain*'s orders and for handling the *cargo;* he is in command of the ship when the *captain* is not on board, is in charge of the *port watch,* and supervises from the *forecastle* when the *crew* is called on *deck.*

chronometer   An instrument for keeping accurate time, particularly used for navigation.

clear, to   To escape from.

cleared for   Prepared for.

clear for running   A rope that has been coiled so that it can run freely.

cleat   Small metal or wooden fitting on which a rope can be tied.

clock calm   When there is so little wind that the water does not even ripple.

close-hauled   Setting a ship's *sails* in such a way as to sail as close to the wind as possible.

coalhole   The *coaling hatchways* in the lower *decks.*

coal bunker   An area for storing the coal used to fuel the engine in a *steamship.*

coaling   Taking on a supply of coal.

coal lighter   A *lighter* used for transporting coal.

coal locker   A container for storing coal for the cook's coal stove.

coal trimmer   *Crew* member assigned to *stow* and *trim* coal.

coal waggon   A derogatory term for a ship carrying a *cargo* of coal.

coamings   Raised metal or wooden edges around *hatches* to prevent water from running down the *hatches* from the *deck.*

cockbilled   An *anchor* suspended and ready to be dropped.

come (a)round, to   To turn toward the wind.

come up, to   While continuing on the same *tack,* to come closer to the wind.

coming to   Coming to a standstill, rest or fixed position.

commodore   A naval rank above a *captain* and below an admiral.

companion   A covering above a ladder or entrance to keep the weather out; sometimes used interchangeably with *companionway.*

companionway   Ladder or stairway connecting one *deck* to another; often referring specifically to a ladder or stairway leading from the *deck* to a *cabin* below.

compass   A device that indicates the direction a ship is traveling.

compass card   Card to which the *compass* needles are attached and with directions and degrees inscribed.

compass lamp   See *binnacle lamp.*

compressors   See *chain compressor.*

consignee of cargo   The person in whose care a consignment of goods is entrusted.

counter   The underside of the overhang of the *stern* above the *waterline.*

cowl Moveable, protective hood usually over a ventilator duct, but Conrad also refers to a cowl over the *binnacle* in *The Shadow-Line*.

coxswain (cockswain) *Crew* member who steers a ship's boat and, after the officer in command, is in charge of the *crew* (pronounced *coxsun*).

crank A ship given to leaning to one side because of loading or construction.

crew All officers and men aboard a ship, a ship's company.

crosshead A supporting piece across the top of a cylinder in a steam engine; also a supporting piece over other types of machinery.

cross swell Similar to a cross sea, a *swell* of water caused by the wind and shifting direction.

cruiser A small *man-of-war*.

cuddy A compartment, often under the *poop*, where officers eat their meals.

davits Crane-like mechanisms for hoisting or lowering a boat.

dead before Straight ahead.

dead calm Completely calm.

deadeye A round, flat wooden *block* with three holes in it, though which *shroud lanyards* are *rove*.

dead water Eddy water below a ship's *counter* that moves slower than the water alongside.

deck Platforms laid over a ship's *beams*.

deckhouse Square or oblong *cabin* on a ship's *deck*.

deep ship A ship that *draws water* extensively.

demurrage Money due to a shipowner for a ship that is delayed beyond the time specified in the *charter party*.

derrick A *spar*, supported by *guys* and *stays*, used for loading and unloading a ship.

dhow A traditional Arab single-masted sailing vessel on the Arabian Sea with triangular *sails*; at times used for any Arab sailing vessel.

discharge When a ship completes its contracted voyage, *cargo* is unloaded and the *crew* disbanded.

dismasted A state in which a ship's *masts* are either blown off by winds or cut off purposely.

dock A location, usually artificial, to which a ship can be *moored* for loading or unloading.

dock, to To draw a ship into place next to a *dock*.

doctor A nickname for a ship's cook, who was also responsible for first aid.

dodger A screen of *canvas* or some other material erected for protection from the elements.

dogwatch Two two-hour periods between 4 P.M. and 8 P.M., sometimes called first and last (or second) dog.

donkeyman The *crew* member responsible for overseeing the auxiliary boiler or donkey boiler and assisting in the *engine room*.

downhaul A rope used to pull or *haul* down a *sail* when *shortening* a *sail*.

draw   To receive enough wind to inflate a *sail*.

draw water   The number of feet of water in which a ship is submerged.

dry dock   A *dock* into which a ship can enter or be pulled and from which the water is evacuated so that repairs can be carried out on it.

earing   A small rope employed to fasten a *sail* to its *yard*.

eight bells   See *bells*.

engineers   *Crew* members in charge of the machinery in *steamships*.

engine room   The room in a *steamship* that contains the engine that drives the ship.

engine-room telegraph   A dial and pointer on the *bridge* that allows signals to be sent to the *engine room*.

even keel   To sail smoothly, with the *keel* appearing not to move side to side or up and down.

fair wind   Favorable wind.

fall   A rope used for lowering or hoisting *cargo*; also, used for the apparatus used to lower or hoist such *cargo*.

fiddle   Strip of wood or cords running through wooden frames and along the edges of a table to prevent objects from sliding off; also may refer to a similar strip surrounding a *hatch*.

fids   Conical pins of hardwood used for opening the strands of rope when *splicing*.

fife rail   The rail around a *mast* that holds *belaying pins*.

fire door   A door to a *steamship*'s engine into which coal is shoveled to be burned as fuel.

fireman   The *crew* member responsible for the fires in the boiler room that provide the power for a *steamship*.

first mate   See *chief mate*.

fishing stakes   Stakes between which nets are secured to catch fish.

flatten in, to   To *haul* in the *aft*-most corner of a sail to allow for greater turning ability.

fluke   One or the other hook of an *anchor*, resembling the tail of a whale.

flywheel   A wheel attached to a rod to regulate motion and/or speed.

fo'c'sle   See *forecastle*.

footrope   Ropes strung under the *yardarm*, *bowsprit*, etc., for the *crew* to stand on.

fore   That part of a ship toward its *stem* or in that direction.

fore and aft   Front to back, *stem to stern, forward* and *aft*.

fore-bitts   *Bitts* in the *fore* part of a ship.

forebrace   Rope attached to the *fore yardarms* for changing the position of the *foresail*.

forecastle   A compartment in the *forward* part of a ship reserved for the *crew*'s quarters (pronounced *foksul*).

forecastle head   The *deck* or roof *forward*.

forecastle ladder   The ladder leading into or out of the *forecastle*.

foredeck   The part of the *deck* from the *foremast* to the *bow*.

forefoot   The *forward*-most part of the *keel* where it meets the lower extremity of the *stem*.

forehatch   The *hatch* in the *fore* part of a ship.

fore lazy tack   A running *bight* on the *tack* of a *fore-and-aft topsail;* it fits around a *stay* to prevent the *sail* from blowing away when hoisted.

foreman   The individual in charge of a group of workers.

foremast   The *forward*-most *mast* of a ship with several *masts.*

foremost   Farthest toward the *fore* of a vessel.

forepart   The *forward* part.

forepeak   The narrowed part of a ship's *hold,* near the *bow.*

forepeak hatch   The *hatch* in the *forepeak.*

fore rigging   *Rigging* in the *fore* part of a ship.

foresail   Main *sail* on *foremast.*

foresheets   The inner part of the *bows,* often fitted with a platform for standing.

foreshore   The part of the shore that lies between the high- and low-water marks.

foreside   The side to the *fore* of a ship.

forestay   The *stay* of the *foremast.*

foretack   The rope used to keep the *windward* or *weather* corner of the *foresail* in place.

fore topsail   The *topsail* on the *foremast.*

fore 'tween-deck   The space between *decks* in the *forward* part of a ship.

foreworks   The *forward* parts of a ship above *deck.*

foreyards   The *yards* or *spars* supporting *sails* on the *foremast.*

forward   Toward the *fore* of a ship.

forward 'tween-deck   See *fore 'tween deck.*

four bells   See *bells.*

freshening gale   A *gale* that is increasing.

friction winch   Mechanical drum apparatus used to pull on lines by the friction created by the line wrapped around it.

full   When the *sails* are fully inflated by the wind.

full and by   Sailing as close to the wind as possible without the *sails* shivering.

funnel   Cylindrical metal pipe through which exhaust from a steam engine escapes; a smokestack.

furl, to   To roll up and tie a *sail* on its *boom* or *yard.*

gaff   A *spar* that extends the *heads* of *fore-and-aft* sails.

gale   A strong wind.

galley   A ship's kitchen.

gangway   A ladder or similar accomodation between a vessel and the shore by which individuals leave or enter a ship.

gantline   A rope passed through a *block* aloft and used for hoisting *sails* or other objects.

gaskets   Rope or other material used for securing *furled sails* to a *yard.*

gather way, to   To start to feel the force of the wind on the *sails* as the ship begins to obey its *helm*.

gear   A generic term for a ship's *rigging*.

gimbals   Two concentric brass rings by which a *compass, chronometer*, or lamp is suspended to counteract the ship's motion.

gin block   See *gins*.

gins   A pulley-like apparatus for hoisting and moving *cargo*.

girder   A heavy supporting *beam*.

good full   Full of wind.

goosewinged   A *sail* that is partially furled (resembling a wing) to avoid the full brunt of the wind.

gunboat   A small boat fitted with one or more cannons in the *bow*.

guy   A rope used for steadying a weight.

half cable   Half the length of a *cable*.

half deck   The space between the foremost steerage's *bulkhead* and the *forepart* of the *quarterdeck*.

half tide   Halfway between high and low tide.

half-tide cavern   A shoreline cave half-covered at *half tide*.

half-tide rock   A rock whose head is visible at *half tide*.

halyards   Ropes employed for hoisting or lowering *sails*.

handspike   A wooden lever (usually made of ash) for moving the *windlass* to pull up the *anchor* or move other heavy objects.

harbor launch   A *steam launch* for transporting harbor officials.

harbor master   The official in charge of seeing that harbor regulations are observed.

harbor office   The office for the administration of maritime affairs in a colonial region.

hard alee   Command to put the *helm* to the *leeward* to change the *tack*.

hard up   To put the *helm* as far over to the *windward* side as possible.

hatch   The covering over a *hatchway*.

hatchway   An opening on a ship's *deck* leading to the interior of a ship.

hatchway ladder   The ladder leading from a *hatchway*.

haul, to   To pull on a rope—to raise a *sail*, for example.

haul out   See *haul, to*.

hawseholes   Holes cut into the *bow* of a ship on both sides of the *stem* through which *cables* are passed and attached to *anchors*.

hawsepipe   A piping placed in the *hawseholes* to prevent *cables* passing through them from cutting into the wood.

hawser   A rope larger than a *cable* but smaller than a *towrope*.

head   The front or top of anything on a ship.

head earings   A rope used to *haul out* the *earings*.

headlands   A steep piece of land jutting out into the water.

head of steam   A confined body of steam kept at a particular pressure to supply the force necessary to run a steam engine.

head sea   A sea where the waves oppose the course of a ship.

head sheets   A chain or rope attached to one or both corners of the *jib* and *staysails* that are *before the mast*.

head wind   A wind blowing directly against the course of a ship.

heave in, to   To shorten the *anchor cable.*

heave short, to   To draw the *anchor cable* in until a ship is nearly over the *anchor* so that the vessel is ready to sail on command.

heel   The junction of the *aft*-end of a ship's *keel* and lower end of the *sternpost.* Also, the lower end of any *boom, mast,* or the *bowsprit.*

heel over   For a ship to lie or incline to one side or the other.

helm   The lever or handle (*tiller*) attached to the *rudder* and used for turning the *rudder* and steering a ship; sometimes used to refer to the entire steering mechanism.

helmsman   *Crew* member responsible for steering a ship.

helm up   See *put the help up.*

hold   A large compartment below the *decks* for stowing *cargo,* provisions, or equipment.

holystone   White sandstone used for scrubbing the *decks.*

hook   A hook and eye that keeps a door partway open and prevents it from swinging back and forth. Sometimes slang for *anchor.*

hooker   Originally a two-masted Dutch ship, later colloquial for any ship.

hook pots   Tin cans fitted to hang on the bars of the galley stove.

house flag   A flag specially designed as the insignia of a shipping company and flown on its vessels.

hove to   To be brought to a standstill.

hulk   A ship no longer seaworthy.

hull   The body or outer frame of a ship.

inboard   Within the ship.

International Signal Code Book   A book containing descriptions of the various signals used in the maritime trade.

jetty   A small *pier* where boats can *dock* or be *moored.*

jib   A large triangular *sail* connected to the *jibboom* and the *foremast.*

jibboom   A *spar* extending *forward* from the *bowsprit.*

joiner   On a ship, a cabinetmaker or worker with finer woodworking tasks than a carpenter.

kalashes   Malay seamen (Malay).

keel   A piece of wood that extends the length of a ship and acts like a backbone to a ship.

keelson   An internal *keel,* built on the floor of a ship just above the *keel,* that connects the floor to the *keel.*

kid   A small, shallow wooden tub, usually circular.

land breezes   Breezes that blow out seaward when the temperature of the land falls below that of the sea.

landlubber   A landsman who knows nothing of nautical matters.

lanyard   A short length of rope fastened to something to make it secure or to serve as a handle.

lanyard knot   A decorative knot tied on the end of a *lanyard,* sometimes called a diamond knot or knife lanyard knot.

lascar An East Indian sailor (Urdu).

lash, to To use a rope to fasten any moveable object on a ship.

lashing A rope used to *lash* something.

lay aft, to To place oneself *aft*. To go *aft*.

lay down Place on the deck to prepare for use.

leading wind A wind *on the quarter* or *abeam*, or a *fair wind* as opposed to a slight wind.

lead line The line attached to the *sounding lead*.

lee The side opposite the direction the wind is blowing.

lee braces The *braces* (used to turn the *yards*) on the *lee* side of the ship.

leech The sloping or perpendicular edge of a *sail*.

leech line A rope fastened to the *leeches* of *sails* to aid in *furling* the *sails*.

lee rail The rail on the *lee* side of the ship.

leeward Toward the *lee*, the side opposite the direction the wind is blowing.

let go, to To cast or release something.

libertymen Seamen on leave.

lifelines Lines stretched around a ship above the *deck* to prevent *crew* members from being washed overboard in bad weather.

lift, to As used in *The Shadow-Line*, the movement of the ship's *hull* upward from the *waterline*.

lifts Ropes that reach from the *masthead* to the ends of its *yardarm*, either to keep the ends at equilibrium or to raise one end higher than the other.

lighter A large, flat-bottomed open boat used to load or unload *cargo* from a ship.

light-screens Screens mounted on navigation lights to restrict the arc of visibility in which the lights could be seen from other vessels.

light-to To stop *hauling* on a *line*.

light vessels Vessels carrying lights to guide ships.

lines A general designation for a variety of small ropes used on a ship.

list, to For a ship to incline or careen to one side.

lobby An apartment or antechamber close to the main *cabin bulkhead*.

log (logbook) The journal in which are recorded the daily important aspects of a sea journey.

lower mast The principal *mast* that carries the other *masts* above it.

low-pressure cylinder A particular cylinder on a reciprocating steam engine.

lubber A new or inexperienced sailor.

main brace The *brace* or rope that connects to the *mainmast* for *trimming* the *sails*.

main hatch See *hatch*.

mainmast The primary *mast* of a sailing ship, located *amidships*.

main pump The largest pump, near the *mainmast*.

mainsail The largest and lowest *sail* on the *mainmast*.

mainsail haul   The order given during *tacking* to *haul* the *after-yards* round when a vessel is almost *head* to wind.

main-topsail   The *mainmast's* second *sail*, above the *mainsail*.

mainyard   The lower *yard* to which the *mainsail* is tied.

Manila line   A rope made from fibers from the abaca banana plant of the Philippines, not subject to rot from seawater and not needing to be *tarred*.

man-of-war   A ship equipped for warfare.

marine boiler   A boiler designed for powering *steamships*.

Marine Office   A section of the Board of Trade in charge of such matters as signing on, paying off, and shipping.

Marine Superintendent   See *harbormaster*.

marlinspike   A pointed iron spike used to separate rope strands for splicing with another rope.

mast   A long, large cylindrical piece of timber positioned at right angles to a ship's *deck*, to which are attached a ship's *sails*, *yard-arms*, and related equipment.

mastheads   The uppermost parts of a *mast*.

master   See *shipmaster*.

Master Attendant   The individual responsible for supervising maritime affairs in a colonial port.

mate   Often used as an abbreviation for the *chief mate* or *first mate*.

mates   The officers next in command to the *captain* or *master*. Mates are divided into *first mate* (*chief mate*), second mate, and *third mate*, in order of seniority.

midship   See *amidships*.

midship-stop   A *stop* near the middle of a *sail*.

mizzen   The *aftermost mast* on a three-masted vessel, the third *mast* from the *fore* end in a ship of four or five *masts*.

mizzenmast (mizenmast)   See *mizzen*.

mizzen rigging   The *rigging* accompanying the *mizzen*.

mizzen topsail   The *topsail* on the *mizzenmast*.

moor, to   To secure a vessel by means of *anchors* to the sea bottom or by ropes or chains to the shore or a buoy.

mooring-bitts   *Bitts* or strong vertical posts on a ship's *deck* or on a wharf (usually in pairs), used for attaching ropes or chains for *mooring* a ship.

muster, to   To assemble the *crew* of a ship.

nip, to   To secure a rope.

offshore tack   A *tack* designed to move a ship away from shore.

old man   Slang for the *master* or *captain*.

old salt   Slang for a well-seasoned sailor.

on the cant   Anything at a slanting position.

on the quarter   Something outside the ship that is visible from a direction near the *stern* but on either side of it.

ordinary seaman   The lowest rank of sailor, competent in a variety of tasks aboard a ship but below the abilities of an *able seaman*.

overhaul, to   To release or take strain off of something.
overhaul the gear   To check, refit, and refasten the *gear*.

paddle wheels   The wheels on either side of a *steamer*, driven by steam, that propel the ship.
paid off   When a ship's *head* falls off from the wind and drops to *leeward*; also when a ship's crew is paid their wages at the end of a voyage.
painter   The rope connected to the *stem* of a boat, used to secure or tow it.
petty officer   The rank between a ship's officers and its *crew*.
pier   A structure of wood or stone built along or at an angle to the water's edge to aid in loading or unloading a vessel.
pier head   The seaward end of *pier*.
pin   See *belaying pin*.
pinnace   A small vessel, often attached to a *man-of-war*.
point   A low promontory of land projecting out into the sea.
pole mast   A *mast* made of a single *spar*.
poop   The raised *deck* in the *afterpart* of a ship.
poop ladder   The ladder leading to the *poop deck*.
port   The left side of the ship when looking forward; also used to refer to a *porthole*.
porthole   Holes in the side of a ship to allow in light and air or for other purposes.
ports   See *porthole*.
port watch   The *watch* on the *port* side of a ship.
pull fair, to   To pull hard.
pump   A mechanism for pumping water into or out of a vessel.
pump leather   Leather used to seal a *pump*.
pump nails   Nails used to nail the leather onto a *pump's* box.
pump-rods   Connecting rods on a *pump*.
punt   A small, flat-bottomed boat.
put her head on, to   To steer a ship directly into oncoming *swells*.
put round, to   To put a ship onto a new *tack*.
put the helm down, to   To position the *helm* so that the *rudder* turns to *windward*.
put the helm up, to   To position the *helm* so that the *rudder* turns to *leeward* (away from the wind).

quay   A strengthened bank or artificial embankment along a water-way for convenient loading or unloading of *cargo*.
quarter   Strictly speaking, the point forty-five degrees *aft* from the *beam* on either side of a ship; more generally referring to any point in that general area.
quarter checks   Ropes extended from each side of a ship to *docks* to keep the ship centered while docked.
quarterdeck   The section of the upper *deck* to the *aft* of the *mainmast*.
quarterdeck capstan   The *capstan* on the *quarterdeck*.
quarterdeck port   A *porthole* on the *quarterdeck*.
quarter hatch   See *hatch*.

ratlines   Small lines horizontally connecting *shrouds*, forming footholds or handholds.

reach   A section of a river, channel, or lake lying between two bends; a straight navigable section of water.

ready about   Command to prepare for *tacking*.

Red Ensign   A red flag with a Union Flag miniature in the upper left corner; the official flag of the British Merchant Marine Service.

reef, to   To take in or roll up part of a *sail* so that a smaller area may be exposed to the wind.

reeve, to   To pass the end of a rope through a block or any opening or cavity.

reeve clear, to   See *to reeve.*

relieving tackle   *Tackle* attached to each side of the *tiller* to relieve stress, particularly during bad weather.

riding light   A light displayed *forward* from sunset to sunrise when a ship is lying at anchor.

rigging   All of the chains, ropes, wire, etc., employed to support the *spars, sails, masts,* and *booms.*

ringbolt   A bolt with a ring attached to fasten *tackle* or ropes.

roads   See *roadstead.*

roadstead   A stretch of water near shore that provides shelter for ships at anchor.

roll   An oscillation of a ship to one side or the other.

roller   A large oceanic *swell.*

rolling   The oscillating motion of a ship from side to side by the force of the waves.

rolling chocks   The *bilge keel.*

rope, to   To sew a rope (called a boltrope) into a *sail, awning,* or some other item made of *canvas* to reinforce it.

round, to be   A ship whose *head* has successfully moved from one side of the wind's direction to the other.

rove, to   See *to reeve.*

royal   The *sail* set next above the *topgallant sail.*

rudder   A flat wooden or metal instrument attached to the *stern* of a ship below water level that can be turned to steer the ship.

rudder casing   A casing that surrounds the *rudder* post, running from the *hull* to the *deck.*

rudder chains   Chains attached to the *rudder* to hold it if it becomes dislodged; also sometimes used for emergency steering.

run   The *after part* of a ship.

running   See *to run.*

running away   Traveling at a rate not to be checked.

run, to   To travel; of a *sail:* to be raised.

run ashore   To run a ship into the shore.

run of the sea   The regular movement of the sea in a particular direction.

run square   See *to square the yards.*

sailcloth Cloth used for making lighter *canvas sails* for lifeboats rather than the *sails* for sailing ships.

sail locker Compartment for storing *sails*.

sailmaker The person in charge of making, altering, or repairing a ship's *sails*.

sails See pp. 337–41.

saloon A public room on a ship.

salt junk Salted meat used as food for lengthy voyages.

sampan A Chinese term used by Europeans for any light boat in the Chinese style.

scend, to When a ship ascends or descends the trough of a wave, often used in the case of high seas as during a storm.

scow A large, flat-bottomed boat with square ends and straight sides, typically used as a *lighter* or as a ferry.

screw-brake The brake on the *windlass,* used to stop the movement of the *chain cable.*

scuppers Openings in a ship's side at *deck* level that allow water to run off into the sea.

seadog An old, seasoned sailor.

seaman A sailor below the rank of an officer.

sea room Space at sea without obstruction so that a ship can be easily maneuvered.

seaway Heavy seas.

secondary battery A set of smaller cannons aboard a warship, as opposed to its primary battery of larger ones.

second engineer The crew member next in responsibility to the *chief engineer* and who is in charge of the *engine room* in the absence of the *chief engineer.* The second engineer's duties are not as well-defined as are those of the chief engineer.

second mate The officer responsible for the *starboard watch;* he leads the crew when they are called on deck and leads their handling of some *sails;* he also assists the *chief mate* in handling cargo.

second officer See *second mate.*

senior apprentice A boy under eighteen bound to a ship's *captain* and trained for a career at sea.

set, to To increase the quantity of a *sail* by letting out the *reefs* or by setting more *sails.*

seven bells See *bells.*

sextant An instrument for making angular measurements, especially of the altitude of celestial or distant terrestrial objects, consisting of a graduated arc, originally of one-sixth of a circle (sixty degrees), and a means of sighting the object (*OED*).

shackle A U-shaped bracket with eyes at both ends through which a bolt can be inserted to attach a chain, usually associated with the *anchor cable.*

sheet A rope or chain attached to a *sail*'s corner(s) or its *boom* for controlling the *sail.*

shellback A jocular term for an experienced or hardened sailor.

shift the helm   Command to move the *helm* to the opposite side of the ship from where it currently is.

ship, to   To join a ship.

shipkeeper   The caretaker of a ship after it has arrived in harbor and the *crew* has been *paid off.*

shipmaster   A ship's *captain.*

shipping master   A person responsible for appointing and discharging sailors from ships.

Shipping Office   Office maintained by the Board of Trade. Sailors are engaged there by the *harbor master.*

ship's articles   The written terms under which a ship's *crew* members sign on for a specific voyage.

ship's bread   Hard biscuits.

ship's head   The *bow* or *fore* section of a ship.

shipwright   Shipbuilder.

shoals   A place where the water is shallow.

shore fasts   A large rope to secure a ship to the *quay, pier,* or *anchor* on shore.

shorten sail, to   To reduce the area of the *sails* that are set by replacing larger *sails* with smaller ones, *reefing* the sails, or taking them in.

show a leg, to   To show that one is awake upon being called.

shrouds   Ropes or *cables* extending from a *masthead* to the ship's sides to support the *mast.*

sick bay   A segment of the *fore* of a ship's *main deck,* used as an infirmary.

side ladder   See *accommodation ladder.*

sidelights   Lights affixed to the sides of a ship, green on the *starboard* and red on the *port,* lit while a ship is *under way.*

signal halyards   *Halyards* for hoisting flag signals.

skids   Timber employed as a roller under a vessel to help in moving it along or timber hung over a ship's side to act as a fender.

skylight   A framework in the *deck* to allow light into rooms below *deck.*

slant   A favorable wind.

slat, to   To flap with extreme force.

slice   On a steamship, an iron bar with a blade attached for clearing away debris in a furnace.

slide   A horizontal slide that comes forward to connect the top of the two vertical doors at the top of the companionway.

sounding   Measuring the depth of the water.

sounding lead   A device for determining the depth of the water.

sounding rod   A rod used for *sounding* the depth of water in a ship's *well* to determine whether it needs to be pumped out.

spanker   A *fore-and-aft sail* set on the *aftermost mast.*

spars   A general term for all *masts, yards, booms, gaffs,* and other similar objects.

speaking tube   A tube reaching from one part of a ship to another, through which one *crew* member can speak to another.

splice The joining of two ropes together by interweaving their strands.

spring tides Tides of greater range that occur near the times of the new or full moon.

spunyarn A rope made by weaving together two or more ropes.

squall A sudden, brief and strong gust of wind that does not necessarily blow in the same direction as the prevailing wind.

square sail Quadrilateral *sail* set from the middle of a *yard;* pivots around a *mast.*

square the yards, to To set a *yard* at right angles to the *mast* and the *keel.*

stamp and go, to To move simultaneously and cheerfully with a *brace, halyard,* etc., often accompanied by a fife, fiddle, or to the sound of a sea shanty.

stanchion Any upright support or post.

stand, to To advance toward or depart from a particular object or direction.

stand by, to To be ready to act.

stand clear, to To stay out of the way.

stand from under Command given to those below to keep out of the way of something coming from above.

stand in, to To approach.

stand up, to When a ship on its *beam ends* turns upright; also, the passage of a ship through a particular body of water.

starboard The right side of a ship when looking *forward.*

starboard rail The rail on the *starboard* side of a ship.

starboard watch The *watch* on the *starboard* side of a ship.

starting-gear Mechanism for starting a steam engine by admitting steam through a smaller valve than the main valves.

stateroom The sleeping *cabin* set aside for the *captain* or another high-ranking officer.

stay, to See *tack.*

stays Ropes that steady a *mast* in the *fore-and-aft* direction.

stays, in A state in which a ship has its *head* into the wind and hangs in that position.

staysail A triangular *sail* extended on a *stay.*

steamboat See *steamship.*

steamer See *steamship.*

steam gauge The gauge that indicates the pressure of steam that powers a *steamship's* engine.

steam gear A device that provides steam power to move a ship's *rudder.*

steam launch A large steam-powered boat for transporting supplies or passengers.

steamship A ship powered by steam.

steam valve A valve for controlling the flow of steam.

steam windlass A *windlass* powered by steam.

steerageway The minimum speed required for a vessel to be maneuvered by the *helm.*

steering gear The various parts of the apparatus necessary for steering a ship, such as the steering wheel or *helm.*

stem   The *foremost* vertical piece of a ship that connects the *bows* together with the *keel* and upon which the *bowsprit* rests on the upper end.

stem to stern   The entire length of a ship, from its *foremost* point to its *aftermost* point.

stern   The back or *afterpart* of a vessel.

stern grating   Grating at the *stern* of a ship.

stern sheets   The section of an open boat between the *stern* and the *aftermost athwart*, usually fitted with seats for passengers.

sternway   The backward movement of a ship with the *stern foremost*.

stevedore   A man employed to load and unload ships.

steward   An officer in charge of a ship's stores and managing the serving of meals. He sometimes helps in other capacities as well.

sticks   Sailor slang for the *masts*.

stoker   See *fireman*.

stokehold   The compartment where the *stokers* attend to the ship's furnace.

stokehold ladder   The ladder leading down to the *stokehold*.

stokehold ventilators   Tubes extending from the *stokehold* up to the main deck to catch wind and send it down to the *stokehold* for ventilation.

stop   A piece of rope used to tie off a *sail*.

stow, to   To put something in its proper place.

stream anchor   Smaller than the main *anchor*, it is often used for steadying a ship.

stream cable   The *cable* attached to the *stream anchor*.

studding sails   Fine-weather *sails* that are set outside the *square sails*.

stunsails   *Sails* for fine weather, set on the outside of square *sails* to extend their area.

suit   An entire set of *sails* for a *mast*, ship, or *spar*.

swab   A mop used aboard a ship.

swell   A rolling wave that usually does not break unless it encounters an object.

swing, to   To move with the movement of the wind or the tide.

tack   A small rope that attaches to the corner of some *sails* for manipulating the *sail*.

tack, to   To change course from *starboard* to *port* by bringing the *head* of a ship into the wind and across it in a zigzag fashion.

tackles   A combination of ropes and *blocks* for leverage in lifting *cargo* or other heavy objects.

taffrail   The *aftermost* rail of a ship; sometimes an extension of a ship's *stern*.

take sail off, to   To take down some of the *sails* on a ship.

take the sun, to   To measure the sun's position with a *sextant*.

tally on, to   To get a hold of.

tar   Sap from pine or fir trees, used for waterproofing *rigging*, *canvas*, etc.

telltale compass   A *compass* hanging face downward from a *beam* in the *captain*'s cabin that shows the direction the ship's *head* is pointing.

third engineer   The crew member who helps the *chief engineer* and *second engineer* with the responsibilities of the ship's engine and machinery.

third mate   The officer belonging to the *port watch;* leads in handling *sails* not coordinated by the *second mate* and takes on some of the *second mate's* duties while in port; not included in every ship's crew.

tide-rode   When a ship at *anchor* is swung by the pull of the tides.

tiller   See *helm.*

topgallant   A quadrilateral *sail,* set above the *topsails.*

topgallant rail   The railing above the *topgallant bulwarks.*

topmast   The *mast* immediately above a *lower mast.*

topping breakers   *Swelling* or cresting *breakers.*

topsail   The second *sail* above the *deck* on a given *mast* (pronounced *topsul*).

topside   All of the ship from the main *deck* and above.

towrope   A heavy *hawser* used for towing a ship.

trim, to   To adjust or arrange the *sails* according to the wind.

trucks   Wooden disks at the top of a *mast* with holes in them for *halyards.*

trysail   A *fore-and-aft sail* used in heavy weather.

tug (tugboat)   A boat used for towing a ship in or out of a harbor.

turn the hands up   To call the *crew* to their work stations.

'tween-deck   The space between two decks, usually between the *main deck* and the *deck* below. It can also refer to a *deck* between the *main deck* and the *hold.*

under bare poles   When a ship has no *sails* set because of heavy weather or for some other reason.

under way   A ship beginning to move through the water.

vang   A rope on either side of a *gaff* running from the top of the *gaff* to a rail, used to stabilize the *gaff.*

waist   The middle part of the main *deck* between the *forecastle* and the *quarterdeck.*

warp, to   To move a ship by means of warps (ropes) attached to *buoys,* other ships, *anchors,* or fixed objects.

wash   The washing action of waves.

washboard   Typically a moveable strake or board that can be attached to a boat to keep water out. In *The Nigger of the "Narcissus,"* the term is also used for a board attached to the bottom of a door to keep water out of the *cabins.*

watch   A four-hour period during which one or more *crew* members keep watch of the ship; also refers to the men working a particular *watch.*

watch below   Those on *watch* below the main *deck.*

watch officer   The officer in charge of a particular *watch*.

water gage   A gage indicating the amount of water in a steam boiler.

waterline   Either the line at which the water meets a ship's *hull* or an actual line marked on a ship's *hull* indicating the appropriate level at which the water meets a ship's *hull* when it is fully loaded.

way   The progress of a ship through the water.

wear ship   To bring a ship onto the other *tack* by bringing the wind around to the ship's *stern*, rather than having the wind facing a ship's *bows*, as is done in *tacking*.

weather   The side of a ship facing the wind.

weather, to   To come safely through a difficulty.

weather cloths   Temporary screens to protect *crew* members from bad weather.

weather ladder   The ladder on the *weather* side of a ship.

weather rail   The rail on the *weather* side of a ship.

well   A space in the bottom of a ship into which water runs.

went off   To go along in a particular direction.

western board (westerboard)   To the western side of a ship.

wharf   See *pier*.

wheel   The wheel used in steering a ship.

wheelbox   The housing for the steering mechanism.

wheelhouse   A small sheltered enclosure around the steering mechanism and associated equipment to protect them and the *helmsman*.

wheelman   See *helmsman*.

whipping up   Hoisting *cargo* by means of a rope or pulley.

winch   A mechanism used for pulling and hoisting, consisting of a barrel around which a rope is wound.

windlass   A barrel or cylinder rotated to lower or raise a ship's *anchor* (pronounced *windless*).

windward   Toward the wind. See *weather*.

wooden fender   A piece of wood hung over the side of a boat to prevent chafing against a *wharf*.

yardarms   The outer ends of a *yard*.

yards   Wooden *spars* hung horizontal to a *mast*, from which a square *sail* is suspended.

Correspondence†

Captain Henry Ellis[1] to Captain C. Korzeniowski

19th January, 1888

This is to inform you that you are required to proceed to day in the s. s. "Melita" to Bangkok and you will report your arrival to the British Consul[2] and produce this memorandum which will show that I have engaged you to be Master of the "Otago" in accordance with the Consul's telegram on a voyage from Bangkok to Melbourne,[3] wages at *fourteen £14 pounds* per month and to count from date of your arrival at Bangkok, your passage from Singapore[4] to Bangkok to be borne by the Ship. Further to receive a passage from Melbourne to Singapore if you are not kept on in the Ship [*PL* 1].

Captain Henry Ellis to E. B. Gould[1]

19th January/ 88

I have the honor to acknowledge the receipt of your telegram "can you engage Master to take 'Otago' from Bangkok to Melbourne

---

† From *A Portrait in Letters: Correspondence to and about Conrad*, ed. J. H. Stape and Owen Knowles (Amsterdam: Rodopi, 1996). Reprinted by permission of Editions Rodopi. Also from *The Collected Letters of Joseph Conrad*, 9 vols. (Cambridge: Cambridge University Press, 1983–2007). *Vol. 1: 1861–1897*, ed. Frederick R. Karl and Laurence Davies (1983). *Vol. 2: 1898–1902*, ed. Frederick R. Karl and Laurence Davies (1986). *Vol. 5: 1912–1916*, ed. Frederick R. Karl and Laurence Davies (1996). *Vol. 6: 1917–1919*, ed. Laurence Davies, Frederick R. Karl, and Owen Knowles (2003). *Vol. 8: 1923–1924*, ed. Laurence Davies and Gene M. Moore (2007). Text of the letters copyright © 1983 the Estate of Joseph Conrad. Introductory material and editorial notes copyright © 1983 Cambridge University Press. Reprinted with the permission of Cambridge University Press. At the end of each letter in this section, the particular source is identified in brackets. Unless otherwise noted, the footnotes are by the editor of this Norton Critical Edition.
1. See p. 59, n. 9.
2. See p. 19, n. 7. "Bangkok": see p. 68, n. 9.
3. The capital of the state of Victoria, in southeastern Australia. "'Otago'": see p. 80, n. 1.
4. See p. 48, n. 7.
1. See p. 67, n. 7.

salary £14 a month to come here by first steamer and sail at once" to which I replied "Master engaged proceed 'Hecate'".[2]

The person I have engaged is M[r]. Conrad Korzeniowski, who, holds a certificate of competency as Master from the Board of Trade.[3] He bears a good character from the several vessels, he has sailed out of this Port.

I have agreed with him that his wages at £14 per month to count from date of arrival at Bangkok, ship to provide him with food and all necessary articles for the navigation of the vessel. His passage from Singapore to Bangkok to be paid by the ship, also on his arrival at Melbourne if his services be dispensed with, the owner to provide him with a cabin passage back to Singapore.

I consider the above terms are cheap, reasonable, and trust will meet with your approval [PL 1–2].

William Willis[1] to Captain C. Korzeniowski

February 1888.

I think it is not out of place on my part that I should state, though not asked by you to do so, to prevent misapprehension hereafter, that the Crew of the Sailing Ship Otago has suffered severely whilst in Bangkok from tropical diseases, including Fever, dysentery and Cholera; and I can speak of my own knowledge that you have done all in your power in the trying and responsible position of Master of the Ship to hasten the departure of your vessel from this unhealthy place, and at the same time to save the lives of the men under your command [PL 2].[2]

[James S. Simpson[1] of] Henry Simpson & Sons to Captain C. Korzeniowski

5[th]. April 1888

Your favors dated Bankok [sic] 2[nd] and 6[th] Feb[ruar]y, latter with postscript dated 7[th] on the eve of sailing, duly reached me, and have been interesting as detailing the melancholy circumstances under which you took charge of the barque "Otago".

2. Possibly the S. S. *Hecate*, a steamer built in 1885 by the Liverpool firm W. H. Porter & Sons for Alfred Holt & Co., of Liverpool. Conrad actually traveled to Bangkok via the *Melita*, not the *Hecate*; see p. 363.
3. See p. 147, n. 6. "Holds a certificate of competency": Conrad passed his exams for this certificate in November 1886.
1. See p. 91, n. 4.
2. The *Otago* set sail on 8 February [original editors' note].
1. Probably the son of Henry Simpson.

The accounts which you enclosed are no doubt at all in order but I have had no means of comparing them with other documents as the late Captain never favored me with the scratch of a pen from the time of leaving Newcastle in August last, and the acting master Mr Born[2] only wrote me a brief note acquainting me with his Captain's death, therefore I am at a loss to know what business was done by the ship after she arrived at Hai-phong[3]—whether she earned, or whether she lost money—In fact other than your documents I have no record whatever of receipts and expenditure— Will you therefore please inform me whether any freight was obtained between Haiphong and Bankok [sic]. If so how much—and generally what business was done by the ship for the few months previous to your assuming command?

I presume the vessel will be entered inwards by the Consignee of cargo, and you will no doubt telegraph your arrival to me— As to what will be done later on, nothing has yet been determined, but probably the late Captain's Executors will wish the vessel sold in the interest of the widow & mortgagees, as his two shares were fully pledged. It is quite likely however that before such sale I shall take a run over to Sydney,[4] in which case I shall have the pleasure of making your acquaintance [PL 3].

*   *   *

Jas. S. Simpson

Henry Simpson & Sons[1] to Captain C. Korzeniowski

April 2nd 1889

April 2nd 1889

Referring to your resignation of the command (which we have in another letter formally accepted) of our barque "Otago", we now have much pleasure in stating that this early severance from our employ is entirely at your own desire, with a view to visiting Europe, and that we entertain a high opinion of your ability in the capacity you now vacate, of your attainments generally, and shall be glad to learn of your future success [PL 5].

---

2. See p. 83, n. 6. "Newcastle": a port city in northeastern England.
3. See p. 86, n. 4. "Captain's death": see p. 84, n. 1.
4. See p. 93, n. 9.
1. Owners of the Black Diamond Line of Colliers, of Port Adelaide in southeastern Australia. The company was established in 1867, by Henry Simpson (1815–1884) and one of his sons, J. L. Simpson. It folded in 1895.

Joseph Conrad to Edward Garnett[1]

[25 November 1896]
* * * My only fear is that I will droop with the end of the "Narcissus". I am horribly dissatisfied with the ideas yet unwritten. Nothing effective suggest[s] itself. It's ghastly [*CL* 1:320]. * * *

Joseph Conrad to Edward Garnett

[29 November 1896]
*   *   *
Of course nothing can alter the course of the "Nigger". Let it be unpopularity if it *must* be. But it seems to me that the thing—precious as it is to me—is trivial enough on the surface to have some charms for the man in the street. As to lack of incident well—it's life. The incomplete joy, the incomplete sorrow, the incomplete rascality or heroism—the incomplete suffering. Events crowd and push and nothing happens. You know what I mean. The opportunities do not last long enough [*CL* 1:321].

*   *   *

Joseph Conrad to Helen Watson[1]

27th Jan. 1897.
*   *   *
The story just finished is called "The Nigger: A Tale of Ship and Men". Candidly, I think it has certain qualities of art that make it a thing apart. I tried to get through the veil of details at the essence of life. But it is a rough story—dealing with rough men and an immense background. I do not ask myself how much I have succeeded; I only dare to hope that it is not a shameful failure; that perhaps, here and there, may be found a few men and women who will see what I have tried for. It would be triumph enough for me [*CL* 1:334].

*   *   *

1. See p. 143, n. 2.
1. Helen Mary Watson (1875–1967) married Conrad's friend Edward Lancelot Sanderson (1867–1939) in 1898. She was originally from Galloway, Scotland.

Joseph Conrad to Edward Garnett

[24 August 1897]

* * *I send You however something else: a short preface to the "Nigger".

I want you not to be impatient with it and if you think it at all possible to give it a chance to get printed. That rests entirely with you. Implicitly the Nigger is *Your* book and besides You know very well I daren't make any move without Your leave. I've no more judgment of what is fitting in the way of literature than a cow. And you must be the herd of that one head of cattle[.] * * *

And let me hear the decree soon to ease my mind. On my eyes be it—I shall not draw one breath till your Sublime Highness has spoken to the least of his slaves. We demand mercy [*CL* 1:375].

* * *

Stephen Crane[1] to Joseph Conrad

Nov 11 [1897]

* * * [T]he book [*The Nigger of the "Narcissus"*] is simply great. The simple treatment of the death of Waite [*sic*] is too good, too terrible. I wanted to forget it at once. It caught me very hard. I felt ill over that red thread lining from the corner of the man's mouth to his chin. It was frightful with the weight of a real and present death. By such small means does the real writer suddenly flash out in the sky above those who are always doing rather well [*PL* 27]. * * *

Joseph Conrad to Stephen Crane

16th Nov. 1897.

I must write to you before I write a single word for a living to-day. I was anxious to know what you would think of the end [*of The Nigger of the "Narcissus"*]. If I've hit *you* with the death of Jimmy [Wait][1] I don't care if I don't hit another man. I think however artistically the end of the book is somewhat lame. I mean after the death. All that rigmarolle [*sic*] about the burial and the ships coming home seems to run away into a rat's tail—thin at the end. Well! It's too late now

---

1. American writer (1871–1900), whose works include *The Red Badge of Courage* (1895), *Maggie: A Girl of the Streets* (1893), and "The Open Boat" (1896). He became a close friend of Conrad before his death, from tuberculosis.
1. See Crane's letter to Conrad of November 11, 1897 (above).

to bite my thumb and tear my hair. When I feel depressed about it I say to myself "Crane likes the damned thing"—and am greatly consoled. What your appreciation is to me I renounce to explain. The world looks different to me now, since our long pow-wow. It was good. The memory of it is good. And now and then (human nature *is* a vile thing) I ask myself whether you meant half of what you said! You must forgive me. The mistrust is not of you—it is of myself: the drop of poison in the cup of life. I am not more vile than my neighbours but this disbelief in oneself is like a taint that spreads on everything one comes in contact with; on men on things—on the very air one breathes. That's why one sometimes wishes to be a stone breaker. There's no doubt about breaking a stone. But there's doubt, fear—a black horror, in every page one writes. You at any rate will understand and therefore I write to you as though we had been born together before the beginning of things. For what you have done and intend to do I won't even attempt to thank you. I certainly don't know what to say, tho' I am perfectly certain as to what I feel [*CL* 1:409–10].

※   ※   ※

Joseph Conrad to [W. L. Courtney][1]

9th Dec. 1897

Allow me to thank you for the thought, the indulgence and the lesson of Your criticism of the "Nigger".[2] Permit me also to say—to you alone—a few words of explanation.

I wrote this short book regardless of any formulas of art, forgetting all the theories of expression. Formulas and theories are dead things, and I wrote straight from the heart—which is alive. I wanted to give a true impression, to present and [*sic*] undefaced image. And You, who know amongst what illusions and self-deceptions men struggle, work, fail—You will only smile with indulgence if I confess to You that I also wanted to connect the small world of the ship with that larger world carrying perplexities, fears, affections, rebellions, in a loneliness greater than that of the ship at sea.

To You, whose mind will sympathise with my feeling, I wish to disclaim all allegiance to realism, to naturalism[3] and—before all—all leaning towards the ugly. I would not know where to look for it. There

1. William Leonard Courtney (1850–1928), English author and editor, edited *The Fortnightly Review* from 1894 until 1928, was the literary editor of *The Daily Telegraph,* and regularly reviewed Conrad's works.
2. Courtney's review appeared in *The Daily Telegraph* on December 8, 1897 (see pp. 399–403).
3. See p. 141, n. 4.

is joy and sorrow; there is sunshine and darkness—and all are within the same eternal smile of the inscrutable Maya.[4] As to the title of the story it's sheer clumsiness of mind. I could not invent anything else.

One word more. I do not think that vice triumphs. It gets the money only. Donkin is an unhappy man. He is the only one of the crowd who is essentially unhappy. The others may suffer but are not unhappy. Jimmy pays with anguish for his want of courage but, till the last moment, is not unhappy. I tried to make so Donkin alone. In my desire to be faithful to the ethical truth I have sacrificed the truth of the individual: I did not bring out that intimate, invincible self-satisfaction which shields such natures from humiliation and despair. And I leave him faced by the contempt of his fellows and shaking with rage. I tried—I failed!

I trust you will forgive me the lenght [sic] of this letter for it declares, as nothing else could, my high appreciation of Your luminous and flattering notice. I am grateful to you for the blame, for the praise, for the kindness that pervades the whole. To pick out the paragraph You have chosen for quotation is more like the inspiration of a true friend than the perspicuous choice of a benevolent critic. And I am most grateful to you for endorsing the words of the end. Twenty years of life went to the writing of these few last lines. "Tempi passati!" The old time—the old time of youth and unperplexed life!

P.S. A preface intended for the Nigger which in deference to my excellent publisher I have withheld has been printed in the last N° of the *New Review*[5] as an Author's note after the final instalment of the story. Is it too much to hope that [you] will find time to look at it [*CL* 1:420–22]?

Joseph Conrad to R. B. Cunninghame Graham[1]

14 Dec. 1897

*   *   *

I've been thinking over the letter you have written me about the *Nigger.* I am glad you like the book. Sincerely glad. It is clear gain to

---

4. In Hindu and Buddhist philosophy, the power through which the universe is manifest; the appearance or illusion of the phenomenal world. This concept appears in the work of the German philosopher Arthur Schopenhauer (1788–1860), whose work appears to have influenced Conrad's thinking.
5. See p. 138, n. 4. "Preface": see pp. 139–42.
1. Robert Bontine Cunninghame Graham (1852–1936) was a Scottish writer, politician, and adventurer. A Liberal Party Member of Parliament (MP) and the first socialist Member of Parliament, he was a swashbuckling figure who served as the model for several literary characters, such as Sergius Saranoff in *Arms and the Man*, by G. B. Shaw (1856–1950). He was also one of Conrad's best friends and confidants.

me. I don't know what the respectable (hats off) part of the population will think of it. Probably nothing. They never think. It isn't respectable. But I can quite see that, without thinking, they may feel an instinctive disgust. So be it. In my mind I picture the book as a stone falling in the water. It's gone and not a trace shall remain. But the words of commendation you and a few other men have said shall be treasured by me as a proof that the book has not been written in vain—as the clearest of my reward.

So You may rest assured that the time you have given to reading the tale and to writing to me has not been thrown away—since, I presume, You do not believe that doing good to a human being is throwing away effort and one's own life. And You have done me good. Whatever may be the worth of my gratitude you have it all; and such is the power of men to show feelings that "helas! Vous ne vous en apercevrez même pas!"[2]

But as I said I've been meditating over your letter. You say: "Singleton with an education". Well—yes. Everything is possible, and most things come to pass (when you don't want them). However I think Singleton with an education is impossible. But first of all—what education? If it is the knowledge how to live my man essentially possessed it. He was in perfect accord with his life. If by education you mean scientific knowledge then the question arises—what knowledge, how much of it—in what direction? Is it to stop at plane trigonometry or at conic sections? Or is he to study Platonism or Pyrrhonism or the philosophy of the gentle Emerson? Or do you mean the kind of knowledge which would enable him to scheme, and lie, and intrigue his way to the forefront of a crowd no better than himself? Would you seriously, of malice prepense cultivate in that unconscious man the power to think. Then he would become conscious—and much smaller—and very unhappy. Now he is simple and great like an elemental force. Nothing can touch him but the curse of decay—the eternal decree that will extinguish the sun, the stars one by one, and in another instant shall spread a frozen darkness over the whole universe. Nothing else can touch him—he does not think.

Would you seriously wish to tell such a man: "Know thyself". Understand that thou art nothing, less than a shadow, more insignificant than a drop of water in the ocean, more fleeting than the illusion of a dream. Would you [*CL* 1:422–23]?

---

2. "Alas! You will not even notice it!" [original editors' note].

W. H. Chesson[1] to Joseph Conrad

13 January 1898

I cannot delay telling you how good I find "The Nigger of the 'Narcis-sus.'" The psychology of the poltroon is traced with a hand so cunning and relentless that there are those who will think it inhuman. And words will not contain my contempt for those who deprecate a lack of story—of plot—in a novel that is alive with all the horrible antics of Fear accompanied by the noise and tumult of the sea.

I dismiss too, cheerfully, the argument that a seaman—a "shell-back" maybe—is not to write that fervid and orchestral style against which the colloquial speech of his comrades sounds with double vitality and increased clearness.

As a work of art the thing seems to me well-nigh faultless. There is no illegitimate interruption of the ironic spectacle, at the end of which you cleverly inveigle the reader into sharing the superstition of the devoted mariners. I expected the breeze to come, and I expected an impediment up to the last. The crawly way of Jimmy's obscene malady of mind demanded the accompaniment of ineffec-tual wind in order that all who served him should be deeply involved in his uncanny night.

Seldom have I talked with sailors, but I have sought to observe them and have been impressed with a curious childlikeness—a chronic state of wonder and submission, which intemperance and bad temper scarcely seem to disturb. You have caught that childlikeness.

One cannot but congratulate you on the romantic force which you apply to a scheme so scientific in its loving inclusion of symptoms. The captain's splendid patience and authority, Singleton's indomita-ble fidelity, flash at me even now when the book is closed. Fine sen-tences, like the first of Chapter IV, march through my mind. The storm, the extrication of Jimmy (wonderful realist to have thought of those nails!), his death (the extinguishing of his eyes), his funeral (the reluctance of the precipitated corpse; the throwing of the Word of God upon the unlistening sea), I am in percipience of it all. And lastly, though I repeat myself in saying so, it takes *shape*, there is a beautiful anatomy, dexterously contrived, under all this display of imagination. "The Nigger" is not an episode of the sea; it is a final expression of the pathology of Fear. At the last you made your vil-lainous oaf Donkin pull it out into an unbearable horror of counte-nance like a gutta percha[2] mask. Is it, I wonder, some shrinking from

---

1. Chesson (1870–1952) worked for T. Fisher Unwin and was one of the two initial read-ers (the other being Garnett) of the manuscript for *Almayer's Folly*. Like Garnett, he recommended publication.
2. Rubberlike substance obtained from trees in the Malay Archipelago.

an Irony made colder, and for a moment less polished than steel, that makes me almost regret Donkin being one of the crew?

One last word; and I know you will forgive me. Why, o friend, will you encourage the asinine critics to prick up their ears by employing "like" when you ought to use *as*! You are sure to have a second edition and I therefore remark that "like" appears for as on pp 144, 170, 187, 214, 222. It is used on p 187 in a conversation where I admit it may be natural enough, as slipshod chitchat.

With my warmest wishes for your very remarkable and power- fully written book[.]

*   *   *

What a lovely vision is that on pp 170–1 [*PL* 30–31].

Joseph Conrad to W. H. Chesson

Sunday 16. Jan 98.

Your unexpected and delightful letter reached me yesterday morn- ing. I would have answered it at once had it not been that the house was in a state of disorganization on account of the arrival of an infant of the male persuasion. However this fuss is over thank God.

Your letter shows such a comprehension of the state of mind which produced the story, that had you given blame instead of gen- erous praise it would still have been a rare pleasure to be thus understood—seized in the act of thinking, so to speak. Of all that has been said about the book this what you say gives the most inti- mate satisfaction, because you not only see what the book is but what it might have been. When you say, "One almost regrets Donkin being one of the crew," I take it as the very highest praise I have received— inconceivably different in its insight within those dark and inarticu- late recesses of mind where so many thoughts die at the moment of birth, for want of personal strenght [*sic*]—or of moral rectitude—or of inspired expression.

One would like to write a book for your reading.

This is what touched me most. The other words of commenda- tion I take as Your recognition of a tendency of mind repulsive to many, understood by few, clearly seen by You—and which I cannot help thinking of as not wholly without merit. But a tendency of mind is nothing without expression and that the expression should please you is in my opinion my very great fortune.

It is to your letter (now incorporated with my copy of the *Nigger*) that in moments of doubt and weariness I shall turn with the greatest confidence as to an infaillible remedy for the black disease of writers. I've read it several times since yesterday.

I have also corrected all the *like* into *as* in my copy. One is so strangely blind to one's own prose; and the more I write the less sure I am of my English. Thanks for going to the trouble of pointing out to me the passages. I don't think the N will have a 2^d Ed: but if—in years to come—it ever has, the corrections shall be made [*CL* 2:19–20].[1]

Joseph Conrad to David Meldrum[1]

31 Oct. 1900

* * * I've not yet finished the *Typhoon* which is to prolong my wretched existence. That infernal story does not seem to come off somehow [*CL* 2:298]. * * *

Joseph Conrad to David Meldrum

6 Dec. 1900.

* * *

The Typhoon is all but finished and pleases me now so that I am sorry it isn't for *Maga*[1] [*CL* 2:308].

* * *

Henry James to Edmund Gosse[1]

June 26th 1902.

* * * *The Nigger of the Narcissus* is in my opinion the very finest & strongest picture of the sea and sea-life that our language possesses— the masterpiece in a whole class; & *Lord Jim* runs it very close [*PL* 36]. * * *

---

1. In 1914, when Nelson Doubleday published a new edition of the novel, Conrad had three of the instances Chesson noted changed from "like" to "as" (pp. 144, 170, and 214).
1. London-based literary advisor (1864–1940) to William Blackwood & Sons, an Edinburgh publishing house that published *Lord Jim* and *Youth: A Narrative and Two Other Stories*, as well as *Blackwood's Magazine*; see p. 255, n. 1.
1. *Blackwood's Magazine*.
1. English poet, author, and critic (1849–1928); he successfully spearheaded an attempt to secure Conrad a grant from the Royal Literary Fund. James (1843–1916), a prominent American novelist and friend of Conrad's, whom Conrad admired intensely, responds to Gosse's request for James's support in this endeavor.

Joseph Conrad to John Galsworthy[1]

[28 October 1912?]

I can't tell you what pleasure you have given me by what you say of the Secret Sharer—and especially of the swimmer. I haven[']t seen many notices—3 or 4 in all; but in one of them he is called a murderous ruffian—or something of the sort.[2] Who are those fellows who write in the Press? Where do they come from? I was simply knocked over—for indeed I meant him to be what you have seen at once he was. And as *you* have seen I feel altogether comforted and rewarded for the trouble he has given me in the doing of him. For it wasn't an easy task. It was extremely difficult to keep him true to type first as modified to some extent by the sea-life and further as affected by the situation [*CL* 5:121–22].

*   *   *

Joseph Conrad to Edward Garnett

5 Nov. '12

*   *   *

Thanks for your letter on the 3 tales—very much of sorts. I dare say Freya[1] is pretty rotten. On the other hand the Secret Sharer, between you and me, is *it*. Eh? No damned tricks with girls there. Eh? Every word fits and there's not a single uncertain note. Luck my boy. Pure luck. I knew you would spot the thing at sight. But I repeat: mere luck [*CL* 5:128].

*   *   *

1. Galsworthy (1867–1933) first met Conrad in 1893, when Conrad was first mate of the *Torrens,* a clipper ship built in 1875 by James Laing of Sunderland. The two became lifelong friends, Conrad naming his second son after Galsworthy. Ironically, both changed careers. Galworthy was an attorney before becoming a successful novelist and dramatist, winning the Nobel Prize for Literature in 1932. He is best known for *The Forsyte Saga* (1922), a series of three novels and two interludes published between 1906 and 1921.
2. The review in *The Daily Telegraph* (October 16, 1912) refers to Leggatt as a "rascal" (p. 16).
1. "Freya of the Seven Isles," the final tale in the three-tale collection *'Twixt Land and Sea,* which appeared on October 14, 1912.

Joseph Conrad to Sir Sidney Colvin[1]

27 Febry 1917

* * *

Very dear of you to write so appreciatively about the little book [*The Shadow-Line*]. But I don't agree that a local-knowledge man would be the right reviewer for it. The locality doesn't matter; and if it is the Gulf of Siam it's simply because the whole thing is exact autobiography. I always meant to do it, and on our return from Austria,[2] when I had to write something, I discovered that this was what I could write in my then moral and intellectual condition; tho' even *that* cost me an effort which I remember with a shudder. To sit down and invent fairy tales was impossible then. It isn't very possible even now. I was writing that thing in Dec 1914 and Jan to March 1915.[3] The very speeches are (I won't say authentic—they are that absolutely) I believe verbally accurate. And all this happened in Mch-April 1887.[4] Giles is a Capt Patterson, a very well known person there. It's the only name I changed. Mr Burns' craziness being the pivot is perhaps a little accentuated. My last scene with Ransome is only indicated. There are things, moments, that are not to be tossed to the public's incomprehension, for journalists to gloat over. No. It was not an experience to be exhibited "in the street". —I am sorry you have received an impression of horror. I tried to keep the mere horror out. It would have been easy to pile it on. You may believe me. J'ai vécu tout cela.[5] However I will tell you a little more about all that when we meet. Here I'll only say that experience is transposed into spiritual terms— in art a perfectly legitimate thing to do, as long as one preserves the exact truth enshrined therein. That's why I consented to this piece being pub^d by itself. I did not like the idea of it being associated with fiction in a vol of stories. And this is also the reason I've inscribed it to Borys—and the others.

PS Re-reading your letter and going over the story I see that the places Bankok [*sic*] and Singapore are distinctly named—but

---

1. A friend of Conrad's (1845–1927), Slade Professor of Fine Arts at Cambridge University, director of the Fitzwilliam Museum, Keeper of Prints and Drawings at the British Museum, and author of biographies of John Keats (1795–1821) and Walter Salvage Landor (1775–1864).
2. In July 1914, Conrad and his family traveled to Poland for a visit. World War I broke out while they were in Poland, and Conrad and his family had to escape via Austria. They eventually traveled to Italy, from where they sailed back to England. "Gulf of Siam": see p. 3, n. 1.
3. See p. 44, n. 4. "To sit . . . now": World War I powerfully affected Conrad and his ability to write; see my "Joseph Conrad's Literary Response to the First World War." *College Literature* 39.4 (Fall 2012): 34–45.
4. Actually, 1888.
5. "I have lived through all that" [original editors' note].

375

obviously they are not named in the right way or in proper context since the mind of an "experienced reader" like yourself is left in doubt. And I must confess that the matter seemed to me of such slight importance in comparison with the subject treated that I really did not consider it at all while writing [CL 6:37–38].

Joseph Conrad to Sir Sidney Colvin

1st Mch 17.

* * * [T]here can be no possible objection to your recognising the autobiographical character of that—piece of writing, let us call it. It is so much so that I shrink from calling it a Tale. If you will notice I call it A Confession on the title page. For, from a certain point of view, it is that—and essentially as sincere as any confession can be. The more perfectly so, perhaps, because its object is not the usual one of self-revelation. My object was to show all the others and the situation through the medium of my own emotions. The most heavily tried (because the most selfconscious) the least "worthy" perhaps, there was no other way in which I could render justice to all these souls "worthy of my undying regard".[1]

Perhaps you won't find it presumptuous if after 22 years of work I may say that I have not been very well understood. I have been called a writer of the sea, of the tropics, a descriptive writer, a romantic writer—and also a realist. But as a matter of fact all my concern has been with the "ideal" values of things, events and people. That and nothing else. The humourous, the pathetic, the passionate, the sentimental *aspects* came in of themselves—mais en vérité c'est les valeurs idéales des faits et gestes humains qui se sont *imposé[e]s* a mon activité artistique.[2]

Whatever dramatic and narrative gifts I may have are always, instinctively, used with that object—to get at, to bring forth les valeurs idéales.

Of course this is a very general statement—but roughly I believe it is true [CL 6:39–40].

Joseph Conrad to Sir Sidney Colvin

[7 or 14 March 1917]

* * *

The Indo-China sheet in any usual Atlas will satisfy your Geographical longings. You will find there Bankok [sic], Cape Liant, and

1. See p. 47.
2. "But the truth is that the ideal values of things and human events have imposed themselves on my artistic activities" [original editors' note].

most likely Koh-ring. From the latter the general direction of the ship was towards the tip of the Malay Peninsula where Singapore is.[1]

No. I don't really want that little piece to be recognised *formally* as autobiographical. It's [*sic*] *tone* is not. But as to the underlying *feeling* I think there can be no mistake. Some reviewers are sure to note that. Others perhaps won't.

I shall try to find the doctor's letter, the agreement, and the Admiralty sheet on which I navigate[d] the ship during those days. I haven't seen these things for years but they must be somewhere in the house. You shall see them, these pièces de conviction,[2] when you come down [*CL* 6:41–42].

Joseph Conrad to W. G. St. Clair[1]

March 31, 1917.

* * *

Yes, I remember Bradbury.[2] It was he who let me off port-dues when I put into Singapore in distress with *all* my crew unfit for duty (1888). It is a very difficult thing to shove everybody into a tale even as auto-biographical as *The Shadow-Line* is. My Capt. Giles was a man called Patterson, a dear, thick, dreary creature with an enormous reputation for knowledge of the Sulu Sea. The "Home" Steward's name[3] (in my time) I don't remember. He was a meagre wizened creature, always bemoaning his fate, and did try to do me an unfriendly turn for some reason or other.

I "belonged" to Singapore for about a year, being chief mate of a steamer owned by Syed Mohsin bin Ali (Craig, master) and trading mostly to Borneo and Celebes[4] somewhat out of the usual beats of local steamers owned by Chinamen.

As you may guess we had no social shore connections. You know it isn't very practicable for a seaman. The only man I chummed with was Brooksbanks [*sic*], then chief officer of the s. s. *Celestial* and

---

1. See p. 48, n. 7.
2. These exhibits.
1. William Graeme St. Clair (1849–1930) was born in Scotland and taught in Burma (now Myanmar). In 1887, he moved to Malaya to edit the *Singapore Free Press*.
2. See p. 133, n. 1.
3. See p. 52, n. 3. "Sulu Sea": see p. 53, n. 9.
4. Now Sulawesi; like its eastern neighbor Borneo, one of the large islands of the Malay Archipelago. "Syed Mohsin bin Ali": see p. 48, n. 9. "Craig, master": see p. 49, n. 5.

later, as I've heard Manager of the Dock at Tan-Jong Pagar.[5] I've heard of course a lot about the men you mention. Old Lingard was before my time but I knew slightly both his nephews, Jim and Jos, of whom the latter was then officer on board the King of Siam's yacht.[6]

In Bangkok when I took command, I hardly ever left the ship except to go to my charterers (Messrs Jucker, Sigg and Co.) and with the chief mate sick I was really too busy ever to *hear* much about shore people. Mr Gould, Consul-General and then Chargé d'Affaires in the absence of Sir E. S[w]atow,[7] was very kind to me during the troubled times I had in port.

Naturally, like everybody else, I was a diligent reader of the excellent and always interesting *Singapore Free Press*[8] then under your direction. I keep my regard for that paper to this day. It was certainly the newspaper of the East between Rangoon and Hong-Kong.[9] Last time Sir Hugh Clifford (a friend of many years) was here we talked appreciatively of the *S. F. P.*[1] I imagine you must have been generally friendly to him on public matters. I wonder what the attitude of the paper was at the time of the B[ritish] F[ederated] Borneo Governorship and resignation.[2] He did not mention it and I did not ask him. We passed on to other memories, for he will never cease to regard his Malayan days.

All my literary life (since 1893) I've been living in the country, coming to town but seldom—and now less than ever. I hope you are recovered by now; and perhaps later, if your health will permit, you will come down here for a day. And then indeed I may hear

5. A section of Singapore. "Brooksbanks": Frederick Havelock Brooksbank (c. 1858–1914), a mariner who was born in West Derby Lancashire but lived much of his life in Singapore. In 1884, Brooksbank married Caroline Lingard, daughter of William Lingard (1829–1888), the model for Tom Lingard, who appears in *Almayer's Folly* (1895), *An Outcast of the Islands* (1896), and *The Rescue* (1920). "s. s. *Celestial*": probably an 840-ton California clipper ship built in 1850 by William H. Webb for Bucklin & Crane, of New York.
6. *Maha Chakkri*. "Old Lingard": William Lingard; see previous note. "Jim and Jos": James and Joshua Lingard. Joshua served as captain of the steamship *Paknam*.
7. Ernest Mason Swatow (1843–1929), British Minister Resident in Bangkok from 1884 to 1887. "Mr Gould": see p. 67, n. 7.
8. An English-language newspaper founded in 1835 as the *Singapore Free Press & Mercantile Advertiser*. The newspaper closed in 1869 but was reestablished as the *Singapore Free Press* in 1884 and ran until 1962, when it merged with *The Malay Mail*.
9. See p. 87, n. 7. "Rangoon": now Yangon, former capital of Burma (Myanmar).
1. Hugh Charles Clifford (1866–1941), a friend of Conrad's, wrote a number of books based on his experience as colonial administrator. He served as British Resident in Malaya and was later Colonial Secretary of Trinidad, as well as Governor of Labuan and North Borneo, the Gold Coast, Nigeria, Ceylon (now Sri Lanka), and the Straits Settlements. Before he met Conrad, Clifford reviewed books for the *Singapore Free Press* for a number of years under the pen name "The Book-Worm." One of these reviews, published on August 30, 1898, considered Conrad's literary career to date and famously suggested that despite the high quality of Conrad's fiction, he actually knew very little about Malaysia or Malays.
2. Clifford was appointed Governor of Labuan and North Borneo in 1899 but became caught in a power struggle with the British North Borneo Company and resigned in 1901.

something really worth knowing about Singapore and the straits of which truly I know very little [*CL* 6:62–63].

Joseph Conrad to Helen Sanderson[1]

[late March–early April 1917]

* * * I want to tell you how much I appreciate the kind things you say about the S-Line. Strangely enough, you know, I never either meant or "felt" the supernatural aspect of the story while writing it. It came out somehow and my readers pointed it out to me. I must tell you that it is a piece of as strict autobiography as the form allowed—I mean the need of slight dramatisation to make the thing actual. Very slight. For the rest not a fact or sensation is "invented". What did worry me in reality was not the "supernatural" character but the *fact* of Mr Burns' craziness. For only think: my first command, a sinister, slowly developing situation from which one couldn't see any issue that one could *try for*, and the only man on board (second in command) to whom I could open my mind, not quite sane—not to be depended on for any sort of moral support. It was very trying. I'll never forget those days [*CL* 6:63–64].

*   *   *

Joseph Conrad to Henry S. Canby[1]

April 7th. 1924.

*   *   *

In the "Nigger" I give the psychology of a group of men and render certain aspects of nature. But the problem that faces them is not a problem of the sea, it is merely a problem that has arisen on board a ship where the conditions of complete isolation from all land entanglements make it stand out with a particular force and colouring [*CL* 8:339]. * * *

1. See p. 366, 2nd n. 1.
1. Henry Seidel Canby (1878–1961), editor of the *New York Evening Post Literary Review,* founder of the *Saturday Review of Literature* (in 1924), and a literature professor at Yale University.

Contemporary Reviews

ROBERT LYND

Mr. Joseph Conrad†

If anyone has doubts of Mr. Conrad's genius he will do well to read "The Secret Sharer," the second story in this volume. I confess repentantly that I once had such doubts. But I had not read "Typhoon" then. None of the three stories in *'Twixt Land and Sea* possesses the cosmic or rather the infernal energy of "Typhoon." In reading "Typhoon" one has constantly, as it were, to catch hold of something solid in order to keep oneself from being swept off one's feet by the fury of the author's sensitive and truthful genius. "The Secret Sharer" is work of a quieter mood. It is as different from "Typhoon" as still water is from a storm. But it is to an equal extent a mastering vision of a world which Mr. Conrad knows and nobody else knows—a world of artistically uncharted seas—a world the seas of which have at once the reality of the seas we know, and something of the still intenser reality of the phantom seas of "The Ancient Mariner."[1]

Everyone who has read Mr. Conrad's stories knows how sensitively and how surely he can create a living atmosphere as he adds nervous sentence to nervous sentence. Every sentence has a nerve: that is one of the distinguishing features of his writing. It is not clever writing—at least, not deliberately so. If his genius fails him, he has none of those glittering reserves of cleverness to fall back upon, such as enable Mr. Kipling[2] always to achieve vividness even when he does

---

† *The Daily News & Leader* (London), October 14, 1912, p. 8. Page references are to this Norton Critical Edition. Robert Wilson Lynd (1879–1949) was Anglo-Irish, born in Belfast. In 1908, he joined the staff of the *Daily News* (London), and he became its literary editor in 1912. He reviewed several of Conrad's works. On more than one occasion, Conrad vigorously complained about Lynd's reviews, as he does of this one; see p. 389, n. 2. See also *CL* 4:107–109, 110–11.
1. See p. 108, n. 4.
2. Rudyard Kipling (1865–1936), English writer best known for his works set in India, such as *Kim* (1901) and *The Jungle Books* (1894, 1895). He received the Nobel Prize for Literature in 1907.

not achieve life. But in what has been called the sense of life, Mr. Conrad is, within his limits, far richer than Mr. Kipling.

The Cosmic Note

It is true that he expresses his sense of life rather through his winds and seas and ships than through his human beings. His human beings are, on the whole, small and eccentric creatures compared to those elements which spring upon them and lie in wait for them like the messengers of gods and devils. His characters, in other words, do not belong to that aristocracy of passion of which Pater wrote.[3] Even though they perform miracles of endurance in their warfare against wind and wave, it is the latter who are the mighty characters of his books. Compared with them, the captains and the sailors seem at times to be just a sort of odd playthings.

Thus his characters have frequently something of the quality of victims. * * *

Studies in Fascination

In his description of human beings subject to some terrible fascination Mr. Conrad excels. "Studies in fascination" would be a not inapt description of the three stories in this book. * * * "The Secret Sharer," * * * which tells of the spell cast upon another captain by a mate charged with murder, who has taken refuge in his ship, is surely a masterpiece. Here Mr. Conrad himself casts a spell.

Ever from that midnight moment, when the captain, lonelily pacing the deck of his anchored ship in islanded eastern seas, looks over the side and beholds the apparently headless body of a man in the phosphorescent water at the foot of the ladder, the story grips one in its quiet, inevitable sentences. There is marvellous psychological insight shown in the way in which the captain, having clothed the man in his clothes and hidden him in his room and heard his strange story, like a secret, in intimate whispers, gradually comes to associate his own identity with the identity of the fugitive. It is the captain and not the fugitive who jumps at sudden sounds and at chances of discovery. The great elation of the story, however, does not arise from its study of the psychology of fascination or curious sense of identity or alarm. All this is necessary to produce it. In his eagerness for the escape of his double, who insists upon dropping over the ship's side at night and swimming to one of the islands where he can live as one

---

3. In his essay "Wordsworth" (1874), Walter H. Pater (1839–1894) refers to certain characters in the poetry of William Wordsworth (1770–1850) as possessing "the true aristocracy of passionate souls" (*Fortnightly Review* n.s. 15 [April 1, 1874]: 460).

dead, a marooned and forgotten man, the captain compels his crew, almost still with horror, to bring the ship right up under the shadow of the land on a pretence of looking for land winds. That scene gives us one of the great thrills of modern literature. "Such a hush had fallen on the ship that she might have been a bark of the dead floating in slowly under the very gate of Erebus. 'My God! Where are we?' It was the mate moaning at my elbow" [40–41]. As the helmsman gives his answers to the captain's orders "in a frightened, thin, childish voice" [41] we, too, are still and tense, like the horror-stricken crew. Then comes the fugitive's escape in the dark water. After that, the escape of that fine ship herself from the shadow, as it were, of the everlasting night—an escape that is one of the wonderful things of the literature of the sea. The elation that we get from this story is the elation which all great literature, even tragic literature, ought to give. Let all the bells of praise ring for so fine a piece of work.

ANONYMOUS

Conrad's Masterpiece†

* * * However keenly one might look forward to all work of Conrad, one was hardly venturesome enough to hope for anything more on that level. Admirable work, of course; that was assured: good to read and keep. But more than that. . . . About all the finest art there is something miraculous. A man can but do what he can: but work and work and work. And for the rest—whoever his gods may be—he can but pray for the divine accident to happen.

The divine accident (with all that it means of life and beauty) has happened in these three stories; supremely in "The Secret Sharer." They are as good as anything Conrad has ever written, tales as good as any man might hope to write. And "The Secret Sharer" is a little better. It is supreme of the three. We say so in no dogmatic spirit. The other two are done as well as they could be done. Many people may for the most admirable reasons prefer them. But "The Secret Sharer" has a quality which seems to us to be the most valuable that any work of art can possess—the quality of spiritual exaltation. Its effect was tremendous and unforgettable.

* * * The story is simple enough, and is told with perfect dexterity. That alone would not make it supreme. The significance of the story itself is the thing: what it tells the spirit. And it sings a gallant song in praise of courage and daring; in praise of friendship; in praise of life which, in spite of everything, if tackled bravely, does not lack

† *The Observer* (London), October 20, 1912, p. 5.

fineness and dignity. From strong foundations of fact the story goes
towering into the sky.

What Conrad knows and what he makes you feel is that the fabric of a story is no more than the wood and ivory of an instrument
from which the music must be drawn—the music which is as necessary to the spirit of man as food is necessary to his body.

ANONYMOUS

From Novels of the Week†

No volume that Mr. Conrad has ever published could offer more
unmistakable proof of his genius than does this collection of three
stories. In his greatest things—in "Typhoon" [1902], in "Youth"
[1898], in *Lord Jim* [1900], in *Nostromo* [1904]—he had big themes,
motifs that lent themselves readily in his hands to great results. In
two of the stories here presented to us there would seem to the
ordinary writer scarcely any theme at all: never before have we
realised so vividly the things that Mr. Conrad can do.

We may acclaim him perhaps as the first king of a new country—
that country of story-tellers who will combine the sense of life proclaimed by the great mid-Victorians with the sense of form discovered
here in England somewhere about 1890. He is as enthralled by the
actual world that he beholds as were ever Dickens or Thackeray; his
prose is as singing and haunting a melody as was ever Meredith's or
Stevenson's.[1] It is when he is concerned with the mean things of life,
as, for instance, the little paper-shop in *The Secret Agent* [1907] or
Jim's fellow criminals on the pilgrim ship in *Lord Jim,* that this startling welding of vision and matter-of-fact is most plainly to be
discerned.

* * * But if the secret of Mr. Conrad's genius is hidden in this first
story ["A Smile of Fortune"], still more is it concealed in the second
tale, "The Secret Sharer." We are inclined to name this as the most
perfect of all Mr. Conrad's stories, although we have not forgotten
"Youth" nor "The Duel" [1908], nor "Typhoon." * * * You are presented with the effect on the captain's mind of the silent and secret
presence of this other man. You are made to feel the rising of that
secret presence through the very boards of the ship, so that the reader
himself, as the ship moves and the tension grows, is almost impelled,
as though he were himself a secret watcher there, to cry out, "Take

† *The Standard* (London), October 25, 1912, p. 7.
1. All prominent Victorian novelists: Charles Dickens (1812–1870), William Makepeace
   Thackeray (1811–1863), George Meredith (1828–1909), and Robert Louis Stevenson
   (1850–1894).

care! Take care!" to the other passengers on the boat. Mr. Conrad places these sensations in the mind of a quite ordinary matter-of-fact man, so that immediately the experience is brought into relation with us all—for all of us that moment may come when the prevailing menace of that Other Self, concealed as we think from the world, threatens us with instant disaster. * * *

ANONYMOUS

Mr. Conrad's New Stories[†]

The triumph of Mr. Conrad's poetic realism was never, surely, more apparent than in the first of the three stories in *'Twixt Land and Sea.* * * * The second story, "The Secret Sharer," will probably prove the most attractive to ordinary taste. A good deal of dramatic incident of an exciting kind forms the warp[1] of the tale, and the very concrete details of the smuggling of a fugitive seaman on board the Liverpool ship *Sephora,* becalmed in the Gulf of Siam, by the ship's captain, and his successful concealment from the officers and crew, will seem "unforgettable." The tale is, indeed, very cunningly told, and the nervous tension of the captain, who here again is the narrator, forms the arch that successfully sustains the down-thrust of the artistic edifice. None the less, the quality of atmosphere does not break into beauty, apart from the first and the last few pages. There is scant time, indeed, for the author's philosophic irony and matchless descriptive power to assert themselves in the bustle and fuss of this game of hide-seek. Of course, no English writer would have treated the incident of a murderer's escape from the law with such psychological sympathy, or have invested the action, at the close, with the haunting spell of high beauty.

The relation of the captain (who is new to his ship) with his uneasy crew is also drawn with much humorous fineness; but the full compass of Mr. Conrad's art cannot be divined from this dexterous performance on two minor instruments. The close of the piece, however, gives the author occasion for a rich orchestration of his motive. No one but he would have dared to make the captain-narrator risk both his ship and his future under the mountain-shadow of the Koh-ring, in the midst of reefs and shoals, out of quixotic interest in the unlucky outcast. * * *

[†] *The Nation* (London), October 26, 1912, pp. 187–88.
1. Strong threads extending lengthwise in a loom that are crossed by other threads to form a woven item.

E[DWIN] F[RANCIS] E[DGETT]

Joseph Conrad: His Three Latest
Stories of Sea and Shore†

Although the three stories in Mr. Conrad's latest volume are of the sea and its people, although their scenes are never far from the shore and are for the most part the decks and cabins of ships, there is in them nothing of the storm and stress of the ocean. Their passions and conditions are of the spirit and the soul of man. * * *

In each of these tales Mr. Conrad is himself ostensibly the narrator as a master-mariner, the calling he followed until he gave up the sea for literature. They are all told in a mood of reminiscence, and they reveal the reflective nature of a man who is prone to ponder upon the motives of human action. He is not content merely to chronicle the doing of man. He strives to reach behind the events themselves to give us something more than a mere surface impression of his characters, to enable us to understand them as they are in real life. And if we fail to understand them, we feel that the story-teller has done his best and has told us all he knows. Mr. Conrad, in fact, relies not a little upon the intelligence of his readers, and he attempts none of the omniscience with which the average novelist weakens his effects and stretches our credulity to the breaking-point. * * *

In "The Secret Sharer," the second of the three stories in *'Twixt Land and Sea*, the situation is exceptional and dramatic. At the same time it is extremely plausible. * * * The entire story is * * * pervaded with an atmosphere of fear, for the captain no less than for the fugitive in hiding. He must not merely be concealed: he must be concealed so that everybody on the boat will have no cognizance of his concealment.

At no moment could the captain feel that he was master of his own vessel. "This is not the place," he says,

> to enlarge upon the sensations of a man who feels for the first time a ship move under his feet to his own independent word. In my case they were not unalloyed. I was not wholly with her. Part of me was absent. That mental feeling of being in two places at once affected me physically as if the mood of secrecy had penetrated my very soul. * * * All unconscious alertness had abandoned me. I had to make an effort of will to recall

† *The Boston Evening Transcript*, January 29, 1913, p. 22. The page reference is to this Norton Critical Edition. Edward Francis Edgett (1867–1946) was the literary editor of the *Boston Evening Transcript* from 1894 until 1938 and regularly reviewed Conrad's works, including *Nostromo, A Personal Record, Chance, Within the Tides, Victory, The Arrow of Gold, The Rescue, Notes on Life and Letters*, and *The Rover*.

myself back from the cabin to the conditions of the moment. I
felt that I was appearing an irresolute commander to those
people who were watching me more or less critically. [30–31]

Thus does Mr. Conrad cause us to enter into and share the feelings
of his characters. His point of view is always the point of view of the
observer. * * *

ANONYMOUS

Stories by Joseph Conrad: Intensely Vivid Descriptions of Life on Asiatic Seas and Shores[†]

Joseph Conrad, that strange genius with a stranger history, the peer
of any living English novelist in the sheer artistry of his use of the
language which he learned largely from the Bible while sailing before
the mast, has produced another striking book, 'Twixt Land and Sea
[1895], with qualities which set it apart from the mass of current fiction. In theme as well as in style it is much what readers of Almayer's
Folly and "Typhoon" have come to expect. It is a volume of three
stories which deal with the Asiatic seas and the mystery-suggesting
river-mouth settlements of the Dutch East Indies.[1] Here Mr Conrad
has returned to the familiar scene of his earliest work. * * *
  In "The Secret Sharer," the second of the three stories in the
present volume and one of the most vivid and remarkably told tales
that have come even from Conrad's pen, the same sentiment finds
expression in such a passage as this, "And suddenly I rejoiced in the
great security of the sea as compared with the unrest of the land, in
my choice of that untempted life presenting no disquieting problems, invested with an elementary moral beauty by the absolute
straightforwardness of its appeal and by the singleness of its purpose" [11]. The episode around which "The Secret Sharer" is constructed is characteristically simple. * * * The story as it continues is
a marvelously minute and vivid psychological study of the strain
that the captain undergoes in keeping knowledge of the refugee's
presence from the crew and finally in venturing so close to an
unknown coast, against the crew's protest, that the refugee can slip
out of a port hole and strike for shore.

---

† Springfield Weekly Republican (Massachusetts), February 20, 1913, p. 5. The page ref-
    erence is to this Norton Critical Edition.
 1. Dutch colonial possessions in the Malay Archipelago, most of which became part of
    modern Indonesia after World War II.

The Malay Archipelago and the neighboring Dutch islands, as Conrad pictures them—and he should know—are the asylum of men of all nations at odds with law and order in their own countries, and are [the] scene of crimes on sea and land that reveal a larger element of intense human passion than in more orderly communities. Mr Conrad has so completely caught the atmosphere of locality that the reader at once senses the presence of these characteristics, although the only guide to them is found in bold sketches of individual persons and their immediate environment. * * *

REVIEWS OF *THE SHADOW-LINE*

ROBERT LYND

Mr. Conrad†

Mr. Conrad will be sixty this year. It is scarcely five years since a London morning paper described him as one of the most brilliant of the younger writers. It was an absurd error, but a happy one, in that it suggested how new a thing Mr. Conrad's genius is. He is a creator and a discoverer. He has discovered the moral and spiritual world of the sea, and has written its legend (as one feels while one reads him) for the first time. He has peopled it with the three races of ships and men and evil spirits. If he had written in the Middle Ages he would have had many marvellous tales to tell of the escapes of ships and sailors from the malice of devils. His ships and sailors— the former are scarcely less alive than the latter—have a way during their voyages of carrying on a running fight with an almost personal devil or league of devils all the way to port. Mr. Conrad's favourite story is that of Christian and Apollyon[1] retold in terms of sailors and ships. His hero is the man that overcomes; his heroine is the ship that pulls through. Has he not written the fable of these things perfectly in "Typhoon" [1902] and "Youth" [1898]?

His new story is, in a sense, the old story over again. Here we have a captain and a ship haunted by devilish influences. It is as though the spirit of the previous captain, a wicked old madman,

---

† *The Daily News & Leader* (London), March 19, 1917, p. 2. Page references are to this Norton Critical Edition. For Robert Lynd, see p. 381, n. †.
1. A reference to the scene from John Bunyan's *The Pilgrim's Progress* (1678) in which Christian battles Apollyon, an angel from the abyss, in the Valley of Humiliation, eventually wounding Apollyon and causing him to flee.

who had died on board, hovered over the ship like a curse.[2] The crew, all but the cook, are fever-stricken on a calm sea, without a breeze to carry them away from the neighbourhood of the pestilential land. Horrors of fever are seen through the eyes of the raving first mate as but the emanations of another horror—the curse of the wicked old man whose body lies at the bottom of the Gulf of Siam at the latitude 8 deg. 20min. Some "purposeful malevolence" [105] seems to be at work to keep the ship from passing the latitude. At night the darkness hangs over the silent ship like death. So thick was it that, according to the captain, "it seemed that by thrusting one's hand over the side one could touch some unearthly substance. There was in it an effect of inconceivable terror and inexpressible mystery" [119].

Mr. Conrad describes the atmosphere of terror and mystery most effectively in his (or the captain's) description of the fever-famished crew moving about mutely at work obeying orders and hauling up the mainsail in the uncanny darkness: "The shadows swayed away from me without a word. Those men were the ghosts of themselves, and their weight on a rope could be no more than the weight of a bunch of ghosts" [120].

One misses the "grue"[3] one has a right to expect, however, when the first mate, crazy with fever, comes out on deck and laughs "a provoking, mocking peal, with a hair-raising, screeching over-note of defiance" [126], and calls on the rest of the crew to laugh with him in order to show the dead man under the sea that they are not afraid of him and his curse. The truth is, *The Shadow Line* is a ghost story which does not quite "come off." It is a story which no one but Mr. Conrad could have written, but it suffers from a tedious introduction, a hero who (though he conquers) gives one the impression of being a spectator rather than a conqueror, and a ship with a less definite personality than most of Mr. Conrad's ships. The central experience of the story is an experience that ages a man rather than an experience that makes a man. Mr. Conrad describes the book as a "confession." Is it the story of his own experience with his first command? If so, it becomes at once an absorbingly interesting document. For it is not necessary that an autobiography should be "convincing" in quite the same sense as a novel must be. * * *

2. Conrad took issue with this review and others like it that wanted to see *The Shadow-Line* in light of the supernatural. In a letter to his agent J. B. Pinker (1863–1922), Conrad remarked, "That donkey Lynd begins his review with the words Mr Conrad will be sixty this year. * * * But I am not calling him a donkey on that account. Imagine he reviews to [*sic*] Shadow-Line from a GHOST-STORY point of view!! Would you believe it? Is it stupidity or perversity, or what?" (*CL* 6:51).
3. Shudder or shiver of horror or terror.

ANONYMOUS

The Great Conrad†

To call an artist "great" nowadays has ceased to be a compliment. There are so many of them, for one thing. And the word has become so much a euphemism of noise, bulk, show, and brag, that to call a mere artist great is something like admiring a mere frog because he has blown himself out to ten times his size. And so when we call Mr. Conrad "great," it is in the antiquated sense of the word, in the sense that we speak of "the great masters." For that is really the only possible way to look at him; nor is it a labored truism to point it out. Criticism is so delivered over to indiscriminate praise that when a genuine master of literature swims into our ken,[1] there is nothing left but to repeat more hoarsely and more stridently the appreciations we have devoted to not a few of his contemporaries. * * *

Before galloping (from lack of space) over *The Shadow Line*, it would not be amiss to underline one aspect of Mr. Conrad's treatment of character. There is a pretty general impression abroad that his characters are highly complex and evasive—an impression natural enough, partly because Mr. Conrad is the greatest living psychologist writing in English, partly because of his method of revealing a personality from every possible angle of vision—as though a number of searchlights set at different and acutely judged distances apart, directed and concentrated differently colored beams upon a single object. It would be truer to say, we think, that on the whole not only are his characters simple, but that their actions are simple and spring from simple motives. It is because he sees that actions and motives, simple in themselves, are tremendously intricate and significant in relation to the universal into touch with which their very simplicity brings them, and what tremendous, untoward, and remote consequences are entailed by these simple motives and actions, that his subtleties seem always to be imposing themselves upon the reader's perception. "He complicated matters by being as simple"[2] [*LJ* 60], he describes one of his own characters. And this complexity of foreground must not be confused with his background of life and character—which, in his grandest work, is as severely simple, elemental, austere, and majestic as the seas which have inspired him.

---

† *The Nation* (London), March 24, 1917, pp. 828, 830. Page references are to this Norton Critical Edition.
1. See p. 12, n. 5.
2. The phrase actually reads slightly differently: "he complicated matters by being so simple."

So lengthy an introduction would be even more tedious were not *The Shadow Line*, to our mind, written at Mr. Conrad's fullest imaginative stretch. The tale, at first glance, is almost disconcertingly bare and unambitious. The first part is occupied partly in relating how a mate got a captaincy. The second describes his first voyage on his new ship, which the malignity of his dead predecessor drives back to port with all his men except the steward (whose heart is too weak for any but slight exertions) down with fever. But it is a great deal more than that. The first thing that strikes you is Mr. Conrad's elfin power of mingling the natural with the supernatural. All the events that happen upon the voyage that is to say—the first mate's obsession of his former captain's dark intent to destroy the ship, the gradual spreading of tropical fever to all the gallant crew, the constant trifling of the winds with the ship in deceptive breezes, the discovery and remorse of the captain that some noxious drug has been substituted for the quinine, the heroic bearing of the steward, the descent of a darkness and silence at night upon the ship like the darkness of primeval chaos, the sick mate crawling up on deck to cast a last defiance at the dead skipper, the final exorcism of the spell and the sailing of the ship by the captain and the steward back to port—all these suggestions, experiences, and episodes might be ascribed *equally* to natural or supernatural causes. The artist reserves his judgment and we reserve ours. All we can feel and express with assurance is the intolerable weight of evil suggestion, the atmosphere of malevolence as menacing and silent as the darkness, "which came over me like a foretaste of annihilation" [119]. The whole thing is as far removed as possible from a vulgar occultism on the one hand and a mere dull concatenation of material impact upon the other. Such a power of invoking the insubstantial is in itself a witchcraft of art, quite apart from the way it throws into relief the broad, fate-opposing, Sophoclean outlines[3] of Ransome, the steward, risking every hardship with heroic cheerfulness, and then, when the strain is removed, breaking into a piteous terror over his diseased heart.

There appears, on the face of it, to be a sharp break between the first and second halves of the story. There would be but for the figure of Captain Giles, who gets the mate his ship, and is threaded, with true artistic instinct, into the last few pages of the book. It is impossible to describe Captain Giles. He is a personality drawn in the finest shades and with that impalpable caress of revelation which is the glory of Henry James.[4] And how can you describe those figures of Henry James? All we can put out is that Captain Giles, so stolid, so heavy, so

---

3. Sophocles (c. 496–406 B.C.E.) was a Greek tragedian. Only seven of his plays survive, most notably *Oedipus Rex*, which chronicles Oedipus's attempts to escape his fate as prophesied by the Oracle.
4. See p. 373, 4th n. 1.

reputable, even stockish, is so impersonal with it, so intimate with his environment and thereby so extraordinarily acute to it, that he can perceive anything that distorts or sends a ripple of the unusual across it, with a ghostly penetration this side second sight—Captain Giles, whose "watch came up from the deep pocket like solid truth from a well" [64]. If there were nothing in the book but Captain Giles, it would be a masterpiece. It is impossible to pick out the method of such a psychology. Such characters seem to happen as a cloud is born instantaneously into a blue sky. For, let there be no mistake about it, *The Shadow Line* is literature—and great literature at that.

ANONYMOUS

A Conrad Hero's Quest for Truth†

Perhaps one reason why Mr. Conrad's novels are not as popular as the romance of their matter and the beauty and clarity of their manner entitle them to be is because they are novels of great quests and of absorbing passions; which is to say that they are not, spiritually speaking, of this day and generation.

For in an era of steam and electricity men have neither time nor patience for quests. As though great experiences were so much merchandise, if the one desired be not immediately at hand we take a substitute and go our way, ignorant of lack. And as for absorbing passions, we distrust them to the point of erecting a barrier betwixt us and them, and labelling our own field "sanity," and the mysterious land beyond, first "eccentricity" and then "delusion."

With Mr. Conrad, on the other hand, whether it be a touch of the Orient in his Slavic blood, or the catching of his dramatic sense by the timeless Arab fatalism of the Malay Archipelago in and out of which he wandered so long, a waiting for the Event is as instinctive as the drawing of breath. The Event is not always, perhaps it is rarely, defined in the soul of the seeker. Sometimes it is love, sometimes the achievement of ambition—this last, by the way, almost always tragically frustrated—sometimes, as in the present tale, it is the crossing of the Shadow Line between untried youth and tested maturity, a line which may be crossed in an hour, but upon which there is no backward turning. Always it is the one event calculated to prove the powers of the individual soul; none other can possibly serve, none other is ever attempted, except to the end of disaster.

† *The New York Times Review of Books*, April 22, 1917, p. 157. Page references are to this Norton Critical Edition.

Linked logically and inevitably with this ideal unity of man and his experience is his capacity for great and consuming passion. Not the passion either of the sentimental or the modern "gripping" school, it is needless to say, but of the antique mold and stature that once led men to the belief in an indwelling demon. Some characters, like Almayer and Willems,[1] too slight or too unworthy by nature for the inhabitation of a god, the demon rends. Others, like the hero of *The Shadow Line,* achieve the fullest measure of manhood. Whether they win or lose, they at least play for great stakes; nothing less than for all they are and can hope to be, in this world and the next.

Long before the cataclysm now whelming the world was dreamed of Mr. Conrad wrote of himself in *A Personal Record* [1912], that most unusual of autobiographies:

> Those who read me know my conviction that the world, the temporal world, rests on a few very simple ideas; so simple that they must be as old as the hills. It rests notably, among others, on the idea of Fidelity. At a time when nothing which is not revolutionary in some way or other can expect to attract much attention I have not been revolutionary in my writings. [*PR* 17]

This statement, made with Mr. Conrad's explicit accuracy in self-analysis, has double significance in relation to his latest work. It is as though the great writer, weary not only with years, but with the madness of the world, had by a supreme effort of the will thrown off the burden of personal anxieties and of hopes and fears for his native and adopted countries, and had gone back to that great passion for the sea that over and over again he has pictured as being the only passion to which a man may give himself unreservedly and gain, not lose, his liberty. In a moment of supreme revolution he has turned from its struggle, not because he is unable to face it, but rather to lay hold upon the permanent things in nature and in the soul of man that underlie it and will outlast it. The cornerstone of his faith is indeed Fidelity.

The Shadow Line is a brief novel, and its action takes place during less than a month in a young man's life. This young man suddenly resigns an excellent berth as a ship's mate, out of whim, as far as apparent reasons go. He could not explain it even to himself, except that all at once, "the past eighteen months, so full of new and varied experience, appeared a dreary, prosaic waste of days. I felt—how shall I express it—that there was no truth to be got out of them" [50].

Perhaps most young people have this feeling at one time or another; its persistence accounts for much of the obscure

---

1. The main characters of Conrad's first two novels, *Almayer's Folly* (1895) and *An Outcast of the Islands* (1896), respectively. Almayer also plays a minor role in *An Outcast of the Islands.*

melancholy of youth. And upon the way in which it is met depends the future—depends that momentous crossing of the Shadow Line, or the frustrate lingering on the hither side, which is all that many a soul knows of life.

But Mr. Conrad's hero, having been faithful to his task before the Call came to him, and faithful to his mistress the sea, is not faithful to himself. He enters upon his quest for the unknown truth blindly indeed, but with a firmness which other men called obstinacy, and a reverence unsuspected even by himself.

His probation was not long, but it was arduous. To the terrors of calm in the tropics and a fever-stricken ship was added the dead hand stretched against them of his predecessor in command, the wicked old captain who had lacked only the power to take the ship and all in it with him on his last dark voyage, as a savage chieftain takes with him his wives and slaves and hunting gear. Day after day, night after night, the silent struggle went on, set upon that vast stage of "stars, sun, sea, light, darkness, space, great waters; the formidable Work of the Seven Days, into which mankind seems to have blundered unbidden. Or else decoyed" [112].

At last one night the stars went out. No one could know what was about to happen, no one could avert it by a hair's-breadth:

> There was still no man at the helm. The immobility of all things was perfect. If the air had turned black, the sea, for all I knew, might have turned solid. It was no good looking in any direction, watching for any sign, speculating upon the nearness of the moment. When the time came the blackness would overwhelm silently the bit of starlight falling upon the ship, and the end of all things would come without a sigh, stir, or murmur of any kind, and all our hearts would cease to beat, like run-down clocks. [119]

In this scene we feel that the young captain crosses his Shadow Line. Here he finds what he has been seeking—his manhood, the place in the world of men and of nature appointed for him from the beginning, which is the final truth.

> "We must try to haul this mainsail close up," I said. The shadows swayed away from me without a word. Those men were the ghosts of themselves, and their weight on a rope could be no more than the weight of a bunch of ghosts. Indeed, if ever a sail was hauled up by sheer spiritual strength it must have been that sail, for, properly speaking, there was not muscle enough for the task in the whole ship let alone the miserable lot of us on deck. [120]

About *The Shadow Line* there is an extraordinary atmosphere of beauty. Not merely in its verbal descriptions of the "gorgeous and barren sea" [107], or of the ship which, "clothed in canvas to her very trucks.* * * seemed to stand as motionless as a model ship set on the gleams and shadows of polished marble" [97], though not even in "Youth" has the author dipped his pen in whiter magic. It is a beauty deeper than mere words go.

Through Mr. Conrad's work has always run the feeling that however much his favourite virtue, fidelity, may profit a man's soul, his earthly existence is largely the sport of circumstances. Over and over again his heroes go down into darkness after a losing fight with villainy or stupidity or mere inertia—dauntless and gallant figures who leave but a name behind to drift upon the light and treacherous airs about obscure gulfs and headlands until in, as it were, some breathless calm, even the name sinks into the forgetful sea.

But in *The Shadow Line* this is not the case. Now and then there is struck a tense note of foreboding, but the anticipated blow never falls. It is as though the gods of disaster are disarmed for once by the youth and courage shining beneath their hand. So, a beauty of human flesh and blood facing triumphantly, if momentarily, the eternal forces of the universe is in the book; the beauty of pause, as though its handful of characters were lifted for an instant and held between heaven and earth as in a crystal sphere; a beauty of independence, of isolation, and of accomplishment. There is something complete, something almost sculptural, about it.

At the beginning of this review it was suggested that the novels of Joseph Conrad lack a general popularity—for the same reason, it may be added, as do Malory's tales of King Arthur,[2] because they are the records of great passions and of desperate quests. The time is near, we believe, when they shall come into their own. Within the past three years hundreds of thousands of young men have gone in search of "the truth that is to be got out of" life or death. They who have gone, those who have remained behind, must, if they had not already done so, have crossed perforce each his Shadow Line. The world, to its own astonishment, has learned anew that passion is not a flame to be avoided but a sword to be grasped; it has learned anew the beauty of quest, and the splendour of fidelity.

After the war is over we shall read more of Sir Thomas Malory than we have done—and more of Joseph Conrad.

---

2. A reference to *Le Morte d'Arthur* (1485), a collection of tales about King Arthur and his court, by the English author Sir Thomas Malory (c. 1415–1471).

E[DWARD] F[RANCIS] E[DGETT]

Joseph Conrad the Supreme Analyst[†]

*His Latest Story a Characteristic Romantic Study
of the Thoughts Flowing through a Man's Mind*

Nothing written by Mr. Conrad during his twenty years of fame as
master of English fiction is more characteristic than *The Shadow
Line*. It is an epitome of his manner and a summary of his method. It
is, to be sure, a direct narrative in which the chief actor is the teller
of his own story, differing thus from the Conradian style of indirec-
tion and circumlocution that has led many readers to misunderstand
him and to speak emphatically of his obscurity. But it is none the less
thoroughly representative of him. Like all the novels and short stories which have revealed him both as a master of English and a master of fiction, its purpose is the dual one of bringing life into a story
by giving emphasis to its reaction upon the mind and soul of man. To
Mr. Conrad as to many of us we live not only through the physical
course of a series of events, but also through the stress of mental
activities that determine them. Thought as well as action is developed by him as contributory to the crises of life.

While other novelists would be content to relate one happening
after another during the progress of a man's life, Mr. Conrad looks
upon men and upon fiction as worth much more than such cursory
treatment. His view of man is that he is a sentient being and that in
any account of what he is and what he does his thoughts should
have first place. It is by this analysis of states of mind, by his records of the currents of thoughts darting through a man's brain, that
the flight of time at many moments of his stories makes practically
no progress whatever, and that for page after page and chapter after
chapter we may have made no temporal advance. Indeed, Mr. Conrad is so eager to delve into the past that he tells many portions of
his tales in such continuous retrospect that they sometimes end at
a point in time antedating their beginning.

Although it is thoroughly in Mr. Conrad's manner, *The Shadow
Line* is from beginning to end a straightforward story. But it moves
slowly, very slowly, through a record of scarcely more than three
weeks. * * *

Men of feeling are to be found in all of Mr. Conrad's stories, but
none is more vitally alive in his deepest emotional instincts than
the hero of *The Shadow Line*. His first sight of the vessel he had

† *The Boston Evening Transcript*, May 5, 1917, part three, p. 6. The page reference is to this
Norton Critical Edition. For Edward Francis Edgett, see p. 386, n. †.

journeyed to Bangkok to command thrilled him. "At first glance," he says, "I saw that she was a high-class vessel, a harmonious creature in the lines of her fine body, in the proportioned tallness of her spars. Whatever her age and her history, she had preserved the stamp of her origin. She was one of those craft that, in virtue of their design and complete finish, will never look old. Amongst her companions moored to the bank, and all bigger than herself, she looked like a creature of high breed—an Arab steed in a string of cart-horses" [80].

When he came to board her his feelings were even stronger and his emotions deeper. * * *

For the remainder of the story the vessel becomes at once both an animate and inanimate object. * * * The young captain put to the test is never for a moment daunted, not even when he discovers that the supply of quinine has vanished. None of his thoughts is kept from us.

Through Mr. Conrad he reveals them all. * * *

No one need pick up *The Shadow Line* with the idea of finding in it merely a sea story. It is a story of the sea and sailors, but it is, like all of Mr. Conrad's stories, much more than that. It is a story of the innermost depths of man, a story of soul trials as well as physical difficulties, a substance of fact embedded in the form of fiction. It makes Mr. Conrad even more than before one of the greatest and most substantial figures in modern English literature.

JOHN MACY

From Kipling and Conrad[†]

* * * Joseph Conrad was well over thirty before he began *Almayer's Folly.* Until then, as he charmingly says in *A Personal Record,* "the ambition of being an author had never turned up among those gracious imaginary existences one creates fondly for oneself at times in the stillness and immobility of a day dream" [*PR* 69]. In the twenty years since the "inexplicable event" of his first book the weathered seaman, who left the sea to enter upon what he calls "the career of the most unliterary of writers" [*PR* 85], has come to be acknowledged, acclaimed by his fellow artists as the chief figure in contemporaneous English prose.

The form is prose. *The Shadow Line* is simply the story of the terrible experience of a young captain; his first command, a fever stricken

† *The Dial,* May 17, 1917, pp. 442–43. Page references are to this Norton Critical Edition. John Albert Macy (1877–1932) was an American author, critic, and poet who regularly reviewed Conrad's works.

ship, is becalmed; when he staggers into port, the captain has crossed the line from youth to manhood. In point of length, method, interest, it groups with "Typhoon," an extended episode somewhere between a short-story and a novel. Like "Typhoon" and other stories of the sea by Conrad, it contains within the prose form qualities which make it in effect as truly a poem as "The Ancient Mariner."

Conrad is a poet of the sea. On land his people move amid the sturdy actualities of life that can be comprehended in unmagical terms. However subtly he unfolds the characters of men, with whatever skill he contrives the adventures, accidents, destinies of terrene humanity, however perfectly his phrases are suited to all occasions, always the daylight actualities ashore, even on strange wild shores, remain on the hither side of that vague line beyond which is more than mystery, more than romance—poetry. When the ship is out of sight of land, the line is crossed, another "shadow-line"; the miracle happens. The ship becomes sentient, a spirit, a will. Common seamen are transformed into the figures of a dream, uncannily repulsive or glorified with an extramundane dignity. The sky above and the sea beneath are endowed, as by a new mythology, with obscure consciousness, purposes benign and malevolent, immensely indifferent to ships and men, yet in curiously personal or personified attitudes toward them. And beauty—always there is the beauty that springs from the poetic use of words, images, cadences, harmonies, whatever the formula is for literary magic.

For Conrad, "the most unliterary of writers" [PR 85], is no more nor no less unliterary than Meredith or Swinburne[1] or Shakespeare. No other writer—I do not except the poets—has a richer variety of verbal resource or uses his power with more careful command. This does not imply over-sophistication; it means that mastery of an imaginative abundance which is the delight and the despair of those who understand literary art, and which, fortunately, makes its effect on those who are merely listening to a story. In the steadily increasing number of Conrad's sea pieces are many storms and many calms, dawns, fogs, and starry nights, and for each he finds new, unrepeated phrases. Not only does he find fresh words to convey the familiar aspects of the sea; but the sea presents to him such manifold wonders that in each new voyage he reveals a mood that even he has not before recorded—as if he could go on writing of the sea forever and exhaust neither the infinity of his mistress nor his power to celebrate her.

In the midst of the waters, like the ship which is his creature and his fragile reliance, is man, adventuresome, romantic in youth,

---

1. Algernon Charles Swinburne (1837–1909), English poet, critic, and novelist, perhaps best known for his collection *Poems and Ballads* (1866); "Meredith": see p. 384, n. 1.

observant, philosophic when he has crossed the shadow-line. "There they are: stars, sun, sea light, darkness, space, great waters; the formidable Work of the Seven Days, into which mankind seems to have blundered unbidden. Or else decoyed. Even as I have been decoyed into this awful, this death-haunted command" [112]. Conrad's men, the truest men that he has drawn, are children of the sea of life, and the god behind the winds that drive the sails toward fortune or disaster is Chance.

REVIEWS OF *THE NIGGER OF THE "NARCISSUS"* AND *CHILDREN OF THE SEA*

W. L. COURTNEY

Books of the Day: *The Nigger of the "Narcissus"*†

Mr. Joseph Conrad does not shrink from the conditions involved in his literary art. He is an unflinching realist and, therefore, has no hesitation in giving to his singularly vivid and powerful tale of the sea the ugliest conceivable title. No one would say that *The Nigger of the "Narcissus"* was a pretty or attractive inscription to stand at the head of an exceedingly careful and minute study; but we know that aesthetic considerations are held to be of no value by those who are determined to paint with exact and merciless severity facts as they know them. I believe that some excellent persons have objected to Captain Marryat's[1] stories of the sea, because his heroes and his heroines use somewhat rough and explicit language, and swear a good deal. Captain Marryat's realism, however, is not a patch upon Mr. Joseph Conrad's—for various reasons, and principally for this, that the latter-day "naturalist,"[2] as we now understand him, had not in his time burst upon an astonished world. Captain Marryat was sometimes inclined to invest a spade with the literary distinction of being an agricultural implement. Mr. Joseph Conrad, inspired by different ideals, remorselessly refers to it as a shovel, with a singularly effective and sanguinary adjective attached. Hence it comes that the seamen of the *Narcissus*—very real, picturesque, and living personages—are heard talking as undoubtedly they ought to talk,

---

† *The Daily Telegraph* (London), December 8, 1897, p. 4. Page references are to this Norton Critical Edition. For W. L. Courtney, see p. 368, n. 1.
1. Captain Frederick Marryat (1782–1848), English naval officer and popular novelist of the sea.
2. See p. 141, n. 4.

and would have talked, without any squeamishness on the part of the author in deference to our sensitive and refined nerves.

There is no doubt an advantage in this form of literal veracity; there is also a disadvantage. A man who is going to delineate an incident, a scene, or the cruise of a merchantship as it actually occurs, will not care for his story as much as for his technique. He is keen to give us the right atmosphere; he will surround his characters with elaborate descriptions of sky and sea, storm and calm; he will spend pages and pages prodigal[3] in careful touches, and deliberate word-painting, so that at the end we may be under the illusion that we have listened to a tale, instead of being invited to a man's studio to see how he works. Mr. Conrad works like an artist—of that we are quite certain when we have finished his book: but we are left with only the vaguest idea of what the story has been all about. The *Narcissus* leaves Bombay, having with some little difficulty made up its complement of sailors, and amongst other hands shipped a picturesque nigger, called James Wait. The man, who was late in arriving, and who seriously upset the equanimity of Mr. Baker, the chief mate, proved a veritable Jonah[4] for the ill-fated vessel. He was apparently far advanced in the declining stages of consumption, but also a skulker by nature, making use of his ailments in order to save himself from the necessity of exertion. Yet, though he was in some senses a *malade imaginaire*,[5] he exercised a kind of tyranny over the whole crew. There belonged to him a magnetic power which fascinated everyone with whom he was brought into contact—with the exception, possibly, of an extremely wideawake cockney, called Donkin, and an aged, taciturn, and morose sailor, named Singleton.

When the *Narcissus* was running south, and encountered a violent storm, she lay for some time on her beam ends, to the imminent peril of everyone on board. Yet the chief preoccupation of the crew was to rescue the nigger, who, as a rule, rewarded his messmates with contemptuous criticism and unmeasured contempt. In fact, James Wait nearly caused a mutiny on board, because on one occasion the captain did not hesitate to tell him what he thought of him. Only the long-headed Singleton knew that there would be no peace until his decease. He dies at last, this uncomfortable, lazy, and consumptive nigger, and the cockney, Donkin, steals the money out of his chest. The crew, however, is plunged into profound grief, only alleviated by the fact that a fair wind at once springs up as soon as Jonah has been thrown overboard. So that *Narcissus* at last comes

---

3. Lavish, copious, generous.
4. A reference to Jonah 1:1–15. Jonah disoboys God and flees in a ship. God sends a raging storm, and Jonah admits to the ship's crew what he has done. The crew then throws him overboard, and the storm ceases.
5. An imaginary invalid (French).

home, the men are paid off, and vice, as personified by Donkin, triumphs. Coming like shadows, the sailors of the Narcissus drift back
again into the vagueness of dreamland, and the reader knows them
no more. It is not a story at all, but an episode, which Mr. Conrad has
chosen to extend to 250 pages, and to adorn with all the resources of
his knowledge, of his artistic skill, and of his unflinching realism.

Everyone will remember what a singular effect Mr. Stephen Crane
produced some little time ago by his *Red Badge of Courage*.[6] Mr.
Joseph Conrad has chosen Mr. Stephen Crane for his example, and
has determined to do for the sea and the sailor what his predecessor had done for war and warriors. The style, though a good deal
better than Mr. Crane's, has the same jerky and spasmodic quality;
while a spirit of faithful and minute description—even to the verge
of the wearisome—is common to both. If we open any page of *The
Nigger of the "Narcissus"* we are told with infinite detail what each
one was doing, what the ship was doing, and what sky and sea were
doing. If Mr. Conrad has to present to us a scene of hesitation, the
angry interval of doubt and self-criticism, which often precedes a
mutiny, he does it in the following fashion:

> What did they want? They shifted from foot to foot, they bal-
> anced their bodies; some pushing back their caps, scratched
> their heads. What did they want? Jimmy was forgotten: no one
> thought of him, alone forward in his cabin, fighting great shad-
> ows, clinging to brazen lies, chuckling painfully over his trans-
> parent deceptions. No, not Jimmy; he was more forgotten than
> if he had been dead. They wanted great things; and suddenly all
> the simple words they knew seemed to be lost for ever in the
> immensity of their vague and burning desire. They knew what
> they wanted, but they could not find anything worth saying.
> They stirred in one spot, swinging at the end of muscular arms
> big tarry hands with crooked fingers. A murmur died out. [228]

This is undeniably effective as a picture of indecision and vagueness,
but Mr. Conrad luxuriates in such effects. He builds up his scenes
piece by piece, never by one large and comprehensive sentence, but
through a mass of commas, semi-colons, and full-stops, especially
when it is his business to depict character or narrate incidents. It is
in those that the example of Mr. Crane is most obvious and potent
upon him. But observe how different the style becomes as soon as
the author turns from man to nature, and gives some scope to that
pictorial instinct of the artist when he is dealing with a large canvas
and big brushes. Here is a passage which Pierre Loti[7] might have
written—and not very frequently even such an artist as he:

6. See p. 367, 1st n. 1.
7. Loti (1850–1923), French naval officer and popular novelist of the sea.

It looked as if it would be a long passage. The south-east trades, light and unsteady, were left behind, and then on the equator, and under a low grey sky, the ship in close heat floated upon a smooth sea that resembled a sheet of ground-glass. Thunder squalls hung on the horizon, circled round the ship, far off and growling angrily like a troupe of wild beasts afraid to charge home. The invisible sun, sweeping above the upright masts, made on the clouds a blurred stain of rayless light, and a similar patch of faded radiance kept pace with it from east to west over the unglittering level of the waters. At night, through the impenetrable darkness of earth and heaven, broad sheets of flame waved noiselessly: and for half a second the becalmed craft stood out with its masts and rigging, with every sail and every rope distinct and black in the centre of a fiery outburst, like a charred ship enclosed in a globe of fire. And, again, for long hours she remained lost in a vast universe of night and silence, where gentle sighs, wandering here and there like forlorn souls, made the still sails flutter as in sudden fear, and the ripple of a beshrouded ocean whisper its compassion afar—in a voice mournful, immense, and faint. [208–09]

There are many scenes of this kind which only a man could paint who knew the sea and was aware of all its changing aspects and beautiful metamorphoses. It is for these, and such as these, perhaps, that some readers will delight in The Nigger of the "Narcissus"; and, indeed, even as a moving panorama of the phases of ocean the book is admirable. But it has a value apart from its picturesque setting. There are few characters among the crew of the Narcissus which do not stand out with vivid and lifelike presentment; we know them all as though we, too, had partaken in the lengthy cruise, and had laughed and grumbled at all their idiosyncrasies and failings. Old Singleton, the Nestor[8] of this company, with his immense knowledge and his impressive taciturnity; blue-eyed Archie, with his red whiskers; Belfast, with his touching fidelity to the nigger; Mr. Baker, the chief mate, with his grunts and his sovereign commonsense; little Captain Allistoun, as hard as nails, and with a will tempered like the finest steel; Donkin, the wastrel and outcast of metropolitan life, shifty, indolent, and sly; and the nigger, James Wait himself, with his mysterious authority and his racking cough—one and all are our familiar friends before the voyage is over. They are not a pleasant lot altogether, yet they are very human—big children in their petulant moods, and heroes in times

---

8. In Greek mythology, the son of Neleus and Chloris, and the King of Pylos. He appears in Homer's The Iliad and is often viewed as a good councilor in his role there.

of crisis. It is Mr. Conrad's merit that we part with them with regret, for, as he says himself, they were a good crowd—"as good a crowd as ever fisted with wild cries the beating canvas of a heavy foresail, or tossing aloft, invisible in the night, gave back yell for yell to a westerly gale" [254].

ANONYMOUS

From Recent Novels†

Mr. Joseph Conrad, whose intimate knowledge of the Malay Archipelago[1] was impressively illustrated in those two powerful but sombre novels, *Almayer's Folly* [1895] and *An Outcast of the Islands* [1896], has given us in *The Nigger of the "Narcissus"* an extraordinarily vivid picture of life on board of a sailing-vessel in the merchant marine. The incidents described all take place during a single cruise from Bombay to London; there is no heroine in the plot—for the excellent reason that there is no woman in the ship's company—no love interest, and practically no hero. The central figure is a negro, who ships as a new hand at Bombay, is soon invalided, but rather than admit the truth—for he is dying of consumption—accuses himself of malingering, and when the captain refuses to let him work, appeals so successfully to the feelings of his shipmates as nearly to stir up a mutiny. Eventually he dies in sight of land, having been robbed while in his death-agony by a villainous guttersnipe named Donkin; and at the very moment his body plunges into the sea the long spell of calm ends and a favouring breeze springs up. "Jimmy Wait," alternately the mascot and the Jonah of the *Narcissus,* is a type of West Indian negro—he comes from St. Kitts—that we confess ourselves wholly unacquainted with, in or out of books, but Mr. Conrad's portraiture in every other instance is so convincing that we are content to admit its accuracy here also. As a picture of rough seafaring life, frank yet never offensively realistic, and illustrating with singular force the collective instincts of a ship's crew, as well as the strange and unlikely alliances that spring up on shipboard, this book is of extraordinary merit. What is more, Mr. Conrad has an abiding sense of the mystery of the immortal sea, and the happy gift of painting her changing moods in words that glow with true poetic fire. Lest this should seem exaggerated praise, let us quote the passage describing the view from the *Narcissus* as she entered the [English] Channel:—

† *The Spectator* (London), December 25, 1897, p. 940. The page reference is to this Norton Critical Edition.
1. See p. 10, n. 9.

Below its [the lighthouse's] steady glow, the coast stretching
away straight and black, resembled the high side of an indestructible craft riding motionless on the immortal and unresting
sea. The dark land lay alone in the midst of the waters, like a
mighty ship bestarred with vigilant lights—a ship carrying the
burden of millions of lives—a ship freighted with dross and with
jewels, with gold and with steel. She towered up immense and
strong, guarding priceless traditions and untold suffering, sheltering glorious memories and base forgetfulness, ignoble virtues
and splendid transgressions. A great ship! For ages had the
ocean battered in vain her enduring sides; she was there when
the world was vaster and darker, when the sea was great and
mysterious, and ready to surrender the prize of fame to audacious men. A ship-mother of fleets and nations! The great flagship of the race; stronger than the storms! and anchored in the
open sea. [247]

Mr. Conrad is a writer of genius; but his choice of themes, and the
uncompromising nature of his methods, debar him from attaining
a wide popularity. Illumined though it is by such shining moments
as the passage just quoted, we own to having found *The Nigger of
the "Narcissus"* at times almost unbearably depressing.

A. T. QUILLER-COUCH

From From a Cornish Window†

Had I to award a prize among the novels of the past season, it should
go to Mr. Joseph Conrad's *Nigger of the "Narcissus."* * * *
    And now I come to Mr. Conrad's *Nigger of the "Narcissus."* I
observe with pleasure that he omits from his volume the "Author's
Note"[1] which decorated the conclusion of the story in the *New Review.*
It contained many just observations, which the reader might have
made for himself, or have been allowed to discover elsewhere. A
good tale needs no author's note; and Mr. Conrad's is a thoroughly
good tale. As folks usually understand the term, it has no "plot." It
is just the narrative of the homeward voyage of a sailing-ship from
Bombay to London Dock. There is no love-making—no word of it.
The *Narcissus* carried no woman on board; but *per contra* she carried a Russian Finn in her crew; which, as every seaman knows, is

---

† *Pall Mall Magazine* (London), March 1898, pp. 425, 428–29. Page references are to this
    Norton Critical Edition. Sir Arthur Thomas Quiller-Couch (1863–1944) was an English
    novelist and poet particularly noted for his compilations *The Oxford Book of English
    Verse 1250–1900* (1900; revised 1939) and *The Oxford Book of Ballads* (1910).
1. What later came to be known as the preface to the novel; see pp. 139–42.

quite enough to account for the foul weather she encountered. Also, she carried a malingering negro, who shammed sick, and kept on shamming it until, within sight of land, he actually died. The fascination exercised upon the crew by this negro and his mysterious state of health is the main motive of the story; and many critics will call this story but an "episode," and compare the book with Mr. Crane's *Red Badge of Courage*. Mr. Conrad has indeed something of Mr. Crane's insistence; he grips a situation, an incident * * *: he squeezes emotion and colour out of it to the last drop * * *. He is ferociously vivid; he knows the life he is writing about, and flings his knowledge at the reader in the truculent fashion we are all growing accustomed to. But he knows the inside of his seamen too: he is no mere counter of buttons. And by consequence the crew of the *Narcissus* are the most plausibly lifelike set of rascals that ever sailed through the pages of fiction; and a good crowd too, as our author assures us in his final sentence: "as good a crowd as ever fisted with wild cries the beating canvas of a heavy foresail; or tossing aloft, invisible in the night, gave back yell for yell to a westerly gale" [254]. No one who has had the honour to scrape acquaintance with the merchant seaman will fail to recognise in Mr. Conrad's portraits the faces of old friends: the pious serious-minded cook; the two Norwegians sitting side by side on a chest, alike and placid, like a pair of love-birds on a perch; Donkin, the impudent rights-of-labour grumbler; Singleton, the oldest able seaman in the ship, who had sailed to the southward since the age of twelve, who in forty-five years had lived no more than forty months ashore, and boasted, with the mild composure of long years well spent, that generally from the day he was paid off from one ship till the day he shipped in another he was seldom in a position to distinguish daylight—an heroic, a patriarchal figure, "the incarnation of barbarian wisdom serene in the blasphemous turmoil of the world" [145]; the "old man," Captain Allistoun, with the iron-grey hair, face coloured like pump-leather, and a sardonic smile when he pronounced his owner's name:—"He shaved every morning of his life—at six—but once (being caught in a fierce hurricane eighty miles south-west of Mauritius) he had missed three consecutive days. He feared naught but an unforgiving God, and wished to end his days in a little house, with a plot of ground attached—far in the country—out of sight of the sea" [162].

These are the men whom Mr. Conrad lets drive through the fierce seas off the Cape: true merchant-seamen; an inarticulate, indispensable, forgotten race; men hard to manage, but easy to inspire; bearing the hardness of their own unique fate; men who know little or nothing of the world, the world which exists "within the frontier of infamy and filth, within that border of dirt and hunger, of misery and dissipation, that comes down on all sides to the water's edge of the incorruptible ocean, and is the only thing they know of life, the only thing they see of surrounding land—those lifelong prisoners of the sea" [146]. For Heaven's sake let us waste no sentiment over them! We have always eaten the fruit of their toil and hardships, and neglected them utterly; and, whatever we may be, they have been the better men for our neglect: men ["]strong and mute; effaced, bowed, and enduring["]—the words are Mr. Conrad's—["]like stone caryatides that hold up in the night the lighted halls of a resplendent and glorious edifice["] [159]; that edifice, my respectable friends, being British Commerce and the Empire that stands upon Commerce.

STEPHEN CRANE

From Concerning the English *Academy*[†]

* * * The novelists did not appear in great force in the discussions which were waged in the columns of the journal previous to the decisions. Many people suggested that the prizes should be given to Mr. Henry James for his *What Maisie Knew*,[1] and to Mr. Joseph Conrad for his *The Nigger of the "Narcissus"*—a rendering which would have made a genial beginning for an English Academy of letters, since Mr. James is an American and Mr. Conrad was born in Poland. However, these two were the only novelists who figured prominently. They were not puny adversaries. Mr. James's book is alive with all the art which is at the command of that great workman, and as for the new man, Conrad, his novel is a marvel of fine descriptive writing. It is unquestionably the best story of the sea written by a man now alive, and as a matter of fact, one would have to make an extensive search among the tombs before he who has done better could be found. As for the ruck of writers who make the sea their literary domain, Conrad seems in effect simply to warn them off the premises, and tell them to remain silent. He comes nearer to an ownership of the mysterious life on the ocean than anybody who has written in this century.

Mr. Conrad was stoutly pressed for the prize, but the editors of the *Academy* judged the book to be "too slight and episodic," although they considered it "a remarkable imaginative feat marked by striking literary power."[2] If one wanted to pause and quibble, one would

† *The Bookman* (New York), March 1898, p. 23. For Crane, see p. 367, 1st n. 1.
1. Crane refers to the journal *The Academy*, which gave out an annual prize for the best book or books published the previous year. For Henry James, see p. 373, 4th n. 1. *What Maisie Knew* is generally considered one of the more important novels of his later literary career.
2. "Our Awards for 1897," *The Academy*, January 15, 1898, 47.

instantly protest against their use of the word episodic, which as a critical epithet is absolutely and flagrantly worthless. * * *

ANONYMOUS

The Children of the Sea†

A new book by a strong and original writer who has already made an impression upon the public by the quality of his work is always welcome. Especially is this true when its advent has been heralded by tantalizingly brief bits of information respecting its merits and meanings. Mr. Joseph Conrad's new story, published in England under title *The Nigger of the "Narcissus,"* had won the English reviewers before it appeared in America this month * * * as *The Children of the Sea*. It was stoutly pressed for the London Academy's[1] hundred guinea prize for the best book of 1897, but the editors of the Academy judged it "too slight and episodic," though they classified it as a "remarkable imaginative feat marked by striking literary power." H. G. Wells and A. T. Quiller-Couch[2] have spoken of it in terms of highest praise, and Stephen Crane, writing to *The Bookman,* says: "Mr. Conrad's novel is a marvel of fine descriptive writing. It is unquestionably the best story of the sea written by a man now alive, and, as a matter of fact, one would have to make an extensive search among the tombs before he who has done better could be found. As for the ruck of writers who make the sea their literary domain, Conrad seems in effect simply to warn them off the premises and tell them to remain silent. He comes nearer to the ownership of the mysterious life on the ocean than anybody who has written in this century" [406].

This smacks somewhat of over-praise, nevertheless *The Children of the Sea* is a remarkable book. It is unique, fascinating, thrilling. Something of the weirdness and mystery of the great Southern Ocean has place in it: it has an exotic quality that differentiates it from all other sea romances. It is a record of the voyage of the *Narcissus* from Bombay to London. "Ships—ships are all right. It is the men in them" [157], says Singleton, the 60-year-old child of the sea.

> Men who knew toil, privation, violence, debauchery—but knew
> not fear and had no desire of spite in their hearts. Men hard to

---

† *The Detroit Free Press*, March 28, 1898, p. 7. Page references are to this Norton Critical Edition.
1. See "Our Awards for 1897," *The Academy* (January 15, 1898), 47.
2. See p. 404. Wells (1866–1946)—English novelist best known for *The War of the Worlds* (1898), *The Time Machine* (1895), and *Tono-Bungay* (1909)—remarked: "*The Nigger of the 'Narcissus'* is, to my mind, the most striking piece of imaginative work, in prose, this year has produced" (*The Academy*, January 8, 1898, p. 34).

manage but easy to inspire—voiceless men—but men enough
to scorn in their hearts the sentimental voices that bewailed the
hardness of their fate. Their generation lived inarticulate and
indispensable, without knowing the sweetness of affections or
the refuge of a home—and died free from the dark menace of a
narrow grave. They were the everlasting children of the mysterious sea. Their successors are the grown-up children of a discontented earth [158],

says Mr. Conrad. It is of the life, the feelings, sympathies, courage
and endurance of these comrades of the ships that he writes, for he
makes his ship a sentient being. "She was beautiful and had a weakness. We loved her no less for that. She wanted care in loading and
handling, and no one knew exactly how much care would be enough.
The ship knew, and would sometimes correct the presumptuous
human ignorance by the wholesome discipline of fear" [175]. When
she rose cleverly to a towering sea the men were proud of her and
praised her. But, asked to do too much, she appeared to lose heart,
refused to rise, and bored her way sullenly through the seas. Off the
Cape of Good Hope the *Narcissus* encountered a fearful gale. The
description of the storm and its effect upon the ship and its crew, the
wreck, and what happened thereafter is a wonderful piece of writing.

> Tremendous dull blows made the ship tremble while she rolled
> under the weight of the seas toppling on her deck. At times she
> soared up swiftly as if to leave this earth forever; then during
> interminable moments fell though a void, with all the hearts
> on board of her standing still, till a frightful shock, expected
> and sudden, started them off again. * * * Now and then, for the
> fraction of an intolerable second, the ship, in the fiercer burst
> of a terrible uproar, remained on her side vibrating and still,
> with a stillness more appalling than the wildest motion. * * * A
> big, foaming sea came out of the mist. * * * It towered close-to
> and high, like a wall of green glass topped with snow. The ship
> rose to it as though she had soared on wings and for a moment
> rested, poised upon the forming crest, as if she has been a
> great seabird. Before we could draw breath a heavy gust struck
> her, another roller took her unfairly under the weather bow,
> she gave a toppling lurch and filled her decks. [177–79]

One more roller and she lay upon her beam ends; half under water,
at the mercy of the storm. What the crew did and said and felt; how
"the nigger" was rescued and expressed his gratitude; how the cook
voiced his most famous speech. "As long as she swims I will cook"
[194], and by standing on his head—almost—to make coffee for the
half-frozen men, and how they passed the hours till the captain

spoke, for the first time in a day and a night, in the peremptory order "Wear, ship!" and was obeyed [196]. Mr. Conrad sets forth so vividly that one can almost feel himself an eye-witness.

Perhaps the secret of his dramatic writing lies in the fact that he so thoroughly knows the life of which he writes. * * * His life has been full of adventure, and his genius enables him to crystallize it in his books. Their unusualness and their familiarity with wild life and strange humanity make *The Children of the Sea*, *The Outcast of the Islands* [sic] and *Almayer's Folly* books decidedly out of the ordinary.

REVIEWS OF *TYPHOON* AND *TYPHOON* AND *OTHER* STORIES

ANONYMOUS

Typhoon: Mr. Conrad's New Book†

It is only a few months since we had the *Youth* volume [1902], and it is perhaps merely an accident of publication that another follows so close upon it. We may well believe, however, that Mr. Conrad is now writing in the fulness of his power and rejoice in a period of fecundity. Certainly there is nothing hasty or perfunctory in these four stories of the sea and seafaring folk, a race generally simple and kindly and yet oppressed with mysteries and terrors; inarticulate, yet here revealed with knowledge and sympathy never brought to their service before. Mr. Conrad has escaped from the tyranny of convention that confines a writer of fiction to short stories or long novels, and two of the pieces in his new volume are of a length that is commonly condemned by the prudent publisher.

Every one of these four pieces is surprisingly good—not that we should anticipate any failure or weakness, but because such fine and original work has the inevitable element of surprise. Mr. Conrad does not begin by idealising his people. They are usually types that may be easily recognised or accepted—individual certainly, but individual in credible, apparent ways. It is under stress of labour and ordeal that they emerge to their human interest and to the heights of their spiritual meaning. The hero of "Typhoon," Captain

† *The Manchester Guardian*, April 23, 1903, p. 10. Page references are to this Norton Critical Edition.

MacWhirr, had "just enough imagination to carry him through each successive day and no more" [260], and it is perhaps Mr. Conrad's single doubtful assumption that this was sufficient to make him run away to sea. It was admitted by Mr. Jukes, his first officer, that he got his ship along all right without worrying anybody, and that he had never been convicted of anything actually foolish. He did what was necessary, and that was all. The useless fripperies with which our lives are embroidered puzzled him. "'I can't understand what you can find to talk about,' says he. 'Two solid hours. I am not blaming you. I see people ashore at it all day long, and then in the evening they sit down and keep at it over the drinks. Must be saying the same things over and over again. I can't understand'" [269]. He "wandered innocently over the waters with the only visible purpose of getting food, raiment, and house-room for three people ashore" [270]. To the ordinary knockabout of the seaman's life he was accustomed, but "he had never been given a glimpse of immeasurable strength and of immoderate wrath" [270] until he commanded the *Nan-Shan* in its voyage northward to the treaty port of Fu-chau with Chinese coolies on board, who were returning home with the savings of their labours. Mr. Conrad's description of the typhoon can hardly be matched, even in his works. It is, indeed, not so much a description as an experience—the curious psychological experience of the first officer who shares the labours and dangers of his less impressionable captain. The great tumult of forces becomes the test of the strong man whose hold on life and identity is never relaxed:

> And again he heard that voice, forced and ringing feebly, but with a penetrating effect of quietness in the enormous discord of noises, as if sent out from some remote spot of peace beyond the black wastes of the gale; again he heard a man's voice—the frail and indomitable sound that can be made to carry an infinity of thought, resolution and purpose, that shall be pronouncing confident words on the last day, when heavens fall, and justice is done—again he heard it, and it was crying to him, as if from very, very far—"All right." [287]

We have not space to quote the scene—perhaps the best show-piece in the book—between the captain, the helmsman, and the second mate, who had "lost his nerve" [301]. The acceptance of all the forces and terrors of the elements, the mad struggle of the Chinamen between decks, the whole disastrous welter of things, is an extravagance of experience that only Mr. Conrad's insatiable imagination could interpret. It is a delirium, a nightmare, with a man in it. And yet the captain does nothing very surprising; if he rises to the occasion it is with no show of exultation; he is kind and business-like, his fortitude has no qualification of fantasy. He conducts affairs by the exercise of small sanities, and we are profoundly affected when he is able, without flurry, to find the matches in the dark. He is well backed, and the engine-room with the second engineer turned stoker, "ripping and raving and all the time attending to his business" [304], becomes a centre of furious labours. The great sea-piece is enveloped in a curious irony when the captain writes home his matter-of-fact account to the "darling wife," who reads it wearily, "reclined in a plush-bottomed and gilt-hammock-chair near a tiled fireplace, with Japanese fans on the mantel and a glow of coals in the grate" [318]. She found the letter rather prosy. * * *

Mr. Conrad will be ranked as a pessimist by those who accept current standards. The heart that is made of penetrable stuff must be wrung by his studies of misery, so splendidly exalted to the measure of tragedy. He takes things hard, and his fortitude, it may be, has not mellowed or weakened to a perfect serenity. His art, original and profound, has qualities of unrest and revolt. It is, nevertheless, based on a philosophy sound and noble, and these stories are a great stimulus and a great enlightenment.

[WILLIAM BEACH THOMAS]

From Fiction[†]

It is always an intellectual stimulus to read Mr. Conrad; and he has written little that is finer than the purple patches in "Typhoon." Not "Q," not even Mr. Kipling,[1] we think, has quite the same power of intense vividness, of insistent concentration. He has the true inspiration of the sea, the real salt savour, and as it were an insight into the elemental forces, and their antagonism in men and nature. * * * The three tales which precede it ["To-morrow"] are in the manner which Mr. Conrad has made his own; and the titular story is both the best and the truest to type. It is as if the author sets out with no other object than to bring before our imagination a typhoon in the China seas; and the only man he can get deliberately to face it is the still, simple, stupid, strong sea captain such as he loves. "The power of the night, the press of the storm"[2] are brought out as vividly as the flashes of lightning through them; and a finer background for the splendid unimaginativeness of the man who fights them could hardly

---

† *The Times Literary Supplement* (London), April 24, 1903, pp. 128–29. Sir William Beach Thomas (1868–1957), English journalist and author, regularly reviewed for *The Times Literary Supplement*—anonymously, as was the practice for that publication.
1. See p. 381, n. 2. "Q": A. T. Quiller-Couch; see p. 404, n. †.
2. A line from "Prospice" (1861) by Robert Browning (1812–1889).

be devised. The mate's account of the prisoned Chinamen fighting through the midst of the storm for the careering money may be compared to the description of the chaining of the vagrant gem in "Quatre-vingt-treize."[3] But how much less great that chapter would have been if it had been put forth by itself on its own merits. As it seems to us, if Mr. Conrad is to advance on himself it is time that he did more than spend his whole energy either on sheer description and the effort after cumulative vividness or on the insistent emphasis of one man's master attribute. Of course, it is good art that the artist should show us in a picture one thing to which all the rest leads us; but the great artist can do this with great accompaniment of subsidiary things or figures. Mr. Conrad could be a greater artist than he dares. * * * The splendid elaboration of the centrepiece claims a larger scheme. In brief, Mr. Conrad writes in this collection as in "Youth" [1898] scenes that lack the proportion of a short story and the construction of a long one. We doubt if his compromise gives to the products of his rare imagination the permanence which they certainly deserve.

ANONYMOUS

A Superb Sea Story by Mr. Conrad[†]

"Typhoon" is one of those books that only too seldom fall into the hands of the reviewer, a book so good that to read it is a peculiar pleasure, to praise it a peculiar privilege. It is good from the first page to the last; it is good through and through. Mr. Conrad knows ships and the sea; no contemporary writer on these subjects is more familiar with them than he is, and one powerful element in this brief narrative of a steamer's experience in passing through a typhoon is the accuracy with which everything about the vessel is described. The author has the technique of the sea at his fingers' ends. But, fortunately, he is a man of imagination, who knows that this technique is of no value for literary purposes except as a means to an end. It is a common fault of writers dealing with the sea that, while insisting upon the immemorial conception of a ship as a living thing, they burden their pages with the technical jargon of their subject. Realism is to be procured, they fancy, by incessant use of the names given to the innumerable parts of the ship, as though verisimilitude could be given to the portrait of man in a novel by constant allusion, in scientific terminology, to his bones and other anatomical belongings.

---

3. An 1874 novel by the French novelist Victor Hugo (1802–1885).
† *The New-York Tribune*, September 14, 1902, Illustrated Supplement, p. 12.

Mr. Conrad rightly keeps all this sort of thing concealed or in the background, with the result that the steamer of his story, the *Nan-Shan*, impresses us as an organism with a soul. She is no less real to us than the captain and his men, and the struggle of these allies, the *Nan-Shan* and her people, with a storm of all but overwhelming power is painted with a vividness that leaves us breathless, as though, in fact, we had passed through that struggle ourselves.

It is an extraordinarily artistic book, spontaneous, natural, full of the air of the sea, but all the time controlled by a sense of balance. Captain MacWhirr, the hero of the great fight, is portrayed with perfect discretion as utterly unconscious of his heroic qualities. He is, indeed, a commonplace man in many ways. Mr. Conrad knows well that if he were to make his man defiant or in any way self-assertive he would make him merely melodramatic and would land in anticlimax. To exhibit him as a conqueror of the typhoon in any spectacular sense would be absurd. MacWhirr, though he lives through it, is always painted with a due sense of proportion; we feel that his companions and his ship owe much to his strong character, but he, like the others and like the ship, remains always a detail in a great picture, which is filled first and last with the might and splendor of the sea in one of its most epical phases. Mr. Conrad's description of that phase bears triumphantly the test of comparison with the thing itself. There are passages in this book which, read in the light of practical experience of the phenomena with which they deal, fit memory like a glove. To read them is to live over again the whole gamut of emotion, the whole scale of visual sensation, experienced in presence of the elements themselves. And the truth is in this book because the author has thought of the truth and of nothing else. There is not a word set down for effect. There is not to be found, even between the lines, a hint of straining after style. It is rather as though Mr. Conrad were a kind of conductor, through which the terror and the beauty of a great storm at sea passed to the printed page as if by some magical process of translation. Only a man of genius could have written "Typhoon" and those other books for which we are indebted to Mr. Conrad.

ANONYMOUS

Joseph Conrad's *Typhoon*[†]

There are at present four conspicuous writers of marine fiction at work in England—W. Clark Russell, the veteran romancer,

[†] *Springfield Sunday Republican* (Massachusetts), September 14, 1902, p. 19. Page references are to this Norton Critical Edition.

W. W. Jacobs, the rollicking humorist, Frank T. Bullen,[1] the expo-
nent of life on a whaler, and Joseph Conrad, who is par excellence
the artist of the sea. Attention was first strongly directed to him
when in 1897 the London Academy "crowned" his *The Nigger of the
"Narcissus"* (known in the United States by the weak and vague title
Children of the Sea) as the best book of the year.[2] Before that he had
been known to a limited circle of readers by certain striking tales of
life in out-of-the-way islands, bound up in volumes entitled *Almayer's
Folly* (1895) and *An Outcast of the Islands* (1896). That the stories
were by no means ordinary was apparent to every discerning reader.
They showed knowledge and unusual power of characterization, and
while the style was still undeveloped it was a style in which the retrospective reader can now see large promise. Still it is doubtful whether
to most readers these stories indicated anything more than a successful echo of the Pacific tales of Louis Becke.[3]

The Nigger of the "Narcissus" was, however, unmistakably the work
of an unusual and very original talent, and the impression was deepened by that extraordinary tale of the sea, *Lord Jim*, which appeared
in 1900, after a volume of minor stories called *Tales of Unrest* (1898).
The Inheritors (1901), written in collaboration with Ford M. Hueffer,[4] was outside the regular line of his development, being a labored
satire on social tendencies, and was a serious mistake, but in his
new story, *Typhoon,* * * * Mr Conrad returns to the field in which he
is unsurpassed, and has fully equaled any of his previous work in
brilliance and interest. As may be supposed from the title, the story
deals exclusively with the sea, where Mr Conrad is as thoroughly at
home as any man, after his long and varied experience as master in
the British merchant service, with voyages to strange seas and distant lands. Yet it is not his knowledge that impresses the reader so
much as his extraordinary gift of style. If the ability to write like
that comes from pacing the bridge in tropic waters and facing wild,
stormy sunsets, there is many a writer that should burn his library

---

1. Frank Thomas Bullen (1857–1915), English author and novelist, whose sea fiction was
particularly popular. W. Clark Russell (1844–1911), English writer, best known for his
nautical fiction, especially for *The Wreck of the Grosvenor* (1877). William Wymark
Jacobs (1863–1943), English fiction writer, is best known for the horror story "The
Monkey's Paw" (1902), but he was also popular for his sea fiction.
2. Conrad won the Academy's prize for *Tales of Unrest* in 1898, not for *The Nigger of the
"Narcissus"* (1897); as noted elsewhere, some felt that he ought to have won the award
in the earlier year; see p. 406.
3. George Lewis Becke (1855–1913), Australian fiction writer, whose sea fiction was especially popular.
4. Hueffer (1873–1939), who changed his name to Ford Madox Ford, was an English
author, best known for his novel *The Good Soldier* (1915) and his tetralogy *Parade's
End*, consisting of *Some Do Not* [1924], *No More Parades* [1925], *A Man Could Stand
Up* [1926], and *Last Post* [1928]). He was a friend of Conrad's and also collaborated
with him on *Romance* (1903) and "The Nature of a Crime" (1909).

forthwith and go off to sea. But it is to be feared that the recipe for good writing is not so simple as that.

Mr Conrad's method is curiously simple. Each of his best books, *The Nigger of the "Narcissus," Lord Jim,* "Typhoon," might be called a monograph in fiction. The first simply tells the story of a long cadaverous negro * * *. Just this and the record of the voyage, with beautiful glimpses of the sea, yet the attention of the reader was miraculously held through the entire book. *Lord Jim* was equally simple * * *, and here again we see the same simple elements—a handful of people standing out with extraordinary vividness against a wonderful background of sea. In these things, then, we see the sources of the author's supremacy in his own narrow field—such a gift in describing and characterizing the sea and its moods as few writers in any language have ever attained, and, second, a no less remarkable faculty of drawing strongly and vividly the people who fit most naturally into this background. This is the chief difference between him and Mr Russell[.] * * * [O]n the one hand his description of calm and storm lack the poetic quality which glows in Mr Conrad's pages, and on the other his characters are for the most part lay figures sketched in to serve the purpose of the romance. Mr Conrad, on the other hand, is primarily an artist, and his romance is not the conventional sea yarn, but the poetry of the great deep itself and the fascinating irony of the contrast between its impressive vastness and the psychology of the human insects that crawl over its wrinkled surface.

Of all his stories, "Typhoon" is the simplest and the most elemental. It is precisely what its title indicates—a record of a great storm at sea, and where such another storm is to be found in literature it would be hard to say. The only deviations from this simple program are to be found in the curious little interludes in which the families of the endangered ship's officers are shown in their homes, and in casual bits of biography thrown in with fine indifference to construction. But everything starts from and comes back to the storm which is the substance of the story and to the little group of people who are the protagonists in the drama. Most admirable is the characterization of Capt MacWhirr on the steamer *Nan-Shan,* the dull heavy man, the routine sailor, slow at book knowledge, who has a huge, bewildered contempt for the theory of rotary storms, and whose only idea is to hammer along and do his duty, but whose solid qualities shine out in the end. This slow, dull-witted man we find in the first chapter confronted by a singular fall of the barometer, and unimaginative enough not to be at all concerned about it: "That's a fall and no mistake," he thought. "There must be some uncommonly dirty weather knocking about" [261]. He must have passed an examination on cyclones, since he was a master, but he remembered nothing of what he had read, and his idea of bad weather did not extend beyond moderate discomfort. So he took no lesson from the barometer:—

> He was, however, conscious of being made uncomfortable by the clammy mist. He came out on the bridge and found no relief to his oppression. The air seemed thick. He gasped like a fish and began to believe himself greatly out of sorts. * * * The smoke struggled with difficulty out of the funnel, and instead of steaming away, spread out like an infernal sort of cloud, smelling of sulphur and raining soot on the decks. [271]

Down in the engine-room the heat went up to 110, and the engineer came climbing up to see why the ventilators were not turned to the wind. The ship rolled heavily in the calm sea:

> At its setting the sun had a diminished diameter and an expiring brown, rayless glow, as if millions of centuries elapsing since the morning had brought it near its end. A dense bank of cloud became visible to the northward; it had a sinister dark olive tint, and lay low and motionless upon the sea, resembling a solid obstacle in the path of the ship. She went floundering toward it like an exhausted creature driven to its death. The coppery twilight retired slowly, and the darkness brought out overhead a swarm of unsteady, big stars that, as if blown upon, flickered and seemed to hang very near the earth. [274–75]

It was at this time that the mate, Mr Jukes, went into the chart-room to write up the ship's log, a feat which he found difficult from the extraordinary way in which the ship rolled:—

> Sprawling over the table with arrested pen, he glanced out of the door, and in that frame of his vision he saw all the stars flying upward between the teakwood jambs on a black sky. The whole lot took flight together and disappeared, leaving only a blackness flecked with white flashes, for the sea was as black as the sky, and sparkled with foam afar. The stars had flown to the roll, and came back on the return swing of the ship, rushing downward in a swarming glitter, not of fiery points, but enlarged in tiny disks, brilliant with a clear wet sheen. [275]

He paused and thought it over, and, having more imagination than Capt MacWhirr, closed his entry with "every appearance of a typhoon coming on" [275]. When he went out on the bridge, where the mean-spirited, second mate was in charge, "The far-off blackness ahead of the ship was like another night seen through the starry night of the earth—a blackness without stars—the night of the immensities beyond the created universe revealed in its appalling stillness through a low fissure in the glittering sphere of which the earth is the kernel" [277]:—

"Whatever these might seem to be about," said Jukes, "we are steaming straight at it."

"You've said it," caught up the second mate. "You've said it, mind, not I."

"And what of that?"

"I've known some real good men get into trouble with their skippers for saying a dam' sight less," answered the second mate furiously. "Oh, no; you don't catch me." [277]

Mr Jukes went in to free his mind and found Capt MacWhirr trying to read a book, standing up and holding to the edge of the book-shelf. He was trying at the last moment to read up on winds, and his head was a muddle of advancing semi-circles, left and right hand quadrants, the probable bearings of the center, the shifts of winds, and the readings of the barometer:—

"It's the confoundest thing, Jukes," he said. "If a fellow was to believe all that's in there he would be running most of his time all over the sea trying to get behind the weather. All these rules for dodging breezes and circumventing the winds of heaven, Mr. Jukes, seem to me the maddest thing when you come to look at it sensibly[.] . . . If the weather delays me—very well. There's your log book to talk straight about the weather. But suppose I went swinging off 300 miles out of my course and came in two days late, and they asked me, 'Where have you been all that time, captain?' what could I say to that? 'Went around to dodge the bad weather,' I would say. 'It must've been dam' bad,' they would say. 'Don't know,' I would have to say, 'I've dodged clear of it.'" [280]

There could hardly be a clearer summary than Mr Conrad gives of the psychology of the stout old British sailor confronted with the necessity of headwork.

After sleeping for a moment the doughty captain was aroused by a loud voice and by a pair of sea boots sliding about the room in a most extraordinary manner. The tumult was frightful, made up of "The rush of the wind, the crashes of the sea, with that prolonged deep vibration of the air, like the roll of an immense and remote drum beating the charges of the gale" [282]. It is a nice touch to his character that his only observation is "There's a lot of weight in this" [282]. Coming out ahead of the ship he saw "a great darkness lying upon a multitude of white fitful, above an immense waste of broken seas, as if seen through a mad drift of smoke" [282]. On the bridge they were putting the shutters in the wheel-house windows for fear the glass would blow in. This seemed the climax. "We must have got the worst of it at once," said Jukes cheerily, shouting with his lips to the captain's ear:—

A faint burst of lightning quivered all round as if flashed into a cavern—into a black and secret chamber of the sea, with a flow of foaming crests. It unveiled for a sinister, fluttering moment a ragged mass of clouds lying low, the lurch of the long outlines of the ship, the black figures of men caught on the bridge, heads formed as if petrified in the act of battering. The darkness palpitated down upon all this, and then—the real thing came at last. [284]

The real thing; no human pen can adequately picture the real thing. Mr Conrad comes as near to it as may be, and to read his book, which leaps at this point into a splendid, sonorous fortissimo, as though all the stops of the full organ had been pulled at once, is the best substitute a landsman may have for the overwhelming sensation of a great storm at sea. And the climax comes when the *Nan-Shan* reaches that deadly center of calm in the very heart of the circular storm, a center out of which only very strong and lucky ships can hope to come safe and sound. The very silence of the brief calm was terrible after the roar of the storm:—

It seemed to them they were talking in a dark and echoing vault. Through a jagged aperture in the dome of clouds the light of a few stars fell upon the black sea, rising and failing confusedly with heavy splashes, all about the ship. * * * Jukes's alert ear caught suddenly the faint, long-drawn roar of some immense wave rushing under that thick blackness which made the appalling boundary of his vision. He saw the stars shining into the pit of black vapors marking the circle of rushing winds and headlong seas. The ship was cut off from the peace of the earth. The wall rose high, with smoky drifts issuing from the inky edge that frowned upon the ship under the patch of glittering sky. The stars, too, seemed to look at her intently, as if for the last time, and the cluster of their splendor sat like a diadem on a lowering brow. [311–12]

And then came the second and most dangerous part of the storm, which Mr Conrad skips, having filled his book handily with the first. "I shouldn't like to lose her" [314], the taciturn Capt MacWhirr had been moved to declare, and he was spared that annoyance. The stout little *Nan-Shan,* with her Siamese flag and her load of Chinese coolies, came through, a wreck, indeed, but safe, and the stolid little Scotch-Irish captain, with his contempt for book knowledge, plays a very heroic figure before the end. The book can hardly be classified—it is neither a novel nor a romance—but there can be no question that it is one of the truest and most artistic works in the whole rich English literature of the sea.

ANONYMOUS

The Quiet Captain[†]

Joseph Conrad's new story would be notable if only for the description of a terrible storm in the China seas, which give it its title "Typhoon." So vivid is the description that you feel you are actually on board the steamer *Nan-Shan* and that you cling to her bulwarks so as not to be blown into the raging waters. We have had of late some inkling what nature can do when an angry mood, and how utterly impotent is man's efforts to resist her.

There is in "Typhoon" very much more than this, however, for the author shows in contrast to the fearful anger of the elements the cool, quiet, deliberate efforts of a man, even a commonplace man, to fight, and fight against what seems inexorable fate, and finally takes the ship from "the Great Beyond, from whence no ship ever returned," into port. She was "so battered incrusted, and gray with salt to the trucks of her masts and to the top of her funnel" that as she slowly made her harbor some smart chap on the dock "offered to give £5 for her as she stood" [317].

Mr. Conrad, in his Captain MacWhirr, has fairly created a new character. Here is a man entirely deficient in imagination. He is not so much matter-of-fact as apparently dull. He is silent because he really has nothing to say. He has no receptivity. The grand traits in the man are his supreme honesty, his sense of duty, more than that, his humanity. It is MacWhirr almost single-handed who fights with the typhoon, though the mate, Jukes, and the engineer, Rout, second him in the ablest manner. Fancy a ship, with her hatches battened down, having 200 coolies on board, and in such a raging storm!

It is not nautical men alone who will appreciate Mr. Joseph Conrad's thorough acquaintance with the ship, but his treatment of the entire subject is one which appeals to a general public.

GEORGE HAMLIN FITCH

From Books That Are New[‡]

In "Typhoon," Joseph Conrad has written one of his best sea stories. It is a mere novelette compared with such long stories as *An Outcast*

---

† *The New York Times Saturday Review of Books and Art*, September 20, 1902, p. 626. The page reference is to this Norton Critical Edition.
‡ *San Francisco Chronicle*, September 28, 1902, Sunday Supplement, p. 4. Fitch (1852–1925), an author, reviewer, and critic, wrote a weekly column for the *San Francisco Chronicle*'s Sunday book page for many years.

of the Islands [1896] and *Lord Jim* [1900], but it is well illustrated * * *. There is practically no plot, the whole book being devoted to an elaborate and intensely graphic picture of a typhoon on the China coast and of the experiences of the tramp steamer *Nan-Shan* in the great storm. These may seem simple materials, but in Mr. Conrad's hands they are ample for the production of a genuine bit of sea literature. In everything that bears on sea life the description is perfect, but what any discriminating reader will resent is the thinness of some of Mr. Conrad's characters. Captain MacWhirr is a colorless mariner. Though he comes out well in the end and shows that he possesses real courage and a strong fund of good horse sense, he is so dry and so commonplace that it requires an effort to take any interest in him. The same may be said of several of the other officers. Only the chief engineer, who drives the steamer through the storm and upon whom the captain relies in the gravest hour, is a real man of flesh and blood. The others strike one as mere abstractions. In all the detail of seamanship the book is well nigh perfect, but what one fails to understand is why so abnormally conscientious a man as Captain MacWhirr should not have changed his course and endeavored to avoid the vortex of the typhoon. Over against this must be placed the admirable figure of the engineer and the irrepressible conflict between the "engine-room" and the "deck." The sketch of the second engineer's fury when he comes on deck to see why the ventilators are not working is finely done. Perhaps the most thrilling thing in the book is the description of the carrying away of the foreworks of the ship, in which were Chinese passengers, and the furious fight of the Celestials over their scattered silver dollars.

Every little detail of the story is so highly wrought that it forms a vital part and goes to make up the total impression of a tremendous battle between the forces of the ocean and the stanch, well-built steamer, with the cool, determined engineer driving her through the mountainous seas, that fall like thunder on her deck. The book is a mere sketch, but it is real literature, because of the combination of minute knowledge of the sea and of seamanship with a style that is the perfection of picturesqueness and strength.

Contemporary Accounts

CHARLES ARTHUR SANKEY

From Ordeal of the *Cutty Sark:* A True Story of Mutiny, Murder on the High Seas[†]

A string of bloody spots spattering on the white deck from aloft interrupted the mate's cursing of the hapless deck hands, and he swung about peering up into the yards overhead, where a knot of incompetent negro sailors were struggling to hoist the mainsail in preparation for the heavy weather making up.

"What the devil are you doing up there, you d— black bunglers?" he bellowed, and immediately caught sight of [John] Francis, grimacing with anguish and gripping a mangled hand, caught in the buntline block as the sail went up.

The mate's [Sidney Smith's] temper, already at boiling pitch from a series of bungles by the inexperienced crew, now snapped all bounds. "Heaven pity me for the pack of useless numbskulls that call themselves a crew!" he shrieked. "Do you call yourself a sailor, yelling over a scratched finger, you malingering swine! Jump overboard and make mincemeat for the whales but get that mains'l up or by the Old Harry[1] I'll have you on deck. Harry I'll have you on deck and flogged!" But Francis, though not too good a sailor, was a powerful truculent man and now he answered the mate in kind.

"Swine yourself!" he shouted, "come up here and we'll see who'll jump overboard."

Insubordination! The bucko[2] mate went white, then red with fury. "All hands down from aloft! Get down on the deck you black swine and take your licking" he roared. An ominous mutter ran through

---

[†] Charles Arthur Sankey (c. 1864–1962) served as an apprentice aboard the *Cutty Sark* from 1880 to 1881. This account was written by his daughter Anna Tillenius (based on Sankey's reminiscences) for the official dedication of the *Cutty Sark* in her dry dock June 25, 1957. This excerpt appeared in the *Winnipeg Free Press* (May 11, 13–15, and 21, 1957), [33]–34, 9, 18, 14, 2.
1. Satan (slang). "Mains'l": mainsail.
2. Swaggering, blustering, or domineering fellow (slang).

the crew forward as not only Francis but all the hands aloft came tumbling down on deck. In a twinkling the mate was surrounded.

As the first sounds of the uproar came aft, Captain Wallace,[3] suddenly made aware of trouble, acted with swift decision. Handing out arms to officers and apprentices, he faced the threatening crew and shouted, "The trouble stops right here, once for all. Francis, apologize to Mr. Smith." Francis' answer was to peel off his jacket and before anyone could move he was on the mate like a tiger.

"All right, let them have it out," the captain growled out, lifting his revolver, "I'll shoot the first man that interferes." His words were lost in the sickening thud of knuckles on bone as the mate's fist smashed down the negro's guard, handicapped as he was with the bloody mangled hand. But even with this disadvantage, the mate could not down him, and after a quarter hour of furious fighting in which the mate more than once took a savage mauling, the captain stopped them. "That's enough," he ordered. "Now get below and the next man I catch abusing his officers I'll clap in irons."

All this time I had stood behind the captain. As senior apprentice, my duty clearly lay with the ship's officers, but since we all had had reason already to fear and despise the bullying mate, my sympathies were undoubtedly with Francis. So it was, though I perhaps alone of the officers heard Francis mutter to his companion as they stumbled below, "I'll lay for him with a capstan bar." I said no word of this. How fervently I later wished I had told the captain, but how could I foresee then the ghastly tragedy that was to make the next two years aboard the *Cutty Sark* a memory to shudder at.

Little did I think, running down the [English] channel aboard the *Fantasie*[4] back from my first voyage, that scarcely a week would pass before I would be again on the high seas trimming sail and eating salt junk. With the other apprentices I had talked of all the great things I would do on shore. But a telegram from Willis and Son[5] calling me to the office at once, took me straightway to London. I was to join the *Cutty Sark*, then lying at Cardiff.[6] * * *

When I reached the float, the *Cutty Sark* was just pulling out of the dock gates into the river at Cardiff, Wales. With the ready assurance and impertinence of youth, I yelled for a boat and ordered them to pull alongside. Catching hold of a wooden fender, worked my way up the ship's side, then, swinging my box over the rail, I clambered on board.

3. Captain James S. Wallace (d. 1880) assumed command of the *Cutty Sark* in 1877.
4. A composite clipper ship built by Alexander Stephen & Sons of Glasgow for C. Shaw & Co. in 1863, originally called *Eliza Shaw* but renamed *Fantasie* when Willis bought it in 1877. The ship was lost at sea in 1884.
5. See p. 4, n. 6.
6. See p. 9, n. 8. For the *Cutty Sark*, see p. 4, n. 6.

She was carrying a cargo of steamer coal consigned to the American Navy in the Pacific and was bound for Anjer in the East Indies[7] to await orders. It was Friday, June 4, 1880, and I was 16 years old. My spirits were fresh and free as the breeze that bellied out our sails—how could I believe that unkind Fate had given me a boost over the rail that morning and that I was just embarking on the most disastrous and adventurous voyage of my life?

Yet there was not lacking a prophet of disaster. On deck old Vanderdecken was pacing endlessly back and forth, "Leave port on a Friday!" he croaked, "We're cursed, we're for it—it's bad luck for this voyage." His old voice quavered. He shook a finger at our snowy white sails now filled with a leading wind giving us our course down the channel, "Bloody red, they'll be!"

We apprentices knew he was weak in the head and laughed uproariously at the spectacle of this queer old man of the sea and his half-crazy croaking—in time, however, we came to fear complete fulfilment of his uncanny prophesies. Though we didn't know it, the component parts were already there and the tragic events that followed live on in a sailor's memory as a hell ship voyage.

Very soon we found out why we had been railroaded off in such a hurry and why they talked so smooth in the office in London. The crew that had been shipped in London had taken the *Cutty Sark* trip to Cardiff and deserted her, after having cashed their advance notes, for they had had "some experiences" with the first mate on the passage round[8] that they didn't want to repeat, but with which we were soon to become familiar. It was extremely hard to get men in Cardiff, as the crews are seldom paid off in that port, so we had to start off with about as mixed a crew as it was possible to pick up—five Englishmen, three Negroes, two Greeks, one Italian, three Danes and one Dutchman made up the forward gang; two Scotsmen, Captain James Wallace, and a first mate Sydney Smith—a hard fibered despotic character more common in the virile days of sail—a rather colourless Englishman as second mate, who was so short-sighted that Captain nearly always stood his watch with him, and the third mate, an apprentice who had failed to pass as second mate and had signed on as ordinary seaman, were in command.

Our berth had been assembled from many other ships and rushed in to fill the crew shortage: Stanton from the *Carlisle Castle*,

---

7. An area now known as the Indian subcontinent, Southeast Asia, and the islands of Oceania and Maritime Southeast Asia. Anjer, or Anyer, is a town in Banten providence, Indonesia.
8. A passage around the Cape of Good Hope to the Far East.

Fullerton from the *Whiteadder*, McCausland from the *Zenobia*,[9] two first voyagers, Bill Barton and Kirby, and myself from the *Fantasie*.

Our carpenter "Chips,"[1] had fallen in love with the ship and signed in her regularly from her first launching. He knew every timber and bolt in her and was a very privileged person. The sail-maker was a big German who answered to the name of Dutchy. We apprentices promptly named him Vanderdecken, The Flying Dutchman.[2] Together with the cook and the steward they completed our crew of 28.

Captain Wallace was a splendid seaman, kindly and interested in the apprentices, with always a friendly word to any of our crowd that happened to go aft or at the wheel, never making any remark if we happened to get a bit off course. The first mate was a regular slave driver who apparently saw only the hardwork side of life. I considered I was lucky not being in his watch—there was never any rest with him on deck.

Long before I joined the *Cutty Sark* she had a world wide reputation and was thought by a great many authorities to be the swiftest clipper afloat, being built especially for the tea racing trade (known in the shipping world as "The Race") which claimed the most wonderful ships, masters and crews that have ever sailed the ocean from China round the Cape to London, but which have been completely spoiled by the cutting of that infernal ditch known as the Suez Canal,[3] which enables steamers to carry tea to Britain by the shorter route. With the loss of this trade the upkeep of these ships had to be reduced to keep expenses down, so it was cutting down sail and shortening crews. * * *

We were barely to sea on that fateful Friday before a wild southwest gale tore up the Bristol Channel with raging seas and howling and we were compelled to anchor in the river Severn[4] for three days.

Old Vanderdecken was triumphant. "It's foul weather all the way, it's doom and damnation for us all," he pronounced. The man never seemed to need sleep. Hour after hour during the night watches he would pad the deck in his bare feet muttering to himself.

---

9. Probably the merchant schooner of that name launched on July 21, 1868, and lost at sea in 1887. The *Carlisle Castle* was a 1344-ton barque owned by J. Robertson and built by R. & H. Green in 1868. The ship sank in 1899 with all hands aboard. The *Whiteadder* was a clipper ship built in 1862 by Bilbe & Co., Rotherhithe, for John Willis & Son. It was taken out of service in 1884.
1. See p. 246, n. 7.
2. Philip Vanderdecken is a character in Marryat's novel *The Phantom Ship*, which explores the legend of the Flying Dutchman; see also p. 108, n. 4.
3. See p. 48, n. 1. "Cape": see p. 173, n. 4.
4. The longest river in the United Kingdom; it flows through Wales, Shropshire, Worcestershire, and Gloucestershire, emptying into the Bristol Channel.

However, we got a fair start with a leading wind down to Cape Finisterre where we picked up the northeast trades, then squaring away the yards we made a run for the Line.[5] Studding sails and every rag of canvas that could be stuck on was ordered set, for we had a record to keep up and another old antagonist. The clipper *Titania*[6] in company with us was bound also for Anjer. We were brought very close together and so we sailed for nearly four days when we drew apart with a challenge for a race to Sunda straits.[7]

Sailing on before the trades we reached the Line where we exchanged our fair wind for squalls and calms, very trying to the temper when coupled with the vertical heat of the sun and further by the discordant elements that made up our crew.

It took only a few days to set the mate abusing and swearing at the negroes, of whom only one was of any use as a sailor. The others he worked up at all sorts of trivial and worrying jobs.

This constant hazing and tormenting began to have its effect. Nerves were strained and tempers shortened day by day, until the fight between Francis and the mate brought the trouble to a head. The captain's firmness seemingly ended the incident, and no inkling of what was to come clouded our anticipation of better sailing weather as we stood out to the south Atlantic.

We headed down the south Atlantic close hauled, making a southwesterly course to latitude 40 degrees south, where we picked up the west wind that forever blows round the southern seas. * * * It was a grand experience showing what a ship like the *Cutty Sark* could do when driven by a captain like ours. Yes, it was cracking on sail all the time!

As usual at such times, in spite of all the squabbles between officers and men everyone seemed keen to make the best of the run and enjoy the excitement. My old knowledge of yacht sailing came in handy and I was counted one of the lucky four Captain Wallace allowed to steer. The first mate demurred at my being at the wheel single-handed at such a time, but I was left on the job, much to my great delight and doing my prettiest. It was no small thing either, as one has to have lots of nerve when a great stern sea comes whizzing up with part of the top coming over the rail and lifting you waist high as the ship rose in grand style and stepped out at her best.

---

5. The equator. Cape Finisterre is a peninsula on the west coast of Galicia, Spain, the westernmost point of the Iberian Peninsula. "Northeast trades": see p. 195, n. 3.
6. A composite clipper ship built in 1866 by Robert Steele & Co., known for its speed during the tea races in the latter half of the 19th century. It later made cargo runs from Great Britain to Vancouver.
7. See p. 18, n. 2.

Now the wind began to come out of the southwest in heavier and heavier squalls and our top gallant sails and chain sheets got a heavy mauling. The men were sent aloft to bend a new lower fore topsail[.] * * *

Up went the topsail in its stops, * * * but it was another thing to bend it. For two hours the men fought aloft, sweating and swearing, the footrope swinging and dipping as they braced against the tilting yard. It seemed an impossible task but set it must be and eventually was as our gallant little ship cleared herself of a green sea which rushed over the stern and swept the length of the deck. During the whole of this strenuous time our little clipper steered beautifully and our entire crew played up most gallantly, wishing only to give the ship the best chance to break the record. It was stand by the whole time, and eat and snooze when we could.

Soon after this event I heard from the second mate that there was some anxiety on account of a variation between our two chronometers and their rating. They had apparently got apart about five minutes of time or seventy miles in longitude. Unlike the *Fantasie*, we used to hear all about the navigation from Captain Wallace. He expected two of our berth to take sights for latitude and longitude on Sundays and then he would invite us down for dinner in his cabin with the officers.

Shortly after we passed the longitude of St. Paul's island,[8] which we gave a wide berth, we hauled northeasterly for Sunda straits and in trimming sail a most serious row occurred.

The mate was trimming sail in the middle watch. So that the sheet could be hauled aloft on the starboard side, he roared out to Francis who was on the lookout at foc'sle head, "Let go-o tack." No movement. Again the mate roared out, "Let go-o tack!" Whether Francis heard him or not, again the order was not obeyed. This was too much for Bucko Smith, who saw red where Francis was concerned, and went for him on the jump,[9] "You god-damned . . ."

What occurred in the next few seconds, no one saw. We heard a sharp crack, a blood curdling yell, followed by a dull thud, as we rushed forward. Francis was down, out cold.

The mate's story was that Francis had met him with an upraised hand spike.[1] In the struggle the mate managed to get hold of it and brought it down with such force that he knocked the darky senseless. He was taken down to the bosun's[2] deck aft, but it was evident that his skull was fractured. He never regained consciousness and

8. Or Île Saint-Paul, an island in the southern Indian Ocean and a territory of France.
9. See p. 77, n. 5.
1. The *Times* (July 5, 1892) account lists Francis's weapon as a marlinespike and Smith's as a capstan bar; see p. 433.
2. Boatswain.

died three days later. The ship was hove to and we lowered the body over the side, Captain Wallace reading the service.

After this the mate kept [to] his cabin. The ship suddenly became quiet, the men going about their work in sullen silence with bitterness in their hearts and never a chanty to buck them up at the most tedious task. Though Francis was far from being popular among us, the mate was openly despised. Old Vanderdecken's gloom enveloped the ship. Her run of bad luck had now fairly started. Captain Wallace took over the mate's watch till we arrived at Anjer, from which we were about ten days sail.

Arriving off the islands of Sumatra and Java[3] the error in chronometers succeeded in fooling us badly. For though it does not matter being a bit out of position when there is lots of sea room, it does not do to run chances of going on the rocks. So we kept well away from the entrance of the straits until we had attained the latitude, then went running due east for Java Head.[4]

Through the portals of these straits the fleets of sailing ships to and from China have made their way for many years. Situated almost on the Line, the southeast trade winds[5] are broken up at its entrance, and dependence has to be put in every favourable slant of breeze or squall. While no high seas are met, it takes the highest class of seamanship to navigate from this point to various destinations in the China Seas[6] and eastern Pacific ocean.

We were very unfortunate in making the land fall. The fresh wind that we were carrying and which should have lifted us up the Straits died away just as we made the entrance. Strange to say, our antagonist, *Titania*, just managed to take advantage of the same wind. The result was, that while we lay becalmed off Krakatoa Island,[7] she was passing through. Had our chronometers been correct we would have either won the race or at least sailed up the Straits together.

At Anjer we came to anchor to enquire for orders. There were none waiting, Jock Willis scarcely expecting his cut-down clipper to make such a quick passage—69 days from Lundy island.[8] So we remained a week at anchor.

One night a number of bumboats came alongside to starboard to sell bananas, pineapples, bunches of small onions and packets of jaggery.[9]

3. Large islands of Indonesia, southwest and south of Malaysia respectively. See p. 336. See p. 17, n. 9.
4. See p. 17, n. 9.
5. See p. 205, n. 1.
6. See p. 109, n. 7 and p. 263, n. 4.
7. A volcanic island located in the Sunda Strait, best known for a cataclysmic eruption in 1883.
8. The largest island in the Bristol Channel.
9. A coarse, dark-brown Indian sugar, produced by evaporating the sap of various kinds of palms.

Captain Wallace supplied the hands with money and soon we were carrying on a noisy brisk bargaining with the gesticulating natives.

But on the port quarter a different scene was being enacted. The mate had evidently persuaded the captain to help him escape. Arrangements had been made with the captain of an American ship, the *Colorado*, which had just arrived from Hamburg,[1] to take the bucko mate on board. Under cover of the excitement to starboard, the mate sneaked up on deck, dropped into a boat sent from the *Colorado* and was off. The steward reported him missing when he went to fix up his berth at 9 p.m.

When the crew found out that the mate had slipped away, they were not long in putting two and two together. Led by Old Vanderdecken, they declared they would do no more work on the ship until he was found. The captain, to pacify them, took a number of men ashore to see the authorities. They sent out some native police to search the ships and made a big investigation, but really did nothing. They would not let one of our crew go with them to help in the hunt, knowing full well that it would be no trouble for sailors to rout him out of a ship.

At this critical moment our belated orders came—"Proceed to Yokohama."[2] The captain called our berth, carpenter, cook and steward to work the ship out. Some of the men started to interfere but we were all armed, the captain ordered four of the ringleaders to be put in irons, and we were left alone. After a long dreary heave we got the anchor up and some sails set by using the capstan to hoist the top sails, and with a light fair wind stood up the Straits and out into the Java sea.[3]

All might have gone well, but unfortunately we were becalmed—a clock calm which lasted for three days. Old Vanderdecken would parade the decks croaking about disaster, "She'll have no luck until that murdering mate is brought to book[4]—I'll hunt him out—he'll hang for that bloody murder—I'll find him if I have to sail the seas till Doomsday!"

Captain Wallace had no sooner helped the mate to escape when he realized the position he had placed himself in. He knew there would be an official investigation when he got to Yokohama and with little doubt he would be held responsible for the mate's escape. The least he could expect would be to lose his certificate. He had an old mother and a young wife dependent on him in Scotland and the outlook was indeed very black.

1. A port city located on the River Elbe in northern Germany.
2. A port city on the east coast of central Japan.
3. See p. 19, n. 6.
4. Made accountable (slang).

I don't think the captain took any sleep from the time we left Anjer. With bowed head he walked the poop night and day or stood gazing unseeing over the water. The ship had lost all life, nothing stirred but the everlasting flapping of the becalmed sails as she rolled to the swell, with scarce an odd puff of wind but fierce heat all day and all night and Vanderdecken's gloomy predictions forever ringing in our ears.

There seemed to be a foreboding of things to happen. The crew kept forward in a sullen angry mood, our berth doing the best we could to carry on, praying for a wind that did not come. This tension could not keep up much longer. Captain Wallace was becoming totally indifferent to all around him, his mind and body would soon crack under the strain, we knew but we were powerless to assist him.

On the fourth day from Anjer our berth had just been called at 4 a.m., when the captain was standing at break of the poop with the faithful Chips. "Is the mate up?" he asked.

"Comin' up, sir" answered Chips.

Captain Wallace turned and went aft. "Check your course," he directed the helmsman. Then deliberately he stepped on to the taffrail and jumped overboard!

Far out abeam of the ship a black triangular fin, a shape ominous as doom, suddenly broke surface and came slicing through the water towards the ship. Another, another and yet another! Shaking with horror, the man at the wheel put down the helm, tore two life-buoys from their place and hurled them overboard into the milling maelstrom below where tigerish shapes churned the waves to froth.

The echoes of the wheelsman's shriek, "Sharks!" were still ringing over the deck when the crew, near to mutiny an hour before, flung themselves into the boat which had been used at Anjer and was still in the davits. With a great splash it struck the water. The ship had been sneaking along making about two knots before the gentle breeze, and the life-buoys were clearly visible a short distance astern. But around and below them white water churned in the wake of the great grey shapes of death that milled and fought furiously over something in the sea beneath. What was it? The heartsick crew, shaken to their depths by the suddenness of the tragedy knew only too well.

Though they rowed tirelessly, back and forth in ever-widening circles, in their innermost hearts they knew, and in their blanched faces could be read the bitter knowledge of all. Captain Wallace was gone from them forever, and in the mind of each man this thought was uppermost—we drove him to it. The splendid seaman, the kind considerate friend to our berth we would see no more, and it was with heavy hearts we at last gave over the useless search and rowed back to the ship.

The crew took this greatly to heart and blamed themselves for being the indirect cause of his death, and we of the half deck knew that never again would we likely sail under such a man, who had sacrificed his position and life to assist an unworthy shipmate in trouble. Surely Old Vanderdecken's prophesies were coming true. The ship had sailed on a Friday and now we were in for it for the rest of the voyage.

As soon as all hope was given up for the captain and the boat was hoisted up, a consultation was held. The crew wanted the second mate to proceed to Yokohama, but he would not undertake the responsibility. His knowledge of navigation was shaky, and his weak eyesight prevented him from taking observations. "Sankey, you'll assist me taking sights. We'll put back to Anjer," he decided.

There was evidently nothing else to do but to put back to Anjer, and in this light wind area it took four days. And it was not without incident! A heavy current caught us just west of Thwart-the-Way Island[5] and took us round stern first, on the northwest side. In this volcanic region the rocks and islands sheer out of the water from great depths and it was lucky for us that there were no outlying reefs. We had to brace up the yards to keep from striking against towering cliffs.

We were completely becalmed, the current carrying us along at about eight knots and we could not get soundings with the deep sea lead line. We sorely missed the direction of Captain Wallace! After getting clear away, a nice slant of wind allowed us to make the anchorage of Anjer, though the hook, dropping on a shelving rock, had to be taken up again and we had to warp in closer to shore.

I can imagine the consternation of Jock Willis in London when he received the cable announcing our disastrous condition, for he knew nothing of the killing of Francis, the escape of the mate or the death of Captain Wallace! Of course he didn't want to stand the loss of the consigned coal to Yokohama, but the second mate wisely would not take on the responsibility of command, so after many telegrams we were ordered, "Proceed to Singapore[6] in charge of Dutch pilot."

This trip was a regular yachting experience, no deck work, and for the most part a light fair wind prevailed. We worked the ship under "calashee" watch, which meant that we stood by at all times ready for a call. We had one close shave, being caught in a tide and the wind about all gone. The strong current rushed us past a line of reefs so close that a biscuit could have been thrown on to their ragged edges.

5. Sangiang, an island midway in the Sunda Strait between Sumatra and Java.
6. See p. 48, n. 7.

The port of Singapore was all agog at the cause of the famous *Cutty Sark*'s first visit to the port and the news began to get abroad of her sailing prowess, notorious crew and bucko mate. Indeed, the stories became so embroidered from repeated telling in foc'sle yarning that Joseph Conrad the celebrated sea novelist, describes (in *Lord Jim*) this incident of the mate's escape from the *Cutty Sark*, stating that the mate "swam" to the *Colorado*.[7] This he could not have done. Wind and tide out of the Java Sea was running against him as the *Colorado* was up the Straits toward Thwart-The-Way Island. And there were sharks, plenty of them.

An enquiry into the recent disaster was now held on shore by the port authorities. The crew was given the option of taking their discharge, which a few did. It was with great relief to most of us that Old Vanderdecken went, for we began to think he was uncanny, and we believed his evil influence was partly the cause of our trouble. Even as he bundled over the rail we heard him muttering, "I'll hunt him down—I'll have him swung at the yardarm[8]—the ship will have no luck till that murderer is caught and the blood washed away." I never heard of him again.

About a week after this a new captain came on board to take charge. His name was Bruce[9]—a rather singular one to follow Wallace, like a return to Scottish history. But there the similarity ended and the contrast began. A short stout man with an uneasy look, and a habit of sliding around the deck and wheel that suggested distrust of officers and men. He had been the first mate on the *Hallowe'en*, one of our line that was lying at Hong Kong,[1] and had been sent down from there to take charge. Our second mate was promoted to first mate, and we shipped another second mate and enough crew to make up our number. * * *

But through a mist of memory, "old salts" (the last of their breed—God bless them!) will see her storming the Atlantic, riding out a gale or fighting her way through the China seas, will hear a rousing chanty break forth as slowly, rhythmically, an anchor is heaved up; will taste again pea soup, boiled salt horse, weevil-flavored biscuit. And as salt spray wets their cheeks will softly utter that old sea truth—"Ships are all right: it's the men in 'em!"[2]

---

7. Sankey means of course Conrad's *The Secret Sharer*; however, Conrad does seem to take some of the events surrounding Captain Wallace's suicide as raw material for Captain Brierly's suicide in *Lord Jim* (1900).
8. Hanged from the yardarm. "Bundled": went off hurriedly and unceremoniously.
9. Captain Bruce commanded the *Cutty Sark* from 1880 until 1882. He eventually had his nautical certificate suspended for brutality.
1. See p. 87, n. 7. "*Hallowe'en*": a 920-ton iron clipper ship built in 1870 by Maudslay, Son & Field at Greenwich for John Willis. The ship was wrecked in South Devon in 1887. "Our line": the shipping line of John Willis and Son.
2. Singleton says this in *The Nigger of the "Narcissus"*; see p. 157. See also *The Mirror of the Sea* (pp. 128–29).

[The *Cutty Sark*][†]

The British barque *Cutty Sark*, arrived this morning from Anjer in charge of the second officer. He reports that the chief officer of the vessel struck one of the crew, a European, at that port[1] and he died soon afterwards from the effects of the blow, it is supposed. The Captain appears to have assisted the chief to escape on board of an American ship bound for Saigon[2] and afterwards, whether from pangs of conscience or fear of future trouble, he threw himself overboard and was drowned. The authorities here will, probably, issue a warrant for the chief officer's arrest to-day, and his extradition will be demanded.

[The Trial of Sidney Smith][‡]

At the Thames Police-court, John Anderson [alias Sidney Smith], at present second mate of the ship *Marianne Gottebohm* [actually the *Ann Nottabohn*], lying in the South-West India Dock, was charged before Mr. Lushington[1] with feloniously killing and slaying John Francis by striking him on the head with a capstan-bar on the British ship *Cutty Sark* while on the high seas. Inspector Wildey,[2] of the Criminal Investigation Department, watched the case. John Somers, a young man, said he was a steward out of employment. He was a steward on the *Cutty Sark*, which sailed from London on May 15, 1880, having on board the prisoner as chief officer, and John Francis as cook and steward. The night they were rounding the Cape of Good Hope[3] the sailmaker ran into the witness's cabin and said the chief officer had knocked Francis down. There had been a little ill-feeling between the prisoner and Francis because he could not do his work as a seaman. On going forward the witness saw Francis being carried aft, and blood flowing from a wound on his head. The captain[4] dressed the wound. On the following morning the prisoner said "I have done for him; he will never lift the capstan-bar to me again." Francis died the same night, and was buried on

---

† *The Singapore Free Press*, September 18, 1880, p. 2.
1. The incident actually occurred at sea, some distance removed from Anjer.
2. Capital city of Cochinchina (now southern Vietnam).
‡ From "Police," *The Times* (London), July 5, 1882, p. 6 col. d.
1. Possibly Vernon Lushington (1832–1912), deputy judge advocate general. "South-West India Dock": The southernmost dock, later known as South Dock, was constructed in the 1860s.
2. Inspector Wildey is probably Detective-Inspector R. Wildey.
3. See p. 173, n. 4.
4. James S. Wallace (d. 1880).

the following day. In the beginning of September the ship was lying in the roads at Anjer. One night a boat was seen under the bows, and the prisoner disappeared from the ship. The second day after the ship left Anjer the captain committed suicide by jumping overboard into the sea. The ship was taken back to Anjer by the second mate, who telegraphed to the agents at Singapore.[5] In answer to a question by the prisoner, the witness said he did not see how the affair happened. He was told of it. Mr. Lushington read an entry from the official log-book, which was to the effect that when the chief mate came on the poop Francis grossly insulted him, refused to obey orders, and on the chief officer going to expostulate with him, he made a blow at his head with a marline-spike. Anderson hit him on the head with a capstan-bar in self-defence. The captain said "This is awful work," and the mate said, "Well, what could I do, it was to be killed or to kill." Mr. Lushington remanded the prisoner for a week.

[Sidney Smith's Indictment][†]

John Anderson, 31, seaman [alias Sidney Smith], was indicted for the wilful murder of John Francis.

Mr. Poland and Mr. Montagu Williams prosecuted for the Treasury; Mr. Edward Clarke, Q. C.,[1] and Mr. Besley appeared for the defence.

The accused, it appeared, was chief mate on board a tea clipper called the *Cutty Sark*, which sailed from the port of London in May, 1880. The deceased, who was a coloured man, shipped as an able seaman, and it was stated that he soon afterwards incurred the displeasure of the prisoner in consequence of his incompetency. About the 9th or 10th of August, 1880, the vessel had just rounded the Cape, and at a quarter to 9 o'clock the prisoner was in command of the watch. The night was dark and dirty, and the watch was occupied in hauling the sail round. The deceased not being competent to perform seaman's duty, had been placed on the forecastle on the look out. The watch on hauling the ropes found that the "fore lazy tack" was fastened, and the prisoner called out to the deceased to let the tack go. The deceased replied "Very well," or, according to the prisoner's version, "Go to the devil." Immediately afterwards the deceased let go the lazy tack, but instead of doing so

5. See p. 48, n. 7.
† From "Central Criminal Court, August 3," *The Times* (London), August 4, 1882, p. 4 col. f. (Before Mr. Justice Stephen.)
1. Queen's Counsel. Montagu Stephen Williams (1835–1892) was a barrister and well known for his work as a defense lawyer. In 1879, he became a prosecutor. "Edward Clarke" is probably Edward George Clarke (1841–1931), a prominent lawyer who represented such notable figures as Oscar Wilde.

as an able seaman would, he let the end go overboard. The prisoner said, "Thou has done that out of spite." The deceased retorted, "Well, you told me to let it go," and the prisoner exclaimed "I will come on the forecastle and heave you overboard, you nigger." The deceased replied, "If you come up here I have got the capstan bar waiting for you." The prisoner then went on to the forecastle and was seen to raise the capstan bar, with which he struck the deceased on the head. The blow knocked the man over the forecastle on to the deck, and he never spoke again. The prisoner said to the watch, "Did you see that nigger lift the capstan bar to me," but the men replied that they did not. The prisoner said, "He will lift no more capstan bars to me, for I have knocked him down," and he added, "I have knocked him down like a bullock; he never gave a kick." The account given by the prisoner was that he did it in self-defence. The captain of the vessel attended to the deceased, but he remained insensible till the following day, when he expired from the injuries he received, and was buried at sea. Before the arrival of the ship at Anjer the accused, with the connivance of the captain, made his escape. The vessel proceeded thence to Singapore, and during the passage the captain committed suicide by jumping overboard, having previously dropped into the sea the capstan bar used by the prisoner. At Singapore the matter was reported to a magistrate, who, in due course, instituted an inquiry. The prisoner was arrested in London.

It was stated in cross-examination that the deceased man Francis had on several occasions threatened the prisoner's life, and once he sharpened his knife upon the grindstone for the purpose of carrying his threat into execution.

Mr. Edward Clarke, addressing his Lordship at the close of the case, submitted that the evidence could not sustain the Court charging the prisoner with murder.

Mr. Justice Stephen concurred; and

Mr. Clarke said that, in those circumstances, he could not resist a verdict of manslaughter. The learned counsel addressed the Court in mitigation of punishment, pointing out that the vessel had been under-manned, and that at the time in question the accused had had an important manœuvre to perform with respect to the sail. The deceased behaved in an insolent and "lubberly" manner, and it was absolutely necessary that the prisoner should assert his authority.

Numerous witnesses were then called on the part of the defence to show that the prisoner bore an excellent character and was a man whose disposition was humane and kindly.

The jury, by his Lordship's direction, then returned a verdict of manslaughter against the accused.

Mr. Justice Stephen, in passing sentence, told the prisoner he had considered the case with anxious attention and with very great pain, because the evidence which had been given showed that he was a man of good character generally speaking and of humane disposition. He was happy to be able to give full weight to the evidence given in his favour. The deceased had certainly acted in a manner which was calculated to make the prisoner very angry, but it must be clearly understood that the taking of human life by brutal violence, whether on sea or on land, whether the life be that of a black or a white man, was a dreadful crime, and deserving of exemplary punishment. He sentenced the prisoner to seven years' penal servitude.

G. JEAN-AUBRY

[Conrad and the *Narcissus*]†

* * * From Madras he [Conrad] went to Bombay to look for a new commission. He was first offered one on board a mail boat of the British-India line, navigating in the Persian Gulf,[1] but he was reluctant to serve on board a steamer if he could possibly avoid it. One evening he was sitting with other officers of the Mercantile Marine on the veranda of the Sailors' Home in Bombay,[2] which overlooks the port, when he saw a lovely ship, with all the graces of a yacht, come sailing into the harbour. She was the *Narcissus*, of 1,300 tons, built by a sugar refiner of Greenock[3] nine years before. Her owner[4] had originally intended her for some undertaking in connection with the Brazilian sugar trade. This had not come off, and subsequently he had decided to employ her in the Indian Ocean and the Far East.[5] Some days later, Joseph Conrad Korzeniowski became her second mate.

She left Bombay on April 28th, and was dismantled at Dunkirk[6] on the 17th of October following. Her name, the *Narcissus*, is, of course, familiar to all who know the work of Joseph Conrad. It has been immortalized in *The Nigger of the "Narcissus,"* one of his indisputable masterpieces describing ships and the sea. The spirit of that book is

---

† From *Joseph Conrad: Life and Letters*, 2 vols. (Garden City, NY: Doubleday, Page, 1927), 1:76–78.
1. A gulf located between Iran and the Arabian Peninsula and leading out into the Indian Ocean. Madras, now Chennai, is a city in southeastern India and the capital of Tamil Nadu State. It lies on the Bay of Bengal, the northern section of the Indian Ocean.
2. The Royal Alfred Sailors' Home, built from 1872 to 1876, served sailors until 1928 when it was sold to the government and has since served various purposes. It is currently the headquarters for the Maharashtra state police.
3. A town in central Scotland, on the southern shore of the Firth of Clyde. For *Narcissus*, see p. 143, n. 3.
4. See p. 143, n. 3.
5. Information given me by Conrad himself [Jean-Aubry's note].
6. A part city in northern France, on the English Channel.

not only the creation of the writer's genius, it also owes much to his memory. *The Nigger of the "Narcissus"* is really a realistic and lyrical record of six months of Conrad's life during the year 1884.

I obtained from Conrad himself some details as to the extent to which the novel follows fact, and I write them down here just as he gave them to me in conversation a little before his death:

> The voyage of the *Narcissus* was performed from Bombay to London[7] in the manner I have described. As a matter of fact, the name of the Nigger of the *Narcissus* was not James Wait, which was the name of another nigger we had on board the *Duke of Sutherland*, and I was inspired with the first scene in the book by an episode in the embarkation of the crew at Gravesend[8] on board the same *Duke of Sutherland*, one of the first ships the crew of which I joined. I have forgotten the name of the real Nigger of the *Narcissus*. As you know, I do not write history, but fiction, and I am therefore entitled to choose as I please what is most suitable in regard to characters and particulars to help me in the general impression I wish to produce. Most of the personages I have portrayed actually belonged to the crew of the real *Narcissus*, including the admirable Singleton (whose real name was Sullivan), Archie, Belfast,[9] and Donkin. I got the two Scandinavians from associations with another ship. All this is now old, but it was quite present before my mind when I wrote this book. I remember, as if it had occurred but yesterday, the last occasion I saw the Nigger. That morning I was quarter officer, and about five o'clock I entered the double-bedded cabin where he was lying full length. On the lower bunk, ropes, fids and pieces of cloth had been deposited, so as not to have to take them down into the sail-room if they should be wanted at once. I asked him how he felt, but he hardly made me any answer. A little later a man brought him some coffee in a cup provided with a hook to suspend it on the edge of the bunk. At about six o'clock the officer-in-charge came to tell me that he was dead. We had just experienced an awful gale in the vicinity of the Needles, south of the cape,[1] of which I have tried to give an impression in my book. . . . As to the

---

7. Since Conrad ended his own voyage aboard the *Narcissus* in Dunkirk, he is referring here to the fictional destination of the *Narcissus*.
8. A town on the southern bank of the River Thames in the southeastern English county of Kent. The *Duke of Sutherland* was a 1,047-ton clipper ship built in 1865 by John Smith of Aberdeen for Louttit & Co. of Wick. Conrad worked as an ordinary seaman on a voyage from London to Sydney from October 1878 to January 1879. The ship ran aground in 1882 in Timaru, New Zealand.
9. See p. 145, nn. 1, 6, and 7.
1. I.e., south of the Cape of Good Hope; see p. 173, n. 4. The Needles are Cape Agulhas, a rocky promontory in the Western Cape province of South Africa, the southernmost point of the African continent.

conclusion of the book, it is taken from other voyages which I made under similar circumstances. It was, in fact, at Dunkirk, where I had to unload part of her cargo, that I left the *Narcissus*.[2]

From this beautiful book and *The Mirror of the Sea* [1906] we know what Conrad's life was like, not only during the voyage of the *Narcissus* but during the twenty years he spent on board sailing ships. The atmosphere, the dangers, the fatigues of that life, become real to us; also its arduous beauty, which appealed intimately to Conrad, brought up from childhood, as he was, to be familiar with the sentiment of the sublime and with struggle against odds.* * *

2. These notes were taken in June, 1924, at Oswald's, Bishopsbourne, Kent, after a conversation with Joseph Conrad about *The Nigger of the "Narcissus,"* apropos of a new edition of Robert d'Humières' [1868–1915] translation of that book into French [Jean-Aubry's note].

CRITICISM

ROBERT W. STALLMAN

From Conrad and "The Secret Sharer"†

✻ ✻ ✻

The single Conrad work which best illuminates the primal plan of all his imaginative works is *The Secret Sharer*. *Heart of Darkness* and *The Secret Sharer* belong, I think, to the top of the basket—with the greatest short stories ever written. One of the supreme achievements in all fiction, *The Secret Sharer* is at once the microcosm of Conrad's works and a perfection in the technique of symbolism. ✻ ✻ ✻ *The Secret Sharer* ✻ ✻ ✻ treats the ✻ ✻ ✻ themes of fidelity and spiritual disunity or moral and aesthetic isolation. [The] story [has] multiple meanings— ✻ ✻ ✻ psychological, ethical, and aesthetic. ✻ ✻ ✻

Everything in *The Secret Sharer* is charged with symbolic purpose. It is this symbolic part of the business that eludes the reader, if not the moral and psychological intention since these meanings, which attach to the narrative or surface level, are less likely to be missed. On a first reading it appears perhaps as simply a spectacular story about a young, newly appointed sea-captain who risks his ship and his career in order to rescue a refugee who happens to bear a striking resemblance to himself. He is a fugitive from the legal consequences of an act of manslaughter; he has killed a man in a desperate scrape, but he is "no homicidal ruffian" [15]. The captain, recognizing their connection in thoughts and impressions, identifies the stranger with himself, guesses his guilt and shares his conscience. He hides him in his cabin and takes extraordinary pains to conceal him from the crew. He risks everything for the sake of this stranger. To help him reach land so that he can begin a new life, the captain takes his ship as close into land as possible, and, while the swimmer makes for shore, he watches in terror the approaching mass of land shadows which threatens to engulf the ship. What saves him is the warning marker left by the swimmer ("the saving mark for my eyes" [42]). It is the captain's own hat, by which he can tell that the ship has gathered sternway. The ship is saved, and the captain at last is fitted for his task. He has established perfect communion with his ship. As he catches a last glimpse of his hat, the captain senses again that mysterious identity with the secret sharer of his cabin and of his thoughts. He describes him as though he were describing himself: "a free man, a proud swimmer striking out for a new destiny" [42].

† From "Conrad and 'The Secret Sharer,'" *Accent* 9.3 (Spring 1949): 134–43. Reprinted by permission of the Estate of Robert W. Stallman. Unless otherwise specified, page references are to this Norton Critical Edition.

441

Conrad's most characteristic works are stories of action: *Nostromo, The Secret Agent, Victory, Suspense.* In *The Secret Sharer* the external action consists almost solely in the drama of the ship in the moment of the captain's crisis. Action and plot are subsidiary to the analysis and exhibition of a psychological process. This psychological or internal action, from which the external drama is projected, prepares for its counterpart and at the climactic moment coincides with it. The whole story may be defined as a prolonged analysis of a series of tensions anticipating one culminating moment, the moment of the captain's crisis and triumph. The story is charged, however, not only with suspense and impending crisis but also with meaning. * * * The real fact is that Conrad has contrived his story with a secret intention. We can get at it only through the story itself. We can work it out, to start with, by questioning certain central motives—the facts basic to the why and the wherefore of what happens in the story.

Even the reader who reads only for "the story" is likely to ask some of the questions, the key ones being these: (1) Why does the captain undertake the risk to his ship for this particular stranger, a risk which he would not impose upon her for any other? (2) Why must he take the ship as close into land as possible?

If we, as Conrad's readers, happen to think in the manner of the chief mate ("He was of a painstaking turn of mind. As he used to say, he 'liked to account to himself' for practically everything that came in his way . . ."), we certainly will try to evolve a theory about the captain and his secret sharer. But to do so, in emulation of the chief mate we had better "take all things into earnest consideration" [9]. We had better answer our question first of all at the narrative or literal level. It's a fact that what the youthful sea captain does for this fugitive, whose mishap was not entirely of his own making, is what any other young sea captain might do, out of common decency, in order to save a decent young chap. He feels impelled to do this out of a moral necessity, his relationship to the fugitive being that of host to guest. But why does he make this commitment?—why for the sake of this particular stranger? Well, the fact that the captain bears an uncanny resemblance to him—Leggatt's similarity not only in appearance and age but in background and experience and in situation— provides us one answer. (It's this sense of identity that prompts the remark: "I saw it all going on as though I were myself inside that other sleeping-suit" [15].) Besides, the captain recognizes not alone this physical identity but also a psychic one. "He appealed to me as if our experiences had been as identical as our clothes" [15]. Each feels that he is "the only stranger on board" [9], and each feels that he has, as it were, "something to swim for" [19]. Each stranger is isolated and wholly alone, pitted against the world and being tested by it. What impelled Leggatt to swim out to the ship was his lonesomeness ("I wanted to be seen, to talk with somebody, before I went on" [21]), and the same impulse motivates the captain and prompts him to greet the newcomer so hospitably. Hospitality, welcome, and self-recognition are stressed from the start. "A mysterious communication was established already between us two—in the face of that silent, darkened tropical sea" [13]. Later in thinking back to this moment Leggatt confides: "It's a great satisfaction to have got somebody to understand. You seem to have been there on purpose" [35]. The same confession could have come from the captain. Each stranger feels the same urgency to communicate with somebody in order to unburden his plight.

It is this mutual, sympathetic understanding of what the other's plight means to him that bolsters and morally fortifies their spiritual being, Leggatt's no less than the captain's. "And then you speaking to me so quietly—as if you had expected me—made me hold on a little longer" [21]. Leggatt's "calm and resolute" [13] voice induces in the captain a corresponding state of self-possession. Through Leggatt that initial mood of calm and resolute self-confidence with which the captain begins and ends his arduous enterprise is gradually reinstated. Leggatt, as we later get to know him, is bold and enterprising, proud and stubborn, determined in moral fiber. While the captain's remark "You must be a good swimmer" [13] has reference to the fact that the nearest land is as far distant as the land at the very bottom of the sea, there is also an implied ethical judgment in these words of encouragement and appraisal. To be "a good swimmer" is to be "a strong soul" [13]. What the captain marvels at in his double is "that something unyielding in his character which was carrying him through so finely" [34]. The overconfident soul of the swimmer stands in contrast to the self-questioning, Hamletlike soul of the newly appointed captain. He observes about the fugitive that there was nothing sickly in his eyes or in his expression, and, with this telling reflection about himself, he notices that "he was not a bit like me, really; yet, as we stood leaning over my bed-place, whispering side by side, with our dark heads together and our backs to the door, anybody bold enough to open it stealthily would have been treated to the uncanny sight of a double captain busy talking in whispers with his other self" [17]. When Leggatt happens to rest a hand "on the end of the skylight to steady himself with, and all that did not stir a limb" [16], the captain simultaneously rests a hand too on the end of the skylight. When on a later occasion the captain made a move "my double moved too" [38]. As "the double captain" [38] is about to slip from the ship into the sea, the captain, struck by a sudden thought, snatches his hat and rams it "on my other self" [39]. He visualizes Leggatt's plight as his own: "I saw myself," he says, "wandering barefooted, bareheaded, the sun beating on my dark poll" [39]. Again and again "[W]e, the two strangers in the ship, faced each other in identical attitudes" [21]. And in identical clothes. It is the captain's secret self that is "exactly the same" as the fugitive, who, dressed in "the ghostly gray of my sleeping suit" (the garb of the unconscious life) [14], must always remain concealed from the eyes of the world.

In terms of the ethical allegory in *The Secret Sharer,* Leggatt is the embodiment of the captain's moral consciousness. His appearance answers the captain's question—"I wondered how far I should turn out faithful to that ideal conception of one's own personality every man sets up for himself secretly" [9]. In darkness he first appears, mysteriously "as if he had risen from the bottom of the sea" [12], and "the sea-lightning played about his limbs at every stir; and he appeared in it ghastly, silvery, fish-like" [12]. At the first sight of him "a faint flash of phosphorescent light, which seemed to issue suddenly from the naked body of a man, flickered in the sleeping water with the elusive, silent play of summer lightning in a night sky" [11–12]. And at the last sight of him, when the secret sharer is making for the shore of Koh-ring (an unknown island), there issues from the discarded hat the same mysterious light: "White on the black water. A phosphorescent flash passed under it" [42]. It's all very mysterious. Leggatt's emerging in a sudden glow from "the sleeping water" [12] seems very much like the flash of an idea emerging from the depths of the subconscious mind. "It was, in the night, as though I had been faced by my own reflection in the depths of a somber and immense mirror" [14]. That dark glassy sea mirrors the captain's *alter ego.* In terms of the psychological allegory, Leggatt represents that world which lies below the surface of our conscious lives. Just before he makes his appearance the riding-light in the fore-rigging burns, so the captain imagines, "with a clear, untroubled, as if symbolic, flame, confident and bright in the mysterious shades of the night" [11]. These moral qualities, though the captain attributes them to the riding-light, belong with equal and very suggestive appropriateness to the captain's as yet undisclosed second self. The captain's subconscious mind has anticipated, in the fiction of the symbolic flame, the idea of a second self—the appearance, that is, of someone untroubled, unyielding, self-confident. (The captain is just the opposite, being of a mind troubled and filled with self-doubt.) The symbolic flame materializes in human form. Leggatt bodies forth the very commonplace upon which the whole story is built: no man is alone in the world, for he is always with himself. Leggatt, this other self, becomes the psychological embodiment of the reality, the destiny, the ideal of selfhood which the captain must measure up to. He provides him the utmost test.

All this, in sum, answers our first question: Why is it that the captain risks his ship for this particular stranger? The initial matter-of-fact answer prepared us for, or rather teased us into making, the allegorical one. In answering the first question we have anticipated the answer to the second: Why is it that the captain must take his ship as close into shore as possible? To begin with a fact, the ship, as the story opens, is anchored inside the islands at the mouth of the river Meinam and is lying cleared for sea. (Her location and voyage can be traced on a map.) She is in dead calm and waits for "the slightest sign of any sort of wind" [10]. "There was not a sound in her—and around us nothing moved, nothing lived, not a canoe on the water, not a bird in the air, not a cloud in the sky" [8]. At last there's enough wind to get under way with, and then for four days she works down "the east side of the Gulf of Siam, tack for tack, in light winds and smooth water. . . ." [32]. When the wind comes and the ship first moves to his own independent word—precisely at this point it is that the captain begins to come to terms with his ship. At midnight of the fourth day out she is put round on the other tack to stand in for shore, and still at the following noon she has had no change of course. The captain has by now attained enough self-confidence to dare this risky maneuver—"to stand right in. Quite in—as far as I can take her" [36]. His excuse for the order to the mate is that the ship isn't doing well in the middle of the gulf, and at the mate's terrified protest he retorts: "Well—if there are any regular land breezes at all on this coast one must get close inshore to find them, mustn't one?" [36]. And this is why, *literally* why, he must shave the land as close as possible.

It is not solely in order to shorten Leggatt's stretch to shore. For Leggatt, that expert swimmer, is capable of making it from almost two miles out. (From the islet to the ship, he figured, "That last spell must have been over a mile" [20].) It's not a test of Leggatt. It's a test of the captain. "The youngest man on board (barring the second mate), and untried as yet by a position of the fullest responsibility. . . ." [9]. He is "the only stranger on board . . . a stranger to the ship; and if all the truth must be told, I was somewhat of a stranger to myself" [9]. For four days the ship has had a captain who has not been "completely and wholly with her. Part of me was absent" [31]. Though she has had "two captains to plan her course for her" [37], nevertheless she is still, so to speak, a ship without a captain. The time has come for the irresolute commander to command—to prove to the crew, to the world, and to himself that he is fitted for his task. It is time that he put to trial that secret conception of his ideal self, to reckon, in sum, with that destiny which from the start he has anticipated with such intensity. For four days the ship has had very little wind in her sails. Instead of waiting for the wind to come to him he determines now to go after it. It's *his* conscience that is on trial ("on my conscience, it had to be thus close—no less" [41]). It's not a test of the crew—"They had simply to be equal to their tasks; but I wondered how far I should turn out faithful to that ideal conception of one's own personality every man sets up for himself secretly" [9]. "All a man can betray is his conscience," Conrad wrote in *Under Western Eyes* [*UWE* 36]. The captain does not betray, even though the entire world seemed leagued against him. Everything—"the elements, the men were against us—everything was against us in our secret partnership; time itself—for this could not go on forever" [29]. And "It was now a matter of conscience to shave the land as close as possible—for now he must go overboard whenever the ship was put in stays. Must! There could be no going back for him" [39]. Nor for the captain: "I had to go on" [40]. Not to let Leggatt strike out for land would be "a sort of cowardice" [35]; it is cowardice not to face up to one's destiny. Like Leggatt, who has "something unyielding in his character" [34], the captain is tenaciously determined not to compromise his soul. There are limits to self-knowledge, however, and beyond this dividing mark of self-knowledge no man dare go. We are told that "all the time the dual working of my mind distracted me almost to the point of insanity" [23]. "On that enormous mass of blackness there was not a gleam to be seen, not a sound to be heard" [40]. The black hill of Koh-ring hangs right over the ship "like a towering fragment of the everlasting night" [40], and such a hush falls upon her "that she might have been a bark of the dead floating in slowly under the very gate of Erebus" [40]. It is the ship, but it is also the captain's soul, that is almost swallowed up beyond recall. "I think I had come creeping quietly as near insanity as any man who has not actually gone over the border" [34]. "My God! Where are we?" cries the terrified mate [40]. "Lost!" [41]. The captain has Leggatt to fortify him, whereas the terrified mate hasn't even "the moral support of his whiskers" [41]. The transferred moral quality of Leggatt has infused itself into the captain's soul and it is this transaction—symbolized in the spot of white hat—that saves him. (The hat is Conrad's symbol for his theme of fidelity.) It is by virtue of his fidelity to that ideal of selfhood that the captain triumphs, and at that decisive moment of his destiny when he measures up to it a new existence begins for him—a spiritually unified one. It begins for him when the cabin is emptied and Leggatt, the secret sharer of his cabin and of his thoughts, has been deposited into that once dark and mysterious but now sunlit sea.

*   *   *

ALBERT J. GUERARD

["The Secret Sharer" and the Other Self]†

* * *

[Conrad's works] seem to say and indeed do say important things about our puzzled and striving human nature: about our capacity for idealism and our capacity for deterioration; about our desire for brotherhood and our propensity to solitary crime. These stories of adventure and romance nearly always suggest long vistas of experience beyond themselves, and their lonely heroes face no less than our common human destiny. Marlow's slow journey up the Congo into the heart of darkest Africa is a journey into the heart of man's darkness. And Leggatt, the secret sharer and fugitive, is more than mere flesh and blood. Most of Conrad's better novels thrust inward toward psychological complexity and outward toward moral symbolism. This is particularly true of [*Heart of Darkness* and *The Secret Sharer*].

Conrad's long stories and short novels are far more experimental and more "modern" than his full-length novels. *The Secret Sharer* and *Heart of Darkness* are among the finest of Conrad's short novels, and among the half-dozen greatest short novels in the English language. * * * *The Secret Sharer* is forthright in structure and simple in style, as direct and immediate and frightening as any very personal diary. * * *

* * * *The Secret Sharer,* much the more exciting and more direct of the two, is also the more difficult to analyze and understand. Both are realistic accounts of things that actually happened—or an actual tragedy at sea; of an actual expedition that Conrad made, in 1890, into the heart of Africa. But both stories are also dramas of consciousness and conscience, symbolic explorations of inward complexity. They are * * * stories of youth's initiation into manhood and knowledge, dramatized testings of personal strength and integrity, psychological studies in half-conscious *identification*. Why does Marlow seek out and remain loyal to the unspeakable and savage Kurtz in *Heart of Darkness*? Why does the narrator (the "I") of the *The Secret Sharer* protect the criminally impulsive Leggatt? Both have identified themselves, temporarily, with these outcast and more primitive beings; lived vicariously in them. In the unconscious mind of each of us slumber infinite capacities for reversion and crime. And our best chance for survival, moral survival, lies in frankly recognizing these capacities. At the beginning of *Heart of Darkness*, Marlow

† From "Introduction," Heart of Darkness *and* The Secret Sharer by Joseph Conrad (New York: Signet Classics, 1950), 7–15. Page references are to this Norton Critical Edition.

does not "know himself"; at the beginning of *The Secret Sharer,* the narrator is naively confident of success in the sea's "untempted life" [11]. The two men must come to know themselves better than this, must recognize their own potential criminality and test their own resources, *must travel through Kurtz and Leggatt,* before they will be capable of manhood . . . manhood and "moral survival." The two novels alike exploit the ancient myth or archetypal experience of the "night journey," of a provisional descent into the primitive and unconscious sources of being. At the end of *Heart of Darkness* and *The Secret Sharer,* the two narrators are mature men. And as Marlow and the young captain both sympathize with and condemn these images or symbols of their potential selves, so too does the novelist Conrad. It is this conflict between sympathy and a cold purifying judgment that gives intensity to the stories as works of art.

These are matters which need not concern us on a first reading of the stories. But eventually these questions come back to haunt us. Many critics and readers have liked *The Secret Sharer,* but few of them have cared to say what the story is "about." And they may have been wise to be so cautious. For every great work of art operates on multiple levels of meaning and suasion. And a work of art as general as *The Secret Sharer,* and as personal, may have something very particular to say to every new reader.

On the first level of meaning, there is no difficulty at all. A young officer named Leggatt, trying to save the *Sephora* in a storm, knocks down and accidentally strangles a mutinous member of his crew, an "ill-conditioned snarling cur" [14]. Put under arrest by his legalistic captain, Leggatt jumps overboard and swims several miles to the unnamed ship of our unnamed narrator. He is taken aboard by this young captain, a man of about his own age and background, and hidden in his cabin. The captain sympathizes at once with Leggatt's plight, and eventually helps him escape by taking the ship dangerously close to the shore of a barren land. The captain even gives the fugitive three pieces of gold, and his own hat to protect him from the tropic sun. At the end of the story we see Leggatt, who has lowered himself into the water, ready to take his solitary punishment: "a free man, a proud swimmer striking out for a new destiny" [42]. He is, I suppose, the hero of this first reading of the story—a courageous man who killed a "cur" without intending to. But there is also the sympathizing young captain who tells the story, and who shows a Christian nobility and pity.

Some readers may not care to go beyond this first meaning. And yet this was clearly not Conrad's meaning, nor the meaning which holds after further readings. If we go outside the novel, to look at Conrad's life and at his other fiction, we see that he was a deeply conservative man, profoundly attached to the rigid laws and pitiless traditions of the sea. A crime on shipboard, whether intended or not, was simply and irrevocably a crime. Conrad deeply distrusted easy sympathy and pity, which he regarded as egoism in disguise. And even if we do not go outside *The Secret Sharer,* we observe that Leggatt is a rather dubious hero. We learn, for instance, that he got his job on the *Sephora* through family influence and not on his merits. And what are the daily consequences of the narrator's protective sympathy? He is so distracted by his efforts to keep Leggatt hidden he has no chance to get to know his officers and crew. As a captain he is dangerously irresponsible; until the very end he does not have the "feel" of his ship. We begin to see, now, that the real moral dilemma is *his,* not Leggatt's, and that he will not be truly master of his ship until the shadowy Leggatt has left it.

Our problem, therefore, is to read the story again, but this time with the narrator or "I," the young captain, as hero and center of interest. And we find then that the purely adventurous story of rescue and escape has become a psychological and symbolic story of self-exploration, self-recognition, and self-mastery. We find that Leggatt, however real his physical presence, is also the captain's ghostly "double" or twin. What does this unreflective and immediate sympathy for a "double" mean but sympathy for one's second, irrational self? The captain hides and protects Leggatt because he vaguely realizes—for the first time in his life—that he too might have stumbled into such a crime. An officer should be able to act unreflectively, yes. But not so unreflectively as to strangle a member of his crew in anger. In the end the narrator has benefited from his dangerous traffic with Leggatt, benefited from this symbolic journey through an underground self. He has wholly outgrown the naive optimism which could rejoice in the "great security of the sea," in its "untempted life presenting no disquieting problems" [11]. The end of wisdom, for Conrad, was pessimism: an awareness that we are eternally menaced, and most of all by ourselves.

The Secret Sharer is what is known as a "double" story. In Poe's *William Wilson* and Dostoevsky's *The Double,* the second selves of the heroes are embodiments of the accusing conscience. In *The Secret Sharer,* our "double" (Leggatt) is rather the embodiment of a more instinctive, more primitive, less rational self. How does the narrator meet Leggatt in the first place? By irrationally dismissing the anchor-watch, and so leaving a rope ladder to hang over the side of the unmoving ship. And what is his first impression of Leggatt? "He was complete but for the head. A headless corpse!" [12]—a being, that is, without intellect. Leggatt is ghostly, silvery and fishlike as he swims in the water—that water which has been, since the beginnings of literature and symbolism, an image for the unconscious life. The captain gives him a sleeping-suit like his own, proper clothing for one who must live as in a dream. Small wonder that the narrator will soon begin to lose all sense of personal identity, and that he cannot draw the green serge curtains across the bed where his double lies. "It was, in the night, as though I had been faced by my own reflection in the depths of a somber and immense mirror" [14]. He has descended, at his peril but for his final instruction, into the depths of the unconscious. The psychologist Jung was to argue, some years later, that only such a descent, only such a traffic with the unknown within, can permit integration and enrichment of the personality.

Reading the story thus, as a brilliant counterpart to the findings of modern psychology, we are likely to be puzzled by its last sentence. If Leggatt is symbolically a lower self capable of crime, fortunately expelled at last—why is he also "a free man, a proud swimmer striking out for a new destiny" [42]? This is a dark question, to which many answers may be given and all of them uncertain. My own partial answer is to recall that Leggatt is the captain's double and symbol for his unconscious, *but also a man of flesh and blood*. By seeing his own dilemmas and difficulties in Leggatt, the captain has turned this man into symbol and spirit, has deprived him of his humanity and "mere flesh" [42]. But at the end, emerging from his self-examination, the captain can see Leggatt as a separate and real human being. He lends the fugitive his hat, to protect him from the burning sun. And this hat—marking the division between the two selves—saves the captain and his ship; it is a marker, floating on the night sea. "And I watched the hat—the expression of my sudden pity for his mere flesh. It had been meant to save his homeless head from the dangers of the sun. And now—behold—it was saving the ship, by serving me for a mark to help out the ignorance of my strangeness" [42]. The captain, having overcome his necessary but egoistic identification with Leggatt, and seeing him now as flesh rather than shadowy spirit, restores to the stranger his identity. In this sense, at least, each is now "a free man, a proud swimmer striking out for a new destiny" [42].

*   *   *

The two stories, using slightly different symbolist techniques, are in fact the same story, and have the same mythical theme—the theme of initiation and moral education, the theme of progress through temporary reversion and achieved self-knowledge, the theme of man's exploratory descent into the primitive sources of being. Conrad believes, with the greatest moralists, that we must know evil—our own capacities for evil—before we can be capable of good; that we must descend into the pit before we can see the stars. But a price must be paid for any such perilous journeys and descents; we must atone for even temporary alliance with the powers of darkness.

This, I take it, is the significance of the curious endings of these two novels. The captain of *The Secret Sharer* takes his ship dangerously close to the reefed shore of Koh-Ring, far closer than is necessary to permit Leggatt's escape. He must take the full risk. "He was able to hear everything—and perhaps he was able to understand why, on my conscience, it had to be thus close—no less" [41]. * * *

Conrad, like Marlow, had a passion for truth—including the dark truth concerning our human nature—and a hatred of complacent egoism. He was a pessimist as well as an idealist, yet his pessimism has a consoling solidity. * * *

DAPHNA ERDINAST-VULCAN

[The Seductions of the Aesthetic: "The Secret Sharer"][†]

*   *   *

I would argue that 'The Secret Sharer' enacts the return of auto-biographical desire. * * * 'The Secret Sharer' was written in an attempt to reclaim the ground lost in the writing of the novel [*Under Western Eyes*], to regain the (non-existent) internal territory of the subject and its sovereignty. * * * [T]he narrator of 'The Secret Sharer' tries—with a degree of *méconnaissance* which applies to the author himself—to aestheticize and frame himself; to reclaim, or rather fabricate, an autonomous topos of subjectivity.

It is hardly surprising that 'The Secret Sharer' should have become so widely anthologized, given its extremely neat structural and formal symmetries, its ostensible treatment of ethical questions, and its equally ostensible concern with psychology, all within the very manageable scope of a short story. But this combination of narrative mastery and apparent thematic weightiness, striking as it undoubtedly is, has produced a rather disturbing work, whose formal elegance 'not only aestheticizes but actually anaestheticizes the call for ethical action'.[1] There is much about the narrator's interpretation of his own motivation and state of mind which is unconvincing; the conflict of loyalties in which he is caught is not resolved by any clear-cut choice; the ostensible act of liberation (whether of himself or of the fugitive is unclear) is highly ambivalent or downright morally suspicious; and the triumphant cadences on which the

---

† From *The Strange Short Fiction of Joseph Conrad: Writing, Culture, and Subjectivity* (Oxford: Oxford University Press, 1999), 36–43, 44–45, 50. Reprinted by permission of Oxford University Press. Page references are to this Norton Critical Edition.
1. Cedric Watts, 'The Mirror-tale: an Ethico-structural Analysis of Conrad's "The Secret Sharer", *Critical Quarterly*, 19, no. 3 (1977), 36.

narrative concludes sound rather hollow when one realizes that the elegance of the resolution is aesthetic rather than ethical. The narrator Captain has put the lives entrusted to him at risk in the most outrageous way in order to save the life of his secret sharer; his future standing with his justly mistrustful crew is by no means assured; and it is only through an amazing stroke of undeserved good fortune (rather than navigational mastery) that his final act does not end disastrously for his ship and her crew.

However, even readers who have refused to be anaestheticized by the neat structural symmetries of the story have only addressed the narrator's unreliability, exempting the author under the implicit assumption that there must be a good moral to a good story; that behind, or above, or below the conflicting elements there is an authorial/authoritative principle of organization; that the ambivalence of the narrative can be relegated to one phase in the dialectics of art and is eventually resolved on a higher, more sophisticated level of authorial construction. Neat as such a resolution would be, there is little in the story to warrant it. The text seems to endorse the position of the narrator by default: there is no rhetorical dissociation of the story from the narrative; no authoritative embodied other who would dispute or challenge the narrator's interpretation and judgment; no hint of retrospective self-doubt in the narrator's discourse; no point of anchorage for that wishful assumption of higher organization.

Like *Under Western Eyes*, its 'other' text, 'The Secret Sharer' explores the idea of borderlines, divisions, and boundaries. But the ubiquity of border states in the story, discussed in an excellent study by James Hansford, does not necessarily indicate an inner rift which needs to be mended as Hansford suggests.[2] I believe that it is precisely the obverse, a state of psychic 'borderlessness', which lies at the core of the narrator's anxiety; that the obsession with boundaries and their inscription is a symptom of the narrator's need to stake out a spurious territory of selfhood. The man who feels like 'a stranger' to himself is already deeply troubled at the outset of the narrative by his inability to make out the lines of division between land and sea, between rocks and ruins:

> On my right hand there were lines of fishing stakes resembling a mysterious system of half-submerged bamboo fences, incomprehensible in its division of the domain of tropical fishes, and crazy of aspect as if abandoned for ever . . . there was no sign of human habitation as far as the eye could reach. To the left a group of barren islets, suggesting ruins of stone walls, towers, and block houses. . . . I saw the straight line of the flat shore

---

2. James Hansford, 'Closing, Enclosure and Passage in "The Secret Sharer"', *The Conradian*, 15, no. 1 (1990), 30–55.

joined to the stable sea, edge to edge, with a perfect and unmarked closeness. [7]

The narrative moves in a cinematic fashion from the panoramic (the view of the land) to the scenic (the ship and her crew), and finally closes up on the perceiving individual. But that movement, normally designed to place and orientate the subject, only compounds the sense of physical and psychological disorientation as it removes all the potential points of reference outside the self and positions the narrator within three concentric circles of uncertainty: the mysterious aspect of the physical surroundings, the unknown ship and her crew, and his own self as captain.[3]

It is this spatial anxiety, this threatening loss of 'selfhood', which generates the need to reinscribe the lines of division, to frame the self as an integral, distinct object. * * * In 'The Secret Sharer', * * * there is no staircase. There is a stepladder which can be pulled up or lowered down into the water at the narrator's will. It is not a permanent avenue for the subject's traffic with the other, but a means of enclosure for the subject. The very same 'anxiety of borderlessness' is shared * * * by the author himself.

Put into a Bakhtinian frame of reference, the narrator's initial state of mind is clearly that loss of the 'inner stance', which is the enabling condition for all action.

> A man who has grown accustomed to dreaming about himself in concrete terms—a man who strives to visualize the external image of himself, who is morbidly sensitive about the outward image impression he produces and yet is insecure about that impression and easily wounded in his pride—such a man loses the proper, purely inner stance in relation to his own body. He becomes awkward, 'unwieldy,' and does not know what to do with his hands and feet. This occurs because an indeterminate *other* intrudes upon his movements and gestures.[4]

Like other Conradian characters—most notably Lord Jim—who have lost the 'inner stance', the narrator would revert to an aesthetic modality of consciousness. In order to recover a sense of his own selfhood, he would try to objectify and 'author' himself exotopically as an 'other', an object of perception, a hero in a text—whole, autonomous, and clearly delineated. He would need, in other words, to devise a human mirror for himself.

3. In his reading of the story, Jeremy Hawthorn has rightly noted the 'split between perceiving and perceived self.' *Multiple Personality and the Disintegration of Literary Character*' (London: Edward Arnold, 1983), 85. It is, I believe, an observation that can apply not only to the process within the text, but to the dynamics of subjectivity 'outside' it.
4. Mikhail Bakhtin, 'Author and Hero in Aesthetic Activity', in *Art and Answerability: Early Philosophical Essays by M. M. Bakhtin*, trans. and notes by Vadim Liapunov, ed. Michael Holquist and Vadim Liapunov (Austin: University of Texas Press, 1990), 59–60.

With Leggatt's arrival on board, the human mirror materializes. There is very little in the narrated events to justify the sense of inexorable fate, the mysterious coincidences, and the suggestions of the uncanny with which the narrative is so heavily fraught. These effects are produced entirely by the narrator's insistence on the bond of doubleness which seems to exist, a priori, between himself and the fugitive. Both men are young and similarly built; they have both been to the same school and are members of the same social class. But the resemblance ends there, and would certainly not justify the assumption of doubleness or the structural symmetry which is so heavy-handedly imposed on the narrative.[5] The narrator's observation of the general physical resemblance between himself and his 'double' is suspiciously overblown:

> He had concealed his damp body in a sleeping suit of the same grey-stripe pattern as the one I was wearing and followed me like my double on the poop. Together we moved right aft, barefooted, silent. [13]

> My sleeping suit was just right for his size. [14]

> The shadowy, dark head, like mine, seemed to nod imperceptively above the ghostly gray of my sleeping-suit. It was, in the night, as though I had been faced by my own reflection in the depth of a sombre and immense mirror. [14]

A few minutes after their first encounter, the narrator begins to refer to Leggatt—with no qualifying quotation marks in the text—as 'my double', my 'other self', the 'secret sharer', etc. [16, 17, 20, 21, 24 ff.]. It is precisely that insistence, the 'overkill' effect of the narrative, which calls for a suspicious reading and produces what appears to be a generic ambiguity in the text.[6] But the sense of the uncanny which looms so large over the story is epistemological rather than ontological: Leggatt, the man, is real enough. It is the perception of Leggatt as the Captain's double which corrodes the substance of the tale.

The projection of identities goes both ways. The narrator Captain looks at his 'double' believing that 'anybody would have taken him for me' [24], superimposing this fabricated interchangeability on his dealings with the skipper of the *Sephora* and with his own crew [26–27]. The more interesting and less explicit process which takes place is the Captain's willed identification with the fugitive. It

---

5. This has been discussed in detail by David Eggenschwiler in 'Narcissus in "The Secret Sharer": A Secondary Point of View,' *Conradiana* 11, no. 1 (Spring 1979), 23–40.

6. In his discussion of the *doppelgänger* motif in the story Paul Coates argues that 'The Secret Sharer' is 'a key example of the way in which the transition from realism to modernism generates uncertainty in writers'. ° ° ° *The Realist Fantasy: Fiction and Reality since Clarissa* (New York: St Martin's Press, 1983), 115.

is, in fact, *he* who takes on the other man's identity; it is *he* who becomes, in fact, the mirror of the other so that the other might become his 'double'. In his need to objectify himself, to view himself from without in the absence of that 'inner stance' which is the necessary condition for all action, he fabricates and literally stage-manages this doubleness as he begins to mime the gestures of the other.

> He rested a hand on the end of the skylight . . . and all that time did not stir a limb, so far as I could see. . . . One of my hands, too, rested on the end of the sky-light; neither did I stir a limb, so far as I knew. It occurred to me that if old 'Bless my soul—you don't say so' were to put his head up the companion and catch sight of us, he would think he was seeing double, or imagine himself come upon a scene of weird witchcraft; the strange captain having a quiet confabulation by the wheel with his own gray ghost. [16]

Like Gentleman Brown in *Lord Jim*, another fictitious double who preceded Leggatt by a decade, the outlaw intuitively plays on this assumed doubleness, and the Captain narrator readily and uncritically responds:

> You know well enough the sort of ill-conditioned snarling cur—He appealed to me as if our experiences had been as identical as our clothes. And I knew well enough the pestiferous danger of such a character [i.e. the dead man] where there are no means of legal repression. And I knew well enough that my double there was no homicidal ruffian. I did not think of asking him for details, and he told me the story roughly in brusque, disconnected sentences. I needed no more. I saw it all going on as though I were myself inside that other sleeping-suit. [15]

Neither a reliable character witness nor an impartial judge in his readiness and need to acquit Leggatt, the narrator seems to be oddly insensitive to the distinct note of callousness in the other's account:

> It's clear that I meant business, because I was holding him by the throat still when they picked us up. He was black in the face. . . . I wonder they didn't fling me overboard after getting the carcass of their precious ship-mate out of my fingers. [15]

Though clearly aware of the temperamental and moral disparity between the fugitive and himself, the narrator Captain chooses to suppress it. But his occasional slips indicate that he is, in fact, conscious of Leggatt's potential for violence.[7] His reaction to a near discovery

---

7. Michael Murphy rightly notes that the narrator wilfully suppresses the Skipper's different version of the incident on board the *Sephora*, judging it 'unworthwhile' to record it. Michael Murphy, '"The Secret Sharer": Conrad's Turn of the Winch', *Conradiana* 18, no. 3 (Autumn 1986), 196.

(when the steward enters the bathroom unexpectedly and there seems to be no way to avert an encounter) indicates the extent of his self-deception: 'My voice dies in my throat and I went stony all over. I expected to hear a yell of surprise and terror, and made a movement, but had not the strength to get on my legs. Had my second self taken the poor wretch by the throat?' [33]. This is clearly at odds with his repeated assertion that 'my double there was no homicidal ruffian' [15].

When the skipper of the *Sephora* comes on board, the narrator meets his tenacious adherence to the law with derision:

> His obscure tenacity on that point had it something incompre-
> hensible and a little awful; something, as it were, mystical,
> quite apart from his anxiety. . . . Seven-and-thirty years at sea,
> of which over twenty of immaculate command, and the last fif-
> teen in the *Sephora* seemed to have laid him under some pitiless
> obligation. [26]

The young Captain narrator cannot see that he too should have been under the same 'pitiless obligation' which comes with the position of command. Having invested his sense of selfhood in this 'double', the narrator reduces the terms of the ethical dilemma into a bogus equation:

> It was all very simple. The same strung-up force which had
> given twenty-four men a chance, at least, for their lives, had, in
> a sort of recoil, crushed an unworthy mutinous existence. [30]

Eggenschwiler notes that his equation is reversed at the end of the story, when the narrator risks the lives of the crew to save the life of one man.[8] But this equation is unacceptable even if one chooses to believe Leggatt's version of the murder. If the supreme value of the communal ethos is that of discipline (hence the unworthiness of the 'mutinous existence' and the justification for the killing), isn't Leggatt himself guilty of mutiny in his refusal to let the law take its course?

In his need to 'find refuge in the other and to assemble—out of the other—the scattered pieces of [his] own givenness, in order to produce from them a parasitically consummated unity',[9] the narra-tor has trapped himself within the aestheticized mode of conscious-ness. The other has become, in Bakhtin's terms again, a 'usurping double', forcing the narrator to articulate a position in conflict with the communal ethos to which he is committed by vocation. The fabricated mirror-relationship born out of the psychic need for self-objectification now becomes a question of what Bakhtin would call 'axiological authority'. What, we should ask, is the source of axio-logical authority for the subject who is inevitably constructed

---

8. David Eggenschwiler, 'Narcissus in "The Secret Sharer"', 32, 35.
9. Mikhail Bakhtin, 'Author and Hero', 126.

within the narrative of the other? What kind of agency may be assumed if there is no such thing as an autonomous, sovereign topos of subjectivity? What guarantees do we have for the benevolence of the authorial Other?

* * *

The apparent turning-point in the story is reached when the time comes for the ship to get under way and for the Captain to take action. * * * [It] becomes clear that the Captain narrator has reached the 'dead point' of action.

> It's to no commander's advantage to be suspected of ludicrous eccentricities. But I was also more seriously affected. There are to a seaman certain words, gestures, that should in given conditions come as naturally, as instinctively as the wincing of a menaced eye. A certain order should spring to his lips without thinking; a certain sign should get itself made, so to speak, without reflection. But all unconscious alertness had abandoned me. [31]

In order to set himself free from a psychic paralysis, the narrator Captain paradoxically needs to take the assumption of doubleness to its ultimate conclusion. The floppy white hat which he puts on the exposed head of his 'double' becomes a metaphoric vehicle for that cast-off identity.

> All at once my strained, yearning stare distinguished a white object floating . . . I recognized my own floppy hat. . . . Now I had what I wanted—the saving mark for my eyes. But I hardly thought of my other self, now gone from the ship. . . . The hat was meant to save his homeless head from the dangers of the sun. And now—behold—it was saving the ship, by serving me for a mark to help out the ignorance of my strangeness. [42]

Miraculously and improbably, the trope of identity becomes a mark of distinction. The discarded hat is no longer a vehicle for transposed identities, but a distinct physical object whose very separateness from the perceiving subject turns it into a reference point outside the self, an aid marking the position of the ship, enabling the narrator to recover his subject position as a member of the community.

If one feels uncomfortable with this triumphant and neat conclusion of the narrative, it is no doubt because of the double bind which seems to operate here. The young Captain narrator seems at last to reject the aestheticizing fantasy of selfhood, to realign himself with the voice of the authorial/authoritative collective other. But at the very point where he sets out to exorcize the double, the narrative swerves once again in the direction of the uncanny: the ship is not saved through his navigational skills but by a most unlikely miracle, which belongs to the same order of phenomena as the appearance of the mysterious double, the improbable avoidance of discovery, and other projections of fantasy. The exorcism of the usurping double is not a truly liberating act; it is little more than an empty gesture performed by a narrator who is still deeply captivated in the realm of the aesthetic.

*   *   *

'The Secret Sharer' is indeed a good story with a good moral. But it is not yet another compact version of the *Bildungsroman*, a coming into one's own. What it offers is a perception of subjectivity as a Möbius strip, where the desire for an illusory kernel of being, an 'aestheticized' or 'authored' selfhood, traverses and surfaces through an ethical, 'yet-to-be' mode of consciousness, which offers no respite from responsibility. The tensile relation between these two modalities may be the missing link in the Postmodernist critique of the transcendental subject. The need for grounding is a concomitant of our innate non-self-sufficiency; it emerges out of our very constitution as discursive, responsive beings, creatures who live on their borderlines. The need to be authored and authorized from without cannot easily be thrown overboard as dead metaphysical ballast. Having lost our moorings, the need for anchorage is still with us.

BRIAN RICHARDSON

Construing Conrad's "The Secret Sharer":
Suppressed Narratives, Subaltern Reception,
and the Act of Interpretation[†]

Conrad was fascinated by issues of interpretation and misinterpretation and regularly staged such dramas in his works; "The Secret Sharer" is probably Conrad's most audacious drama of narration and reception. The work seems at first to be profoundly multivalent, even to the point of self-contradiction. It is at the same time both a writerly text that invites a wide variety of incompatible interpretations and, curiously, a readerly text that is quite explicitly about accuracy in interpretation as it repeatedly stages and evaluates interpretive acts. The critical literature, however, has generally tended to exemplify the first of these aspects rather than explore implications of the latter. The paradox in this treatment of the text is that the

[†] From *Studies in the Novel* 33.3 (Fall 2001): 306–21. Copyright 2001 by the University of North Texas. Reprinted with permission of Johns Hopkins University Press. The author revised the essay for this Norton Critical Edition; unless otherwise specified, page references are to this edition.

larger hermeneutical principles it ultimately affirms cast doubt on the validity of many of the interpretive stances it seems to have solicited. The widely recognized multiplicity of different readings this text indulges is itself threatened by a profound skepticism that the work invites us to assume. This story of the fortunes of interpretation serves as a good beginning point for this study's more extended investigations into the subject.

We may start with a look at some of the various acts and tropes of reading, interpretation, and understanding that are present in the text. As the narrative opens, the ship is at anchor in the Gulf of Siam, far from harbor. The first character that the captain-narrator introduces us to is the first mate, who is characterized by his fascination with interpretation: "His dominant trait was to take all things into earnest consideration. * * * As he used to say, he 'liked to account to himself' for practically everything that came in his way" [9].[1] This depiction comes in the middle of and is occasioned by an interpretive situation: the captain, having just spotted the mastheads of another ship, announces its presence (surprising the reader as much as the characters), and the mates set to work trying to explain the ship's unexpected presence. The chief mate's hypothesis, that the vessel drew too much water to cross the sandbar except at the "top of the spring tides," is immediately corroborated by the second mate—whose accurate but unexpected knowledge is itself in need of additional explanation ("The tugboat skipper told me when he came on board for your letters, sir" [10]).

Wondering whether his peremptory dismissal of his officers from the deck would be construed not as generosity but rather eccentricity ("Goodness only knew how that absurdly whiskered mate would 'account' for my conduct" [11]), the captain himself walks into a mystery. The side ladder is down; more strangely, it can't be pulled up. The captain is astounded and, just like "that imbecile mate," tries "to account for it" [11]. In the water at the bottom of the ladder is yet another enigma in the naked figure of a man named Leggatt, whom the captain shortly learns has escaped from the brig on the other ship and is now seeking some kind of asylum.

Just who he is and exactly what he has done is not as obvious as might appear on a first encounter. Among the uncontested facts of the case are the following. There is no question that Leggatt killed a man on the *Sephora* during a storm, that he was imprisoned on board, and that he later escaped overboard and swam to the

---

1. Mark Ellis Thomas briefly discusses various interpreters in this text, and remarks perspicaciously, "What more fitting double for the careful, critical reader than the chief mate, whose 'dominant trait was to take all things into earnest consideration'" ("Doubling and Difference in Conrad: 'The Secret Sharer,' *Lord Jim,* and *The Shadow-Line,*" *Conradiana* 27.3 [Autumn 1995]: 224).

narrator's own ship. Leggatt claims to have saved his vessel by his
actions and to have acted rightly according to a higher morality of
the code of the sea that transcends the petty calculus of good and
evil meted out by law books and courtrooms. The dead man, presented by Leggatt as a contemptible wretch, threatened the survival
of the crew and in the crisis had to be dealt with swiftly and deci-
sively. Leggatt claims he saw what had to be done, was trying to set a
reefed topsail, throttled the blackguard that tried to hinder him,
saved the ship, and was then imprisoned for his efforts. The narrator
buys this story in toto, and even helps Leggatt produce it. One need
only observe the dialogue in which the killing is announced to see
the peculiar dynamics of this narration and its reception. The
captain, after hearing Leggatt say he was the mate of the *Sephora*,
immediately inquires,

"Aha! Something wrong?"
"Yes. Very wrong indeed. I've killed a man."
"What do you mean? Just now?"
"No, on the passage. Weeks ago. Thirty-nine south. When I say a
    man—"
"Fit of temper," I suggested, confidently.
The shadowy, dark head, like mine, seemed to nod imperceptibly.
    [14]

As indeed it might: the captain has just provided the killer with a
sympathetic ear and an acceptable motive. Leggatt continues in the
vein suggested by the captain—a good man in an unfortunate bind.
It works well. Within a few more lines, the captain states, "He
appealed to me as if our experiences had been as identical as our
clothes. * * * I knew well enough also that my double there was no
homicidal ruffian. I did not think of asking him for details, and he
told me the story roughly in brusque, disconnected sentences. I
needed no more" [15]. With the evidence that the narrator has at
this point, he has no plausible ground to make such a judgment,
either according to the logic of legitimate interpretation already
established in the text, or by the ordinary standards of appropriate
inference: if you were to meet a largely naked stranger outside a bus
depot who admits he's just killed a man, you would not be so quick
to offer him clothing, a hiding place, and excuses for his act.

   Throughout the piece, the narrator seems determined that no
fact or set of facts will tamper with the flattering conception he has
so quickly formed of Leggatt. The vast majority of this novella's
interpreters have—often equally uncritically—trusted the judgment of the narrator on this point. But despite the fact that alternative accounts of this affair are generally suppressed, they
nevertheless leave some significant traces that call into question

Leggatt's version. Two of the comments of Archbold, one reported by the narrator, the other recounted by Leggatt, fail to jibe with Leggatt's version. Archbold's observation that, in the course of his thirty-seven years at sea, he has "never heard of such a thing happening in an English ship" [25], does not make much sense when applied to the noble act of impassioned duty described by Leggatt, which is after all an occurrence that would not be so uncommon; nor is it the kind of act that would normally cause someone to express his wonder that Leggatt can sleep at night after what he's done, as Archbold says to Leggatt's face [19]. The same is also true of the unrecorded account provided by the crew of the *Sephora*, which elicits from the first mate the comments "a very extraordinary story," "horrible enough for me," and "[b]eats all these tales we hear about murders in Yankee ships" [29]. These statements too make no sense unless directed to a much more spectacular act of criminality than any Leggatt will ever admit to.

And how bad were these acts historically? American ships had a well-earned reputation for brutality in the 1880s and '90s. Joseph Goldberg writes:

> The "Red Record" of American maritime industry drawn up by the Sailors' Union of the Pacific listed charges by over 100 ships' crews over a period of 11 years of 15 deaths from maltreatment; instances of loss of limbs, eyes, or teeth; other injuries of a permanent character, including insanity; and several suicides attributable to persecution. It was reported that only seven convictions were obtained against the officers involved, with punishments largely nominal. Although flogging had been prohibited by statute in 1850, corporal punishment was not prohibited, the effect being "merely to change its character from the specific to the general: it prohibited the cat; and by implication authorized the use of the belaying-pin and handspike."[2]

It wasn't until 1898—several years after the setting of the tale—that the White Act prohibited corporal punishment "such as that meted out by the 'bully mates' who hitherto had relied on their fists, belaying pins, and handspikes to enforce discipline,"[3] often in an arbitrary or brutal manner. Again we must wonder, just what did Leggatt actually do? This of course leads to the corollary question of just how far off the narrator's perceptions and judgments really are.

On strictly epistemic grounds, the narrator can be described as very strange. As J. D. O'Hara has pointed out, he demonstrates his

2. Joseph P. Goldberg, *The Maritime Story: A Study in Labor-Management Relations* (Cambridge, MA: Harvard University Press, 1958), 11.
3. Jack K. Bauer, *A Maritime History of the United States* (Columbia: University of South Carolina Press, 1988), 285.

irresponsibility by leaving his post as watch to go below for a cigar, then leaving it again as Leggatt climbs the ladder unwatched while he goes back for some clothes. This is indeed "wildly improbable as a description of an English captain coping with such a strange visitor in a foreign land,"[4] particularly if we recall that the official punishment for abandoning one's watch in the British and American navies of the period was death; furthermore, the captain leaves his watch three times that night. Nearly as dubious is the parallel dereliction of his duty to his men when he gives Leggatt half the money intended to buy fresh fruit and vegetables for the crew—provisions as important for morale as nutrition on a long voyage before the advent of refrigeration.

The narrator is justly famous in critical circles for his feelings of isolation, of being a stranger; when he says, "I felt that it would take very little to make me a suspect person in the eyes of the ship's company" [21], he may well be underestimating the distance between himself and his justifiably apprehensive crew. His odd behavior, starting with his admittedly unusual taking of that fateful watch and continuing with the strange actions designed to protect Leggatt, does cause some perfectly understandable apprehension, most palpably when he feigns deafness while Archbold is trying to apprehend a fugitive and, at the end, when the narrator nearly runs the ship aground for no apparent reason (and for no good reason, given that Leggatt was such an admirable swimmer).

The captain's discourse is curiously charged with descriptions of his own mental instability: "the dual working of my mind distracted me almost to the point of insanity" [23], "It was very much like being mad" [23], "part of me was absent" [31], "my nerves were so shaken that I could not govern my voice" [32], "I had come creeping quietly as near insanity as any man who has not actually gone over the border" [34]. The repeated references to madness strongly suggest that something much more substantial than mere unreliability is afflicting the narrator; coming from the mouth of the one most desirous of maintaining his credibility, they would seem to constitute an unwitting admission of genuine and severe mental instability.

In one revealing passage, he comments on the mate's tapping his forehead with his forefinger while talking with "a confidential air" to the ship's carpenter. He goes on to explain that although it was too far to hear a word, he nevertheless had no doubt that this pantomime "could only refer to the strange new captain" [32]. Again, there is no compelling rational foundation for this inference: there are many other equally plausible explanations for this gesture—one

---

4. J. D. O'Hara, "Unlearned Lessons in 'The Secret Sharer,'" *College English* 26.6 (March 1965): 447.

that indeed is unremarkable coming from a man who likes to get to the bottom of things. The captain's interpretation is closer to paranoia than probability. This is also the case when he hears Archbold's statement of Leggatt's unfitness: "I had become so connected in thoughts [with Leggatt] that I felt as if I, personally, were being given to understand that I, too, was not the sort that would have done for the chief mate of a ship like the *Sephora*" [26]. The captain admits, that is, that his feeling of resentment has its source in his own psychic projections rather than in any identification Archbold may have suggested.

This behavior in turn may well suggest a nautical intertext that would resonate powerfully in the minds of many of the period, particularly those connected to the sea. I am referring here to the events—real and imagined—on the American brig, the *Somers*, which one historian calls "the most discussed mid-nineteenth century naval episode of any that bore the imprint of mutiny."[5] This is a historical narrative that itself continues to engender and defy interpretation, and involves unreliable narrators, unrecorded counternarratives, and crucial events that may never have taken place. As James E. Valle writes: "The *Somers* mutiny may not, in fact, have been a mutiny at all." It is not clear whether the three men condemned and hanged at sea were really plotting to capture a U.S. vessel and murder her officers, or whether they were simply "the victims of an overwrought commanding officer with a hyperactive imagination. * * * The facts we do know are utterly baffling and include evidence to support either hypothesis." Some of the damning "evidence," it might be noted, included "a good deal of tense whispering in odd corners of the berth deck."[6] The oddities of the behavior of the captain would thus carry additional ominous overtones to the crew, who might have to pay for his hyperactive imagination with their flesh; I believe that any suspicion they may feel toward the captain is entirely justified. I'd like to suggest here that for a seaman of the period, the commander of the *Somers* would probably come quickly to mind as a kind of bitter potential double of the story's narrator-captain. We should also treat the captain's self-serving interpretations with appropriate skepticism, and try to listen to the muted voices of the ordinary seamen that Conrad so respected.

The simultaneous importance and unreliability of the imagination has been a staple of Conrad criticism since Guerard, as has a sensitivity to the limited perspectives of first-person narrators; nevertheless, the vast majority of interpreters have in varying degrees

5. Leonard F. Guttridge, *Mutiny: A History of Naval Insurrection* (Annapolis, MD: Naval Institute Press, 1992), 116.
6. James E. Valle, *Rocks and Shoals: Order and Discipline in the Old Navy, 1800–1861* (Annapolis, MD: Naval Institute Press, 1980), 108–09.

been seduced by the rhetoric of this captain-narrator.[7] To get to the other, obscured narratives in the work (and to the class-inflected sensibilities of those that try to utter them) it is necessary first to move beyond the captain's "point of view"—and I use this term in both its psychological and narratological senses. We may revisit two earlier and rather neglected critics of "The Secret Sharer," Robert D. Wyatt and Michael Murphy, whose arguments have not been adequately appreciated or developed as fully as they deserve to be.[8]

Murphy argues that the captain "is in some important respects an unreliable narrator";[9] Murphy does not claim the narrator "is lying, but simply that he is not telling the whole story."[1] A major piece of evidence for this interpretation (also noted by Wyatt) is the determination of the narrator to suppress all rival accounts of Leggatt and his activities on the *Sephora*. As Murphy explains, Archbold, the captain of the *Sephora*, "raises his voice to tell his story. What is that story? Oh, 'it is not worthwhile to record that version.' We should be the judges of that, but we do not get the chance. All we get are bits, though Conrad makes sure they are significant bits."[2] In addition, the alternative account provided by the crew of the other ship who knew Leggatt and witnessed the killing also goes unrecorded. Murphy concludes that Conrad's narrative method "forces us to remain ignorant of both" of these different versions.[3]

We may now inquire more deeply into the nature, motives, and appropriateness of the narrator's identification of himself with Leggatt. At its outset, the case made for their similarity is extremely rapid and not particularly rational. Based at first on what he calls "pure intuition" and "a mysterious communication" [13], the captain quickly imagines an entire psychology and, soon after, a personal history for the brusque stranger before him who is said to speak in "disconnected sentences" [15]. This resembles more the infatuation of an imaginative new lover than the appropriate behavior of a vigilant commander. The captain goes on to innocently believe every

7. Jakob Lothe, for example, simply states: "Although the narrator's vivid imagination and extreme egocentricity make him less than reliable, his unreliability is delimited by the absence from the text of firmer indications of authorial authority" (*Conrad's Narrative Method* [Oxford: Oxford University Press, 1989], 70–71).
8. Michael Murphy, "'The Secret Sharer': Conrad's Turn of the Winch," *Conradiana* 18.3 [Autumn 1986]: 193–200; Robert D. Wyatt, "Conrad's 'The Secret Sharer': Point of View and Mistaken Identities," *Conradiana* 5.1 (January 1973): 12–26.
9. Murphy, 193.
1. Murphy, 194. Murphy notes that he is building on an earlier article by J. D. O'Hara, whose position is somewhat tamer than Murphy's, as well as that of Robert D. Wyatt, who is in many respects more thorough. I will be citing both of these neglected critics in the course of this article. Some of their points are also taken up by Daniel R. Schwarz, who however prefers to call the narrator "imperceptive" rather than unreliable ("A Critical History of 'The Secret Sharer,'" in *The Secret Sharer* by Joseph Conrad, ed. Daniel R. Schwarz [Boston: Bedford/St. Martin's Press, 1997], 70).
2. Murphy, 195–96.
3. Murphy, 199.

statement and claim put forth by Leggatt, never wanting or daring to scrutinize the other's discourse critically: "I had not interrupted him. There was something that made comment impossible in his narrative, or perhaps in himself; a sort of feeling, a quality, which I can't find a name for" [20]. It is precisely these kinds of romantic, unnameable qualities, I suggest, that often do not exist at all.

A close reading of the descriptive passages in which the narrator identifies physical resemblances between the two men can also reveal much about their actual relation. An early mention of their similarity is literally shrouded in darkness: "The shadowy dark head, like mine, seemed to nod imperceptibly above the ghostly grey of my sleeping suit. It was, in the night, as though I had been faced by my own reflection in the depths of a somber and immense mirror" [14]. It is certainly a very opaque mirror, through which the narrator can see only darkly and fitfully. Later on, the captain makes the somewhat unusual observation that, "with his face nearly hidden, he must have looked exactly as I used to look in that bed" [21]. This "double" would seem to be strangely deficient in the quality of uniqueness: perhaps half the men in the ship, had their faces been similarly obscured, might have looked like him, too.

The oddest statement of all comes after the narrator, remarking on the expression of Leggatt's face, admits, "He was not a bit like me, really" [17]. This disclosure utterly undercuts all other affirmations of identity; I can conclude only that any similarities, physical or psychological, are largely projections of the narrator onto the other man, a series of fabrications that have little or no objective validity. As Robert Wyatt puts it, "there is almost no factual evidence for the narrator's felt sense of identification, other than their shared youth and the coincidence that they are both *Conway* boys. Whatever identification the narrator feels is more the consequence of his imagination than any similar, objective conditions."[4] There is consequently little reason to wonder why the captain fears Archbold's alternative interpretations, characterizations, and counternarratives: "If he had only known how afraid I was of his putting my feeling of identity with the other to the test!" [27], the captain writes, and he is correct in feeling alarm at the idea of such an investigation because it is a test he cannot expect to pass. Mark Ellis Thomas has convincingly argued, based on his analysis of parallel figures in *Lord Jim,* "The Secret Sharer," and *The Shadow Line,* that "Conradian doubling is a red herring, a false hermeneutic trail."[5] We may assent entirely concerning "The Secret Sharer."

4. Wyatt, 18. Or, as Mark Ellis Thomas observes, "Conrad's doubles fasten onto similarity as the salient factor in their doubling relationships and so ignore the more important differences" (223).
5. Thomas, 230.

Daniel R. Schwarz has observed that the captain's "flattering description of Leggatt is continually modified until it is almost contradicted," and that "the process of idealizing his double . . . is arbitrary and noncognitive."[6] Schwarz's analysis can also help explain the captain's crucial flaw. Just before encountering Leggatt, the captain wonders how faithful he would prove "to that ideal conception of one's personality every man sets up for himself secretly" [9]. It is an undue obsession with this ideal that makes the narrator so vulnerable and subject to the most egregious misprisions. Conrad, always so keen to expose the various catastrophes that follow directly from every form of idealism, even sees fit to puncture overly zealous idealizations of a favorite Conradian virtue, responsibility—an unexpected twist that no doubt has led many interpreters astray.

The many affirmations of understanding in the tale can themselves be read as a continuous ironic narrative that recapitulates the larger interpretive dynamics of the work as a whole. The first one comes from Leggatt shortly after he has come on board: "He appealed to me as if our experiences had been as identical as our clothes" [15], and this is an appeal that the narrator cannot resist, no matter how unjustified it might be. Later, when the captain of the *Sephora* comes on board, he explains that Leggatt was not at all the type of man for the job of mate, and adds the phrase "You understand" [27]. The narrator rejects this notion of shared comprehension as vigorously and as arbitrarily as he had earlier embraced Leggatt's appeal. Listening to Leggatt's revised tale of his mishap after the other captain has left, the narrator, instead of asking any hard questions, merely states, "I quite understand," thereby precluding any sustained examination of the discourse [30].

Throughout, Leggatt expresses his doubts that any jury would adequately judge his character and his narrative; they would lack the necessary context to properly comprehend the story. Appropriately, he thanks the captain in the end for an understanding that may well have been entirely spurious: "It's a great satisfaction to have got somebody to understand. You seem to have been there on purpose" [35]—or to have been jockeyed into position by Leggatt's maneuverings and the demands of his own insecurities. In the end, the original situation is reversed; it is now the captain who says, "I only hope I have understood, too" [38] as Leggatt (who, whatever his real identity may be, has certainly understood the captain from the start) is now the one invested with epistemic supremacy and granted the moral stature to judge the reach of the captain's empathy.

6. Daniel R. Schwarz, "'The Secret Sharer' as an Act of Memory," in *The Secret Sharer* by Joseph Conrad, ed. Daniel R. Schwarz (Boston: Bedford/St. Martin's Press, 1997), 105.

The ultimate basis of the captain's identification with the fugitive may be simple class prejudice. As Cedric Watts points out, both men "are ex-*Conway* boys, and thus members of a British social and maritime elite; both have the tone, style, phraseology and assumptions of gentlemen rather than of the working class," and are thus "privileged 'officer material' from the start of their careers."[7] Consequently, they are objects of resentment to both their crews, having been appointed to positions of command by decrees in high places "over the heads of older and possibly more experienced seamen" who instead had to laboriously work their way through the ranks.[8] It hardly needs to be added that the same class identification is a common feature of middle-class readers' responses to this narrator, and may partially explain why the captain's version of the events is so rarely questioned in any fundamental way.

Who then is the curious fugitive? If the discourse of the narrator is streaked with images of insanity, that of Leggatt keeps returning to killing: "Miserable devils that have no business to live at all" [14]; "somebody else might have got killed—for I would not have broken out only to get chucked back" [18]; "Somebody would have got killed for certain, and I did not want any of that" [20]; "Do you think that if I had not been pretty fierce with them I should have got the men to do anything?" [30]. Ultimately, this language even begins to infect the narrator's speech: after the steward goes into the captain's inner cabin, where Leggatt is hiding, not a sound is heard; the narrator himself can't help wondering, "Had my second self taken the poor wretch by the throat?" [33].

We too may speculate just what he might do in any given situation. We are not able to say for certain what Leggatt is, but we can be sure that he is not nearly as good as the rather Byronic story he provides for himself. Beyond that he is merely a blank slate on which the narrator traces the figure he needs to find. We know, that is, exactly what the narrator wants Leggatt to be, but we can never know what he is in himself. He may simply be a reckless devil with a smooth tongue who is skilled in telling the right lie to the right person. But there is insufficient evidence to ever determine whether he is or is not "a murderous ruffian," to use a phrase Conrad himself explicitly rejected (*CL* 5:121; see p. 374: Editor). In the end, we have very little more than the captain's "edition" of Leggatt's narrative, itself internally consistent but unable to account for the numerous anomalies, elisions, and contradictions that surround it. The narrative of Leggatt's life is both more ambiguous and more amenable to distinctively

7. Cedric Watts, "The Mirror Tale: An Ethico-Structural Analysis of Conrad's 'The Secret Sharer,'" *Critical Quarterly* 19.3 (1977): 27.
8. Watts, 27.

modernist interpretive strategies than has generally been accepted, even more so than Schwarz and Wyatt have suggested.

As might be expected in a work that consistently stages and thematizes narrative interpretation, there are a great number of potentially self-reflexive statements concerning speech, tale-telling, and narrative genres. It is after all the quality of Leggatt's voice that first predisposes the captain to believe Leggatt's words ("The voice was calm and resolute. A good voice" [13]). Leggatt is motivated by his dread of being trapped within an inaccurate but inescapable story; the mere facts, once related on shore, are certain to be misunderstood and thrust into the service of a very different narrative context: as we have noted, his is a "sufficiently fierce story to make an old judge and respectable jury sit up a bit" [15]; it is hardly a "[n]ice tale for a quiet tea party" [16]. Leggatt's request to be marooned is first objected to on narrative grounds ("We are not living in a boy's adventure tale" [35]), but, as is often the case in Conrad, men do often act as if they lived in such a fictitious universe. In any event, the choice is sealed with Leggatt alluding to another narrative, the biblical story of Cain—a most unusual intertext for one who claims he has merely committed justifiable homicide. At one point, the narrator refers to "the chapter of accidents that counts for so much in the book of success" [30], an apt metaphor of the confused action of the tale, whose full import the narrator literally cannot imagine.

As the tale ends, the now self-assured captain affirms, "Nothing! no one in the world should stand now between us * * * the perfect communion of a seaman with his first command" [42]. He has all the confidence that youth and idealism can engender. He has deserted his watch, alienated his crew, harbored a killer, hidden him from the authorities, given him money that was to have bought fresh food for his crew, and nearly destroyed his first command and marooned his own men for no good reason. He is entirely ignorant of the situation around himself.

The tale's narrator is a prisoner of a hermeneutic circle that he has both constructed and snared himself within. He has invented a noble and resolute personality for Leggatt, for which there is no compelling evidence, and perceived an identity between them that probably does not exist: "He was not a bit like me, really" [17]. He is so obsessed with his own inner drama that he has lost touch with reality to the point of being partly delusional. "The Secret Sharer" is not a last, tired reworking of the by then rather hackneyed theme of the doppelgänger but, I suggest, a skeptical parody of this familiar Romantic topos. This position, though admittedly at the far end of the range of existing critical interpretations, nevertheless offers, I believe, the most comprehensive explanation of the relevant events, images, and figures of this rich text.

A consequence of my overall reading of this text is that we should take a more complexly nuanced look at the many readings that presuppose an easy correspondence between the author and the narrator; such readers have been as uncritically accepting of the narrator's account as the credulous narrator was of Leggatt's version of events. This entire cycle of identifications is extremely dubious and unlikely to withstand a critical investigation. Nowhere else in Conrad is the distance greater between the implied author and the fallible narrator, and perhaps nowhere is it better hidden. Those looking for a simple autobiographical correspondence should perhaps reflect on the surprise experienced by Conrad's wife, Jessie, who had also assumed such a relation to exist: "I remember bitterly reproaching my husband for not having ever spoken of this episode [i.e., that dramatized in 'The Secret Sharer'] to me before he wrote the story. He gave a hoot of delight, and then as soon as he recovered from his unusual outburst of mirth, gave me a great hug and exclaimed: 'My dear, it is pure fiction. I don't know where the idea came from, but I've taken you in beautifully. Hurrah.'"[9]

"The Secret Sharer" both stages and invites basic questioning concerning the interpretation of any sequence of events, as the interpretive choices and class perspectives within the story are doubled by the critical interpretations that the tale engenders. It demands in the end both a more rigorous textual scrutiny and closer attention to the actual literary and social history that circumscribes it. This text ultimately eludes the models of reading suggested by the three most prominent positions currently in use: the objective implied reader of Wayne Booth, the subjectivist reader of Norman Holland, and the changing communities of readers of Stanley Fish.[1] Instead, we will find that a neglected concept of Umberto Eco that is situated between these opposites in fact describes Conrad's text more accurately: it is one of the works that "tell stories about the way stories are built up. In doing so these texts are much less innocuous than they seem: their deep theme is the functioning of that basic cultural machinery which, through the manipulation of our beliefs (which sublimate our wishes), produces ideologies, contradictory world visions, self-delusion."[2] It is a text that inscribes at least two contradictory readings, the most transparent of which is a trap for the unwary. In this, it embodies a depth and a playfulness typical of high modernism, one that criticism needs to more fully acknowledge.

9. Jessie Conrad, *Joseph Conrad and His Circle* (London: Jarrolds, 1935), 95.
1. On the other hand, Peter Rabinowitz's discussion of the frequent opposition between what he calls "authorial" and "narrative" audiences is extremely helpful for analyzing this text (*Before Reading: Narrative Conventions and the Politics of Interpretation* [Ithaca: Cornell University Press, 1987], 97–104).
2. Umberto Eco, *The Role of the Reader: Explorations in the Semiotics of Texts* (Bloomington: Indiana University Press, 1984), 256.

LILLIAN NAYDER

[History and Gender in Conrad's Maritime Fiction]†

* * *

A Victorian sailor as well as a novelist, Conrad participated in the industrial revolution that transformed the British merchant marine in the second half of the nineteenth century—the gradual replacement of sailing ships with the more reliable and profitable steamers. For Conrad, as for many of his contemporaries, the industrialization of the merchant marine appeared to have dire social consequences. On the one hand, the transformation from sail to steam was held responsible for the declining caliber of the men, who no longer seemed willing or able to respond to emergencies at sea—who had, in effect, lost the skills, endurance, and courage possessed by those "trained before the mast."[1] "A few months in steam rusts a sailor," Frank T. Bullen explained in 1900, for "what is wanted in a steamer is only a burly labourer who is able to steer."[2] On the other hand, problems of class conflict and social unrest in the merchant marine were attributed to the introduction of the "black gangs" hired to work the new steam engines.

* * *

Conrad responded to this revolution at sea by idealizing life on the sailing ship. Rewriting history in such a way that the harsh realities of life under sail are obscured, Conrad promotes an ideal that both maritime historians and literary critics have set out to demythologize. Complaining of the "nostalgic sentimentality" with which Conrad treats his sailing ships, on which the men are consistently unified, content, and obedient, they have undertaken to reconstruct the social history that underlies Conrad's glorified "distortions," pointing to the dangers, degradation, and isolation to which Victorian sailors were exposed, as well as to the growing problems of incompetence and undermanning.[3] They describe Conrad's idealized vision of social

---

† From "Sailing Ships and Steamers, Angels and Whores: History and Gender in Conrad's Maritime Fiction," in *Iron Men, Wooden Women: Gender and Seafaring in the Atlantic World, 1700–1920,* ed. Margaret S. Creighton and Lisa Norling (Baltimore: Johns Hopkins University Press, 1996), 190–203. Copyright 1996 The Johns Hopkins University Press. Reprinted with permission of Johns Hopkins University Press. Unless otherwise specified, page references are to this Norton Critical Edition.

1. Frank T. Bullen, *The Men of the Merchant Service: Being the Polity of the Mercantile Marine for 'Longshore Readers* (New York: Frederick A. Stokes, 1900), 257–259. * * *

2. Bullen, 259, 274.

3. Robert Foulke, "Life in the Dying World of Sail, 1870–1910." *Journal of British Studies* 3.1 (November 1963): 105, 109, 133.

obedience and solidarity at sea as a wish fulfillment of sorts, "a plea for order and community . . . in the face of the 'modernizing habits' of individualism and class antagonism."[4] As Fredric Jameson notes, the sea in Conrad's fiction is "the privileged place of the strategy of containment," a place where threatening social realities are repressed. The dreary life of the capitalist workplace and its antagonistic class relations are left behind by Conrad's mariners, among whom "human relations [are] presented in all their ideal formal purity."[5]

What these critics and historians fail to note, however, is that Conrad retells and recasts maritime social history by sexualizing his social anxieties as well as by idealizing and repressing class relations. In response to what he perceives as the socially destructive transition from sail to steam, Conrad not only mythologizes the solidarity and obedience of sailors; he also transforms class conflicts at sea into problems of gender relations. Adhering to an ideological pattern well established in English fiction by the late nineteenth century, Conrad assuages his primary, social anxieties by feminizing the working class. In Conrad's maritime fiction, as in the domestic fiction of Dickens and the Brontës, "class conflict comes to be represented as a matter of sexual misconduct," a problem more easily solved than that of social unrest, by means of the discipline and surveillance of women.[6]

Throughout his sea narratives, Conrad draws on the polarized stereotypes of Victorian womanhood in order to provide a reassuring explanation of the shift from sail to steam. Although he conceives of this shift in socioeconomic terms, as the inevitable change from traditional, pre-capitalist social relations to the antagonistic class relations of an industrialized economy, he represents this shift in sexual terms. In effect, the difference between sail and steam becomes the difference between two types of feminine behavior, that of the angel and the whore.[7] Confronted with the specter of social unrest and the rise of a resentful proletariat at sea, Conrad resolves his fears by imagining class relations as marital relations. He turns from the political conflicts between a captain and his men to the romantic conflicts between a captain and his ship, displacing the dangers of working-class resentment with the threat of female insubordination. Although Conrad's maritime world is generally understood to

4. Michael Levenson, "The Modernist Narrator on the Victorian Sailing Ship," *Browning Institute Studies* 11 (1983): 101–102.
5. Fredric Jameson, *The Political Unconscious: Narrative as Socially Symbolic Act* (Ithaca: Cornell University Press, 1981), 210 [506, this edition: Editor].
6. Nancy Armstrong, *Desire and Domestic Fiction: A Political History of the Novel* (Oxford: Oxford University Press, 1987), 178.
7. For discussions of these dichotomous female stereotypes, see Lynda Nead, *Myths of Sexuality: Representations of Women in Victorian Britian* (Oxford: Basil Blackwell, 1988); and Kate Millet, "The Debate over Women: Ruskin vs. Mill," in *Suffer and Be Still: Women in the Victorian Age*, ed. Martha Vicinus (Bloomington: Indiana University Press, 1967), 121–139.

be an "exclusively masculine community" where "women have no entry,"[8] Conrad invites us to read his adventure stories as domestic narratives that explore the tensions between captains and their troublesome "wives."

* * *

Conrad critics have long noted his antipathy to steamers, attributing it to the industrial nature of these ships. Observing that Conrad's maritime fiction consistently disparages steamships, they point out that he watched as steam power replaced sailors with engineers, and thus brought to sea the conflicts characteristic of factory life on shore. "There is not much difference now between a deck and a factory hand," Conrad complained to his friend Captain A. W. Phillips in 1924 [CL 8:272]. In particular, the sounds of the steamer's engine room in Conrad's stories are menacing; they remind us that the ship has been industrialized, and that a party of disgruntled workers is present below deck. In Lord Jim, for example, "short metallic clangs burst . . . out suddenly in the depths of the ship, the harsh scrape of a shovel, the violent slam of a furnace-door, exploded brutally, as if the men handling the mysterious things below had their breasts full of fierce anger" [LJ 16].

But if the "short metallic clangs" from below serve to acknowledge unpleasant social realities, the sexualized throbbing of the engine room serves to obscure them—to divert our attention from social to sexual dangers. Operated by an engineer who is "flushed" and "feminine" in appearance, the machinery—with its "slow," "gentle," yet "powerful movements"—recalls "the functions of a living organism" [302]. Characterized by her "big body," the steamer "pulsates" and "throbs" as she "shoulders [her] arrogant way against the great rollers" [MS 37, 64–65]. Thus, if the engine room in Conrad's steamer is the site of class unrest, it is also the locus of a threatening female sexuality.

As both literary critics and historians have shown, female sexuality was perceived as a subversive source of power in the Victorian period. Figures of sexually powerful yet demonic women abound in Victorian writing, where they challenge and resist patriarchal authority. The ideal Victorian woman was a de-eroticized being, her sexual activity limited to a purely reproductive function within the bounds of marriage. The so-called angel in the house, a Victorian icon, is meek and self-sacrificing, an asexual woman who serves rather than threatens the patriarchal status quo. Although her husband's sexual drive is active and spontaneous, her own is dormant. Only women considered pathological or deviant exhibit the sexual aggression allotted to men. * * *

8. Bernard C. Meyer, Joseph Conrad: A Psychoanalytic Biography (Princeton: Princeton University Press, 1967), 307.

In light of such beliefs, it seems only appropriate that the narrator of *The Shadow-Line* chooses to "divorce" a sexualized steamer at the outset of his story. Despite the seemingly irrational nature of his decision, he has good reason to "chuck his berth" [48]: "she was a steamship and therefore, perhaps, not entitled to . . . [his] loyalty" [48]. In particular, the narrator explains, it is the steamer's "internal propulsion" that has driven him away: "if it had not been for her internal propulsion," he observes, she would have been "worthy of any man's love" [49].

An emblem of female sexuality—powerful, autonomous, and devouring—the steamer's "internal propulsion" renders her "unworthy" of love in Conrad's eyes; what Conrad dislikes about the steamer, he explains in *The Mirror of the Sea* (1906), is "the power she carries within herself" [*MS* 63]. Adapting for his own ends the stereotype of the powerful, sexualized female, Conrad engenders his social concerns in *The Shadow-Line*. At the outset of the narrative, Conrad refers to the "rebellious discontent" of those on board the steamer [51] and dramatizes a hostile encounter between the first mate and the second engineer [50]. When his protagonist leaves the steamer and assumes command of a sailing ship, he meets a more experienced captain, who warns him of the deskilling caused by the advent of steam and fumes about mariners who are "afraid of the sails" [67]. But these issues of incompetence and insubordination in the merchant marine are no sooner raised than they are obscured. Although the new captain "can't muster more than three hands to do anything" on board his sailing ship [115], Conrad attributes the noncompliant state of the men to disease rather than inability or insurrection. Rather than pursuing the class implications initially raised by his narrative—the captain's fear that his men want to tear him "limb from limb" [111]—Conrad recasts it as a cautionary tale about female empowerment and rebellion.

In *The Shadow-Line*, Conrad's fear of female sexuality and the threat it poses to male authority is suggested by his depiction of the steamer, with her "internal propulsion." But informing his treatment of the steamer is a powerful, sexualized woman on shore. This woman has seduced the captain of a sailing ship—the man whom the narrator is hired to replace. Recounting the story of his predecessor's seduction, as it was told to him by the first mate, Mr. Burns, the narrator simultaneously acknowledges and displaces the class anxieties that inform Conrad's fiction:

> In Haiphong . . . [the captain] got himself, in Mr. Burns' own words, "mixed up" with some woman. Mr. Burns had had no personal knowledge of that affair, but positive evidence of it existed in the shape of a photograph taken in Haiphong. Mr. Burns found it in one of the drawers in the captain's room.

> In due course I, too, saw that amazing human document (I
> even threw it overboard later). There he sat with his hands repos-
> ing on his knees . . . and by his side towered an awful, mature,
> white female with rapacious nostrils and a cheaply ill-omened
> stare in her enormous eyes. She was disguised in some semi-
> oriental, vulgar, fancy costume. She resembled a low-class
> medium or one of those women who tell fortunes by cards for
> half-a-crown. And yet she was striking. A professional sorcer-
> ess from the slums. [86]

Although this passage articulates Conrad's fears of the urban working class and the power its members have assumed over traditional
figures of authority, his anxieties are expressed in a pointedly sexual
way. "Towering" over the captain, the "low-class. . . . sorceress" has
established her dominion over the man who, in Conrad's view, should
be her master. In comparing her to a "low-class medium. . . . from the
slums," Conrad draws upon a figure familiar to his original readers,
one in whom the dangers of working-class revolt are linked with those
of feminist rebellion. In the spiritualist movement of the late nineteenth century, the seance served a subversive political function: it
enabled women to appropriate the power and autonomy generally
reserved for men. By assuming a masculine or an upper-class per-
sona, the female medium could circumvent the rigid Victorian norms
of social class and gender and could speak with the voice of authority.
Furthermore, the medium's trance—her possession by various
spirits—helped to redefine conceptions of female sexuality, extending
the limits of women's sexual life in a socially acceptable way.[9]

Unlike the captain who has preceded him, and who is seduced
and emasculated by a sexualized woman, the narrator of *The
Shadow-Line* maintains his authority by associating with an asexual and angelic female figure. Having divorced an internally powered steamer, he wisely "remarries" a sailing ship the second time
around. Whereas Conrad represents the steamer as a demonic and
rebellious female body, he imagines the sailing ship as an angelic
and subservient female soul. Sailing ships "lead . . . a sort of unearthly
existence," Conrad tells his readers. Made of "gossamer," they are
angelic beings "held to obedience"—wholly dependent on the masculine winds and on the seamen for their movements. They thus
provide a marked contrast to the steamer, which is largely independent of "man power" [MS 37, 64] and is both autonomous and pro-
miscuous in Conrad's eyes. Like a "loose" woman, the steamer can be
"loaded" by anyone, and in virtually any way: "Her cargo is not stowed
in any sense; it is simply dumped into her through six hatchways,

---

9. Alex Owen, *The Darkened Room: Women, Power, and Spiritualism in Late Victorian
England* (Philadelphia: University of Pennsylvania Press, 1990), 4, 11, 218.

more or less . . . with clatter and hurry and racket and heat, in a cloud of steam and a mess of coal-dust." But the sailing ship resembles a "modest bride," "diffident, lying very quiet, with her side nestling shyly against the wharf," and must be "loaded" with care [*MS* 47, 132].

In Conrad's fiction, this female ideal serves an important, though largely unspoken, function—it enables the captain to bolster his patriarchal authority in the face of diminishing social control. Thus, in *The Shadow-Line*, Conrad's idealized conception of the "modest" sailing ship allows him to "solve" the problem of unrest and disaffection among the men. Although the captain "can't muster more than three hands to do anything" [115], the ship is ready to serve her master. When the narrator gains his appointment as captain and is introduced to his "lover" [78], he is immediately empowered by her, since her will is utterly subordinate to his own: "A ship! My ship! She was mine, more absolutely mine for possession and care than anything in the world; an object of responsibility and devotion. She was there waiting for me, spellbound, unable to move, to live, to get out into the world (till I came), like an enchanted princess" [73].

Like his predecessor's relationship to the human seductress, the narrator's relationship to his ship is described in sexual terms. Nonetheless, their physical intimacy is rendered nonthreatening: while the narrator receives physical satisfaction from his ship, the ship herself—like the de-eroticised and subservient Victorian wife—merely suffers through her "loading":

> That illusion of life and character which charms one in men's finest handiwork radiated from her. An enormous baulk of teakwood timber swung over her hatchway; lifeless matter, looking heavier and bigger than anything aboard of her. When they started lowering it the surge of the tackle sent a quiver through her from water-line to the tucks up the fine nerves of her rigging, as though she had shuddered at the weight. It seemed cruel to load her so. . . .
>
> Putting my foot on her deck for the first time, I received the feeling of deep physical satisfaction. Nothing could equal the fullness of that moment, the ideal completeness of that emotional experience. . . . My rapid glance ran over her, enveloped, appropriated the form concreting the abstract sentiment of my command. . . . In all the parts of the world washed by navigable waters our relation to each other would be the same—and more intimate than there are words to express in the language. [80–81]

Utterly passive and dependent on her male lover, the sailing ship waits for him, "unable to move, to live" until he arrives. An object that can be "enveloped," "appropriated," and "possessed," she provides only the "illusion" of life, and thus the captain can safely enjoy her charms; she gives concrete form to his "abstract sentiment of . . . command" [80].

She is, furthermore, not simply an object, but a "man made" one at that, an example of "men's finest handiwork" [80]. As such, she defuses the dangers posed to social order by the growth of industrialism and by what Conrad perceives to be the uncontrollable force of female nature. As fine handiwork, Conrad's sailing ship is distinguished from the manufactured steamers, whose parts came from iron foundries and whose construction required highly specialized manufacturing facilities that gradually destroyed the local shipbuilding communities that Conrad valued. At the same time, the ship's "man-made" status safely mediates her femininity; she is the product of male culture rather than a threatening manifestation of female nature. Subscribing to the patriarchal ideology that associates women with nature and men with culture, Conrad speaks of woman as "a force of nature, blind in its strength and capricious in its power." Like electricity, she can be "captured" by a man and used to "light . . . him on his way," to "warm . . . his home," and to "cook his dinner for him"; yet "the greater demand he makes on [her] . . . the more likely [she] is to turn on him and burn him to a cinder" [C 327] But ships, unlike women, are born of men, and hence dissociated from the destructive force of Mother Nature; Conrad describes them as a "perfect brood" to which "the thundering peal of hammers beating upon iron . . . gives birth" [175]. Indebted to their fathers rather than their mothers for life, they bear witness to the strength of patriarchy instead of undermining it.

Despite her preindustrial and patriarchal origins, however, the sailing ship in *The Shadow-Line* temporarily behaves like the rapacious woman on shore; once under way, she too resists the captain's control. He feels "bewitched" [103] because he has difficulty sailing her beyond the Island of Koh-ring, and because once he succeeds in getting her out to sea, so many of his men have been laid low by fever that she threatens to "take the wheel out of [the helmsman's] hands" [121]. "We won't be able to do anything with her," the captain warns his men: "She's running away with us now. All we can do is to steer her" [129]. Yet if *The Shadow-Line* registers the threat posed to the captain's authority, it ultimately affirms his ability to put down insubordination. Despite the captain's anxieties about "handling" the "wildly rushing ship full of dying men" [129], her struggle for autonomy is foiled by her very design. Unlike a steamer operating upon her own power, by means of "internal propulsion," the sailing ship depends upon men for her movement. Thus, the captain can control his ship by manipulating her sails. "Haul[ing] the mainsail close up," "squar[ing] the mainyard," fastening the leech-line, and "letting go all the sheets and halliards by the run," he safely brings the ship into port [120, 131].

In *The Shadow-Line*, the physical anatomy of the sailing ship ensures her subordination; so, too, does her economic purpose. Unlike the engineers and firemen on Conrad's steamers, who persistently complain of their wages, and who jealously compare their earnings to those of sailors and officers, his idealized ship is a female worker who selflessly labors for the good of her master. "Backed by the fidelity of ships"—"willing" and "untiring servants"—men "wrest from [the ocean] the fortune of their house, the dominion of their world" [MS 120, 136–37]. Though, in *The Nigger of the "Narcissus"* (1897), Mr. Baker tells his men that they must "take care of the ship" [193], the ship ultimately serves the men, and Conrad compares her labor to "the unselfish toil of a delicate woman" [174]. As we will see, such "unselfish toil" is rare among Conrad's women, who serve to displace not only the threat of class unrest in the merchant marine but also the problem of economic exploitation as well.

*   *   *

Representing the transition from sail to steam as if it reenacts the Fall of mankind, Conrad attributes the loss of maritime "innocence" in the nineteenth century to the construction of the Suez Canal. * * * Yet insofar as Conrad idealizes the economic "innocence" of life under sail, he misrepresents this transition. Although the merchant marine always operated for profit and made possible the lucrative expansion of the empire, Conrad suggests that before the advent of steam, those who "followed the sea" had higher motives: childlike, faithful, and content with their hard lot, they were above financial calculations. For the sailors in his sea fiction, work is an end in itself, an "artistic" activity undertaken for pleasure rather than profit. Obscuring the economic and power relations among masters, officers, deck hands, and shipowners, and eliding the turbulent labor history of the merchant marine, Conrad promotes a spiritual ideal of sail in which mariners and shipowners follow a "calling" or "vocation" and are alike "untainted by the pride of possession" [MS 31, 136]:

> No seaman ever cherished a ship, even if she belonged to him, merely because of the profit she put in his pocket. No one, I think, ever did; for a ship-owner, even of the best, has always been outside the pale of that sentiment embracing in a feeling of intimate, equal fellowship the ship and the man, backing each other against the implacable, if sometimes dissembled, hostility of their world of waters. [MS 137]

Into this "intimate, equal fellowship" between man and sailing ship at sea, the captain's wife intrudes, bringing with her the divisions and antagonisms that Conrad associates with the advent of steam, the profit motive, and claims to private property. While the men on Conrad's sailing ships are financial innocents, their wives certainly are not, and to them Conrad attributes the exploitation of maritime labor. Insofar as Conrad acknowledges the existence of exploited workers under sail, they are men victimized by greedy female "masters." Thus, while Conrad displaces class conflict with feminist rebellion, he also depicts women as members of a powerful leisure class, the unproductive "passengers" on board his ship of state. The wives in Conrad's maritime fiction are often characterized as heartless managers, and their husbands as the laborers whom they oppress and exploit.

Not surprisingly, the labor problems that Conrad associates with industrialism are most obvious on his steamers. Yet even here the wife is held responsible for the exploitation of the men. In "Typhoon" (1902), the sufferings of the working class on board the steamer *Nan-Shan* are suggested in two ways—by the condition of the men in the engine room, who are choked with ashes and who "toil . . . mutely, as if [their] tongue[s] had been cut out" [307], and by the injuries sustained during a violent storm by the two hundred coolies whom Captain MacWhirr is transporting to their homes in Fo-Kien "after a few years of work in various tropical colonies" [261]. But instead of criticizing the merchant marine as an agent of industry and empire—for treating those in the engine room as mute beasts of burden, and the coolies as human "cargo" [323]—Conrad discredits these figures by feminizing them and recasts the problem of exploitation as a marital one. Conrad portrays the languid coolies on the deck of the *Nan-Shan* as they pose in "girlish" attitudes, plaiting their hair [271], and he notes that the third engineer below, with coal dust settled on his eyelids, has "something of a feminine, exotic and fascinating aspect" [302]. He then collapses the economic and social distinctions among those characters who retain their masculinity by shifting our attention to the exploitation of men by women—in particular, that of the working-class captain by his socially superior wife. While her husband risks his life at sea in order to finance her pleasures, Mrs. MacWhirr spends her days shopping and luxuriates in her suburban home at his expense:

> He paid five-and-forty pounds a year for [her house], and did not think the rent too high, because Mrs. MacWhirr . . . was admittedly ladylike, and in the neighborhood considered as "quite superior." . . . She reclined in a plush-bottomed and gilt hammock-chair near a tiled fireplace, with Japanese fans on the mantel and a glow of coals in the grate. Lifting her hands, she glanced wearily here and there into the many pages [of her

husband's letter]. . . . She had a movement of impatience. He was always thinking of coming home. He had never had such a good salary before. What was the matter now? [267, 318]

The exploitation of male workers by the members of this female leisure class is even more apparent in those stories in which Conrad's captains bring their wives to sea.* * *

But while Conrad represents the wives on his ships as queens who dominate and divide the male community, he represents the ships themselves as female workers who serve their masters rather than exploiting them. Although Conrad characterizes the ship in *The Shadow-Line* as "a high-class vessel" [80], she is "high-class" in a very restricted sense—as "a creature of high-breed" [80]. What the narrator perceives as her superiority over the "low-class" woman from the slums [86] is, in reality, the mark of her subservience to him: "Amongst her companions," "all bigger than herself, she looked like an Arab steed in a string of cart-horses" [80].[1] And while, in "Typhoon," Mrs. MacWhirr reclines in luxury, the *Nan-Shan* "labor[s] heavily in . . . mountainous black waters" [312], "paying with [her] hard tumbling the price of her life" [316]. Like Mrs. MacWhirr, she is described in the act of "spending," yet her expenditure is the mark of her self-sacrifice.

Furthermore, the ship—unlike the wife—is shared by all the men on board her and is passed on from one captain to the next. Unlike the exclusive relation between a captain and his wife, which "taints" the male community with conceptions of private property, the relation between the ship and men is polyandrous. As common property, she enables the male community to remain stable and brotherly. A ship "bonds" men together, Conrad explains in *The Mirror of the Sea*: "and therein a ship, though she has female attributes and is loved very unreasonably, is different from a woman" [MS 19] Unlike a wife, a ship provides a home to all the men aboard her, and as a result they feel a common pride in their beloved rather than fighting among themselves for possession of her. "We all watched [the ship]," the narrator in "The Nigger of the *Narcissus*" notes. "We loved her. . . . We admired her qualities aloud, we boasted of them to one another, as though they had been our own" [175]. As anthropologists and social historians point out, such polyandrous societies are generally matriarchal in structure, with the power of women based on "mother-right" (matrilineality), the right of the mother rather than the father

---

1. Jeremy Hawthorn notes in his introduction to *The Shadow-Line* that Conrad's novel suggests that "the world would be better if women were like well-made ships: beautiful to look at and under the control of an appreciative captain" (Oxford: Oxford University Press, 1985), xxii.

to lay claim to the children. But in Conrad's stories, the polyandrous community is patriarchal rather than matriarchal. This is the case because the ship produces rather than reproduces; although she has a multitude of husbands, she can lay no claim to mother-right.

In Conrad's fiction, the idealized conception of life under sail seems imperiled not by class unrest and exploitation but by a woman's presence; by replacing ungovernable women with subservient ships in his sailors' affections, Conrad maintains his maritime ideal. In "Youth" (1898), the captain's wife is deposited on shore, and her feminine functions are assumed by the *Judea*, a ship that mothers all the men on board her; "it seemed as though we had been born in her, reared in her," the narrator remarks [Y 21].

* * * Understood as a response to the problems of industrialization and the transition from sail to steam, Conrad's maritime fiction shows that these strategies² operate in a literary realm too often defined as purely masculine. Read as domestic narratives of a sort, his seafaring tales reveal the ideological uses to which sexual stereotypes are put in nineteenth-century literature; in so doing, they collapse the polarity critics have traditionally established between masculine adventure stories and domestic fiction, with its presumably "feminine" concerns. It may appear that Conrad's heroes are "free from the complexities of relations with . . . women."³ Yet their relations with their ships, under both sail and steam, demonstrate that tales of maritime adventure and stories of courtship and marriage can be one and the same.

MARK D. LARABEE

"A Mysterious System": Topographical Fidelity and the Charting of Imperialism in Joseph Conrad's Siamese Waters†

Not long after the publication of his novel *The Shadow-Line*, Joseph Conrad wrote a letter to Sidney Colvin cautioning him against reading too much into the presentation of setting in that tale. "Very dear of you to write so appreciatively about the little book," Conrad

2. I.e., to free his sea stories from troubling political realities by sexualizing them [*Editor*].
3. Patrick Brantlinger, *Rule of Darkness: British Literature and Imperialism, 1830–1914* (Ithaca: Cornell University Press, 1988), 11.
† *Studies in the Novel* 32. 3 (Fall 2000): 348–68. Copyright © 2000 by the University of North Texas. Reprinted with permission of Johns Hopkins University Press. The author revised the essay for this Norton Critical Edition. Unless otherwise specified, page references are to this edition.

tells him, "But I don't agree that a local-knowledge man would be the right reviewer for it. The locality doesn't matter; and if it is the Gulf of Siam it's simply because the whole thing is exact autobiography" [*CL* 6:37; see p. 375: Editor]. Conrad sought to reveal the artistic verities that lie outside, or underneath, empirical or visible reality—as he explains in the preface to *The Nigger of the "Narcissus,"* where he defines art "as a single-minded attempt to render the highest kind of justice to the visible universe, by bringing to light the truth, manifold and one, underlying its every aspect" [139]. According to Conrad's line of reasoning, the author subordinates the verifiable aspects of a story's basis to the truths that the story reveals, coincidentally implying that artistic truths exist not only independent of empirical reality, but sometimes in spite of the constraints that mere facts might impose.

In Conrad's letter to Colvin, the author seems to put the matter of factual accuracy firmly to rest. But we might also draw the opposite conclusion: namely, that Conrad sounds like an author with something to hide. Despite his best efforts to draw attention away from the factual basis of his fiction, moreover, Conrad cannot but attract that very same critical curiosity he hopes to avoid through his dismissive tone. Yet this relegation of historical facts to relative unimportance garners support from none other than Norman Sherry in his landmark study *Conrad's Eastern World.*[1] * * * Sherry, like Conrad, prefers the notion of an artistic truth that manifests itself in man's actions; as a revelation of mental and emotional life, this special kind of transcendent truth does not depend on a faithful representation of "the original 'true' incident" [*CEW* 273] Sherry underlines his point by quoting Aristotle's *Poetics* to illustrate Conrad's treatment of artistic truth, which does not "relate such things as have actually happened, but such as might have happened—such as are possible, according either to probable or necessary consequence" [*CEW* 272]. As Aristotle, Conrad, and Sherry insist on the greater significance of what "might have happened," compared with an historical context that is not only superficial but open to alteration, evaluating the fidelity of *The Shadow-Line* to the factual basis of the Gulf of Siam seems a pointless exercise.

Nevertheless, if we closely examine this novel's setting (against Conrad's wishes), we will find it to be considerably less than "exact autobiography" and more significant than Conrad leads us to believe; in fact, his expression of artistic truth depends on a deliberate and systematic manipulation of a supposedly unrelated historical reality. To demonstrate the largely neglected importance of the

---

1. Norman Sherry, *Conrad's Eastern World.* Cambridge: Cambridge University Press, 1996.

topographical element of factual analysis, I will focus on the setting of *The Shadow-Line*, with additional consideration of how the Gulf of Siam appears in "Falk" and "The Secret Sharer." I have drawn on nineteenth-century British Admiralty charts, pilot guides, and travel narratives, among other materials, to reconstruct the factual setting of these tales and evaluate the author's fidelity to that setting—revealing how Conrad alters specific details of the seascape in order to reinforce the major themes of his art.

Examining Conrad's alteration of the East takes on an added dimension given the recent resurgence of interest in Conrad's fiction within the context of Orientalism and British imperialism. An awareness of geography plays a key role in this reconsideration of Conrad's colonial world; for example, Marlow's boyhood fascination with maps in "Heart of Darkness" has come under the scrutiny of numerous critics interested in imperialism. Yet when Conrad makes such assertions as those in his evasive-sounding letter to Sidney Colvin, critics tend to take Conrad at his word—finding much to consider in Conrad's portrayal of the landscape but neglecting to examine how factually accurate that portrayal really is. As I will demonstrate, the discrepancy between the factual and fictive Gulf of Siam matters very much indeed, for Conrad's misrepresentation of historical reality can be seen as conforming to an imperialist reading of the observable world.

Conrad based *The Shadow-Line*, "Falk," and "The Secret Sharer" partly on a series of actual events. While at Singapore in 1888 (having just left his billet as first mate in the *Vidar*), he accepted an offer to take command of the *Otago*, a sailing merchantman lying at Bangkok. He was to take the place of the ship's previous master, who had recently died at sea. Conrad traveled to the Siamese capital as a passenger on the steamship *Melita* and took charge of a crew laid low by fever. After fighting a series of delays in Bangkok, he eventually descended the Meinam River to the Gulf of Siam; over the next three weeks, baffling calms slowed the ship to a torturous crawl and further sickness incapacitated the crew. He finally managed to bring the *Otago* into Singapore as one of the few physically able men left aboard.[2] (See Figure 1 for a contemporary map of the area.)

The narrator in *The Shadow-Line* travels from Singapore to Bangkok to take command under the same circumstances. He brings his unnamed ship down the Meinam and across the gulf to Singapore,

2. Jerry Allen, *The Sea Years of Joseph Conrad* (New York: Doubleday, 1965), 245–253. "Meinam" (or "me nam") means "river." The river in these stories, the Me Nam Chao Phraya, is variously called the Me Nam Chao Praya, the Chow Phya Menam, the Bangkok River, the river Menam, the Menam river, the Meinam River, or the Meinam, in the nineteenth-century materials cited in this article. For simplicity, I refer to it as the Meinam or the Meinam River.

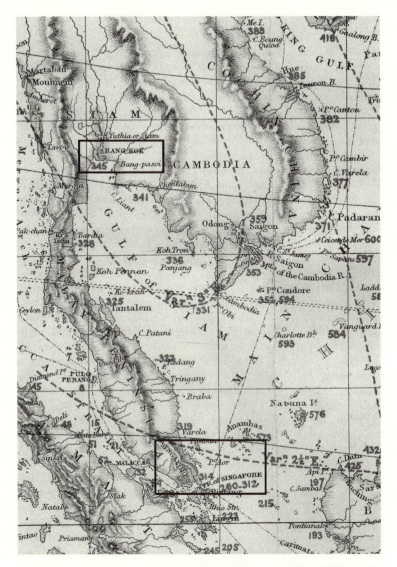

Figure 1. The Gulf of Siam Region. Reproduced from Alexander G. Findlay, *A Directory for the Navigation of the Indian Archipelago and the Coast of China, from the Straits of Malacca and Sunda, and the Passages East of Java, to Canton, Shanghai, and the Yellow Sea, and Korea, With Descriptions of the Winds, Monsoons, and Currents, and General Instructions for the Various Channels. Harbours, Etc.,* 3rd ed. (London: Richard Holmes Laurie, 1889), facing title page. Boxes added by Mark D. Larabee.

battling similar calms and sickness in a harrowing cruise that tests his competence and moral stature. Conrad makes the descent of the river the setting of "Falk"; in "The Secret Sharer," he shows us a voyage from the river's mouth to an island off the Cambodian coast. These three stories, while set in slightly different locations within the same general area, share several key elements of setting that are susceptible to a revealing comparison with their historical counterparts— for several puzzling inconsistencies arise when we closely examine Conrad's descriptions of the details of the gulf.

In *The Shadow-Line*, Conrad gives us our first glimpse of Siam just after his narrator, having come from Singapore onboard the *Melita*, crosses the bar at the mouth of the Meinam River. In the 1889 edition of the *Directory for the Navigation of the Indian Archipelago and the Coast of China*, a standard pilot guide, Alexander Findlay describes in great detail the actual hazards of this bar: its three-foot minimum depth, "extensive banks of sand and mud," sunken wrecks, scarcity of navigational aids, swift currents, and irregular tides.[3] A number of contemporary travel accounts corroborate Findlay's assessment of the dangers.[4] This bar represented such a hazard that Conrad's narrator in "Falk" describes it as "a great nuisance to the shipping" [*TOS* 164]. In the manuscript version of that story, he goes further to call the bar "a crying shame" and an "impediment to civilisation" [*CEW* 233]. Yet passing this significant obstacle in *The Shadow-Line* merits only the most perfunctory remark: Conrad's narrator says simply "One morning early, we crossed the bar" [78].

Dismissing the significance of the bar in this particular story seems incredible when we remember Conrad's characterization of this tale as "exact autobiography." Moreover, we may justifiably wonder why the author would pass up the opportunity to exploit the Tennysonian connotations of bar-crossing in a novel so laden with symbolism of life and death. The minimization of this obstacle in *The Shadow-Line* is no accident; nor can it simply be the result of the narrator's attempt at brevity. Already, with the first significant topographical description, we can see a conscious reshaping of physical reality—the start of a pattern that will consistently develop throughout the novel, and which I will disclose in further detail.

After passing the oddly shrunken hurdle of the sand bar, the narrator describes how, "while the sun was rising splendidly over the flat spaces of the land [they] steamed up the innumerable bends, passed under the shadow of the great gilt pagoda, and reached the outskirts

3. Alexander G. Findlay, A *Directory for the Navigation of the Indian Archipelago and the Coast of China* * * *, 3rd ed. (London: Richard Holmes Laurie, 1889), 347.
4. See Frank Vincent, *The Land of the White Elephant* (London: Sampson Low, Marston, Low & Searle, 1873), 117, and H. Warington Smyth, *Five Years in Siam from 1891 to 1896*, 2 vols. (London: John Murray, 1898), 1:2.

of the town" [78–79]. Bangkok lies twenty-five miles up the winding Meinam, which flows by what H. Warington Smyth, in his travel narrative, calls "The Pagoda in the River."[5] Conrad ascribes varying locations to this pagoda, which appears in all three stories. Judging from the description in *The Shadow-Line*, the temple seems to be near the end of the twenty-five-mile river transit; we see it only after having passed "innumerable bends." Yet in the opening scene of "The Secret Sharer," set on a ship at the anchorage outside the river's mouth, Conrad writes of the narrator being able to see the pagoda (surrounded by a grove) "far back on the inland level," yet definitely within view [7]. The narrator in "Falk" (also on a ship at that very same anchorage) can clearly discern the details of the pagoda's "shining curves and pinnacles," seeing the structure as though it were quite near [*TOS* 166]. When we compare the placement of the pagoda in *The Shadow-Line* with its location in "Falk" and "The Secret Sharer," we can see that Conrad situates the pagoda in two distantly-separated positions—neither of which corresponds to historical fact.

In "Falk" and "The Secret Sharer," Conrad effectively moves the pagoda to a location much closer to the water than it actually occupied. Seen through the narrators' eyes, the structure dominates the horizon surrounding the shallow water outside the Meinam. However, we may reasonably question how those narrators can possibly have seen the temple from their vantage point. The narrators' ships would not have anchored just anywhere, but within a specified anchorage—a relatively small, circumscribed location appearing on charts and in pilot guides, in fact almost ten miles from the pagoda (see Figure 2).[6] Both the presence of intervening trees on the shoreline and the curvature of the earth lead us to question how much of the pagoda could have been seen at that distance.

More importantly, pilot guides (both Conrad-era and modern) fail to mention the pagoda—and it would have been a conspicuous and useful aid to navigation if, as in "Falk" and "The Secret Sharer," its spire dominated the surrounding jungle. Additionally, travel narratives imply the pagoda could not be seen from outside the river's mouth.[7] While these clues do not conclusively rule out the ability of

5. "One of the prettiest and most characteristic things of the kind in the country." Smyth, 1:7.
6. The anchorage is clearly marked on the British Admiralty chart *China Sea: Gulf of Siam, Sheet II, Koh Ta Kut to Cape Liant (Chart No. 2720)* (London: Hydrographic Office, 1860, large corrections up to 1880, small corrections up to 1908); see Findlay, 347, and Smyth, 7.
7. See Findlay, 347; see also United States, Defense Mapping Agency Hydrographic/ Topographic Center, *Pub. 161. Sailing Directions (Enroute): South China Sea and Gulf of Thailand,* 7th ed. (Washington: DMA, 1998), 140, and Maxwell Sommerville, *Siam on the Meinam from The Gulf of Atyuthia, Together with Three Romances Illustrative of Siamese Life and Customs* (London: Sampson Low, Marston, 1897), 17.

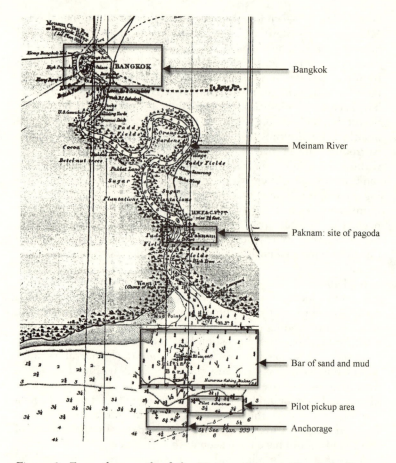

Bangkok

Meinam River

Paknam: site of pagoda

Bar of sand and mud

Pilot pickup area

Anchorage

Figure 2. From the mouth of the Meinam River to Bangkok. Reproduced from Great Britain, Admiralty, *China Sea: Gulf of Siam, Sheet II, Koh Ta Kut to Cape Liant (Chart No. 2720)* (London: Hydrographic Office, 1860, large corrections to 1880, small corrections to 1908). Boxes added by Mark D. Larabee.

the narrator in "The Secret Sharer" to glimpse the pagoda's "mitre-shaped hill" [8], they at least make unlikely the possibility of the narrator in "Falk" to descry its "shining curves and pinnacles" [TOS 166] from a distance of ten miles. Most significantly, in both cases Conrad leaves the reader with the impression that the pagoda stands closer to the sea than it actually does.

While the author seems to place the pagoda too close to the river's mouth in these two stories, in *The Shadow-Line* the pagoda lies too far up the Meinam. After the narrator covers the great distance implied by the words "innumerable bends," the pagoda is the last object he sees just before reaching Bangkok. But as we can see from Figure 2, the river's bends are hardly "innumerable"; furthermore, the turns in the Meinam appear *after* passing the pagoda rather than before. Something odd is going on here, for the pagoda cannot be at the beginning *and* the end of the Meinam passage, as Conrad implies when we compare all three accounts. It is possible that Conrad might simply have forgotten the temple's location; he wrote "Falk" and "The Secret Sharer" thirteen and twenty years, respectively, after having traveled to Bangkok, and he wrote *The Shadow-Line* an additional seven years after "The Secret Sharer." On the other hand, the migration of this important landmark serves Conrad's purposes well because the structure functions differently in each narrative.

The pagoda appears in the opening scene of "The Secret Sharer," where the narrator describes the sensation of isolation and abandonment he feels at the start of his voyage. As he gazes at his surroundings, he keeps seeing false clues of a human presence. The opening sentence portrays lines of fishing-stakes jutting haphazardly from the water, "resembling a mysterious system of half-submerged bamboo fences, incomprehensible in its division of the domain of tropical fishes, and crazy of aspect as if abandoned for ever by some nomad tribe of fishermen now gone to the other end of the ocean; for there was no sign of human habitation as far as the eye could reach." The narrator persists in searching for those signs, however; he sees "a group of barren islets" that seem man-made, "suggesting ruins of stone walls, towers, and blockhouses." A steam tug, proceeding away up the river, appears to "[steam] right into the land," becoming "lost to [his] sight, hull and funnel and masts, as though the impassive earth had swallowed her up without an effort, without a tremor." Only "the grove surrounding the great Paknam pagoda" provides relief for eyes employed in "the vain task of exploring the monotonous sweep of the horizon." The smoke from the tug grows more faint and distant until it becomes lost behind the pagoda's "mitre-shaped hill." "And then," the narrator concludes, "I was left alone with my ship, anchored at the head of the Gulf of Siam" [8].

In this passage from "The Secret Sharer," the pagoda serves two functions. It symbolizes the last presence of humanity in a setting that makes the narrator responsible for his fellow-men while surrounded by the hostile, empty seascape. Second, by hiding the fading smoke of the tug it suggests the triumph of timeless oriental antiquity over temporary western intrusion. In these two roles, the pagoda stands as a particularly apt object of the narrator's searching gaze—alien and ancient, man-made but not truly inhabited, a Buddhist structure but shaped like a bishop's miter, the temple serves as a fitting witness to the start of a journey that will explore themes of solitude vs. community and identity vs. the other. In this respect, then, Conrad does well to move the pagoda closer to the river's mouth, where it can be seen by the narrator from his ship on the cusp of voyage.

On the other hand, the pagoda serves a different symbolic purpose in *The Shadow-Line*. Conrad describes the approach to the heart of Bangkok through a series of images that steadily carry the eye from the "flat spaces of the land" past the "brown houses . . . sprung out of the brown soil," up past the "crowded mob of low, brown roof ridges" to the "great piles of masonry" that "towered" above [78–79]. In this progression from undeveloped land to "gorgeous and dilapidated" [79] structures, from the low-lying ground to the tall buildings, the pagoda fits in better towards the end. There it can announce, through its very foreignness, the final approach to the Siamese capital—"Oriental and squalid," the symbolic opposite of civilized Singapore [96].

Not only does Conrad place the pagoda in different locations in these stories, but he significantly alters its appearance. Six eyewitness accounts from the nineteenth century describe the Paknam pagoda, most agreeing on its size and elaboration.[8] (Most usefully, Smyth offers a drawing of how it appeared during his 1891–96 trip.) Yet this appearance, like the pagoda's location, varies from tale to tale in accordance with the requirements of Conrad's different narratives.

---

8. See Carl Beck, *Temples and Elephants: The Narrative of a Journey Exploration Through Upper Siam and Lao* (London: Sampson Low, Marston, Searle, & Rivington, 1884), 2. See also Benajah Ticknor, *The Voyage of the "Peacock."* ed. Nan Powell Hedges (Ann Arbor: University of Michigan Press, 1991), 233–235; W. S. W. Ruschenberger, *A Voyage Round the World, Including Embassy to Muscat and Siam, in 1835, 1836, and 1837* (Philadelphia: Carey, Lea, and Blanchard, 1838), 263; Henri Mouhot, *Travel in the Central Parts of Indo-china (Siam), Cambodia, and Laos, During the Years 1858, 1859, and 1860,* 2 vols. (London: John Murray, 1864), 1:41; Vincent, 118; and Sommerville, 17.

The portrayal of this temple in "Falk" seems true to life; Conrad writes of how the temple appears "uprising lonely and massive with shining curves and pinnacles like the gorgeous and stony efflorescence of tropical rocks" [TOS 166]. In The Shadow-Line, in contrast, he mentions passing "the great gilt pagoda" [79] and leaves the description unfinished. In "The Secret Sharer," he writes only of the "mitre-shaped hill" that obscures the retreating tug's smoke, and of the grove that surrounds the temple [8].

In addition to the purposes served by the pagoda's varying location, its differing appearance supports the dissimilar themes of each story. In "The Secret Sharer," the temple's featureless, alien bulk effectively contrasts with the smoke that so vividly represents the receding comforts of companionship. In "Falk," the pagoda stands as the only thing on which the narrator's eye can rest while he awaits the loading of his ship's cargo; by describing the pagoda's appearance in great (almost florid) detail, Conrad thus dresses up the principal item of scenery on his otherwise empty stage. Finally, in The Shadow-Line he shrewdly restricts himself to the words "great gilt pagoda" for an important reason. The edifice serves only to announce the nearness of Bangkok—which, as the center of disease and delay, receives a more extensive description from the author.

Upon his arrival at the Siamese capital, the narrator boards his ship and soon confronts the disturbed chief mate, Mr. Burns. After the previous master died while the ship was near the mouth of the Gulf of Siam, Burns brought the ship north to Bangkok rather than south to Singapore—a closer port and the regional British shipping center. In the course of his conversation with the resentful Burns, it dawns on the narrator that the chief mate had sailed to Bangkok because he hoped the lack of qualified replacements in the Siamese capital would allow him to succeed to command. "But his naive reasoning forgot to take into account the telegraph cable reposing on the bottom of the very Gulf up which he had turned that ship," the narrator concludes, "Hence the bitter flavour of our interview" [89]. But no submarine cable linked Bangkok and Singapore—neither in 1888 during Conrad's actual trip, nor by 1915 when he wrote his novel. In fact, even by 1927 (three years after his death) no submarine cable had yet been laid.[9] Contemporary accounts make clear that messages from Singapore to Bangkok would have gone either by mail, or by a combination land-sea telegraph route via

9. F. J. Brown, The Cable and Wireless Communications of the World (London: Sir Isaac Pitman & Sons, 1927), frontispiece map.

Saigon.[1] A telegraph cable on the bottom of the Gulf of Siam, however, was pure fiction.

Given the time Conrad spent in these waters, we may presume he knew of the actual arrangements. As a matter of fact, his own appointment to the *Otago* also came about thanks to a telegram: Captain Ellis, the Master-Attendant of Singapore, received a message from the British Consul in Bangkok informing him of the need for a replacement captain.[2] The historical telegram must have come to Singapore via the combination land-sea route around the Gulf of Siam rather than through its depths, but Conrad chooses a more ironic path for the fictional telegram in *The Shadow-Line*. In that story, the telegraph makes possible the selection of a new captain rather than the promotion of Burns to that position; thus the author enhances the "bitter flavour" of the relationship between Burns and the narrator by having the message sent back down the very gulf up which Burns thought to have escaped his replacement.

After getting his ship on its way down the Meinam, Conrad's narrator emphasizes the relief he feels at escaping the pestilential atmosphere of Bangkok. To describe the passage down to the sea, though, he mentions only how "the ship's head swung down the river" [96]. The narrator leaves out an essential part of the story— that the ship would have been towed down the river by a steam tug. Unlike the *Melita*, which could steam up or down the river on its own, the sailing ship in *The Shadow-Line* could not easily navigate the Meinam by wind power.[3] Conrad makes use of this need in "Falk," devoting an entire page of that story to the episode of procuring a tow downriver. As the exasperated narrator tells it, "The whole procedure was an unmitigated bore" (*TOS* 165). The narrator goes on to complain of the various charges involved, the annoyance of dealing with the tug master, and the careless way his ship gets jerked out of her berth. The need for a tug plays a crucial role in "Falk"; in *The Shadow-Line*, however, the tug does not appear at all. Furthermore, that very dangerous bar at the river's mouth merits even less description on the downriver transit than it does on the upriver trip: "About mid-day," the narrator tells us, "we anchored a mile outside the bar" [96]. This second minimized description, like the first—and like the absence of the tug—is the result of a conscious effort on Conrad's part to enhance the essential theme of maturation in this novel. Only his depiction of the gulf passage

1. See Frederick G. D. Bedford, *The Sailor's Handbook: Containing Information in a Concise Form which the Sailor Will Find Useful in All Parts of the World* (Portsmouth: Griffin & Co., 1890), 264, 291; see also Findlay, 346, and Brown, 16.
2. Allen, 245.
3. According to Jerry Allen, Conrad himself faced the same situation when he made the trip in the *Otago*; see Allen, 248.

remains to be considered before we may draw the strands of this thematic argument together.

Conrad's narrator gets his ship underway into the gulf, beginning the novel's climactic struggle against fickle winds, "mysterious currents" [102], and an increase of illness among his crew—made more grave by the discovery that his supply of quinine had been sold off and a useless white powder put in its place [102]. This struggle causes the captain much soul-searching and offers the trial of moral and psychological strength that cements his maturity. All the while, the narrator keeps to the eastern side of the Gulf of Siam, following the cryptic advice given to him in Singapore by Captain Giles, who had called the gulf "[a] funny piece of water" [76]. The narrator, never having traveled the gulf, does not know quite how to respond:

> Funny, in this connection, was a vague word. The whole thing sounded like an opinion uttered by a cautious person mindful of actions for slander.
> I didn't inquire as to the nature of that funniness. There was really no time. But at the very last he volunteered a warning.
> "Whatever you do, keep to the east side of it. The west side is dangerous at this time of year. Don't let anything tempt you over. You'll find nothing but trouble there."
> Though I could hardly imagine what could tempt me to involve my ship amongst the currents and reefs of the Malay shore, I thanked him for the advice. [77]

This passage serves a crucial role in the narrative, for it establishes the mysterious, almost supernatural atmosphere that dominates the story. From this brief exchange, Conrad would have us conclude not only that the western side of the gulf conceals specific dangers, but some unnamed hazard imperils any traverse of the gulf at all.[4]

Despite Conrad's cryptic description, the Gulf of Siam had been fairly well charted by the late 1800s. As hydrographers discovered, two separate monsoon seasons dictate two different passages to take when crossing the gulf. Sailing directions published at the time point out that the southwest monsoon starts around the middle of May and continues through September; during this season, strong winds from the southwest indicate the advisability of southwesterly passage, along the Malay shore. During the northeast monsoon, whose northeasterly winds blow from November to

4. See Sir Archibald Day, *The Admiralty Hydrographic Service 1795–1919* (London: H. M. Stationery Office, 1967), 68, and Findlay, v, 313.

January, conditions make a more easterly passage, hugging the
Cambodian coast, the more prudent option (see Figure 3).[5]

We may draw two conclusions from these sailing directions and
the charts they illuminate. First, while Conrad does not specify the
time of year in *The Shadow-Line*, we can infer that the action takes
place during or close to the November-to-January northeast monsoon season because Captain Giles advises an easterly passage, saying that "The west side is dangerous at this time of year" [77]. The
narrator's track down the gulf therefore closely follows that of Conrad himself, who slowly paralleled the Cambodian coast during his
February 1888 passage in the *Otago*.[6]

So Conrad's narrator, were he traveling during the northeast monsoon season, merely followed good seasonal advice by staying to the
east. But the vaguely sinister nature of Giles's unfinished warning
makes the western side of the gulf seem unnaturally dangerous.
Conrad disposes us towards placing considerable faith in Giles's
opinion, for the narrator describes that captain as:

> an expert. An expert in—how shall I say it?—in intricate navi-
> gation. He was supposed to know more about remote and
> imperfectly charted parts of the Archipelago than any man liv-
> ing. His brain must have been a perfect warehouse of reefs,
> positions, bearings, images of headlands, shapes of obscure
> coasts, aspects of innumerable islands, desert and otherwise.
> [54]

And the narrator, in his response, concurs in believing the western
side of the gulf especially hazardous whatever the season; he "could
hardly imagine what could tempt [him] to involve [his] ship amongst
the currents and reefs of the Malay shore" [77]. In making the far
shore dangerous, Conrad follows the long-standing European myth
associating the west with death. Beyond this symbolic consideration, however, it is clear from contemporary descriptions of the
gulf that the west coast held no more hazard than the east—perhaps
even less.[7] Yet Captain Giles and the narrator in *The Shadow-Line*
express an ungrounded fear of the western shore, and Giles's cryptic
description of the gulf makes the area as a whole seem even more
hazardous than it really was.

5. See Findlay, 1313–14, 1367; also Philippe de Kerhallet, *General Examination of the
   Indian Ocean, together with Directions for the Navigation of Torres Straits and Nautical
   Directions or Avoiding Hurricanes*, trans. R. H. Wyman (Washington: Government
   Printing Office, 1870), 169–170.
6. Allen, 252.
7. See Findlay, 1343–44, 313, 332–333, and United States, *DMA, Pub 161, Sailing Directions*, 127.

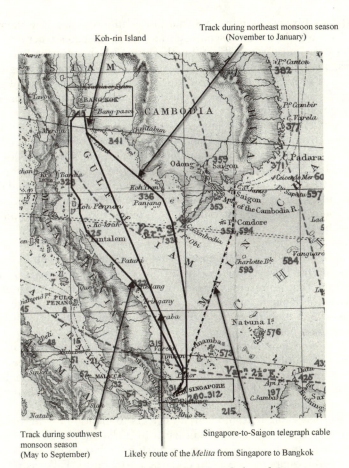

Figure 3. Seasonal tracks between Bangkok and Singapore, with location of Singapore-Saigon cable. Reproduced from Alexander G. Findlay, *A Directory for the Navigation of the Indian Archipelago and the Coast of China,* facing title page. Boxes added by Mark D. Larabee.

We have by now observed that the landmarks in the Gulf of Siam undergo significant alteration in *The Shadow-Line,* "Falk," and "The Secret Sharer." One may justifiably wonder why these alterations should in themselves attract our attention, however. Fiction, after all, is not nonfiction, and Conrad does what all authors do when he adjusts the details of this world to create his fictive one. But these particular changes are not simply for convenience; Conrad

shapes his seascape in ways that powerfully reinforce the themes
of his art. As we have seen, Conrad places the cable where it can
have the most ironic effect. Furthermore, he changes the Paknam
pagoda's appearance and location to enhance its symbolic significance in each of these three stories. His major alteration of the
gulf's seascape, however, supports the issues of transformation
and responsibility at the heart of *The Shadow-Line*.

Let us return to that dangerous sandbar at the mouth of the Meinam River, whose considerable hazards receive no mention at all in
The Shadow-Line. At the moment of the narrator's first crossing of
the bar, the account may owe its brevity to something more purposeful than a desire to hasten the story along. To comprehend the
significance of this lacuna we should keep in mind the author's
principal theme; in his Author's Note to the text, Conrad proposes
to "[present] . . . certain facts which certainly were associated with
the change from youth, care-free and fervent, to the more self-
conscious and more poignant period of maturer life" [44]. In composing his *Bildungsroman*, the author emphasizes the part of the
voyage that represents the severe moral trial for his protagonist:
from the moment of assuming command of the ship, through the
passage of the gulf, to the arrival at Singapore. On the way upriver,
Conrad's narrator crosses the bar as a mere passenger in the
Melita—without responsibilities and quite naturally disinterested in
the difficulties of judging the tides and securing the assistance of a
river pilot. As difficult as the bar crossing may have been in reality,
it does not directly challenge the fictional narrator and therefore
merits no elaboration in the story.

For the same reason, Conrad neglects to mention the necessary
steam tug that figures so prominently in "Falk," and he leaves out of
his account any description of recrossing the bar on the ship's exit
from the Meinam. If we can take the portrayal in "Falk" as representative, the steam tug would have towed the ship all the way to
the anchorage outside the bar. Or perhaps, for some reason, the
sailing ship proceeded across the bar on its own; in this case the
captain would have relied on the services of a pilot—as would have
happened in reality, according to written pilot guides.[8] Engaging a
pilot relieves the captain of some of the responsibility for his ship and
crew—an obligation otherwise total.[9] In Conrad's fictional account,

8. "Owing to the shifting pasture of the bar, it is not safe to enter without a pilot": Findlay,
   347. "There is generally a pilot boat at anchor outside the bar * * * The pilots are European, and should be engaged": Bedford, 291.
9. See Richard Henry Dana Jr., *The Seaman's Friend* (1851; reprint, Delmar: Scholars'
   Facsimiles & Reprints, 1979), 187; see also A. C Boyd, *The Merchant Shipping Laws*
   (London: Stevens & Sons, 1876), 301.

consequently, the pilot must stay in the background because his presence while crossing a dangerous obstacle diminishes the moral isolation and sense of lonely responsibility that a captain—real or fictional—might feel.

Conrad manipulates the hazards of the gulf passage for a similar reason. After leaving the bar at the mouth of the Meinam, the narrator begins the phase of his journey that will test his ability as a leader and a seaman; hence an exaggeration of the dangers he faces makes his trial seem more profound. First, Conrad leads us to place credence in the opinion of that "expert in intricate navigation" [54], Captain Giles, whose cryptic pronouncement on the perils of the "funny piece of water" [76] makes the gulf seem an unusually dangerous passage for a new captain. The narrator soberly recognizes the challenges he will face, applying what little knowledge he has of the area to agree with Captain Giles that the western side of the gulf should be avoided at all costs. In this exchange, Conrad skillfully plays on the reader's reaction to mystery; the less we know of the gulf, the more perilous it appears to be. As the location of the narrator's most important test, therefore, the gulf passage becomes transformed under Conrad's hand into the ideal arena for moral trials carried out under the influence of supernatural powers.

So we may see Conrad's manipulation of the gulf's topography as an essential part of his thematic expression. The question remains, however: why is this alteration any different from any other author's rearrangement of the factual world to create a fictive one? In short, why does the lack of factual accuracy in this story matter, if it serves only to permit the foregrounding of certain themes? First, we should recognize how this systematic manipulation of geographical reality is all the more astonishing in light of a claim Conrad makes in his 1924 essay "Geography and Some Explorers": "the honest maps of the nineteenth century nourished in me a passionate interest in the truth of geographical facts and a desire for precise knowledge which was extended later to other subjects" [LE 11]. Conrad reveals a fundamental contradiction by stressing a passion for geographical truth after having relied on a calculated alteration of reality—a reality he dismisses elsewhere as irrelevant, and an alteration he claims not to have made. Moreover, larger consequences follow from the acknowledgment of Conrad's topographical distortion: the new information in this study opens the way for a revaluation of Conrad's fiction in the contexts of Orientalism and imperialist representations of the world.

It should not surprise us that Conrad reshapes the reality of the Gulf of Siam in ways he would not do to London or Europe. The

significance of the gulf area in the British Imperial system requires
a certain kind of "imaginative geography" to describe it, as Edward
Said discusses in *Orientalism*. Said points out how mid-nineteenth-
century conceptions of the Orient made the East "wonderfully
synonymous with the exotic, the mysterious, the profound, the
seminal"—certainly the kind of atmosphere that imbues Conrad's
Gulf of Siam.[1] Furthermore, while "the *geographical space* of the
Orient was penetrated, worked over, taken hold of," Said explains
that "What was important in the latter nineteenth century was not
whether the West had penetrated and possessed the Orient, but
rather *how* the British and French felt that they had done it."[2]
Conrad's recasting of the Gulf exemplifies one kind of possessive,
self-aware act carried out by the West: a remapping of the East
that imposes a desired construct of the Orient over its actual
contours.

This spirit of "imaginative geography" that Said describes
appears in Conrad's essay "Geography and Some Explorers" as "militant geography[,]" whose only object was the search for truth"
[*LE* 9]. Conrad's choice of terminology reveals quite a bit more than
he might have intended. Like "the single-minded explorers of the
nineteenth century" he credits for fathering "militant geography"—
whose discoveries in fact paved the way for the application of imperial power—Conrad imposes his own version of "truth" on the
colonial landscape [*LE* 9]. "Militancy" is particularly apt here, for
Conrad joins the explorers he praises in seeing the East as territory
ripe for aggressive remapping.

Consequently, Conrad's alteration of topography makes perfect
sense when considered from the standpoint of Orientalist constructions of the East. One can argue that Conrad's process of mystifica-
tion serves primarily to give his protagonists a suitably ambiguous
environment as the backdrop for initiation. The supernatural world
surrounding the narrator in *The Shadow-Line* certainly establishes
the ideal conditions for a story of initiation. However, it is also possible that the factual discrepancies in Conrad's Gulf of Siam result
from a colonialist textual strategy that is the logical extension of an
Orientalist perspective. In this reading, the imperialist project dic-
tates Conrad's peculiar and deliberate misrepresentation of physical setting, turning the known world into a mysterious one in order
to justify its exploration by the West.

In *Shadowtime: History and Representation in Hardy, Conrad, and
George Eliot*, Jim Reilly analyses the representation of history in a

---

1. Edward Said, *Orientalism* (New York: Vintage, 1979), 51.
2. Said, 211.

number of Conrad's works, demonstrating the deliberate obscurity Conrad employs in depicting colonial history. As Reilly points out, the language Conrad uses in "Heart of Darkness" to describe colonial explorers and developers—"'Hunters', 'pursuers', 'bearers', 'messengers' [*HD* 5]—slides from a sense of an *activity* of colonialism to a mere sense of *mediation*."[3] This shift results from the unknowable nature of the colonial sphere into which imperial agents penetrate: in Conrad's words, "the mystery of an unknown earth" [*HD* 5]. This crucial lack of knowledge also informs the geography of *Nostromo*, whose explorers Conrad describes as "speculators" [*N* 174]; according to Reilly, "'speculation' . . . has [in this usage] been completely stripped of its root meaning of 'observation'. History is here precisely that which is *not* observed . . . doubly 'speculation'—an entrepreneurial venture and an unverifiable conjecture."[4] This link between history and the representation of the unrepresentable has profound consequences for our understanding of Conrad's topographical alterations.

For Conrad, the description of place (as a representation of historical reality) pulled in two directions. On one hand, he felt drawn to relate in accurate detail his characters' fictive surroundings. In an 1897 letter to Edward Garnett, he admits, "It is evident that my fate is to be descriptive and descriptive only. There are things I *must* leave alone" [*CL* 1:387] Similarly, in the author's note to *An Outcast of the Islands* he writes, "For the life of me I don't see that there is the slightest exotic spirit in the conception or style of that novel . . . The mere scenery got a great hold on me as I went on" [*OI* ix]. But in attempting to treat "the mere scenery" with language that is "descriptive only," Conrad faces a dilemma; underneath that scenery is the mysterious world of the other, whose portrayal preoccupies Conrad and whose penetration and examination constitutes the essential strategy of the colonialist project.

The only way to connect the superficial and underlying worlds is to make the observable world mysterious and unknowable. Conrad reveals the necessity of this solution in his 1905 essay "Books":

> In truth every novelist must begin by creating for himself a world, great or little, in which he can honestly believe. This world cannot be made otherwise than in his own image: it is fated to remain individual and a little mysterious, and yet it must resemble something already familiar to the experience,

---

3. Jim Reilly, *Shadowtime: History and Representation in Hardy, Conrad, and George Eliot* (New York: Routledge, 1993), 136–137.
4. Reilly, 137–138.

the thoughts and the sensations of his readers. At the heart of fiction, even the least worthy of the name, some sort of truth can be found. [*NLL* 11]

The fictive world, Conrad tells us, must be sufficiently faithful to the real world to be recognizable on the part of his readers, yet it must also contain a mystery in order to be "true" in the eyes of both Conrad and his fellow imperialist observers. In *Shadowtime*, as we have seen, Jim Reilly argues persuasively that Conrad deliberately obscures colonial space in order to justify its penetration and enlightenment by colonial powers. If we accept the mismatch between the factual and fictive Gulf of Siam as representing the topographical dimension of Conrad's enhancement of mystery, then examining Admiralty charts and pilot guides adds significantly to the work of Reilly, Said, and other critics interested in Conrad's colonialist mapping.

For example, Christopher GoGwilt, in *The Invention of the West: Joseph Conrad and the Double-Mapping of Europe and Empire*, analyzes numerous examples of mapping in Conrad's works to develop the thesis that Conrad reveals a "scramble for the *representation* of imperialism" at the same time the scramble for territory was underway.[5] The importance of Samburan's placement at the center of the Eastern Hemisphere in *Victory*, Marlow's "blank spaces" on the globe and the "darkness" (*HD* 8) they become, and the multicolored map of partitioned Africa on the Company's wall in *Heart of Darkness* (*HD* 10) lies primarily in how they all reflect the construction of a "Western" identity. * * * An examination of real maps, as this study has done, substantially extends GoGwilt's argument by revealing how the shifted contours of Conrad's Gulf of Siam tell us much about the author's Western identity.

Conrad constructs the topography of his Gulf of Siam according to an organization as subtle and evocative as the "mysterious system" [7] of bamboo fences that confronts the bewildered narrator's eyes at the beginning of "The Secret Sharer." * * * The information provided by nautical charts, pilot guides, and travel narratives allows us to draw illuminating comparisons between factual and fictive geography, significantly furthering our understanding of this author's "funny piece of water" [76]. Examining such invaluable but hitherto virtually neglected materials can yield a completely new, fuller vision into the depths of Conrad's art.

---

5. Christopher GoGwilt, *The Invention of the West: Joseph Conrad and the Double-Mapping of Europe and Empire* (Stanford: Stanford University Press, 1995), 67.

MORTON DAUWEN ZABEL

[*The Nigger of the "Narcissus"*]†

* * *

[T]here was another realm, more elemental even than the subtle and barbaric East, that Conrad had come to know during his years as a mariner in the British Merchant Service. It, too, was a world that appealed to the inmost forces of his nature and it gave him an even more radical medium and symbol for the exercise of his moral imagination. It was the Sea; and now, in *The Nigger of the "Narcissus,"* he dramatized it for the first time in the splendor, violence, and intimacy by which he had known it.

His account with the Sea, like his account with the East, was never to be fully closed. It preoccupied him throughout his career. * * * But here, in *The Nigger of the "Narcissus,"* he wrote not only in the full freshness and immediacy of his material but with a personal passion and vividness of memory that kindled his imagination to its first full powers of poetic vision. When Henry James said of the book in 1902 that it "is in my opinion the very finest and strongest picture of the sea and sea-life that our language possesses—the masterpiece of a whole great class,"[1] he recognized that vision and paid the work a tribute which many readers have since seconded. And when Conrad himself called it "the book by which, not as a novelist perhaps, but as an artist striving for the utmost sincerity of expression, I am willing to stand or fall," and said that "its pages are the tribute of my unalterable and profound affection for the ships, the seamen, the winds and the great sea—the moulders of my youth, the companions of the best years of my life" [137], he testified to the intense emotion with which he wrote it and to the ineradicable impression made upon him by the experiences it records.

* * *

The East and the Sea: it is not often that a novelist finds himself endowed by practical experience with two subjects of such rich and suggestive possibilities, subjects which enter his life from outside the conditions of his race and birth, striking his senses and imagination during his years of keenest impressionability, and offering themselves to so rich a dramatic and symbolic use. * * *

---

† From "Introduction," in *The Nigger of the "Narcissus"* by Joseph Conrad (New York: Harper & Brothers, 1951), viii–xxxi. Copyright 1951 by Harper & Brothers. Reprinted by permission of HarperCollins Publishers. Unless otherwise specified, page references are to this Norton Critical Edition.
1. Letter to Edmund Gosse, June 26, 1902 (*PL* 36) [Editor].

Conrad was, on one side of his nature, a self-confessed romantic. He probably felt the attraction of the remote and the unreal as strongly as any modern author. But two factors operated to save him from the risks of his material. One was a ruthless moral instinct that forced him to identify himself, sympathetically and morally, with even the most extravagant of his adventures. The other was the practical condition of his case—of his life as an exile and seaman.

His moral sense was made acute by his solitude, his deracination, his estrangement from family and homeland. * * *

Conrad's material, whether that of the East or of the Sea, first came to him in terms the reverse of aesthetic. It came to him as fact, as the data of serious and responsible experience. However romantic or adventurous the emotion he took with him as a young man into the Merchant Service or the Orient, he knew those worlds first as worlds to be met and conquered by dint of hard labor, scrupulous industry, skill in the technique of his trade and cunning in his dealings with men. * * * He had to learn, know, and accept his subject matter on its own terms before he could see it in terms of art. When, years later, he came to make fiction of it, the integrity of the material acted as a discipline for the artist.

* * *

[The struggle to digest and express new things] is evident through the first half at least of Conrad's career. * * * When he wrote *The Nigger of the "Narcissus"* he was in the thick of his problem. But here, more than in his first two books, his romantic impulse joined with the strictest realism he had ever known. The book illustrates what he once said, in an important passage, about his work:

> I have not sought for special imaginative freedom or a larger play of fancy in my choice of characters and subjects. The nature of the knowledge, suggestions, or hints used in my imaginative work has depended directly on the conditions of my active life. It depended more on contacts, and very slight contacts at that, than on actual experience; because my life as a matter of fact is far from being adventurous in itself. Even now, when I look back on it with a certain regret (who would not regret his youth?) and positive affection, its coloring wears the sober hue of hard work and exacting calls of duty; things which in themselves are not much charged with a feeling of romance. If these things appeal strongly to me even in retrospect, it is, I suppose, because the romantic feeling of reality was in me an inborn faculty. This in itself may be a curse, but, when disciplined by a sense of personal responsibility and a recognition of the hard facts of existence shared with the rest of mankind, becomes but a point of view from which the

very shadows of life appear endowed with an internal glow. And such romanticism is not a sin. It is none the worse for the knowledge of truth. It only tries to make the best of it, hard as it may be; and in this hardness discovers a certain beauty.

    . . . My subjects are not medieval, and I have a natural right to them because my past is very much my own . . . the mere fact of dealing with matters outside the general run of everyday experience laid me under the obligation of a more scrupulous fidelity to the truth of my own sensations. The problem was to make unfamiliar things credible. . . . This was the hardest task of all and the most important, in view of that conscientious rendering of truth in thought and fact which has always been my aim. [*WT* 5–6]

The truth of fact served Conrad when he wrote *The Nigger of the "Narcissus."* * * *

* * *

When Conrad wrote his tale in 1897 it was that ship [the *Narcissus*] and memory he commemorated. * * * The *Narcissus* * * * herself becomes an actor in the drama, more so than the ships in *Typhoon* and *The Shadow-Line*. She and her crew join their forces against the fury of the storm. To save themselves the crew must save her. She is, so to speak, the heroine of the tale, as the crew is its collective hero. When they leave her at last in the port of London, she has become an inseparable part of their lives, as she had become part of Conrad's.

* * *

Conrad is doing more than writing a tribute to his old brothers of the days of sail. * * * He is making of the *Narcissus* and her crew a world, an image of humanity on its hazardous voyage into the elements, the future, the unknown. That world will hold what Conrad always dreaded—its "plague spots," its falsehood, meanness, and evil, its Donkin. It will also hold the steadfast faith of a Singleton and, somewhere above, its code-ruled, self-effacing, steady captains, its Allistouns. Yet what these are worth may not be apparent until the test is imposed on them, and in *The Nigger of the "Narcissus"* two such tests are imposed.

* * *

His ship and crew are a microcosm of mankind. His plot is shaped less by human motives and conflicts than by a strife of elements. These elements lie outside man and oblige him to pit his strength against them, but they also lie within him. "Both men and ships live in an unstable element," Conrad said in *The Mirror of the Sea* [*MS* 27]. When the crew man their ship, obey her impersonal regimen, submit their wills to the will of their Captain, they identify themselves with her and with the craft she exacts of her manipulators. When she advances out of fair weather into foul, and thus into the fury of the storm, they become one with her life. They must bend every ounce of their strength to save her from the concerted fury of natural forces—water, wind, cold, rain—that appears intent on destroying the tiny barque and her frail load of humanity. But another instability threatens them: their disunity as men, their secret fears and cowardice, the insecurity that competes with their tough and almost mindless tenacity as sailors who are closer to brutes than to civilized beings.

That insecurity lives among them in the Negro. He has come from no one knows where. He belongs to another world than Europe's. He becomes their charge and their child as illness overtakes him and makes him the object of their pity and dread. The fear, hatred, and love they feel for him as he fights his battle are the dread and reverence they feel in their own lives as they hang frailly between the anger of the storm and the doom of the sea.

What comes forward in the book, what makes it important as the work in which Conrad first defined the central motives of his art, are several of the primary conceptions that were to be developed and given their full complexity of realization in his future novels. There is first the sea itself, now for the first time imaged by Conrad as a symbol of unconscious nature—a nature which woos man into its mindlessness but which proves, once he faces its reality, to test his capacity to save and declare himself against its nihilism. The sea is thus a cognate of the East. It is a realm of elemental nature in which the conscious personality and egoism of man dissolve on encountering a force unbroken to the reason and assertive will of civilized life. At grips with it, life resumes the terms of a primary hostility and danger. It symbolizes for Conrad the anti-human—cleansing, purging, primitive, but destructive too, what Stein in *Lord Jim* calls "the destructive element" [*LJ* 129] and with the simplest condition of man's fate implicit in it.

There is, too, that drama of man's destiny which Conrad repeatedly emphasized: the conflict between his isolation as an individual, the incommunicable secrecy of the self which begins and ends in loneliness, and his need to share his life with others, the force of that "solidarity" which Conrad insistently invoked as a human necessity, a mode of salvation from the nihilism of the isolated temperament. An "unavoidable solidarity," he called it, "the solidarity in mysterious origin, in toil, in joy, in hope, in uncertain fate, which binds men to each other and all mankind to the visible world" [141]. What we get in *The Nigger of the "Narcissus"* is a forecast, under the primitive conditions of sea life, of the complex versions of this drama which were to come in *Lord Jim, Nostromo,* and *Typhoon,* in *Under Western Eyes, Chance,* and *Victory.*

We get also a third factor, here embodied in the role played by James Wait. He plays it, it first seems, unconsciously, but perhaps he is not wholly unconscious of it. It is the role which Marlow, the narrator of *Lord Jim,* "Heart of Darkness," and *Chance,* plays with intent purpose; the role also which Leggatt, of "The Secret Sharer," enacts for the young captain of the ship on which he finds refuge as a murderer, "a fugitive and a vagabond on the earth, with no brand of the curse on his sane forehead to stay a slaying hand" [42]. This tale names the role. Leggatt, like Wait, like Marlow, like Nostromo, becomes the secret sharer of the weakness, the guilt, fear, and ignorance which all men harbor within themselves. He is the man they fear to be, but who they find they must be and are—the man alone in life or death, too proud to be rescued from his fate by the subterfuges of life. He is the man all men must finally know, whose secret they must share, if they are to prove themselves worthy of life. Leggatt with his guilt seeks refuge in the sea. He comes out of the sea at midnight, naked. He must live in hiding on the strange ship, concealed by the captain, sleeping in the captain's bed, wearing the sleeping-suit the captain lends him, the garb of the unconscious life. Finally he will be given back to the sea again, "a free man, a proud swimmer striking out for a new destiny" [42]; but he will leave the captain, who has sinned against his seaman's code by hiding him, possessed of a knowledge of his own secret nature he never had before. So Wait, weakening, protesting, dying, shares his secret with the men who curse and try in vain to help him. When his body is committed to the sea, he leaves his secret with the men. It will weaken or strengthen them according to their natures.

Lastly, there is the way in which the drama of the Negro joins with that of the sea itself. Conrad strove, as his work progressed, to bring the fact of human isolation out of its confinement in egoism into the "hard facts" of man's life and condition on earth. His greater novels all move in the direction of a larger social morality, even a political morality, which exacts its price in every man's life. That morality is present in microcosmic form in the community and regimen of a ship. Yet whatever community of purpose a ship requires of its crew, the sea will also have its special test for every single man aboard. He may hide his ordeal. He may never confide the knowledge it has yielded to him to another man. But that knowledge will be born in him, and he will emerge from peril, if he measures up to the test, a man worthy of his fate as a man. For Conrad the ordeal is a measure of a man's fitness for his destiny as a human being. He put its meaning into words when he described Captain MacWhirr of the *Nan-Shan,* in *Typhoon,* before he enters upon his cataclysmic voyage across the China Sea—the stolid Scot who has never in a lifetime's service met the full fury of the ocean.

*   *   *

As the storm is the test and symbol of life, so James Wait becomes the test of the crew's ability to face another, an equally inevitable, form of destiny—death. Conrad meant him to act as such: "In the book he is nothing; he is merely the centre of the ship's collective psychology and the pivot of the action" [137]. When, after Wait dies and his body, about to be lowered into the deep, clings reluctantly to the planks, Belfast shrieks passionately, "Jimmy, be a man!" [245] he speaks for the crew and for the wisdom they have wrested from their agony. To be men worthy of a man's destiny, it is not only life that must be faced and conquered; it is also death.

The reader is bound to feel that in this book Conrad was testing himself and his powers more intimately than he had yet done. * * * [I]n *The Nigger* the exotic gives way to another and more salient simplicity—that of nature and her elements as the seaman knows them. * * * *The Nigger of the "Narcissus,"* suffused by its own kind of sentiment, gains something new from the conditions of practical reality it portrays. Here, long before he became vexed by "that infernal tail of ships and that obsession of my sea life" which had led him, unjustly he felt, to become classified by critics as a "'spinner of sea yarns—master mariner—seaman writer' and so forth" [*CL* 8:130], rather than as a serious novelist, Conrad was writing out of the direct immediacy of his maritime experience and memory. The rudimentary conditions of life on a ship gave him a special advantage. It permitted him to arrive at the truth of effect which by this time he had made his special purpose as a novelist, and which he asserted as his aim in the "Preface" he wrote when the novel was finished, his credo as an artist:

> A work that aspires, however humbly, to the condition of art should carry its justification in every line. And art itself may be defined as a single-minded attempt to render the highest kind of justice to the visible universe, by bringing to light the truth, manifold and one, underlying its every aspect. . . . Confronted by the same enigmatical spectacle the artist descends within himself, and in that lonely region of stress and strife, if he be deserving and fortunate, he finds the terms of his appeal. . . . He speaks . . . to the subtle but invincible conviction of solidarity that knits together the loneliness of innumerable hearts,

to the solidarity in dreams, in joy, in sorrow, in aspirations, in
illusions, in hope, in fear, which binds men to each other,
which binds together all humanity—the dead to the living and
the living to the unborn. . . . My task, which I am trying to
achieve, is by the power of the written word to make you hear,
to make you feel—it is, before all, to make you *see*. That—and
no more, and it is everything. [139–41]

The Nigger of the "Narcissus" was dedicated to this task, to a rendering of life in terms of specific conditions, and to making the
reader see them. * * * The book is also addressed to the other task he
defined for himself: the task of invoking the "invincible conviction"
of moral community in men. When the crew of the *Narcissus* gathers
for the last time on Tower Hill in London before life blows them
apart again, they stand "a dark knot of seamen," like "castaways
making merry in the storm and upon an insecure ledge of a treacherous rock," while "the roar of the town resembled the roar of topping breakers, merciless and strong." Before they drift away, "the
sunshine of heaven" falls "like a gift of grace on the mud of the
earth, on the remembering and mute stones, on greed, selfishness;
on the anxious faces of forgetful men" [254].

But these men—except for Donkin, whom destiny disdains—will
not forget the voyage they have made. "Haven't we, together and
upon the immortal sea, wrung out a meaning from our sinful lives?"
Nor is the reader, any more than Conrad himself, likely to forget "a
shadowy ship manned by a crew of Shades" [254]. What he has just
read will remain for him, if not the richest experience Conrad can
give him in some of his other books, a memory of descriptive powers
and suggestive writing at one of their highest points of artistry in
English fiction. Here and in *Typhoon* Conrad made his drama of
the sea in storm, as in "The Secret Sharer" and *The Shadow-Line*
he made it of the sea in its other aspect of danger—calm. * * * Unified as is the impression the tale leaves, poetic as are its conception
and rendering from first to last, it unquestionably arrives at its fullest strength in its powerful third chapter—the great scene of the
storm. There Conrad not only reaches the height of his descriptive
art; he also brings the whole complexity of his theme into brilliant
fusion—the ship, the men, the doomed Negro, the thundering seas,
the deadly contest between the crew and the elements; and in their
midst, "swaying upon the din and tumult of the seas, with the
whole battered length of the ship launched forward in a rolling
rush before his attentive face" [199], Singleton at the wheel: he who
knew from the first the truth about Wait—"Why, of course he must
die" [170]—and who also knows that the ship must survive the

storm and that its crew will live. "In front of his erect figure only the two arms moved crosswise with a swift and sudden readiness, to check or urge again the rapid stir of circling spokes. He steered with care" [199].

FREDRIC JAMESON

[The Sea as Strategy of Containment in *The Nigger of the "Narcissus"* and *Lord Jim*]†

The privileged place of the strategy of containment in Conrad is the sea; yet the fact of the sea also allows us to weigh and appreciate the relative structural difference between the "nascent modernism" that we will observe in these texts and the more fully achieved and institutionalized modernisms of the canon. For the sea is both a strategy of containment and a place of real business: it is a border and a decorative limit, but it is also a highway, out of the world and in it at once, the repression of work—on the order of the classic English novel of the country-house weekend, in which human relations can be presented in all their ideal formal purity precisely because concrete content is relegated to the rest of the week—as well as the absent work-place itself.

So the sea is the place from which Jim can contemplate that dreary prose of the world which is daily life in the universal factory called capitalism:

> His station was in the fore-top, and often from there he looked down, with the contempt of a man destined to shine in the midst of dangers, at the peaceful multitude of roofs cut in two by the brown tide of the stream, while scattered on the outskirts of the surrounding plain the factory chimneys rose perpendicular against a grimy sky, each slender like a pencil, and belching out smoke like a volcano. [*LJ* 9]

Jim's externality to this world, his absolute structural distance from it, can be measured by a process to which we will shortly return, namely the impulse of Conrad's sentences to transform such realities into impressions. These distant factory spires may be considered the equivalent for Jim and, in this novelistic project, for Conrad, of the great Proustian glimpses of the steeples of Martinville (with the one obvious qualification that the latter are already sheer impression and

† From *The Political Unconscious* (Ithaca: Cornell University Press, 1981), 210–18. Copyright 1981 by Cornell University. Used by permission of the publisher, Cornell University Press. Unless otherwise specified, page references are to this Norton Critical Edition.

need neither aesthetic transformation, nor the Archimedean point of a structural externality, all the energy of Proustian style now being invested in the meditation on the object itself).

Two comments on this geographical strategy of containment need to be made before we do justice to its historical ambiguity. First of all, in a certain sense Jim tries to reverse one of Marx's classical ideological models (the repetition in pure thought of concrete social situations) and to reenact in reality what his father achieves symbolically, in speech and idea. His father's vocation, as ideologue in the characteristic British class system (he is an Anglican parson), is carefully underscored in the paragraph that precedes the one quoted above:

> Jim's father possessed such certain knowledge of the Unknowable as made for the righteousness of people in cottages without disturbing the ease of mind of those whom an unerring Providence enables to live in mansions. [*LJ* 8]

From our point of view, and from the logic of its insertion in Conrad's text, this ideological function of religion is also to be grasped in terms of containment and totality; the geographical vision of cottage, mansion, and "little church" (the place of the production of the ideology that harmonizes them) requires that neither class position be able to focus or indeed to see the other. Jim's method for living this geography, harmonized by ideological blindness, is an uncommon one: choosing a vocation such that he can step completely outside all three class terrains and see them all equally, from over a great distance, as so much picturesque landscape.

Yet if Jim's choice of the sea as space and as vocation is a kind of unconscious denunciation of ideology by way of its enactment and its reversal, it is no less dependent for its realization on a rather different level of ideological production, namely, that of the aesthetic. We must, indeed, carefully stress, as does Conrad in these preparatory pages, Jim's *bovarysme*, the relationship between his work and the "course of light holiday literature" [*LJ* 8] that first suggests it to him:

> On the lower deck in the babel of two hundred voices he would forget himself, and beforehand live in his mind the sea-life of light literature. He saw himself saving people from sinking ships, cutting away masts in a hurricane, swimming through a surf with a line; or as a lonely castaway, barefooted and half-naked, walking on uncovered reefs in search of shell-fish to stave off starvation. He confronted savages on tropical shores, quelled mutinies on the high seas, and in a small boat upon the ocean kept up the hearts of despairing men—always an example of devotion to duty, and as unflinching as a hero in a book. [*LJ* 9]

Nowhere in Conrad are the Flaubertian accents stronger than in such a passage, which reproduces at a lower level of verbal intensity the great cadences of the Flaubertian lyric illusion,*** Yet precisely here we have not only the transition from the naive naming of the outside world in realism to the presentation of the image, a transition to modernism and impressionism which is itself dependent on the very ideology of the image and sense perception and the whole positivist pseudo-scientific myth of the functioning of the mind and the senses; we also have a preselection of narrative material such that thought can be fully realized in images, that is to say, a rejection of the conceptual in favor of the two great naturalist psychic and narrative texts of daydreaming and hallucination. Where Conrad marks an "advance," if that is the right term to use about this historical process, is in his own mesmerization by such images and such daydreaming. *Madame Bovary* invented a register of impressionistic daydreaming in order then sharply to differentiate its own "realistic" language from the other, to use the first register of language as the object to be demystified by the second, to create a decoding machinery which does not have its object external to itself but present within the system—and a presence which is no longer merely abstract, in the form of the "illusions" and ideals of the Balzacian or Stendhalian heroes, but stylistic and molecular, of a piece with the text and the life of the individual sentences. The force of Flaubert lies in the nonrealization of the image***

Thus the non-place of the sea is also the space of the degraded language of romance and daydream, of narrative commodity and the sheer distraction of "light literature." This is, however, only half the story, one pole of an ambiguity to whose objective tension we must now do justice. For the sea is the empty space between the concrete places of work and life; but it is also, just as surely, itself a place of work and the very element by which an imperial capitalism draws its scattered beachheads and outposts together, through which it slowly realizes its sometimes violent, sometimes silent and corrosive, penetration of the outlying precapitalist zones of the globe. Nor is the sea merely a place of business; it is also a place of labor, and clearly we will say nothing of consequence about the author of *The Nigger of the "Narcissus," Typhoon,* and *The End of the Tether* if we overlook the "realistic" presentation of working life at sea, of which all these narratives give a characteristic glimpse. Yet strategies of containment are not only modes of exclusion; they can also take the form of repression in some stricter Hegelian sense of the persistence of the older repressed content beneath the later formalized surface.*** In this respect, too, Conrad, as a merely emergent moment in such a strategy, has suggestive and emblematic things to show us, as witness the following supremely self-conscious art-sentence, whose Flaubertian triplication is a virtual allegory of manifest and latent levels in the text:

> Above the mass of sleepers, a faint and patient sigh at times floated, the exhalation of a troubled dream; and short metallic clangs bursting out suddenly in the depths of the ship, the harsh scrape of a shovel, the violent slam of a furnace-door, exploded brutally, as if the men handling the mysterious things below had their breasts full of fierce anger: while the slim high hull of the steamer went on evenly ahead, without a sway of her bare masts, cleaving continuously the great calm of the waters under the inaccessible serenity of the sky. [*LJ* 16]

Ideology, production, style: on the one hand the manifest level of the content of *Lord Jim*—the moral problem of the "sleepers"—which gives us to believe that the "subject" of this book is courage and cowardice, and which we are meant to interpret in ethical and existentializing terms; on the other, the final consumable verbal commodity—the vision of the ship—the transformation of all these realities into style and the work of what we will call the impressionistic strategy of modernism whose function is to dereal-ize the content and make it available for consumption on some purely aesthetic level; while in between these two, the brief clang from the boiler room that drives the ship marking the presence beneath ideology and appearance of that labor which produces and reproduces the world itself, and which, like the attention of God in Berkeleyan idealism, sustains the whole fabric of reality continu-ously in being.

*   *   *

So this ground bass of material production continues underneath the new formal structures of the modernist text, as indeed it could not but continue to do, yet conveniently muffled and intermittent, easy to ignore (or to rewrite in terms of the aesthetic, of sense per-ception, as here of the sounds and sonorous inscription of a reality you prefer not to conceptualize), its permanencies ultimately detect-able only to the elaborate hermeneutic geiger counters of the politi-cal unconscious and the ideology of form.

This reality of production is, of course, at one with the intermit-tent vision of the sea's economic function, and with Conrad's unquestionable and acute sense of the nature and dynamics of imperialist penetration. We will shortly see how even awareness of this latter historical and economic type is "managed" in the text itself. As for the productive relationship of human beings to nature, I will argue that Conrad's consciousness of this ultimate building block of social reality (as well as of its class content under capitalism—the "fierce anger" of the muffled sounds) is systematically displaced in two different ways. The first is by a recoding of the human pole of the labor process in terms of the whole ideological myth of *ressentiment*. Indeed the narrative of *The Nigger of the "Narcissus,"* with its driving power and ideological passion, may in this respect be characterized as one long tirade against *ressentiment;* the work concludes with the transformation of its villain, Donkin, the epitome of the *homme de ressentiment*, into a labor organizer (who "no doubt earns his living by discussing with filthy eloquence upon the right of labour to live" [254]). The other pole of the labor process, that nature which is its material object and substratum, is then strategically reorganized around one of great conceptual containment strategies of the day, one which we have come to call existentialism, and becomes the pretext for the production of a new metaphysic—a new myth about the "meaning" of life and the absurdity of human existence in the face of a malevolent Nature. These two strategies—*ressentiment* and existentializing metaphysics—allow Conrad to recontain his narrative and to rework it in melodramatic terms, in a subsystem of good and evil which now once again has villains and heroes. So it is no accident that Jim's first experience of the violence of the sea is at once coded for us in existential terms, the sea, the source of this mindless violence, becoming the great adversary of Man * * * :

> Only once in all that time he had again the glimpse of the earnestness in the anger of the sea. That truth is not so often made apparent as people might think. There are many shades in the danger of adventures and gales, and it is only now and then that there appears on the face of facts a sinister violence of intention—that indefinable something which forces it upon the mind and the heart of a man, that this complication of accidents or these elemental furies are coming at him with a purpose of malice, with a strength beyond control, with an unbridled cruelty that means to tear out of him his hope and his fear, the pain of his fatigue and his longing for rest: which means to smash, to destroy, to annihilate all he has seen, known, loved, enjoyed, or hated; all that is priceless and necessary—the sunshine, the memories, the future,—which means to sweep the whole precious world utterly away from his sight by the simple and apalling act of taking his life. [*LJ* 11]

But if you believe this version of the text, this particular rewriting strategy by which Conrad means to seal off the textual process, then all the rest follows, and *Lord Jim* really becomes what it keeps telling us it is, namely a tale of courage and cowardice, a moral story, and an object-lesson in the difficulties of constructing an existential hero. I will argue that this ostensible or manifest "theme" of the novel is no more to be taken at face value than is the dreamer's immediate waking sense of what the dream was about. * * * I will simply suggest, at this point, that our business as readers and critics of culture is to "estrange" this overt theme in a Brechtian way, and to ask ourselves why we should be expected to assume, in the midst of capitalism, that the aesthetic rehearsal of the problematics of a social value from a quite different mode of production—the feudal ideology of honor—should need no justification and should be expected to be of interest to us. Such a theme must mean *something else*: and this even if we choose to interpret its survival as an "uneven development," a nonsynchronous overlap in Conrad's own values and experience (feudal Poland, capitalist England).

At any rate, with the problematic of existentialism and the heroic confrontation with the malignant absurdity of Nature, we are obviously very far from that productive process with which we began; the capacity of the new strategy to displace unwanted realities thereby becomes clear. We will return to the strategic function of the ideology of *ressentiment* later on; for the moment one reflection may be in order about the paradoxical relationship between labor and that non-space, those places of strategic narrative containment (such as the sea) which are so essential in what the Frankfurt School called the "degradation" of mass culture (that is, the transformation of formerly realistic materials into repetitive diversions which offer no particular danger or resistance to the dominant system). The paradox lies in the relationship between the peculiarly unpleasant narrative raw materials of the sea—not only that of sheer physical exertion and exposure to the elements, but also that of isolation, sexual privation, and the like—and the daydreaming fantasies of the mass public, for whom such "diversions" are destined. * * *

Analogous problems arise, therefore, wherever we choose to articulate the generic discontinuities in the text of *Lord Jim*: whether we understand its stylistic modernism as the repression of a more totalizing realism both expressed and recontained or managed within the narrative as a whole; or, on the contrary, register the emergence of something like the nascent mass-cultural discourse of a degraded romance from that quite different high-cultural or textual discourse of the *Patna* episode. * * * The categories of periodization employed in such readings * * * are meaningful only on condition we understand that they draw on a linear fiction or diachronic construct solely for the purpose of constructing a synchronic model of coexistence, nonsynchronous development, temporal overlay, the simultaneous presence within a concrete textual structure of what Raymond Williams calls "residual" and "emergent" or anticipatory discourses.

* * *

JEREMY HAWTHORN

From Race and Class in *The Nigger of the "Narcissus"*†

[T]here are two linked problems which make of *The Nigger of the 'Narcissus'* Conrad's problem work: technical confusions in the manipulation of narrative perspective and distance, and ideological uncertainties relating to Conrad's attitudes to the life he is depicting. But what strikes the modern, first-time reader of the novella is perhaps a more pressing and particular problem. When first I read *The Nigger of the 'Narcissus'* as part of an undergraduate course in English literature, what I wanted most of all was a reaction to that word 'nigger' in the title and body of the work—either from within the work itself, or from critical responses to it. Why does Conrad make a black man the centre of this story, and draw attention to him and his blackness in its title? What is the narrative attitude to Wait and his blackness? What is the significance of Conrad's use of the word 'nigger' here? I knew that the word could be used in a relatively neutral manner at the time Conrad was writing. * * * And it is only in comparatively recent years that the issue of James Wait's race, and of the significance which this is made to carry in *The Nigger of the 'Narcissus'*, has been discussed by literary critics. * * * Wait's portrayal seemed so clearly to feed off many stereotypical racist prejudices, and no clear narrative rejection of such elements could be found in the work.

As I read more of Conrad I found this increasingly puzzling, for Conrad's record on racism is generally a very honourable one, especially when seen in the light of his time and circumstances. The Author's Note to *Almayer's Folly* is an admirable assertion of the common humanity of all races, and although, subsequently, I was able to understand the basis of [Chinua] Achebe's description of the Conrad of *Heart of Darkness* as a racist,[1] I could never accept that a fully contextualized reading of this work could justify such an accusation.

From *Joseph Conrad: Narrative Technique and Ideological Commitment* (London: Edward Arnold, 1890), 101–32. Copyright Jeremy Hawthorn. Reprinted by permission of the author. Unless otherwise specified, page references are to this Norton Critical Edition.
1. 'An Image of Africa: Racism in Conrad's *Heart of Darkness*,' *Massachusetts Review* 18.4 (Winter 1977): 782–94. [See *HD* 336–49.]

I still find this element of *The Nigger of the 'Narcissus'* problematic, but in a rather different way. The figure of James Wait seems to me to be the visible tip of an iceberg of narrative indecision in this work, a narrative indecision that stems from ideological contradictions and uncertainties in Conrad but which manifests itself most obviously in terms of technical unclarities and blurrings. Of all Conrad's works, *The Nigger of the 'Narcissus'* seems to me to be the most perfect example of the manifestation of ideological problems on the narrative plane. And it now seems to me that Conrad's artistic instinct led him to choose the figure of the Negro as the central character in this work with good grounds, for if anything symbolized contradiction and unclarity in the late Victorian popular mind it was the figure of the Negro. After all, although there were many black sailors in Conrad's time (and Conrad had sailed with some), there seems no obvious reason on realist grounds why Conrad should make one the villain of a story designed to say something summarizing about a particular nautical era, especially when the tale also included the figure of Donkin. * * *

I refer to *The Nigger of the 'Narcissus'* as Conrad's problem work not to suggest that the work is a failure, or of no artistic value. Indeed, it is precisely because there is so much that is fine—and quintessentially Conradian—about the novella that it represents a problem for us. * * * *The Nigger of the 'Narcissus'* is a problem not just because so much that is good in it is mixed in with much that is not, but more because the novella is packed with incoherences, with, literally, failures to cohere, to hang together. I am not referring to the sort of ambiguities and tensions so prized by the New Critics—ambiguities and tensions which can be seen to contribute to a deeper, more complex, artistic unity—but to more fundamental disunities which present the reader with insoluble and, finally, artistically unrewarding puzzles, rather than with aesthetically productive challenges. Graham Hough has pointed out that the reader is sent back to consider the intentions of a writer far more by an unsuccessful than by a successful work,[2] and perhaps the sort of work that leads us on repeated and frustrating sorties back to the author is that which, like *The Nigger of the 'Narcissus'*, seems to consist of elements which may be unproblematic in themselves, but which fail to hang together, which cannot be combined to produce a satisfying and coherent whole.

* * *

2. Graham Hough, *An Essay on Criticism*, London, Duckworth, p. 60.

I have always found *The Nigger of the 'Narcissus'* to contain * * * 'apparently anomalous parts',[3] and have never succeeded in the sort of successful prediction that would justify the attribution of Cedric Watts's term 'imaginative intentionality' to the novella, either on first or on subsequent readings.

*   *   *

[E]ven with a highly modernist novel such as Robbe-Grillet's *The Voyeur*, one can still find a *consistency of artistic purpose*—what Watts refers to as imaginative intentionality. The contradictions in this work confuse the reader on first acquaintance, but before long one realizes that this is what the writer wants—or, at least, the presentation of elements designed to produce such disorientation in the reader gives the work a sort of unity. And, using Watts's yardstick, after a while even the first-time reader of *The Voyeur* can *predict* that the rest of the novel will follow this pattern. It is this consistency of artistic purpose, this sense of comprehensive imaginative intentionality or control, that seems to me to be lacking in *The Nigger of the 'Narcissus'*.

Indeed, attempts to discover such a unity of purpose or of control seem, finally, to create even more problems, ending up by imposing a coherence or consistency on the work which the text cannot justify. * * * [I]t is only comparatively recently that some critics, rather than trying to discover a principle of unity in the work, have instead sought to relate the incoherences to unresolved ideological tensions and contradictions in Conrad the writer. * * * My aim is to carry this sort of analysis further—particularly with regard to the importance of James Wait's race—and, briefly, to suggest ways in which Conrad appears to have been able to advance his art by apparently learning from the incoherences of this work, to find ways of producing coherent and thematically unified works out of his own divisions and uncertainties.

It is time now to give chapter and verse, to list what I would claim are fundamental incoherences to be found in the novella.

Hardly any critic of *The Nigger of the 'Narcissus'* has failed to observe that there are inconsistencies in Conrad's manipulation of point of view in the novella, and this critical recognition is paralleled by a comparable unease on the part of the common reader. It is worth starting with this issue, for although I see it as secondary rather than primary in essence, it may be more apparent to the reader than are what I see as the underlying ideological causes.

---

3. Cedric Watts, *'Heart of Darkness': A Critical and Contextual Discussion* (Milan: Mursia International, 1977), 159 [Editor].

Artistic incoherence is not necessarily produced by technical inconsistency in the manipulation of point of view. Many of Conrad's major works exhibit such technical inconsistencies. In *Under Western Eyes*, for example, the teacher of languages tells the reader things which, by his own account of the sources of his information, he could not actually know. And if we accept (which Conrad did not) that Marlow talks for far longer than it is realistic to believe he could possibly have done in *Lord Jim*, then we have another technical inconsistency here, but one which few readers of the novel would deem a significant artistic problem.

It is clearly not inevitably a problem if two characters in a literary work hold different opinions, or if the opinion of one is at variance with that of a personified or non-personified narrator. Nor is it necessarily the case that a work which makes it impossible for the reader to determine between what is supposed objectively to have happened, and what a character merely imagines took place, is artistically flawed—as we see in *The Voyeur*. What generates incoherence is the belief or suspicion that irreconcilable views or perceptions are being presented to the reader in an artistically uncontrolled manner, in a way that either conceals or ignores their irreconcilability, or which even suggests that this irreconcilability is neither artistically planned nor controlled.

From the earliest reviews of the novella mention has been made of the fact that the work appears to have a single narrator who mainly adopts the viewpoint and perspective of an ordinary crew-member of the 'Narcissus', but who sometimes sounds more like an officer and who even becomes omniscient on a number of occasions—at least to the extent of granting us access to the private thoughts of Creighton [156]; Singleton [204–05]; Donkin [234–35; 237; &c.]); and James Wait [237–38]. The reader is also made privy to private conversations between the captain and the mate, and between Donkin and James Wait. There are, too, regular shifts between the narrative use of 'we' and 'they' to refer to the crew of the 'Narcissus', often in the same paragraph [c.f. 185], and in the final four pages of the work the narrator becomes, for the first time, 'I'.

* * *

Conrad's use of Free Indirect Discourse (FID) does not normally avail itself of the potentialities for ambiguity implicit in the technique. And yet in *The Nigger of the 'Narcissus'* FID is on crucial occasions accompanied by ambiguity, such that it is frequently impossible to be sure whether a particular sentiment should be ascribed to a character or rather to a commenting narrating voice—whether omniscient or personified. Indeed, from what I have said before it should be clear that there is no single narrating 'voice' to which sentiments can unproblematically be ascribed. This creates no difficulties when it is with the description of events or of characters and their thoughts and opinions that we are concerned, but it does when we are interpreting narrative opinions and attitudes. If we are satisfied that James Wait actually said and thought what he is described as having done, then from what source our information comes is of less importance. But when it comes to opinions concerning the crew, or relating to the significance of Wait's race, then the source becomes very important indeed, because it is crucial for the reader to know whether such views are to be ascribed to a crew member or to a narrator with whose values the reader is expected to sympathize.

* * *

Reynold Humphries has drawn useful attention to other techniques used in the novella, in particular, the use of passive formulations in such a way as to create a similar ambiguity to that produced by Conrad's use of FID. The use of passive formulations is, of course, a classic means whereby the source of opinions or instructions is concealed. Humphries suggests that the text tries to solve the problem of having a crewman narrator who is both 'a subject of the *énoncé* like any other member of the crew [and] also a subject of the *énonciation* within this *énoncé* inasmuch as he *narrates*'. He suggests that the text tries to solve this dilemma by quite simply pretending that '*there is no narrator at all*', so that 'the events on board ship are often presented as if nobody were relating them, the text disavowing its own activity and encouraging the reader to do the same'.[4] To repeat a point made earlier, I would suggest that *events* cause rather fewer problems than do *opinions* and *interpretations*, for it is in these latter cases that an isolable source is most needed, and it is here that ideological factors are most important.

On a number of occasions passive formulations or FID are used in transitional or linking passages, so that we move between passages which can unambiguously be attributed to a specific source or sources, via 'grey areas', passages of indeterminate authority and origin. A classic example of this is to be found in the description of Wait's face as

> a face pathetic and brutal: the tragic, the mysterious, the repulsive mask of a nigger's soul. [154]

---

4. Reynold Humphries, 'How to Change the Subject: Narrative, Reader and Ideology in *The Nigger of the "Narcissus"*', *Recherches Anglaises et Américaines*, 15, 1982, 41.

Immediately before these words Conrad's use of FID has taken the reader inside James Wait's consciousness, into his private thoughts. We emerge from Wait's mind into—what? Is it a crew member who expresses the racially prejudiced view quoted above? An officer? Or an omniscient narrator to whom we are expected to grant our assent, a narrator expressing views which the novella as a whole underwrites? My own feeling is that my last suggestion comes closest to the way in which most readers read the words in question, for which reason the passage is a very disturbing one. And yet this authorial voice is impossible satisfactorily to pin down; as a result of the ambiguities of point of view in the novella we can rarely make a confident attribution of any views to a narrator who is clearly authorial and reliable.

I will now move on to detail what seem to me to be more specifically ideological incoherences in *The Nigger of the 'Narcissus'*. I would stress, however, that problems of point of view and ideological irresolution are very often hard to separate, are very often two sides of the same coin.

*   *   *

It is with regard to James Wait, however, that incoherences are to be found in the greatest abundance. As I have argued, Wait is the visible part of a fault-line that spans the whole of the work, the nodal point at which more far-reaching contradictions are displayed and made apparent. Wait is

(i) *a malingerer but also genuinely sick*

Critics of *The Nigger of the 'Narcissus'* are still unable finally to make up their minds whether Wait is genuinely sick, and pretending to be a malingerer so as to conceal the fact of his impending death from himself, or whether he actually believes himself to be shamming sickness. The majority opinion at the present time seems to be that Wait is pretending to be shamming so as to avoid recognizing that he is dying. But Seiji Minamida's recent glossary on the novella, commenting upon the captain's statement that Wait has 'been skulking nearly all the passage' [219], argues that

> Captain Allistoun learned from his discharge Jimmy's bad record in his last ship, and had been sure all along that the latter was shamming ill.[5]

Other critics have seen Allistoun's comment as a sympathetic gesture towards Wait, pretending to accept his imposture so as to help him

5. Seiji Minamida, 'The Nigger of the "Narcissus", Explanatory Notes and Glossary', b-20, *Journal of the College of Arts and Sciences Chiba University*, November 1987, 143.

to delay recognition of his impending death. Both explanations are, it seems to me, possible. David Manicom, in an article on *The Nigger of the 'Narcissus'* * * *, outlines what are essentially these two alternatives in great detail, and concludes:

> Neither of these two hypotheses concerning Wait's 'illness' can be proven or disproven. The novel's narrative levels allow the two different 'meanings' to play tantalizingly at being the truth behind the lies.[6]

Cedric Watts gives us an equally plausible third alternative which straddles those already mentioned.

> Throughout the voyage, as the text makes clear, [Wait] suffers from tuberculosis (on the first night his 'roaring, rattling cough . . . shook him like a hurricane' [158]); but when his illness is relatively mild, he exaggerates it in order to malinger, while when the illness becomes mortal, he lies to others and to himself that he is fit.[7]

Conrad seems to go to great lengths to preserve uncertainty; we might think that once it becomes clear that Wait really is dying then the ambiguity would be cleared up, but just about this point comes Wait's confession to Donkin that he has 'done this afore' [213], an admission that might seem to confirm that Wait is, at least in part, malingering. Typically, it is just at this point that Wait coughs violently, thus overlaying the impression of malingering with a reminder of real physical illness. The reader can never be sure whether or not Wait is a malingerer.

* * *

(iv) urbane yet also primitive

This particular collision is nowhere better illustrated than in the following passage.

> He stopped short. The folly around him was confounded. He was right as ever, and as ever ready to forgive. The disdainful tones had ceased, and, breathing heavily, he stood still, surrounded by all these white men. He held his head up in the glare of the lamp—a head vigorously modelled into deep shadows and shining lights—a head powerful and misshapen with a tormented

6. David Manicom, 'Tru Lies/False Truths: Narrative Perspective and the Control of Ambiguity in *The Nigger of the "Narcissus"*,' *Conradiana* 18.2 (Summer 1986), 115 [Editor].
7. Cedric Watts, *The Deceptive Text: An Introduction to Covert Plots*, Brighton, Harvester, 1984, 59–60.

and flattened face—a face pathetic and brutal: the tragic, the mysterious, the repulsive mask of a nigger's soul.

[154]

The first part of this passage clearly includes represented thought, taking us into Jimmy's consciousness (note the giveaway use of *'these* white men' rather than *'those'*). The resources of FID are utilized to give the reader both the impression that here we have an accurate depiction of Wait's thoughts, and also that the narrator is contemptuous of Wait's pretensions. But even in this first part of the extract the narrative situation is complex, however, as the words 'The disdainful tones had ceased, and, breathing heavily' clearly come from a narrator rather than from Jimmy, who *is* disdainful but does not *think of himself* being so any more than he *thinks* of himself breathing heavily. We then move, however, from Jimmy as sneering aristocrat to Jimmy as distorted brute—a movement which almost inevitably brings along Satanic associations which tie in with other associations of Wait with the devil.[8] It is at this point that the lack of specificity with regard to point of view becomes important. *Who* is it who sees Jimmy's face as brutal and repulsive?

In the course of *The Nigger of the 'Narcissus'* the following words are all applied to or associated with Wait: swagger [153]; disdainful [154]; condescended [154]; contemptuously angry [165]; overbearing [165]; casual [167]; fastidious (used with regard to his appetite: [167]); languor [209]; contempt [206, 232]; superb (assurance [238]).

All of these words are such as are normally associated with upper-class or aristocratic pride and assurance—or with the devil. And yet in contrast we find the following:

He was afraid to turn his head, he shrank within himself; and there was an aspect astounding and animal-like in the perfection of his expectant immobility. A thing of instinct—the unthinking stillness of a scared brute.

[218]

We are led either to the conclusion that Wait is a Satanic figure combining contemptuous self-assurance and pride with animal-like brutality (although Wait's alleged fear does not square with this), or to the conclusion that Wait's refined manner is a thin veneer over his essential brutishness. Or, finally, that Conrad's presentation of Wait is artistically confused, and hovers between irreconcilable allegorical and realistic strategies, strategies which are further complicated by the influence of racially stereotypical elements.

* * *

8. Wait is associated with the devil on pages [154, 188, 216, and 218] of the novella. We should also bear in mind that this 'intruder' causes a fruit pie to be stolen!

(vi) both loved and hated by his fellows

'We hesitated between pity and mistrust'; '(We all lovingly called him Jimmy, to conceal our hate of his accomplice)': this on the same page as mention of 'this obnoxious nigger' [165]! During the rescue Belfast shouts to Wait, 'Knock! Jimmy darlint! . . . Knock! You bloody black beast!' [165]. During the rescue Wait is described as a 'hateful burden' [188], and as his death nears we read 'Donkin, watching the end of that hateful nigger' [241]. Frequently a single sentence will include contradictory elements: 'We knew he was dry and comfortable within his little cabin, and in our absurd way were pleased one moment, exasperated the next, by that certitude' [176]. Note how phrases like 'in our absurd way' manage to combine two perspectives here, either those of the crew at the time along with the crew-member's later hindsight, or that of the crew at the time along with an implied authorial narrator. (The crew clearly did not think that their way was absurd at the time.) In this example then the contradictory attitudes towards Wait are recognized by the narrative, are typified as 'absurd', and are attributed to the crew. But this is far from being always the case.

What explanations are there for so many complex and interlocking inconsistencies and incoherences in this work? I do not believe that there is a single, or a simple, available explanation. On one level of argument I would suggest that The Nigger of the 'Narcissus', although by no means Conrad's first work, can still in many ways be seen as an apprentice piece. It is a far more ambitious work than Conrad's first two novels, and this ambition seems to have presented Conrad with problems and difficulties of an order different from those encountered earlier on in his writing career. In particular, during the writing of The Nigger of the 'Narcissus' Conrad had to learn how to produce a work that can contain and depict contradictory visions whilst not being mastered by them, uniting them by means of some larger artistic conception. Subsequently Conrad learned, for example, how to displace such tensions and contradictions into a narrator such as Marlow, thereby anchoring them in a way that they are not anchored in The Nigger of the 'Narcissus'.

What are these root contradictions which Conrad fails to master in The Nigger of the 'Narcissus' and which underlie this work's incoherences? I would wish to isolate two rather different underlying factors: firstly, Conrad's hesitation between what we can term romanticism and realism, and secondly his failure fully to come to terms with Victorian Britain's schizophrenic attitude to the Negro.

Many commentators have found an oscillation between a roman-
ticized and a realistic view of nineteenth-century sailing life in *The
Nigger of the 'Narcissus'*. Some have suggested that this oscillation
reflects Conrad's own inability to decide what exactly his view of—
and relations towards—this life were. It is certainly possible that
one reason why Conrad remained so fond of this particular work to
the end of his life was that it did hold very different attitudes towards
his sea-life in a sort of suspension; not reconciling their contradictions, but effecting some sort of cohabitation between them.

* * *

In *The Nigger of the 'Narcissus'* we find no admission that both
illusion and reality, romance and actuality are engendered by the
sea—*and that they are opposites and irreconcilable*. The work, by concealing, effectively attempts to deny the existence of such a tension.
Lord Jim, in contrast, explores and analyses it.

James E. Miller Jr has suggested that

> The iconography of *The Nigger of the 'Narcissus'* was not accom-
> plished without a dangerous compromise between the natural-
> istic, biographical material and its symbolic transformation.[9]

Conrad's own comments on the work, made at the time of its compo-
sition, are evidence of a duality in his intentions. In a letter written
while he was writing the work he speaks of producing 'a respectable
shrine for the memory of men with whom I have, through many hard
years lived and worked'.[1] In another such letter he uses similar
words, stating that he 'must enshrine my old chums in a decent
edifice'.[2] And by 1903 he can write that

> As a work of fiction *The Nigger* puts a seal on that epoch of the
> greatest possible perfection which was at the same time the end
> of the sailing fleet.[3]

'Shrine', 'perfection'; Conrad's terminology in these letters is very
revealing. But of course it doesn't really square up all that satisfactorily with what Conrad actually wrote, with the evidence of the
text. As we can remember, the epoch of greatest possible perfection
is seen in *The Nigger of the 'Narcissus'* as that to which Singleton
and his contemporaries belonged. The sailors with whom Conrad
sailed might, had they read *The Nigger of the 'Narcissus'*, have found

---

9. James E. Miller, Jr, 'Trial by Water: Joseph Conrad's *The Nigger of the "Narcissus"'*.
   Reprinted in John A. Palmer (ed.), *Twentieth-Century Interpretations of 'The Nigger of
   the "Narcissus"'*, Englewood Cliffs, Prentice-Hall, 1969, 37.
1. Letter to T. Fisher Unwin, 19 October 1896. (*CL* 1: 308–9)
2. Letter to Edward Garnett, 25 October 1896. (*CL* 1: 310)
3. Letter to Kazimierz Waliszewski, 5 December 1903 (*CL* 3: 89)

Conrad's 'shrine' a little less than totally complimentary about themselves. What Conrad appears to be doing here is confusing a subjective perfection—the experiences of his youthful years—with an objective one—the end of the sailing fleet. In 'Youth' the distinction is recognized; in *The Nigger of the 'Narcissus'* it is not.

Elsewhere however Conrad refers to the work in rather different terms. Writing again to Edward Garnett, 29 November 1896, he remarks:

> As to lack of incident well—it's life. The incomplete joy, the incomplete sorrow, the incomplete rascality or heroism—the incomplete suffering. Events crowd and push and nothing happens. You know what I mean. The opportunities do not last long enough.
>
> Unless in a boy's book of adventures. Mine were never finished. They fizzled out before I had a chance to do more than another man would. [CL 1:321]

* * * In *The Nigger of the 'Narcissus'*, in contrast, the conflict is not so much the subject of the work as one of the sources of its incoherence. Commenting upon the final pages of the novella, Michael P. Jones argues that

> Rather than a commentator or a critic, [Conrad] has become an elegist, a kind of pastoral poet singing the praises of a mythical and imaginary past. In the end, Conrad cannot and will not reconcile the detachment of an ironist with the emotional involvement of a participant. And therein lies the final conflict in point of view.[4]

This seems to me to be very well said, but I think that the ideological underpinnings of Conrad's irony and of his realism in *The Nigger of the 'Narcissus'* need to be detailed. In this work narrative irony is never directed towards the officers of the 'Narcissus', but always towards some or all of the crew; it is premised upon highly conservative and hierarchical assumptions. * * * Conrad's irony in *The Nigger of the 'Narcissus'*, then, seems in tension with his declared aim of enshrining his old chums in a decent edifice. This aim seems actually to have been mastered by a stronger, ideological impulse in the work at times, and these times are characteristically marked by Conrad's use of irony.

Raymond Williams has drawn our attention to the fact that if there is one sure thing about the Golden Age, it is that it has always gone. The further back in time one proceeds, the further back its date is displaced. One aspect of Conrad's contradictory attitude

---

4. Michael P. Jones, *Conrad's Heroism: A Paradise Lost*, Ann Arbor, UMI Research Press, 1985), 62 [Editor].

towards the crew in the novella seems to be that it varies very much according to whether Conrad is picturing himself among the crew. Of course, 'Conrad' is not a character in the work; nevertheless, Conrad's real-life attitudes towards the seamen of his sailing days are clearly projected into the work. But the seamen *also* serve a very different function. If at one time they are Conrad's 'old chums', it is apparent that at other times they play a more *representative* rôle in the work, and it is at these times that ideological factors become more intrusive. David Manicom puts the matter as follows.

> The Nigger of the 'Narcissus' is a carefully drawn realistic novel that nevertheless continually gazes toward the allegorical. It is possible to accomplish this so convincingly because, as in *Lord Jim* and *Heart of Darkness*, our narrator is both living in *and* interpreting the story.[5]

The difference between *The Nigger of the 'Narcissus'* on the one hand and both *Lord Jim* and *Heart of Darkness* on the other, however, is that Marlow's double attitude towards the events narrated is explained and incorporated into the artistic structure of the works. He admits to it, and tries to tackle its implications. In *The Nigger of the 'Narcissus'*, partly because this work does not have a fully personified intra-mimetic narrator, the contradictions are not explained in terms of the experience and viewpoint of the narrator. Indeed, they are not acknowledged at all. * * * To resolve these problems their ideological roots have to be uncovered by the reader with little help from the work. * * *

At the time of writing *The Nigger of the 'Narcissus'* Conrad seems still to have been hovering between a conservative-paternalist view of the working class (seen at its purest in the admiring description of Singleton, the hard worker who is totally dedicated to his job, is unthinking and accepts authority unquestioningly, and who abandons himself to mindless drunkenness off-duty), and a rather different conservative-reactionary view most apparent in the treatment of Donkin and of his fellow seamen when they are under his influence. This conservative-reactionary ideology is most visible in the younger Conrad, and it tends to disappear and to be replaced by the conservative-paternalist view in his older years. It is expressed in its purest form in Conrad's letter to Spiridion Kliszczewski. The ideology lying behind this outburst is, surely, the same that gives rise to the sarcastic narrative comments in *The Nigger of the 'Narcissus'* about the seamen, who

> inspired by Donkin's hopeful doctrines . . . dreamed enthusiastically of the time when every lonely ship would travel over a

serene sea, manned by a wealthy and well-fed crew of satisfied skippers. [208]

Donkin himself is the parody of the working-class agitator that such an ideology has to create to justify itself. Again, the language used to describe him comes from the same stable as that in Conrad's letter. Donkin is

> The man who can't do most things and won't do the rest. The pet of philanthropists and self-seeking landlubbers. The sympathetic and deserving creature that knows all about his rights, but knows nothing of courage, of endurance, and of the unexpressed faith, of the unspoken loyalty that knits together a ship's company. The independent offspring of the ignoble freedom of the slums full of disdain and hate for the austere servitude of the sea. [149]

The passage is rich in ideological polemic. Note how the faith and loyalty that knit together the organic community of the ship have to be *unexpressed and unspoken*; there is here a recognition on the part of the ideology that *it must not speak itself*, a recognition that helps to explain why it is that *The Nigger of the 'Narcissus'* cannot confront its own contradictions and incoherences. Indeed, the work itself mirrors this ideology's view of the ship and—clearly, by implication—of society at large. *It will not confront its own divisions and contradictions*, but asserts an organic unity that is revealed as spurious by the hysterical nature of this protestation itself. This is why Singleton has to be 'unthinking', for were he capable of thought he would recognize the incompatibilities in his implicit view of the world. And what is it that is so feared? 'The *independent* offspring of the ignoble *freedom* of the slums full of disdain and hate for the austere *servitude* of the sea'. What is feared is that the exercise of rational thought on the part of the working class will lead to a preference of freedom and independence over servitude. And of course on one level Conrad knows that the seamen do have legitimate grievances: how else can we explain how quickly Donkin persuades his listeners, listeners who we have been told already 'know him' very well? Singleton, incidentally, is just as likely to have come from a slum as is Donkin. It is not really Donkin's origins that Conrad is concerned to attack, but his potential rôle in leading his fellow seamen to stop being 'unthinking' and to begin rationally to consider their situation. * * *

Such tensions also enter the portrayal of James Wait, although in his case there are additional factors to be considered. Wait is both the symbolic, dark, satanic intruder into the prelapsarian Eden of the ship that represents that 'epoch of the greatest possible perfection', and also the realistically depicted Afro-Caribbean, suffering from a non-symbolic tuberculosis. On the one hand he is the symbolic 'weight' which holds back the ship and makes it 'wait' (his name, in cockney pronunciation, also suggests 'white'). On the other hand, as an unnamed member of the crew observes, 'The man's a man if he is black' [220], or as the Captain adds later on, 'He might have been half a man once' [224]—a comment which partly concedes that before the onset of his disease Wait was as good a human being as any of his white mates.

Such an approach perhaps helps to explain why *The Nigger of the 'Narcissus'* needs *two* agents of corruption: Donkin and Wait. Donkin generally functions as agent of corruption on a realistic level, while Wait performs the same function on a symbolic/mythic plane. It is notable that when he is with Donkin, Wait is realistic Afro-Caribbean, but his relations with the rest of the crew operate on an appreciably less realistic level. * * *

An additional problem seems to be, however, that even at sea these two aspects of Wait's rôle leak into one another. And this is partly because of the other factor which makes of Wait such a problematic character in the novella. So many myths concerning the Negro held sway in Victorian England, that portraying a Negro in a purely realistic manner would probably have been impossible. Even the more realistic side of the depiction of Wait contains numerous mythic elements which seem to have their origin in wider social myths about the Negro in Victorian England. And these combine with ideological views of the working class in complex ways. There was, after all, a firm basis for a realistic description of a black sailor in Conrad's time. I have already mentioned that Conrad had sailed with black seamen, and one estimate from 1878 puts the number of coloured sailors engaged in long voyages for the British Merchant Service at 20,000—of whom 5,000 were Lascars working for the Peninsular and Orient Company.[6]

But this objective basis was overlaid in Victorian public opinion by a mass of myths relating to imperialism and colonialism. Not just this, but even more liberal views—those opposing slavery and colonial brutality, for instance—were often heavily paternalistic in form. And thus paternalism could function as the bridge which joined views of black people and views of the native European working class.

Victorian views of the Negro have been well-documented in recent years, and can be quickly summarized. Firstly, the Negro was seen as racially inferior.

> By unanimous consent, said the *Encyclopaedia Britannica*, the African Negro occupied the lowest position in the evolutionary scale, his abnormal length of arm, prognathism and light-weight brain supposedly affording the best material for 'the

6. Douglas A. Lorimer, *Colour, Class and the Victorians*, Leicester, Leicester UP, 1978, 40.

comparative study of the highest anthropoids and the human species'. The Victorian fixation with the notion of a 'missing link' becomes apparent here.[7]

Brian Street reports discussion in the Anthropological Society of London about Negro intelligence, suggesting that the Negro child developed until the age of twelve, when the 'sutures' then closed and intelligence stultified.[8]

*   *   *

The alleged childishness of the Negro is another bridge reaching over to that native working class represented by the white seamen of the 'Narcissus'. Writing of *The Nigger of the 'Narcissus'* in *Notes on Life and Letters*, Conrad declares of the seamen of his seagoing years that, 'their simple minds had a sort of sweetness' [*NLL* 145]. It is clear that a paternalist attitude needs a child or children. *   *   *

In *The Nigger of the 'Narcissus'* Conrad's paternalistic conservatism finds an object in his childlike seamen and in the childish James Wait. *   *   * Conrad seems always to have found it easier to escape from cultural preconceptions with Malays than with Africans.

*   *   *

*   *   * According to [Christine] Bolt

the abolitionist and missionary attempt to demonstrate the essential equality of all men before God seemed disproved by this supposed example of the innate savagery of the Negro—a savagery which permitted, even made essential, savage counter-measures on the part of the superior white race.[9]

Of particular interest is Brian Street's comment that

Characters who crossed the racial, national and environmental boundaries were important to the Victorians because they helped to define those boundaries . . . Victorians were suspicious, not only of biological hybrids but of those 'cultural hybrids' who had inherited one background but tried to adopt another. These characters, the white man in Africa and the black man in European clothes, present a dilemma which is central to Victorian conceptions of race and culture . . . [1]

It seems clear that such views as I have outlined above have a complex ideological origin. Firstly, they offer a justification for European behaviour in Africa. And secondly, the black man is used as the con-

7. Christine Bolt, *Victorian Attitudes to Race*, London, RKP, 1971, 133.
8. Brian Street, *The Savage in Literature: Representations of 'Primitive' Society in English Fiction 1858–1920*, London, Routledge, 1975, 73. Street's source is *Anthropological Review*, 2, 1964, 386.
9. Bolt, 92.
1. Street, 111.

cealed ideological representative of the native working class, the pastoral scapegoat who can justify the treatment of these native inferiors.

It is no surprise that Conrad is able most effectively to confront and question such views when, in literary terms, he returns to one of these two roots—in 'An Outpost of Progress' and *Heart of Darkness*. The black person subject to most authorial irony in 'An Outpost of Progress' is Makola—who has been westernized. A similar point can be made of Marlow's helmsman in *Heart of Darkness*. Wait's portrayal in *The Nigger of the 'Narcissus'* needs to be seen in the light of complex ideological pressures: not only has he crossed 'racial, national and environmental boundaries', to quote Brian Street, but this in turn allows him to have all sorts of domestic European problems projected on to him in the classic manner of the scapegoat. This seems to be the reason why his portrayal is markedly different from that of Africans and of Malays in other works of Conrad, who are not called upon to bear the sins of Europe in quite the same way. The fact that Victorian society displaced many of its own problems and guilts—especially concerning social class—onto the figure of the Negro, constitutes a key element in the link between Donkin and Wait.

*   *   *

A recent study by Catherine Gallagher has confirmed that from a very early date in nineteenth-century Britain, debates about American Negro slavery became intertwined with arguments concerning the native British working class.[2] Again, the link between Donkin and Wait may be seen to represent complex ideological connections available to the Victorians only in mythic form.

*   *   *

Michael Pickering confirms Douglas A. Lorimer's point that stereotypes of the Negro in Victorian Britain were full of contrasts and contradictions.

> From one side the 'negro' was the faithful, deferential servant; from another the indolent, undisciplined labourer. Turn him again, 'jis so', and one confronts the natural Christian, opposed from an opposite angle by the image of an unregenerate sinner; yet another pair of antithetical popular conceptions show him as a patient, suffering forbearing slave on the one hand, and on the other a brutal, lustful, vengeful savage.[3]

2. Catherine Gallagher, *The Industrial Reformation of English Fiction 1832–1867*, London, Chicago UP, 1985.
3. Michael Pickering, 'White Skin, Black Masks: "Nigger" Minstrelsy in Victorian Britain'. In J. S. Bratton (ed.), *Music Hall: Performance and Style*, Milton Keynes, Open UP, 1986, 85.

We can summarize much of the foregoing and say that for the Victorians the stereotype of the Negro contained a range of contradictions, many of which were exaggerated displacements of views held of the native working class.

* * *

It is no surprise that James Wait's name is represented by a blur in the novella; Conrad's presentation of him reproduces many of the contradictions and incoherences contained in the Victorian stereotype of the Negro.

I have already noted that Conrad seems to have found it far less problematic to escape from the racism of his age when dealing with Malays. We have the splendid Author's Note to *Almayer's Folly* to witness here, and we can also note how, in *The Rescue*, it is the unsympathetic Shaw who refers to Malays as 'niggers', and is the clear recipient of authorial scorn for so doing. There is unambiguous internal evidence in *The Nigger of the 'Narcissus'* that the term 'nigger' was considered to be offensive.

> 'You wouldn't call me nigger if I wasn't half dead, you Irish beggar!' boomed James Wait, vigorously. [193]

Lorimer cites Mayhew to confirm that certainly in 1862 black people found this term offensive.[4] Christine Bolt uses the fact that this word gained currency as a term of abuse in India after 1857 to establish the level of Victorian racial prejudice against the Negro. Moreover, in April 1897, a matter of four months before *The Nigger of the 'Narcissus'* started to be serialized, Conrad's friend-to-be Cunninghame Graham published a bitingly sarcastic article entitled 'Bloody Niggers', from which Cedric Watts has quoted the following extract:

> 'Niggers' who have no cannons, and cannot construct a reasonable torpedo, have no rights. 'Niggers' whose lot is placed outside our flag, whose lives are given over to a band of money-grubbing miscreants (chartered or not) have neither rights nor wrongs. Their land is ours, their cattle, fields, their houses, their poor utensils, arms, all that they have; their women, too, are ours to use as concubines, to beat, exchange, to barter for gunpowder and gin . . . Cretans, Armenians, Cubans, Macedonians, we commiserate, subscribe, and feel for . . . But 'niggers', 'bloody niggers', have no friends.[5]

As Watts points out, Conrad read Graham's article in *The Social-Democrat,* and remarked, 'very good, very telling' [CL 2:69]. How

4. Lorimer, 43.
5. Quoted by Cedric Watts in his introduction to the Penguin edition of *The Nigger of the 'Narcissus'*, Harmondsworth, 1988, p. xxv.

then do we explain Conrad's own quite different attitude to the word 'nigger' in *The Nigger of the 'Narcissus'*? Cedric Watts has suggested that the influence of both Rudyard Kipling and of W. E. Henley may possibly be seen in Conrad's novella. Henley was the editor of the *New Review*, which had agreed to publish *The Nigger of the 'Narcissus'* while Conrad was still writing it, and he was an admirer of Kipling. Henley's opinions were, in Watts's phrase, 'patriotic, royalist, and imperialistic'. A letter from Conrad to the Chairman of a committee formed to establish a memorial to Henley after the latter's death would seem to confirm this. Referring to letters he had written Henley, Conrad adds

> It seemed impossible to tell him on paper that the story he accepted for the Review was written with an eye on him—and yet with no idea that it would ever meet his eye. And that is the strict truth. [*CL* 3:115]

Whatever the reason, in *The Nigger of the 'Narcissus'* not only is the word 'nigger' used by crew members, but also by the narrator—both when speaking as 'we' and also when adopting a more detached and omniscient perspective. And his use betrays no evidence of Conrad's having been affected by Cunninghame Graham's article. * * *

According to Kenneth Little's book *Negroes in Britain* (first published in 1948), the end of the nineteenth century was a period in which attitudes towards, and notions concerning, the Negro 'seem to have undergone a considerable change'.

> An object for pity becomes very often an object for condescension. The difficulty was that by emancipation the Negro had theoretically ceased to be either. It was no longer possible to regard him merely as the faithful black, a typification of servile devotion and fidelity. It was as if in becoming a 'man and a brother', as one anonymous commentator puts it, 'he forthwith ceased to be a friend'.[6]

It is this 'neither one thing nor the other' sort of attitude which seems to be reflected in *The Nigger of the 'Narcissus'*, and reflected rather than reflected upon; Conrad seems unable to make this indecision the *subject* or focus of the work. Rather, it becomes an element which, because it is not fully recognized and artistically controlled, renders the text of the work unstable and lacking full coherence.

* * *

6. Kenneth Little, *Negroes in Britain: A Study of Racial Relations in English society*, revised edn with a new Introduction by Leonard Bloom, London, RKP, 1972, 229.

What Conrad seems to have learned about his art from writing *The Nigger of the 'Narcissus'* can be summed up as the realization that he had to be able to dramatize uncertainties and contradictions rather than to attempt to resolve or deny—and thus to be mastered by—them. Conrad's inner conflicts and ambiguities of belief did not disappear upon completion of *The Nigger of the 'Narcissus'*, although he certainly appears to have resolved some of them, as the portrayal of black people in *Heart of Darkness* bears testimony to. But many tensions and contradictions in his mental furniture remained—as they do in all of us. Clearly Marlow was of immense value to Conrad's artistic development. A personified narrator framed by an outer narrator allowed for tensions and uncertainties to be displaced down a narrative chain and thus themselves subjected to scrutiny. And where Conrad does not make use of personified narrators or framed narratives his narrative voices are far more consistent than is the case in *The Nigger of the 'Narcissus'*: think of *Nostromo* and *The Secret Agent*.

Beyond the development of such technical resources, however, it seems as if this work of Conrad's forced him to confront and think through certain inadequately considered attitudes. The conservative-reactionary voice that we find in the letter to Kliszczewski and in the depiction of Donkin appears hardly at all in Conrad's works after *The Nigger of the 'Narcissus'*. And there is a world of difference in the way the Marlow of *Heart of Darkness* comments about those 'with slightly flatter noses than ourselves' [*HD* 7] and the comments about James Wait's physiognomy in *The Nigger of the 'Narcissus'*. By this time Conrad seems more concerned to perceive the humanity that unites black and white. It is true that his recognition of the humanity of non-Europeans seems always to be more complete in the case of Malays than of Africans, and yet his two African works mark his supersession of a range of myths and prejudices which lie at the heart of the incoherences of *The Nigger of the 'Narcissus'*.

CESARE CASARINO

From The Labor of Race; or, Heterotopologies of the Third Man[†]

We return to this text, however, not without casting yet another parting glance in the direction of *The Secret Sharer*. * * * [M]uch like

[†] From *Modernity at Sea: Melville, Marx, Conrad in Crisis* (Minneapolis: University of Minnesota Press, 2002), 235–44. Reprinted with permission of the University of Minnesota Press. In the previous chapter, Casarino argues for a homoerotic relationship between the narrator and Leggatt in "The Secret Sharer," upon which the argument in

the narrator of *The Secret Sharer* abjures the desires of his own narrative in the end, I wish to push his and my desires also in a different direction here. To undo *The Secret Sharer* in a different manner entails no less than rethinking the sublime of the closet by articulating its historical-political conditions of possibility within modernity. Whereas the previous chapter focused primarily on the modalities of being of the romance between the narrator and Leggatt, I want now to investigate the narrative presuppositions of that romance: in that chapter, I read what was there on the page for all to see rather than what had already taken place behind the narrative scenes. Here, we turn to the question of Leggatt's murder: it is about that murder— about whom, why, and how Leggatt killed—that questions need to be formulated so as to read *The Nigger of the "Narcissus"* as the racial unconscious and the political archaeology of *The Secret Sharer*.

This murder constitutes as much of a *fons et origo*[1] as *The Secret Sharer* will ever have: it is because Leggatt has killed a man that he runs away from his ship and into the eager arms of the narrator in the first place. So eager is the narrator, and for so long must he have been awaiting one such as Leggatt, and so well predisposed is he already to his arrival, that the news that Leggatt is a murderer makes the latter not only more attractive to the narrator but also altogether more like the narrator. You might also recall how "confidently" the narrator excuses Leggatt's murder, that is, how "confidently" [14]. the question of this crime is at once allowed to emerge in the narrative and evaded thereafter: "'Fit of temper,' I suggested, confidently." The narrator's omnipotent confidence nonetheless does need this murder for his infinitely paranoiac imagination to be triggered into motion and for all the ensuing plots of romance to get off the narrative ground. It is amusing to see such a confidence in a character who has no self to speak of—let alone self-confidence— and whose self-described hysteric countenance is constantly on the brink of physical and mental collapse. It is crucial to emphasize, in other words, how it is precisely and only about the conjoined questions of Leggatt's murder and moral integrity that the narrator can have any confidence at all. Paranoia is henceforth Conrad's preferred and indeed obligatory narrative form.

Why should this murder be posited as the primal scene of such a form? Let us pose this question to Leggatt himself:

> ". . . [The murdered sailor] was one of those creatures that are just simmering all the time with a silly sort of wickedness. Miserable devils that have no business to live at all. He wouldn't do

---

this chapter builds. Unless otherwise noted, page references are to this Norton Critical Edition.
1. Source and origin (Latin) [Editor].

his duty and wouldn't let anybody else do theirs. . . . You know well enough the sort of ill-conditioned snarling cur. . . ." And I knew well enough the pestiferous danger of such a character where there are no means of legal repression. And I knew well enough that my double there was no homicidal ruffian. I did not think of asking him for details, and he told me the story roughly in brusque, disconnected sentences . . .

"It happened while we were setting a reefed foresail, at dusk. Reefed foresail! You understand the sort of weather. The only sail we had left to keep the ship running; so you may guess what it had been like for days. . . . He gave me some of his cursed insolence at the sheet. I tell you I was overdone with this terrific weather. . . . I believe the fellow himself was half crazed with funk. It was no time for gentlemanly reproof, so I turned round and felled him like an ox. He up and at me. We closed just as an awful sea made for the ship. All hands saw it coming and took to the rigging, but I had him by the throat, and went on shaking him like a rat, the men above us yelling, 'Look out! look out!' Then a crash as if the sky had fallen on my head. . . . It was a miracle that they found us, jammed together behind the forebitts. It's clear that I meant business, because I was holding him by the throat still when they picked us up. He was black in the face. It was too much for them. It seems they rushed us aft together, gripped as we were, screaming 'Murder!' like a lot of lunatics. . . . They had rather a job to separate us, I've been told. A sufficiently fierce story to make an old judge and a respectable jury sit up a bit." [14–15]

And so it is that a narrative of male homoerotic tenderness and affection has its origin and complement in a narrative of brutal violence between men. All that touching, holding, and gripping each other in the sublime closet of the narrator's cabin has its grotesque and just as homoerotic counterpart in this strangulation—a strangulation that is furiously protracted well beyond the call of duty ("I had him by the throat, and went on shaking him like a rat"; "they found us, jammed together"; "[i]t's clear that I meant business, because I was holding him by the throat still when they picked us up"; "gripped as we were . . . [t]hey had rather a job to separate us") [15]. Leggatt—who, mind you, is "no homicidal ruffian" [15]—revels nonetheless in recounting in graphic and gruesome detail the frenzied horrors of the macho prowess of which he seems to be quite frankly proud: his feat, after all, is a "sufficiently fierce story to make an old judge and a respectable jury sit up a bit." The most arresting horror in Leggatt's edifying vignette of robust virility is the fact that his unrepentant and defiant pride is met by the narrator with an attitude of complete understanding and indulgence, which makes it abundantly clear that the narrator thought this to be a perfectly excusable and justified use of violence, even though such a violence is most significantly characterized by unaccounted intensity, vehemence, frenzy, and hysteria that make it well congruent with that systemic homophobic violence identifiable as homosexual panic.[2] Leggatt constitutes the shared element, the pivotal hinge, and the translating apparatus between these two complementary narratives—namely, the narrative of his murder and the narrative unfolding in the enclosure of the cabin—that belong thus in a continuum of gender and sexual production. This is a continuum in which Leggatt can afford openly to express affection for and be physically intimate with another man only because he has already amply proven himself to be a man, as well as gained that other man's respect, by killing a third man, who is one of those "[m]iserable devils that have no business to live at all" [14], that is, who does not deserve to exist because he is all that a man must at all costs not be.

Who *is* this third man who, on the one hand, defies so despicably the normative definition of masculinity, and, on the other hand, is indispensable for this romance to take place, since it is precisely his murder that brings the narrator and Leggatt together (each as double of the other, and both as perfect replicas, examples, and incorporations of that normative definition of masculinity)? Who is this sailor who "is simmering all the time with a silly sort of wickedness," who "wouldn't do his duty and wouldn't let anybody else do theirs," who is an "ill-conditioned snarling cur" constituting a "pestiferous danger . . . where there are no means of legal repression?" [14]. One has surely met him before, in an earlier novel. His name is Donkin. His ship is the *Narcissus*. And this is his story:

> Another new hand—a man with shifty eyes and a yellow hatchet face . . . observed in a squeaky voice: 'Well, it's a 'omeward trip, anyhow. Bad or good, I can do it on my 'ed—s'long as I get 'ome. And I can look after my rights! I will show 'em!' All the heads turned towards him. . . . He stood repulsive and smiling in the sudden silence. This clean white forecastle was his refuge; the place where he could be lazy; where he could wallow, and lie and eat—and curse the food he ate; where he could display his talents for shirking work, for cheating, for cadging; where he could find surely someone to wheedle and someone to bully— and where he would be paid for doing all this. They all knew him. Is there a spot on earth where such a man is unknown, an

2. The analytic category of "homosexual panic" is homonymous with the psychiatric term at times used in trials so as to advocate leniency for gay-bashers; see Eve Kosofsky Sedgwick, *Epistemology of the Closet* (Berkeley: University of California Press, 1990), 19–21, but see also 200–201 and more generally 182–212 for a discussion of the dangers involved in using "homosexual panic" as a central category of a antihomphobic inquiry.

534   CESARE CASARINO

ominous survival testifying to the eternal fitness of lies and
impudence? . . . He was the man that cannot steer, that cannot
splice, that dodges the work on dark nights; that, aloft, holds on
frantically with both arms and legs, and swears at the wind, the
sleet, the darkness; the man who curses the sea while others
work. The man who is the last out and the first in when all
hands are called. The man who can't do most things and won't
do the rest. The pet of philanthropists and self-seeking landlubbers. The sympathetic and deserving creature that knows all
about his rights, but knows nothing of courage, of endurance,
and of the unexpressed faith, of the unspoken loyalty that
knits together a ship's company. The independent offspring of
the ignoble freedom of the slums full of disdain and hate for
the austere servitude of the sea. [148–49]

If, as Jameson suggests, Donkin is "the epitome of the *homme de ressentiment*" and "*The Nigger of the 'Narcissus'* . . . may be characterized
as one long tirade against *ressentiment*",[3] such a tirade—of which this
passage is an exemplary moment—seems to borrow its acrimonious-
ness from the very *ressentiment* against which it is directed. The reactionary virulence of such a philippic is as relentless as Leggatt's
murderous violence—and they are both aimed at the same historical
subject. At the very end of *The Nigger of the "Narcissus"*, the narrator—
who turns out to be an officer aboard the *Narcissus*—actually imagines Donkin "who never did a decent day's work in his life, no doubt
[to be earning] his living by discoursing with filthy eloquence upon
the right of labour to live" [254] Donkin, the "independent offspring
of the ignoble freedom of the slums" [149], is the personification of an
urban proletariat in social ascent through its increasing involve-
ment in the politics of unionism and socialism—a politics that saw
its confrontational and official culmination in the arena of British
public discourse with the foundation of the Labour Party in 1900,
three years after the publication of *The Nigger of the "Narcissus"*.
Donkin is the compendium of all the proclivities, behaviors, and
beliefs that for Conrad are antinomial to any definition of masculinity and that can be conveniently summarized as the refusal to work,
as the rejection of the mystique of labor. In Conrad, real men work.
Donkin—the modern political subject of an antagonistic working
class that is "full of disdain and hate for the austere servitude of
the sea" [149] that, in other words, is determined to resist ruthless
exploitation—resurfaces at the beginning of *The Secret Sharer* in the
guise of the nameless murdered sailor, so as to be promptly sacrificed

3. Fredric Jameson, *The Political Unconscious: Narrative as Socially Symbolic Act* (Ithaca,
N.Y.: Cornell University Press, 1981), 215–16 [510, this edition: Editor].

as a body of aberrant masculinity on the altar of a consecrated male-male romance whose spectacle is about to unfold. In this respect, *The Secret Sharer* completes what in *The Nigger of the "Narcissus"* constituted an unfinished project. In Conrad, a nostalgic as well as reactionary mystique of labor and a homoerotic as well as homophobic mystique of the male body are produced as one set of discursive practices. Donkin is the epitome of that emergent subject who—even though he is a man . . . but not really, and even though he is a worker . . . but not fully—can no longer be forced to work for either of those two symbiotic mystiques.

The real men—that is, the men like Leggatt, the men who proudly and silently endure their hard fate as well as "the austere servitude of the sea," the men both the narrator of *The Nigger of the "Narcissus"* and the narrator of *The Secret Sharer* love to love—are a dying race:

> [Singleton, the *Narcissus's* oldest sailor] was only a child of time, a lonely relic of a devoured and forgotten generation. He stood, still strong, as ever unthinking; a ready man with a vast empty past and with no future, with his childlike impulses and his man's passions already dead within his tattooed breast. The men who could understand his silence were gone—those men who knew how to exist beyond the pale of life and within sight of eternity. They had been strong, as those are strong who know neither doubts nor hopes. They had been impatient and enduring, turbulent and devoted, unruly and faithful. Well-meaning people had tried to represent those men as whining over every mouthful of their food; as going about their work in fear of their lives. But in truth they had been men who knew toil, privation, violence, debauchery—but knew not fear, and had no desire of spite in their hearts. Men hard to manage, but easy to inspire; voiceless men—but men enough to scorn in their hearts the sentimental voices that bewailed the hardness of their fete. . . . Their generation lived inarticulate and indispensable. . . . They were the everlasting children of the mysterious sea. Their successors are the grown-up children of a discontented earth. They are less naughty, but less innocent; less profane, but perhaps also less believing; and if they had learned how to speak they have also learned how to whine. But the others were strong and mute; they were effaced, bowed and enduring, like stone caryatides that hold up in the night the lighted halls of a resplendent and glorious edifice. They are gone now—and it does not matter. The sea and the earth are unfaithful to their children: a truth, a faith, a generation of men goes—and is forgotten, and it does not matter! Except, perhaps, to the few of those who believed the truth, confessed the faith—or loved the men. [158–59]

What can one add to such an infantilizing, patronizing, romanticizing, effacing, and yet stunning elegy to the laboring male body? What can one ask of the eloquent and sentimental heights that are reached here in order to speak of these "strong and mute" "caryatides" and "voiceless men" who were "men enough to scorn in their hearts the sentimental voices that bewailed the hardness of their fate"? And how is one to understand the relations that bind in secret partnerships the quasi-religious reverence for silence, the passionate veneration of masculine strength, and the contradictory position that this garrulous narrator occupies vis-à-vis that reverence and that veneration, since he, unlike those "strong" men who are silent and don't need to speak, is the one who does so much talking and representing? Here, I would like to rupture further the already uneven historical faultline that is the political voice of the narrator in *The Nigger of the "Narcissus"*—a faultline that will be restaged even more unevenly in the narrator of *The Secret Sharer*. In between these two generations of men and the two eras of labor and masculinity to which they belong—the first and premodern one constituted by the men who are "strong and mute," and the second and modern one constituted by the men who, having "learned how to speak," had "also learned how to whine"—stand "the few of those," like the narrator of *The, Nigger of the "Narcissus"*, who remember, because they "believed the truth, confessed the faith—or loved the men." The men in between are inextricably caught in that modern double bind of representation within which to remember and to write longing elegies in honor of the "forgotten" laboring male body of yore is already to be its historical executioner. * * * But if the narrator of *The Nigger of the "Narcissus"* is in between these different bodies as well as in between these apparently mutually exclusive eras of labor, if he is constituted as a faultline between the Donkins and the Leggatts and their respective worlds, he is not as yet constituted as a faultline between the nostalgic as well as reactionary mystique of labor and the homoerotic as well as homophobic mystique of the male body. In *The Nigger of the "Narcissus"*, these two mystiques can still come into being as completely coextensive strata of ideology, since the narrator is able, for the most part, to deploy successfully both of them at the same time and in the same space without as yet unleashing their explosive contradictions. In *The Nigger of the "Narcissus"*, these mystiques somehow can still usefully exploit each other for the realization of a common ideological capital. It is in *The Secret Sharer*, instead, that a new interstitial position is added to the previous ones and that the narrator becomes a more uneven faultline between increasingly irreconcilable libidinal economies. The narrator of *The Secret Sharer* is precisely in between Leggatt and the ship and is constituted as the unstable interference between suddenly antinomial worlds: on the one hand, the world of Leggatt, of the "strong and mute" men who devoted their lives to the sea and its ships, of the homoerotic as well as homophobic passions for such men, and, on the other hand, the world of the ship, of its demands of labor and discipline, of its heteronormative as well as homophobic adult libidinal forms. In *The Nigger of the "Narcissus"*, both these worlds were the symbiotic halves of a whole apparatus of labor and desire: there, to love the men was in no contradiction whatsoever with and was actually indispensable to the world of the ship and its injunctions. In *The Secret Sharer*, however, the narrator is split by the opposite vectors of precisely these two trajectories of desire: while according to his definitions and expectations these trajectories should have been perfectly compatible with each other, they now seem at once increasingly semiautonomous and mutually exclusive as well as increasingly bound to each other's fates. The narrator of *The Secret Sharer* marks the intuition of a profound and perhaps ultimately indomitable modern crisis in the mode of production: this is a crisis in which the production of bodies and of their desires proceeds by enlarging the distance as well as by intensifying the antagonism between—at once increasingly self-enclosed and atomized, and increasingly interdependent and interrelated—libidinal economies such as labor and capital, and such as homosexuality and heterosexuality. The narrator of *The Secret Sharer* constitutes the ever-widening gap between the opposite polarities of the dialectic that are produced more and more as both monads *and* fragments, as both spaces of absolute enclosure *and* spaces of absolute relationality, as both times of the event *and* times of the teleological: he embodies the tendentially unexchangeable, unexploitable, and unco-optable crisis of modernity.

Let us return now one last time to Leggatt's murder, so as to begin, in the end, to tell yet another story. In *The Secret Sharer*, Conrad rewrote an event that at the time had caused quite a sensation in the maritime world of East Asia: the murder of a sailor by an officer aboard the *Cutty Sark*. Conrad often refers to that event as one of the sources for *The Secret Sharer*. In a letter, for example, he writes:

> [Leggatt] himself was suggested to me by a young fellow who was 2d mate (in the '60) of the *Cutty Sark* clipper and had the misfortune to kill a man on deck. But his skipper had the decency to let him swim ashore on the Java Coast as the ship was passing through Anjer Straits. The story was well remembered in the Merchant Service even in my time.[4]

4. See Appendix A in Sherry (*CEW* 295) [See *CL* 6:99]; see also Conrad's "Author's Note" to *'Twixt Land and Sea* [4].

This last recollection is possibly even more chilling than Leggatt's own account of the murder. In between misplaced "misfortune" and misplaced "decency," Conrad stands here as a cartographer of capital and disciplinary power: in the end, he is always on the side of the officers. In Conrad's rewriting of this event in *The Secret Sharer* as well as in his letters, however, there is a crucial omission: the murdered sailor was black. In *The Log of the Cutty Sark*, we learn not only that the murdered sailor was black but also that the officer who murdered him "was apparently a despotic character with a sinister reputation"—a far cry, in other words, from the narrator's portrayal of Leggatt—and that the incident culminating in the murder had started as the black sailor's attempt to challenge the officer's authority.[5] This sailor was a resistant black man—and it was as such that he was killed. The fact that the enabling event of a narrative of romance between two white men is the murder of a sailor who was not only the embodiment of the antithesis of Conrad's definitions of the laboring male body but also a resistant black man—such a fact marks the emergence of same-sex desire in *The Secret Sharer* also as the articulation of lethal anxieties about racial difference.

Furthermore, the fact that the matter of race is thoroughly erased in Conrad's rewritings of the murder also indicates the extent to which *The Secret Sharer* is a completion of the projects of *The Nigger of the "Narcissus"*. In the latter, in fact, there was a sailor whose isolation and ostracism lubricated the delicate machinery of labor, discipline, and homosocial cohesion even better than the isolation and ostracism of Donkin. That sailor's name is James Wait—the only black sailor aboard a ship of white men, to whom the title of the novel refers. Around his illness, agony, and death, the other sailors coalesce as one cohesive, compliant, efficient, and homoerotically charged body of labor. Conrad, who was an officer aboard the *Narcissus*, thus remembers James Wait in the preface to the novel's American edition:[6]

> From that evening when James Wait joined the ship . . . to the moment when he left us in the open sea, shrouded in sailcloth, through the open port, I had much to do with him. He was in my watch. A negro in a British forecastle is a lonely being. He has no chums. Yet James Wait, afraid of death and making her his accomplice was an impostor of some character—mastering

---

5. See Appendix A in Sherry's summary of Basil Lubbock's *The Log of the "Cutty Sark"* in *CEW*, 256–57; for a more extensive account of Conrad's sources in *The Secret Sharer*, see also 253–269.
6. Casarino is referring to the introductory remarks, "To My American Readers," that prefaced the 1914 Doubleday edition of the novel, not to what has come to be known as the "Preface" to *The Nigger of the "Narcissus"*; see pp. 137–38 [Editor].

our compassion, scornful of our sentimentalism, triumphing over our suspicions.

But in the book he is nothing; he is merely the centre of the ship's collective psychology and the pivot of the action. Yet he, who in the family circle and amongst my friends is familiarly referred to as the Nigger, remains very precious to me. For the book written round him is not the sort of thing that can be attempted more than once in a life-time. [137]

As Conrad only too precisely puts it, *The Nigger of the "Narcissus"* is indeed "written round" James Wait—who is at once "nothing" and "merely the centre of the ship's collective psychology and the pivot of the action." But what does it mean for somebody to be at once "nothing" and "the centre" of everything but that these two distinct modalities of being are nonetheless mutually determining and dialectically determined? And yet, what could it possibly mean to write that this "nothing" is not only "the centre" and "the pivot" but also "merely" so? How can anything and even a "nothing" be "the centre" and "the pivot" "*merely*"? This dialectic is decidedly tilted: while the condition of being "nothing" is given as pure and unqualified, the condition of being "the centre" and "the pivot" is qualified by an adverb that retracts at least as much as it concedes, and that hence expresses a certain reluctance and ambivalence at having to grant that James Wait is "nothing" precisely to the extent to which he is not only the most important element in this narrative but also "very precious" to Conrad after all this time. With the insertion of this adverb, Conrad attempts a reversal of this dialectic as soon as he realizes that he has cornered himself into admitting that this dialectic is actually reversed the other way around. In other words, rather than being "the centre" because he is "nothing," James Wait is turned into "nothing" precisely because he is "the centre."

Ultimately, Conrad's preface to *The Nigger of the "Narcissus"* is more accurate as a description not of this novel but rather of *The Secret Sharer*. This preface indexes an as yet unfinished project that comes to its logical and complete fruition only in *The Secret Sharer*. In *The Nigger of the "Narcissus"*, after all, James Wait still *is* something and somebody, Conrad's claims to the contrary notwithstanding. In *The Nigger of the "Narcissus"*, the explosive question of racial difference is still allowed to be present as no less than the historical-political condition of possibility for the complex apparatus of labor, discipline, and same-sex desire—even if such a presence takes the form of a reiterated process of sublation. *The Secret Sharer* does what *The Nigger of the "Narcissus"* could not yet do: it entirely erases the body of racial difference, it completely elides the fact that it is over a murdered black body that white men stand to love each

other. An inverse proportionality guides the passage from the first
to the second novel: as the representation of sexual desire between
white men emerges more clearly and crystallizes into a full-fledged
narrative in the second text, the elision of the racial condition of
possibility of such a narrative becomes increasingly successful to
the point of its absolute disappearance from the representational
field of that text. It is regarding *The Secret Sharer* that one can say
what Conrad had already claimed regarding *The Nigger of the "Narcissus"*: there, the male body of racial difference is really "nothing"
and yet all the more "the centre" of everything. Or, more accurately,
in *The Secret Sharer*, the male body of racial difference is that
negated "nothing" that constitutes "the centre" of everything that
matters to the white body. There is finally something far more pernicious about the way in which *The Secret Sharer* negates the dialectical whirlwind of the *Aufhebung* that relentlessly sweeps the decks of
the *Narcissus*. While *The Secret Sharer* is able to short-circuit and
circumvent all sorts of dialectical processes * * * nonetheless it is not
able to circumvent the dialectics of racial constitution: in *The Secret
Sharer*, we witness a negation of this dialectic rather than an escape
from it—and this is a negation that reasserts the power of such a
dialectic all the more ruthlessly in the end. * * * The faint and nonetheless overpowering trace of such a negation can be sensed in the
textual fabric of *The Secret Sharer* only as a foundational and
peremptory gesture of effacement, that is, only as violence and murder. *The Secret Sharer* brings back from *The Nigger of the "Narcissus"* both Donkin and James Wait so as to incorporate them into one
single, negated body of labor and racial difference: it is the murder
of such a body that enables the coming-into-being of what is nonetheless a liberating narrative of same-sex desire.

*   *   *

PETER LANCELOT MALLIOS

[On Lost Causes, Political Narrative, and *The Nigger of the "Narcissus"*][†]

*   *   *

The Nigger of the "Narcissus" is set at a moment of disturbing
social transition: one Jacques Berthoud has described in terms of
the (enormously consequential) transition from sail to steam in the

† From *Our Conrad* (Stanford: Stanford University Press, 2010), 342–46. Copyright by
the Board of Trustees of the Leland Stanford Jr. University. All rights reserved. Used
with the permission of Stanford University Press, www.sup.org. The author has slightly
revised the essay for this Norton Critical Edition. Page references are to this edition.

British merchant marine in the later nineteenth century; one Ian Watt discusses in terms of a shift in social organization from *Gemeinschaft* ("community": a preindustrial mode predicated on traditional hierarchies and organic customs) to *Gesellschaft* ("society": an urbanized, atomized, liberalized, and class-conscious mode); one Cesare Casarino locates in a shift in Western mode of production from mercantile capitalism to industrial capitalism; and one that may also be linked to the rise of the "New Imperialism" in Africa in the 1880s and 1890s.[1] Amid this palimpsest of interlocking historical sea changes, and without taking away from Berthoud's claim that there are uniquely valuable ways in which Conrad's text registers the historicity of the sea in his moment,[2] I think we may also follow Fredric Jameson's line of argument that the *Narcissus* is something of a stay against time: a vehicle of delaying, "derealizing" and "displac[ing] unwanted realities" associable with modernity.[3] Though it exists in a world whose "land" has already been thoroughly transformed to "modern" urban-industrial terms, and though it has already been irremediably infiltrated by contagious related conceptions of individual rights, class consciousness, and organized resistance that the novel tendentiously vocalizes and vilifies in the figure of Donkin, the *Narcissus* sails at a scrupulously maintained distance from "land" and is manifestly a figurative attempt at what Conrad knows is the "lost cause" of forestalling, containing, and sealing off the momentum of modernity. The text almost lovingly itemizes and valorizes all the various aspects of "old custom" [160], "resumed routine" [161], "etiquette of the forecastle" [169], "discipline" [172], "force of habit" [196], "pace" [172], "place" [161], and "the half-hourly voice of the bells [that] ruled our lives" [161], which constitute the preindustrial (organic, hierarchical) traditions and social order of sail—and which the book attests, against the overdetermined adversary of the sea, are necessary for the ship's smooth operations and survival. Similarly, the "modern" Donkin has a curious way of speaking both to and for certain elements of discontent within the ship's crew, and then being ultimately produced—by text and crew alike—as an absolute other. Furthermore, the very intensity of the novel's "impressionist" aesthetics—its vivid attention to the cascading surfaces of sky and sea, which form the boundaries of the "great circular solitude" [161] that the novel incessantly draws around itself and

1. Jacques Berthoud, "Introduction," in *The Nigger of the "Narcissus"* by Joseph Conrad (Oxford: Oxford University Press, 1984), xiv–xix; Ian Watt, *Conrad in the Nineteenth Century* (Berkeley: University of California Press, 1979), 112–15; Cesare Casarino, *Modernity at Sea: Melville, Marx, Conrad in Crisis* (Minneapolis: University of Minnesota Press, 2002), 3–9.
2. Berthoud, vii–viii.
3. Fredric Jameson, *The Political Unconscious: Narrative as Socially Symbolic Act* (Ithaca: Cornell University Press, 1981), 214, 217 [509, 511, this edition: Editor].

the *Narcissus*, and that Conrad "makes us *see*" precisely as a function of making it very difficult to see *beyond* them—manifestly
inscribes a will to distance and obscure "land" and its "modern"
coordinations.

Jameson comments, in the context of *Lord Jim* but in a charge that
also reverberates for the problems of social value at issue in *The Nigger of the "Narcissus"*: "Why should we be expected to assume, in the
midst of capitalism, that the aesthetic rehearsal of the problematics
of a social value from a quite different mode of production—the feudal ideology of honor—should need no justification and should be of
interest to us? Such a theme must mean *something else*: and this
even if we choose to interpret its survival as an 'uneven development,'
a nonsynchronous overlap in Conrad's own values and experience
(feudal Poland, capitalist England)."[4] One answer to this question is
that it depends on who "we" are. Writing from the perspective of the
contemporary metropolitan West, tellingly elided in "interest" with
late nineteenth-century imperial "capitalist England," Jameson min-
imizes as personal ("Conrad's own values and experiences") the very
kind of "nonsychronous overlap" that in postpartition Poland and the
postbellum South—and, as Said extends the analogy in the important
essay "On Lost Causes," the more recent experiences of many Pales-
tinians, Vietnamese, Cubans, South Africans, Angolans, Arme-
nians, American Indians, Tasmanians, Gypsies, and Jews[5]—was a
primary cultural mode: an ideological resistance-formation whose
principal "interest" and "justification" lay precisely in its "uneven"
relation to adjacent modes of ostensibly insuperable domination;
a resistant and "residual" matrix of ideology that must primarily
"mean something else" only to a perspective unwilling to consider
the marvel, priority, and perils of its resurgent autonomy in its own
terms.

Such residual tenacity and struggle under the shadow of Death,
in any event, comprise not only the project of *The Nigger of the
"Narcissus"*—which is related by an obviously invested (and notori-
ously unstable) "narrator" long after the *Narcissus* and its brood are
gone—but the essence of its plot as well. Old Singleton, the ideal
sailor of the old order, incarnates something of both the book's and
the ship's embattled struggle to keep what can only be called the
hegemony of the *Narcissus*—for as we shall see, what is fundamentally at issue is the instrumentations of its power relations—alive:

> "Old Singleton" . . . through half a century had measured his
> strength against the favours and the rages of the sea. He had

4. Jameson, 217 (emphasis in original) [511, this edition: Editor].
5. Edward W. Said, "On Lost Causes," in *Reflections on Exile* (Cambridge, MA: Harvard
   University Press, 2002), 543.

never given a thought to his mortal self. He lived unscathed, as though he had been indestructible, surrendering to all the temptations, weathering many gales. He had panted in sunshine, shivered in the cold; suffered hunger, thirst, debauch; passed through many trials—known all the furies. Old! It seemed to him he was broken at last. And like a man bound treacherously while he sleeps, he woke up fettered by the long chain of disregarded years. He had to take up at once the burden of all his existence, and found it almost too heavy for his strength. Old! He moved his arms, shook his head, felt his limbs. Getting old . . . and then? He looked upon the immortal sea with the awakened and groping perception of its heartless might; he saw it unchanged, black and foaming under the eternal scrutiny of the stars; he heard its impatient voice calling for him out of a pitiless vastness full of unrest, of turmoil, and of terror. He looked afar upon it, and he saw an immensity tormented and blind, moaning and furious, that claimed all the days of his tenacious life, and, when life was over, would claim the worn-out body of its slave. . . . [205]

Among the infinite riches of this passage (to which we will return shortly) is its presentation of Singleton's embattled incarnation of the "old" order through images of him "fettered" by a "long chain," tormented in the "worn-out body" of a "slave," and gazing into the "black" mirror of the sea. These tropes pointedly connect Singleton and the backward-looking ideological project he epitomizes in and for the novel to the single black character who gives Conrad's novel its name: James Wait, the eponymous "nigger" of the *Narcissus.* * * * Conrad's prototype stages its essentially "realist" presentation of a social world in "a passing phase of life" [141] in relation to a central, spectral, dying character who coordinates the novel as a matter of collective psychology and social mechanism. Conrad's Wait—his name implies residual hailing ("Wait!" [153]) and psychosocial burden ("weight")—enters Conrad's novel with the manifest symptoms of a shockingly "sick man" [168]—and the "idea of stalking death" [165] ever around him. Though there is an important question of whether Wait is "shamming," the crucial issue of *doubt* is whether the central character is actually dying, with all the various *ambivalences* of anger and pity, attraction and repulsion, renunciation and resuscitation that surround the spectacle of his dying. Moreover, *The Nigger of the "Narcissus"* nonetheless rigorously blocks off (with one exception) Wait's subjectivity from other characters and the reader; and Wait is repeatedly presented as a species of the fundamental evasiveness that he constitutes for the novel as a matter of form: a "hollow" man [169]; an "empty man—empty—empty" [215]; "nobody" [239]; "no one at all" [239]; a "black phantom" [240]; an "empty cask" [189]; "all his

inside . . . gone" [215]; "distrustful of his own solidity" [232]; someone who "did not like to be alone in his cabin, because, when he was
alone, it seemed as if he hadn't been there at all" [237]. Wait, one
might say, is less a "character" than the amorphous mirror and tangled intersection of a social condition—and this Conrad *does* say
(though trust the tale, not the teller) in his American preface to the
novel: "He is nothing . . . merely the centre of the ship's collective
psychology and the pivot of the action" [137]. "Immaterial like an
apparition" [231], Wait slides through many different and radically
inconsistent postures, each varying with the specific audience he is
reflecting—the evangelist cook, for instance, believes Wait is a
"black devil" [218] and genuinely dying as a function of the cook's
own missionary zeal; Donkin believes Wait is shamming because of
the cynical self-interest that underlies his (Donkin's) every action—
while everyone on board, including the captain [224], the officers
[171], and Donkin [241], are generally compelled by the anxieties of
death he elicits from, intermingles for, and reflects and deflects in
them. The mortal vulnerability of the ship's traditional structures of
cohesion exist under the "fit emblem" of Wait's "moribund carcass"
[221] and the collective psychology of the ship that he not only
emblematizes but centralizes and organizes. And the very contours
of Conrad's novel are determined by a "return" voyage "home" in
which the social community waits for and wonders if this central-
ized character is going to die.

*   *   *

F. R. LEAVIS

["Typhoon" and *The Shadow-Line*]†

*   *   *

The sailor in him [Conrad], of course, is rightly held to be a main
part of his strength. * * * It is time to ask where the strength may be
found in its purest form. There will, I think, be general approval of the
choice of *Typhoon* as a good example. But I am not sure that there is as
general a recognition of just where the strength of *Typhoon* lies. The
point may be made by saying that it lies not so much in the famous
description of the elemental frenzy as in the presentment of Captain
MacWhirr, the chief mate Jukes and the chief engineer Solomon

---

† From *The Great Tradition* (New York: George W. Stewart, [1948]), 183–89. Copyright
1951 by Harper & Brothers. Reprinted by permission of Faber and Faber Ltd. Page
references are to this Norton Critical Edition.

Rout at the opening of the tale. Of course, it is a commonplace that Conrad's distinctive genius comprises a gift for rendering the British seaman. But is it a commonplace that the gift is the specific gift of a novelist, and (though the subtler artist doesn't run to caricature and the fantastic) relates Conrad to Dickens? Consider; for instance, this:

> He was rather below the medium height, a bit round-shouldered, and so sturdy of limb that his clothes always looked a shade too tight for his arms and legs. As if unable to grasp what is due to the difference of latitudes, he wore a brown bowler hat, a complete suit of a brownish hue, and clumsy black boots. These harbour togs gave to his thick figure an air of stiff and uncouth smartness. A thin silver watch-chain looped his waistcoat, and he never left his ship for the shore without clutching in his powerful, hairy fist an elegant umbrella of the very best quality, but generally unrolled. Young Jukes, the chief mate, attending his commander to the gangway, would sometimes venture to say, with the greatest gentleness, "Allow me, sir,"—and, possessing himself of the umbrella deferentially, would elevate the ferrule, shake the folds, twirl a neat furl in a jiffy, and hand it back: going through the performance with a face of such portentous gravity, that Mr. Solomon Rout, the chief engineer, smoking his morning cigar over the skylight, would turn away his head in order to hide a smile. "Oh! aye! The blessed gamp. . . . Thank 'ee, Jukes, thank 'ee," would mutter Captain MacWhirr heartily, without looking up. [259–60]

Consider the exchanges between Captain MacWhirr and Jukes over the Siamese flag, deplorably, poor Jukes feels ('Fancy having a ridiculous Noah's ark elephant in the ensign of one's ship' [263–64]), substituted for the Red Ensign. Consider the accounts of the home backgrounds of MacWhirr and the chief engineer.

It is to be noted further that these backgrounds in their contrast with the main theme of the tale afford a far more satisfactory irony (it is, in fact, supremely effective) than that, in *Heart of Darkness*, of the scenes at Brussels. At the same time it is to be noted that there is in *Typhoon* no sardonic Marlow, commenting on an action that he is made to project; whereas, though *Heart of Darkness* is given from the point of view of the captain of the steamboat, that captain *is* Marlow—Marlow, for whom Conrad has more than one kind of use, and who is both more and less than a character and always something other than just a master mariner. For comment in *Typhoon* we have the letters home of Solomon Rout, the chief engineer, and the letter of Jukes to his chum. In short, nothing in the story is forced or injected; the significance is not adjectival, but resides in the presented particulars—the actors, the incidents and the total action: we are given the ship, her cargo and her crew of ordinary British seamen, and the impact on them of the storm.

The ordinariness is, with a novelist's art, kept present to us the whole time; the particular effect of heroic sublimity depends on that.

> And again he heard that voice, forced and ringing feeble, but with a penetrating effect of quietness in the enormous discord of noises, as if sent out from some remote spot of peace beyond the black wastes of the gale; again he heard a man's voice—the frail and indomitable sound that can be made to carry an infinity of thought, resolution and purpose, that shall be pronouncing confident words on the last day, when heavens fall, and justice is done—again he heard it, and it was crying to him, as if from very, very far—"All right". [287]

Conrad can permit himself this, because the voice is that of the unheroically matter-of-fact Captain MacWhirr, whose solid specific presence, along with that of particularized ordinary sailors and engineers, we are never allowed to forget:

> A lull had come, a menacing lull of the wind, the holding of a stormy breath—and he felt himself pawed all over. It was the boatswain. Jukes recognized these hands, so thick and enormous that they seemed to belong to some new species of man.
>
> The boatswain had arrived on the bridge, crawling on all fours against the wind, and had found the chief mate's legs with the top of his head. Immediately he crouched and began to explore Jukes' person upwards, with prudent, apologetic touches, as became an inferior. [290]

                              *   *   *

The seamen are their ordinary selves, the routine goes forward in the engine-room, and the heroic triumphs of the *Nan-Shan* emerge as matters-of-fact out of the ordinariness:

> "Can't have . . . fighting . . . board ship", [296]

says Captain MacWhirr through the typhoon, and down into the 'tween-deck, into the human hurricane of fighting coolies, go Jukes and his men as a routine matter-of-fact course, to restore order and decency:

> "We have done it, sir," he gasped.
> "Thought you would," said Captain MacWhirr.
> "Did you?" murmured Jukes to himself.
> "Wind fell all at once," went on the Captain.
> Jukes burst out: "If you think it was an easy job—"
> But his captain, clinging to the rail, paid no attention.
> "According to the books the worst is not over yet". [311]

And the qualities which, in a triumph of discipline—a triumph of the spirit—have enabled a handful of ordinary men to impose sanity on a frantic mob are seen unquestionably to be those which took Captain MacWhirr, in contempt of 'Storm-strategy' [281], into the centre of the typhoon. Without any symbolic portentousness the Captain stands there the embodiment of a tradition. The crowning triumph of the spirit, in the guise of a matter-of-fact and practical sense of decency, is the redistribution—ship devastated, men dropping with fatigue—of the gathered-up and counted dollars among the assembled Chinese.

In *The Shadow Line*, also in common recognition one of Conrad's masterpieces (it is, I think, superior to *Heart of Darkness* and even to *Typhoon*), we have the same art. It has been acclaimed as a kind of prose *Ancient Mariner*, and it is certainly a supremely sinister and beautiful evocation of enchantment in tropic seas. But the art of the evocation is of the kind that has been described; it is not a matter of engendering 'atmosphere' adjectivally, by explicitly 'significant' vaguenesses, insistent unutterablenesses, or the thrilled tone of an expository commentator, but of presenting concretely a succession of particulars from the point of view of the master of the ship, who, though notably sensitive, is not a Marlow, but just a ship's master; an actor among the other actors, though burdened with responsibilities towards the crew, owners and ship. The distinctive art of a novelist, and the art upon which the success of the prose *Ancient Mariner* essentially depends, is apparent in the rendering of personality, its reactions and vibrations; the pervasive presence of the crew, delicately particularized, will turn out on analysis to account for the major part of the atmosphere. The young captain, entering the saloon for the first time and sitting in the captain's chair, finds he is looking into a mirror:

> Deep within the tarnished ormolu frame, in the hot half-light sifted through the awning, I saw my own face propped between my hands. And I stared back at myself with the perfect detachment of distance, rather with curiosity than with any other feeling, except of some sympathy for this latest representative of what for all intents and purposes was a dynasty; continuous not in blood, indeed, but in its experience, in its training, in its conception of duty, and in the blessed simplicity of its traditional point of view on life. . . .
>
> Suddenly I perceived that there was another man in the saloon, standing a little on one side and looking intently at me. The chief mate. His long, red moustache determined the character of his physiognomy, which struck me as pugnacious in (strange to say) a ghastly sort of way. [82]

The disobliging and disturbing oddity of the mate turns out to be due to the sinister vagaries and unseemly end of the late captain:

> That man had been in all essentials but his age just such another man as myself. Yet the end of his life was a complete act of treason, the betrayal of a tradition which seemd to me as imperative as any guide on earth could be. It appeared that even at sea a man could become the victim of evil spirits. I felt on my face the breath of unknown powers that shape our destinies. [89]

The sinister spell that holds the ship is characteristically felt in terms of contrast with the tradition and its spiritual values, these being embodied in the crew, a good one, who carry on staunchly against bad luck and disease. The visiting doctor himself is 'good' in the same way. The story ends, it will be noted, on the unexpected parting with the faithful Ransome, the exquisitely rendered seaman with a voice that is 'extremely pleasant to hear' [118] and a weak heart:

> "But, Ransome," I said, "I hate the idea of parting with you."
> "I must go," he broke in. "I have a right!" He gasped and a look of almost savage determination passed over his face. For an instant he was another being. And I saw under the worth and the comeliness of the man the humble reality of things. Life was a boon to him—this precarious, hard life—and he was thoroughly alarmed about himself.
> "Of course I shall pay you off if you wish it."
> 'I approached him with extended hand. His eyes, not looking at me, had a strained expression. He was like a man listening for a warning call.
> "Won't you shake hands, Ransome?" I said gently. He exclaimed, flushed up dusky red, gave my hand a hard wrench— and next moment, left alone in the cabin, I listened to him going up the companion stairs cautiously, step by step, in mortal fear of starting into sudden anger our common enemy it was his hard fate to carry consciously within his faithful breast. [135–36]

These things are worth many times those descriptions of sunsets, exotic seas and the last plunge of flaming wrecks which offer themselves to the compilers of prose anthologies.

This is at any rate to confirm the accepted notion of Conrad to this extent: that his genius was a unique and happy union of seaman and writer. If he hadn't actually been himself a British seaman by vocation he couldn't have done the Merchant Service from the inside. The cosmopolitan of French culture and French literary initiation is there in the capacity for detachment that makes the intimate knowledge uniquely conscious and articulate. We are aware of the artist by vocation, the intellectual who doubles the seaman, only when we stop to take stock of the perfection of the rendering and the subtle finish of the art.

*   *   *

JOSEPH KOLUPKE

Elephants, Empires, and Blind Men: A Reading of the Figurative Language in Conrad's "Typhoon"†

Joseph Conrad's "Typhoon" presents a curious case: a story celebrated for its wealth, indeed its plethora, of figurative language, yet a story dominated by a hero who is explicitly anti-figurative in his conception of human communications:

> "It's the heat," said Jukes. "The weather's awful. It would make a saint swear. Even up here I feel exactly as if I had my head tied up in a woolen blanket."
> Captain MacWhirr looked up. "D'ye mean to say, Mr. Jukes, you ever had your head tied up in a woolen blanket? What was that for?"
> "It's a manner of speaking, sir," said Jukes, stolidly.
> "Some of you fellows do go on! What's that about saints swearing? I wish you wouldn't talk so wild. What sort of saint would that be that would swear? No more saint than yourself, I expect. And what's a blanket got to do with it—or the weather either. . . . The heat does not make me swear—does it? It's filthy bad temper. That's what it is. And what's the good of your talking like this?" [274]

It is, indeed, a story that seems to focus on the very nature of signs and human knowledge, a fact that may be obscured for readers by the comic tone in which this aspect of the work is conveyed. "Fancy having a ridiculous Noah's Ark elephant in the ensign of one's ship" [263–64], Jukes complains to the chief engineer, referring to the Siamese flag under which the ship is sailing. His more oblique protest to the Captain that the flag looks "queer" results in the comic spectacle of the literal-minded MacWhirr checking the International Signal Code-Book to verify its correctness. And indeed it is correct: a white elephant on a red field. And at this point, if we are reading carefully,

† From *Conradiana* 20.1 (Spring 1988): 71–83. Copyright © 1988 Texas Tech University Press. All rights reserved. Reprinted by permission of the publisher. Unless otherwise specified, page references are to this Norton Critical Edition.

we must pause. International Code-Book. White elephant. *White elephant?* But in English that means something else, something different! What sort of invitation is Conrad offering to his readers, or at any rate to those more inquisitive than the stolid MacWhirr? * * *

What did he imagine himself to be doing in "Typhoon"? * * *

> At its first appearance "Typhoon," the story, was classed by some critics as a deliberately intended storm-piece. Others picked out MacWhirr, in whom they perceived a definite symbolic intention. Neither was exclusively my intention. Both the typhoon and Captain MacWhirr presented themselves to me as the necessities of the deep conviction with which I approached the subject of the story. It was their opportunity; and it would be vain to discourse about what I made of it in a handful of pages, since the pages themselves are here, between the covers of this volume, to speak for themselves. [256]

Experienced readers of the prefaces will immediately recognize here a characteristic Conradian evasion, in which the dilemma of symbolic versus literal interpretation is cloaked in a dark phrase, "necessities of a deep conviction." Nor will they be overly surprised to learn that the reference to the symbol-hunting critics may well be as much a product of Conrad's imagination as the story itself: in the reviews we know of, at least, there is not a whisper of any symbolic reading whatever. What emerges most clearly from Conrad's preface is the sense that the story must *not* be taken merely as a realistic description of a storm. Indeed, there is something absurdly ironic in the tendency of early critics to do so. Later commentators have pointed out at length the extraordinary figurative richness of "Typhoon," even for a Conrad story.[1]

The question, then, lies in the significance of this wealth of figuration. It is easy to see, of course, how this aspect of the story would escape notice by readers predisposed to view Conrad as a more or less literal chronicler of the sea. Figurative expression, even elaborately fanciful figurative expression, has traditionally been taken for granted as a normal tool of descriptive prose. It is not ordinarily interpreted as evidence of symbolic intent unless, by one means or another, it calls attention to itself. Moreover, recent critical theory tends to confirm the traditional practice in the sense that it sees all language as radically figurative and hence cases such as that of "Typhoon" as merely representing a difference of degree rather than of kind. Nevertheless, it seems to me that we are justified in asking

---

1. Perhaps the most comprehensive such attempt is that by Lawrence S. Graver, "*Typhoon*: A Profusion of Similes," *College English*, 24.1 (October 1962): 62–64. For a powerful synthesis from a religious point of view, see Thomas J. Rice, "*Typhoon*: Conrad's Christmas Story," *Cithara*, 14.2 (1975): 19–35.

why the excess is there. Does it add up to anything in symbolic terms? Does it contain, as I have already hinted, a kind of meta-linguistics of its own? I would like to argue that the seemingly wild flight of figures does signify something, or at least very nearly signi-fies something, but that the story also contains a recognition of the limits of this signification, a recognition that tends to undermine any ultimate allegorical codification of its elements. Further, that it is no accident that Conrad has chosen the linguistically limited MacWhirr for his protagonist. * * *

Let us, then, examine the figurative elements to see if we can establish a consistent pattern of meaning. Careful readers are prob-ably aware, at least subliminally, of Conrad's tendency to describe the storm in terms of a mob or an unruly army. In a passage describ-ing the beginning of the most violent phase of the typhoon, for exam-ple, we are told: "The seas in the dark seemed to rush from all sides to keep her [the *Nan-Shan*] back where she might perish. There was hate in the way she was handled, and a ferocity in the blows that fell. She was like a living creature thrown to the rage of a mob" [289]. Nor is this an isolated example; in fact, references to the sea as an anar-chic mob are so frequent as to make quotation of them all impracti-cal here. Some of the more prominent:

> It was tumultuous and very loud—made up of the rush of the wind, the crashes of the sea, with that prolonged deep vibra-tion of the air, like the roll of an immense and remote drum beating the charge of the gale. [282]

> The *Nan-Shan* was being looted by the storm with a senseless, destructive fury . . . [286]

> The mutter of the winds drew near apace. In the forefront could be distinguished a drowsy waking plaint passing on, and far off the growth of a multiple clamour, marching and expand-ing. There was the throb as of many drums in a vicious rushing note, and like the chant of a tramping multitude. [316]

The last, we might note, is the final figurative characterization of the storm before MacWhirr's memorable understatement, "I wouldn't like to lose her" [316].

It is, I think important to note here that this imagery character-izes the ship's enemy not just as an unorganized mob (though the first example might suggest this), but as a kind of rapacious, revolu-tionary army, rag-tag and undisciplined, to be sure, but formidable nonetheless. In other words, these are not merely the images of natural anarchy, but of organized revolution. Were they merely iso-lated impressions of an angry sea, one might well write them off as unconscious expressions of Conrad's well-known distrust of revolu-tions and revolutionaries. As William R. M. Hussey has observed, however, the sea imagery is linked to the descriptions of the coolies between decks[2]—linked, one might add, in a subtle, naturalistic fashion in which the figurative language of the storm description becomes the literal denotation of the struggling coolies: "When the boatswain threw open the door it seemed that an eddy of the hurricane, stealing through the iron sides of the ship, had set all these bodies whirling like dust: there came to them a confused mutter, gusts of screams dying away, and the tramping of feet mingling with the blows of the sea" [308]. Indeed, the equation even penetrates the psychology of the characters: Jukes, the first mate, having subdued the coolies, feels "that in his mad struggle down there he had overcome the wind somehow" [309].

I would suggest from this evidence alone (and there are numerous other corroborating elements in the story) that a major aspect of the meaning of "Typhoon" is political; that in fact the *Nan-Shan* is a very familiar kind of literary symbol: the ship as ship-of-state, a political microcosm.

What is the topography, so to speak, of this microcosm? The ship and its crew, of course, represent the basic body politic: in this respect, the challenge to the leadership of MacWhirr, obliquely by Jukes, the first mate, and more directly by the unnamed second mate, is a confrontation of a traditional authoritarianism by, respectively, a more imaginative, "enlightened" ideological attitude, and by a sort of anarchic nihilism. The rest of the officers and crew presumably stand for the range of human types, with an odd specimen or two that invite speculation: the ape-like boatswain and the taciturn chief engineer, Solomon Rout, are especially interesting in this regard * * * . While one might argue as to the precise shade of political meaning to attribute to these characters, there can be little controversy over their general function in the scheme.

* * * Two other matters, however, offer some difficulty: the Chinese passengers (*pace*, Captain!) and the insignia of the ship itself. If the rapacious storm is the sign for the political problems facing the nation of the *Nan-Shan*, what do the coolies stand for (keeping in mind their symbolic identification with the storm)? There are, I think, two answers to this question. The more obvious is that the coolies are the symbolic link between the ship and the larger environment of sea and storm. In narrow terms, they are the colonial peoples under the direct rule of the leadership represented by MacWhirr and his officers. The other answer is that there is a dramatic advantage for Conrad in having actual human beings on board, because their presence enables him to show MacWhirr's literal as well as symbolic relationship to these subject

2. William R. M. Hussey, "'He was spared that annoyance,'" *Conradiana*, 3.2 (1971–72): 21.

peoples. Nevertheless, it is important to note that the equation of the literal to the figurative introduces dissonance, contradiction, and redundancy.

The fact that the ship is sailing under the Siamese flag is more difficult. Conrad goes to some trouble to point out that this is a considerable anomaly, as Juke's complaint makes clear. Jukes's reference to a "Noah's Ark elephant" appears to reinforce the microcosmic symbolism associated with ships of state (all of humanity in one boat). It seems nearly inevitable that Conrad here is also playing on the idiomatic meaning of the term "white elephant" in its basic sense of a useless but expensively maintained possession, his implication being that the duties of empire constitute, to use Kipling's more vulgar term, a white man's burden. Of course, the white elephant in this Noah's ark is the human cargo between decks, or more generally, the European responsibility for the economic and social well-being of the peoples under its control.

What of the action of the story? In symbolic terms, we see the political-cultural system represented by the Captain, the officers, and the crew, faced with a crisis, a rebellion of the multitudes against its order and authority. The chief symbol of this rebellion is, of course, the storm; secondarily, it is the destructive anarchy between decks as the coolies fight among themselves for the loose silver dollars, a literal survival-of-the-fittest struggle. The question posed by the story has to do with attitudes toward leadership: what sort of leader is likely to prevail under these circumstances? In this sense, Conrad has deliberately limited the options. Answered in the abstract, we should all say, "Why, a decent, enlightened, intelligent, *imaginative* leader, of course! Someone who sees the subtleties, the nuances, the far-reaching implications of a course of action. Someone not unlike Jukes, if we must pick among those on board the *Nan-Shan*." But we know that for Conrad such a man, if he exists at all, is the wrong man, the kind of man who, faced with a crisis, will be paralyzed into delay and inaction—a Lord Jim, whose typological cousin Jukes is. The choice, in fact, appears, in this instance, to be limited to two types:

> "For my part," Solomon was reported by his wife to have said once, "give me the dullest ass for a skipper before a rogue. There is a way to take a fool; but a rogue is smart and slippery." [268]

Of course, we needn't take the chief engineer's judgment of Mac-Whirr at face value, since a major thrust of the story is the vindication of MacWhirr's intellectual qualities in the light of actual experience. MacWhirr lacks imagination, but he is not, as events demonstrate, a mere fool. Or to put it another way, MacWhirr's devotion to the literal, the factual, and to duty, though undeniably a handicap under some circumstances, turns out to be the quality that saves the ship and brings justice to the passengers.

Not that MacWhirr is always and invariably the servant of the prescribed ways of doing things. This is made clear just before the onset of the typhoon, when he chooses to ignore not only Jukes's advice but that of his navigation book and the experience of his fellow captains in their counsel to take evasive maneuvers. His decision is in part a matter of rationalization (MacWhirr is overwhelmed by the complexity of the advice in the book), but primarily a matter of general principles and temperamental preference:

> "A gale is a gale, Mr. Jukes . . . and a full-powered steam-ship has got to face it. There's just so much dirty weather in the world, and the proper thing is to go through it with none of what old Captain Wilson of the *Melita* calls 'storm strategy.'" [280–81]

Now, as nautical practice this may seem more than a little obtuse, but if read as a political attitude it becomes comprehensible as a conventional (though, of course, debatable) strategy: meet trouble head-on, don't temporize, don't be unduly swayed by the feelings or short-term discomforts of those under your protection. That, in fact, appears to be the gist of MacWhirr's disregard of Jukes's concern for the comfort of the coolies; his open contempt for any consideration of them as "passengers" (i.e., persons) reveals the ugly, racist side of this outlook, but in the long run we see that the coolies are at least as well off under MacWhirr's regime as they would be under any other; though MacWhirr's attitudes may seem unfeeling, his basic adherence to principles of common sense and fairness works to the benefit of all in the end. (And he is, of course, correct in his rejection of Captain Wilson's storm strategy, as Jukes acknowledges in the grip of the crisis [315].)

Jukes's inadequacy (his name can mean, according to the *OED*, to lie at rest or asleep, or to dodge or hide from a blow), Conrad makes clear, is a matter of both temperament and age:

> Jukes remained indifferent, as if rendered irresponsible by the force of the hurricane, which made the very thought of action utterly vain. Besides, being very young, he had found the occupation of keeping his heart completely steeled against the worst so engrossing that he had come to feel an overpowering dislike towards any other form of activity whatever. He was not scared; he knew this because, firmly believing he would never see another sunrise, he remained calm in that belief. [291]

And later the Captain reproves him, though in a positive, friendly manner, for this negative feature of his personality:

> "You are always meeting trouble half way, Jukes," Captain Mac-
> Whirr remonstrated quaintly. "Though it's a fact that the second
> mate is no good. D'ye hear, Mr. Jukes? You would be left alone
> if. . . ." [315]

It is clear, of course, that MacWhirr's concern is less for Jukes personally than for the fate of the ship in the event that Jukes should
have to take command. And he is correct: Jukes in command would
be a disaster. Even after the storm is past, Jukes, who had been so
concerned for the comfort of the "passengers," now has no solution
to the problem they pose other than to keep them confined, to let
them fight it out for the money, and to turn them over to the authority of the local despots in Fu-Chou.

Jukes's heavy dependence upon the strength of MacWhirr is symbolized by his physical embrace of the Captain during the initial
onslaught of the storm. We are told that the unique feature of a
destructive wind, as opposed to other natural disasters, is to separate
men: "it isolates one from one's kind" [284]. Conrad may have had in
mind here Carlyle's dictum in the "Captains of Industry" chapter of
Past and Present, "Isolation is the sum-total of wretchedness to
man,"[3] where the context is explicitly political. In any case, Jukes,
washed about by a massive wave and thinking that "the whole China
sea had climbed on the bridge" (note the personification), by chance
finds MacWhirr:

> as soon as he commenced his wretched struggles he discovered
> that he had become somehow mixed up with a face, an oilskin
> coat, somebody's boots. He clawed ferociously all these things
> in turn, lost them, found them again, lost them once more, and
> finally was himself caught in the firm clasp of a pair of stout
> arms. He returned the embrace closely round a thick solid body.
> He had found his captain. [285]

The force of the last sentence, with the use of the possessive form of
the personal pronoun, is quite clearly to make a statement of great
psychological and symbolic importance: it is Jukes's confession of
faith, tantamount (for Jukes has been praying) to a religious
affirmation.

The manner in which Jukes finds the captain is also significant.
Jukes blindly *feels* his way to this discovery, an action that is repeated
by the boatswain when he arrives with the news of the struggle
between decks:

> then a hand gripped his [Jukes's] thigh. A lull had come, a men-
> acing lull of the wind, the holding of a stormy breath—and he

---

3. Thomas Carlyle, *Past and Present*, ed. Richard D. Altick (Boston: Houghton Mifflin,
1965), 271.

felt himself pawed all over. It was the boatswain. Jukes recognized these hands, so thick and enormous that they seemed to belong to some new species of man.

The boatswain had arrived on the bridge, crawling on all fours against the wind, and had found the chief mate's legs with the top of his head. Immediately he crouched and began to explore Jukes' person upwards with prudent, apologetic touches, as became an inferior. [290]

This substitution of touch for language suggests once more a figurative or symbolic attitude toward the discovery of reality. The fact that it occurs under the insignia of an elephant calls to mind the very old folktale of the blindmen and the elephant. This story, which exists in many versions, is summarized by the folklorist Stith Thompson as follows: "Four blind men feel an elephant's leg, tail, ear, and body, respectively, and conclude it is like a log, a rope, a fan, and something without beginning or end."[4] We do not, of course, have a literal reenactment of the story in "Typhoon" but the motif of the limitations of human perception and insight as a guide to the nature of reality is plainly relevant to Conrad's story. Opinions of MacWhirr's qualities vary considerably, and Jukes's overtly superior attitude is plainly contradicted in this key scene, where he discovers a new MacWhirr, the MacWhirr that is *his* captain, just as the boatswain shortly afterward discovers his superior in Jukes. (In the light of this scene, Jukes's final condescending judgment of MacWhirr as a "stupid man" represents a considerable weakness of character on his part—it is as if the truth he discovered in the moment of crisis has been replaced by his former glib notions, a blindness more reprehensible in the light of his new stock of experience. We are left to conclude that he still does not know MacWhirr.)

The elephant flag and its reflection in the folktale parallel invite further speculation on the importance of this element to the story. We note first of all that if the flag serves the usual purpose of identifying the nationality of the ship, then the political entity represented cannot be British but must be seen as in some sense a protectorate or client state of the western power.[5] Thus MacWhirr's response to Jukes's complaint about the foreign flag is quite straightforward: it makes no difference "as long as *we* are on board" [321]. Second, this attitude accords with the idiomatic meaning of the phrase "white elephant," though of course the notion that the possessions of empire really were, in economic terms, white elephants, is, to say the least,

4. Stith Thompson, *Motif-Index of Folk Literature*, 6 vols. (Bloomington: Indiana University Press, 1955–58), 4:144.
5. Siam, modern Thailand, was at the time of the story an essentially independent nation, though dependent on France and England for various trade arrangements.

debatable. Third, if we follow out the logic of the folktale motif, then MacWhirr is in some sense identified with the elephant, which is in turn identified with reality itself* * *. At this point the possibility of a consistent allegorical rendering begins to recede, though it is very hard to resist the notion that this is part of the essential meaning of "Typhoon": MacWhirr's final importance seems to depend in large part upon one's perspective, and one's perspective seems to depend upon one's response to the figurative language.

The natural question in all of this concerns the foundation of the political attitude embodied in the story. Why did Conrad invest such a heavy significance in the half-comic figure of MacWhirr? There is, of course, the possibility of satire, though this, it seems to me, is insupportable in light of the ending of the story, of which more presently. As we know from the biographical facts, Conrad distrusted progressive notions of government, but he was no blind defender of hereditary privilege or racial superiority as such. His political convictions grew out of his pessimism over the prospects of human survival and represented not a preference for past glories but an instinctive caution concerning the human capacity for reasoned choice and action. For a man of his imaginative constitution, the various prevailing optimisms of the time offered doubtful comfort. There was, of course, the "optimism" represented by social Darwinism and a variety of other evolutionary philosophies that placed humanity at the forefront of a parade of progress, but "Typhoon," it seems to me, is a considered rejection of this sort of "applied science." The struggle of the coolies in the hold is an implicit indictment of the notion that human competition conduces inevitably to social betterment: the description of the coolies as "streaming like a mass of rolling stones down a bank," a mass which then metamorphoses into "the hatchway ladder . . . loaded with coolies swarming on it like bees on a branch" [298], is as nice a reduction of the human social struggle into geo-biological terms as one could wish—a thoroughly horrible one that we are gratified to see ended by the firm but humane order of MacWhirr and the action of his first mate.

The message is very simple: if humanity is facing ultimate extinction as a matter of the natural course of things, then, by God, as MacWhirr might say, we can at least face it in an orderly manner. That, of course, is the point of Conrad's reporting MacWhirr's reaction to Jukes's actions:

> He was glad the trouble in the 'tween deck had been discovered in time. If the ship had to go after all, then, at least, she wouldn't be going to the bottom with a lot of people in her fighting teeth and claw. That would have been odious. And in that feeling there was a humane intention and a vague sense of the fitness of things. [313]

And, of course, it is also the point of setting the story on Christmas Eve. In this utterly un-Western, un-Christmaslike setting, one genuinely Christian value is affirmed—that men shall not be allowed to struggle like beasts for survival, but that they shall face their fate with charitable regard for one another as human beings. We are speaking here of the ethics of Christianity rather than its metaphysics, an ethics so basically humanistic that one might reasonably question the use of the adjective Christian at all, but obviously Conrad wished us to couple the significance of Christian ethics with the saving of the ship through MacWhirr's agency.

The use of animal imagery in the description of the other crew members confirms this implicit rejection of reductive "scientific" notions of human social relationships. The boatswain, for example, despite his simian appearance, is a man committed first of all to his duty as an officer; he risks the wrath of the crew and the ravages of the storm to bring his report of the coolies' struggle to the attention of MacWhirr. And the second mate, whom the boatswain discovers "lying low, like a malignant little animal under a hedge" [296], is not thereby excused his perfidious behavior in this crisis. Men may resemble lower animals in all sorts of ways, but, at least from Mac-Whirr's (and, one assumes, Conrad's) point of view, they remain men nonetheless. Thus the boatswain is no O'Neillian Hairy Ape, but a humorous figure who, worried what his "old woman" might think of his predicament [297], brings us a measure of comic relief in the midst of the grim struggle—an affirmation of his distinctively human place in Conrad's universe.

The presence of Solomon Rout, the Chief Engineer, raises some important questions, largely because of his name. One might speculate that Conrad was engaging in a kind of metonymic playfulness here, because, plainly, what "Solomon says" is little more than lively gossip. It is MacWhirr who, by his equitable distribution of the silver dollars, displays the only genuinely Solomonic wisdom. Rout's practical function in the story is, of course, to keep the engines running. Here again there is a homology between the engines, whose articulation is likened to a human skeleton, and the crew: "Sometimes all those powerful and unerring movements would slow down simultaneously, as if they had been the functions of a living organism, stricken suddenly by the blight of languor . . ." [302]. Which, of course, parallels the periodic spells of inactivity and hopelessness that afflict the crew and Jukes. Any doubt of the importance of this characterization of the engines as living things is dispelled by the further description of the engine room as an organic whole: "The whole loftiness of the place, booming hollow to the great voice of the wind, swayed at the top like a tree, would go over bodily, as if borne down this way and that by the tremendous blasts" [303].

These organic filaments connecting the various elements of the story serve to reinforce the sense that one is witnessing here not just a story of unfortunate sailors, but a socio-political model of humanity as a whole. In delineating these features, however, I do not mean to imply that the story represents in any way a considered political treatise or recommended model of government of any kind. Conrad's whole outlook would argue against such a simplistic reading. Rather, I would argue, the story is a dramatization of certain kinds of political and social realities that confront humanity in times of crisis. The importance of attitudes and behavior that counteract the natural drift to nihilism and anarchy is, it seems to me, the essential theme of "Typhoon." The need for action is seldom if ever presented under ideal conditions, a fact that makes necessary a practical and affirmative stance not overly attentive to ultimate questions. Hence MacWhirr's simple pragmatism on the matter of the flag puts aside ideological questions in favor of the need for immediate and responsible action.

Let us turn now to some special aspects of the handling of figures of speech in this remarkable story, a handling that, as noted earlier, has been the occasion of much commentary. In addition to the profusion of figures, we also see, in a number of places, some peculiar play of imagery, as in the crucial scene of physical embrace between Jukes, MacWhirr, and the boatswain, where MacWhirr's voice above the wind is said to be "like a ship battling against the waves of an ocean" [289]. The same odd sort of reversal occurs in the description of the discovery of the coolies' plight, where the boatswain confuses the sounds of their struggle with those of the storm:

> He was vaguely amazed at the plainness with which down there he could hear the gale raging. Its howls and shrieks seemed to take on, in the emptiness of the bunker, something of the human character, of human rage and pain—being not vast but infinitely poignant. . . . Was it the wind? Must be. It made down there a row like the shouting of a big lot of crazed men. [294]

This passage is still another example of the identification, noted earlier, of the coolies with the storm. But in its employment of an apparently figurative vehicle that is in fact a literal description of what the boatswain hears, it seems to go beyond symbolic function to a kind of commentary on the nature of figurative language itself. The profusion of similes tells us that language plays a vital role in the interpretation of any experience, be it confronting a storm at sea or conceptualizing the concrete nature of leadership in human society. It seems to say that it is in the nature of literary language to expand in this fashion, symbol and symbolized, vehicle and tenor, mirroring one another, even exchanging places as we scrutinize them ever more carefully.

MacWhirr, in his antifigurative attitudes, comes very close to representing the very antithesis of the usual protagonist of the novel. As J. Hillis Miller has noted, what customarily undoes the heroes of many novels is their tendency to see their lives as a series of repetitions. Trapped in this fashion by linguistic conceptualizings of events that are in fact unique, they misinterpret their experience and assure their own failure.[6] In this respect, MacWhirr may represent at least a partial exception; his distrust of language predisposes him to a more direct kind of action, best represented by his ignoring of the navigation book's advice on storm strategy. In political terms, this amounts to a rejection of history as a guide to political action in favor of an abstract set of principles, those articulated by MacWhirr in his lecture to Jukes.

Nevertheless, as Conrad clearly tells us, though there may be times when a radical skepticism toward language can be salutary, there is, ultimately, no escape from it. For human beings, language and reality are inseparably joined, may in fact be the same thing. This is stated plainly in a key passage that Conrad would later echo in another context:

> And again he heard that voice, forced and ringing feebly, but with a penetrating effect of quietness in the enormous discord of noises, as if sent out from some remote spot of peace beyond the black wastes of the gale; again he heard a man's voice—the frail and indomitable sound that can be made to carry an infinity of thought, resolution and purpose, that shall be pronouncing confident words on the last day, when heavens fall and justice is done—again he heard it, and it was crying to him, as if from very, very far—"All right." [287]

This sense of the story's special emphasis on the human voice (complementary, one might say, to the despairing existential voice of the dying Kurtz in *Heart of Darkness*. "A voice! a voice! It rang deep to the very last" [*HD* 67]) is confirmed by a remarkable similarity to another passage in Conrad's writings. Because of William Faulkner's paraphrase in his Nobel Prize acceptance speech, we are all familiar with Conrad's observations on the end of humanity in his 1905 essay on Henry James:

> When the last aqueduct shall have crumbled to pieces, the last airship fallen to the ground, the last blade of grass have died

---

6. J. Hillis Miller, *Fiction and Repetition: Seven English Novels* (Cambridge, MA: Harvard University Press, 1982), 13.

upon a dying earth, man, indomitable by his training in resistance to misery and pain, shall set this undiminished light of
his eyes against the feeble glow of the sun. The artistic faculty, of which each of us has a minute grain, may find its voice
in some individual of that last group, gifted with a power of
expression and courageous enough to interpret the ultimate
experience of mankind in terms of his temperament, in terms
of art. . . . He is so much of a voice that, for him, silence is
like death; and the postulate was, that there is a group alive,
clustered on his threshold to watch the last flicker of light on
a black sky, to hear the last word uttered in the stilled work-
shop of the earth. It is safe to affirm that, if anybody, it will be
the imaginative man who would be moved to speak on the eve
of that day without tomorrow—whether in austere exhortation or in a phrase of sardonic comment, who can guess? [*NLL*
16–17]

The voice in the first passage is, of course, MacWhirr's. A casual
glance would suggest that there is a fundamental divergence between
the two passages in that the one from "Typhoon" appears to refer to
the Last Judgment. Looking more closely, however, we see that the
phrase "justice is done" can be read to mean either "justice is rendered" or "justice is ended, abolished." The fact that "the heavens
fall" suggests that the second meaning is the one intended for the
careful reader—this is the end of everything human, which, practically speaking, is everything—this is, one is tempted to say, the final
aporia.

The sense of both passages is unmistakably clear. Language may
be an illusion, the ultimate illusion or source of illusion, but it is also
the only thing that sustains human existence. MacWhirr's naive
belief in the literal allows action, including political action, from
simplicity of motive; his arbitrary arrest of language allows for a kind
of arrest of reality. And this is shown to be necessary: the confident
voice, the artist or weaver of linguistic illusion in every person, even
the inarticulate MacWhirr, is always already calling us back to life,
to hope, no matter what the circumstances, even including the ultimate catastrophe poetically evoked in these passages. In Conrad's
universe there is no transcendental signifier, only a human voice saying, against all evidence to the contrary, "All right."

For this reason, if no other, I would argue that "Typhoon" increasingly must be seen as a story in no way inferior to Conrad's other
major works. * * * Its radical questioning of the whole range of human
action, from the physical to the linguistic, must place it among the
indispensable works we must know if we are to understand the
nature of Joseph Conrad's achievement.

JAKOB LOTHE

From "Typhoon": Thematically Productive Narrative Simplicity[†]

Critical evaluations of 'Typhoon'***can be grouped in two broad categories. First, there are the critics who underestimate the work—either implicitly by limiting their critical attention to other Conrad texts,[1] or through their explicit commentary on this particular narrative. In her early study of Conrad, M. C. Bradbrook considers 'Typhoon' a mere 'yarn'.[2] Douglas Hewitt finds that in this novella 'Nothing happens which . . . seems "to throw a kind of light" on moral or spiritual issues'.[3] Guerard admires the text for its characterization and evocative prose, but claims that its 'preoccupations are nearly all on the surface . . . Thus *Typhoon* requires no elaborate interpreting'.[4] F. R. Leavis too regards 'Typhoon' as a minor work, yet interestingly goes on to single it out as a text in which Conrad's 'strength may be found in its purest form'.[5]

This appreciation, one of the first influential ones of the novella, establishes a point of transition to the more favourably-disposed view characteristic of the second group of critics. John H. Wills emphasizes what he calls the 'organic nature' of 'Typhoon', and gives an unconvincing formulation of the story's thematic concern: 'the ironic victory of modern society over a world it cannot understand'.[6] It must be added, however, that Wills also observes that 'Typhoon' 'is a complex of centrifugal, as well as centripetal forces' and that 'Theme is dissolved also in the structural and stylistic elements of the novel.'[7] Combined with the useful analysis of Jukes's function and

---

[†] From *Conrad's Narrative Method*. Oxford: Clarendon Press, 1989, 102–116. Reprinted by permission of Oxford University Press. Page references are to this Norton Critical Edition.

1. Jacque Berthoud, for instance, does not discuss 'Typhoon' (*Joseph Conrad: The Major Phase*. Cambridge: Cambridge University Press, 1978), and neither does C. B. Cox; see his *Joseph Conrad: The Modern Imagination* (London: Dent, 1974). A recent exception to the general tendency to dismiss the novella is Francis A. Hubbard, *Theories of Action in Conrad* (Ann Arbor, MI: UMI Research Press, 1984). Hubbard provides an extended discussion of 'Typhoon' in his first chapter, 1–22, before proceeding to 'Heart of Darkness' and *The Secret Agent*.
2. M. C. Bradbrook, *Joseph Conrad: Poland's English Genius* (Cambridge: Cambridge University Press, 1941), 32.
3. Douglas Hewitt, *Conrad: A Reassessment* (Cambridge: Bowes & Bowes, 1952), 113.
4. Albert J. Guerard, *Conrad the Novelist* (Cambridge, MA: Harvard University Press, 1958), 294.
5. F. R. Leavis, *The Great Tradition: George Eliot, Henry James, Joseph Conrad* [544, this edition: Editor].
6. John H. Wills, "Conrad's *Typhoon*: A Triumph of Organic Art," *North Dakota Quarterly* 30 (1962): 62.
7. Wills, 69.

personal growth, such observations firmly place Wills in the second group, to which critics such as Paul S. Bruss and H. M. Daleski also belong.[8] Following Wills, they are both eager to revaluate the thematic importance of Jukes in the story. Of the two essays Daleski's is clearly the more perceptive. Arguing that 'Typhoon' brings to an end the phase in which Conrad was 'primarily concerned with the question of physical self-possession',[9] he makes the important, if rather obvious, point that 'the crew of the *Nan-Shan*, like that of the *Patna*, are subjected to a sudden and unexpected test',[1] and that this particular test (the typhoon) not only reveals what is hidden in a character, 'but also exposes hitherto unrealized dimensions of the universe in which he lives'.[2]

✳   ✳   ✳

Such a provisional grouping into two main critical attitudes to 'Typhoon' makes it easier to delineate the critical focus of this chapter. My critical concern remains narrative method, which in this particular case essentially means investigation of the diversified functions of the text's authorial narrative. Even if it is true that 'Typhoon' is a relatively straightforward Conrad text, still its omniscient authorial narrator performs functions more varied and sophisticated than critics have generally noted. Once the particular form of narrative sophistication which 'Typhoon' evinces is appreciated, then the thematic generalizations briefly summarized above are revealed as simplifying or even misleading. The main critical focus is on Jukes and MacWhirr. As much of the novella's central action revolves around these two characters, and as they receive about the same amount of authorial commentary, they gradually emerge as the two main characters of the text. There is a particular thematics attached to each of them; a larger and more ambiguous thematics arises from the striking contrast between these two personalities, and from their divergent relations to the crew and to the typhoon with which the ship is confronted.

I

At 100 pages, 'Typhoon' consists of six chapters of approximately equal length. Several critics have noted that Chapters 1 and 6 frame the novella's central action, which is basically constituted by the ordeal of the typhoon which Captain MacWhirr decides to meet head-on. Wills finds that the first and last chapters are 'primarily

8. Paul S. Bruss, "*Typhoon*: The Initiation of Jukes," *Conradiana* 5.2 (1973): 46–55; H. M. Daleski, *Joseph Conrad: The Way to Dispossession* (London: Faber & Faber, 1977), 104–12.
9. Daleski, 105.
1. Daleski, 105.
2. Daleski, 107.

comprised of observations by others upon the character and actions of MacWhirr'.[3] In actual fact, however, these two chapters are really quite different. It is thematically significant that the novella ends with Jukes's letter, with no authorial comment appended to it. In the first chapter, in contrast, authorial prominence is striking and must be considered in some detail, but first the narrative pattern of the beginning of the text must be discussed.

The first paragraph immediately establishes an authorial narrative situation where attention is focused on MacWhirr in order to give an introductory characterization of him. The authorial omniscience becomes apparent at once: MacWhirr's 'physiognomy . . . was the exact counterpart of his mind: it presented no marked characteristics of firmness or stupidity; it had no pronounced characteristics whatever; it was simply ordinary, irresponsive, and unruffled' [259]. This early example of authorial omniscience prefigures what is gradually established as one of the chief narrative characteristics of the novella. Its effects are, as we shall see, varied. A general point to be made already, however, is that in this text there is a crucial linkage between authorial omniscience and narrative authority: there is no narrative instance or device in the text which gives the reader reason to doubt the veracity of the authorial narrator's pronouncements. To emphasize the narrator's authority—which is strengthened, but not directly verified, by his omniscience—is not to suggest that all his statements and views should be accepted uncritically. Still, most of the narrative and thematic effects of 'Typhoon' are intimately related to the authority of the authorial narrative.[4]

In this connection I shall draw attention to a sentence in the third paragraph whose significance critics appear to have overlooked. Having given a preliminary characterization of MacWhirr as non-imaginative, reliable and factual, the narrator adds: 'Yet the uninteresting lives of men so entirely given to the actuality of the bare existence have their mysterious side' [260]. If narrative authority is taken, as it must be, to include the view of MacWhirr and his likes voiced here, then the sentence not only gives a partial explanation of the authorial narrator's sincere interest in the type of character and work ethic MacWhirr represents, but also advises the reader not to take too dismissive a view of MacWhirr (and certainly not, as both Wills and Bruss tend to do, to ridicule him by way of contrasting him with Jukes). At this early stage of the narrative these implications may seem strained, but we shall see that they are borne out

---

3. Wills, 69.
4. Thus, it is debatable if Bruss is justified in talking, for example, about MacWhirr's 'verbal absurdity'—a phrase the authorial narrator would never have employed. See Bruss, 46.

by its development, and also that the generalization is effectively related to the novella's curiously modified use of irony.

More immediately, however, it introduces an analeptic narrative movement outlining MacWhirr's background. The function of this analepsis is essentially twofold. First, it incorporates the first of the several letters which throughout the novella serve as an important, though somewhat mechanical, variant on the authorial narrative. The length and thematic significance of the letters, which in a relatively unsophisticated manner provide personal perspectives on the events related by the authorial narrator, vary greatly. The first one belongs, with the next two following suit, among the shortest: 'We had very fine weather on our passage out' [260]. In addition to the narrative variation it provides, the letter represents, with the following description of the parents' reaction to it, an early example of humour in 'Typhoon'. Secondly, the analepsis establishes a contrast which is to be substantiated later on in the narrative, that between life ashore and aboard the *Nan-Shan*. This contrast serves as a structural basis for two of the novella's thematic concerns, the problems of human communication and loneliness.

The analepsis is followed by a strikingly economical 'reach':[5] 'All these events had taken place many years before the morning when, in the chart-room of the steamer *Nan-Shan*, he stood confronted by the fall of a barometer he had no reason to distrust' [261]. This transition to the novella's main narrative focus introduces a distinct element of suspense, which is simply but effectively generated by the warning the fall of the barometer gives. Generally, the narrative function of suspense is less intricate here than in 'The Secret Sharer'. One reason for this relative simplicity is suggested by the early authorial characterization of MacWhirr and made almost excessively explicit in the authorial commentary following the quotation; already at this early stage of the narrative it seems doubtful whether even a violent storm can bring about any profound change in the main character. Suspense thus becomes externalized; it is focused principally on what will happen to the ship, only secondarily on the possibility of some profound alteration in the character of MacWhirr. However, with the introduction of Jukes, the contrastive character to MacWhirr, the function of suspense is nuanced and extended.

In the remaining part of Chapter 1 information is provided on the *Nan-Shan*, her chief engineer Solomon Rout, and her first mate Jukes. The quarrel over the change of flag (from British to Siamese)

---

5. 'Reach' corresponds to Genette's term *'portée'*, which indicates the temporal distance or extension of the anachronic variation in a narrative, whether into the past or into the future. The concept is thus closely related to both analepsis and prolepsis. See Gérard Genette, *Narrative Discourse*, trans. Jane E. Lewin (Oxford: Basil Blackwell, 1980), 48.

is exceptionally well rendered. Even if MacWhirr's inability to under-stand Jukes's consternation seems to reveal an almost incredible naïvety, the captain's attitude is still quite consistent with the initial authorial characterization of him. Furthermore, the scene gives Conrad the opportunity to exploit the humorous aspects of the tale. The comedy of the failure of the ship's two senior officers to under-stand each other also accentuates the problem of communication. Thus suspense is increased: we wonder whether the two men can work together if the ship is exposed to danger, as the falling barometer indi-cates she will be. As the narrative progresses the challenge of the typhoon leads to a diversification of the problem of communication.

Of the two letters which bring Chapter 1 to its conclusion, Jukes's is by far the more interesting, particularly if related to the authorial commentary that accompanies it. Sharing with a friend his impres-sion of MacWhirr, Jukes considers his captain 'jolly innocent' [269] and elaborates upon his dullness and queerness. His description sub-stantiates rather than contradicts the earlier authorial characteriza-tions. The phrase 'He doesn't do anything actually foolish' [269], for instance, is consonant with the authorial 'his mind . . . presented no marked characteristics of firmness or stupidity' [259]. Once Jukes's letter is given (in full, presumably), the authorial narrator proceeds to comment to it:

> Thus wrote Mr. Jukes to his chum in the Western ocean trade, out of the fullness of his heart and the liveliness of his fancy.
>   He had expressed his honest opinion. It was not worth while trying to impress a man of that sort . . . He was not alone in his opinion. [270]

This is somewhat clumsy and qualitatively uneven writing for the mature Conrad, but it tells much about the way in which the autho-rial commentary functions in this text. Although Jukes may appear closer to the authorial narrator than the other characters are, yet the narrator takes care to distance himself from him. Then the awk-wardly explicit 'He had expressed his honest opinion' is followed by a passage of narrated monologue, which again serves as starting-point for authorial reflections. What is interesting about the narrated monologue applied to Jukes here ('It was not worth while trying to impress a man of that sort') is that it seems to indicate authorial distance from Jukes, and to subject his views to irony by imitating them. Authorial attitude to Jukes is curiously suspended at this stage of the narrative; and the narrator's evaluation of MacWhirr is similarly indeterminate.

Starting from Jukes's 'opinion', the authorial reflections of the final paragraph of Chapter 1 explicity confirm that in spite of his wide and varied experience MacWhirr has never been put to the test. The authorial narrator does not himself use the word 'test', but the implication of the pointedly direct commentary is clear enough:

> Captain MacWhirr had sailed over the surface of the oceans as some men go skimming over the years of existence to sink gently into a placid grave, ignorant of life to the last, without ever having been made to see all it may contain of perfidy, of violence, and of terror. There are on sea and land such men thus fortunate—or thus disdained by destiny or by the sea. [270]

The reader's sense of suspense is obviously reinforced here, and extended from a mere outward indication (falling barometer) of a major challenge approaching the story's main character. Equally if not more intriguing is the suspense related to the tension which is established between the authorial narrator's description of Mac-Whirr's ignorance of life and his inarticulateness. Building on the first chapter alone we cannot, for instance, know whether MacWhirr will experience the challenge *as* a test; and although this may be a minor difficulty, it is clearly one which is related to Conrad's use of authorial narrative.

The most notable achievement of Chapter 2 is to establish a gradually strengthened impression of looming threat, the ominously approaching typhoon. The manner in which this effect is obtained is similar to that already observed in Chapter 1. There is, however, one important addition to the text's narrative method, constituted by two atmospheric authorial descriptions of the *Nan-Shan* as she draws nearer and nearer to the storm. The narrative technique of these descriptions must be considered in some detail.

> (*a*) At its setting the sun had a diminished diameter and an expiring brown, rayless glow, as if millions of centuries elapsing since the morning had brought it near its end. A dense bank of cloud became visible to the northward; it had a sinister dark olive tint, and lay low and motionless upon the sea, resembling a solid obstacle in the path of the ship. She went floundering towards it like an exhausted creature driven to its death. The coppery twilight retired slowly, and the darkness brought out overhead a swarm of unsteady, big stars, that, as if blown upon, flickered exceedingly and seemed to hang very near the earth. At eight o'clock Jukes went into the chart-room to write up the ship's log. [274–75]

> (*b*) The far-off blackness ahead of the ship was like another night seen through the starry night of the earth—the starless night of the immensities beyond the created universe, revealed

in its appalling stillness through a low fissure in the glittering
sphere of which the earth is the kernel. [277]

Passage (*a*) is striking for its efflorescence of similes. The sun looks
smaller and has 'an expiring . . . glow', 'as if millions of centuries
elapsing since the morning had brought it near its end'; there is a
bank of cloud 'resembling a solid obstacle in the path of the ship',
which she approaches 'like an exhausted creature driven to its death',
while the stars 'as if blown upon, flickered exceedingly and seemed
to hang very near the earth'. The most obvious function of the imagery employed here is to intensify the reader's sense of imminent
drama and danger. In this capacity it functions effectively as an integral part of the novella's narrative method, whose sophistication is
thus enhanced. To start with the simplest simile, the strictly factual
second one prefigures the dispute MacWhirr and Jukes later have as
to whether the ship should turn eastward or continue north towards
the 'solid obstacle'. The way in which this matter-of-fact simile is
interposed between the others increases the proximity of all of them
to the story of the *Nan-Shan*. Suggesting a return to this story, the
second simile delimits the implications of the first, which would
otherwise have seemed more contrived. As they now stand, modified not only by the second simile but also by the narrative preceding and following them, the first and third similes significantly
widen the thematic scope of the novella by giving it a more universal or cosmic dimension of ominous finality. In a sense it is surprising that such a range of problems can be suggested in what is for
Conrad a rather simple narrative, but at the same time it is precisely
the simplicity of the setting which assures that this can be done
without too great a loss of credibility.

The third simile is also remarkable. As the final 'its death' echoes
and extends 'its end' of the first, the cosmic or universal dimension
of the ship's confrontation with the typhoon is brought closer to the
narrative itself. Furthermore, the sense of seriousness and danger
is intensified both through the suggested link between the first and
third similes and through the content of the third one. Then the final
simile of passage (*a*) suggests increased authorial affinity with Jukes's
frame of mind. It becomes noticeable in the verb *seem* and in the
description of the 'big stars', which are also watched by Jukes [275].
Although this authorial slanting into Jukes's perspective illustrates
a problematic element in the novella's narrative method, it serves
here as a transition from the descriptive interlude back to the narrative proper.

The imagery of passage (*b*) extends the thematic implications of
the first. Its apocalyptic aspects are related to an existential anguish
provoked by the threat of the typhoon. When a Conrad character is

put to the test, the problematic and enigmatic nature of his or her life experience tends to be accentuated. In spite of the authorial basis for the description, there is here, too, an authorial slanting into Jukes's thought. We have just been told that 'Jukes reflected rapidly . . .' [277]; and although these reflections concern the second mate and not the image itself, his following comment is—for all its casualness—clearly related to the content of the imagery. It would seem, then, that the imagery identified and briefly discussed here not only intensifies and extends the thematic range of 'Typhoon', but also modulates the authorial narrative by suggesting a strangely intimate relationship with Jukes.

This authorial alliance with the first mate increases his narrative and thematic importance. MacWhirr's position is correspondingly weakened; there is a shift of emphasis and Jukes appears to emerge as the central character of the novella. This change seems confirmed by the curious theory MacWhirr advances about facing the storm: 'A gale is a gale, Mr. Jukes . . . and a full-powered steam-ship has got to face it' [280]. This 'gale philosophy', to which the captain returns in Chapter 5 [316], is consistent with the earlier authorial descriptions of MacWhirr, but becomes more problematic now, since the narrator has meanwhile established greater intimacy with Jukes, who is a more reflective and well contrasted character.

In the next chapter, however, the authorial descriptions are better balanced in that while attitudinal distance between the narrator and Jukes increases somewhat, that between the narrator and MacWhirr appears to decrease. The way in which this decrease is achieved is quite sophisticated, and has at least two constitutive aspects. First, the characterization of MacWhirr changes. If, as Daleski finds, his 'decision to meet the typhoon head-on must be adjudged rash to the point of irresponsibility',[6] his actions and perseverance during the ordeal are portrayed as consistent with the decision, for which he is ready to take full responsibility. This responsibility, which includes both the ship and her crew, is coupled with the 'deep concern' [292] he has for the Chinamen when informed by the boatswain that they have started fighting amongst themselves. The concern indicated here, which is verified by Jukes's realization that he will have to obey orders and attempt to solve the problem presented by the Chinamen, is an important addition to the previous authorial characterization of MacWhirr. It is surprising when compared with his earlier outburst: 'The Chinamen! . . . Never heard a lot of coolies spoken of as passengers before. Passengers, indeed!' [278]; and it goes quite far to present MacWhirr as a

6. Daleski, 107.

character whose qualities should be appreciated on the basis of his actions and attitudes rather than his words. As the narrator says, 'To be silent was natural to him, dark or shine' [284].

Secondly, a certain rehabilitation of MacWhirr's textual position is also suggested indirectly through an increased attitudinal distance between the authorial narrator and Jukes. This distance, which is related to a difference in age and experience, is particularly notice-able at the beginning of Chapter 4:

> Jukes, however, had no wide experience of men or storms. He conceived himself to be calm—inexorably calm; but as a mat-ter of fact he was daunted; not abjectly, but only so far as a decent man may, without becoming loathsome to himself . . . Jukes was benumbed much more than he supposed. [291]

A related constituent aspect of this increased distance is that if Jukes has previously appeared to be more concerned about the Chinamen than his captain, the tables are now turned: 'Jukes remained indiffer-ent, as if rendered irresponsible by the force of the hurricane, which made the very thought of action utterly vain' [291]. At this stage, MacWhirr seems to be passing the test better than Jukes.

In Chapter 3, then, the descriptions and generalizations are more independently authorial than previously. Authorial slanting into Jukes's perspective is less apparent; and this has the effect of quali-fying the earlier impression of Jukes's privileged proximity to the narrator. The sixth paragraph of Chapter 3, for instance, is obvi-ously connected with Jukes in the sense that he is mentioned both before and after it, but it is authorially authoritative in a manner more reminiscent of Chapter 1 than Chapter 2; and this tendency is further strengthened in the succeeding paragraph:

> It was something formidable and swift, like the sudden smash-ing of a vial of wrath. It seemed to explode all round the ship with an overpowering concussion and a rush of great waters, as if an immense dam had been blown up to windward. In an instant the men lost touch of each other. This is the disintegrat-ing power of a great wind: it isolates one from one's kind. [284]

As one of the most poignant generalizations in 'Typhoon', the final sentence of this quotation pinpoints both the narrative and the the-matic significance of the authorial narrator's commentary. Not just descriptive but also interpretative, the generalization emphasizes the utmost seriousness of the human drama enforced on the crew by the typhoon. Furthermore, it forms the constitutive basis for a central paradox which is established and affirmed through the new sense of companionship and mutual respect MacWhirr and Jukes come to experience. If the wind creates barriers among the men that appear insurmountable, leaving each isolated with his fear, it also unites them as they realize that it is only through common effort they can possibly survive. As MacWhirr is inevitably the pivot of this effort, his position at the centre of the narrative is strengthened.

If part of the funtion of the authorial narrative here is to suggest a more balanced attitude to, and evaluation of, the two main characters, it also provides a convincing description of the violent storm. The most important additional narrative variant is the use of personification:

1. 'The *Nan-Shan* was being looted by the storm with a senseless, destructive fury . . .' [286]
2. 'They held hard. An outburst of unchained fury, a vicious rush of the wind absolutely steadied the ship . . .' [288]
3. 'There was hate in the way she was handled, and a ferocity in the blows that fell. She was like a living creature thrown to the rage of a mob: hustled terribly, struck at, borne up, flung down, leaped upon.' [289]
4. '[MacWhirr] had to fight the gale for admittance . . .' [299]

When we consider these descriptive, authorial passages we must conclude that the personifications help to intensify the typhoon as human challenge and drama. It is one of the potential effects or implications of personification as a rhetorical device that authorial description becomes invested with an unidentified personal element, which is here related to the crew and to the personified *Nan-Shan*. * * * It serves essentially to strengthen the sense of alliance between crew and ship. Both are engaged in a desperate attempt to survive the fight against what the personifications—through a blend of authorial and unidentified personal perspective—portray as a mighty adversary endowed with human feelings of fury and hatred.

The culmination of the storm comes at the beginning of Chapter 5:

> Nobody—not even Captain MacWhirr, who alone on deck had caught sight of a white line of foam coming on at such a height that he couldn't believe his eyes—nobody was to know the steepness of that sea and the awful depth of the hollow the hurricane had scooped out behind the running wall of water . . . She dipped into the hollow straight down, as if going over the edge of the world. [306]

Part of the climactic effect of this passage obviously depends on the intensification of earlier descriptions, but it is also generated through the authorial insistence on a more exhaustive knowledge of the storm's dimensions than that possessed by any character, including MacWhirr. The imagery in the following paragraph confirms this stress on authorial knowledge. The information provided about the characters is marked by pointed authorial distance, even from Jukes, whose face is 'like the face of a blind man' [306].

The middle section of Chapter 5 is taken up with Jukes's attempt to settle the fight (which has aspects of the absurd, the grotesque, and the comic) which the Chinamen have started over some 'scattered dollars' [309]. It could be argued that these passages, where the authorial narrative is related first to the perspective of the boatswain and then to that of Jukes, are shallow and monotonous compared to the intensity of the storm description. The section does, however, widen the thematic scope of the novella. The fact that the human drama enacted below the deck of the *Nan-Shan* is only superficially described seems at first to increase the affinity of the perspective of the authorial narrative and that of the crew. When the row has been settled the sailors are relieved: 'There is something horribly repugnant in the idea of being drowned under a deck' [310]. Yet in this narrative statement the distance between the authorial narrator and the crew again seems to increase. Far from suggesting a derogatory view of the Chinamen, the authorial implication is that their suffering during the ordeal of the typhoon must have been even greater than that of that crew. An implied sympathy on the part of the authorial narrator with the crew does not necessarily mean that he vouches for all the views they pronounce. Moreover, an interesting shift of perspective is observable in the middle of the account of the Chinamen's struggle: 'The coming of the white devils was a terror. Had they come to kill?' [309]. This narrated monologue provides an illuminating narrative variation: although the perspective does not remain with the Chinamen for long, the shift is clearly sufficient to indicate that the authorial narrator's knowledge and sympathy exceed that of the crew.

The last part of the chapter returns to MacWhirr in order to modify and extend authorial characterization of him. This applies in particular to the passage which starts with the 'incredibly low' [312] reading of the barometer and then proceeds to give the most extended characterization of MacWhirr in the whole novella. Three aspects of the narrative method of this passage may be noted. First, omniscient authorial observation of MacWhirr's reading of the barometer is accompanied by effectively interposed narrated monologue: 'Perhaps something had gone wrong with the thing!' [312]. Combined with the authorial observations, the instances of narrated (and quoted) monologue are then employed as a basis for explanatory reflection: 'These instantaneous thoughts were yet in their essence heavy and slow, partaking of the nature of the man' [313]. The persuasiveness of this

comment is enhanced by its textual position: it summarizes a quality of MacWhirr's character that the action has already dramatized.

More importantly, the passage makes the reader more aware of
MacWhirr's loneliness and sense of responsibility. This is achieved
through a narrative combination of the authorial reflections with
the third constitutive aspect of the passage, the sparing but effective use of quoted monologue. If we introduce a potentially useful
distinction here between quoted thought and quoted monologue,
then we can immediately note two instances of the former, '"It'll be
terrific," he pronounced, mentally' and '"I wouldn't have believed it,"
he thought' [313]. But then these two examples of quoted thought
are followed by two of quoted monologue that are not only distinctly
less cumbersome, but also indicative of a substantial maturing of
MacWhirr's character: '"I shouldn't like to lose her," he said half
aloud' and 'Then a murmur arose. "She may come out of it yet"' [314].
The banality of the first remark is striking; yet paradoxically so is its
narrative effect because of MacWhirr's deeply ingrained taciturnity
and because the remark comes just after an authorial statement on
MacWhirr: 'By this awful pause the storm penetrated the defences of
the man and unsealed his lips. He spoke out in the solitude and the
pitch darkness of the cabin, as if addressing another being awakened
within his breast' [314]. Combined with this powerful authorial statement, the remark not only improves the reader's understanding of
MacWhirr's sense of responsibility and sincere concern for his ship,
but also suggests increased self-knowledge on his part.

In addition to these modulations of quoted thought and monologue, the most noteworthy aspect of narrative method here is the
omission of a second gale description. Conrad seems to have concluded, and no doubt rightly, that it would not have added substantially to the very effective first one but would instead, unavoidably,
have seemed anticlimactic. As the second half of the ship's struggle
with the typhoon is passed over in silence, the reader is left to
infer—on the basis of the description of the first part of the ordeal—
what it must have been like. Temporally, the ellipsis must be located
in the reach between the fifth and the last chapter, which takes the
form of an epilogue to the story proper.

In this final chapter, the description of Mrs MacWhirr and her
daughter ironically reaffirms and strengthens the contrast between
two extremely different ways of life that has already been indicated
earlier in the novella. Irony mingles with humour and resignation; the
two parties are in every sense—not just geographically—miles apart.
Underneath the humorous presentation of the failure to communicate, however, a more serious implication can be detected in this particular approach to what is a major problem in Conrad: his fiction

contains few examples of genuine and mutually rewarding human communication. Considering these relatively rare instances, it does not take long to notice that they are often related to a sense of communication through shared work—not least in the well-defined and limited setting of a ship. It is important, therefore, that MacWhirr and Jukes, who embody very different personal characteristics, are helped, if not forced, to co-operate and communicate during such a major crisis as that of the typhoon.

Once the crisis is over, however, former positions are all too easily resumed—as Jukes's seems to be in the letter of his which effectively concludes the narrative of 'Typhoon'. The use of letters—both Mac-Whirr's and Jukes's—is an important variation in a narrative that at times appears somewhat monotonously authorial. Providing both information and personal views, Jukes's concluding letter reduces authorial focus on MacWhirr, but not without stressing his crucial role and impressive professional skills. The very last sentence again contains an example of curiously modified irony. There is an obvious authorial distance from Jukes here, for MacWhirr's performance during the storm clearly does not correspond with Jukes's adjective 'stupid' [324]; and yet there is some truth in the characterization, as the simplicity of MacWhirr's 'face it' philosophy may appear to verge on stupidity. It seems just right that Jukes's letter concludes the novella; Conrad wisely refrained from adding an authorial comment to it.

Francis Hubbard argues that MacWhirr is fundamentally changed by his experience of the typhoon.[7] If my interpretation of the novella suggests agreement with Hubbard's thesis, it has also—through the critical focus on the modulations of the text's authorial narrative, and the thematic effects of these modulations—shown in greater detail than Hubbard does how MacWhirr's change is indicated and dramatized. Although the narrative method of 'Typhoon' is distinctly less sophisticated than that of, say, 'Heart of Darkness', the various constituent aspects of this method—the authorial omniscience, the shifts of perspective, the use of letters, imagery, and personification—present several thematic concerns that are both persuasive and suggestive. In the narrative discourse of 'Typhoon', thematic simplicity promotes thematic suggestiveness: as the elemental drama of the *Nan-Shan* struggling with the typhoon accentuates human qualities such as courage, perseverance, and the ability to face up to loneliness, so it is precisely this lone, test-like fight on the part of MacWhirr that constitutes the basis for his change and makes him emerge as a wiser and more imaginative human being at the end of the novella.

7. Hubbard, 11–12.

NELS PEARSON

"Whirr" Is King: International Capital and the Paradox of Consciousness in *Typhoon*[†]

Much critical reception of *Typhoon*—which pits a ship's captain incapable of figurative speech against a "great wind" that "disintegrate[s]" the linguistic economy of his vessel into "shreds and fragments of forlorn shouting"—has focused on its remarkable, and perhaps prototypically modernist, insight into the twentieth century's theoretical interest in the contingency of the linguistic sign [282–83]. As Sooyoung Chon notes, the story can be read as "a parable about narrative art" wherein Captain MacWhirr's effort to "maintain [. . .] civilized order on a ship in crisis" reflects how the "imaginative language [of] good narrative" struggles to maintain "contact with the humane and the real" that lie at the elusive heart of what a narrative endeavors to convey (34–5). Similarly, for Joseph Kolupke, *Typhoon* is about "a ship of state, a political microcosm" whose pragmatic leader arrests "the natural drift to nihilism and anarchy" in a "universe [in which] there is no transcendental signifier" (74, 81, 83 [552, 559, 561, this edition: Editor]).

Such interpretations are well deserved, for the text clearly demonstrates Conrad's effort to draw an extended parallel between the great storm encountered by the unimaginative and "literal" Captain MacWhirr and a turbulent, knowledge-threatening slippage between utterance and understanding [272]. After all, at the height of the storm at sea, the fierce swirling winds fragment the dialogue (at times stealing speech at the moment of utterance), leave the crew "whirled a great distance" from their central voice of authority, and cause the first mate to consider "the very thought of action utterly vain" [291] until he hears the "resisting voice" [289] of the "literal MacWhirr" [272] as if it were "sent out from some remote spot of peace beyond . . . the gale" [287]. As Ted Billy rightly observes, *Typhoon* thus "dramatize[s] the limitations of all human systems based on verbal constructs" (100). But I would argue that the tale's foresight into the twenty-first century's theoretical concerns lies in its more complex struggle to comprehend how material, and specifically global-economic, forces are intimately bound together with those of language and consciousness. Indeed, what Conrad's own inconclusive wrangling with semiotic ambiguity in *Typhoon* ultimately discloses is a

† Reprinted from *Conradiana* 39.1 (Spring 2007): 29–37. Copyright © 2007 Texas Tech University Press. All rights reserved. Reprinted by permission of the publisher. The author has slightly revised the article for this Norton Critical Edition. Page references are to this edition.

deep-rooted link between crises of meaning or knowledge, loosely understood as modern, and the volatile interdependence of interests that drive the incipient global phase of imperial capitalism.

Although it has not been analyzed in due detail, the ship upon which the plot of *Typhoon* unfolds, a newly built steamer named the *Nan Shan*, stands out among the sailing vessels in Conrad's *oeuvre* as a forceful symbol of industry and capitalist modernity.[1] The partial but frequent glimpses Conrad gives us of the vessel unfailingly depict it as a composite of "excellen[t] instrument[s]" [261], a marvel of the division of labor that "embod[ies] all the latest improvements" [262]. During the storm, the brief close-ups of the ship's machinery are accelerated into a visual effect that anticipates the use of montage in Sergei Eisenstein's *Potemkin*, Fritz Lang's *Metropolis*, and Wyndham Lewis's Vorticism:

> Gleams, like pale long flames, trembled upon the polish of metal; from the flooring below the enormous crank-heads emerged in their turns with a flash of brass and steel—going over; while the connecting rods, big-jointed, like skeleton limbs, seemed to thrust them down and pull them up again with an irresistible precision [while] discs of metal rubbed smoothly against each other, slow and gentle, in a commingling of shadows and gleams. [302]

Arguably, the "irresistible precision" of the machine even anticipates a futurist paradox, as industry here churns against *and* with nature, in turns suppressing and harnessing what Conrad, in his "Author's Note" to the novella, terms the "elemental fury" of the typhoon [256].

Intervening with these tensions of modernity, however, is the equally relevant fact that the *Nan Shan* is a product, a material symbol, of empire and its burgeoning economies. In fact, what Edward Said notes of *Heart of Darkness*, that it "emphasiz[es] the fact that during the 1890s the business of empire, once an adventurous and often individualistic enterprise, had become the empire of business," is even more true of *Typhoon* (23). For it is not just "all Europe," but a broad range of Eastern and Western interests that have, quite literally, "contributed to the making of" the *Nan Shan* (*HD* 49). The construction of the ship is funded by a British company based in uncolonized, trade-opened Siam, a location that allows the ship owners to sail under the Union Jack or, when they "judged it expedient," the Siamese ensign [263]. The ship was built by laborers in

---

1. As Susan Jones has argued, Maurice Grieffenhagen's illustrations for the serial publication of "Typhoon" in *Pall Mall Magazine* are decidedly modernist in their "representation of discontinuity or dislocation" (201). See Jones's "Conrad on the Borderlands of Modernism: Maurice Geiffenhagen, Dorothy Richardson, and the Case of *Typhoon*," 195–211.

Dumbarton, Scotland, in the region near Glasgow where, as Eric Hobsbawm reminds us, "the erosion and collapse of [Scottish] native institutions, [. . .] educational system and religion" was the price for becoming an industrial engine of empire (308–9). The ship is, in turn, hired from Siam-based Sigg and Son by the Chinese Bun-Hin Company, who use the ship to transport coolie laborers. These workers, returning from their "few years of work in various tropical colonies," represent the ease with which imperialist economic interests substituted coolie trafficking for the recently illegalized slave trade [261]. The ship's captain, meanwhile, is a transient native of Belfast who has effectively abandoned his family business; and his crew is a compelling, untraceable mixture of middle and lower classes from the British Isles. Thus, the vessel is indeed a "political microcosm," as Kolupke argues, but it is considerably more complex than a "ship of state" (74 [552, this edition: Editor]). Considering both the mode of producing the composite machine that is the *Nan Shan* and the *Nan Shan*'s function within economic production, we should recognize that the ship embodies a much more slippery entity: the deterritorializing drive for commodity and surplus. Here I would agree with Stephen Ross, who, although surprisingly without any mention of *Typhoon*, argues in his recent study *Conrad and Empire* that "the Conrad of the major phase almost obsessively presents us with a [. . .] depiction of imperialism as global-capitalist (rather than nation-statist) [. . . .] and international casts of characters whose hybridity often renders any accurate genealogy impossible" (14).

It is thus difficult to accept Chon's contention that the "moral kernel of the story"—the message that "story-telling is the only way of transcending [. . .] the realm of actual events and action"— renders the "colonial dominations represented" in the tale "not all that significant" (25–6, 32). For, given the incipient globalization that Conrad's narrative makes a very literal effort to contain, the opposite may be true, namely, that the material content of *Typhoon* helps to *determine* the reflexivity of its inquiry into meaning. Such is certainly the case with one of *Typhoon*'s most compelling aesthetic maneuvers, its use of the whirling storm both as a symbol of epistemological ambiguity *and* as the vehicle in metaphoric descriptions of the "tempestuous tumult" of Chinese laborers fighting over the coins that are strewn about their cargo hold during the storm [308].[2] Although critical attention has been paid to the "subtle, naturalistic fashion in which the figurative language of the storm description becomes the literal denotation of the struggling coolies," interpretations tend to engage this manifold trope only on its

2. In the "Author's Note," Conrad underscores this equation by describing the storm as an "elemental fury" and the coolies as the "human element below [the] deck" [255].

NELS PEARSON

more abstract valences (Kolupke 73 [551, this edition: Editor]). As Kolupke puts it,

> the identification [. . .] of the coolies with the storm [. . . is] a kind of commentary on the nature of figurative language itself. [. . .] It seems to say that it is in the nature of literary language to expand in this fashion, symbol and symbolized, vehicle and tenor, mirroring one another, even exchanging places as we scrutinize them ever more carefully. [. . .] For human beings, language and reality are inseparably joined, may in fact be the same thing. (81–2 [559–60, this edition: Editor])

Kolupke further posits that what *Typhoon* dramatizes, via MacWhirr's pragmatic responses to such semiotic entanglements, is the human effort to "counteract," by way of insistence upon purposeful utterance, "the natural drift to nihilism and anarchy" that "confront[s] humanity in times of crisis" (81 [559, this edition: Editor]). However, such a reading abstracts, and thus naturalizes, the specific function of the ship and the manner in which that function is restored by the operation of language as an objective medium of exchange. The narrator explains that "Old Mr. Sigg liked a man of few words;" hence, the ship's owner is comfortable with MacWhirr at the helm [263]. But because a chief function of the Sigg and Son ships is the trafficking of coolie labor, then the challenge of a literal mind stabilizing epistemological disjuncture aboard these ships is, by the same logic, analogous to the challenge of legitimizing or narratologically comprehending a slave trade—of operating within a system that requires not just labor, but some kind of *trade* in that labor, to support its expansion of a surplus-based economy.

Paradoxically, one way to resolve this challenge is to depict the reality of an en masse commodification of humans with more consumable figures of speech: to represent them as teeming masses of primitive humanity, as racial others of a unified consciousness, or as the very embodiment of one's own sense of incomprehension. We might argue, then, that what is really offered in the text's equation of the storm with epistemological uncertainty *and* with the "confused uproar" of coolie laborers, whose "gusts of screams [. . .] mingle with the blows of the sea" as they fight over their storm-strewn coins, is evidence of Conrad's own struggle to ascertain a metaphysical understanding of the human consequences of imperial and capitalist ideology [308]. Indeed, among Conrad's conscious concerns in *Typhoon* is to wrestle not just with the slippage between language and meaning, but with the unconscious "forces" that drive human beings and the systems of value and exchange, including language, which they create. It seems to want, like Captain MacWhirr, "to penetrate the hidden intention [of the storm] and guess the aim and

force of the thrust" [282]. But just as MacWhirr is himself a component of this force—a sharer in the inscrutable intention of an expansive capitalist endeavor that presumably motivates the individual and
the collective at once—so too is *any* mode of consciousness or expression aboard the *Nan Shan* already complicit with the mobile gale of
ambiguity that it presumes to contest.

Indeed, the "force" welling up to "disintegrate" the false objectiv-
ity of meaning and systematic functionality aboard the *Nan Shan*—
the "senseless, destructive fury" of the storm that "loot[s]" the
ship—is, or is inseparable from, the attempt to sustain, through
networked interests and well-divided labor, a permutation of slave
trading [286]. As the boatswain descends to the cargo hold at the
height of the storm, the volatile rhetorical core of this attempt—
the representation of coolies as both literal victims and figurative
symbols of the natural forces that drive the global market—is
confronted:

> down there he could hear the gale raging. Its howls and shrieks
> seemed to take on [. . .] something of the human character,
> of human rage and pain—being not vast but infinitely poi-
> gnant. [. . .] He pulled back the bolt: the heavy iron plate
> turned on its hinges; and it was as though he had opened the
> door to the sounds of the tempest. A gust of hoarse yelling met
> him: [. . .] a tumult of strangled, throaty shrieks that pro-
> duced an effect of desperate confusion. [294–95]

Perhaps part of the intent here, as in *Heart of Darkness*, is to employ
the racial other in the critique of the imperial project—as a primitive
test-case for the human propensity to develop or accept the various
signs (such as money, words, or manners) that mediate desire and
fulfillment and therefore develop (naturally?) into expansive market
economies. Like the cannibalistic Congo natives in Marlow's recollection, *Typhoon*'s "Chinamen" are sometimes perceived as showing
what Marlow calls "restraint," and at others basic desire, which in
turn reflects the philosophical inquiry into the forces of nature that
the story puts in conflict (*HD* 41). But if so, then what is also evident is that in *Typhoon*, as in *Heart of Darkness*, the system of imperialism that Conrad exposes also proves to "ha[ve] the power of a
system representing as well as speaking for everything within its
dominion," as is especially evident in the appropriation not simply
of the consciousness, but the incomprehensibility, of the other
(Said 24). In the case of *Typhoon*, the result is that the human figures who represent exploitation by the system also represent the
"incomprehensible" or "confus[ing]" forces of nature that somehow
drive it, and this paradox is in turn internalized or interpreted to
stand for a modern crisis of meaning [310, 295].

Much like the theme of the novel, its ambiguous centerpiece Captain MacWhirr, whom Conrad envisioned as "a leading motive [to] harmonize all these violent noises, and [. . .] put all that elemental fury in its place," is also an inseparable component of the contingent forces of global imperialism that he presumes to navigate [256]. Prior to the storm, Conrad's narrator makes a crucial allusion that connects the unconscious "motives" of MacWhirr to the theistic force that, in Adam Smith's formulation, propels the division of labor: for MacWhirr to have "run away to sea [. . .] at the age of fifteen," says the narrator, "was enough [. . .] to give you the idea of an immense, potent, invisible hand thrust into the antheap of the earth [. . .] and setting the unconscious faces of the multitude towards inconceivable goals" [260]. As the storm hits, both above and below deck, Smith's conundrum of nature and consciousness morphs into its Marxist opposite, concerning altruistic species-being: fearing that a "Mischievous hand" would be at work if the ship went down while the coolies fought over money, MacWhirr contemplates "the nature of man," and the "heart, which [. . .] even before life itself—aspires to peace" [291]. Herein he makes his decision to "face" both the human storm below deck, by equally dividing the money, and the typhoon itself [315–16].

Unfortunately, it is not possible to determine the degree of unmediated consciousness that motivates the captain against ambiguity and greed, or to evaluate objectively his actions as protests against modernity and imperialism, for MacWhirr, whose name can literally mean "son or offspring of a spinning motion," is indeed only derivative of the very crisis he navigates. Whether or not MacWhirr's act of distributing wealth among the warring coolies is understood as species-being altruism ("hope to have done the fair thing") or as a perfectly task-oriented adherence to his role in a division of labor ("for the sake of all concerned"), the act nonetheless serves to sustain the burgeoning economic system of which the ship, crew, and human cargo are a part [319, 322]. After all, this is a system that, exactly like MacWhirr, "is unable to grasp what is due to the difference of latitudes" [259].

From the standpoint of Marx's writings on capitalism and imperialism, it is worth noting that what the "unimaginative" MacWhirr most closely corresponds to is the "division of mental and material labor" in *The German Ideology*. Marx asserts that the perpetuation of ideology requires the distinct but complementary roles of the "thinkers [or] active, conceptive ideologists" and the more task-oriented bourgeoisie who "have less time to make up illusions and ideas about themselves," and whose "passive and receptive" relationship to a reigning ideology helps to sustain it (173). The former, we might say, are in the business of figurative language, while the latter expound the virtues of the literal, but as long as the material field of reference for word usage remains the same, then the difference in modalities of expression matters little. At best, then, MacWhirr's heroic indifference to any signification beyond the material is a mere simulacrum of the ultimate indifference of global-capitalist imperialism to any of the cultural, moral, or philosophical principles that, especially in Conrad's era, presumably functioned as the centers of nation-state ideologies. Conrad in fact seems to anticipate, or verify, much more recent developments in the critique of the global permutation of capitalist ideology, such as the definition of Empire as a "postmodern [. . .] global economy" offered by Michael Hardt and Antonio Negri:

> In contrast to imperialism, Empire establishes no territorial center of power and does not rely on fixed boundaries or barriers. It is a *decentered* and *deterritorializing* apparatus of rule that progressively incorporates the entire global realm within its open, expanding frontiers. Empire manages hybrid identities, flexible hierarchies, and plural exchanges through modulating networks of command. The distinct national colors of the imperialist map of the world have merged and blended in the imperial global rainbow. (xii–xiii)

Typhoon's Captain MacWhirr cannot be an opponent of this apparatus, because he is an uncanny personification *of* it. Two important defenses for this belief lie in his complicity in the primitive symbolism attached to the coolies, as explained above, and his resistance to the metaphysical symbolism of the Siamese flag, as discussed below.

According to Eberhard Griem, MacWhirr's comical lack of concern for what the Siamese flag represents politically (for he is only concerned that the flag matches the picture in his Signal Code book) "express[es] the view that what really counts in the responsible command of the ship are the people in command, rather than the abstract authority indicated by the flag" (27). James Hansford, on a similar but more theoretical note, points to MacWhirr's insistence on the formal correctness of the Siamese ensign as evidence of the captain's laudable "emphasis on the reality of experience, not upon the signifying system under which it provisionally functions" (149). I propose, however, that the "arbitrary nature of the signifying system" is the "authority" in command of the ship, and that the arbitrary nature of representation does not obscure, but rather *determines*, the "reality of experience" aboard the *Nan Shan* (Hansford 149). MacWhirr's stance against figurative expression matters little, that is to say, because the ensign, like its British counterpart, is *already* an arbitrary signifier, functioning as mere disguise within the hegemony of capital interests. MacWhirr's presumed triumph of presence against a gale of indeterminacy—of "mere holding on to existence within the excessive tumult"—may be no more than a confirmation of the unfathomable resilience of market forces, which adjust to moral paradoxes and linguistic turbulence as easily as the Siggs can raise or lower the more "expedient" national flag [291, 263]. To be sure, the contending forces that would appear, on one level, to be pitted against one another throughout *Typhoon* can also be seen, upon more thorough analysis, to derive from the same pervasive, expansive, and motive-disregarding force of the increasingly global economies of Empire. Whether or not closure or certainty are achieved by the multiple letters that the crew members write, attempting to explain or comprehend MacWhirr's actions at sea, the system embodied by the voyage rolls on, equally inscrutable. Hence the subtlety of Mrs. MacWhirr's response to the triumphantly unimaginative letter her husband had written from the eye of the storm:

> "He's well," continued Mrs. MacWhirr languidly. "At least I think so. He never says." She had a little laugh. The [daughter's] face expressed a wandering indifference, and Mrs. MacWhirr surveyed her with fond pride. "Go and get your hat," she said after a while. "I am going out to do some shopping. There is a sale at Linom's." [319]

Works Cited

Billy, Ted. *A Wilderness of Words: Closure and Disclosure in Conrad's Short Fiction.* Lubbock: Texas Tech University Press, 1997.

Chon, Sooyoung. "'Typhoon': Silver Dollars and Stars." *Conradiana* 22 (1990): 25–43.

Griem, Eberhard. "Rhetoric and Reality in Conrad's Typhoon.'" *Conradiana* 24 (1992): 21–32.

Hansford, James. "Money, Language, and the Body in 'Typhoon.'" *Conradiana* 26 (1994): 135–55.

Hardt, Michael, and Antonio Negri. *Empire.* Cambridge, MA: Harvard University Press, 2001.

Hobsbawm, E. J. *Industry and Empire.* New York: Penguin, 1978.

Jones, Susan. "Conrad on the Borderlands of Modernism: Maurice Greiffenhagen, Dorothy Richardson, and the Case of *Typhoon.*" *Conrad in the Twenty-First Century: Contemporary Approaches and Perspectives.* Eds. Carola M. Kaplan et al. New York: Routledge, 2005. 195–211.

Kolupke, Joseph. "Elephants, Empires, and Blind Men: A Reading of the Figurative Language in Conrad's Typhoon.'" *Conradiana* 20 (1988): 71–85.

Marx, Karl, and Friedrich Engels. "The German Ideology" (Part 1). *The Marx-Engels Reader.* 2nd ed. Ed. Robert C. Tucker. New York: Norton, 1978. 146–200.

Ross, Stephen. *Conrad and Empire.* Columbia: University of Missouri Press, 2004.

Said, Edward. *Culture and Imperialism.* New York: Vintage, 1993.

Joseph Conrad: A Chronology

1857	December 3	Joseph Conrad is born as Józef Teodor Konrad Korzeniowski in Berdyczów in Ukraine to Apollo Korzeniowski and Ewelina Bobrowska Korzeniowska
1862	May	Apollo Korzeniowski and his wife exiled to a remote region of Russia; Conrad accompanies them
1865	April	Ewa Korzeniowska dies of tuberculosis
1868		Korzeniowski allowed to return to Poland
1869	February	Korzeniowski and Conrad move to Cracow
	May	Korzeniowski dies of tuberculosis
1874		Conrad moves to Marseille to study to be a sailor
1875		Apprentices on the *Mont-Blanc*
1876–77		Apprentices on the *Saint-Antoine*
1878		Attempts suicide and later joins the *Mavis* and travels to England for the first time. Joins the crew of the *Skimmer of the Sea*
1878–80		Sails aboard the *Duke of Sutherland* and the *Europa*
1880	June	Passes examination for second mate
1880–81		Sails as third mate on the *Loch Etive*
1881–84		Sails as second mate in the *Palestine*, the *Riversdale*, and the *Narcissus*
1884	December	Passes examination for first mate
1885–86		Sails as second mate on the *Tilkhurst*
1886		Possibly submits "The Black Mate" to *Tit-Bits* competition; becomes a British subject and passes an examination for master and receives Certificate of Competency

1886–87		Sails as second mate on the *Falconhurst*
1887–88		Sails as first mate on the *Highland Forest*, and the *Vidar*
1888–89		Becomes captain of the *Otago*
1889		Begins *Almayer's Folly*
1890		Sails to the Congo and second-in-command and temporarily captain of the *Roi des Belges*
1891–93		Sails as first mate on the *Torrens*
1893		Visits his uncle Tadeusz Bobrowski in Ukraine; later signs on as second mate of the *Adowa*
1894	January	Signs off *Adowa* when planned voyage does not materialize
1895	April	*Almayer's Folly* published
1896	March	*An Outcast of the Islands* published; later marries Jessie George
1897	December	*The Nigger of the "Narcissus"* published
1898		Meets Ford Madox (Hueffer) Ford and H. G. Wells
1899	February–April	"The Heart of Darkness" published in *Blackwood's Edinburgh Magazine*
1900	September	Accepts J. B. Pinker as literary agent
	October	*Lord Jim* published
1901	June	*The Inheritors* (with Ford) published
1902	September	*Typhoon* published in United States
	November	*Youth: A Narrative and Two Other Stories* published
1903	April	*Typhoon and Other Stories* published
	September	*Falk, Amy Foster, To-Morrow: Three Stores* published in United States
	October	*Romance* (with Ford) published
1904	October	*Nostromo* published
1905	June	*One Day More* staged in London
1906	October	*The Mirror of the Sea* published
1907	September	*The Secret Agent* published
1908	August	*A Set of Six* published
	October	*The Point of Honor* ("The Duel") published in United States
1911	October	*Under Western Eyes* published
1912	January	*Some Reminiscences* published (as *A Personal Record* in United States)

	October	*'Twixt Land and Sea* published
1914	January	*Chance* published
1915	January	*A Set of Six* published in United States
	February	*Within the Tides* published
	September	*Victory* published
1917	March	*The Shadow-Line* published
1919	August	*The Arrow of Gold* published
1920	June	*The Rescue* published
1921	January–April	Collected editions begin publication in England (Heinemann) and in United States (Doubleday)
	February	*Notes on Life and Letters* published
1922	November	*The Secret Agent* staged in London
1923	May–June	Visits United States at request of F. N. Doubleday
	December	*The Rover* published
1924	May	Declines knighthood
	August 3	Dies and is buried in Canterbury
	September	*The Nature of a Crime* (with Ford) published
	October	*The Shorter Tales of Joseph Conrad* published
1925	January	*Tales of Hearsay* published
	September	*Suspense* (unfinished) published
1926	March	*Last Essays* published
1928	June	*The Sisters* (unfinished) published

Selected Bibliography

• indicates items included or excerpted in this Norton Critical Edition

Bibliographies

Ehrsam, Theodore G. *A Bibliography of Joseph Conrad*. Metuchen, NJ: Scarecrow Press, 1969.
Knowles, Owen. *An Annotated Critical Bibliography of Joseph Conrad*. New York: St. Martin's Press, 1992.
Peters, John G. *Joseph Conrad's Critical Reception*. Cambridge: Cambridge University Press, 2013.
Teets, Bruce E. *Joseph Conrad: An Annotated Bibliography*. New York: Garland Publishing, 1990.
————, and Helmut E. Gerber. *Joseph Conrad: An Annotated Bibliography of Writings about Him*. De Kalb: Northern Illinois University Press, 1971.

Biographies

Baines, Jocelyn. *Joseph Conrad: A Critical Biography*. London: Weidenfeld & Nicolson, 1959.
Karl, Frederick R. *Joseph Conrad: The Three Lives, A Biography*. New York: Farrar, Straus, Giroux, 1979.
Meyer, Bernard C. *Joseph Conrad: A Psychoanalytic Biography*. Princeton: Princeton University Press, 1967.
Najder, Zdzisław. *Joseph Conrad: A Life*. Trans. Halina Carroll-Najder. Rochester, NY: Camden House, 2006.
Sherry, Norman. *Conrad's Eastern World*. Cambridge: Cambridge University Press, 1966.
————. *Conrad's Western World*. Cambridge: Cambridge University Press, 1971.
Stape, John. *The Several Lives of Joseph Conrad*. London: William Heinemann, 2007.
Watts, Cedric. *Joseph Conrad: A Literary Life*. New York: St. Martin's Press, 1989.

Correspondence

Conrad, Joseph. *The Collected Letters of Joseph Conrad, 1861–1897*. Ed. Frederick R. Karl and Laurence Davies, et al. 9 vols. Cambridge: Cambridge University Press, 1983–2007.

Introductions

Karl, Frederick R. *A Reader's Guide to Joseph Conrad*. Rev. ed. New York: Farrar, Straus & Giroux, 1969.

Peters, John G. *The Cambridge Introduction to Joseph Conrad*. Cambridge: Cambridge University Press, 2006.
Simmons, Allan H. *Joseph Conrad*. New York: Palgrave Macmillan, 2006.
Watts, Cedric. *A Preface to Conrad*. 2nd ed. London, Longman, 1993.

General Commentaries

Armstrong, Paul B. *The Challenge of Bewilderment: Understanding and Representation in James, Conrad, and Ford*. 1–25, 109–85. Ithaca: Cornell University Press, 1987.
Berthoud, Jacques. *Joseph Conrad: The Major Phase*. Cambridge: Cambridge University Press, 1978.
Bonney, William W. *Thorns & Arabesques: Contexts for Conrad's Fiction*. Baltimore: Johns Hopkins University Press, 1980.
Cox, C. B. *Joseph Conrad: The Modern Imagination*. London: J. M. Dent & Sons, 1974.
Crankshaw, Edward. *Joseph Conrad: Some Aspects of the Art of the Novel*. London: John Lane, 1936.
Daleski, H. M. *Joseph Conrad: The Way of Dispossession*. London: Faber & Faber, 1977.
Donovan, Stephen. *Joseph Conrad and Popular Culture*. New York: Palgrave Macmillan, 2005.
Erdinast-Vulcan, Daphna. *Joseph Conrad and the Modern Temper*. Oxford: Clarendon Press, 1991.
———. *The Strange Short Fiction of Joseph Conrad: Writing, Culture and Subjectivity*. Oxford: Oxford University Press, 1999.
Fleishman, Avrom. *Conrad's Politics: Community and Anarchy in the Fiction of Joseph Conrad*. Baltimore: Johns Hopkins University Press, 1967.
GoGwilt, Christopher. *The Invention of the West: Joseph Conrad and the Double-Mapping of Europe and Empire*. Stanford: Stanford University Press, 1995.
Gordan, John Dozier. *Joseph Conrad: The Making of a Novelist*. Cambridge: Harvard University Press, 1940.
Graver, Lawrence. *Conrad's Short Fiction*. Berkeley: University of California Press, 1969.
Greaney, Michael. *Conrad, Language, and Narrative*. Cambridge: Cambridge University Press, 2002.
Guerard, Albert J. *Conrad the Novelist*. Cambridge: Harvard University Press, 1958.
Hampson, Robert. *Joseph Conrad: Betrayal and Identity*. London: Macmillan Press, 1992.
Harpham, Geoffrey Galt. *One of Us: The Mastery of Joseph Conrad*. Chicago: University of Chicago Press, 1996.
Hawthorn, Jeremy. *Joseph Conrad: Language and Fictional Self-Consciousness*. London: Edward Arnold, 1979.
———. *Joseph Conrad: Narrative Technique and Ideological Commitment*. London: Edward Arnold, 1990.
Hay, Eloise Knapp. *The Political Novels of Joseph Conrad: A Critical Study*. Chicago: University of Chicago Press, 1963.
Hervouet, Yves. *The French Face of Joseph Conrad*. Cambridge: Cambridge University Press, 1990.
Hewitt, Douglas. *Conrad: A Reassessment*. Cambridge: Bowes & Bowes Publishers, 1952.
Jameson, Fredric. *The Political Unconscious: Narrative as a Socially Symbolic Act*. 206–280. Ithaca: Cornell University Press, 1981.
Jones, Susan. *Conrad and Women*. Oxford: Clarendon Press, 1999.

Leavis, F. R. *The Great Tradition: George Eliot, Henry James, Joseph Conrad.* 17–23, 173–226. New York: George W. Stewart, 1948.

Lothe, Jakob. *Conrad's Narrative Method.* Oxford: Clarendon Press, 1989.

Mallios, Peter Lancelot. *Our Conrad: Constituting American Modernity.* Stanford: Stanford University Press, 2010.

Miller, J. Hillis. *Poets of Reality: Six Twentieth-Century Writers.* 13–67. Cambridge: Harvard University Press, 1965.

Morf, Gustav. *The Polish Heritage of Joseph Conrad.* London: Sampson Low, Marston & Co., 1930.

Moser, Thomas C. *Joseph Conrad: Achievement and Decline.* Cambridge: Harvard University Press, 1957.

Nadelhaft, Ruth L. *Joseph Conrad.* Atlantic Highlands, NJ: Humanities Press International, 1991.

Parry, Benita. *Conrad and Imperialism: Ideological Boundaries and Visionary Frontiers.* London: Macmillan Press, 1983.

Peters, John G. *Conrad and Impressionism.* Cambridge: Cambridge University Press, 2001.

Roberts, Andrew Michael. *Conrad and Masculinity.* New York: St. Martin's Press, 2000.

Ross, Stephen. *Conrad and Empire.* Columbia: University of Missouri Press, 2004.

Said, Edward W. *Joseph Conrad and the Fiction of Autobiography.* Cambridge: Harvard University Press, 1966.

Schneider, Lissa. *Conrad's Narratives of Difference: Not Exactly Tales for Boys.* New York: Routledge, 2003.

Schwarz, Daniel R. *Conrad: "Almayer's Folly" to "Under Western Eyes."* Ithaca: Cornell University Press, 1980.

———. *Conrad: The Later Fiction.* London: Macmillan Press, 1982.

Thorburn, David. *Conrad's Romanticism.* New Haven: Yale University Press, 1974.

Watt, Ian. *Conrad in the Nineteenth Century.* Berkeley: University of California Press, 1979.

Watts, Cedric T. *The Deceptive Text: An Introduction to Covert Plots.* Brighton: Harvester Press, 1984.

White, Andrea. *Joseph Conrad and the Adventure Tradition: Constructing and Deconstructing the Imperial Subject.* Cambridge: Cambridge University Press, 1993.

Wollaeger, Mark A. *Joseph Conrad and the Fictions of Skepticism.* Stanford: Stanford University Press, 1990.

• Zabel, Morton Dauwen. *Craft and Character: Texts, Method, and Vocation in Modern Fiction.* New York: Viking Press, 1957.

Commentary on The Secret Sharer

Benson, Carl. "Conrad's Two Stories of Initiation." *PMLA* 69.1 (March 1954): 46–56.

[Berthoud, Jacques]. "Introduction." In *'Twixt Land and Sea* by Joseph Conrad. Ed. Jacques Berthoud, Laura L. Davis, and S. W. Reid. xxxi–xlii, lxii–lxxi, xcix–cxvi. Cambridge: Cambridge University Press, 2008.

Bidwell, Paul. "Leggatt and the Promised Land: A New Reading of the 'Secret Sharer.'" *Conradiana* 3.2 (1971–1972): 26–34.

Brown, P. L. "'The Secret Sharer' and the Existential Hero." *Conradiana* 3.3 (1971–72): 22–30.

Burjorjee, Dinshaw M. "Comic Elements in Conrad's 'The Secret Sharer,' *Conradiana* 7.1 (January 1975): 51–61.

Casarino, Cesare. *Modernity at Sea: Melville, Marx, Conrad in Crisis.* 186–87, 208–44. Minneapolis: University of Minnesota Press, 2002.

Cohen, Michael. "Sailing through *The Secret Sharer*: The End of Conrad's Story." *Massachusetts Studies in English* 10.2 (Fall 1985): 102–09.

Cox, C. B. *Joseph Conrad: The Modern Imagination*. 137–50. London: J. M. Dent & Sons, 1974.

Curley, Daniel. "Legate of the Ideal." In *Conrad's Secret Sharer and the Critics*. Ed. Bruce Harkness. 75–82. Belmont, CA: Wadsworth Publishing, 1962.

———. "The Writer and His Use of Material: The Case of *The Secret Sharer*." *Modern Fiction Studies* 13.2 (Summer 1967): 179–94.

Daleski, H. M.. *Joseph Conrad: The Way to Dispossession*. 171–83. London: Faber & Faber, 1977.

David, W. Eugene. "The Structures of Justice in 'The Secret Sharer.'" *Conradiana* 27.1 (Spring 1995): 64–73.

Devers, James. "More on Symbols in Conrad's 'The Secret Sharer.'" *Conradiana* 28.1 (Winter 1996): 66–76.

Dilworth, Thomas R. "Conrad's Secret Sharer at the Gate of Hell." *Conradiana* 9.3 (Autumn 1977): 203–17.

Dobrinsky, Joseph. "The Two Lives of Joseph Conrad in 'The Secret Sharer.'" *Cahiers Victoriens et Edouardiens* 21 (April 1985): 33–49.

Dussinger, Gloria R. "'The Secret Sharer': Conrad's Psychological Study." *Texas Studies in Literature and Language* 10.4 (Winter 1969): 599–608.

Eggenschwiler, David. "Narcissus in 'The Secret Sharer': A Secondary Point of View." *Conradiana* 11.1 (Spring 1979): 23–40.

Emmett, Paul J. "Conrad's Secrets: Narrative Suppression and Dream Distortion in 'The Secret Sharer.'" *Journal of Evolutionary Psychology* 25.3–4 (August 2004): 154–69.

• Erdinast-Vulcan, Daphna. *The Strange Short Fiction of Joseph Conrad: Writing, Culture, and Subjectivity*. 30–50. Oxford: Oxford University Press, 1999.

Evans, Frank B. "The Nautical Metaphor in 'The Secret Sharer.'" *Conradiana* 7.1 (January 1975): 3–16.

Foye, Paul F., Bruce Harkness, and Nathan L. Marvin. "The Sailing Maneuver in 'The Secret Sharer.'" *Journal of Modern Literature* 2.1 (September 1971): 119–23.

Freeman, Linda A. "The Secret Sharer' through Eastern Eyes." *Conradiana* 43.1 (Spring 2011): 85–95.

French, Warren. "'The Secret Sharer': Film Confronts Story in Face to Face." In *Conrad on Film*. Ed. Gene M. Moore. 93–103. Cambridge: Cambridge University Press, 1997.

Goonetilleke, D. C. R. A. *Joseph Conrad: Beyond Culture and Background*. 111–17. New York: St. Martin's Press, 1990.

Gramm, Christie. "The Dialectic of the Double in *Lord Jim* and 'The Secret Sharer.'" *The Conradian* 37.2 (Autumn 2012): 80–94.

Graver, Lawrence. *Conrad's Short Fiction*. 149–158. Berkeley: University of California Press, 1969.

Guerard, Albert J. *Conrad the Novelist*. 30–33. Cambridge: Harvard University Press, 1958.

• ———. "Introduction." *Heart of Darkness & The Secret Sharer* by Joseph Conrad. Ed. Albert J. Guerard. 8–15. New York: Signet Classics, 1950.

Hampson, Robert. *Joseph Conrad: Betrayal and Identity*. 191–95. New York: St. Martin's Press, 1992.

Hansford, James. "Closing, Enclosure and Passage in 'The Secret Sharer.'" *The Conradian* 15.1 (Spring 1990): 30–55.

Harkness, Bruce, ed. *Conrad's "Secret Sharer" and the Critics*. Belmont, CA: Wadsworth, 1962.

Hewitt, Douglas. *Conrad: A Reassessment*. 70–79. Cambridge: Bowes & Bowes, 1952.

Hoffmann, Charles G. "Point of View in 'The Secret Sharer.'" *College English* 23.8 (May 1962): 651–54.

Johnson, Barbara, and Marjorie Garber. "Secret Sharing: Reading Conrad Psychoanalytically." *College English* 49.6 (October 1987): 628–40.

Johnson, Bruce. *Conrad's Models of Mind.* 126–39. Minneapolis: University of Minnesota Press, 1971.

Kaplan, Carola M. "Women's Caring and Men's Secret Sharing: Constructions of Gender and Sexuality in 'Heart of Darkness' and 'The Secret Sharer.'" In *Approaches to Teaching Conrad's 'Heart of Darkness' and 'The Secret Sharer.'* Ed. Hunt Hawkins and Brian Shaffer. 97–103. New York: Modern Language Association of America; 2002.

Leavis, F. R. "*The Secret Sharer.*" In *Anna Karenina and Other Essays* by F. R. Leavis. 111–20. London: Chatto & Windus, 1967.

Leiter, Louis H. "Echo Structures: Conrad's 'The Secret Sharer.'" *Twentieth Century Literature* 5.1 (January 1960): 159–75.

Levenson, Michael. "Secret History in 'The Secret Sharer.'" In *The Secret Sharer* by Joseph Conrad. Ed. Daniel R. Schwarz. 163–74. Boston: Bedford/St. Martin's Press, 1997.

Lothe, Jakob. *Conrad's Narrative Method.* 47–71. Oxford: Clarendon Press, 1989.

Maisonnat, Claude. "Whiskers and Whispers: Metafictional Negotiations in *The Secret Sharer.*" *L'Epoque Conradienne* 38 (2012): 45–57.

Martinière, Nathalie. "Symbolic Space and Narrative Focus: The Cabin in Conrad's Sea Stories." *The Conradian* 27.1 (Spring 2002): 24–38.

Miller, J. Hillis. "Sharing Secrets." In *The Secret Sharer* by Joseph Conrad. Ed. Daniel R. Schwarz. 232–52. Boston: Bedford/St. Martin's Press, 1997.

Moore, A. Luyat. "Conrad's Technique of 'The Secret Sharer.'" *L'Epoque Conradienne* 3 (1977): 35–53.

Murphy, Michael. "'The Secret Sharer': Conrad's Turn of the Winch." *Conradiana* 18.3 (Autumn 1986): 193–200.

O'Hara, J. D. "Unlearned Lessons in 'The Secret Sharer.'" *College English* 26.6 (March 1965): 444–50.

Paccaud, Josiane. "The Alienating Imaginary and the Symbolic Law in Conrad's *The Secret Sharer.*" *L'Epoque Conradienne* 13 (1987): 89–96.

———. "Under the Other's Eyes: Conrad's 'The Secret Sharer.'" *The Conradian* 12.1 (Spring 1987): 59–73.

Perel, Zivah. "Tranforming the Hero: Joseph Conrad's Reconfiguring of Masculine Identity in *The Secret Sharer.*" *Conradiana* 36.1–2 (Spring–Summer 2004): 111–29.

Phelan, James. *Narrative as Rhetoric: Technique, Audiences, Ethics, Ideology.* 119–31. Columbus: Ohio State University Press, 1996.

———. "Reading Secrets." In *The Secret Sharer* by Joseph Conrad. Ed. Daniel R. Schwarz. 128–44. Boston: Bedford/St. Martin's Press, 1997.

Phillips, Gene D. *Conrad and Cinema: The Art of Adaptation.* 81–89. New York: Peter Lang, 1995.

Ressler, Steve. *Joseph Conrad: Consciousness and Integrity.* 80–97. New York: New York University Press, 1988.

• Richardson, Brian. "Construing Conrad's 'The Secret Sharer': Suppressed Narratives, Subaltern Reception, and the Act of Interpretation." *Studies in the Novel* 33.3 (Fall 2001): 306–21.

Said, Edward W. *Joseph Conrad and the Fiction of Autobiography.* 125–32, 156–58. Cambridge: Harvard University Press, 1966.

Schenck, Mary-Low. "Seamanship in Conrad's 'The Secret Sharer.'" *Criticism* 15.1 (Winter 1973): 1–15.

Schneider, Lissa. *Conrad's Narratives of Difference: Not Exactly Tales for Boys.* 33–40. New York: Routledge, 2003.

Schwarz, Daniel R. *Conrad: The Later Fiction.* 1–10. London: Macmillan Press, 1982.

———. "'The Secret Sharer' as an Act of Memory." In *The Secret Sharer* by Joseph Conrad. Ed. Daniel R. Schwarz. 95–111. Boston: Bedford/St. Martin's Press, 1997.

Scott, Bonnie Kime. "Intimacies Engendered in Conrad's 'The Secret Sharer.'" In *The Secret Sharer* by Joseph Conrad. Ed. Daniel R. Schwarz. 197–210. Boston: Bedford/St. Martin's Press, 1997.

Simons, Kenneth. *The Ludic Imagination: A Reading of Joseph Conrad.* 95–140. Ann Arbor: UMI Research Press, 1985.

Simmons, J. L. "The Dual Morality in Conrad's *The Secret Sharer.*" *Studies in Short Fiction* 2 (1965): 209–20.

• Stallman, R. W. "Conrad and 'The Secret Sharer.'" *Accent* 9.3 (Spring 1949): 131–43.

Stape, J. H. "Topography in *The Secret Sharer.*" *The Conradian* 26.1 (Spring 2001): 1–16.

Steiner, Joan E. "Conrad's 'The Secret Sharer': Complexities of the Doubling Relationship." *Conradiana* 12.3 (Autumn 1980): 173–86.

Thomas, Mark Ellis. "Doubling and Difference in Conrad: 'The Secret Sharer,' *Lord Jim,* and *The Shadow Line.*" *Conradiana* 27.3 (Autumn 1995): 222–34.

Thorburn, David. *Conrad's Romanticism.* 140–46. New Haven: Yale University Press, 1974.

Toker, Leona. *Towards the Ethics of Form in Fiction: Narratives of Cultural Remission.* 143–56. Columbus: Ohio State University Press, 2010.

Troy, Mark. "'. . . Of No Particular Significance Except to Myself': Narrative Posture in Conrad's 'The Secret Sharer.'" *Studia Neophilologica* 56.1 (1984): 35–50.

Watts, Cedric. *The Deceptive Text: An Introduction to Covert Plots.* 84–90. Brighton, UK: Harvester Press, 1984.

———. "The Mirror-Tale: An Ethico-Structural Analysis of Conrad's *The Secret Sharer.*" *Critical Quarterly* 19.3 (Autumn 1977): 25–37.

Wexler, Joyce. "Conrad's Dream of a Common Language: Lacan and 'The Secret Sharer.'" *Psychoanalytic Review* 78.4 (Winter 1991): 599–606.

White, James F. "The Third Theme in 'The Secret Sharer.'" *Conradiana* 21.1 (Spring 1989): 37–46.

Williams, Porter Jr. "The Matter of Conscience in Conrad's *The Secret Sharer.*" *PMLA* 79.5 (December 1964): 626–30.

Wyatt, Robert D. "Joseph Conrad's 'The Secret Sharer': Point of View and Mistaken Identities." *Conradiana* 5.1 (January 1973): 12–26.

Yelton, Donald C. *Mimesis and Metaphor: An Inquiry into the Genesis and Scope of Conrad's Symbolic Imagery.* 272–98. The Hague: Mouton, 1967.

Commentary on The Shadow-Line

Berthoud, Jacques. "Introduction: Autobiography and War." *The Shadow-Line* by Joseph Conrad. Ed. Jacques Berthoud. 7–24. London: Penguin Books, 1986.

Bock, Martin. "Conrad's Voyages of Disorientation: Crossing the Shadow-Line." *Conradiana* 17.2 (Summer 1985): 83–92.

———. *Joseph Conrad and Psychological Medicine.* 181–88. Lubbock: Texas Tech University Press, 2002.

Burns, Allan. "The Opening of *The Shadow-Line.*" *English Studies* 80.6 (December 1999): 518–26.

Collits, Terry. *Postcolonial Conrad: Paradoxes of Empire.* 57–62. London: Routledge, 2005.

Cox, C. B. *Joseph Conrad: The Modern Imagination.* 150–58. London: J. M. Dent & Sons, 1974.

Erdinast-Vulcan, Daphna. *Joseph Conrad and the Modern Temper.* 127–38. Oxford: Oxford University Press, 1991.

Geddes, Gary. *Conrad's Later Novels.* 81–113. Montreal: McGill-Queens University Press, 1980.

GoGwilt, Chris. "The Interior: Benjaminian Arcades, Conradian Passages, and the 'Impasse' of Jean Rhys." In *Geographies of Modernism: Literatures, Cultures, Spaces*. Ed. Peter Brooker and Andrew Thacker. 65–75. London: Routledge, 2005.

Goonetilleke, D. C. R. A. *Joseph Conrad: Beyond Culture and Background*. 117–22. New York: St. Martin's Press, 1990.

Graham, Kenneth. *Indirections of the Novel: James, Conrad, and Forster*. 142–53. Cambridge: Cambridge University Press, 1988.

Graver, Lawrence. *Conrad's Short Fiction*. 178–92. Berkeley: University of California Press, 1969.

Guerard, Albert. *Conrad the Novelist*. 29–33. Cambridge: Harvard University Press, 1958.

Hawthorn, Jeremy. "Introduction." *The Shadow-Line* by Joseph Conrad. Ed. Jeremy Hawthorn. xi–xxxiii. Oxford: Oxford University Press, 2003.

———. *Sexuality and the Erotic in the Fiction of Joseph Conrad*. 47–54. London: Continuum, 2007.

Hewitt, Douglas. *Conrad: A Reassessment*. 112–17. Cambridge: Bowes & Bowes, 1952.

Jaudel, Philippe. "The Calm as Initiation: A Plural Reading of *The Shadow-Line*." *L'Epoque Conradienne* (1988): 129–35.

Kerr, Douglas. "Conrad and the 'Three Ages of Man': 'Youth,' *The Shadow-Line*, 'The End of the Tether.' " *The Conradian* 23.2 (Autumn 1998): 27–44.

Knowles, Owen. "Introduction." In *The Shadow-Line* by Joseph Conrad. Ed. J. H. Stape and Allan H. Simmons with Owen Knowles. xxv–lvii. Cambridge: Cambridge University Press, 2013.

Krasnow, Charles G. "Joseph Conrad's *The Shadow Line*: From Late Adolescence to Adulthood." *Adolescent Psychiatry* 16 (1989): 202–15.

Larabee, Mark D. " 'A Funny Piece of Water': The Altered Seascape of Joseph Conrad's Gulf of Siam." *CEA Critic* 63.1 (Fall 2000): 36–46.

• ———. " 'A Mysterious System': Topographical Fidelity and the Charting of Imperialism in Joseph Conrad's Siamese Waters." *Studies in the Novel* 32.3 (Fall 2000): 348–68.

Le Boulicaut, Yannick. "To Cross or Not to Cross the Shadow-Line." In *Conrad in France*. Ed. Josiane Paccaud-Huguet. 107–25. Boulder, CO: Social Science Monographs, 2006.

• Leavis, F. R. *The Great Tradition: George Eliot, Henry James, Joseph Conrad*. 187–89. New York: George W. Stewart, 1948.

———. "Joseph Conrad." *Sewanee Review* 66.2 (Spring 1958): 179–200.

Lothe, Jakob. *Conrad's Narrative Method*. 117–32. Oxford: Oxford University Press, 1989.

Manocha, Nisha. "Reading Documents: Embedded Texts in *The Professor's House* and *The Shadow-Line*." *Studies in the Novel* 44.2 (Summer 2012): 186–207.

Miczka, Tadeusz. "Literature, Painting, and Film: Wajda's Adaptation of *The Shadow-Line*." In *Conrad on Film*. Ed. Gene M. Moore. 135–50. Cambridge: Cambridge University Press, 1997.

Moser, Thomas. *Joseph Conrad: Achievement and Decline*. 137–43. Cambridge: Harvard University Press, 1957.

Moutet, Muriel. "Ghost Words: Negative Initiation and Poetic Enunciation in *The Shadow-Line*." In *Conrad in France*. Ed. Josiane Paccaud-Huguet. 149–75. Boulder, CO: Social Science Monographs, 2006.

• Nayder, Lillian. "Sailing Ships and Steamers, Angels and Whores: History and Gender in Conrad's Maritime Fiction." In *Iron Men, Wooden Women: Gender and Seafaring in the Atlantic World, 1700–1920*. Ed. Margaret S. Creighton and Lisa Norling. 193–98. Baltimore: Johns Hopkins University Press, 1996.

Paccaud-Huguet, Josiane. " 'Another Turn of the Racking Screw': The Poetics of Disavowal in *The Shadow Line*." In *Conrad, James and Other Relations*.

Ed. Keith Carabine, Owen Knowles, and Paul Armstrong. 147–70. Boulder, CO: Social Science Monographs, 1998.

———. "Reading Shadows into Lines: Conrad with Lacan." *The Conradian* 22.1–2 (Spring–Autumn 1997): 144–77.

Romanick, Debra. "*The Shadow-Line*." In *A Joseph Conrad Companion*. Ed. Leonard Orr and Ted Billy. 236–51. Westport, CT: Greenwood Press, 1999.

Said, Edward W. *Joseph Conrad and the Fiction of Autobiography*. 165–97. Cambridge: Harvard University Press, 1966.

Schwarz, Daniel R. "Achieving Self-Command: Theme and Value in Conrad's *The Shadow-Line*." *Renascence* 29.3 (Spring 1977): 131–41.

———. *Conrad: The Later Fiction*. 81–94. Macmillan: London, 1982.

Sherry, Norman. "'Exact Biography' and *The Shadow-Line*." *PMLA* 79.5 (December 1964): 620–25.

Shidara, Yasuko. "Conrad and Bangkok: Another Excursion to his 'Eastern World.'" In *Journeys, Myths and the Age of Travel: Joseph Conrad's Era*. 76–96. Karlskrona, Sweden: University of Karlskrona/Ronneby, 1998.

———. "*The Shadow-Line*'s 'Sympathetic Doctor': Dr William Willis in Bangkok, 1888." *The Conradian* 30.1 (Spring 2005): 97–110.

Sulik, Boleslaw. *A Change of Tack: Making "The Shadow Line."* London: British Film Institute, 1976.

Texier-Vandamme, Christine. "*The Shadow-Line*: Condensation, Line of Flight and Fascination with Death." In *Conrad in France*. Ed. Josiane Paccaud-Huguet. 127–47. Boulder, CO: Social Science Monographs; 2006.

Watt, Ian. "Story and Idea in Conrad's *The Shadow-Line*." *Critical Quarterly* 2.2 (Summer 1960): 133–48.

Watts, Cedric. *The Deceptive Text: An Introduction to Covert Plots*. 90–99, 119–25. Brighton: Harvester Press, 1984.

Yelton, Donald C. *Mimesis and Metaphor: An Inquiry into the Genesis and Scope of Conrad's Symbolic Imagery*. 299–322. The Hague: Mouton, 1967.

Zuckerman, Jerome. "The Architecture of *The Shadow-Line*." *Conradiana* 3.2 (1971–72): 87–92.

Commentary on The Nigger of the "Narcissus"

Adams, David. *Colonial Odysseys: Empire and Epic in the Modernist Novel*. 118–23. Ithaca: Cornell University Press, 2003.

Ambrosini, Richard. *Conrad's Fiction as Critical Discourse*. 18–31, 65–70. Cambridge: Cambridge University Press, 1991.

Ash, Beth Sharon. *Writing in Between: Modernity and Psychosocial Dilemma in the Novels of Joseph Conrad*. 19–73. New York: St. Martin's Press, 1999.

Berthoud, Jacques. "Introduction." *The Nigger of the "Narcissus"* by Joseph Conrad. Ed. Jacques Berthoud. vii–xxvi. Oxford: Oxford University Press, 1984.

———. *Joseph Conrad: The Major Phase*. 23–40. Cambridge: Cambridge University Press, 1978.

Bock, Martin. "Joseph Conrad and Germ Theory: Why Captain Allistoun Smiles Thoughtfully." *The Conradian* 31.2 (Autumn 2006): 1–14.

Bongie, Chris. *Exotic Memories: Literature, Colonialism, and the Fin de Siècle*. 165–71. Stanford: Stanford University Press, 1991.

Bonney, William W. "Semantic and Structural Indeterminancy in *The Nigger of the 'Narcissus'*: An Experiment in Reading." *ELH* 40.4 (Winter 1973): 564–83.

Bruss, Paul. *Conrad's Early Sea Fiction: The Novelist as Navigator*. 31–46. Lewisburg, PA: Bucknell University Press, 1979.

Burgess, C. F. "Of Men and Ships and Mortality: Conrad's *The Nigger of the 'Narcissus.'*" *English Literature in Transition 1880–1920*. 15.3 (1972): 221–31.

• Cesarino, Cesare. *Modernity at Sea: Melville, Marx, Conrad in Crisis*. 19–23, 25–28, 235–44. Minneapolis: University of Minnesota Press, 2002.

Christensen, Tim. "Racial Fantasy in Joseph Conrad's *Nigger of the 'Narcissus*,'" *Ariel* 37.1 (January 2006): 27–43.

Clark, Lorrie. "Rousseau and Political Compassion in *The Nigger of the 'Narcissus.'* " *Conradiana* 31.2 (Summer 1999): 120–30.

Curle, Richard. "The History of *The Nigger of the 'Narcissus*': Human, Literary, Bibliographical." In *Conrad in the Public Eye: Biography, Criticism, Publicity.* 127–46. Ed. John G. Peters. Amsterdam: Rodopi, 2008.

Daleski, H. M. *Joseph Conrad: The Way to Dispossession.* 26–50. London: Faber & Faber, 1977.

Davis, Kenneth W., and Donald W. Rude. "The Transmission of the Text of *The Nigger of the 'Narcissus.'*" *Conradiana* 5.2 (May 1973): 20–45.

DeKoven, Marianne. *Rich and Strange: Gender, History, Modernism.* 68–70, 75–78. Princeton: Princeton University Press, 1991.

Deresiewicz, William. "Conrad's Impasse: *The Nigger of the 'Narcissus*' and the Invention of Marlow." *Conradiana* 38.3 (Fall 2006): 205–27.

Donovan, Stephen. *Joseph Conrad and Popular Culture.* 42–62. New York: Palgrave Macmillan, 2005.

Echeruo, W. J. C. "James Wait and *The Nigger of the 'Narcissus.'*" *English Studies in Africa* 8 (1965): 166–80.

Fleishman, Avrom. *Conrad's Politics: Community and Anarchy in the Fiction of Joseph Conrad.* 129–32. Baltimore: Johns Hopkins University Press, 1967.

Foulke, Robert. "Creed and Conduct in *The Nigger of the 'Narcissus.'*" *Conradiana* 12.2 (Summer 1980): 105–28.

———. "Postures of Belief in *The Nigger of the 'Narcissus.'*" *Modern Fiction Studies* 17.2 (Summer 1971): 249–62.

Gekoski, R. A. *Conrad: The Moral World of the Novelist.* 56–71. New York: Barnes & Noble, 1978.

Goonetilleke, D. C. R. A. *Joseph Conrad: Beyond Culture and Background.* 97–105. New York: St. Martin's Press, 1990.

Gordan, John Dozier. *Joseph Conrad: The Making of a Novelist.* 54–57, 135–41, 226–40. Cambridge: Harvard University Press, 1941.

Graver, Lawrence. *Conrad's Short Fiction.* 63–70. Berkeley: University of California Press, 1969.

Guerard, Albert J. *"The Nigger of the 'Narcissus.'"* *Kenyon Review* 19.2 (Spring 1957): 205–32.

Gurko, Leo. "Death Journey in *The Nigger of the 'Narcissus.'*" *Nineteenth-Century Fiction* 15.4 (March 1961): 301–11.

Hampson, Robert. *Joseph Conrad: Betrayal and Identity.* 101–06. New York: St. Martin's Press, 1992.

• Hawthorn, Jeremy. *Joseph Conrad: Narrative Technique and Ideological Commitment.* 101–32. London: Edward Arnold, 1990.

Hay, Eloise Knapp. *The Political Novels of Joseph Conrad.: A Critical Study.* 230–35. Chicago: University of Chicago Press, 1963.

Henricksen, Bruce. *Nomadic Voices: Conrad and the Subject of Narrative.* 23–46. Urbana: University of Illinois Press, 1992.

Hervouet, Yves. *The French Face of Joseph Conrad.* 39–49. Cambridge: Cambridge University Press, 1990.

Humphries, Reynold. "How to Change the Subject: Narrative, Reader and Ideology in *The Nigger of the 'Narcissus.'*" *Recherches Anglaises et Américaines* 15 (1982): 39–50.

• Jameson, Fredric. *The Political Unconscious: Narrative as Socially Symbolic Act.* 213–17. Ithaca: Cornell University Press, 1981.

Johnsen, William A. "'To My Readers in America': Conrad's 1914 Preface to *The Nigger of the 'Narcissus.'*" *Conradiana* 35.1–2 (Spring–Summer 2003): 105–22.

Johnson, Bruce. *Conrad's Models of Mind.* 24–40. Minneapolis: University of Minnesota Press, 1971.

Jones, Michael P. "Judgment and Sentiment in *The Nigger of the 'Narcissus.'*" *Conradiana* 9.2 (Summer 1977): 159–69.

Juhász, Tamás. *Conradian Contracts: Exchange and Identity in the Immigrant Imagination.* 177–99. Lanham, MD: Lexington Books, 2011.

Kane, Michael. "Insiders/Outsiders: Conrad's *The Nigger of the 'Narcissus'* and Bram Stoker's *Dracula.*" *Modern Language Review* 92.1 (January 1997): 1–21.

Kimbrough, Robert, ed. *The Nigger of the "Narcissus"* by Joseph Conrad. New York: Norton, 1979.

Kirschner, Paul. *Conrad: The Psychologist as Artist.* 102–09, 200–205, 272–74. Edinburgh: Oliver & Boyd, 1968.

Land, Stephen K. *Paradox and Polarity in the Fiction of Joseph Conrad.* 49–63. New York: St. Martin's Press, 1984.

Larabee, Mark D. "Joseph Conrad and the Maritime Tradition." In *A Historical Guide to Joseph Conrad.* Ed. John G. Peters. 55–60. New York: Oxford University Press, 2010.

Lester, John. "Conrad's Narrators in *The Nigger of the 'Narcissus.'*" *Conradiana* 12.3 (Autumn 1980): 163–72.

Levin, Yael. *Tracing the Aesthetic Principle in Conrad's Novels.* 26–34. New York: Palgrave Macmillan, 2008.

Livingston, Robert Eric. "Seeing through Reading: Class, Race and Literary Authority in Joseph Conrad's *The Nigger of the 'Narcissus.'*" *Novel* 26.2 (Winter 1993): 133–50.

Lothe, Jakob. *Conrad's Narrative Method.* 87–101. Oxford: Clarendon Press, 1989.

• Mallios, Peter Lancelot. *Our Conrad: Constituting American Modernity.* 352–71. Stanford: Stanford University Press, 2010.

Manicom, David. "True Lies/False Truths: Narrative Perspective and the Control of Ambiguity in *The Nigger of the 'Narcissus.'*" *Conradiana* 18.2 (Summer 1986): 105–18.

Marcus, Miriam. "Writing, Race, and Illness in *The Nigger of the 'Narcissus.'*" *The Conradian* 23.1 (Spring 1998): 37–50.

McDonald, Peter. "Men of Letters and Children of the Sea: Conrad and the Henley Circle Revisited." *The Conradian* 21.1 (Spring 1996): 15–56.

Messenger, Nigel. "'We Did Not Want to Lose Him': Jimmy Wait as the Figure of Abjection in Conrad's *The Nigger of the 'Narcissus.'*" *Critical Survey* 13.1 (2001): 62–79.

Miller, James E. Jr. "*The Nigger of the 'Narcissus'*: A Re-Examination." *PMLA* 66.6 (December 1951): 911–18.

Morgan, Gerald. "The Book of the Ship *Narcissus.*" In *The Nigger of the "Narcissus"* by Joseph Conrad. Ed. Robert Kimbrough. 201–12. New York: Norton, 1979.

Moyne, Ernest J. "Wamibo in Conrad's *The Nigger of the 'Narcissus.'*" *Conradiana* 10.1 (Spring 1978): 55–61.

Mudrick, Marvin. "The Artist's Conscience and *The Nigger of the 'Narcissus.'*" *Nineteenth-Century Fiction* 11.4 (March 1957): 288–97.

North, Michael. *The Dialect of Modernism: Race, Language & Twentieth-Century Literature.* 37–58. New York: Oxford University Press, 1994.

Packer-Kinlaw, Donna. "'Ain't We Men?': Illusions of Gender in Joseph Conrad's *The Nigger of the 'Narcissus.'*" *Conradiana* 38.3 (Fall 2006): 247–65.

Palmer, John A., ed. *Twentieth Century Interpretations of* The Nigger of the "Narcissus": *A Collection of Critical Essays.* Englewood Cliffs, NJ: Prentice-Hall, 1969.

Peters, John G. "'What's in a name?': Conrad's *The Nigger of the 'Narcissus.'*" *L'Epoque Conradienne* 33 (2007): 41–48.

Pinsker, Sanford. "Selective Memory, Leisure, and the Language of Joseph Conrad's *The Nigger of the 'Narcissus.'*" *Descant* 15.4 (Summer 1971): 38–48.

Polloczek, Dieter Paul. "Case and Curse: Confinement, Legal Fiction, and Solidarity in Conrad's *The Nigger of the 'Narcissus.'*" *Conradiana* 30.3 (Fall 1998): 183–202.

Pulc, I. P. "Two Portrayals of a Storm: Some Notes on Conrad's Descriptive Style in *The Nigger of the 'Narcissus'* and 'Typhoon.'" *Style* 4.1 (Winter 1970): 49–57.

Redmond, Eugene B. "Racism, or Realism? Literary Apartheid, or Poetic License? Conrad's Burden in *The Nigger of the 'Narcissus.'*" In *The Nigger of the "Narcissus"* by Joseph Conrad. Ed. Robert Kimbrough. 358–68. New York: Norton, 1979.

Richardson, Brian. "Conrad and Posthumanist Narration: Fabricating Class and Consciousness onboard the *Narcissus*." In *Conrad in the Twenty-First Century: Contemporary Approaches and Perspectives*. Ed. Carola M. Kaplan, Peter Lancelot Mallios, and Andrea White. 213–22. New York: Routledge, 2005.

Robin, Christophe. "The One and the Multiple: The Question of Hybridity in *The Nigger of the 'Narcissus.'*" *L'Epoque Conradienne* 29 (2003): 41–49.

Ross, Stephen. "The Ancien Régime and Fetishistic Politics in *The Nigger of the 'Narcissus.'*" *Conradiana* 39.1 (Spring 2007): 3–16.

———. "*The Nigger of the 'Narcissus'* and Modernist Haunting." *Novel* 44.2 (Summer 2001): 268–91.

Roussel, Royal. *The Metaphysics of Darkness: A Study in the Unity and Development of Conrad's Fiction.* 72–79. Baltimore: Johns Hopkins University Press, 1971.

Rude, Donald W., and Kenneth W. Davis. "The Critical Reception of the First American Edition of *The Nigger of the 'Narcissus.'*" *The Conradian* 16.2 (Spring 1992): 46–56.

Saveson, John E. "Contemporary Psychology in *The Nigger of the 'Narcissus.'*" *Studies in Short Fiction* 7.2 (Spring 1970): 219–31.

Schneider, Lissa. *Conrad's Narratives of Difference: Not Exactly Tales for Boys.* 63–66, 73–88. New York: Routledge, 2003.

Schwarz, Daniel R. *Conrad: "Almayer's Folly" to "Under Western Eyes."* 35–51. Ithaca: Cornell University Press, 1980.

Scrimgeour, Cecil. "Jimmy Wait and the Dance of Death: Conrad's *Nigger of the 'Narcissus.'*" *Critical Quarterly* 7 (1965): 339–52.

Simmons, Allan H. "*The Nigger of the 'Narcissus'*: History, Narrative, and Nationalism." In *Joseph Conrad: Voice, Sequence, History, Genre*. Ed. Jakob Lothe, Jeremy Hawthorn, and James Phelan. 141–59. Columbus: Ohio State University Press, 2008.

———. "Representing 'The Simple and the Voiceless': Story-Telling in *The Nigger of the Narcissus.*" *The Conradian* 24.1 (Spring 1999): 43–57.

Smith, David R. *Conrad's Manifesto: Preface to a Career, the History of the Preface to* The Nigger of the "Narcissus" *with Facsimiles of the Manuscripts.* Philadelphia: Philip H. and A. S. W. Rosenbach Foundation, 1966.

———. "'One Word More' about *The Nigger of the 'Narcissus.'*" *Nineteenth-Century Fiction* 23.2 (September 1968): 201–16.

Stape, J. H. "'History' and Fiction: Composite Sources and *The Nigger of the 'Narcissus.'*" *The Conradian* 10.1 (Spring 1985): 47–49.

Verleun-van de Vriesenaerde, Jetty, ed. *Conrad Criticism 1965–1985*: The Nigger of the "Narcissus." The Netherlands: Phoenix Press, 1988.

Watt, Ian. "Conrad Criticism and *The Nigger of the 'Narcissus.'*" *Nineteenth-Century Fiction* 12.4 (March 1958): 257–83.

———. *Conrad in the Nineteenth Century.* 68–125. Berkeley: University of California Press, 1979.

———. "Conrad's Preface to *The Nigger of the 'Narcissus.'*" *Novel* 7.2 (Winter 1974): 101–15.

Watts, Cedric. *The Deceptive Text: An Introduction to Covert Plots.* 59–74. Brighton, UK: Harvester Press, 1984.

Weston, John Howard. "*The Nigger of the "Narcissus"* and Its Preface." In *The Nigger of the "Narcissus"* by Joseph Conrad. Ed. Robert Kimbrough. 339–53. New York: Norton 1979.

Wexler, Joyce Piell. "Conrad and the Literary Marketplace." In *A Historical Guide to Joseph Conrad.* Ed. John G. Peters. 83–88. New York: Oxford University Press, 2010.

Willy, Todd G. "The Conquest of the Commodore: Conrad's Rigging of 'The Nigger' for the Henley Regatta." *Conradiana* 17.3 (Autumn 1985): 163–82.

Yelton, Donald C. *Mimesis and Metaphor: An Inquiry into the Genesis and Scope of Conrad's Symbolic Imagery.* 272–98. 127–30, 137–39, 154–62. The Hague: Mouton, 1967.

Young, Vernon. "Trial by Water. Joseph Conrad's *The Nigger of the 'Narcissus.'*" *Accent* 12.2 (Spring 1952): 67–81.

Commentary on Typhoon

Acheraïou, Amar. "Floating Words: Sea as Metaphor of Style in 'Typhoon.'" *The Conradian* 29.1 (Spring 2004): 27–38.

———. *Joseph Conrad and the Reader: Questioning Modern Theories of Narrative and Readership.* 89–93. New York: Palgrave Macmillan, 2009.

Baldwin, Debra Romanick. "The Voice of Comedy in Conrad's *Typhoon* and Primo Levi's *The Monkey's Wrench.*" *Conradiana* 39.1 (Spring 2007): 17–28.

Billy, Ted. *A Wilderness of Words: Closure and Disclosure in Conrad's Short Fiction.* 92–105. Lubbock: Texas Tech University Press, 1997.

Bonney, William W. *Thorns & Arabesques: Contexts for Conrad's Fiction.* 31–50. Baltimore: Johns Hopkins University Press, 1980.

Brown, Carolyn B. "Creative Combat in 'Typhoon.'" *The Conradian* 17.1 (Autumn 1992): 1–16.

Bruss, Paul S. "'Typhoon': The Initiation of Jukes." *Conradiana* 5.2 (May 1973): 46–55.

Carabine, Keith. "'In the Light of the Final incident: Re-Reading *Typhoon*." In *Joseph Conrad: Between Literary Techniques and Their Messages.* Ed. Wiesław Krajka. 73–91. Boulder, CO: East European Monographs, 2009.

Daleski, H. M. *Joseph Conrad: The Way of Dispossession.* 104–12. London: Faber & Faber, 1977.

Donovan, Stephen. *Joseph Conrad and Popular Culture.* 175–82. New York: Palgrave Macmillan, 2005.

Dryden, Linda. "'The Times Indeed Are Changed': Conrad, 'Typhoon,' and *Pall Mall Magazine.*" *Conradiana* 41.2–3 (Fall–Winter 2009): 132–52.

Forman, Ross G. "Coolie Cargoes: Emigrant Ships and the Burden of Representation in Joseph Conrad's *Typhoon* and James Dalziel's 'Dead Reckoning.'" *English Literature in Transition 1880–1920* 47.4 (2004): 398–428.

Foulke, Robert. "From the Center to the Dangerous Hemisphere: *Heart of Darkness* and *Typhoon*." In *Conrad's Literary Career.* Ed. Keith Carabine, Owen Knowles, and Wiesław Krajka. 127–51. Boulder, CO: East European Monographs, 1992.

Goonetilleke, D. C. R. A. *Joseph Conrad: Beyond Culture and Background.* 105–12. New York: St. Martin's Press, 1990.

Graver, Lawrence. *Conrad's Short Fiction.* 94–99. Berkeley: University of California Press, 1969.

Griem, Eberhard. "Rhetoric and Reality in Conrad's 'Typhoon.'" *Conradiana* 24.1 (Spring 1992): 21–32.

Guerard, Albert J. *Conrad the Novelist.* 294–99. Cambridge: Harvard University Press, 1958.

Hansford, James. "Money, Language, and the Body in 'Typhoon.'" *Conradiana* 26.2–3 (Fall 1994): 135–55.

Hewlett, Douglas. *Conrad: A Reassessment.* 112–14. Cambridge: Bowes & Bowes, 1952.

SELECTED BIBLIOGRAPHY 599

Hubbard, Francis A. *Theories of Action in Conrad*. 1–22. Ann Arbor: UMI Research Press, 1984.

Hussey, William R. M. "'He was spared that annoyance.'" *Conradiana* 3.2 (1971–72): 17–25.

Jones, Susan. "Conrad on the Borderlands of Modernism: Maurice Greiffenhagen, Dorothy Richardson and the Case of *Typhoon*." In *Conrad in the Twenty-First Century: Contemporary Approaches and Perspectives*. Ed. Carola M. Kaplan, Peter Lancelot Mallios, and Andrea White. 195–211. New York: Routledge, 2005.

Juhász, Tamás. *Conradian Contracts: Exchange and Identity in the Immigrant Imagination*. 53–72. Lanham, MD: Lexington Books, 2011.

Kerr, Douglas. "Chinese Boxes: 'Typhoon' and Conrad's History of the Chinese." *CLIO* 39.1 (Fall 2009): 29–52.

Kirschner, Paul. *Conrad: The Psychologist as Artist*. 110–18. Edinburgh: Oliver & Boyd, 1968.

• Kolupke, Joseph. "Elephants, Empires, and Blind Men: A Reading of the Figurative Language in Conrad's 'Typhoon.'" *Conradiana* 20.1 (Spring 1988): 71–85.

• Leavis, F. R. *The Great Tradition: George Eliot, Henry James, Joseph Conrad*. 183–87. New York: George W. Stewart, 1948.

• Lothe, Jakob. *Conrad's Narrative Method*. 102–16. Oxford: Oxford University Press, 1989.

Luyat, Anne. "Voyage to the End of Strangeness in *Typhoon* (1901)." *L'Epoque Conradienne* 17 (1991): 35–45.

Maisonnat, Claude. "Narrativity and the Ethics of Interpretation in 'Typhoon.'" In *Conrad in France*. Ed. Josiane Paccaud-Huguet. 177–88. Boulder, CO: Social Science Monographs, 2006.

Manocha, Nisha. "Conrad's Tidalectic Sea Tales." *The Conradian* 38.2 (Autumn 2013): 36–52.

• Pearson, Nels C. "'Whirr' Is King: International Capital and the Paradox of Consciousness in *Typhoon*." *Conradiana* 39.1 (Spring 2007): 29–37.

Purdy, Dwight H. "Conrad at Work: The Two Serial Texts of *Typhoon*." *Conradiana* 19.2 (Summer 1987): 99–119.

Rapin, René. "*Typhoon*: Conrad's Tacit Recessional." *Conradiana* 35.1–2 (Spring–Summer 2003): 123–32.

Rice, Thomas J. "*Typhoon*: Conrad's Christmas Story." *Cithara* 14.2 (May 1975): 19–35.

Roberts, Andrew Michael. *Conrad and Masculinity*. 66–67, 74–82. New York: St. Martin's Press, 2000.

Said, Edward W. *Joseph Conrad and the Fiction of Autobiography*. 114–16. Cambridge: Harvard University Press, 1966.

Schwarz, Daniel R. *Conrad: "Almayer's Folly" to "Under Western Eyes."* 111–18. Ithaca: Cornell University Press, 1980.

Walsh, Dennis M. "Conrad's 'Typhoon' and the *Book of Genesis*." *Studies in Short Fiction* 11.1 (Winter 1974): 99–101.

Watt, Ian. "Comedy and Humour in *Typhoon*." In *The Ugo Mursia Memorial Lectures: Papers from the International Conrad Conference, University of Pisa, September 7th–11th, 1983*. 39–56. Ed. Mario Curreli. Milano: Mursia International, 1988.

Webster, H. T. "Conrad's Changes in Narrative Conception in the Manuscripts of *Typhoon and Other Stories* and *Victory*." *PMLA* 64.5 (December 1949): 953–62.

Wegelin, Christof. "MacWhirr and the Testimony of the Human Voice." *Conradiana* 7.1 (January 1975): 45–50.

West, Russell. *Conrad and Gide: Translation, Transference and Intertextuality*. 66–98. Amsterdam: Rodopi, 1996.

Wills, John H. "Conrad's *Typhoon*: A Triumph of Organic Art." *North Dakota Quarterly* 30 (1962): 62–70.